Prosperity in Rural Africa?

The book challenges many of the established truths about rural Tanzania. And it does so based on a series of revisits by researchers with their feet on the ground and with long-term knowledge of the respective communities. It is not an anthology in in the common sense, but a collective project with methodological clarity. Based on its actual empirical material, it breaks new ground without following a pre-set formula with expected outcomes.

Mats Widgren, University of Stockholm

This book is a classic in the making, dealing with the significance of assets in understanding differentiated outcomes alongside rising prosperity across rural Tanzania. The first few chapters will be of tremendous use to researchers and students across a wide range of fields, with the case study chapters that follow being of huge interest to people working in those particular areas. The main contributions are written in a direct and engaging style and the work is enriched with the authors' unusual personal field work histories. Overall this is a fantastic compendium, and a tremendous achievement by the editors (and central contributors) to have drawn these different studies out, and pulled them together.

Kathy Homewood, University College London

Cogent and compelling, this book tells how rural Tanzania has changed substantially for the better in recent decades, more so than some may imagine. Most rural households, almost all engaged in smallholder farming, have accumulated assets: better housing, more consumer goods, more education. In the process, many have become more able to manage their lives—uwezo. A combination of (modest) public investments, the vigour of private traders, but above all the efforts of farming households has made this so. For anyone who wonders if and how rural Africa can prosper, please read this book. You will be pleasantly surprised.

Steve Wiggins, Overseas Development Institute

This series of longitudinal studies from Tanzania de-bunk common but poorly informed narratives about Africa's rural economy, which is far from stagnant! The many people surveyed by these rich case studies have been remarkable, innovative, and strategic in their grasp of new market opportunities, bringing substantial increases in incomes and wealth in diverse parts of the country. The different chapters make clear the ways in which some people are much better able than others to take advantage of new opportunities and the sequence of new investments and activities which unfurl over time. This book will be a central, long-lived part of the development economics canon, not only for illuminating rural development pathways in Tanzania, but also for its lively discussion of research methods in practice.

Camilla Toulmin, International Institute for Environment and Development

Prosperity in Rural Africa?

Insights into Wealth, Assets, and Poverty from Longitudinal Studies in Tanzania

Edited by

DAN BROCKINGTON AND CHRISTINE NOE

OXFORD
UNIVERSITY PRESS

OXFORD
UNIVERSITY PRESS

Great Clarendon Street, Oxford, OX2 6DP,
United Kingdom

Oxford University Press is a department of the University of Oxford.
It furthers the University's objective of excellence in research, scholarship,
and education by publishing worldwide. Oxford is a registered trade mark of
Oxford University Press in the UK and in certain other countries

First Edition published in 2021

Impression: 1

Published in the United States of America by Oxford University Press
198 Madison Avenue, New York, NY 10016, United States of America

British Library Cataloguing in Publication Data
Data available

Library of Congress Control Number: 2021931942

ISBN 978–0–19–886587–2

DOI: 10.1093/oso/9780198865872.001.0001

Printed and bound by
CPI Group (UK) Ltd, Croydon, CR0 4YY

Contents

List of Figures

List of Tables

List of Boxes

A Guide to Using the Book

This book provides the findings of a large collaborative project that explored long-term change in a variety of sites in rural Tanzania. There are people who will read this cover to cover—and thanks for doing so! But we realize that there will not be many of those. Rather, most people will be reading individual chapters—and downloading these chapters individually also. In particular we realize that any students reading this book will be focusing on individual chapters rather than the whole thing.

Accordingly we have written this book to facilitate that sort of reading. Each chapter should stand alone. You should be able to read each chapter and understand it without having to read the others. And, at the same time, we have indicated where arguments mentioned in particular chapters can be followed up.

But, if you are reading it from cover to cover please be warned that you will find some of the arguments repetitive. They are framed in the same way, and draw on similar literatures. Please just skip the bits which say the same thing.

To get the best out of this book read the introductory chapter, and Chapter 2, which explains why we measure what we measure. And then take your pick of any of the other chapters. You will find a guide to them in the introductory Chapter 1. And whichever of the case studies you pick, please make sure you also read the 'back-story' that lies behind them that you will find in the Epilogue. It is not often that you will get to read such honest and frank accounts of the business of doing fieldwork as these provide. We hope you enjoy them.

Biographies of Principal Authors

Agnes Andersson Djurfeldt is Professor of Human Geography at Lund University. Her research interests focus on rural-based processes of transformation within and outside agriculture in sub-Saharan Africa involving changing rural and multi-spatial livelihoods, gender-based access to productive resources, and intra-household division of labour and income. She uses a mixed-methods approach combining the use of quantitative data with qualitative field work.

Torben Birch-Thomsen is Associate Professor at the Department of Geosciences and Natural Resource Management, Section of Geography, University of Copenhagen, Denmark. He is trained as a human geographer, and his research interests fall within the fields of environmental and socioeconomic effects of land use change and intensification. Particular interests are within the relations between livelihood strategies of rural communities, farming system, land use changes, and rural-urban linkages with special reference to East, West, and southern African conditions. He has more than twenty-eight years' experience of participation in interdisciplinary research, educational, and capacity-enhancement projects in East, West, and southern Africa as well as South East Asia and Oceania. A particular close connection to Tanzania has been characteristic for his work. It started in Njombe District, collecting data for his M.Sc. thesis just south of Makambako in 1987, and continued by extended fieldwork in Rukwa in 1990–2 linked to his PhD study (which also includes Northern Province in Zambia). During 1994–2001 fieldwork in Mazombe/Ismani (Iringa) took place—data that are referred to in this book. Within the past ten years, he has conducted extended fieldwork in relation to research on rural-urban linkages in Iringa/Njombe, Morogoro, and Dodoma Regions.

Monique Borgerhoff Mulder is Distinguished Professor Emerita at the University of California at Davis in the Department of Anthropology, and a senior scientist at the Max-Planck Institute for Evolutionary Anthropology in Leipzig. She primarily studies demography, family, marriage, health, social networks, and inequality from an evolutionary perspective with particular interest in comparative analysis. She also works in the field of conservation science. Most of her fieldwork has been in East Africa—with Kenyan Kipsigis, with pastoralists in the Eyasi Basin of Tanzania, in Rukwa, and now on Pemba Island (Zanzibar). She co-authored, with Peter Coppolillo, *Conservation: Linking Ecology, Economics and Culture* in 2005, and most recently co-edited the *Evolution of Female-Biased Kinship* (2019). Most of all she enjoys fieldwork, and the experiences, friendships, and challenges of living in communities so different from that in which she was raised.

Dan Brockington is co-Director of the Sheffield Institute of International Development. He studied for his PhD thesis at UCL with Kathy Homewood and has worked on aspects of natural resource management and livelihood change in East Africa based on long-term fieldwork in remote locations. His books include *Celebrity Advocacy and International*

Development, Fortress Conservation and *Nature Unbound* (with Rosaleen Duffy and Jim Igoe). He has recently published (with Peter Billie Larson) *The Anthropology of Conservation NGOs*.

Ernestina Coast is Professor of Health and International Development at the London School of Economics and Political Science. Her research is multidisciplinary and she is a social scientist with training in demography and anthropology. Her research uses mixed methods (quantitative and qualitative) and has two main foci: the production and consumption of evidence for policy, and sexual and reproductive health and rights.

Esbern Friis-Hansen is Senior Researcher at the Department of Natural Resources and Development, Danish Institute for International Studies (DIIS). Esbern has thirty-seven years' experience with development research and consultancy focusing on smallholder agricultural development and political economy of natural resource management in East and southern Africa, with occasional projects in Asia and Latin America. He has participated and coordinated research programmes with a focus on domestic investments in non-industrial private forest; climate change adaptation and rural institutions; farmer organizations; agricultural research and extension reform; local governance of service provision; and empowerment through transformative learning. Esbern has extensive experience with undertaking fieldwork-based research in Tanzania and is currently co-coordinating the Timber Rush Research Program at Sokoine University of Agriculture. Esbern has authored or edited four books, including *Democratic Rural Organizations: Thresholds for Evolution in Africa and Asia* (2018) and *Decentralized Governance of Adaptation to Climate Change in Africa* (2017).

Olivia Howland is an ethnographer, anthropologist, painter, and professional gypsy, with roots in the English traveller community. She gained her PhD in 2016 in Applied Anthropology, and has been based in East Africa for the past twelve years. Olivia's home is in rural Kenya, which she built in 2012, on the side of a very beautiful mountain. She currently works in Kenya and is a researcher by day on a project for the University of Liverpool.

Vesa-Matti Loiske is a Human Geographer from Stockholm, Sweden. He wrote his PhD in Hanang District in Tanzania on socio-economic reasons behind land degradation in the 1990s. He has continued research and teaching in the Manyara area during his whole career and came to dedicate his professional life to the area. As director for the Coastal Management Research Center at Södertörn University in Stockholm he was a member of the Sida-funded MASMA programme committee (Marine Science for Management) that resulted in more than two hundred research projects in the Western Indian Ocean area between 2000 and 2006. He is now retired and continues his efforts in Manyara as project leader for Manyara Organic Farming Initiative (MOFI), which is a Sida-funded NGO project with the aim to convert small-scale farmers to organic farming and counteract the interests of transnational conventional agricultural companies.

Anna Mdee is Professor in the Politics of Global Development at the University of Leeds. She is a social anthropologist working on the aid industry, livelihoods, and local governance, primarily in Tanzania. She has a particular focus on water governance and work in Tanzanian villages with members of her extended family.

Joseph Mduma is Chief Conservator of Mount Hanang Nature Forest Reserve, Tanzania. He has been conservation officer at Mt Meru forest reserve, and for almost two decades he worked as forester and soil conservation specialist in Kondoa District for a major land rehabilitation intervention, the Hifadhi Ardhi Dodoma (HADO) project, run by the Tanzanian Ministry of Natural Resources and Tourism.

Christine Noe is currently an Associate Professor at the University of Dar es Salaam. She trained for her PhD at the University of Cape Town where she graduated in 2009. Her research and teaching are mostly on conservation and development politics, land tenure and rights, and rural livelihood changes. She is currently involved in collaborative research projects on New Partnerships for Sustainability (NEPSUS) (with Copenhagen Business School, Roskilde University, and University of Sheffield); Greenmentality (with Department of International Environment and Development Studies, Norwegian University of Life Sciences), and Livelihood Change in Tanzania (with University of Sheffield). Her growth as an African scholar, mentor, and research leader benefitted from early involvement in competitive grants. She received the Five College Young African Scholars program (in 2004 at the University of Massachusetts), All Africa House Fellowship (in 2012 at the University of Cape Town), and a Visiting African Fellowship (in 2015/16 at the University of Cambridge). She headed the University of Dar es Salaam's Directorate of Research and Publication (January 2018–April 2019) where she strengthened her skills on research management. Christine believes that strong collaborations are the foundation on which solid African scholarship can be supported.

Wilhelm Östberg is Associate Professor of Social Anthropology, currently affiliated researcher at the Department of Human Geography, Stockholm University, Sweden. He is a former curator of African Studies at the Museum of Ethnography, Stockholm, and was for a number of years co-editor-in-chief of *Ethnos. Journal of Anthropology.*

Stefano Ponte is Professor of International Political Economy and Director of the Centre for Business and Development Studies at Copenhagen Business School. He is primarily interested in economic and environmental governance, with focus on overlaps and tensions between private governance and public regulation. Stefano examines governance dynamics and economic and environmental upgrading trajectories in global value chains—especially in Africa. He is particularly interested in sustainability trajectories, in how sustainability standards, labels, and certifications shape agro-food value chains, and in how different forms of partnerships affect sustainability outcomes and rural livelihoods. He is also involved in projects critically examining the role of celebrities and branding in these processes, new forms of corporate social and environmental responsibility, and cause-related marketing initiatives that 'sell' suffering Africans to Western consumers. Stefano has authored or edited ten books, including *Business, Power and Sustainability in a World of Global Value Chains* (2019) and *Farmers and Markets in Tanzania* (2002).

Sara Randall was trained in demography at the London School of Hygiene and Tropical Medicine and has worked in the UCL Anthropology department since 1991. Along with understanding the demographic dynamics of rural West African populations her recent research focuses on using anthropological approaches to unpacking and understanding concepts, data, and metrics used in quantitative data collection and analyses and thus for policy-making.

Katherine A. Snyder is Professor and Director of the Master's in Development Practice Program at the University of Arizona, School of Geography and Development. She has over twenty-five years of experience in East and southern Africa carrying out research on rural livelihoods, gender and development, land-use change, and sustainable agriculture.

Cosmas Sokoni is a Senior Lecturer at the Department of Geography, College of Social Sciences, University of Dar es Salaam, Tanzania, where he has worked for more than thirty-three years. He wrote his PhD thesis at the University of Dar es Salaam titled: 'The Influence of Agricultural Marketing Reforms on Highland Farming Systems in Tanzania. The Case of the Uporoto Highlands, Mbeya Region.' He is trained as a human geographer and his research interest is in farming systems, rural livelihoods, rural settlement development, and rural-urban interactions. He has published some articles in these areas. He has researched on the Uporoto Highlands, on Rungwe, Kilimanjaro, and on the Usambara Mountains.

Emmanuel Sulle is a Research Associate and PhD Graduate at the Institute for Poverty, Land Agrarian Studies, University of the Western Cape, South Africa. His research focuses on the politics of inclusive business models in land-based investments, land tenure, and rural livelihoods.

Verdiana Tilumanywa is a Lecturer at the Department of Geography, College of Social Sciences, at the University of Dar es Salaam, Tanzania. She obtained her PhD in Geography and Environmental Studies from Stellenbosch University in South Africa in 2013 and her Master's and Bachelor's degrees from the University of Dar es Salaam. Verdiana has received a number of scholarships, the SIDA SAREC full-funded scholarship for her Master's degree from 2005 to 2007 at the University of Dar es Salaam; the Partnership for Africa's Next Generation of Academics (PANGeA) scholarship for her PhD studies from 2010 to 2012 at Stellenbosch University; and finally the SSRC under the Next Generation Social Science programme for a dissertation completion fellowship in 2012. In 2017 she was a Fellow under the Climate Impact Research Capacity and Leadership Enhancement in Sub-Saharan Africa programme (CIRCLE). Since September 2016 till now, Verdiana has been the Deputy Principal of the College of Social Sciences at the University of Dar es Salaam. Her research interests include environmental analysis, GIS and mapping, application in land cover and land use studies and change detection, environmental change, land use change, climate change and variability, analysis and management of special environments (mountains), livelihoods, tourism and development, and potential, management, and impact analysis.

Acknowledgements

General

All the authors want to thank all the different individuals, families, and communities who have taken part in this research and engaged with them as informants, critics, commentators, and friends. All this work has only been possible because of their support and participation. We would similarly like to thank the national and district government officers who have supported this work through granting research permission, as well as meetings, interviews, and other forms of support during the fieldwork phases. We have also benefitted from several stakeholder meetings and the generous commitments of time and critical commentary that participants at those meetings provided. This work was funded by the DFID-ESRC Growth Research Program, jointly funded by the UK Department for International Development (DFID) and ESRC, grant number ES/L012413/2. The findings and conclusions contained in the chapters are those of the authors and do not necessarily reflect positions or policies of the UK government, DFID, or ESRC. We also acknowledge the support of the Research Council of Norway through the Greenmentality project. It has been particularly well supported throughout by the ODI, in part with financial support and especially the critical commentary and engagement of Steve Wiggins and Louise Shaxson. We thank Mats Widgren for kicking this whole thing off by gifting a copy of Vesa-Matti's thesis to Dan Brockington. And we thank Moses Mnzava for multiple forms of work, support, and input and Cathbert Mwanyika and Einhard Mwanyika for all their hard work in multiple locations.

Monique

First many thanks to the people of Mirumba for their persistent tolerance of a full census across the years, and the many delightful friendships they offered. Thanks also to the Louis Leakey Foundation, the National Science Foundation, and the University of California at Davis for funding. Research was conducted with ethical clearance from the University of California at Davis Institutional Review Board.

Christine

I am most grateful to the late Rolf Larson whose footsteps I followed in this project. It is because of the meticulous order in which he kept his data and a chance encounter with his former colleagues that I have been able to re-study Meru. I am very grateful to Göran Djurfeldt, Rolf's supervisor, for making this possible. I would also like to acknowledge the initial idea of getting me to join the project team. Thank you to Dan Brockington who has continuously built my confidence that there was much to find out in a place I call home—and that I could bring a different voice into Rolf's data. I have indeed enjoyed and learned a great deal.

Anna

Thanks to the villagers of Uchira who have hosted me for all these years and endured my idiotic questions. Most especially to Ernest Msuya, village councillor and merciless research facilitator, with whom I endlessly walked the hills and lowlands and shared many beers, and our first assistants, Rhoda Mdee (a distant relation) and Yusuphu Mfinanga, still in touch although now far from Uchira. And also to my husband, Chris Mdee, and brothers-in-law, Gasper and Erast Mdee, for their research assistance, love, and friendship.

Torbern and Esbern

We are grateful for the financial and academic support allowing re-surveying study sites from back in the mid-1990s. It has been a fantastic and unique opportunity to compare datasets, to enhance understanding of processes of social and agricultural change, and to document well-being changes and livelihood outcomes. Furthermore, we are very grateful for the strong support, hospitality, and invaluable assistance provided by the communities, local assistants, and village authorities of Ilambilole and Ikuwala as well as the Ilula Township. Particularly we would like to thank the households in Ikuwala and Ilambilole villages, who welcomed us back after more than twenty years! Thank you for hosting us and sharing your experience of change.

Dan

My thanks to all the contributors to this volume who have worked so hard on the data collection, analysis, writing, and general conviviality that is required in a federated project like this. Particular thanks to all in Gitting and Gocho and my friends and acquaintances in Mtowisa who were so generous and welcoming during my revisits, particularly to Noeli Kilatu and Sylvie Ngomeni.

Agnes

The work presented in Chapter 11 was funded by the DFID-ESRC Growth Research Program, jointly funded by the UK Department for International Development (DFID) and ESRC, grant number ES/L012014/1. The findings and conclusions contained in the chapter are those of the authors and do not necessarily reflect positions or policies of the UK government, DFID, or ESRC. The authors wish to thank the participants in the Afrint study sites in Kilombero for their long-standing contributions to the study—in some cases spanning nearly two decades! We also wish to thank the research assistants involved in data collection in November 2017.

Permissions and Disclaimer

A number of previously published papers have been refashioned for this collection and we have reproduced them with permission here. Our thanks to the editors and reviewers of those journals whose critical input substantially improved our work. The papers we have used, and the main chapters they appear in, are listed below.

D. Brockington, O. Howland, V.-M. Loiske, M. Mnzava, and C. Noe (2019). 'Assets and Poverty Dynamics: The Methodological Challenges of Constructing Longitudinal Surveys in Tanzania.' *Tanzanian Development: A Comparative Perspective.* D. Potts. Woodbridge, Boydell and Brewer. (Chapter 1)

O. Howland, D. Brockington, and C. Noe (2021). 'The Multiple Meanings of Prosperity and Poverty: A Cross-Site Comparison from Tanzania.' *Journal of Peasant Studies* 48: 180–200. (Chapter 3)

D. Brockington, E. Coast, O. Howland, A. Mdee, and S. Randall (2021). 'Assets and Domestic Units: Methodological Challenges for Longitudinal Studies of Poverty Dynamics.' *Journal of Peasant Studies* 48: 159–79. (Chapter 4)

K. A. Snyder, E. Sulle, D. A. Massay, A. Petro, P. Qamara, and D. Brockington (2019). '"Modern" Farming and the Transformation of Livelihoods in Rural Tanzania.' *Agriculture and Human Values* 37: 33–46. (Chapter 6)

O. Howland, D. Brockington, and C. Noe (2020). 'Women's Tears or Coffee Blight? Gender Dynamics and Livelihood Strategies in Contexts of Agricultural Transformation in Tanzania.' *Agrarian South, Journal of Political Economy* 9(2): 171–96. (Chapter 7)

D. Brockington (2021). 'Persistent Peasant Poverty and Assets. Exploring Dynamics of New Forms of Wealth and Poverty in Tanzania 1999–2018.' *Journal of Peasant Studies* 48: 201–20. (Chapter 8)

D. Brockington, O. Howland, V.-M. Loiske, M. Mnzava, and C. Noe (2018). 'Economic Growth, Rural Assets and Prosperity. Exploring the Implications of a Twenty Year Record of Asset Growth in Tanzania.' *Journal of Modern African Studies* 56(2): 217–43. (Chapter 9)

W. Östberg, O. Howland, J. Mduma, and D. Brockington (2018). 'Tracing Improving Livelihoods in Rural Africa Using Local Measures of Wealth: A Case Study from Central Tanzania, 1991–2016.' *Land* 7(44): 1–26. (Chapter 10)

S. Ponte and D. Brockington (2020). 'From Pyramid to Pointed Egg? A Twenty-Year Perspective on Poverty, Prosperity and Rural Transformation in Tanzania.' *African Affairs* 119(475): 203–23. (Chapter 12)

1
Understanding Long-Term Change in Rural Tanzania

Dan Brockington and Christine Noe

The Insistent Farmer

We had to talk to Erick. He would not let us carry on with the other interviews we had planned for that day until we had visited him. We wanted to say that we were conducting a stratified random sample of families in this village and that he was not on the list. But that did not translate too well into Swahili. Also it was not appropriate to use a sample frame as an excuse not to meet someone. And Erick was interesting.

He and his wife, Paulina, wanted to tell us about the transformations that they had experienced in their lives in the last fifteen years or so. It had not begun well. He had been imprisoned for bad debt. But he had cleared himself of it, and his family's fortunes had transformed since. He and Paulina had farmed their land—a relatively small plot of a few acres growing maize, sunflower, and sesame. They had sold their crops at various times to buy goats, an ox, a plough, and its chain and to build a new brick house with a metal roof. They were pleased and proud of all the changes that they had brought to their lives.

Erick and Paulina lived in Mtowisa, in a remote part of Tanzania. When we had first met, in 2000, they were immersed in poverty. There was no electricity, no passable roads in the wet season. Crops were difficult to move out of the village, and goods expensive to move in. The region itself had no tarred roads connecting it to the rest of the country. It was distant and isolated. Children died young, relatively few villagers made it to old age. The village clinic was poorly equipped, the secondary school (build by villagers' initiative) was crumbling and barely functioning.

But now it was completely different—there were roads, regular bus services, telecommunications towers, a hospital with an operating theatre and a huge, vibrant secondary school. The village was transformed, and not just to our eyes. In our initial focus group discussions, we were told to expect to find a village that had 'lifted itself' because of the myriad stories like Erick's—of people working themselves out of some of the forms of the poverty they experienced by virtue of their farming.

Dan Brockington and Christine Noe, *Understanding Long-Term Change in Rural Tanzania* In: *Prosperity in Rural Africa? Insights into Wealth, Assets, and Poverty from Longitudinal Studies in Tanzania.* Edited by: Dan Brockington and Christine Noe, Oxford University Press. DOI: 10.1093/oso/9780198865872.003.0001

The encounter with Erick and Paulina was one of hundreds that the researchers in this collection have undertaken as part of a large research project that tried to do something deceptively simple. We re-visited families who had been surveyed as part of research projects some twenty to thirty years previously and we explored what had changed in their lives since then. It is difficult work to do well, but when, as in Tanzania, there are few data available which can track change over the last three decades, then it can be useful.

Erick and Paulina's story, and the complexities and nuances which come with it, matter a good deal in a continent plagued by poor data and data gaps. If their story is repeated widely then it may require rethinking how we measure and value progressive change. Specifically, revisits such as this can provide insights into the debate on the consequences for rural poverty of economic growth and on the nature, condition, and basis of prosperity in rural Africa.

Tanzania provides an excellent lens with which to examine this issue. The country has experienced strong economic growth in recent decades (from the 1990s onwards). But it is not clear what that growth had done to rural areas, and there is sharp disagreement as to what is happening in the Tanzanian countryside. As we show in the next chapter, radical critics insist that economic growth is not benefiting rural areas. The profits of new economic change are confined to urban areas, or particular sectors (such as mining or tourism) which export most of the wealth they create. Indeed, the problem may be far worse than a simple failure to distribute the benefits of growth. Present-day capitalism, it is alleged, can actively impoverish the rural poor in Africa. Some forms of investment require land alienation and loss of the very resources upon which the rural poor depend. Other changes bring rural differentiation and class formation in villages that maintain significant deprivation.

Exultant advocates of market solutions and stronger capitalism welcome the economic revolution Tanzania has witnessed because they perceive it to be part of a broader transformation of a backwards continent. The fourth Tanzanian government under President Jakaya Kikwete in particular announced grand new policies (SAGCOT, Kilimo Kwanza, Big Results Now) that would, it believed, cut through the problems of obdurate, slow-moving, smallholder farmers and create welcome forces for change in rural areas. With the fifth government under President John Pombe Magufuli, industrialization and infrastructure development (including rural electrification) were to add impetus to the wave of rural transformation. The changes that radical critics deplore are welcomed with equal vehemence by these analysts. Moving smallholders out of agriculture and into productive labour serving capital lies at the heart of their vision of progressive change.

Erick and Paulina's story challenges both camps. Because neither the critics who decry persistent poverty despite growth, nor the progressives who seek transformation and replacement of smallholder farming, are good at seeing the welcome changes that smallholders bring to their own lives through investment in rural assets. Their story asks both sides: are they measuring the right thing? Are they looking at the changes which count to the people who matter? What does economic prosperity look like for the rural poor? What sort of changes do rural Africans, and particularly rural Tanzanians, welcome? And what are the epistemological and methodological difficulties of trying to track these changes?

The purpose of this book is to explore these questions. In the chapters that follow we consider the role of assets, the significant purchases of which Erick and Paulina were so proud, as markers of wealth and poverty in rural societies. We consider why they matter and why they may have been overlooked in current debates about rural poverty. We discuss the challenges of tracking change in assets over time, and we present twelve cases studies which have tried to do this. We glean general lessons, methodological and substantive, that others will find useful.

In the rest of this chapter we provide the key building blocks that you will need to understand this collection. First, we state our argument. Second we present the methods we used to build up the collection of case studies. Finally we provide an outline of each of the chapters in the book as a whole.

The Argument

We contend that if we are to understand poverty dynamics in rural African societies then we must examine changes to the assets that people control. We define assets broadly as things which provide revenue streams. They matter because they are the sources of income and consumption which are the more frequently used measures of poverty and prosperity. They matter also because when we talk to rural Tanzanians about what wealth and poverty means those Tanzanians tell us about assets. Assets are crucial to local perceptions of what the good life is. And assets are systematically excluded from the most commonly used measure of poverty (consumption data). The first part of our argument is that we need to pay more attention to rural people's assets.

The second part is that, in Tanzania, when we do look at assets, rural people are richer than we were expecting them to be. In case after case we have found transformations in rural people's lives as viewed through the assets they have been able to build up. If there is one general tendency that emerges from this collection it is that Erick's story is, if anything, the norm. To our surprise most of the people we revisited, in most of the places, tended to be better off than they had been, as measured by their assets.

It does not follow, however, that rural Tanzanians are in fact wealthy and not poor because of the growth in their assets. That is the third part of the argument.

Poverty and prosperity are multi-faceted. We have to look at all their dimensions. Owning a plough and a cow and building a new house—in short, improving your assets—does not necessarily make you rich. It does not mean that your children are healthier or better educated. It does not mean you will be free from hunger. The transformations we describe in this volume are inscribed in lives which also continue to experience other forms of harm and deprivation.

People are not 'really' wealthy if they have been able to invest in assets. In fact they may have been able to invest in assets despite their poverty, or even by going hungry and reducing day-to-day expenditure. Assets matter because they are important locally and have been overlooked by commonly used measures of poverty and prosperity. But documenting assets does not provide *the* answer to problems of data poverty. There can be no such single answer. Rather it behoves us to try and understand better the nature of the relationship between these different dimensions of wealth and poverty.

But given that assets are part of the story, and given that their growth has surprised most of the researchers in this collection, what might explain this apparent prosperity in assets? Here we have to be careful. It is tempting to say that the story here is that there is no story. The timing of the changes we have documented, the crops involved, the social relations, the infrastructural changes, all are different from place to place.

But in all this diversity there are some consistent common threads, which are further supported by other research across the country and broader continent, and these concern the abilities of smallholders to realize the changes that they want to achieve. Tanzanian peasants have long been dismissed in policy circles, national and international, as being dominated by subsistence practices that were slow to change, unproductive, and therefore mired in poverty. Change requires outside investors and the transfer of land and water to them. More radical commentators have been vocal in their concerns about such changes. They warn that the invasion of market forces can unleash forces of commoditization and social differentiation that will build inequality, dispossession, and disadvantage.

But we dispute both views. Smallholders are engines of growth and rural prosperity. They have seized the opportunities that new markets have afforded. This does not always result in disadvantage and want that the radical critics feared.

The final element of our argument is that the growth of markets for crops across the country has spread prosperity and locally valued change. We make this argument with caution. Longstanding cash crops have suffered price fluctuations; new high-value crops will do too. But we believe this remains the case even when we bear in mind the considerable exclusions and limits our methods present. This begs the question what broader conditions and circumstances—infrastructural changes and policy support—are conducive to bringing such rural transformations? We attend to these in the conclusion.

Methods in Longitudinal Survey Research: Exploring Assets in Tanzania

If trends in assets are an important source of information how might we study them? Long-term data sets that track change in asset ownership over time are hard to find. They require longitudinal data sets which can comprise restudies (of particular places), revisits (returning to specific people and domestic units), or panels (in which cohorts are recruited for repeated revisits to the same people or families) (Vandergeest and Rigg 2012). Panels tend to have shorter time intervals between their visits, whereas decades can elapse between revisits and restudies (Baulch and Hoddinott 2000, Dercon and Shapiro 2007, Dercon et al. 2009, Baulch 2011).

Longitudinal studies, as Burawoy (2003) observed, have to cope with four types of change (see also Kloos 1997). As well as the changes to internal dynamics and external pressures in the places studied that we have reported above, there are also changes to the researcher (on which see Ponte in the Epilogue p. 387), and the theoretical contexts in which they are thinking (Himanshu et al. 2016). Vandergeest and Rigg neatly capture how in Asian and South East Asian research theoretical foci have shifted from self-contained 'villages' to 'communities' and to larger concerns of political economy.[1] Revisits conducted now have to cope with the theoretical frames of earlier village-contained baseline surveys (Vandergeest and Rigg 2012). Similarly earlier approaches may have used concepts like 'household' in ways which hid important dynamics. As Vandergeest and Rigg put it: 'there was [in our original studies] a tendency to expect individual voices to emerge, unbidden, from the household context' (ibid.: 15).

There is a niche literature in longitudinal research that we review in the final chapter of this collection. Suffice to say here that it is a small niche, and there are surprisingly few studies of this sort in African contexts. There are more in Asia and Latin America. In the global north governments frequently sponsor large-scale panel surveys which makes the need to look for longitudinal studies less pressing.

Tanzania is not blessed with many longitudinal studies or panels. Pat Caplan's decades of engagement in Mafia island provide detailed and intimate accounts with one community using largely qualitative data (Caplan 1992, 1997). For more quantitative data there are three studies. There is the Kagera Health and Demographic Study (hereafter the Kagera study) which spans 1994 and 2004 (de Weerdt 2010, Beegle et al. 2011); the AFRINT study which covers ten villages in Iringa and Morogoro from 2002 to 2016 (Djurfeldt et al. 2011, and see Chapter 10 in this volume), and the Living Standards Measurement Survey (LSMS) data from 2008 to the present for a sample of 3,000 families (Christiaensen 2017). So the older

[1] The village frame is clearly visible in some longitudinal works—such as Epstein's (1973, and Epstein et al. 1998).

studies cover few regions (just three) and the nationally representative case is recent. Altogether they do not provide a good basis to understand the changes that have been brought by the economic growth that has persisted since the late 1980s. Stefan Dercon's call for more longer-term insights into the fortunes of rural households during periods of growth remains as relevant as ever in Tanzania (Dercon 2006).

The problem is not confined to Tanzania. The World Bank, with Gates Foundation support, are expanding panel data collection in a number of African countries. This is why the LSMS was established in Tanzania. It is already yielding some results but cannot fill historical gaps and help us to understand changes that happened in the early years of economic growth.

Moreover analyses of panel data have suffered from a problematic conceptualization of poverty. This arises where analyses focus primarily on the qualities of households and individuals, and quantitative analyses of the same, and pay less attention to the politics of poverty creation and reduction (Harris 2009). Such an approach risks seeing poverty as a condition of the poor alone. It misses its production through broader local, national, and international relations, which have, as Schaffer has observed, been a 'blindspot in applied microeconomic causal analysis' (Shaffer 2012a: 1779).

Our response to this lack of data has been to take one-off surveys conducted in the late 1980s to early 2000s and turn them into longitudinal surveys by re-surveying the same families. It is similar to methods which ask respondents to reconstruct change over time from the present (turning survey data 'upside down' as Dercon and Shapira put it, 2007: 30), except that it does not rely on those memories for its baseline. The baseline is provided by the first survey. This gives it an advantage as recall can suffer from rose-tints and inaccuracy, a risk, for all its insights, in the 'stages of progress' method (Krishna et al. 2004, Krishna 2006, Krishna 2010). We rely instead on actual observations recorded some twenty years ago.

To undertake this work we had to build up a suitable list of sites that could be revisited. We had two essential criteria. The researcher had to have first visited their study sites between 1985 and 2005, and they had to have a list of the named domestic units (aka families or households) that they had interviewed in their first survey. 1985 was the lower limit because after that problems of recall and domestic unit integrity (on which more below) make the method problematic. 2005 is the upper limit because after that there are panel data in the form of the LSMS. The list of family names was necessary because our method hinges upon re-visiting the actual families visited in the original survey in order that we can see how asset ownership changes over time.

We constructed a list of sixteen different researchers who have worked in thirteen regions, twenty-six districts, and in over seventy villages (see Figure 1.1). This is fewer than we expected to find. We had thought that there would be many more

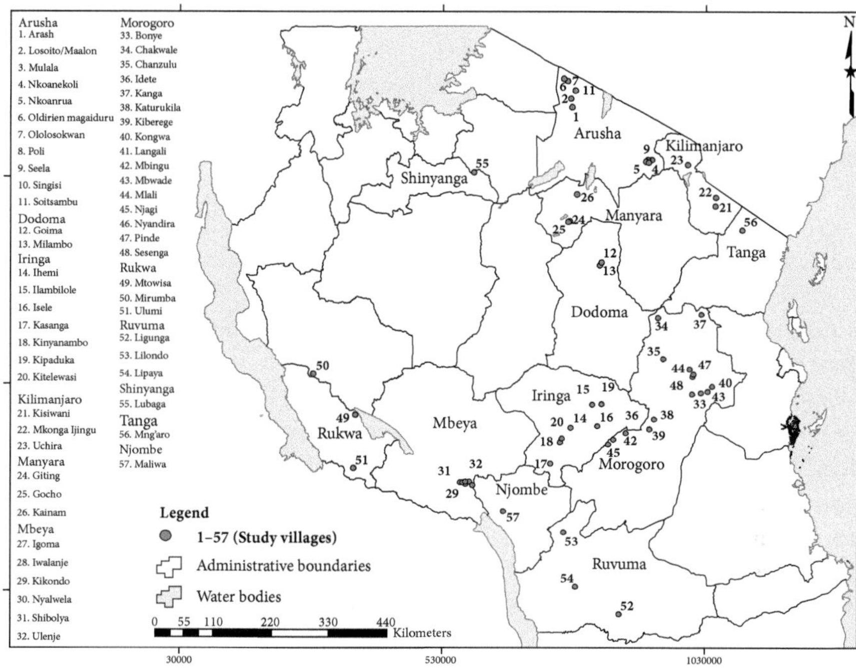

Figure 1.1 Sites identified for possible revisits.

researchers and that we would be able to select a good variety of studies to revisit. This has not been the case. There was no comprehensive list of researchers upon which to draw. COSTECH records (which provide research permission to overseas researchers) and the East Africana library (holding theses written by Tanzanians) proved less forthcoming than we had hoped. We relied on our own networks and connections and our own readings to identify the surveys we used. Fortunately the network of researchers in Tanzania is strong, and it was possible to find out about possible studies using snowballing and word of mouth enquiries.

We do not think that we have identified all possible surveys. And we have certainly not identified a nationally representative sample. There are obvious gaps here (no coastal areas, none in the south-east and far west of the country) and there is a selection bias arising from researchers' accumulated preference for sites along the main roads out of Dar es Salaam. The central eastern regions of Morogoro and Iringa are over represented. Just four of the surveys are in remoter locations: (Katherine Snyder, Vesa-Matti Loiske, Dan Brockington, and Monique Borgerhoff Mulder). Others were in remoter locations (Stefano Ponte in Songea, Esbern Friis-Hansen in Njombe) which are now more accessible.

Another disappointing aspect is that too few of the researchers who are listed here are Tanzanians. It seems that here we were confronting different cultures of research practice that made recovering the records we required to undertake the surveys unusually problematic. Northern-based researchers rarely throw away their PhD or post-doc data. These are kept in boxes and attics awaiting possible re-use. The collector's ethos is rather deeply engrained. Tanzanian researchers were more likely to have suffered lost data, sometimes inadvertently, on other occasions because it did not seem particularly important to keep it at the time. There was at least one heart-breaking story of questionnaires disposed of when they had been safely stored (because the room they were stored in was re-allocated to another use) or of data lost with stolen computers and failed back-ups.

Finally, despite the prominence of land alienation and displacement in the literature on rural Tanzania (Bluwstein et al. 2018), only one of the sites we have covered has been subject to active land loss. In this instance some villagers in Mbeya have suffered as a result of the creation of Kitulo National Park (see Chapter 14). This has had a significant impact on people's livestock keeping practices, restricting many to zero grazing. However other sites have not experienced these new restrictions. The relative absence of incidents of land loss in our work does not mean that the claims about land alienation in Tanzania are overblown or stated (on that topic please see Locher and Sulle 2014). Indeed the overlapping amalgamation of alienations (Bluwstein et al. 2018), both existing and portending are in and of themselves concerning. This gap in our work simply means that we cannot report on the consequences of that sort of change. As we hope is clear from Brockington's and Noe's other works, land loss and eviction pose extremely serious problems (Brockington 2002, Noe 2013, Kangalawe and Noe 2015, Noe and Kangalawe 2015, Olwig et al. 2015). They deserve a great deal of attention. Their absence in this volume is an accident of the case studies we were able to find, not a deliberate choice, nor a good indication of the experience of land alienation more generally.

Notwithstanding these gaps we believe that we have identified enough studies to make this collection worthwhile. Indeed the insights they afford can be wonderful. They are testimony to years of committed research. For example, Monique Borgerhoff Mulder had visited her community in Pimbwe every two years since 1995 and rigorously surveyed the entire community each time. The quality of those data sets the standard for all others. Similarly Katherine Snyder and Emmanuel Sulle's work in Kainam is one of the most intimate and engaged possible. Sulle was born and bred in Kainam, Snyder has been working there for thirty years including a number of extended stays of over one or two years for her PhD and subsequently. Both have also been collaborating continuously since. The survey they repeated was first conducted in 1994 and came at the end of five years of research work when respondents were already comfortable with the researchers and their questions. Anna Mdee is reporting from families in a village which she has been visiting since the mid-1990s, as researcher and also having married into the village. Wilhelm Östberg's work built on previous revisits prior to our own with other collaborators (Slegers and Östberg 2008, Östberg and Slegers 2010).

Similarly Agnes Andersson Djurfeldt's work (part of the AFRINT project afore mentioned) already takes the form of a panel data-set which has been surveyed three times (2002, 2008, and 2016). Again the depth of quantitative data available here will make these data a useful sounding board against which to test other findings.

But the single-visit studies are remarkable too. Friis-Hansen's re-survey entails revisiting families with whom he worked in the mid-1980s when there were high levels of poverty and deprivation. He had already begun revisiting these families before we contacted him. Brockington's work in Rukwa entailed a survey of over four hundred households from one village, Mtowisa B (and nearly as many from its immediate neighbour, Mtowisa A). Cosmas Sokoni was re-visiting villages where he was both raised and studied for his PhD.

Finally there is the case of the Rolf Larson's survey from Meru, whose work is being followed up posthumously by Christine Noe. This story is hard to tell and is best expressed in the words of Christine's blog:

> The research reported here is unusual for a couple of reasons. First, the original work was undertaken by the late Rolf Larson in the mid-1990s. I am, in some ways, following in his footsteps, and how I have come to do so is a moving and difficult story. Rolf was killed in a road accident in Tanzania in 2004, on his way to revisit Meru and the sites of his original research. He had kept his data in meticulous order, however, and a chance encounter with his former colleagues has meant that I have been able to access it and use it. I am [we are] very grateful to Rolf and Göran Djurfeldt for making this possible.
>
> The second is that, in other ways, Rolf was walking where I had trod when he did his research. Unlike most researchers in this livelihood change project, the work in Meru is a return to my homeland, the place where I was born and grew up. I was born in Poli-Ndatu village and studied at Makumira primary and secondary school for thirteen years. My village is among the nine villages that Rolf Larson studied in 1994/1998. Part of my excitement with this project is that I am so well placed to contribute to the interpretation of change in Meru due to my personal experience, the local network, language fluency and connection to the landscape.[2]

In fact the technique we used, of building a network of federated studies each exploring slightly different aspects of change, proved to be one of the joys of the project. It brought together people with decades of experience living and working in the country and all with similar interests in rural economic and livelihood

[2] http://livelihoodchangeta.wixsite.com/tanzania/single-post/2016/06/20/Coffee-BreakPotentials-and-Pitfalls-for-Meru-Farmers-Prosperity visited 15/12/16.

change. The researchers involved in this project have met twice to discuss findings and progress and present their work. We have also shared findings with government officials, multilateral institutions, and NGO staff in two stakeholder workshops in 2017 and 2018. The work in this collection is therefore the collective product of decades of engagement by numerous people, some of whom have been working in the country all their lives, others all their professional lives, and many of whom have enjoyed lasting relationships with the places they have studied and know as home. It is also the result of a comparative engagement with each other's work and experience. The Epilogue to this book presents a recorded discussion of what it was like for us as individuals to undertake that work.

Through this network of researchers, and others who contributed their data (such as Fred Ellis and Ntengua Mdoe) we covered thirty-seven villages (see Figure 1.2 and Table 1.1). Our work used a mixture of quantitative and qualitative methods building on our own experience, and others (Lawson et al. 2003, Adato et al. 2007, Howe and McKay 2007, de Weerdt 2010, Shaffer 2012b, Muyanga et al. 2013). For each visit we undertook focus groups to discuss the meaning of wealth, and its changes over time. We met with key informants and government officials to talk about the changing history of the village, and wherever possible we used ranking exercises to explore the distribution of wealth in each village. We then revisited all the domestic units that we could find from the original surveys (the highest attrition rate was 40 per cent, 10–20 per cent was more normal). Finally, wherever possible, we returned to the villages after our work to discuss findings with them.

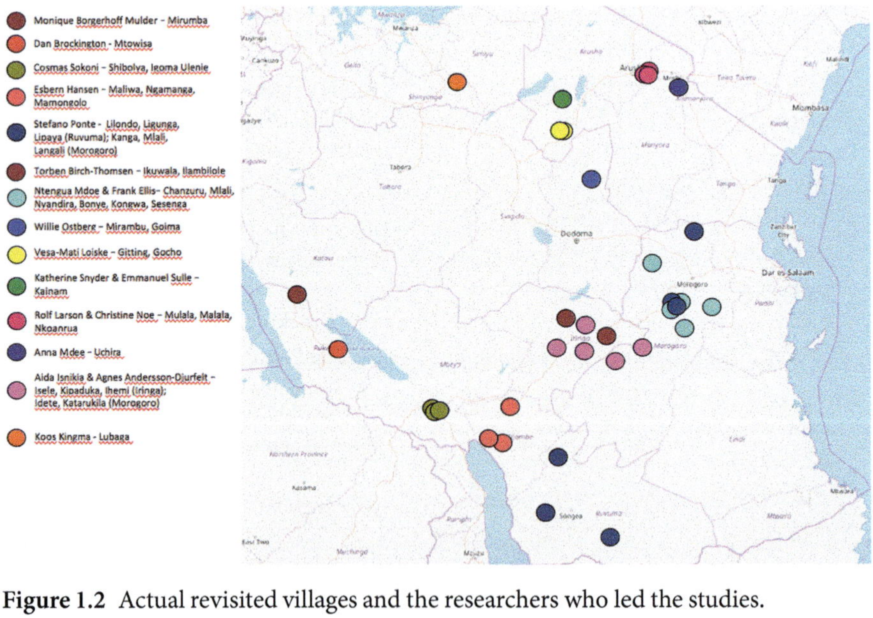

Figure 1.2 Actual revisited villages and the researchers who led the studies.

Table 1.1 List of study sites re-visited

Region	District	Village	Researcher	Sample size
Arusha	Arumeru	Malala	Christine Noe/Rolf Larsson	54
		Mulala	Christine Noe/Rolf Larsson	57
		Nkoanrua	Christine Noe/Rolf Larsson	50
Dodoma	Chemba	Goima	Wilhelm Östberg	34
		Mirambu	Wilhelm Östberg	41
Iringa	Iringa Rural	Ilambilole	Torben Birch-Thomsen	21
		Ihemi	Agnes Andersson Djurfeldt	27
	Kilolo	Ikuwala	Torben Birch-Thomsen	26
		Isele	Agnes Andersson Djurfeldt	26
		Kipaduka	Agnes Andersson Djurfeldt	21
Katavi	Mlele	Mirumba	Monique Borgerhoff Mulder	267
Kilimanjaro	Moshi Rural	Uchira	Anna Mdee	15
		Koresa	Anna Mdee	15
Manyara	Hanang	Gitting	Vesa-Matti Loiske	40
		Gocho	Vesa-Matti Loiske	36
	Mbulu	Kainam	Katherine Snyder	180
Mbeya	Mbeya Rural	Igoma	Cosmas Sokoni	21
		Shibolya	Cosmas Sokoni	25
		Ulenje	Cosmas Sokoni	21
Morogoro	Kilosa	Chanzuru	Fred Ellis, Ntengua Mdoe	67
	Morogoro Rural	Bonye	Fred Ellis, Ntengua Mdoe	27
		Kongwa	Fred Ellis, Ntengua Mdoe	27
		Sesenga	Fred Ellis, Ntengua Mdoe	27
	Mvomero	Kanga	Stefano Ponte	13
		Langali	Stefano Ponte	13
		Mlali	Stefano Ponte/Fred Ellis, Ntengua Mdoe	32
		Nyandira	Fred Ellis, Ntengua Mdoe	30
	Kilombero	Idete	Agnes Andersson Djurfeldt	36
		Katarukila	Agnes Andersson Djurfeldt	41
Njombe	Makete	Maliwa	Esbern Friis-Hansen	12
	Njombe	Ngamanga	Esbern Friis-Hansen	18
	Njombe Rural	Mamongolo	Esbern Friis-Hansen	16
Rukwa	Sumbawanga	Mtowisa B	Dan Brockington	64
Ruvuma	Madaba	Lilondo	Stefano Ponte	15
	Namtumbo	Ligunga	Stefano Ponte	18
	Songea Rural	Lipaya	Stefano Ponte	17
Shinyanga	Kishapu	Lubaga	Koos Kingma	10
Totals				
Regions	Districts	Villages	Researchers	Domestic Units
12	21	37	16	1460

The Organization of This Book and How to Use It

Assembling this book has been something of a challenge because it comprises many voices. We have tried to write this such that each chapter is comprehensible on its own, without reading all the others. This is necessary because few people will read the book all the way through. Many will just study individual chapters. We have tried to make that easier for readers.

At the same time this also means that there will be an element of repetition across some of the chapters. In order to stand alone each chapter is anchored in particular research debates, and sometimes these have overlapped across different chapters. This can happen across Chapters 5 to 16 in which we dwell on different case studies. Where they find that to be the case, readers are advised to concentrate on the methodological and substantive findings which are unique to each chapter.

However we have ensured that there is no overlap in the introductory chapters and final conclusion which frame and conclude these case studies. Chapters 2 to 4 examine substantive and methodological debates that surround assets—the touchstone of this collection. Chapter seventeen presents our substantive conclusions on that topic. Readers who have time to dip into more than one chapter are advised to attempt these chapters before they explore the case studies.

Finally some readers will appreciate the Epilogue which explains candidly what it was like actually to do the research which lead to the different case studies. In case that is difficult to read all the way through, we have explained which pages of the Epilogue match to which chapter.

To guide readers through the different chapters they may wish to explore we present here a summary of all the chapters. The chapters in Part 1 examine more carefully the key concepts and methods on which this collection is built. In Chapter 2 Dan Brockington and Christine Noe consider the importance of assets as markers of wealth and poverty in rural economies. They summarize findings which show why assets are so important for understanding poor rural societies and explain why they may have been overlooked in current data and debates about economic and social change in many African countries.

Chapter 3 examines one particular aspect of assets in more detail—the question of asset indices, and how they fit empirically with the geographically variable prioritization of different assets across Tanzania. Using data from focus groups Olivia Howland, Christine Noe, and Dan Brockington consider how assets were actually reported to matter as notions of wealth and poverty vary across different parts of Tanzania. The authors compare these findings, from different villages and for men and women and charts the common ground and differences. The collection of villages on which this work draws were largely agricultural—it missed fishing villages and more pastoral villages. But despite that similarity this comparison of different grounded notions of wealth and poverty produces considerably different definitions and interpretations of prosperity in different parts of the country. It also produces a different list of meaningful items from that normally found in the shorter asset indices usually used to determine wealth in large samples.

The challenge of identifying and tracking 'domestic units' required for our methods is not trivial. We used domestic units because many of the assets described here (land, houses, livestock) are effectively owned and managed by social units larger than individuals. Their benefits, or the problems of their loss, are experienced collectively, if not equally. However, it is well established, but inadequately recognized, that domestic units contain and can obscure considerable inequalities, power struggles and differences between intersections that include gender and age. These can be fundamental to understanding the nature and reproduction of poverty and prosperity. This issue is compounded in longitudinal research because domestic units are not static entities. Their membership, location, activities, and both internal and external power relations can change substantially and rapidly. In Chapter 4 Dan Brockington, Ernestina Coast, Anna Mdee, Olivia Howland, and Sara Randall explores the challenges of using assets to understand dynamics of poverty and prosperity within and across domestic units over time. They argue that in some respects changes in assets cannot be attributed to individuals alone—they belong to, distribute benefits to, and are managed by domestic units. But this introduces a number of interesting challenges with respect to the difficulties of tracking changes to those domestic units over time, and changes to the assets in these domestic units. This chapter explores the circumstances through which change to assets could be tracked over time through longitudinal studies of domestic units.

The second part of the book then presents the different case studies. In Chapter 5 Monique Borgerhoff Mulder presents her extraordinary work from Mirumba, in **Katavi** Region. Monique visited this village seven times over a fifteen-year period and conducted a full village census every time. It is in terms of its quantitative data, as well as many of its other insights, the most authoritative longitudinal study of which we are aware. Moreover Monique first began working in Tanzania since 1979. Mirumba is but one of several long-term engagements she has had with different parts of the country. One of the advantages of her approach is that, despite working in a poor village with high rates of migration, family breakdown and divorce, she is able to trace change in highly unstable social environments. She shows clearly that there has been a significant improvement in different types of asset for most domestic units. She also shows that improvement in assets is, in this instance, well correlated with other measures of well-being, such as farm productivity, decreased stress, education, and health. She also shows that significant levels of poverty remain.

Chapter 6 presents the work of Emmanuel Sulle and Katherine Snyder on Kainam, in **Manyara** Region. This village was remote and isolated. It was quite self-sufficient and known for its productivity, but it was cut off from the rest of the country. Now it is much more thoroughly integrated into the rest of the economy, and in many ways, as measured by local indices, villagers appear wealthier. But all this new wealth, and all the assets associated with it, also bring unwelcome change in social practices and social cohesion which means that people do not feel richer.

Christine Noe, Olivia Howland, and Dan Brockington in Chapter 7 take up the case of Meru villagers, close to Arusha town and in **Arusha** Region, who grew rich on coffee from the 1950s onwards—and on male control of female labour to produce it. The demise of coffee from the 1990s and rise of market gardening and urban employment opportunities is welcomed by women and sustains new forms of prosperity and new meanings of wealth. The result is an interesting tale of villagers who have, in many respects, lost assets (they farm less and they have fewer cows); however the returns on their farming, and the things that they count as wealth, have changed too, and the results may be livelihoods that are more empowering for women than was previously the case.

Dan Brockington's work in Mtowisa in **Rukwa** Region began in 1999–2000 and features in Chapter 8. His work explores a boost to local economies caused by sesame seed price rises which have transformed the appearance of the village and the lives of sesame farmers. At the same time the closing of the land frontier means no new farms are easily available, which heralds much greater inequality. Part of the value of this contribution is that it is based on a full census survey that was undertaken in late 2000 (n > 400), this presents a more complete picture of the changes in subsequent years.

Chapters 9 and 10 bring out some of the sharpest contrasts in these case studies. Wilhelm Östberg and Joseph Mduma's work in **Dodoma** Region in Chapter 9 demonstrates the benefits, but also dangers, of expanding agricultural activity through extensification. In the mid-1990s he worked in two remote communities characterized by small farms, long fallows, and abundant land and forests. Now he has found much wealthier families, much improved infrastructure, and substantially reduced forests. Families appear wealthier due to increased inequality (because newly wealthy entrepreneurs and philanthropists are improving village infrastructure and equipment), transformed national infrastructure (roads and buses), and better crop prices. There has also been dramatic decline in forest cover.

But all this is the obverse of Vesa-Matti Loiske's findings in Chapter 10 from Gitting and Gocho in **Manyara** Region. He also found much improved living standards, by local measures of wealth, but this has occurred in the absence of any locally available land to distribute, because of increasing equality, which has reduced oppressive practices by local big men and without any change in national infrastructure provision. The one common denominator with Chapter 9 is that improved crop prices seem to have driven the higher returns to farming activity that underpin asset acquisition.

Chapter 11 reports findings from the AFRINT dataset (Djurfeldt et al. 2011, Andersson Djurfeldt et al. 2018) which has built up a longitudinal dataset across six countries with three visits between 2002 and 2017. The findings and insights possible from this dataset are remarkably rich. In this chapter Agnes Andersson Djurfeldt, Ellen Hillbom, and Elibariki Msuya examine two villages in Kilombero District, **Morogoro** Region, which have been transformed by improvements in rice irrigation. It examines the driving forces of these changes, locating them within current theories of change to irrigation practices. The authors argue that smallholder farmers have been responding to price improvements nationally and have been facilitated by improving technology and extension services. They also note that the transformations in rice cultivation were fuelling a strong demand to rent land, and that this was benefitting women who were able to keep the revenues from lands they rented, but less able to control income from family farms.

In Chapter 12 we return to Stefano Ponte's work in **Morogoro** which he first began in 1996. That research formed the basis of a series of substantial contributions to our understanding of rural economies through his publications on farmers and markets and on rural value chains. We have been able to revisit these study sites, and combine these findings with others from neighbouring villages (surveyed in the LADDER project). We show that, despite earlier published fears of agricultural involution, pathways to prosperity (in terms of assets) do exist, which are sufficiently inclusive to produce proportionately larger middle groups of relatively wealthy villagers, with the poor being relatively few. On the basis of this work the authors chart different livelihood trajectories which characterize the transformations in these regions.

Chapter 13 reports changes in the longest-running study of all, led by Esbern Friis-Hansen. Friis-Hansen's work is the longest study as he first began his research in these villages in the mid-1980s. It is also a story of the greatest transformation as he encountered extreme levels of poverty when he first arrived, and is now recording landscapes and societies which have become wealthy through emigration and tree planting. Villagers in **Njombe** Region were desperately poor in the mid-1980s with even clothing scarce. Many emigrated and found prosperity elsewhere, sending money home. Those who have remained have become remarkably wealthy from the trees they have planted. The changes derive in the first instance from rural transformation—services and income from remittances improved the welfare of residents. Only later did agricultural transformation, driven by potatoes and trees, bring the substantial increases in wealth he found.

Cosmas Sokoni conducted his PhD in 1999 visiting six villages in **Mbeya** Region, where he himself grew up as a child. His family remains there. In

Chapter 14 Cosmas Sokoni and Verdiana Tilumanywa report on the findings of revisits to three of these villages. The story is mixed in that there are signs of increasing wealth in the form of housing quality. There are more opportunities to take part in the growing urban economy of nearby Mbeya town, and there are changes to the cash crops from which people have grown wealthy. However people in this area are also constrained by the decreasing availability of land due the presence of forest reserves, forestry plantations, and the national park. Farm sizes are smaller than before and there are signs that poorer families are being squeezed out of farming lifestyles.

We present further research from the south of Tanzania in which draws on Torben Birch-Thomsen and Esbern Friis-Hansen's decades of work in **Iringa**. Chapter 15 shows how, despite a closing land frontier, improved infrastructure and opportunities to develop cash crops for urban markets have benefitted farmers with the social and economic capital to invest in these new crops. These requirements exclude other families from joining and so creates new divisions of wealth and poverty.

Anna Mdee's work in Chapter 16 is one of several in this collection which provides a mixture of professional engagement with personal insight. She has been associated with Uchira village (**Kilimanjaro** Region) since the mid-1990s in the form of various research projects. But she also married into the village, into the family of the then village chairman which has enhanced her understanding of the place. This case study is also important because it bucks the trend in the rest of the study. People are not richer in Uchira; there has been stasis and decline. The local economy has suffered from adverse climate and a collapsed cattle economy. There is money coming into the village from people seeking to buy now expensive plots of land. Uchira is close to the growing town of Moshi and its reliable water supplies and good connections to the town make it suitable for rich urbanites. But this injection of wealth is patchy and episodic and does not benefit the large groups of people in the ways that we have seen in other study sites.

Chapter 17 concludes the book. In this chapter the editors draw together the experience of the case studies to consider what they collectively imply for our understanding of rural economies, and what their implications are for current debates about land grabs, investment and smallholder farming, and policies pertaining to them. We consider here the surprises of this work, and why they should exist, and what generalizable lessons we can draw from this analysis

Finally, at our writing workshops that have created this collection we recorded discussions of our own fieldwork experiences, our understanding of what we learned, and the effect it had on our lives. In the Epilogue we present an edited transcript of those discussions. This is a crucial element of the book. It shows, pretty much warts and all, what doing this work was like and how we have struggled, and thrived on it.

References

Adato, M., F. Lund, and P. Mhlongo (2007). 'Methodological Innovations in Research on the Dynamics of Poverty: A Longitudinal Study in KwaZulu-Natal, South Africa.' *World Development* 35(2): 247–63.

Andersson Djurfeldt, A., F. M. Dzanku, and A. C. Isinika (2018). *Agriculture, Diversification and Gender in Rural Africa: Longitudinal Perspectives from Six Countries*. Oxford, Oxford University Press.

Baulch, B. (2011). *Why Poverty Persists: Poverty Dynamics in Asia and Africa.* Cheltenham, Edward Elgar.

Baulch, B. and J. Hoddinott (2000). 'Economic Mobility and Poverty Dynamics in Developing Countries.' *The Journal of Development Studies* 36(6): 1–24.

Beegle, K., J. De Weerdt, and S. Dercon (2011). 'Migration and Economic Mobility in Tanzania: Evidence from a Tracking Survey.' *The Review of Economics and Statistics* 93(3): 1010–33.

Bluwstein, J., J. F. Lund, K. Askew, H. Stein, C. Noe, R. Odgaard, F. Maganga, and L. Engström (2018). 'Between Dependence and Deprivation: The Interlocking Nature of Land Alienation in Tanzania.' *Journal of Agrarian Change* 18: 806–30.

Brockington, D. (2002). *Fortress Conservation: The Preservation of the Mkomazi Game Reserve, Tanzania.* Oxford, James Currey.

Burawoy, M. (2003). 'Revisits: An Outline of a Theory of Reflexive Ethnography.' *American Sociological Review* 68 (October): 645–79.

Caplan, P. (1992). 'Socialism from Above: The View from Below.' *The Tanzanian Peasantry: Economy in Crisis*. P. G. Forster and S. Maghimbi. Aldershot, Avebury: 103–23.

Caplan, P. (1997). *African Voices, African Lives: Personal Narratives from a Swahili Village.* Abingdon, Routledge.

Christiaensen, L. (2017). 'Agriculture in Africa—Telling Myths from Facts: A Synthesis.' *Food Policy* 67: 1–11.

de Weerdt, J. (2010). 'Moving out of Poverty in Tanzania: Evidence from Kagera.' *The Journal of Development Studies* 46(2): 331–49.

Dercon, S. (2006). 'Economic Reform, Growth and the Poor: Evidence from Rural Ethiopia.' *Journal of Development Economics* 81: 1–24.

Dercon, S., D. O. Gilligan, J. Hoddinott, and T. Woldehanna (2009). 'The Impact of Agricultural Extension and Roads on Poverty and Consumption Growth in Fifteen Ethiopian Villages.' *American Journal of Agricultural Economics* 91(4): 1007–21.

Dercon, S. and J. Shapiro (2007). 'Moving On, Staying Behind, Getting Lost: Lessons on Poverty Mobility from Longitudinal Data.' Global Poverty Research Group GPRG-WPS-075.

Djurfeldt, G., E. Aryeetey, and A. C. Isinika (2011). *African Smallholders: Food Crops, Markets and Policy*. Wallingford, CABI.

Epstein, S. (1973). *South India: Yesterday, Today and Tomorrow. Mysore Villages Revisited.* London, Macmillan.

Epstein, S., A. P. Suryanarayana, and T. Thimmegowda (1998). *Village Voices: Forty Years of Rural Transformation in South India*. London, Sage.

Harris, J. (2009). 'Bringing Politics Back into Poverty Analysis: Why Understandings of Social Relations Matters More for Policy on Chronic Poverty than Measurement.' *Poverty Dynamics: Interdisciplinary Perspectives.* T. Addison, D. Hulme, and R. Kanbur. Oxford, Oxford University Press: 205–24.

Himanshu, P. Jha and G. Rodgers (2016). 'Introduction.' *The Changing Village in India: Insights from Longitudinal Research.* P. Jha Himanshu and G. Rodgers. Oxford, Oxford University Press: 1–19.

Howe, G. and A. McKay (2007). 'Combining Quantitative and Qualitative Methods in Assessing Chronic Poverty: The Case of Rwanda.' *World Development* 35(2): 197–211.

Kangalawe, R. Y. M. and C. Noe (2015). 'Biodiversity Conservation and Poverty Alleviation in Namtumbo District, Tanzania.' *Agriculture, Ecosystems & Environment* 162: 90–100.

Kloos, P. (1997). 'Restudies in Anthropology: Modalities, Limitations and Alternatives.' *The Village in Asia Revisited.* J. Breman, P. Kloos, and A. Saith. New Delhi, Oxford University Press: 229–46.

Krishna, A. (2006). 'Pathways out of and into Poverty in 36 Villages of Andhra Pradesh, India.' *World Development* 34(2): 271–88.

Krishna, A. (2010). *One Illness Away: Why People Become Poor and How They Escape Poverty*. Oxford, Oxford University Press.

Krishna, A., P. Kristjanson, M. Radeny, and W. Nindo (2004). 'Escaping Poverty and Becoming Poor in Twenty Kenyan Villages.' *Journal of Human Development* 5(2): 211–26.

Lawson, D., A. McKay, and J. Okidi (2003). 'Poverty Persistence and Transitions in Uganda: A Combined Qualitative and Quantitative Analysis.' Working Paper 38. University of Manchester, Chronic Poverty Research Centre.

Locher, M. and E. Sulle (2014). 'Challenges and Methodological Flaws in Reporting the Global Land Rush: Observations from Tanzania.' *Journal of Peasant Studies* 41(4): 569–92.

Muyanga, M., T. S. Jayne, and W. J. Burke (2013). 'Pathways into and out of Poverty: A Study of Rural Household Wealth Dynamics in Kenya.' *Journal of Development Studies* 49(10): 1358–74.

Noe, C. (2013). 'Contesting Village Land: Uranium and Sport Hunting in Mbarang'andu Wildlife Management Area, Tanzania.' *Utafiti* 10(1): 19–39.

Noe, C. and R. Y. M. Kangalawe (2015). 'Wildlife Protection, Community Participation in Conservation, and (Dis) Empowerment in Southern Tanzania.' *Conservation and Society* 13(3): 244–53.

Olwig, M. F., C. Noe, R. Kangalawe, and E. Luoga (2015). 'Inverting the Moral Economy: The Case of Land Acquisitions for Forest Plantations in Tanzania.' *Third World Quarterly* 36(12): 2316–36.

Östberg, W. and M. F. W. Slegers (2010). 'Losing Faith in the Land: Changing Environmental Perceptions in Burunge Country, Tanzania.' *Journal of Eastern African Studies* 4(2): 247–65.

Shaffer, P. (2012a). 'Post-development and Poverty: An Assessment.' *Third World Quarterly* 33(10): 1767–82.

Shaffer, P. (2012b). 'Ten Years of "Q-Squared": Implications for Understanding and Explaining Poverty.' *World Development* 45: 269–85.

Slegers, M. F. W. and W. Östberg (2008). 'The Strength of the Land and the Missing Rains: Environmental Change in Goima, Tanzania, and Farmers' Growing Concerns.' *Exploring Farmers' Perceptions of Drought in Tanzania and Ethiopia.* M. F. W. Slegers. Wageningen, Wageningen University: Erosion and Soil & Water Conservation Group: 129–50.

Vandergeest, P. and J. Rigg (2012). 'The Restudy "Problem" and Agrarian Change: Revisiting Rural Places in Southeast Asia.' *Revisiting Rural Places: Pathways to Poverty and Prosperity in Southeast Asia.* J. Rigg and P. Vandergeest. Singapore, Singapore University Press and Hawaii University Press: 1–24.

PART I

THE ROLE OF ASSETS IN UNDERSTANDING SOCIAL CHANGE IN RURAL TANZANIA

Theoretical and Methodological Reflections

2
Assets, Prosperity, and Data in Rural Africa

Dan Brockington and Christine Noe

Is economic growth good or bad for prosperity? The question is not crazy. Economic growth is calculated by measuring change to GDP, a number which we know does not capture really important aspects of our lives. In fact, worse still, it counts as progress things that harm us (Stiglitz et al. 2010, Fioramonti 2017). GDP puts together all the unwelcome economic activity (expensive medical procedures following accidents, rebuilding homes and businesses after fires and disasters, pollution clean-ups, insurance claims) and all the welcome activity (organic vegetable markets, toy shops, universities, sales at co-operative art galleries) and counts them all as one thing. If all the toy shops, co-operatives, and organic vegetable markets burned down and were replaced by casinos, plastic factories, and chemical waste depots, then disastrous as these would be for their customers and owners, it would make a great contribution to GDP.

The evidence is fairly clear that many forms of poverty decline with economic growth. But we are not interested in this book in just poverty reduction. We are concerned with well-being and prosperity. And the relationship between these and economic growth is much more opaque.

Moreover even if we were certain that larger economies might be able to generate more prosperity it is not at all clear how we get there. Do we invest in the livelihoods that people currently pursue, even if they are lowly, unproductive forms of agriculture? Or do we encourage a shift to more productive sectors of the economy? This could entail violence and dislocation, if, for example, the more productive sectors require land and resources currently occupied by less productive peasants. Where there is economic growth in poor countries does it generate beneficial change for those who need it most? And how are we to measure this progress (or regress)?

These debates are at the core of this book. In trying to understand what has happened using retrospective longitudinal research we ask fundamental questions about the nature and measurement of welcome change. In this chapter we tackle these questions. We outline a vigorous debate about the nature of economic change in rural African economies and whether or not it benefits rural Africans. We consider if indeed economic growth could depend on their displacement. Then we question the type of data that have been used to sustain those arguments.

Dan Brockington and Christine Noe, *Assets, Prosperity, and Data in Rural Africa* In: *Prosperity in Rural Africa? Insights into Wealth, Assets, and Poverty from Longitudinal Studies in Tanzania.* Edited by: Dan Brockington and Christine Noe, Oxford University Press. © Dan Brockington and Christine Noe 2021. DOI: 10.1093/oso/9780198865872.003.0002

We suggest that analysts on both sides of the argument may in fact be looking at the wrong thing. This is because the data which they are using does not count the forms of wealth—assets—which matter a great deal to rural Tanzanians. We explain, using case studies and economic theory, why we need to pay more attention to assets when trying to understand rural change.

Transforming Africa or Leaving Rural Areas Behind?

Rapid economic growth is transforming many African economies (Radelet 2010). Sustained high rates of growth (despite downturns and austerity elsewhere in the world), macro-economic stability, relatively low inflation, and growing investment and infrastructural development are seeing numerous countries become more prosperous. Some observers are celebrating a rising continent that will be known for its growth, peace, and stability (Chuhan-Pole and Angwafo 2011). Jayne and colleagues have recently described a general economic transformation of numerous (but not all) poor African countries that is built on increased rural productivity and associated prosperity (Jayne et al. 2018).

These trends are exemplified in Tanzania. Observers are quick to praise Tanzania's economic success over the last twenty years (Edwards 2014, Adam et al. 2017). According to Edwards, in Nyerere's last years in power, the country was suffering from stagnant agriculture and manufacturing, productivity in 'free fall', and a 'sky-rocketing' trade deficit (Edwards 2014: 81). The broad social vision that drove his policies (such as free universal primary education) were suffering from a basic absence of state funds. Since then, with reforms and structural adjustment, the economy has been transformed. Nord and colleagues summarize the changes as a 'remarkable turnaround', compared to the want and scarcity that characterized the country in the 1980s. Now there is low inflation, a 'buoyant' economy which has averaged 7 per cent annual growth and real per capita income has risen 50 per cent (Nord et al. 2009: 1). Robinson and colleagues describe a period of accelerated growth since 1996 that has seen macro-economic stability and increased public spending (Robinson et al. 2011). Arndt and colleagues found that indices of education, shelter, and water provision had improved in Tanzania from 1990 (Arndt et al. 2017). As we were working on the final version of this book, Tanzania was deemed by the World Bank to have become a lower-middle income country, graduating from its low income status five years ahead of expectations.[1]

Is all this growth inclusive and pro-poor? This is less obvious (Barrett 2011). Robinson and colleagues note that agriculture has not really contributed to

[1] https://blogs.worldbank.org/africacan/what-does-tanzanias-move-lower-middle-income-status-mean. Viewed 21 October 2020.

economic growth, which is a 'cause of concern' given that agriculture is the economic mainstay of rural areas where most people, and most of the country's poor people, live (Robinson et al. 2011: 26–7). Globally agriculture appears to be one of the best ways of reducing poverty among the poorest of the rural poor (Christiaensen et al. 2011). But in several African countries agricultural growth is not correlated with poverty reduction (Jayne et al. 2018). Far deeper change appears to be necessary to reduce poverty (Barrett et al. 2017).

For the most severe critics, the deprivation in rural areas despite years of economic growth is particularly damning. Mashindano and colleagues compared change in poverty statistics using Household Budget Survey data with GDP growth data. They conclude that there has been substantial economic growth, but that this growth has not reached the poor; if anything it has passed them by (Mashindano et al. 2013: 126). They suggest that:

> [i]n Tanzania the critical question is why has rapid growth in Tanzania not been accompanied by a corresponding fall in poverty? Why have the numbers of impoverished risen? (Mashindano and Shepherd 2013: 3)

The gap is particularly stark after 2000 when GDP growth outstripped population growth considerably, but was not matched by a commensurate fall in rural poverty. Edwards, using the same data, notes that poverty decline has been far slower in Tanzania than in other countries (Edwards 2014: 251). Arndt and colleagues also observe that the growth in GDP from 1990 to 2007, but a slow decline in poverty over the same period, was a conundrum (Arndt et al. 2017). The indications are that most households (and particularly most rural households) were not benefitting from the continued economic growth that the country was experiencing in this period.

The poor performance of agriculture, which has not seen significant increases in productivity, and the consequent inability of smallholders to get wealthier in appreciable numbers, is particularly sobering. This reflects low productivity of smallholders in absolute terms—they cannot produce enough to feed themselves, let alone prosper (Jayne et al. 2010, Bryngelsson et al. 2012). Analyses of the 2007 Household Budget Survey data reported signs that agricultural livelihoods are proving particularly unprofitable (Hoogeveen and Ruhinduka 2009). These analyses suggest that Tanzanians were diversifying out of agriculture in order to improve their wealth, and investment in agricultural assets (livestock, ploughs, and hoes) declined between 2001 and 2007. Indeed the analysts go so far as to state that 'it is difficult to make a decent living out of agriculture' (ibid.: 29).

Further there are signs that social dynamics in rural areas can enhance poverty. Some studies point to increased inequality and poverty as rural labour markets and land and resource poverty fuel differentiation within villages (Mueller 2011, Greco 2015). Studies of changes to land-holdings at the national scale suggest a slow insidious growth of larger farms at the expense of smaller farms, with wealthy urbanites purchasing increasing amounts of land and a growth in landless rural families (Jayne et al. 2016).

More recent waves of the Household Budget Survey suggest that there has been a reduction of poverty in recent years (between 2007 and 2011), and that growth has become more inclusive (World Bank 2015). But poverty remained concentrated in rural areas. Rural areas held 68 per cent of the population, but 84 per cent of the poor (World Bank 2015). That had barely declined (to 81 per cent) in the most recent surveys for 2017–18 (URT 2019).

However even if there has been an improvement in rural wealth after 2007, that cannot explain the persistent rural poverty, despite strong economic growth, before that year. The poor connectivity between national economic growth and rural poverty remains a conundrum. For around two decades since 1990, Tanzania's economic growth appears not to have been sufficiently inclusive, and substantial parts of the population, especially in rural areas do not appear to be getting richer in proportion to economic growth (Figure 2.1). Many Tanzanians have only been able to enjoy their country's growing prosperity vicariously.

There are several different perspectives on the reasons for such persistent rural poverty. For some observers this simply reflects the fact that smallholders are just unproductive compared to other sectors of the economy. Economic growth hinges on adding value through investment and labour. If the labour is wielding hand hoes, and land owners are too poor to buy fertilizer, then such a sector cannot produce enough to generate meaningful economic change. Bluntly put, peasants are backward. The best way to obtain economic growth is for people to leave agriculture and find employment in other sectors. This view is most effectively expressed in Paul Collier's and Stefan Dercon's writings (Collier and Dercon 2014, Dercon and Gollin 2014).

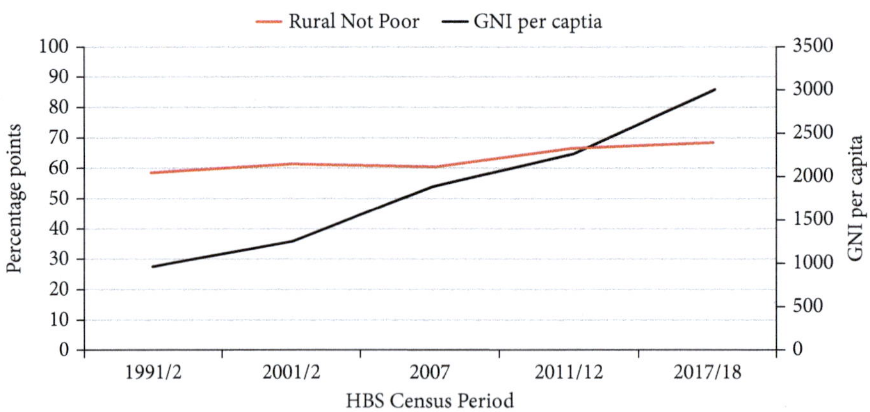

Figure 2.1 Key trends in GNI and poverty in Tanzania.

Others profoundly oppose this thinking. For some this view is just wrong-headed because it does not appreciate the value of rural livelihoods and lifeways for rural people. Pauline Peters captures this best:

> The villagers in southern Malawi where I've lived and researched for many years…express satisfaction in work well done on the land—a fine field of maize or pigeon peas, a good tobacco harvest for sale, fat goats and laying chickens, a healthy stand of trees for fruit and timber, well-brewed sorghum beer—these are appreciated not only as material goods but as aesthetic and cultural values to be cherished. (Peters 2013: 556)

For others the key constraint is not peasant productivity, but peasant poverty. Peasants cannot gain from their productivity because of the way surplus is extracted from them. This view underpins Shivji's following remarks:

> In spite of the low rate of surplus, the peasant is subjected to a high degree of exploitation. How is this possible? It is possible only because exploitation digs into the necessary consumption of the peasant. The peasant yields to capital not only surplus labour, but part of his necessary labour as well by depressing his requirements to a subhuman level. It is through superhuman labour and subhuman existence that the peasantry satisfies the rapacious demands of capital. Peasants wear rags; eat the coarsest kind of food, forego education and medical care and put the whole family, men, women and children, to work to satisfy the insatiable greed of imperialism and its local allies…. Since the surplus is sizeable there is very little accumulation in agriculture…. What is preserved and reproduced, therefore, is an impoverished, starving middle and poorer peasantry which forms the backbone of agricultural production and the source of surplus for capital. (Shivji 1992: 129, 143)

In the field of peasant studies the persistent problem of peasant poverty has been a leitmotif for decades. The question has two dimensions—why are peasants poor, and why do they persist in their poverty? For many of these critics the answers to both in African contexts hinge on the invasions and depredations of capital, historic and contemporary (Rodney 1972, Bond 2006, Wuyts 2008). They see land loss and insecurity in rural areas as driving immiseration and increasing poverty. Rural poverty may be enhanced *because* of the growth strategies being advocated by mainstream economists (Borras et al. 2011, Gardner 2012). A number of authors have argued that rural populations are suffering as a result of diverse forms of dispossession, primitive accumulation, and forms of rural differentiation and growing inequality that happen when overseas investment hits the ground (Hall 2011, Scoones et al. 2013, Wolford et al. 2013, Ansoms and Hilhorst 2014, Greco 2015, Hall et al. 2015, Hall et al. 2017).

Specifically in Tanzania problems of land alienation are marked. Green grabs for wildlife conservation (Fairhead et al. 2012) and REDD+ (Benjaminsen and Bryceson 2012, Svarstad and Benjaminsen 2017) are combining with mining concessions and agricultural investment corridors to render large swathes of the country inhospitable to rural residents (Bluwstein et al. 2018). The stark maps showing how swathes of the country are becoming off-limits in Bluwstein and colleagues' work and the detail of how this dispossession concentrates disadvantage on more vulnerable and marginalized groups is disturbing (Homewood et al. 2020).

The critics of these processes are convinced that a disaster is unfolding. Just over thirty years ago Shivji predicted that the consequences of economic transformation and capital investment in Tanzania would include concentration of prime agricultural land into the hands of foreign corporations, rapid development of a 'landless peasantry', massive migration to urban areas, and high inequality with 'sprawling cities full of luxury consumer goods' with 'millions of marginalised unemployed masses on the verge of starvation' (Shivji 1987: 128, cited in Shivji 2017: 5–6).[2]

Those same views of 1987 were repeated in 1992 when that essay was reprinted. As the quotation above makes clear, for Shivji, peasants are super-exploited either directly by capital or indirectly by states. That exploitation leaves them, in his words, in rags, and starving. Further exposure of peasant resources and societies to capital will lead to further exploitation, and their ultimate disenfranchisement.

Writing much more recently, Shivji thinks that his prediction of thirty years ago was too close to the mark. 'One wishes...one would have proved wrong!' (Shivji 2017: 6). He feels these predictions have 'come close' to fulfilment in Tanzania and is uncannily close to reality for Africa as a whole. Elsewhere he speaks of the peasantry being 'flushed' out of land, and of processes of primitive accumulation driving marginalization, rather than proletarianization (Wuyts 2008: 1088). Plans for Africa's economic 'development' will simply mean that rural people will lose access to resources with no industrial development to absorb their labour.[3]

How Do We Know about Rural Poverty?

Another way of thinking about this dispute is not in terms of the nature of social and economic processes taking place in the countryside, but rather as a question of evidence and data. How do we know what changes are happening to whom?

[2] Technically a peasantry is, by definition, not landless. But Shivji's meaning is clear.

[3] Shivji's views typify a gloomy outlook that pervades the writing of radical critics on the outlook for rural peasants. Michael Watts completed his magnum opus *Silent Violence* thus: 'For the peasants...Barrington Moore is probably right when he says that under capitalism "sooner or later they are its victims." I suspect that what we are witnessing in Nigeria is the beginning of what John Berger refers to as a final act of historical elimination' (Watts 1983: 513).

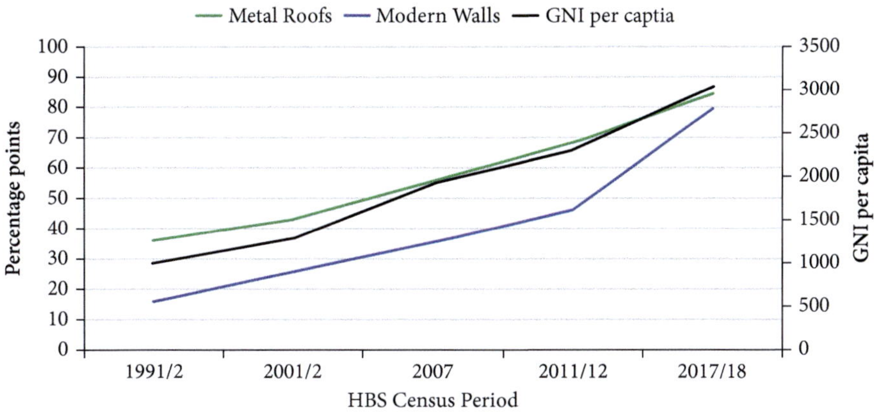

Figure 2.2 Key trends in GNI and house construction in Tanzania.

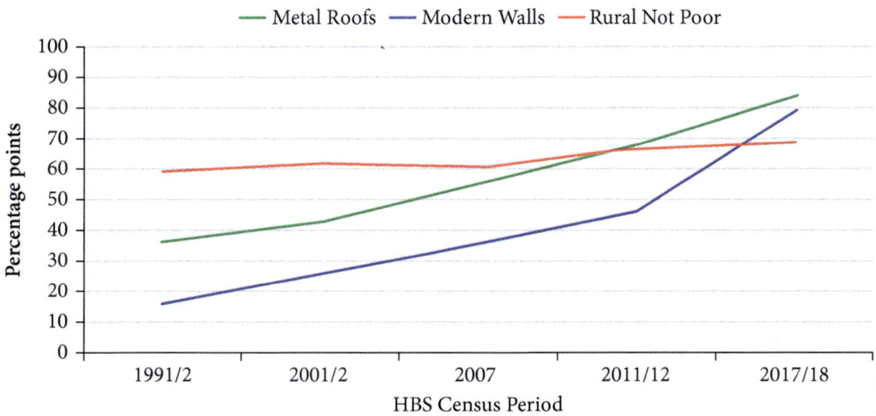

Figure 2.3 Key trends in poverty levels and house construction in Tanzania.

The problem of data is indicated by the same Household Budget Surveys that seem to depict obdurate, slowly declining poverty. There are apparent inconsistencies in the trends these surveys capture. At the same time as poverty is declining slowly, house quality is improving considerably—and at rates which match economic growth (Figure 2.2). If has poverty persisted, how can poor peasants build so many (relatively) good-quality houses (Figure 2.3)?

Another way of putting this question is: what are the forms of poverty that peasants experience? We know that the insults and injuries of poverty are multidimensional (Green and Hulme 2005, Alkire and Foster 2011). They have many different expressions which will require different sources of data to comprehend. Yet that complexity has yet to filter through into debates about peasant poverty.

For example, the central premise of a recent edited collection on peasant poverty *Peasant Poverty in the 21st Century* (Boltvinik and Mann 2016b) is that there is no doubt that peasant poverty has persisted, if not increased, in recent decades. The constitution of that poverty was not a significant concern of the book. As the editors themselves observed, poverty measurement was not their 'central object' (ibid.: 7). They establish the basic facts of peasant poverty briefly and succinctly using poverty line data. They argue that problems with World Bank poverty-line data in fact mean that levels of poverty globally, as determined by these lines, have not fallen as widely as the Bank claims (Boltvinik and Mann 2016a). Similarly Mashindano and Shepherd's claim that poverty persists in rural Tanzania is also based on an analysis of poverty-line data.

But poverty-line data, if they are based on consumption patterns, are not a good way of tracking change in poor rural societies.[4] They deliberately exclude aspects of life, wealth, and poverty that can be particularly important for peasant families. To understand how this is the case we need to examine more carefully how poverty lines are calculated.

A poverty line is a measurement of how much people spend over a particular time period. It captures the 'cost of attaining a given level of economic welfare or "standard of living"' (Ravallion 2016: 183). The famous notion that you are poor if you are living on less than $1 per day (or, more recently, $1.25 or $1.90) is made on the basis of poverty lines. Distributions of daily expenditure across nations are drawn up and anyone deemed to be spending less than particularly low levels per day are deemed to be poor.

From this measure the World Bank and others insist that fewer people are poor because the proportion (and in many places the number) of people below that line is declining. 35.9 per cent of people in the world used to live below the international poverty line (World Bank 2018). Now 10 per cent live below the line. In absolute terms this is a decline from 1.9 billion to 736 million. By this measure a capitalist world economy and economic growth have reduced poverty in the last few decades.

Boltvinik and Mann dispute the validity of this decline in two ways. Taking the numbers at face value, they insist that the line is too low, and a more realistic measure of poverty would be $2.50 per day (Boltvinik and Mann 2016a). The proportion of people in that category increased by 13 percentage points between 1980 and 2005.[5] By this measure the capitalist world economy which flourished in those twenty-five years has increased the number of poor people.

More fundamentally they also dispute the validity of the construction of such lines. Here they draw on Pogge and Redde's conceptual and practical critique of the methodology of making historical and geographical comparisons required for

[4] Poverty lines can also be based on income data, rather than expenditure data. These are not the focus of our discussion.

[5] Chen and Ravallion note the same pattern (Chen and Ravallion 2010) and see Pogge for a short and biting rejoinder to the political significance of poverty lines which are set too low (Pogge 2008).

international poverty lines (Reddy and Pogge 2010). The adjustments required to make prices in different countries, and times, comparable are just much harder to do well than the World Bank has allowed. Ravallion has offered a spirited defence of international poverty lines in response, but without necessarily dealing with all the criticisms (Ravallion 2010).[6]

We do not dispute the problems of setting poverty lines too low, or the challenges of making poverty lines drawn from one place and time comparable with others. But we need also to recognize the limits that pertain to the *sorts* of poverty that poverty lines can capture. This is an entirely different critique to that we have discussed so far.

The poverty lines we have discussed are only concerned with the money that people spend on day-to-day needs. They are constructed from Household Budget Survey data using measures of consumption.

> The basis for assessing income poverty is a measure of households' consumption expenditure.... This is compared with a poverty line, which represents the cost of a basic basket of consumption. Households that fall below the poverty line are poor; individuals are classed as poor if they live in a poor household.
>
> (URT 2007: 47)

However, not all expenditure undertaken by a family is included in this measure of household consumption. *These calculations deliberately exclude all production costs.* That is, they exclude all costs entailed in creating any income. If a farmer is managing a 100-acre farm, then the survey will not try to capture her costs of ploughing, planting, weeding, or harvesting it. It captures (consumptive) use of the income resulting from such activity. The survey would also similarly not record any purchase of new land, or ploughs or oxen, or seeds or labour for smaller farmers. These too are production costs.

The instructions with respect to production costs are unambiguous. The World Bank's guidance states that:

> Care must be taken not to interpret spending that is made for inputs into household production, including outlays for tools or other inputs like fertilizer, water, or seed in agricultural production, as spending for consumption or as income. If we included spending on in-puts in the consumption or income aggregate, we would overstate the actual welfare levels achieved by households.
>
> (Coudouel et al. 2002: 32)

[6] A further issue arises with respect to the availability of adequate data with which to track changes in poverty-line data. Even if the methods for comparing between countries were sound they require good data to work with. In the most recent assessment of the data Beegle and colleagues found that, as of 2012, only twenty-seven of forty-eight countries had two comparable surveys since 1990 (!) which could be used to track changes in poverty lines (Beegle et al. 2016).

In Tanzania's 2011/12 Household Budget Survey the nature of the exclusions is clearer from the schedule of 'COICOP' codes used.[7] This provides an exhaustive list of all different types of expenditure recorded in a consumption survey, including food, clothing, house costs, furniture, education, water, electricity, insurance, and even money spent employing sex workers.

But this same code list does not include any purchase of land. Nor does it allow for the purchase of ploughs, power tillers, or tractors. Livestock purchase is only recorded if the animal is to be used for meat. Veterinary services are only recorded for pets, not herds, and fertilizer and other inputs for gardens, not farms. It is impossible to mention investment in productive assets because there are no codes for them.

Investment in productive assets is not the only thing that would be missed. As we have pointed out elsewhere (Brockington et al. 2018), expensive purchases are excluded because they are outliers, and skew the data.[8] Indeed in the published COICOP codes there is no entry for house construction. So if a family invests in building a new house, or putting a new roof on it, then that cannot be captured in this survey.

There are good reasons for these omissions. A Household Budget Survey is just that—surveys of household budgets, not business budgets. But this means that a frugal family, which was restricting day-to-day expenditure in order to save for assets, would appear poor, even if it was also purchasing land, oxen, ploughs, and diverse inputs.[9] It is therefore problematic to use poverty-line data based on consumption to track poverty dynamics in rural areas. These data cannot see some improvements in rural prosperity that are important for rural people.

Taking a critical look at data on economic growth in Tanzania therefore presents a problem. On the one hand the vibrant economic growth of the last twenty years appears to have been a largely urban phenomenon which is simply not enjoyed by the bulk of the population, the rural poor, who need most to see some change. On the other hand the measures which raise this alarm are in themselves incomplete. If assets are an important part of rural livelihoods then it may be premature to conclude, as Mashindano and others have done, that economic

[7] COICOP refers to 'Classification of Individual Codes by Purpose' for the purposes of recording consumption (see https://unstats.un.org/unsd/class/revisions/coicop_revision.asp, viewed 14 March 2019). A copy of the list of COICOP codes used in Tanzania is in the first author's possession.

[8] Indeed our 2018 publication was mistaken. In it we claimed that investment in assets, such as land or large livestock, might be excluded if the asset was expensive, and so the expenditure would appear as an outlier. They would be excluded, but for the prior reason that any expenditure on such assets would be classified as productive. In discussing these findings with colleagues we have been struck how often understanding of the exclusions of poverty-line data were known only by people with a good background in economics.

[9] Investment in agricultural assets is recorded elsewhere in the survey, but these are not assigned COICOP codes and are not included in the indices of family consumption. The full surveys and their explanations are in the first author's possession.

growth in Tanzania has excluded the poor. The measure of poverty they were used did not look at change in the productive assets in which rural Tanzanians will be so keen to invest.

Assets in Rural Livelihoods

What do we mean by assets? They are crucial to our argument and the book as a whole. More restricted definitions refers to things which are owned, bought, saved, and disposed of—land, livestock, houses, and domestic goods. In rural African contexts assets can refer to land, livestock, and businesses, or equipment like ploughs, boats, or fishing nets.

Many definitions of assets are broader, indeed Carter and Barrett (2006) describe assets as the things which generate income or a livelihood, without specifically offering a definition. A number of papers on assets have included a variety of other measures of prosperity as 'assets' (Sahn and Stifel 2000, Booysen et al. 2008, Young 2012). Barrett and colleagues recently defined assets

> broadly...as the state/stock variables used to generate income, including future income against which one might borrow. This includes both public and private goods and encompasses financial, human, natural, and social capital. (2016: 5)

This definition includes broad aspects of prosperity such as levels of education, health, or more hard-to-measure notions of social connections or happiness, such that, as Johnston and Abreu observed, the term 'assets' has come to be more a measure of well-being than assets per se, and can sometimes be used in a way which makes it synonymous with 'sustainable livelihoods' (Scoones 1998) or 'capabilities' (Sen 1999).[10] Ellis (2000: 296) explicitly equates assets to the five forms of capital outlined in the sustainable livelihoods framework. Bebbington treats assets and capitals synonymously:

> assets—or what I call capitals in this framework—are not simply *resources* that people use in building livelihoods: they are assets that give them the *capability* to be and to act. (Bebbington 1999: 2022 emphasis in the original)

Even when broadly defined, assets are useful for exploring poverty dynamics because they allow researchers to distinguish between different sorts of income poverty, according to the asset profiles that underlie them (Barrett et al. 2006).

[10] We are mainly concerned in this paper with tangible assets that can be bought, used, and sold because we are interested in the social units that are engaged in the processes of acquiring and distributing them. This means that we will use a more restrictive definition of assets.

Those without assets or much income are structurally poor or else endure persistent poverty (Naschold 2012). Assets are also a good measure to use because they are relatively easily counted—there is less room for the sort of errors that can arise when trying to count income (Johnston and Abreu 2016).

Assets can be divided into 'productive assets' which produce food or income (land or livestock), and 'non-productive assets' which do not normally do so (phones, televisions, and fridges). However the productive and non-productive distinction can break down when non-productive assets also generate income. Fridges can be used to store medicines or sodas and ice cubes for sale in informal shops. Televisions attract customers to bars. Use of phones (normally a non-productive asset) is also sold—as calls reduce time spent on long journeys. A domestic unit with electricity will charge neighbour's phones for a small fee. Likewise land can be kept unused or become infertile and oxen can be rested; productive assets are not always productive.

Assets, and change in assets, can provide a number of insights into poverty dynamics. In the first instance they can be used to construct asset indices—this topic we tackle in the next chapter. Further, one of the most important insights is that ownership and control of assets are fundamental to the definitions of poverty and wealth that are used by poor people (Narayan 2000). As we discuss in the next chapter, when focus groups in Tanzanian villages discuss the meaning of wealth they tend to focus on the quality of houses, amount of land farmed, size of herds and the abilities and freedoms that derive from owning these things, rather than income per se. Similarly poverty is defined, in part, by the lack of ownership of or access to important assets. Assets provide a means of providing sustained long-term income, and an insurance against risk and loss.

Poverty researchers have frequently observed this phenomenon. The 'Voices of the Poor' study undertaken by the World Bank found that assets were particularly important for the poor's own understanding of their poverty and desired wealth (reported in Meinzen-Dick et al. 2011). Wanjala and Muradian similarly conclude, based on a study of the Millenium Village Project in Kenya that 'accumulation of productive assets—and particularly land—is fundamental for poor households to increase their income and escape poverty' (2013: 157). Andrew Shepherd observes that the '[k]ey to success in agriculture is accumulating assets—land, oxen, and ploughs' (Mashindano et al. 2013: viii). Barrett and Carter's work on poverty traps examines the possibility that some families may be trapped in poverty because they cannot accumulate assets (Carter and Barrett 2006).

Conversely sale of assets can also be important signs of stress and immiseration. Assets, particularly productive assets, are usually the things which poorer people experiencing immiseration hold onto for the longest (De Waal 1989). Better to go hungry than sell the cow that could sustain you when the rains return

(Behnke and Scoones 1993). The sale of (important) productive assets therefore is a good indicator that things have got bad, and are about to get worse.

One of the reasons why assets feature so prominently in rural definitions of prosperity is that, especially in rural areas with few shops and poor banking services, assets are a useful means of storing and saving wealth in agricultural societies where income is lumpy and infrequent because it depends on harvests (Van der Ploeg 2014). Injections of cash will be targeted at acquiring assets rather than everyday consumption. This is captured by the following focus-group statement:

> We get money seasonally. Some people…after the harvest they buy a TV, or solar panels, or all manner of things and they have a good life. But [later] although she's got her television, if she… needs 50,000 shillings she'll have to wait 5 months. In July if you want to borrow a million shillings she will give it, but go to them in November and ask to borrow 200,000…and they will tell you I have nothing, I have bought a TV, I've bought a plot, I've bought bricks. Focus Group Kilwa 22 February 2017 (50,000 shillings is about $20)

The statement reflects a key aspect of rural life. When people are experiencing a rise in their fortunes they will often invest in assets and capabilities rather than day-to-day expenditure (Scott 2010). If fortunes improve, you do not necessarily start enjoying meat meals or a bottled soda every day. Rather you might invest in education, sewing machines, livestock, a better home, and so on. Assets provide for the long-term future of households. That is why owning assets is a good indication of long-term prospects, and selling assets a sign of impending problems (cf. De Waal 1989). They make families more resilient to shocks and problems, and better able to prosper from good fortune.

The salience of assets in local meanings of wealth and poverty is underlined by the centrality of assets in understanding longitudinal poverty dynamics (Carter and Barrett 2006, Dercon et al. 2012, Naschold 2012). Barrett and colleagues observe that meagre asset bases yielding poor income streams result in behaviour that reinforces poverty (see also Barrett and Swallow 2006, Barrett and Carter 2013, Barrett et al. 2016). Growth which is accompanied by loss of assets, inability to use them well, or a failure to acquire new assets (such as education) among the poor will not be inclusive (McKay and Lawson 2002, Naschold 2012).

A number of useful case studies underlines the importance of asset investment for poor people in poor countries. Adato and colleagues have shown that poor asset bases and weak social capital limit economic mobility for the South African poor (Adato et al. 2006, Adato et al. 2007). Changing assets can be a more sensitive measure to increases in wealth than, for example, changes to diet. Liverpool-Tasie and Winter-Nelson found from panel data in Ethiopia that asset-based measures of wealth were much better at predicting future expenditure and asset portfolios than expenditure-based measures of wealth (Liverpool-Tasie and Winter-Nelson 2011). Carter and Lybbert (2012), exploring panel data from Burkina Faso in the mid-1980s, found two different responses to weather shocks with respect to assets that neatly captures the significance and role of assets in poverty dynamics. They observed that households who were poor with respect to their productive assets (herd sizes of less than 15.5 Tropical Livestock Units—TLU) conserved their assets, and experienced declines in every-day consumption due to weather shocks. Conversely those who were productive asset rich (more than 24.1 TLU) were able to offset consumption declines with herd sales, and readily did so. Nguyen and colleagues observe similar behaviour in rural households in Vietnam (Nguyen et al. 2019). Productive assets therefore are a crucial means of becoming wealthy in rural areas in poor countries and rural people save in order to invest in them.

We should also note that this manner of local asset accumulation is also consistent with primitive accumulation by capital, as defined by Shivji: '*a process of surplus extraction by capital based on expropriation of a part of necessary consumption of the producer*' (Shivji 2017: 11, italics in the original). They are consistent because it is possible both for peasants to yield surplus to capitalists, and to save for assets. But this fact means that, contra Shivji, these processes are not characterized only by peasants' immiseration. It is still possible, slowly, and with difficulty, for poor rural families to acquire forms of wealth which are meaningful to them. Himanshu and colleagues observed in Palanpur, an Indian village that has been studied for sixty years, that one of the most marked changes, even in a population characterized by considerable poverty, was investment in assets and people's houses (Himanshu et al. 2018).[11] As Lord Stern, one of Himanshu's co-authors, put it at a book launch, it is remarkable how the poorest people are still able to save and invest. Measures of poverty which only capture weekly expenditure cannot capture changes in assets. This is why we insist that we need a richer understanding of the nature of peasant poverty that includes assets, better to understand its dynamics.

The importance of assets does *not* mean that families who are, by dint of repeated denial, able to accumulate assets are actually well-off and just 'look' poor according to consumption data. As we will show below, and as should be plain anyway, having to scrimp and save to acquire or conserve assets is an aspect of poverty. When Chayanov observed that the best adapted peasant farmer 'knows how to starve' (1991 (1927): 40), then that farmer's condition is characterized by her occasional starvation as much as her adaptation. So, while assets matter a great deal for understandings of rural poverty, they can be problematic if

[11] Half of the population of Palanpur was at or below the international poverty line in 2008/9 while this wealth was being accrued.

understanding of prosperity is reduced only to assets. As we shall see in the next chapter, this is a risk when using assets to derive asset indices.

Finally interest in assets and debates about African poverty has risen following Alwyn Young's controversial paper which argued that trends in assets available from DHS data indicated that Africa was experiencing a 'growth miracle' (cf. Sahn and Stifel 2000, Young 2012). These findings have been disputed. Harttgen and colleagues argue that the countries which drive this pattern have experienced more than normally high economic growth, and that there are problems with building in depreciation costs (Harttgen et al. 2013). But this criticism still makes it possible for individual countries to have experienced a growth miracle, if not the continent as a whole. And if economists find it hard to capture depreciation, that should not detract from the continued use-value Africans enjoy from their assets.

More fundamentally, Johnston and Abreu (2016) have argued that it is not always safe to assume that wealth (or well-being) is correlated with assets (and see Chapter 3 p. 46 for more discussion on this topic). Asset ownership may reflect cultural preferences rather than wealth per se. It can also contain elements of social signalling, or marking distinction or aspiration, for example where teachers should have a certain type of house or clothes. Beegle and colleagues similarly find that asset indices are difficult to use in international comparisons and are not good proxies for monetary poverty (Beegle et al. 2016).

There are dangers, therefore, in inferring too much from asset data alone. Accordingly, in this book we do not use assets as proxies for other forms of wealth. Rather we use definitions of wealth and poverty that hinge on how these assets are combined by different socially recognized wealth classes. As we show in this book, for specific communities across Tanzania, assets matter in terms of their own definitions of what it means to be rich and poor. We have shown in this chapter, work on peasant poverty has omitted, inadvertently, attention to these assets by virtue of the measures it used. We therefore will explore what can be learned from assets in Tanzania contexts.

Conclusion

We have argued in this chapter that assets matter a great deal to rural Tanzanians. We have shown that assets are not adequately counted by traditional measures of poverty built on counting consumption. Indeed assets are systematically excluded from these measures. We have also shown why, from a variety of studies, this will be a problem and will not help us to understand poverty dynamics in Tanzania.

But we need now to take a less theoretical approach. Assets matter to rural Tanzanians—but which assets, and what are the patterns in the assets that Tanzanians count in different parts of the country? That is the task of the next chapter.

References

Adam, C. S., P. Collier, and B. Ndulu (2017). *Tanzania: The Path to Prosperity*. Oxford, Oxford University Press.

Adato, M., M. R. Carter, and J. May (2006). 'Exploring Poverty Traps and Social Exclusion in South Africa Using Qualitative and Quantitative Data.' *Journal of Development Studies* 42(2): 226–47.

Adato, M., F. Lund, and P. Mhlongo (2007). 'Methodological Innovations in Research on the Dynamics of Poverty: A Longitudinal Study in KwaZulu-Natal, South Africa.' *World Development* 35(2): 247–63.

Alkire, S. and J. Foster (2011). 'Understandings and Misunderstandings of Multidimensional Poverty Measurement.' *Journal of Economic Inequality* 9(2): 289–314.

Ansoms, A. and T. Hilhorst (2014). *Losing Your Land: Dispossession in the Great Lakes*. Woodbridge, James Currey, Boydell and Brewer.

Arndt, C., V. Leyaro, K. Mahrt, and F. Tarp (2017). 'Growth and Poverty: A Pragmatic Assessment and Future Prospects.' *Tanzania: The Path to Prosperity*. C. S. Adam, P. Collier, and B. Ndulu. Oxford, Oxford University Press: DOI:10.1093/acprof:oso/9780198704812.003.0009.

Barrett, C. (2011). 'Assisting the Escape from Persistent Ultra-Poverty in Rural Africa.' Stanford Symposium Series on Global Food Policy and Food Security in the 21st Century, https://fse.fsi.stanford.edu/zh-ch/multimedia/assisting-escape-persistent-ultra-poverty-rural-africa-0.

Barrett, C., T. Garg, and L. McBride (2016). 'Well-Being Dynamics and Poverty Traps.' Centre for Climate Change Economics and Policy Working Paper No. 250 Grantham Research Institute on Climate Change and the Environment Working Paper No. 222, London, LSE.

Barrett, C. B. and M. R. Carter (2013). 'The Economics of Poverty Traps and Persistent Poverty: Empirical and Policy Implications.' *Journal of Development Studies* 49(7): 976–90.

Barrett, C. B., M. R. Carter, and P. D. Little (2006). 'Understanding and Reducing Persistent Poverty in Africa: Introduction to a Special Issue.' *Journal of Development Studies* 42(2): 167–77.

Barrett, C. B., L. Christiaensen, M. Sheahan, and A. Shimeles (2017). 'On the Structural Transformation of Rural Africa.' *Journal of African Economies* 26 (AERC Supplement 1): i11–35.

Barrett, C. B. and B. M. Swallow (2006). 'Fractal Poverty Traps.' *World Development* 34(1): 1–15.

Bebbington, A. (1999). 'Capitals and Capabilities: A Framework for Analyzing Peasant Viability, Rural Livelihoods and Poverty.' *World Development* 27(12): 2021–44.

Beegle, K., L. Christiaensen, A. Dabalen, and I. Gaddis (2016). *Poverty in a Rising Africa*. Washington DC, The World Bank.

Behnke, R. H. and I. Scoones (1993). 'Rethinking Range Ecology: Implications for Rangeland Management in Africa.' *Range Ecology at Disequilibrium: New Models of Natural Variability and Pastoral Adaptation in African Savannas*. R. H. Behnke, I. Scoones, and C. Kerven. London, ODI: 1–30.

Benjaminsen, T. A. and I. Bryceson (2012). 'Conservation, Green/Blue Grabbing and Accumulation by Dispossession in Tanzania.' *Journal of Peasant Studies* 39(2): 335–55.

Bluwstein, J., J. F. Lund, K. Askew, H. Stein, C. Noe, R. Odgaard, F. Maganga, and L. Engström (2018). 'Between Dependence and Deprivation: The Interlocking Nature of Land Alienation in Tanzania.' *Journal of Agrarian Change* 18: 806–30.

Boltvinik, J. and S. A. Mann (2016a). 'Introduction.' *Peasant Poverty and Persistence in the 21st Century: Theories, Debates, Realities and Policies*. J. Boltvinik and S. A. Mann. London, Zed Books.

Boltvinik, J. and S. A. Mann (2016b). *Peasant Poverty and Persistence in the 21st Century: Theories, Debates, Realities and Policies*. London, Zed Books.

Bond, P. (2006). *Looting Africa: The Economics of Exploitation*. London, Zed Books.

Booysen, F., R. B. Servaas van der Berg, and M. von Maltitz (2008). 'Using an Asset Index to Assess Trends in Poverty in Seven Sub-Saharan African Countries.' *World Development* 36(6): 1113–30.

Borras, S. J., R. Hall, I. Scoones, B. White, and W. Wolford (2011). 'Towards a Better Understanding of Global Land Grabbing: An Editorial Introduction.' *Journal of Peasant Studies* 38(2): 209–16.

Brockington, D., O. Howland, V.-M. Loiske, M. Mnzava, and C. Noe (2018). 'Economic Growth, Rural Assets and Prosperity: Exploring the Implications of a Twenty Year Record of Asset Growth in Tanzania.' *Journal of Modern African Studies* 56(2): 217–43.

Bryngelsson, D. K., A. Åhlén, C. Azar, and U. M. Persson (2012). 'The Effect of Food-Price Movements on African Households.' *International Journal of Agricultural Resources, Governance and Ecology* 9(3/4): 121–46.

Carter, M. R. and C. B. Barrett (2006). 'The Economics of Poverty Traps and Persistent Poverty: An Asset-Based Approach.' *Journal of Development Studies* 42(2): 178–99.

Carter, M. R. and T. J. Lybbert (2012). 'Consumption versus Asset Smoothing: Testing the Implications of Poverty Trap Theory in Burkina Faso.' *Journal of Development Economics* 99: 255–64.

Chayanov, A. V. (1991 (1927)). *The Theory of Peasant Co-operatives*. Columbus, Ohio State University Press.

Chen, S. and M. Ravallion (2010). 'The Developing World Is Poorer Than We Thought, but No Less Successful in the Fight against Poverty.' *Quarterly Journal of Economics* 125(4): 1577–1625.

Christiaensen, L., L. Demery, and J. Kuhl (2011). 'The (Evolving) Role of Agriculture in Poverty Reduction—An Empirical Perspective.' *Journal of Development Economics* 96: 239–54.

Chuhan-Pole, P. and M. Angwafo (2011). *Yes Africa Can: Success Stories from a Dynamic Continent*. Washington DC, The World Bank.

Collier, P. and S. Dercon (2014). 'African Agriculture in 50 Years: Smallholders in a Rapidly Changing World?' *World Development* 63: 92–101.

Coudouel, A., J. S. Hentschel, and Q. T. Wodon (2002). 'Poverty Measurement and Analysis'. *A Sourcebook For Poverty Reduction Strategies*. J. Krugman. Washington DC, The World Bank: 29–70.

De Waal, A. (1989). *Famine That Kills: Darfur, Sudan, 1984–1985*. Oxford, Clarendon Press.

Dercon, S. and D. Gollin (2014). 'Agriculture in African Development: Theories and Strategies.' *Annual Review of Resource Economics* 6: 471–92.

Dercon, S., J. Hoddinott, and T. Woldehanna (2012). 'Growth and Chronic Poverty: Evidence from Rural Communities in Ethiopia.' *The Journal of Development Studies* 48(2): 238–53.

Edwards, S. (2014). *Toxic Aid: Economic Collapse and Recovery in Tanzania*. Oxford, Oxford University Press.

Ellis, F. (2000). 'The Determinants of Rural Livelihood Diversification in Developing Countries.' *Journal of Agricultural Economics* 51(2): 289–302.

Fairhead, J., M. Leach, and I. Scoones (2012). 'Green Grabbing: A New Appropriation of Nature?' *The Journal of Peasant Studies* 39(2): 237–61.

Fioramonti, L. (2017). *The World after GDP: Politics, Business and Society in the Post Growth Era*. London, Polity Press.

Gardner, B. (2012). 'Tourism and the Politics of the Global Land Grab in Tanzania: Markets, Appropriation and Recognition.' *Journal of Peasant Studies* 39(2): 377–402.

Greco, E. (2015). 'Landlords in the Making: Class Dynamics of the Land Grab in Mbarali, Tanzania.' *Review of African Political Economy* 42(144): 225–44.

Green, M. and D. Hulme (2005). 'From Correlates and Characteristics to Causes: Thinking about Poverty from a Chronic Poverty Perspective.' *World Development* 33(6): 867–79.

Hall, R. (2011). 'Land Grabbing in Southern Africa: The Many Faces of the Investor Rush.' *Review of African Political Economy* 38(128): 193–214.

Hall, R., I. Scoones, and D. Tsikata (2015). *Africa's Land Rush: Rural Livelihoods and Agrarian Change*. Woodbridge, James Currey, Boydell and Brewer.

Hall, R., I. Scoones, and D. Tsikata (2017). 'Forum: Land and Agricultural Commercialisation in Africa. Plantations, Outgrowers and Commercial Farming in Africa: Agricultural Commercialisation and Implications for Agrarian Change.' *Journal of Peasant Studies* 44(3): 515–37.

Harttgen, K., S. Klasen, and S. Vollmer (2013). 'An African Growth Miracle? Or: What Do Asset Indices Tell Us about Trends in Economic Performance?' *Review of Income and Wealth* 59 (Special Issue, October 2013): s37–61.

Himanshu, P. Lanjouw, and N. H. Stern (2018). *How Lives Change: Palanpur, India and Development Economics.* Oxford, Oxford University Press.

Homewood, K., M. R. Nielsen, and A. Keane (2020). 'Women, Wellbeing and Wildlife Management Areas in Tanzania.' *The Journal of Peasant Studies*, doi.org/10.1080/03066150.2020.1726323.

Hoogeveen, J. and R. Ruhinduka (2009). 'Lost in Transition? Income Poverty Reduction in Tanzania since 2001.' Paper Prepared for the Research and Analysis Working Group, United Republic of Tanzania.

Jayne, T. S., J. Chamberlin, and R. Benfica (2018). 'Africa's Unfolding Economic Transformation.' *Journal of Develoment Studies* 54(5): 777–87.

Jayne, T. S., J. Chamberlin, L. Traub, N. Sitko, M. Muyanga, F. K. Yeboah, W. Anseeuw, A. Chapato, A. Wineman, C. Nkonde, and R. Kachule (2016). 'Africa's Changing Farm Size Distribution Patterns: The Rise of Medium-Scale Farms.' *Agricultural Economics* 47: 197–214.

Jayne, T. S., D. Mather, and E. Mghenyi (2010). 'Principal Challenges Confronting Smallholder Agriculture in Sub-Saharan Africa.' *World Development* 38(10): 1384–98.

Johnston, D. and A. Abreu (2016). 'The Asset Debates: How (Not) to Use Asset Indices to Measure Well-Being and the Middle Class in Africa.' *African Affairs* 115(460): 399–418.

Liverpool-Tasie, L. S. O. and A. Winter-Nelson (2011). 'Asset versus Consumption Poverty and Poverty Dynamics in Rural Ethiopia.' *Agricultural Economics* 42: 221–33.

Mashindano, O., K. Kayunze, L. da Corta, and F. Maro (2013). 'Growth without Poverty Reduction in Tanzania—Reasons for the Mismatch.' *Translating Growth into Poverty Reduction: Beyond the Numbers.* F. Kessy, O. Mashindano, A. Shepherd, and L. Scott. Dar es Salaam, Mkuki na Nyota: 121–42.

Mashindano, O. and A. Shepherd (2013). 'Introduction: Translating Growth into Poverty Reduction.' *Translating Growth into Poverty Reduction: Beyond the Numbers.* F. Kessy, O. Mashindano, A. Shepherd, and L. Scott. Dar es Salaam, Mkuki na Nyota: 1–9.

McKay, A. and D. Lawson (2002). 'Assessing the Extent and Nature of Chronic Poverty in Low Income Countries: Issues and Evidence.' *World Development* 31(3): 425–39.

Meinzen-Dick, R., N. Johnson, A. Quisumbing, J. Njuki, J. Behrman, D. Rubin, A. Peterman, and E. Waithanji (2011). 'Gender, Assets, and Agricultural Development Programs. A Conceptual Framework.' CAPRi Working Paper No. 99.

Mueller, B. E. T. (2011). 'The Agrarian Question in Tanzania: Using New Evidence to Reconcile an Old Debate.' *Review of African Political Economy* 38(127): 23–42.

Narayan, D. (2000). *Voices of the Poor: Can Anyone Hear Us?* Washington DC, The World Bank.

Naschold, F. (2012). '"The Poor Stay Poor": Household Asset Poverty Traps in Rural Semi-Arid India.' *World Development* 40(10): 2033–43.

Nguyen, G. T. N., B. White, and C. Ma (2019). 'When Faced with Income and Asset Shocks: Do Poor Rural Households in Vietnam Smooth Food Consumption or Assets?' *Journal of Develoment Studies* 55(9): 2008–23.

Nord, R., Y. Sobolev, D. Dunn, A. Hajdenberg, N. Hobdari, S. Maziad, and S. Roudet (2009). 'Tanzania: The Story of an African Transition.' Washington DC, IMF.

Peters, P. E. (2013). 'Land Appropriation, Surplus People and a Battle over Visions of Agrarian Futures in Africa.' *The Journal of Peasant Studies* 40(3): 537–62.

Pogge, T. (2008). 'Where the Line Is Drawn: A Rejoinder to Ravallion.' *International Poverty Centre. One Pager* 69 (October 2008).

Radelet, S. (2010). *Emerging Africa: How 17 Countries Are Leading the Way.* Washington DC, Centre for Global Development.

Ravallion, M. (2010). 'How Not to Count the Poor? A Reply to Reddy and Pogge.' *Debates on the Measurement of Global Poverty*. S. Anand, P. Segal, and J. E. Stiglitz. Oxford, Oxford University Press: 86–101.

Ravallion, M. (2016). *The Economics of Poverty: History, Measurement and Policy.* Oxford, Oxford University Press.

Reddy, S. G. and T. Pogge (2010). 'How Not to Count the Poor.' *Debates on the Measurement of Global Poverty*. S. Anand, P. Segal, and J. E. Stiglitz. Oxford, Oxford University Press: 42–85.

Robinson, D. O., M. Gaertner, and C. Papageorgiou (2011). 'Tanzania: Growth Acceleration and Increased Public Spending with Macroeconomic Stability.' *Yes Africa Can: Success Stories from a Dynamic Continent*. P. Chuhan-Pole and M. Angwafo. Washington DC, The World Bank: 21–49.

Rodney, W. (1972). *How Europe Underdeveloped Africa*. London, Bogle-L'Ouverture Publications.

Sahn, D. E. and D. C. Stifel (2000). 'Poverty Comparisons over Time and across Countries in Africa.' *World Development* 28(12): 2123–55.

Scoones, I. (1998). 'Sustainable Rural Livelihoods: A Framework for Analysis.' IDS Working Paper 72. Brighton, IDS, University of Sussex.

Scoones, I., R. Hall, S. M. Borras, B. White, and W. Wolford (2013). 'The Politics of Evidence: Methodologies for Understanding the Global Land Rush.' *Journal of Peasant Studies* 40(3): 469–83.

Scott, L. (2010). 'Giving Assets: An Effective Approach for Reducing Vulnerability and Building Livelihoods? The Case of the Chars Livelihoods Programme.' PhD Thesis, Manchester University.

Sen, A. (1999). *Development as Freedom*. Oxford, Oxford University Press.

Shivji, I. G. (1987). 'The Roots of Agrarian Crisis in Tanzania: A Theoretical Perspective.' *Eastern African Social Science Review* 3(1): 111–31.

Shivji, I. G. (1992). 'The Roots of an Agrarian Crisis in Tanzania: A Theoretical Perspective.' *The Tanzanian Peasantry: Economy in Crisis*. P. G. Forster and S. Maghimbi. Aldershot, Avebury: 124–50.

Shivji, I. G. (2017). 'The Concept of "Working People".' *Agrarian South: Journal of Political Economy* 6(1): 1–13.

Stiglitz, J. E., A. Sen, and J.-P. Fitoussi (2010). *Mismeasuring Our Lives: Why GDP Doesn't Add Up*. New York, The New Press.

Svarstad, H. and T. A. Benjaminsen (2017). 'Nothing Succeeds Like Success Narratives: A Case of Conservation and Development in the Time of REDD.' *Journal of Eastern African Studies* 11(3): 482–505.

United Republic of Tanzania (URT) (2007). 'Household Budget Survey 2007 Main Report.' Dodoma, National Bureau of Statistics.

United Republic of Tanzania (URT) (2019). 'Tanzania Mainland. Key Indicators Report. 2017–18 Household Budget Survey.' Dodoma, National Bureau of Statistics.

Van der Ploeg, J. D. (2014). *Peasants and the Art of Farming: A Chayanovian Manifesto*. Bourton on Dunsmore, Practical Action Publishing Ltd.

Wanjala, B., and M. and R. Muradian (2013). 'Can Big Push Interventions Take Small-Scale Farmers Out of Poverty? Insights from the Sauri Millennium Village in Kenya.' *World Development* 45: 147–60.

Watts, M. (1983). *Silent Violence: Food, Famine & Peasantry in Northern Nigeria*. Berkeley, University of California Press.

Wolford, W., S. M. J. Borras, R. Hall, I. Scoones, and B. White (2013). 'Governing Global Land Deals: The Role of the State in the Rush for Land.' *Development and Change* 44(2): 189–210.

World Bank (2015). 'Tanzania Mainland Poverty Assessment.' Washington DC, The World Bank.

World Bank (2018). 'Piecing together the Poverty Puzzle.' Washington DC, The World Bank.

Wuyts, M. (2008). 'Issa Shivji. Interviewed by Marc Wuyts.' *Development and Change* 39(6): 1079–90.

Young, A. (2012). 'The African Growth Miracle.' *Journal of Political Economy* 120(4): 696–739.

3

The Multiple Meanings of Prosperity and Poverty in Tanzania

Olivia Howland, Christine Noe, and Dan Brockington

Introduction

We saw in the last chapter that the consequences of economic growth in Tanzania are contested. Mainstream researchers celebrate the consequences of economic growth. More radical critics fear that these are built on displacement and marginalization.

Yet despite these substantial differences, the two camps, and indeed all observers of social and economic change hold one important view in common. They believe there is a shared story to be told. They look for common experiences arising from contemporary dynamics that affect many groups of people. Such accounts, be they of the benefits of economic growth (Young 2012, Jayne et al. 2018), or of the sacrifices that growth has entailed because of land loss (Shivji 2017, Bergius et al. 2018), have to be based on generalizable measures that capture locally valued meanings of wealth, poverty, dignity, and well-being.

Given the focus in this collection on assets, one of the most obvious means of telling a common story would be to use the widespread technique of constructing asset indices to examine patterns in wealth and poverty. However this presents a problem for our project. Ours is a granular study: we have proceeded village by village. And we have also grounded our perceptions of change that matters in villagers' perceptions of what poverty means and what prosperity entails. But asset indices are not built on these principles. As we shall see they entail two essential assumptions: first, that they can be compiled at a national scale (they are constructed for large national-scale samples), and second that asset ownership correlates with 'wealth'.

Too often, however, asset indices are used without a good empirical understanding of how the value and meaning of assets actually vary across space. Specifically, few studies have tried to explore how local meanings and definitions of wealth can vary within particular countries. This is explicitly recognized in the literature and there are recently published calls to examine how the meaning of wealth and poverty can vary at the national scale (Johnston and Abreu 2016). This chapter addresses that call.

Olivia Howland, Christine Noe, and Dan Brockington, *The Multiple Meanings of Prosperity and Poverty in Tanzania* In: *Prosperity in Rural Africa? Insights into Wealth, Assets, and Poverty from Longitudinal Studies in Tanzania*. Edited by: Dan Brockington and Christine Noe, Oxford University Press.
DOI: 10.1093/oso/9780198865872.003.0003

To explore this we present findings of a series of focus groups that we conducted as part of the restudies in 2016–17 from seventeen villages in Tanzania. We focus on the spatial variation in importance of different assets in the present day. As we have seen in the previous chapter these attributes are also noticeable for their absence in official statistics monitoring change in wealth in the country, and debates about persistent peasant poverty.

We argue it is possible to discern a cluster of attributes that broadly signify wealth across many parts of Tanzania. However a definitive list would be hard to construct because precisely how much, and what forms of, wealth any given variable signifies changes from place to place. It is also clear that, although assets are frequently used to construct asset indices, many aspects of life that do matter locally are not tracked by current asset indices because they do not include the right assets.

A Brief Introduction to Asset Indices

Given that the previous chapter showed that assets are omitted by poverty-line data, then the obvious tool to use to compensate for this gap should be asset indices. Asset indices impute differences in household wealth from the different bundles of assets they own. The bundles are weighted according to principal component analyses (or factor or multiple correspondence analysis), which looks for structures and patterns in the asset ownership data.

Asset indices can be used to group populations (quintiles, quartiles, etc.) and make comparisons between these groups. Asset indices are also used to check the accuracy of new proxies of poverty, such as mobile phone records (Blumenstock et al. 2015), or remotely sensed images (Jean et al. 2016, Watmough et al. 2019). Thus one set of proxies of wealth (social media data, built infrastructure visible from space) is used to verify another (asset indices).

Asset indices are valued for their speed and ease of construction (Filmer and Pritchett 2001, for reviews see Howe et al. 2009, Howe et al. 2012). The advantage of such indices is that their data are easily collected, for few variables are required. Indeed recent attempts try to do so using as few variables as possible. For example Chakraborty et al. (2016: 152) developed simplified asset indices which could use as few as six questions (Table 3.1). Blumenstok and colleagues (2015) found that an asset index comprising just six assets (ownership of a fridge, bicycle, television, motorbike/scooter, radio, and electricity in the house) could be used to test measures of wealth in Rwanda based on mobile phone data.

The assets owned in such short lists are affected by broader infrastructural provision (such as the availability of electricity), which leads to the well-recognized urban bias of asset indices. They can differentiate urban populations from rural populations (as the six assets Blumenstok used would suggest) but not necessarily

Table 3.1 Simplified and minimized asset indices

Bangladesh	Benin	Tanzania
Does your household have: –electricity; –a television; –an electric fan; –an almirah/wardrobe; –a refrigerator?	Does your household have: –electricity; –a television; –a VCD or DVD player?	Does your household have: –a television; –a radio; –an iron?
What is the main material used in your house walls?	What is the main material used in your house walls?	What is the main material of the floor of your dwelling?
What is the main material used for your house floor?	What is the main fuel you use for cooking?	What is the main material of the exterior walls of your dwelling?
Does any member of this household have a bank account?	What type of toilet do members of your household use?	What is the main material of the roof of your dwelling?
		What type of fuel does your household mainly use for cooking?
		What is the main source of energy for lighting in the household?
		Does any member of this household have a bank account?

Source: (Chakraborty et al. 2016: 152) and http://www.equitytool.org/tanzania/ accessed 16th February 2018.

indicate the wealth of rural families, who may prioritize different asset bundles, based on land, livestock, and agricultural technology (Howe et al. 2012).

Asset indices can identify patterns that are statistically meaningful. But whether these correspond to locally recognized wealth is a different issue. Underpinning these lists is the assumption that ownership of those assets provides locally meaningful and sensitive markers of differences in wealth.

Johnston and Abreu (2016) observe that the relationship between an asset index and wealth is a key assumption of the makers of the index. It is not an empirical observation. Researchers assume that the feature that allows families to accumulate assets is wealth, and that asset bundles co-vary with wealth. But, they point out, this is not always the case. Other dimensions of culturally determined choice that prevent the purchase of some goods, and hasten the purchase of others, will shape asset ownership irrespective of wealth. Moreover the core assumption of asset indices—that assets correlate with wealth—is more likely to be violated if indices are used to cover large geographical areas and long periods of time. This is because differences in infrastructure provision (determining the availability of electric goods and cost of building materials), and local values and cultural priorities, are more likely to become important at these larger scales.

Johnston and Abreu then make three recommendations that need to be addressed before assets can be reliably used over larger scales. These are:

> (1) indices should be constructed and compared over limited geographic scales and time periods; (2) the choice of assets should be based on an understanding of what it means to be wealthy or poor in a particular place; and (3) that the choice of assets in an index should reflect the kind of well-being to be measured. (ibid.: 417–18)

This chapter considers the first two of the recommendations made by Johnston and Abreu. We explore what assets mean to different definitions of wealth and poverty, and how local understandings of poverty and wealth vary geographically. We want to understand whether national comparisons are possible or simply ruled out by the difference we find. We also explore the meaningfulness of using the abbreviated asset indices that have been suggested by other observers.

These questions could have considerable consequences for debates about the distribution of benefits of economic growth with which we began. If we find that, broadly, the same assets matter across the country, then it will be possible to use asset indices to explore poverty dynamics nationwide. Likewise if we find that the assets used in abbreviated asset indices are also locally meaningful, then these abbreviated indices will provide robust means of tracking change. But if the meaning and value placed in assets vary across the country then these methods are flawed. It may be possible to derive statistically robust relationships within asset indices, but they will not tell us much about locally important change. They will not provide a good lens for understanding wealth and poverty or changes to them.

Methods

The data presented here derive from a sub-sample of seventeen villages that we surveyed from seven regions from a variety of parts of the country, with data collected in 2016 and 2017 (Table 3.2). The data we use cover contemporary local definitions of wealth and poverty; we have not tried to compare how definitions have changed over time across our different study sites. As we have seen earlier, our methods bind us to sites which have been previously visited. We cannot set out systematically to sample different parts of the country. However, we are fortunate that the sites we have reached do provide us with good coverage which captures different parts of rural Tanzania, with different social, economic, and physical geographies.

Table 3.2 The study sites covered in this paper

Region	District	Village count
Arusha	Meru	2
Dodoma	Chemba	2
Iringa	Iringa Rural	2
	Kilolo	3
Mbeya	Mbeya Rural	2
Morogoro	Mvomero	4
Rukwa	Sumbawanga Rural	1
Shinyanga	Kishapu	1

There are some aspects of diversity across Tanzania that we have been able to capture. There is environmental difference. We have mountainous regions characterized by limited land availability, good rainfall and good soils (Arusha, Mbeya), and mountainous sites also well watered and crowded, where soils are poorer (Morogoro). We also have flatter regions, which are less well watered and with a mixture of poor soils (Iringa, Shinyanga) and good soils (Rukwa). Across these environmental gradients we cover also a variety of ethnic groups from matrilineal Luguru societies in Morogoro to strongly patriarchal societies of the Meru people in Arusha and Sukuma-Nyamwezi in Shinyanga, to Fipa societies not marked by strong gender differences in Rukwa.[1]

Across this social and environmental diversity there are also very different histories of development. Our sites in Morogoro, Arusha, and Iringa are close to major towns and well-maintained roads. These are also sites which have benefitted from historical investment either from the state (when the Southern Highlands were the breadbasket of the country) or from farmers' associations (when Meru coffee farmers were making substantial investment in farms and crops). In contrast sites in Rukwa, Dodoma, and Shinyanga have only recently (within the last ten years) enjoyed improved infrastructure and still remain distant from larger towns and markets. Historically they have suffered from lack of investment, poverty, and emigration.

These differences are considerable but there are still others we missed. Our study sites were only rural. Our method (revisiting families surveyed long ago) did not bring up any urban surveys.[2] We have missed (because few researchers went there) significant geographical regions such as the south-east and west of Tanzania.

[1] We did not collect data on ethnicity as part of our surveys, and do not know what ethnic groups our focus groups represented. The point we are making is that there are a variety of cultures and values which can be found across the regions in which our work has been conducted.

[2] Our method, revisiting the same families, is unlikely to work well in areas of high mobility.

Another notable omission is the general lack of pastoralist groups and fisher-people. These groups are often marginalized in Tanzania. Their lives and livelihoods are considered unruly by a Tanzanian state long bent on their 'modernization' (Homewood 2008, Benjaminsen and Bryceson 2012). Their absence from this work limits our conclusions in some respects, and creates important tasks for any follow-up. However that absence also strengthens our findings. Working with different agriculturalist groups should make it more likely to find constant notions of wealth and poverty across the different sites. The differences we report therefore become more compelling.

Focus groups were organized by village representatives and consisted of between six and fifteen participants. Men's and women's focus groups were conducted separately. Most groups involved much lively debate and discussion. They were conducted in Swahili and led mostly by Olivia Howland and the project assistant, Cathbert Mwanyika, as well as some lead by Dan Brockington and our research partners.

The focus groups considered generally open-ended questions about what wealth and poverty mean and what were the characteristics of poor and wealthy people. We did not have an exhaustive list of variables that we wanted people to cover or mention; rather we let the groups define things for themselves. This method produces a list of the salient properties of wealth for each focus group—the things that they think matter. It does not produce a definitive list of all the characteristics of wealth and poverty. Thus if one group mentions something (such as owning a motorbike), and another fails to, this does not mean that motorbike ownership is not an attribute of wealth for the second group. A different set of techniques would be required to determine that. Our purpose was to see what, unprompted, wealth meant locally.

We took a mixture of transcripts or notes according to the preferences of the groups. These transcripts were analysed to bring out the commonalities and differences that we describe below using Nvivo software. When examining the signifiers of wealth and poverty we have examined how people talked about wealth and poverty generally, and then examined what characteristics stand out as characteristics for poor and wealthy groups. We have analysed these for similarities and differences across study sites.

In the results we summarize the main themes which emerge and illustrate with the apposite phrases and remarks taken from focus groups in boxes associated with each theme. We have not listed everything that every focus group said in the boxes. Rather we have chosen the most apposite phrases to illustrate what is meant by particular concepts. Separate lines denote separate focus groups and the origins of phrases from women's groups and men's groups is given by '(W)' and '(M)' respectively after each statement. We have grouped findings across men and women because we found that they were broadly similar, except that women tended to provide more detail as to the nature of good assets (especially houses) than men.

Variations in Wealth and Poverty across and within Study Sites

The general pattern across these studies is that there are broad areas of agreement as to what wealth constitutes. The Swahili term that we used in our discussions was 'uwezo', which literally translates as 'ability' or 'means'. It refers to the wherewithal to get things done, to cope with the misfortunes and happenstance that can happen at any moment while also being able to plan ahead far enough for the various projects they are engaged in to succeed.

One group went into considerable detail on the meaning of uwezo, touching upon many common themes:

> Uwezo is the ability to work, to have strength in your body to farm your land, and to have good health. It is the ability to do whatever you need to do, and to be able to farm without problems or issues. It could be someone who also runs a business without problems. It is being able to use your brain to solve issues. Someone who has a car has more uwezo, but this is a different type of uwezo. This is uwezo of money. But the other meaning is uwezo in your body. Uwezo to do your work well. It is about strength.
>
> Good seeds, modern fertilizer and chemicals—these inputs are an indicator of uwezo, so if you have no uwezo you cannot use them. Cash crops and market access are also factors in uwezo. A man with uwezo will be a quick thinker. He does not have to be really educated but educated enough for his own job. Cars, shops, businesses, several houses, maybe he himself has not studied more than primary school but he invests in things which bring returns on money. Things that bring in more money all the time. A house built with bricks and a metal roof is an indicator of uwezo. Schooling is more important than housing though. They might have left improving their home until all the children have been educated. Uwezo is about prioritizing what matters.
>
> Uwezo is someone with good health but also if they get sick, they can afford to go to hospital, or they think to go to hospital. If you have no children then you have no uwezo, but if you have many children then this is not uwezo—however, if you can send them all to school and afford their healthcare, then you have uwezo. It is about supporting your family. (Morogoro men's focus group)

From this and other groups it was plain that typically a wealthy family in rural Tanzania enjoys a number of similar attributes (shown in Box 3.1). However, as we shall see, there are also important differences in the way that the elements of wealth are described, quantified, and assembled from place to place. A wealthy

Box 3.1 General characteristics of wealth and poverty

Wealth
Good quality houses
Ability to hire in labour
Good access to farmland
Use of modern inputs which increase agricultural productivity
Control over businesses and undertaking business-orientated farming
Livestock ownership
Educated children
Being a source of support and loans
Ability to pay for medical needs (to remain mentally and physically healthy)

Poverty
Having to work for other people to secure basic needs
Not being able to use land productively
Dependence on others
Inadequate food

family in one place may not have been considered wealthy in all respects elsewhere. In addition the list also differs in important ways from some of the existing literature. Poverty obviously entails not having these characteristics. But participants also mentioned a number of other aspects, that did not feature so frequently in definitions of wealth, as shown at the bottom of Box 3.1. We will discuss these in detail, and then consider their broader implications.

Housing

One of the most salient and common features of wealth and poverty was the quality of the home (Box 3.2). A good home had a metal roof (pitched) with cement or burned bricks, cement rendering, a cement or even tiled floor, and had good windows and doors. These were the most common features. Also mentioned was the fact that the best homes even had water and electricity (with solar power increasingly common), or South African roofing material. Some groups also stipulated that houses would be large with enough rooms to sleep in and a living room.

Conversely the houses of poor people were in poor condition, with grass or leaf roofs, or old, tired metal sheets and without solar power. The walls would be

Box 3.2 Rich peoples' houses

Arusha:
Housing—self-contained (toilet, kitchen, water), sofa, South African roofing materials, tiles, grills and glass, television, electricity. (W)

Dodoma:
They live in a big house with eight rooms or more. The house has an iron sheet roof and has tiles inside. (M)

Iringa:
Their homes are built with burned bricks, iron sheet roof, glass in the windows, and modern inside toilets. (M)

They live in a modern house with electricity and water, a modern toilet, a pitched metal roof and burned bricks. (W)

Mbeya:
Wealth is someone with a modern house, burned bricks, plastered floor, and a metal roof. Someone with a proper toilet and a house maybe with more than four big rooms. They would have a sitting room, modern toilet with a brick lined hole and a cement floor, a sink. (W)

Morogoro:
Has a good house: baked bricks, inside toilet, nice doors, electricity or solar panels. (M)

Rukwa:
Has a good house with a tiled floor and electricity (solar). Has water inside the house. (W)

Shinyanga:
They build their houses with bricks and roofing with iron sheets. (W)

made of wattle and daub, or if using bricks then they would be merely sun-dried, not burned, and the walls would not be plastered. The houses would be small, with inadequate rooms, and would be vulnerable to the weather, letting the rain in, or being damaged during storms. The very poorest were those who had no home of their own but rented rooms in other peoples' houses.

We should note here that renting is common among immigrants but that different sorts of village immigrants will have different sorts of social and economic status from that of other villagers. For example, social workers (teachers, nurses, extension officers) rent houses but are often respected for their profession, the services they offer, and the salaries that they earn. Migrant agricultural labourers will rent the meanest houses and barest rooms.

Labour

The rich were defined as those who could pay other people to work for them (Box 3.3). This was partly because this indicated that such families had both the means and liquidity to hire labour (often in cash-poor times of the year, before harvests). But this also denoted wealth because of the lifestyle that went with, being, effectively, a farm manager (or a 'veranda farmer'), rather than a farm worker.

Conversely the poor were those who had to work for other people for daily needs, and often at a cost to their own longer-term needs (Box 3.4). It is important to note that it is not the condition of working for others per se which denotes poverty. When villagers drew up wealth groups for their villages there

Box 3.3 'Veranda' farmers pay others to farm for them

Dodoma:

They do not do day labouring themselves. They employ day labourers on their farm. (M)

They are veranda farmers—they can sit on the veranda and instruct other people to do the work. They might also have livestock but they are herding not themselves. (W)

Iringa:

They are using day labourers on the farm. (M)

Mbeya:

They plough with hired labour and cows, use chemicals and hired labour to spray crops. They are not doing any of this themselves. (W)

Morogoro:

Hires labour not only for farming but also to help in other jobs. Does not farm him/herself. (M)

Rukwa:

Pays for hired labour work to do his/her weeding. (M)

Box 3.4 Poor people have to work for other people for their basic needs

Dodoma:

Poor people have to do day labouring as there is no other way to get money. (W)

Iringa:

Most of their time they have to spend doing day labour for others. They must work for others to get money for food, or are paid in food. (M)

They cannot cultivate their farm. They must work for others, but then they cannot farm their own land because there is not enough time. (W)

Mbeya:

The poor have to do daily labour work to buy soap. This is only surviving, doing daily labour work and renting out their own farm because they need the money and cannot farm it themselves. (M)

Morogoro:

They do not have enough food to last them in a year so they work to the rich people as labour so as to get food. (M)

Rukwa:

The poorest people do lots of casual work. (M)

was often a group (or groups) in the middle who were less able to hire in labour, and who might, in order to build up capital or invest in assets, perform labour for other people. Rather it is *why* people work for others that matters. Having to work for others for daily food or soap was a sign of poverty. But working to raise capital to invest in your own projects was not; it just meant not being wealthy already.

Land

Land was frequently mentioned as a condition of wealth, although the quantity varied. In some villages it would be 100 acres, in others twelve. But in mountainous crowded areas smaller farm sizes (3–7 acres) denoted wealth. Importantly this need not be owned land, but rather land that wealthy people could access through rental or sharecropping arrangements.

Poverty, on the other hand was not necessarily marked by landlessness. The poorest groups identified could have neither land nor a home, or they could have particularly small plots (less than 1 acre in crowded villages). However a far more common feature of poverty than landlessness was the inability of poor families to make their land productive (Box 3.5). This was because they did not have the capital to purchase the inputs required (pesticide, fertilizer, ploughing services), access to high-value marketable varieties, or were unable to choose the planting time (for want of access to their own ploughs). It was particularly apparent in places where poor soil fertility made extra inputs essential for decent returns. Another common reason that made farms unproductive was that they had to invest their labour into other people's farms rather than on their own projects. Sometimes poor families' farms could be quite large (up to 10 acres), but they just could not be worked or managed properly. Alternatively the lands had to be hired out to other people to bring in money for daily needs, as farms without inputs are worth little.

Box 3.5 Poor people's insufficiently used land

Dodoma:

They are renting out their land to others because they cannot use it all. (M)

They have a small farm but are unable to farm it properly because they have to keep going to look for work, for money, for food for the family, and this means there is no time for farming their own land. (W)

Iringa:

They have 3 to 10 acres of land but their farms are poorly managed. They don't use fertilizers and other agrochemicals because they can't afford to buy them and so they plant without tilling the land. They rent their farms to other people. (M)

Mbeya:

Everyone has a farm but some cannot afford any inputs so they harvest very little. (W)

Morogoro:

They have farms but they unable to cultivate and so they rent their farms to other people. (M)

Inputs

If land without inputs made people poor, then being able to use inputs on land was a clear sign of wealth (Box 3.6). This came up frequently. In part it referred to land preparation and was signified by owning tractors (the most wealthy) but more frequently being able to access ploughing services, renting in tractors, and owning or renting oxen. Poverty in contrast was marked by having to prepare fields for planting using hand hoes. In part it referred to what was put on the fields—it meant being able to use the modern seed varieties which could be high yielding, and the corresponding chemicals required (fertilizer, pesticide).

Box 3.6 Wealthy people's agricultural inputs

Dodoma:

Wealthy people are able to use inputs: buying improved seeds, fertilizer, pesticides. (W)

Iringa:

They are able to grow any type of crop that they want because they have enough capital to run their farming projects. (M)

Using manure as well as chemical fertilizer. They can farm 10 acres of tomatoes and all types of inputs that they might need. They use a tractor (either their own, or they rent) or they use oxen to plough. (W)

Mbeya:

The difference is not the crops but how much land they have combined with how well they can farm it. They plough with hired labour and cows, use chemicals and hired labour to spray crops. (W)

The wealthy are able to buy inputs of all types, at the time they need them. They invest in things. The biggest thing making people poor is lack of inputs, and so those who can afford them have more wealth. (M)

Morogoro:

The wealthy have at least 5–8 acres of farming and uses tractors for land preparation. They use chemical fertilizer and other agrochemicals. (M)

Businesses

Wealthy people however were not just industrious farmers, they were multi-tasking entrepreneurs who were able to generate funds from diverse sources (Box 3.7). Their farming was commercial, which meant growing cash crops and selling them far afield. If they had the resources they could even invest in vehicles which would allow them to sell directly in towns and bypass the middlemen, thus improving their farm gate returns. But in addition to the cash crops wealthy people were frequently said to have other business interests. Shops were

Box 3.7 Rich people's ventures

Arusha:
A wealthy man should have more than three projects e.g. shops, chickens, farm. (M)

Dodoma:
They own a milling machine; they have shops; they have a business selling crops. They send their harvests to Arusha, Moshi, and Dodoma to market. These are the higher value crops. (W)

Iringa:
They own small businesses, like small grocery shops. Often they have more than one house, because they are renting houses out to other people. (W)

Mbeya:
Someone who has a small business has wealth: selling clothes, rice, cooking oil, sodas, and vouchers. They have their own shops. (W)

Someone with a milling machine and/or a shop. If someone has a house in the centre of the village, they can rent it out. (M)

Morogoro:
A rich person has one or more motorbikes, some also rented out to young men to drive. (M)

Shinyanga:
Renting out houses means wealth because each time the owner receives money. (W)

mentioned in many places, or milling machines, and owning houses to rent to others also mattered.

Livestock

Owning cattle, goats, sheep, pigs, and chickens was often considered an attribute of wealth. But the number of livestock required to make people wealthy varied considerably from place to place (from less than ten to one thousand or more, see Box 3.8). It was also recognized that livestock ownership could correlate in different ways with wealth. In some cases it might be the form of wealth and was not used to purchase other forms. In other instances it provided liquidity. Being poor meant not having cattle, or sometimes neither cattle or smallstock and just

Box 3.8 Variations in livestock and wealth

Arusha:
Three or four cows regularly milking, each producing around 10 litres per day. Goats for milking each producing around five litres a day. Local variety chickens selling eggs getting around 20 eggs a day. (M)

Dodoma:
More than 50 cattle means somebody is wealthy but they still might have a poor house and might not eat three times a day. Some people might have no cows but a modern house. More than 50 acres is more important than cows because cows can get lost in the bush.... You might own a lot of cattle but not know how best to use them. Therefore it does not matter how many cattle you own, more how you care for them and their uses. Somebody might not have a good place to sleep, but he looks after his cows well. It depends on each person. For some the house is important, for others livestock is important. (M)

Iringa:
They have cows starting from 300 and more, 100 to 200 goats, 100 pigs, and 50 chickens for eggs. (W)

Mbeya:
Someone with cows also is a sign of wealth: 4 pigs, more than 15 chickens kept inside, goats, guard dogs, 2 zero-grazing cows. (W)

Continued

Morogoro:
They have more than 1000 cows. (W)

Rukwa:
60 cows as well as goats and some pigs. (M)

Shinyanga:
Cows means wealth because people with cows are not much affected with hunger as they just sell their cows and get money to buy food. (W)

having a few chickens. In some cases it could also mean having unproductive livestock (cattle without milk or chickens without eggs for sale and exchange for other goods).

Residents of more mountainous villages seem to have fewer cattle since there is not the space or grazing for them, and saw smaller livestock, such as sheep, goats, or fowl, as important. In places where geographical constraints make ownership of larger livestock difficult, it is not the number of livestock which are important, but the variety, and whether they are improved stock or not, as we see in the mountainous Meru villages, or the higher altitude Morogoro villages in the study.

Supporting Others and Being Supported

One of the most marked and frequently mentioned aspects of poverty was not being able to support oneself and being reliant on others (Box 3.9). Deeper poverty was experienced when people did not have the normal networks (children and relatives) needed to support them when they got old and sick. Alternatively poverty could also be marked by not being wealthy enough or reliable enough to be loaned to. Poor families would need to borrow money, for example to invest in their farms at particular times of the year or to meet health or educational expenses, but their reputation or circumstances made them too risky a prospect for local money lenders. In contrast wealth was marked by the ability to give loans and provide support. This is both a mark of esteem (helping others) and also a business venture (money lending at high local interest rates).

Education

The wealthy educated their children and educated them well, to higher levels (university) and in good institutions (private schools). The poor could only manage primary school, if that (Box 3.10). At the time of the research education in

Box 3.9 Support and dependence

Wealthy people support and lend to others

Dodoma:

You can ask wealthy people for loans for small businesses. In return, you give them a small percentage of your business, and repay your loan. (M)

Iringa:

Someone who has ability is somebody who can help others. (M)

Shinyanga:

Wealthier persons are also lending money to others to help them solve their problems such as buying food. However, the interest rate is high as it is 100 per cent per year. . . . So wealthy men give loans with interests, poor people cannot access this money. (W)

Being rich means for the men that they are approached to give loans and requests to help others. (M)

Poor people have to ask for support

Dodoma:

The people right at the bottom cannot farm, can barely eat, and rely on others to feed them. (M)

Children might have to sleep elsewhere with neighbours or extended family. (W)

Those in the lowest group depend on others because they are disabled or old or completely unable to work. They live in someone else's house and cannot look after themselves. (W)

Iringa:

If they have health problems they have to ask neighbours to help. (W)

Morogoro:

They depend on getting assistance from their relatives, neighbours and TASAF. (W)

Box 3.10 Contrasting educational experiences

Wealthy Families

Arusha:
Children go to international schools and reach the university. (W)

Dodoma:
They send their children to private schools, and up to university. (W)

Iringa:
Their children go to school here in the village for primary school, but by the time they go to secondary school they are sent to private school or the expensive school. (W)

Mbeya:
They send all their children to school if they are wealthy. It doesn't matter if they themselves have not been to school, but they send their children up to university. (W)

Poor families

Dodoma:
Children are not able to go to school, they have no clothes for school, there is no food at home. (W)

Iringa:
Their children are only able to attend primary school. (M)

Mbeya:
They might be able to educate their kids up to form 4 but mostly only finish primary school. (W)

Rukwa:
Children only go to primary school not secondary school—although free secondary schooling now makes that easier. (M)

secondary school was free in terms of school fees up to form four. However there were other costs (uniform, text books, and lost family labour) which meant that going to school beyond primary was difficult for poor families. Education is a relatively new aspect of wealth in that many groups pointed out that wealthy people were often themselves unschooled.

Food, Possessions, and Clothes

Finally wealth and poverty was also about day-to-day conditions—about having enough to eat (three meals a day for the rich), and not enough to last the year, or to have more than one or two meals per day for the poor. Being rich meant having good clothes. It was also indicated in good transport arrangements, cars for the most wealthy, motorbikes for well-off families (and especially in mountainous areas). Being poor meant simply not having much stuff at all—few possessions, nor furniture.

What Counts and What Does Not: Are Abbreviated Asset Indices Counting the Right Thing?

Expected aspects of poverty such as poor diet and lack of possessions are clearly present in the transcripts above. These in turn are likely to be driven by low levels of daily and weekly expenditure. Or in other words, they are the consequences of patterns in expenditure and consumption which are already captured in the Household Budget Surveys used to construct poverty lines. But, for most focus groups, these consumption indicators were but one aspect of wealth and poverty. Often they were not the most important thing which animated them. The more important aspects were land use, livestock, and farming activities. Food, clothing, and possessions were consequences of deeper causes of poverty (cf. Brockington et al. 2018, Östberg et al. 2018).

Similarly, income was rarely mentioned. Only in Meru—a peri-urban area on the edge of Arusha, was monthly income (over 1 million shillings) stipulated as one of the conditions of wealth. In almost every other focus group it was simply not mentioned. The ability to access money to make farms productive, run businesses, pay for labour, and make loans mattered. But this was not thought of in terms of 'income'.

Instead, prominent in these definitions from rural settings are the factors which make agriculture productive—land, labour, livestock, inputs as well as the liquidity to run businesses. Many of these attributes could be called assets, according to the definition used by economists of:

> broadly...as the state/stock variables used to generate income, including future income against which one might borrow. This includes both public and private goods and encompasses financial, human, natural, and social capital.
>
> (Barrett et al. 2016: 5).

But where assets are used in constructing abbreviated asset indices then *they appear to be using the wrong assets from the perspective of rural Tanzanians.* Televisions, irons, and fridges do not feature much in rural Tanzanian focus groups. The list of assets reported for abbreviated asset indices in Table 3.1 does not match well with the assets reported in our boxes. The fault lines in rural Tanzanian society are defined differently. Fuel or energy sources were also not mentioned. Both the latter depend on the availability of electricity and wood supplies locally in the first instance. Their role in determining wealth or poverty is predetermined by geography and infrastructure.

This means that the abbreviated asset indices, while they might report patterns in particularly large samples, and especially when comparing urban to rural societies, simply do not mean much when applied to rural Tanzanian society. They do not monitor aspects of life which matter to many rural Tanzanians. They cannot give sensitive understandings of differences in wealth and poverty.

Table 3.3 Gender difference in the salience of attributes of wealth

Gender Group	Things mentioned by men not women / women not men	Things mentioned by most men and a few women / most women and a few men	Things mentioned in common by both men and women
Women	Painted house; television; donkeys; flowers in the garden; gated compound; forward planning; life without problems; access to a vet	Private health care; private education; solar electricity; water; enough food; children educated to university; ploughing with oxen; ability to work; selling milk; milling machine; ability to farm land; renting extra land; growing potatoes/tomatoes	A good house; electricity; metal roof; glass windows; modern toilet; burned-brick walls; plastered walls; using paid labour; farm size; improved livestock varieties; ploughed fields; modern inputs in farms; commercial tree crops; external crop market; business owner; property investments; cows; sheep/goats; fowl; pigs; car; tractor; motorbike; eat three times per day; educate children to form IV and above; sofa set; social networks; salaried job; fewer children
Men	Bank account; livestock well cared for; land well managed	*We could not populate this cell with any attributes.*	

Instead the assets which matter (subject to the caveats below) are house quality (particularly a combination of good attributes), livestock (although the quantity varies considerably), land worked (note not land owned), modern agricultural inputs, vehicles, and businesses. These assets matter because they are (in the main) productive, they yield income streams, or in the case of houses, substantial benefits to the well-being of those who enjoy them.

There are also a series of attributes which are better described as forms of social capital rather than assets per se (cf. Bebbington 1999 and the discussion in the previous chapter). These include the ability to educate children, being respected, and being a source of loans and support. Similarly a prominent theme in the condition of poverty was dependence on others.

This view of assets should come as little surprise to economists who have explored how assets can be the focus of investment strategies for poor people, who will save to accumulate them, and reduce consumption to avoid selling them (Carter and Barrett 2006, Scott 2010, Liverpool-Tasie and Winter-Nelson 2011, Carter and Lybbert 2012,Barrett and Carter 2013). We explored this in the previous chapter. Asset ownership becomes one of the means by which we can distinguish between 'shallow' and 'deep' poverty (cf. Wuyts 2006). The latter refers to those in poverty, the former those who are vulnerable to it, should they lose their assets.

Nonetheless it is surprising how discussions about class formation and social distinction in writings about Tanzanian peasantry so rarely cover all these dimensions of wealth and poverty. Land worked is a pre-eminent concern and labour is similarly mentioned (Mueller 2011). But the other attributes that were so important in our focus groups are not so frequently covered.

Variation in the Meaning of Assets and Their Implications for Asset Indices

We found some diversity in the meaning of assets within and between study sites. In particular men and women tended to talk about assets in different ways in that women were much more detailed and specific when discussing the assets that mattered, particularly with respect to homes, than were men (Table 3.3).

Across study sites some assets that people mentioned signified different things in different places. A metal roof, we were told in Mbeya, meant nothing these days as they were so common. A good house must be good in all its aspects if it is to signify wealth. Furthermore what levels of wealth are indicated by what sort of house will vary in different parts of the country as the price of basic inputs (cement, glass, and metal sheeting) vary. Tanzania is still characterized by weak infrastructural links and long retail chains (many middle men and women) which can substantially raise the costs of provisions. The cost of building materials is much cheaper close to well-connected urban areas. It costs more to build well in remote rural areas.

Livestock present obvious problems for measuring wealth. The availability of cattle in some parts of the country (such as the south-east) has been historically restricted because of tsetse fly and other diseases. Pigs are rare in predominantly Muslim areas. But even where cattle are present and welcome then, even within a single village, these animals can be both a correlate of wealth, and its ultimate measure. Some respondents noted that people could be wealthy in livestock, but not use that wealth to invest in houses or education. Livestock (cattle) were wealth for such respondents. For others they were a means of providing liquidity—a resource to be turned to when need arose.

Livestock are also interesting because the numbers entailed could vary so much from place to place. In Meru a really wealthy family might send their children to international school, work overseas, *and* have as many as five cattle. In Morogoro the wealthy numbered their herds in the thousands. Clearly livestock would be difficult to operationalize in any nationally comparative asset index.

Land signifies wealth and poverty in somewhat surprising ways. The Demographic and Health Surveys ask only about land ownership.[3] But, according to our informants, ownership per se does not signify wealth. Owning small areas of land was not a problem if rich people could access other peoples' farms through rental agreements or sharecropping. Likewise a common characterization of poverty was not landlessness, but rather the inability properly to use land assets for productive gains. This was either because of incapacity, or because people lacked the capital to make their land productive, or because they had to use their labour on other people's farms to satisfy daily needs. They could not invest their labour time in their own lands. Either way the relevant criteria to determine wealth would be use of the more advanced means of farming (ploughs, improved seeds, and fertilizers). These are not covered in the Demographic and Health Surveys.

Labouring for other people was generally and commonly an indication of poverty. This is also found in recent work which finds that engagement in casual work (universally called kibarua) is an indication of poverty (Homewood et al. 2020). However, as we shall see in later chapters (on Dodoma and Meru), while kibarua is associated with and created by poverty, it is also a means of enrichment. It can be used as part of an investment strategy.

More generally, while similar things appear in the meaning of wealth and poverty across the country, it is difficult to put together a list of assets that has *the same meaning* across the country. Here our findings match other similar studies. Keane and colleagues in wealth-ranking work in focus groups from twelve villages in north and south Tanzania found that the:

[3] https://dhsprogram.com/pubs/pdf/DHSQ7/DHS7_Household_QRE_EN_16Mar2017_DHSQ7.pdf, accessed 26 February 2018.

> criteria chosen to define wealth categories differed substantially from village to village and made sense given what is known of local livelihoods. For example, villages in the north give greater prominence to the importance of cattle, reflecting their well-established cultural and economic importance, while some villages in the south did not refer to cattle at all in their wealth rank definitions.
>
> (Keane et al. 2020: 231)

We have therefore, a response to Johnston and Abreu's challenge posed at the beginning of the paper. They insisted that asset 'indices should be constructed and compared over limited geographic scales and time periods; [and that] the choice of assets should be based on an understanding of what it means to be wealthy or poor in a particular place' (2016: 417–18). Our results clearly show that the national scale is too large a canvas for the limited geographic scales Johnston and Abreu call for. This means that where we have comparative data that crosses several sites within one country then we must presume that any asset index constructed from these data cannot be generalized beyond particularly similar places (villages or neighbouring villages). Instead a meaningful asset index will have to be built up from the ground up—starting with localized asset indices derived from the smallest scale, and generalizing to include other areas only if there is significant similarity.

It follows too that where we have studies of change as observed through assets then these too need to be localized studies. As we have tried to show in the accompanying papers, we need to build up a plethora of different case studies in order to understand how different societies respond to new economic opportunities and constraints in terms of adjusting their asset portfolios.

This point is reinforced if we consider the limitations of our site selection. All the societies we visited were mainly agricultural. They were not herders, not fisher-people, and not running small businesses in towns. Were we to include these other groups then the differences we found are likely to grow. Agriculturalists might be expected to share more similarities. The fact that they do not emphasises the difficulties of finding common measures of locally meaningful wealth and poverty.

Conclusion

We have examined variations in the local meaning of wealth and poverty for men and women in seventeen rural locations from seven different regions in Tanzania. Our data come from a variety of social, economic, and environmental settings, all of them rural, but all primarily agricultural (not pastoral or fishing communities). We undertook this work in order to explore the recommendations made by

Johnston and Abreu (2016) as to the geographical limits of asset indices and the need for asset indices that reflected local understandings of wealth.

We found that, across Tanzania, assets feature prominently in local definitions of wealth and poverty for rural Tanzanians who were pursuing agricultural livelihoods. This poses two challenges. First, if we are to follow asset ownership over time then with what social units do we track assets? Assets are rarely owned solely by individuals. The benefit streams they afford, the work done on them, are shared (unequally) by families. Tracking assets over time requires tracking these domestic units over time too—and this presents significant methodological issues. We tackle this problem in the next chapter.

The second challenge is that while assets are good indicators of local level change, it is difficult to use change in assets to generalise across cases studies and different regions. There are signs that, across rural Tanzania, quality of housing and access to electricity and electrical goods are generic indicators of wealth. However the value of these elements in distinguishing families will vary from place to place. A fine house with electricity may be relatively common in peri-urban areas; it will be a mark of some distinction in the remoter areas we visited. It is possible also that measures related to farm inputs and livestock can be used across large areas. But again this will depend on the environmental circumstances. Some dryland areas may be more suited to livestock than agriculture; some soils and some crops will require more inputs than others. There are also differing cultural values that surround particular types of livestock that vary regionally.

We have also found that, in rural areas, current commonly used asset indices do not well reflect local interpretations of wealth or poverty. The Demographic and Health Surveys counts land ownership, instead of land use. Conversely, asset indices may count things (irons, televisions, or fridges) that were simply not mentioned in our focus group discussions. Asset indices plainly capture statistically significant difference. But it does mean that these statistical patterns are not good proxies of the changes that rural Tanzanians want to see.

To summarize as briefly as possible, we have found that it is difficult to compile effective asset indices that will work across Tanzania. There is too much variety. This is true for our study sites, and the point is enhanced if we recall the limitations of our sources, which omit large areas of the country and important livelihoods. There is more variety to be found than we have been able to capture. Instead we have to find ways of intelligently combining different indices from different places and livelihoods. For some datasets this will be hard, because the sample size from particular places will not allow sample sizes which are large enough from specific places. For other studies larger sample sizes per village allow such localized constructions. Our response to that challenge in this collection has been to compile a series of different case studies—reported in this collection. But first we have to consider the methodological challenges of undertaking this work, and these we consider in the next chapter.

References

Barrett, C. B. and M. R. Carter (2013). 'The Economics of Poverty Traps and Persistent Poverty: Empirical and Policy Implications.' *Journal of Development Studies* 49(7): 976–90.

Barrett, C. B., T. Garg, and L. McBride (2016). 'Well-Being Dynamics and Poverty Traps.' Centre for Climate Change Economics and Policy Working Paper No. 250, Grantham Research Institute on Climate Change and the Environment Working Paper No. 222. LSE, London.

Bebbington, A. (1999). 'Capitals and Capabilities: A Framework for Analyzing Peasant Viability, Rural Livelihoods and Poverty.' *World Development* 27(12): 2021–44.

Benjaminsen, T. A. and I. Bryceson (2012). 'Conservation, Green/Blue Grabbing and Accumulation by Dispossession in Tanzania.' *The Journal of Peasant Studies* 39(2): 335–55.

Bergius, M., T. A. Benjaminsen, and M. Widgren (2018). 'Green Economy, Scandinavian Investments and Agricultural Modernization in Tanzania.' *The Journal of Peasant Studies* 45(4): 825–52.

Blumenstock, J., G. Cadamuro, and R. On (2015). 'Predicting Poverty and Wealth from Mobile Phone Metadata.' *Science* 350(6264): 1073–6.

Brockington, D., O. Howland, V.-M. Loiske, M. Mnzava, and C. Noe (2018). 'Economic Growth, Rural Assets and Prosperity: Exploring the Implications of a Twenty Year Record of Asset Growth in Tanzania.' *Journal of Modern African Studies* 56(2): 217–43.

Carter, M. R. and C. B. Barrett (2006). 'The Economics of Poverty Traps and Persistent Poverty: An Asset-Based Approach.' *Journal of Development Studies* 42(2): 178–99.

Carter, M. R. and T. J. Lybbert (2012). 'Consumption versus Asset Smoothing: Testing the Implications of Poverty Trap Theory in Burkina Faso.' *Journal of Development Economics* 99: 255–64.

Chakraborty, N. M., K. Fry, R. Behl, and K. Longfield (2016). 'Simplified Asset Indices to Measure Wealth and Equity in Health Programs: A Reliability and Validity Analysis Using Survey Data From 16 Countries.' *Global Health: Science and Practice* 4(1): 141–54.

Filmer, D. and L. H. Pritchett (2001). 'Estimating Wealth Effects without Expenditure Data—or Tears: An Application to Educational Enrollments in States of India.' *Demography* 38(1): 115–32.

Homewood, K., M. R. Nielsen, and A. Keane (2020). 'Women, Wellbeing and Wildlife Management Areas in Tanzania.' *The Journal of Peasant Studies*. DOI: 10.1080/03066150.2020.1726323.

Homewood, K. M. (2008). *Ecology of African Pastoralist Societies*. Athens, OH, Ohio University Press.

Howe, L., B. Galobardes, A. Matijasevich, D. Gordon, D. Johnston, O. Onwujekwe, R. Patel, E. A. Webb, D. A. Lawlor, and J. R. Hargreaves (2012). 'Measuring

Socio-Economic Position for Epidemiological Studies in Low- and Middle-Income Countries: A Methods of Measurement in Epidemiology Paper.' *International Journal of Epidemiology* 41(3): 871–86.

Howe, L., J. Hargreaves, S. Gabrysch, and S. Huttly (2009). 'Is the Wealth Index a Proxy for Consumption Expenditure? A Systematic Review.' *Journal of Epidemiology and Community Health* 63(11): 871–7.

Jayne, T. S., J. Chamberlin, and R. Benfica (2018). 'Africa's Unfolding Economic Transformation.' *Journal of Develoment Studies* 54(5): 777–87.

Jean, N., M. Burke, M. Xie, W. M. Davis, D. B. Lobell, and S. Ermon (2016). 'Combining Satellite Imagery and Machine Learning to Predict Poverty.' *Science* 353(6301): 790–4.

Johnston, D. and A. Abreu (2016). 'The Asset Debates: How (Not) to Use Asset Indices to Measure Well-Being and the Middle Class in Africa.' *African Affairs* 115(460): 399–418.

Keane, A., J. F. Lund, J. Bluwstein, N. D. Burgess, M. R. Nielsen, and K. Homewood (2020). 'Impact of Tanzania's Wildlife Management Areas on Household Wealth.' *Nature Sustainability* 3: 226–33.

Liverpool-Tasie, L. S. O. and A. Winter-Nelson (2011). 'Asset versus Consumption Poverty and Poverty Dynamics in Rural Ethiopia.' *Agricultural Economics* 42: 221–33.

Mueller, B. E. T. (2011). 'The Agrarian Question in Tanzania: Using New Evidence to Reconcile an Old Debate.' *Review of African Political Economy* 38(127): 23–42.

Östberg, W., O. Howland, J. Mduma, and D. Brockington (2018). 'Tracing Improving Livelihoods in Rural Africa Using Local Measures of Wealth: A Case Study from Central Tanzania, 1991–2016.' *Land* 7(44): 1–26.

Scott, L. (2010). 'Giving Assets: An Effective Approach for Reducing Vulnerability and Building Livelihoods? The Case of the Chars Livelihoods Programme.' Manchester University. PhD.

Shivji, I. G. (2017). 'The Concept of "Working People".' *Agrarian South: Journal of Political Economy* 6(1): 1–13.

Watmough, G. R., C. L. J. Marcinko, C. Sullivan, K. Tschirhart, P. K. Mutuo, C. A. Palm, and J.-C. Svenning (2019). 'Socioecologically Informed Use of Remote Sensing Data to Predict Rural Household Poverty.' *Proceedings of the National Academy of Sciences* 116(4): 1213–8.

Wuyts, M. (2006). 'Developing Social Protection in Tanzania within a Context of Generalised Insecurity.' Special paper 06 19. Dar es Salaam, REPOA.

Young, A. (2012). 'The African Growth Miracle.' *Journal of Political Economy* 120: 696–739.

4

Assets and Domestic Units

Methodological Challenges for Longitudinal Studies of Poverty Dynamics

Dan Brockington, Ernestina Coast, Anna Mdee, Olivia Howland, and Sara Randall

Introduction

Throughout this collection we describe repeated instances of transformation. We have frequently found that once-poor families appear to be richer due to better farming technology (ploughs, more oxen, and improved crop breeds), higher crop prices, and changing social relations within villages. Or we find villages that were once remote are now bustling with busy centres, motorbike taxis for hire, frequent bus services, solar-powered electricity, and mobile telephone services. Housing quality has markedly improved.

These stories may appear easy to tell. Changes to farming activity have made people richer and they have invested in their homes and farms. But things are not as simple as that. Before we can claim that there is greater meaningful local prosperity, we have to pay more attention to what has improved, and how it has been experienced. Embedded in any claim about changing prosperity are other important claims about how prosperity should be measured and the social units which experience that prosperity.

As we discussed in the second chapter of this book, many of the changes in wealth described here are best captured by exploring changes to *assets*, not poverty lines, because the latter measure standard baskets of consumption and exclude assets. Describing the transformations we have just reported requires describing changes in asset access, ownership, and control. Assets are particularly important to emic definitions of wealth and well-being.

Any measure of wealth and poverty requires the right analytical social unit to track change. Inseparable from any investigation of assets is the question of what is the appropriate social unit of analysis required to understand change in assets. Many of the assets described here (land, houses, livestock) are effectively owned and managed by social units larger than individuals. Their benefits, or the

Dan Brockington, Ernestina Coast, Anna Mdee, Olivia Howland, and Sara Randall, *Assets and Domestic Units: Methodological Challenges for Longitudinal Studies of Poverty Dynamics* In: *Prosperity in Rural Africa? Insights into Wealth, Assets, and Poverty from Longitudinal Studies in Tanzania.* Edited by: Dan Brockington and Christine Noe, Oxford University Press.
DOI: 10.1093/oso/9780198865872.003.0004

problems of their loss, are experienced collectively, although not equally. They are not, therefore, a good measure of change in individual fortunes. Rather assets will require reference to the families, households, domestic units, or domestic groups who collectively own and manage these assets. We will talk about these social entities as 'domestic units' in this chapter.

However, investigations involving domestic units are difficult. It is well established, but inadequately recognized, that domestic units contain and can obscure considerable inequalities, power struggles, and differences between intersections that include gender and age (inter alia). These can be fundamental to understanding the nature and reproduction of poverty and prosperity. This issue is compounded in longitudinal research because domestic units are not static entities. Their membership, location, activities, and both internal and external power relations can change substantially and rapidly.

In this chapter we explore the conceptual and practical challenges that can arise when trying to use assets, and therefore domestic units, in longitudinal research on wealth and poverty. We contend that exploring the socially embedded dynamics of assets is necessary to understanding changing prosperity, both in and out of poverty.

We argue that this requires examining carefully the nature of the domestic units in which assets are socially embedded. As we will show, in some circumstances the challenges of tracking change by following domestic units can be insurmountable. We will argue that it is useful to examine the circumstances in which instability of domestic units makes working with assets so hard. But we will also identify situations where it is more practical to use assets and domestic units in longitudinal research, if the challenges of so doing are tackled carefully.

We proceed as follows. First, we consider how the complications of exploring assets and wealth change over time. Next we turn to the social units through which changes in assets need to be examined. We show that this needs to work with entities like domestic units, but we then outline the problems of working with such units over time. We conclude with thoughts on the importance of tackling these problems in order to understand dynamics of asset ownership over time.

Assets and Poverty Dynamics over Time

As we explored in the two previous chapters, assets are an essential part of rural definitions of wealth and poverty. They provide income streams upon which day-to-day consumption and strategies for investment and growing wealth depend. They are clearly important to monitor as part of understanding poverty dynamics. But their contribution is probably best described as a necessary complication, rather than a welcome clarification. Assets are central to any robust understanding of wealth and poverty, but how to capture that relationship and its changes over time is fraught with difficulty.

If we try and explore the changing value of assets over time problems arise. The monetary value of assets is hard to capture because asset prices can vary considerably over various time scales both seasonally (livestock) and over years (land or motorcycles). Meaningful depreciation costs of houses, in contexts where houses are rarely bought or sold, and where each domestic unit constructs their own, are hard to calculate. This is particularly true of poorer people's houses, or houses built from naturally and locally available materials. The value of land, especially where markets are dominated by informal exchanges, can be hard to ascertain.

These problems grow when exploring the changing value of assets over the long term. In high inflationary environments converting an asset into a cash value and then subjecting that number to modifications due to inflation and purchasing power parity changes, further adds to the difficulties in determining the worth of assets. Even without these financial considerations, exploring change in asset ownership and wealth is complicated because local interpretations of wealth and the value of assets change over time (cf. Mushongah and Scoones 2012).

Finally, the relationship of assets with more common measurements of poverty is not straightforward. The relationship between income and assets is not linear (Harttgen et al. 2013) and asset indices are not always a good proxy for consumption (Howe et al. 2009, and cf. Friis-Hansen, this volume). A recent study, and one of the few to use longitudinal data, found that income increased in all groups studied, but that over the same time period the value of asset portfolios owned by these groups decreased (de Weerdt 2010, Beegle et al. 2011). Borgerhoff Mulder (this volume) does find good relationships between assets and other measures of well-being, concluding that 'assets tell us a lot about a household' (p. 90). But she also cautions against extrapolating these findings broadly. Assets share the flaws of income, consumption, and other measures in that all are, individually, imperfect measures of welfare.

None of these challenges make historical comparisons using assets futile. Indeed, the very fact that asset dynamics can vary from measures of consumption and nutrition is another reason to include assets—for otherwise the changes they signify will be missed. However our point is that it is no easy task. Indeed, as Angus Deaton and Thomas Pogge have pointed out for poverty-line data, these difficulties attend all international and diachronic measures of poverty (Deaton 2004, Pogge 2004). Attention to assets therefore complicates recognized methodological woes; it does not solve them. But the difficulties of examining assets are not in themselves an objection to trying to use them.

Domestic Units and Poverty Dynamics over Time

If assets are important for understanding wealth and poverty dynamics then the social unit and scale of analysis used to assess assets also has to be considered carefully. The social consequences of access to an asset or a bundle of assets can only be understood in the context of the domestic units that own, access, use, and share them (Meinzen-Dick et al. 2011, Johnson et al. 2016). Domestic units can even be understood as entities that come to exist and form themselves around particular configurations of assets. Their origins, fission, and fusion are signalled by transfers and changes in asset distribution. The classic example of this is livestock in pastoral societies, in which male heads of domestic units may have significant decision-making power over the disposal of cattle, but their wives, and their children and their children's fiancés and prospective in-laws, all have claims of varied importance and priority to different animals. In pastoral societies the transfer of livestock marks moments of engagement, marriage, childbirth, and ties between families (Broch-Due 1990).

If the benefit streams and management costs of assets at any moment in time are controlled by domestic units then it follows that any sort of meaningful claim about changes in wealth based on assets which are owned by domestic units hinges on the conceptualization, composition, and stability of domestic units. For example, consider the claim that a particular village has become richer because the asset ownership of its constituent domestic units has improved—they have more livestock, more televisions, more smartphones, and bigger houses. This single claim has in fact two components: the obvious claim that asset portfolios are better, and, underlying it, the claim that domestic units being compared have been stable enough to merit comparison.

If there is no such stability then the comparison becomes less meaningful. For example, it might be that a village appears to have become richer only because the poor are no longer present. This could be the case if poorer domestic units have died, or their members redistributed, because of their poverty, or been forced out, or been displaced by some process of gentrification. Another possibility might be that the organization of domestic production and the membership of domestic units has changed in ways which have allowed new forms of asset accumulation. There may have been no noticeable immigration or emigration, but the domestic units that people live in have changed.

We must attend to the stability of the social unit used because there is a history of domestic units which has seen the term, and particularly cognate terms like 'household', used carelessly and in ways which disguise important dynamics (cf. van de Walle 2006). Specifically, they conceal inequalities between age groups and gender that make generalizations across 'households' problematic at best. These problems have been recognized for many years (cf. Guyer 1981, Vandergeest and Rigg 2012), but still persist (Randall et al. 2011, Randall and Coast 2015). The problems, serious enough in cross-sectional surveys, are compounded in longitudinal studies which attempt to revisit communities, and in particular the same domestic units more than once, because the sorts of economic activity (of production and consumption) that creates domestic units, and the social life that animates them, will vary considerably over time. They may be, in short, not at all the same units that were originally visited.

Numerous dynamics that have to be accounted for when attempting to use domestic units as a vehicle for understanding social change. Perhaps the most well known is the 'developmental cycle' of domestic groups (Goody 1958). This refers to the stages through which domestic units pass as they age and members are born and die, which, to an extent, determine their residence patterns, control over resources, and membership, as well as their asset base. Fortes used this concept to explain how households from the same ethnic group could appear to adopt different residence patterns, demonstrating that this was simply a function of the 'time factor' that had to be grasped if we are to understand how these societies reproduce themselves (Fortes 1958: 2). As Stenning showed so clearly, the developmental cycle of WoDaabe pastoralists in northern Nigeria was marked by stages of betrothal, child birth, and then the subsequent dispersal and dissolution of the domestic units (Stenning 1958). He also made clear that exigencies of climate, disease, and the internal dynamics of units themselves would mean that units would coalesce and fissure over varying timescales. For the purposes of understanding dynamics in prosperity and wealth with respect to assets, the developmental cycle is essential. It shows how younger units and older units can be expected to be poorer than mature units. Growing prosperity may simply be a sign of a maturing family, and immiseration a sign of senescence.

But the developmental cycle contains important assumptions that, if violated, may limit its usefulness (Murray 1987). First, it assumes a homogeneity in societies to processes of change over time that allows for these generational processes to be observed. Second, the developmental cycle can be distinguished from other forces for change which are occurring over similar time spans. Murray argued that, in southern African contexts in the 1980s, there was too much variety in the form and dynamics of domestic units to generalize in terms of cycles. What people did, and what happened to their residential groups and larger families, was bound up in changes to the migrant labour economy of South Africa, more than it was driven by internal dynamics.

These tensions illustrate that the domestic unit is both a product of cultural expression that reproduces a society (it facilitates stasis), and an expression of the ways that individuals interact through relations of mutual dependence in order to ensure their own survival in a context of varying economic, environmental and political conditions (it helps people to cope with change). Hyden suggests that an economy of affection is characteristic of the peasant mode of production:

> it denotes a network of support, communications and interaction among structurally defined groups connected by blood, kin, community or other affinities, for example, religion. It links together in a systematic fashion a variety of discrete economic and social units which in other regards may be autonomous.
>
> (Hyden 1983: 8)

Whilst the original analysis saw the economy of affection as offering resistance to the capitalist mode of production, Hyden (2015) finds the concept still useful to describe social relations and reciprocity in increasingly urban and capitalist Africa.

Ferguson's recent work on notions of dependence in southern Africa develops the idea that people seek relations of dependence on each other and on collective institutions (Ferguson 2013 and 2015). In apartheid South Africa, the labour market and apartheid laws dominated the domestic networks that could be constituted, with many men migrating to earn wages to send home to their dependents in the homelands. In contemporary South Africa, social protection systems and high unemployment create new forms of dependence, where the recipients of social welfare (the elderly and children) can construct domestic units that do not rely on the waged labour of a male employee. Thus the domestic unit is also buffeted and shaped by wider economic and political forces.

There are common forms of heterogeneity and instability in some societies that make it difficult to talk about developmental cycles, and indeed stymy the whole project of trying to explore change through the lens of domestic groups, particularly if those groups are seen as geographical nodes, rather than as networks of relationships. Membership of domestic units may be highly unstable because of divorce, fostering practices, or migration. Mathew Lockwood describes in detail the sorts of dynamism that occurred in rice growing districts of southern Tanzania that exemplify these difficulties:

> The following is the history of the household in which I lived between December 1985 and September 1986. Before I moved in, the household consisted of a man in his forties, A, his wife, son from a previous marriage, aged about 15, and a daughter aged about 5. In December his wife left him and went to live with relatives in Zanzibar. The daughter went to stay with her grandmother in the village. At this point I moved in. January: a cousin of A's arrives, with her teenage daughter. They start preparing to farm rice in the valley. February: A's son argues with his father and leaves for relatives in Mkongo. A's daughter comes back to the house. April: The visiting cousin moves to a dungu [small hut in the fields

> used when cultivation work is heavy] in the rice fields. Her daughter, together with A's daughter, lives half there and half in the village. A's son returns for a short time and then leaves again. Late May/June: A's cousin and her daughter harvest rice and return to the village. They then go off to a village on the road to Dar es Salaam to visit her husband. Throughout this period, A would go to Dar es Salaam for a few days every month, where he acted as a rent collector for someone. The cousin's husband would also come at weekends from the other village, where he was a teacher. (Lockwood 1998: 143 fn 1)

The relationships and dependencies which make domestic units come to exist in the first place, are themselves dynamic. Units, and their cycles, may experience varied pressures as they take on tasks of educating children (and young adults) or providing migratory labour, or taking on new livelihoods (agriculture, urban occupations). The domestic unit, which was configured around one set of assets, livelihoods and their social relations, may have transformed into differently structured and configured units under new forms of livelihood, opportunity, and constraint, whilst continuing to serve key roles as a site of socialization, care, and support.

When exploring change involving domestic units the stability of the unit becomes key. 'Stability' here does not refer simply to residential stasis, but to social relations within domestic units. Whitehead's experience of working with 'households' in Northern Ghana provides a salutary example of the difficulties of comparing domestic units whose location remains the same, but whose developmental cycles have become so complex and convoluted that understanding how assets benefit different members cannot be understood without delving into the different components of the domestic unit. She describes, for example, (polygamously) married sons remaining with their (polygamously married) father in the same compound, and sometimes continuing to do so after their father had died. As a result:

> Households could have several adults living in them and these adults included closely related married and single men, as well as polygamously married wives and the elderly widows of former male household members. This complex compound was an asset holding and cooperative work unit, although its physical, economic and social organization allowed for the possibility of overlapping circles of individual and collective responsibilities. (Whitehead 2006: 285)

The number of people living in these groups were large, with median 'household' size being over twelve and ranging up to 73. Any assumption that domestic units remain sufficiently constant to compare over time is clearly ambitious in this case. Jane Guyer's longitudinal study of change around Ibadan eschewed domestic units altogether because 'people were mobile from one house to another, and their income earning, including farming, was individuated [so] at the pragmatic level of research method "the household" was unmanageable' (Guyer 1997: 25).

It is possible therefore, that a domestic unit surveyed for one purpose, or at one particular moment, may not be the best vehicle to understand the relationships and dependencies around which different sorts of domestic units come to exist at a later time. This could be because its circumstances have changed so much over time, or it could reflect the nature of the research instrument. A large-scale questionnaire-based survey creates a particular domestic unit through both the definition of the unit designed to guide the interviewers and the questions that are being asked in order to make it visible. The domestic unit produced by a survey may preclude understanding of wider dynamics, resource flows, and relationships. These important dynamics can be beyond the scope of many research projects, as their limited levels of analysis and recording of data precludes understanding such complexity as experienced in daily realities of life. The type of data we, as researchers, want to collect, especially when we need larger scale statistics, are not concerned with the dynamics of domestic unit level changes or fluctuations.

Alternatively there may be so little stability, or even recognizability, in the constitution of domestic units from one period to the next that using domestic units when bounded by geographical location as a lens through which to view change simply makes no sense at all. They are too ephemeral. This is likely to be the case in Mathew Lockwood's study site in Rufiji (Lockwood 1998). Housing structures might remain constant, but who lives in them, how they are related to each other, and, crucially, what assets bring which benefits to whom are too variable to be easily tracked over time.

Even if a once surveyed domestic unit ceases to exist, the relationships of dependence between individuals can still continue in ways largely invisible to the outsider using a survey tool. In 2004–5, Mdee interviewed what she thought were several distinct households located around a public tap in the village of Uchira in Tanzania (see Chapter 16). On marrying into one of those households, and over the course of several visits, she realized that these several households were in fact one domestic unit sharing blood relations, economic interests, and assets. However, a survey of domestic units which assumed domestic units were constituted by housing units would have recorded two elderly female-headed households, and two male-headed households at different life stages. In fact, the 'unit' in the terms defined in this paper is constituted by relations of dependence, obligation, and reciprocity that now extend across continents.

A variation of the scenario that Lockwood describes is that the degree of instability in social relations that constitute domestic units may be a contributing factor to the prosperity of the units. More stable units may experience more prosperity and derive more benefits from their assets. De Weerdt's research on the

Kagera panel study indicates as much (de Weerdt 2010). He used quantitative data to predict which households (as defined by the Kagera study) were more likely to lose and gain assets over time, and then focus group research to explore which households were bucking the expected trends (gaining assets when losses would have been predicted, and vice versa). This produced a number of characteristics that were typically missed by econometric analyses, including the importance of good co-operative relations between spouses for prosperity. Conversely, divorce could be particularly disadvantageous to women, as could widowhood in polygamous marriages.

In instances such as these the dynamism of domestic units becomes a means by which the fortunes of their members can be understood. Such longitudinal data cannot be organized by rows of 'households' in a spreadsheet—with obvious implications for panel data. Rather it is the changes to the definition and functioning of domestic units, and individuals within them, which becomes the focus for analysis. The domestic units become the dependent variable.

Once again the dynamism of the domestic units which come to exist around bundles of assets does not make exploration of asset dynamics impossible. That very dynamism, potentially visible through assets, can make exploring change in assets ever more important. Our point therefore is not that domestic units should not be used, just that they should be used carefully, and, if necessary re-defined should the stability required for meaningful comparison simply be inadequate.

Assets, Progress, and Change

Ben White, in his review of *Revisting Rural Places* captures well the dangers of longitudinal research. They are certainly pleasurable and exciting for the researcher but:

> however promising, many re-studies are ultimately disappointing, showing us 'then it was like that, now it is like this' but unable to tell us much more about how and why things changed, or how these changes have been experienced. To be useful, they must go beyond the presentation of contrasting snapshots or time slices to the more demanding project of writing rural social history, focusing on the processes and mechanisms, rather than just the 'facts' and outcomes, of rural change. (White 2014: 635)

We do not dispute this point. But for longitudinal studies to be taken seriously, there must be room for some more empirically focused approaches. As we saw in Chapter 2 sometimes the facts are disputed, or obscured by techniques used to track change. We need to get a clear understanding of who gets what, or who owns what, as well as what do they do with it (following Bernstein 2010) to understand the role of assets (and not just land ownership) in class dynamics. That means knowing what the 'what' is that Bernstein refers to.

In our case studies the assets we examined are also particularly important for vernacular definitions of wealth and poverty, for, in other words, understanding situated class dynamics. For example, change in Gitting (see Chapter 10), the example with which we began was locally explained by the decline in 'capitalism' (Swahili: ubepare). This was a reference to a broadening of the means of production which had seen ploughs, oxen, and eventually tractors spread from a restricted number of individuals who charged extortionate fees for their use. Greater equality in asset ownership, through local investment, resulted in a general rise in prosperity. As we have seen in Chapter 2 it is precisely this form of investment that poverty-line data omit.

But the opposite proved to be the case in Dodoma, where Östberg worked (see Chapter 9). Here wealthy entrepreneurs' tractors are new arrivals and essential to the larger farms that people are now working. Investment in shared water points has also reduced labour (particularly women's work) in collecting water. Greater inequality, in the form of relatively benevolent wealthy businessmen, has been key to raising productivity generally. The changes to the village have also seen a change in the meaning of daily labour from being solely a sign of penury and disadvantage to also signifying, in some circumstances, the ability to invest in particular projects.

However, while greater attention to assets can provide more sensitive insights into local-level class dynamics it is also possible for attention to assets to be used in ways which obscure change. In tandem with this burgeoning interest in measuring assets lies a significant danger of the 'seduction of quantification' (Merry 2016), with the push to quantify, track, and compare complex social phenomena.

Specifically there is a danger that one or two assets become proxies for 'prosperity'. For example, if the use of iron sheeting as a roofing material (which is helpfully visible to remote sensing) denotes progress (Jean et al. 2016, Watmough et al. 2019), then policy and resources might shift to fulfil this indicator. However, changes to the roofing of a dwelling can conceal all sorts of changes in the social lives of those living in it, and may not be linked to the 'prosperity' of the individuals living under it. Thus a single asset used as an indicator could conceal important dynamics, and become as a proxy for a normative concept (that iron sheeted roofing makes a better home).

If assets can be incorporated into national measures of well-being (Maganga et al. 2016), it is important to understand how such changes might be grounded in specific instances in the lived experiences of particular domestic units in different places. General measures of change in assets across regions or countries may be based in very different experiences of the distribution and enjoyment of those assets in particular places. There remains a strong role for locally based and well-grounded research that can contextualize such change.

Conclusion: Exploring Asset Dynamics in Development Research

We began with apparently straightforward observations of simple changes, and improvements in people's lives that are measurable and locally meaningful because they detail changes that matter, for which people strive. The purpose of our reflections in this chapter is not to invalidate such observations. However, we want to make clear precisely what claims are being made when prosperity is said to have improved because of a change in patterns of asset ownership.

In the first instance the prosperity that assets signify has to be taken in conjunction with other measurements of well-being. In the second, these claims are not just about assets, they also entail claims about the social units which share, benefit from, maintain, and reproduce these assets. We must recognize that there are two things which have happened in numerous examples in this collection: assets have increased, and domestic units have remained sufficiently stable for that to be a visible and meaningful change. Instability in the membership of domestic units would render the comparison over time less meaningful.

If circumstances allow—reasonable membership stability in domestic units—then exploring change in assets can be useful. And if not, then not. In two chapters in this collection (Chapters 13 and 16) other methods have been necessary. But we also suggest that this is, ideally, not the only measure used. The weak relationship between assets and other forms of well-being and prosperity (income, nutrition, wealth) means that it is but one measure among many that needs to be considered. This should be no surprise: poverty is multi-facetted. The main reason why these other measures were not also included in the re-studies we have undertaken is simply that they were not easily accessible in the original survey data.

Researchers of poverty dynamics and long-term change, we submit, need to understand these conceptions of wealth and the social units which wield them. This requires accurate and nuanced evidence and conceptualizations of domestic units that are recognizable to those communities from which we collect our data. An approach to understanding poverty dynamics, dominated by Western academic or policy evidence, cannot claim to understand those changes as experienced within their original context.

More generally, understanding poverty in its many dimensions requires exploring different indicators at a variety of scales—the individual, the domestic unit, the community, region, or nation. For each scale particular indicators are required, and others may be inappropriate. But tracking change over time requires sufficient constancy in the unit of measurement. And if the individuals, households, or communities we are interested in effectively disappear, then we cannot make statements about change over time at those scales, and we may not be able to compare different places for which data at particular scales no longer exist.

Or, to make this point another way: there are some aspects of the world which are simply unknowable because of the ways that they are constituted and because of the ways in which they change. The challenge of research in development is to push the boundaries between what can be known, and what cannot. The changing nature and meaning of assets, and the changing social units which govern and derive benefit from them, will make the location and shape of this research frontier ever interesting.

We believe that tracing assets through domestic units does indeed push the boundaries of our knowledge and understanding of social change, but only if the limitations of what we can learn from assets, and how we treat domestic units, are taken seriously. Attempts to use assets as proxies for change without due care will miss the social contexts that make assets meaningful in the first place. As the consequences of land loss and economic investment strategies are vigorously debated we encourage more researchers to use this sort of longitudinal approach to understand change in rural areas. However progress in understanding will be achieved if researchers recognize the heterogeneity of change and the critical importance of local context and conditions, often at small scales.

References

Beegle, K., J. De Weerdt, and S. Dercon (2011). 'Migration and Economic Mobility in Tanzania: Evidence from a Tracking Survey.' *The Review of Economics and Statistics* 93(3): 1010–33.

Bernstein, H. (2010). *Class Dynamics of Agrarian Change*. Halifx and Winnipeg, Fernwood Publishing.

Broch-Due, V. (1990). 'Livestock Speak Louder than Sweet Words: Changing Property and Gender Relations among the Turkana.' *Property, Poverty and People: Changing Rights in Property and the Problems of Pastoral Development*. P. T. W. Baxter and R. Hogg. Manchester, Manchester University Press: 147–63.

de Weerdt, J. (2010). 'Moving out of Poverty in Tanzania: Evidence from Kagera.' *The Journal of Development Studies* 46(2): 331–49.

Deaton, A. (2004). 'Measuring Poverty.' Princeton Research Program in Development Studies Working Paper. Available at SSRN: https://ssrn.com/abstract=564001 or http://dx.doi.org/10.2139/ssrn.564001.

Ferguson, J. (2013). 'How to Do Things with Land: A Distributive Perspective on Rural Livelihoods in Southern Africa.' *Journal of Agrarian Change* 13(1): 166–74.

Ferguson, J. (2015). *Give a Man a Fish: Reflections on the New Politics of Distribution*. Durham, NC, Duke University Press.

Fortes, M. (1958). 'Introduction.' *The Developmental Cycle in Domestic Groups*. J. Goody. Cambridge, Cambridge University Press: 1–14.

Goody, J. (1958). *The Developmental Cycle in Domestic Groups*. Cambridge, Cambridge University Press.

Guyer, J. I. (1981). 'Household and Community in African Studies.' *African Studies Review* 24(2/3): 81–137.

Guyer, J. I. (1997). *An African Niche Economy: Farming to Feed Ibadan 1968–88*. Edinburgh, Edinburgh University Press.

Harttgen, K., S. Klasen, and S. Vollmer (2013). 'An African Growth Miracle? Or: What Do Asset Indices Tell Us about Trends in Economic Performance?' *Review of Income and Wealth* 59 (Special Issue, October 2013): s37–61.

Howe, L., J. Hargreaves, S. Gabrysch, and S. Huttly (2009). 'Is the Wealth Index a Proxy for Consumption Expenditure? A Systematic Review.' *Journal of Epidemiology and Community Health* 63(11): 871–7.

Hyden, G. (1983). *No Shortcut to Progress: African Development in Perspective*. Berkeley, University of California Press.

Hyden, G. (2015). 'The Economy of Affection.' *Routledge Handbook of African Politics*. N. Cheeseman, D. Anderson, and R. Scheibler. Abingdon, Routledge: 334–45.

Jean, N., M. Burke, M. Xie, W. M. Davis, D. B. Lobell, and S. Ermon (2016). 'Combining Satellite Imagery and Machine Learning to Predict Poverty.' *Science* 353(6301): 790–4.

Johnson, N. L., C. Kovarika, R. Meinzen-Dick, J. Njuki, and B. and A. Quisumbing (2016). 'Gender, Assets, and Agricultural Development: Lessons from Eight Projects.' *World Development* 83: 295–31.

Lockwood, M. (1998). *Fertility and Household Labour in Tanzania: Demography, Economy, and Society in Rufiji District, C. 1870–1986*. Oxford, Oxford University Press.

Maganga, F. P., K. Askew, R. Odgaard, and H. Stein (2016). 'Dispossession through Formalization: Tanzania and the G8 Land Agenda in Africa.' *Asian Journal of African Studies* 40: 3–49.

Meinzen-Dick, R., N. Johnson, A. Quisumbing, J. Njuki, J. Behrman, D. Rubin, A. Peterman, and E. Waithanji (2011). 'Gender, Assets, and Agricultural Development Programs. A Conceptual Framework.' CAPRi Working Paper No. 99.

Merry, S. E. (2016). *The Seductions of Quantification: Measuring Human Rights, Gender Violence, and Sex Trafficking*. Chicago, University of Chicago Press.

Murray, C. (1987). 'Class, Gender and the Household.' *Development and Change* 18: 235–49.

Mushongah, J. and I. Scoones (2012). 'Livelihood Change in Rural Zimbabwe over 20 Years.' *The Journal of Development Studies* 48(9): 1241–57.

Pogge, T. (2004). 'The First UN Millennium Development Goal: A Cause for Celebration?' *Real World Justice. Studies in Global Justice*, vol. 1. A. Follesdal and T. Pogge. Dordrecht, Springer: 317–38.

Randall, S. and E. Coast (2015). 'Poverty in African Households: The Limits of Survey and Census Representations.' *Journal of Development Studies* 51(2): 162–77.

Randall, S., E. Coast, and T. Leone (2011). 'Cultural Constructions of the Concept of Household in Sample Surveys.' *Population Studies* 65(2): 217–29.

Stenning, D. J. (1958). 'Household Viability among the Pastoral Fulani Derrick.' *The Developmental Cycle in Domestic Groups*. J. Goody. Cambridge, Cambridge University Press: 92–119.

van de Walle, E. (2006). *African Households: Censuses and Surveys*. London, Routledge.

Vandergeest, P. and J. Rigg (2012). 'The Restudy "Problem" and Agrarian Change: Revisiting Rural Places in Southeast Asia.' *Revisiting Rural Places: Pathways to Poverty and Prosperity in Southeast Asia*. J. Rigg and P. Vandergeest. Singapore, Singapore University Press and Hawaii University Press: 1–24.

Watmough, G. R., C. L. J. Marcinko, C. Sullivan, K. Tschirhart, P. K. Mutuo, C. A. Palm, and J.-C. Svenning (2019). 'Socioecologically Informed Use of Remote Sensing Data to Predict Rural Household Poverty.' *Proceedings of the National Academy of Sciences* 116(4): 1213–8.

White, B. (2014). 'Revisiting Rural Places: Pathways to Poverty and Prosperity in Southeast Asia.' *The Journal of Peasant Studies* 41(4): 635–38.

Whitehead, A. (2006). 'Persistent Poverty in North East Ghana.' *Journal of Development Studies* 42(2): 278–300.

PART II
CASE STUDIES OF CHANGE

5

Tracing the Relationships between Assets and Well-Being in Complex Social Environments

Monique Borgerhoff Mulder

Epilogue pages 412–414

Introduction

Research on changing poverty and prosperity in African contexts, and in Tanzania specifically, is split. Some authors celebrate a rising continent with healthy economic growth, macro-economic stability, and climbing productivity (Radelet 2010, Chuhan-Pole 2011), or at least elements of such optimism (as in some chapters of Adam et al. 2017). Some have even suggested an 'African Growth Miracle', on the basis of DHS data across numerous African countries showing increases in asset ownership, education, and employment, together with declines in morbidity and mortality (Young 2012). Indeed *The Economist* (3 December 2011) produced the caption 'The Hopeful Continent: Africa Rising' when only eleven years earlier they had dubbed Africa 'The Hopeless Continent' on their cover. Others find many indications that the structural causes of spatially concentrated poverty persist, that economic growth fails to be inclusive of the poor (Barrett 2011, Barrett and Carter 2013) and may indeed merely exacerbate inequality (Benjaminsen and Bryceson 2012). For example, studies of the Tanzanian Household Budget Survey conclude that the economic growth that occurred between 1991–2 and 2000–1 failed to reduce poverty among the poor (Mashindano et al. 2013). Yet other scholars maintain that the economic policies of neoliberalism promote land loss, alienation, and eviction among the poor, leading to the neglect of rural livelihoods, marginalization, and increased impoverishment of vulnerable communities (e.g., Mueller 2011, Bluwstein et al. 2018). In short, emphasizing the recent economic growth in African countries can be a distraction from recognizing persistent poverty and inequality.

Monique Borgerhoff Mulder, *Tracing the Relationships between Assets and Well-Being in Complex Social Environments*
In: *Prosperity in Rural Africa? Insights into Wealth, Assets, and Poverty from Longitudinal Studies in Tanzania.*
Edited by: Dan Brockington and Christine Noe, Oxford University Press.
DOI: 10.1093/oso/9780198865872.003.0005

As Brockington and Noe (Chapter 2) note, the differences between these positions are ideological and epistemological as well as empirical. This chapter turns squarely to the latter. Specifically I address the extent to which inclusive economic growth reflects experience in the lives of villagers living in south-western Tanzania, and I explore how a widely used measure of wealth—material asset holdings—is associated with well-being.

As regards the 'African Growth Miracle' the picture in Tanzania is quite mixed. Two decades of stable economic growth have brought a reduction in non-monetary measures of poverty, contingent on public (and private) investments in education and health. Monetary poverty has nevertheless declined only minimally (38.6 to 35.7 per cent) between 1991 and 2007, with the absolute number of people living in poverty actually rising to 3.3 million (Arndt et al. 2016, based on Household Budget Survey consumption figures that exclude expenditures on durable goods). Furthermore, as regards inequality—well recognized as impeding future economic growth and progress towards poverty reduction (e.g., Ravallion 2014), and now prioritized as one of the seventeen Sustainable Development Goals to guide development over the next fifteen years—the picture is again mixed. Tanzanian society is showing widening wealth inequality between regions, gender, and the rural-urban divide (Maliti 2016, using DHS wealth data 2004, 2007, and 2010), and both increasing and (latterly) decreasing horizontal inequality in education (Hassine and Zeufack 2015, Maliti 2016, using HBS and DHS data respectively). Furthermore different dimensions of inequality (income, education, health, water, and sanitation, Maliti 2018) are both spatially and socially patterned. For example the Gini coefficient in income inequality declined from 0.37 in 2007 to 0.34 in 2012, due primarily to improved distribution of consumption in rural as compared to urban areas. On the other hand the top 20 per cent of income earners in Tanzania accounts for almost half the total income in Tanzania, and 28 per cent of Tanzanians still live below the national poverty line (with 9 per cent classed as 'extremely poor', i.e., below the food poverty line). Furthermore spatial, wealth-based, and gender-based inequities in some health outcomes are still on the rise, as is access to clean water (Maliti 2018). In short, national level data offer no clear narrative of how livelihoods and well-being have changed over the last two decades. Whether this reflects the somewhat patchy quality of national statistics or genuine heterogeneity across the nation is unclear.

This should not be surprising. The problems with depicting shifts in poverty levels using national statistics are well recognized (Jerven 2013). These include inconsistencies in data collection protocols over time, difficulties in finding appropriate price deflators, discrepancies between findings using poverty indices based on consumption as opposed to national PPP1US$/day data, and possible biases against identifying rich households, all recognized as problems for Tanzania (Arndt et al. 2016). In short, country-level analyses can conceal disparities in disadvantage, and hide the specific dynamics entailed in poverty alleviation and/or persistence. Village-level studies, by comparison, can complement national statistics by offering insights into locally relevant features of wealth transitions, insights that national studies might miss on account of their coarse (and typically aggregated) description of economic changes across time and space. As such evidence from village-level studies may have a role to play in both confirming and/or contesting the inferences drawn from national-level studies.

Turning now to measurement issues, there is considerable debate over the nature of the data needed to adjudicate on the nature and drivers of change over time in levels of poverty, well-being, and prosperity. Indeed the principle critiques of Young's conclusions regarding the African Miracle focus on measurement problems, and specifically the use of assets to identify wealth.

Using assets, and assets-based wealth rankings, as indices of changing economic conditions can be problematic, particularly when sites are compared across geographical zones with differing natural resources, infrastructure, and length of value chains, and also when sites are compared over time (Harttgen et al. 2013, Johnston and Abreu 2016). Not only do preferences, prices, as well as quality and mere availability of different items vary across regions and decades, but the very significance of an item (be it a corrugated iron roof, a bicycle, or a mobile phone) changes over time (Howland et al. 2021). More fundamentally, notions of well-being, poverty, and security are hugely variable with respect to their dependency on material wealth, and of course differ on whether they are defined by subjective (emic) or objective (etic) criteria (Tucker et al. 2011). Furthermore, even when focus is restricted to the material domain, expenditure, income, consumption, and assets are often only weakly associated (Howe et al. 2012, Johnston and Abreu 2016, Kaiser et al. 2017), with households handling their stocks (assets) and flows (income) in different ways. For example, when faced with weather shocks, poorer pastoral families in Burkina Faso sought to conserve their assets (herds) and reduce their consumption ('asset smoothers') whereas pastoral families with bigger herds could offset consumption declines by selling cattle ('consumption smoothers') (Carter and Lybbert 2012).

Alternatives to assets indices are measures based on consumption, and measures based on income. For multiple reasons these can also be problematic. As argued by Johnston and Abreu (2016), consumption measures (that typically exclude large/durable expenditures including productive assets so as to avoid rare events that might skew data) fail to capture the key investments rural families make to change their lives, such as a plough, secondary education, or hospital charges after an accident. Using income raises different challenges. Small payments here and there can be hard to quantify. They are also difficult to recall, especially if they are seasonal, and they may also be concealed from other household members, a the interviewee. Furthermore, as discussed below, income can be an indicator of poverty or landlessness rather than wealth.

There is no easy answer to the question of which measures of wealth are most informative. Which measure to use will depend crucially on the question to be asked, the specifics of the study site, and the opportunities for obtaining accurate data. Further considerations are whether the data are to be used for comparison with other sites, and whether the goal of the research is to assess change over time. Given these complexities, it certainly behoves researchers to explore the consequences of their chosen wealth measure for broader individual or family well-being, especially those outcomes that are deemed emically prominent; in other words, to determine whether the measure of wealth selected provides a robust means of tracking locally important changes in well-being (Howland et al. 2021). It is also important to follow the fortunes of rural households during periods of economic growth, and when this growth slows, in order to glean insights into the dynamics of change, as advocated by Dercon (2006).

To address these issues, I use a fifteen-year study in Tanzania's Rukwa (now Katavi) Region to examine changes in well-being over time. Specifically, using data from the village of Mirumba, I tackle two sets of questions. The first asks whether economic livelihoods improved or faltered in Mirumba between 1995 and 2010. More specifically:

- How have farm productivity, land use, and off-farm economic pursuits changed over time?
- How has overall economic well-being changed over time, using locally relevant indigenous wealth categories that are comparable to other studies?
- Are changes in household wealth over time a consequence of selective emigration and/or selective household dissolution?
- Turning from households to individuals, how do individuals prosper or flounder with respect to the indigenous wealth ranking of their household?
- And is there any difference by gender?

The second set of questions address whether wealth measures based on assets, explored in this collection of papers, offer a good indicator of broader well-being. Specifically I ask:

- Are assets associated with farm productivity?
- Are assets associated with absence of stress?
- Are assets associated with educational performance of school-aged children in the household
- Are assets associated with the growth of members under 15 years of age, and with BMI of adult household members?

Briefly, the answer to the first question is: production and asset holdings have generally increased, but with some worrying trends. To the second question, the answer is an unambiguous yes—assets tell us a lot about household well-being.

More generally, with respect to the divergence of views among researchers investigating changes in prosperity over time, I show that both narratives in their more extreme forms probably over-simplify the picture, and that there is considerable power in ethnographically based longitudinal studies, at least to the extent that they can be generalized.

In the next section I give the ethnographic context of the study and the methods used to assess changes in economic livelihoods and consequences thereof. I then turn to answer the two questions concerning changes in economic livelihoods, and the value of wealth measures based on assets, before discussing the findings in their broader context and offering a brief conclusion from the study regarding the African Growth Miracle.

Ethnography and Methods

Introduction to the Village and Nation

The Rukwa Valley (previously Mpanda District, Rukwa Region; now Mlele District, Katavi Region) lies in western Tanzania to the east of Lake Tanganyika below the Ufipa Plateau. The traditional home of the Pimbwe people (Mgawe et al. 2013) its villages are now a mix of Pimbwe and neighbouring Fipa and Rungwa groups (Willis 1966) and, like most other villages in Tanzania, representatives of many other ethnicities. The area is and has for the last one hundred years been poorly served administratively in terms of infrastructure (Mgawe et al. 2013, Seel et al. 2014), labelled as a forgotten corner and administrative backwater of central Africa (Tambila 1981) and still seriously lagging in the 1990s (Jerve and Ntemi 2009). The national neoliberal reforms of the late 1990s were slow to affect life in Rukwa Region, but gradual improvements to the road into the valley (Kisi-Kibaoni, starting most notably around 2005), and efforts to link the regional capital Sumbawanga to the city of Mbeya 350km to its south, have brought greater economic opportunities to the valley, although primarily with respect to the agricultural sector. While Ufipa has long been dubbed a breadbasket of Tanzania, the northern Rukwa Valley (and similarly the communities along the shores of Lake Tanganyika) suffered from poor soils, no transport network, and poor infrastructural development (e.g., Wandel and Homboe-Ottesen 1992, Hadley et al. 2007). Like many other parts of western Tanzania villages in Mpimbwe have received an influx of Sukuma agro-pastoralists who began arriving in the area in the mid-1970s (Salerno et al. 2017). The Sukuma live on the peripheries of villages, and have brought large numbers of livestock, co-operative work parties, new crops (sweet potato, rice), and the use of ox-drawn ploughs, as well as generating new jealousies between the 'indigenous' peoples and the immigrants (for further south in the Rukwa Valley, see Brockington 2001).

Transformation of the agricultural sector from subsistence to commercial production has been at the heart of Tanzanian policy since the early 2000s. Strategic frameworks include the Tanzania Development Vision 2025, the National Strategy for Growth and Reduction of Poverty (NSGRP/MKUKUTA and ZSGRP/MKUZA), Agricultural Sector Development Strategy (ASDS), Agricultural Sector Development Programme (ASDP), Comprehensive African Agriculture (CAADP)-TAFSIP, and SAGCOT, culminating in Kilimo Kwanza launched in 2009. The impact of such programmes on the Rukwa Valley has been limited, but not negligible, due in part to the Pimbwe origins of the nation's Prime Minister serving between 2008 and 2015 and the albeit highly delayed building of a tarmac road into the Rukwa Valley. This road was only effectively linked to the national network in 2016, but it was already making crop marketing much more practicable and profitable by 2006. Furthermore there was no implementation of the pilot phase of the Tanzania Social Action Fund's conditional cash transfers in the study area, an intervention with considerable social and economic benefits for vulnerable families elsewhere in the nation (Evans et al. 2014).

The data presented here were collected using full censuses of every household in the village of Mirumba conducted on seven occasions (always dry season) between 1995 and 2010; (subsequent visits until 2016 did not produce full censuses). As elsewhere in Tanzania the village of Mirumba consists of a varying number of subvillages—all of which were censused unless they were predominantly Sukuma. The data therefore capture the lives of the non-Sukuma inhabitants of Mirumba village over a fifteen-year period, and were virtually exclusively collected by myself, almost always with one or more local assistant.

A household is defined by the identity of its household head(s) rather than physical location. There may be one or two household heads—either a married couple, a single man, or a single woman. Households can re-form across years due to death, migration, marriage, and divorce. In the analyses below a household is considered to be the same household across two consecutive censuses if it is headed by the same individual(s) at both censuses (all paired household heads are in heterosexual unions, unsurprisingly). A household is considered to have disbanded if not found in the village at the next census (although in some cases the household will have moved in its entirety to another village). Finally, a household is considered to be new if it is made up of a new pairing of individuals from within or outside of the village, even if they occupy a pre-existing, but subsequently abandoned, physical structure.

Livelihoods in Mpimbwe

Farm production

Prior to successive expropriation of their traditional homeland primarily for conservation purposes (Borgerhoff Mulder et al. 2007, Seel et al. 2014) cassava production, fishing, and hunting were central to Pimbwe livelihoods. Over the twentieth century cassava, finger millet, and increasingly maize became critical to subsistence, with cash crop production (maize, and in recent years sunflower, rice, finger millet, and sesame) gaining particular prevalence in recent years as opportunities for reliable sale are boosted by the improved road network out of the Rukwa Valley (in the 1990s sacks produced for sale were often found rotting in peoples' homes or on the side of the road). Maize is currently both the primary subsistence crop and the most common cash crop. Typically maize surpluses are sold either directly after harvest or later in the year when prices climb, depending on a family's immediate cash needs. Often, as a result of cash exigencies, a household will sell too much maize at harvest season, such that they run out of maize in their store prior to the next harvest. If this occurs before April/May, there is not yet green maize available for picking in the fields and maize (or maize flour) must be purchased (often for a high price). These observations motivate measures used in this study: the total number of sacks produced (*total sacks [ttsacks]*); and the number of months a household was without maize in the store prior to the next harvest (*months without maize*).

Land in Tanzania is ultimately the property of the village. Accordingly questions about land ownership are poorly understood. Furthermore typically it is access to land (described below) rather than land ownership that is of crucial importance to crop production. Land access is conditioned as much on labour availability, friendly ties to a household with surplus land and/or cash for paying a season's rent as it is on nominal ownership. Typically in any given year well over 90 per cent of households farm. The reasons for not farming are mixed, and include recent arrival in the village, impending departure, or labour shortages arising from sickness, pregnancy complications, or a diverse set of family problems. For example, severe illnesses or accidents, bereavement and witchcraft cases may necessitate long absences from the village that interfere with optimally timed planting and weeding, and can lead to fields being taken over by others and/or invaded by wildlife. Amongst active farmers in any one year, the amount of land in production varies considerably, primarily as a function of labour resources, health, and age; between 10–20 per cent of households cultivate less than an acre in any one year. Households often use multiple plots in any one year. To the extent that land is formally owned, it can be inherited typically from husband's (patri-family) or wife's (matri-family) parents, from the clearing of village bushland, from a direct purchase, or through the bestowal of land via village institutions (for example special dispensation from the school or the village chairman). The majority of farm work is provided by the members of the household, but a small proportion of households hire in paid wage labour for a certain period. Some households rent out land, for very variable rates, and/or simply allow others to farm there for free. Pimbwe claim fear of cattle, do not like to drink milk 'mixed from different cows', and traditionally avoided the use of oxen for ploughing, although the use of ploughing services (with oxen, or very occasionally a tractor or power tiller) has grown in recent years. Goats, chickens, ducks, guinea fowl, and occasionally doves are kept for food, and starting around 2006 a few households keep pigs and/or cattle as sources of protein and cash.

To capture inequalities in land, livestock, and labour this study measures the percentage of households that farm in any one year (*farming households*), acreage in use in any one year (*acres*), source of acquisition of the household's primary agricultural plot (*provenance of plot*), and the suite of household livestock converted into total livestock units (Jahnke et al. 1988) (*TLU*). Unfortunately neither the hiring in of farm labour, the renting out of land, nor the renting and/or use of oxen for ploughing were systematically recorded across all censuses. However, by 2010, between 80–85 per cent of households were still depending exclusively on hand-held hoe (jembe in Swahili) cultivation, less than 5 per cent of households were renting out land for cash on a regular basis, and only 5–10 per cent households had used hired labour on their fields at some time in the year. Furthermore, the use of fertilizer and chemical inputs was rare before 2006, largely because of the common practice of burning last year's straw prior to planting; slightly less than 5 per cent of Pimbwe households were using general (undifferentiated) purchased inputs by 2010, though many families complained of insufficient cash to purchase much-needed improved seeds and modern fertilizers.

Off-Farm activities

Given the highly variable rainfall patterns, crop pests, theft, wildlife damage, problems with household labour, and variable soil quality (data recorded but not presented here) there is high food insecurity in the Rukwa Valley (Wandel and Homboe-Ottesen 1992, Hadley 2005, Hadley and Patil 2006, Hadley et al. 2007), and most families attempt to engage in supplementary off-farm activities. These are of various sorts. Some households rely on the *harvest* of natural resources (fish, meat, grass, bees, timber) and the associated secondary processing (carpentry, honey, baskets, thatch, rope, etc.). Others focus more on the *provision of services*, which might include traditional medicine, sewing, butchery, pottery, brick-making, building, and repairing bicycles, buckets, shoes, hoes, etc. Others engage in small-scale *trading* of crops, dried sardines from Lake Tanganyika (such as dagaa in Swahili), or trade products (cooked food, harvested foods, other goods) either at monthly cattle auction markets (minaada in Swahili) or more informally in the village on temporary stands. In this study all such activities are grouped as *crafts-trade*; no attempt was made to estimate annual income from such activities because it was so evident that this was highly unpredictable. Nevertheless persistent engagement in such activities indicates a household is not entirely vulnerable to the vicissitudes of farming. Households who engage in trade on the basis of more considerable capital investment are considered as engaged in *business*: this includes households with someone running a bar, a small shop (duka in Swahili) or semi-permanent kiosks (fixed locales with stored merchandise for sale), a milling machine, or permanent eating venue (mgahawa in Swahili). Two activities are typically turned to by the more desperate: the provision of day labour (kuhemea in Swahili literally 'shopping') on Sukuma farms—typically weeding in a given area compensated for with food (such as a few sweet potatoes or a scoop of maize or cassava flour, *piecework*), and the brewing (kukoroga in Swahili) of beer from maize (*brewing*). Working for Sukuma can be brutally hard work and is poorly rewarded (reportedly sometimes unrewarded), and brewing is not only exhausting, but entails using precious maize flour destined for family consumption, collecting large logs to support the lengthy boiling period, and disrupting the household on the beer-selling day with drunken revellers (though increasingly beer is now sold to local bars, avoiding this latter inconvenience). Notably, however, brewing is also engaged in by wealthier households, specifically by women seeking to profit from a maize surplus. Accordingly, only households that, as off-farm activities, engage *only* in Sukuma day labour *and/or* brewing are considered as particularly poor in the wealth rankings developed below; households that supplement their economic portfolios with piecework and/or brewing are not necessarily particularly poor.

Wages and salaries

Wages can be earned by working as a farm labourer, assisting in a bar, shop, or milling machine, or serving as a watchman (for example, for the dispensary) or cook; by 2010 such opportunities increased with the arrival of the Chinese road builders; households with individuals engaged in such activities are classed as having *wage labour*. There are in addition a few salaried individuals in the village: these include the village secretary (mtendaji in Swahili), primary school teachers, a nurse attendant, a few men working as rangers for the adjacent national park, and a foreman for a company in the regional town. These households are considered as *salaried*.

Material assets

Household productivity is primarily directed at securing food products (such as oil, salt, sugar, tea, etc.) that require purchase, the health of family members, the education of children, productive assets, luxury items, and better-built (and often more salubrious) houses. To monitor success in the acquisition of material assets a few items were monitored systematically across the years—these include buckets, cooking pots, basic implements, hoes, watches, radios, kerosene lamps, bicycles, drums (for beer brewing); in recent years to this list were added mobile phones, solar panels, TV-DVD sets, motor cycles, modern furniture like sofas, and cupboards. In previous analyses these have been combined in a cash value

(Borgerhoff Mulder and Beheim 2011). While cash assets as a measure of wealth can be problematic (Harttgen et al. 2013), they provide at least a coarse indicator of wealth differences *at any one point in time*. Like Brockington et al. (2018) I view assets as greatly preferable to income or consumption as a potential indicator of family well-being; income suffers from many zero values, poor reporting of potentially sensitive information, and the fact that people with no assets are forced into working for money, such that presence of an income does not necessarily indicate well-being. Consumption expenditures were not measured, and would be extremely difficult for respondents to report (and recall) accurately. For this paper, given our interest in depicting changes over time, I quantify both the total (annually deflated) cash value (in thousand TZ shillings) of household assets (*household assets*), and the distribution of some key assets. Regarding cash value, most items have easily determined village prices identified on an annual basis. Regarding the annual deflation rate, despite the use of the recommended corrected deflators (pers. comm. Emmanuel Maliti) these measures are not ideal for comparing wealth over time. Accordingly I also look at some specific assets, examining separately three items—*bicycles*, *drums*, and the *building material quality* of the primary household residence (if the house is built of mud brick or sticks, of baked brick or improved with cement and/or a tin roof). Bicycles and building material quality are chosen because these are assets to which everyone aspires, for a combination of productivity, comfort and healthy/salubrious living conditions. Large metal drums (or barrels) are important capital for women, given the profits from beer brewing.

Indigenous Household Wealth Category Rankings

No wealth ranking of households was conducted in the field, though individual productivity (work effort and use of alcohol) was characterized for other purposes (Borgerhoff Mulder 2009). Accordingly all household economic data were examined retroactively and fitted into categories (*IWC_cat*) best capturing local classifications easily recognizable among villagers and researchers alike over the years: 'destitute', 'very poor', 'vulnerable', 'struggling', 'satisfactory', 'productive', 'very productive', and 'rich' (described in the first two columns of Table 5.1). For present purposes I aligned my categories with two alternative household wealth-ranking schemas reported for East/South African countries: Dorward and Loiske. Dorward's (2009) categories (*IWC_dorward*) of 'dropping out', 'hanging in', 'stepping up', and 'stepping out', to which two additional categories were added: 'marginally dropping out' and a 'very comfortable' existence (see column 3, Table 5.1). Loiske's categories (*IWC_loiske*), comprised of 'extremely poor', 'poor', 'average farmer', 'above average farmer', 'rich', 'very rich', and 'immensely rich' (Brockington et al. 2018) were also coded from my initial categories for comparative purposes

Table 5.1 Wealth rankings calculated for each census

Wealth ranking (IWC_cat)	My description	Wealth ranking (IWC_Dorward)	Wealth ranking (IWC_Loiske)
Destitute (10)	Destitute and unable to help self, often because ill, old, or alcoholic; nothing to rent out; often marginalized, scavenging, and rely on external help	'dropping out' (1)	[7] Extremely poor; alcohol; sick; very little work
Very poor (11)	Destitute but able to do piecework for Sukuma and/or brewing, but have no assets in house or livestock; very poor agricultural production	'dropping out' (marginal) (2)	[7] Extremely poor; alcohol; sick; very little work
Vulnerable (12)	Struggling through mix of beer brewing or piecework labour for Sukuma, off-farm activities in crafts and/or trade, but with very few assets and no other off-farm activities; erratic income/ productivity and vulnerable to moving into destitute category	'hanging in' (3)	[6] Poor; rents land out; casual labour; few livestock
Struggling (21)	Struggling through piecework for Sukuma, brewing, off-farm activities in crafts and/or trade; supplemented by paid day labour, with some evidence of a few assets that are likely sold off in crisis, and erratic earnings; vulnerable to moving into destitute category, but not poor; no evidence of savings	'hanging in' (3)	[5] Average farmer; a few cattle; farm; no labourers
Satisfactory (22)	Satisfactory condition, with some productivity in farming, off-farm activities in crafts or trade; not typically forced to brew of do piecework for Sukuma; able to accumulate assets and some livestock, and possible investment in very small business enterprise and/or use of higher-quality building material	'stepping up' (4)	[5] Average farmer; a few cattle; farm; no labourers
Productive (31)	Relatively productive farm; effort invested additionally in business, crafts, and or trade, with some accumulation of assets through local production and/or wage labour; possibly use high-quality building materials	'stepping up' (4)	[4] Above average farmer; cattle; farm; some use of labourers

Continued

Table 5.1 Continued

Wealth ranking (IWC_cat)	My description	Wealth ranking (IWC_ Dorward)	Wealth ranking (IWC_Loiske)
Very productive (32)	Productive farm with some paid labour, supplemented with diversified sources of income, such as successful trade or capital-intensive business (like a bar or milling machine, typically in a group); household would typically include a mobile phone owner by 2006 and building materials of high quality	'stepping up & out' (5)	[3] Rich; vibarua, cattle, business
Rich (40)	Look comfortable in terms of farming; considerable modern assets; well-built house with furniture, cement, and maybe even glass; and often a salary and/or capital investment in strong local business	Very comfortable (6)	[2] Very rich; tractor; business; cattle; and [1] Immensely rich (lorries)

(column 4, Table 5.1), although there were no households falling in the highest two categories (since none owned a tractor or a lorry in 2010). The categories used here overlap closely with those of other studies in the region (e.g., Mushongah and Scoones 2012). Despite the retroactive nature of my wealth categories the amount of data collected on each household made decisions over these rankings straight forward. This likely results from my having conducted more than 1,400 households interviews with families with whom I became very familiar over the fifteen-year period.

Additional Data on Education and Growth

To assess the impact of wealth measures (including assets) for household well-being, the data are combined with standard measures of educational performance and anthropometrics as reported elsewhere (Borgerhoff Mulder and Beheim 2011). Educational attainment is measured by the standard/grade of school-aged children in the household for each year, calculated as a standardized residual on the cubic function of age (*educational performance*). As is common in Tanzanian village schools, students 'repeat' a year if they perform badly. Hence whether a child is relatively old or relatively young in a class, as measured here, is a good indicator of a child's performance (and indeed his or her attendance) at school. Health is determined indirectly through the use of anthropometrics (heights and weights) conducted, on a voluntary basis, each census year. From linking these measurements to the household of the individual that year, age and sex-specific residuals for height (*Z-height*) and weight (*Z-weight*) for all household members under 20 years of age at time of measurement can be calculated. For individuals who have passed their twentieth birthday Body Mass Index (BMI) is calculated (*BMI*), as is more appropriate. Since there is as yet very little obesity at the fieldsite, positive BMI measures are taken as indicators of a healthy rather than a diseased body.

Have Economic Livelihoods Improved or Faltered between 1995–2010?

Farming, Land, and Off-Farm Economic Pursuits Compared over Time

Using cross-sectional data, and comparing variables measured at the household level (Table 5.2a), we observe that the mean total number of sacks produced (primarily maize, but also rice, sunflower, and sesame) has increased (notably since 2004) over time (Figure 5.1a). This pattern likely reflects the gradual improvement of transport into the Rukwa Valley, and policies to boost commercial crop production through Kilimo Kwanza and other initiatives. There has also been an increase over time in mean and variance in livestock holdings, most notably starting in 2006 (Table 5.2a, Figure 5.1b). Perhaps most notably, total value of household assets, and the variability in this measure (as measured by the coefficient of variation) have increased steeply since 2004 (Table 5.2a, see also Figure 5.1f), reflecting purchase of mobile phones, basic furniture, solar panels, and in three instances motorcycles (Figure 5.1f).

Despite this indication of greater productivity in the agricultural and livestock sector, the mean number of acres used (and variability therein) has remained quite stable (Table 5.2a), as has the proportion of households actively farming (Table 5.2b). Furthermore, despite considerable inter-annual variability in households that farm less than 1 acre, the percentage hovers at a little above 10 per cent (Table 5.2b). This cross-sectional perspective therefore gives evidence of greater farm productivity and no indication of consequential loss of access to land, or proletarization. While many Sukuma families (not included here) have arrived in the village since 1995, typically they establish farms outside of the village, only rarely taking possession of land formerly farmed by Pimbwe. Finally (data not shown) there is no noticeable change in the source of household land, with the majority (~40 per cent) acquiring their primary plot of land from the husband's family, approximately 20 per cent from the wife's family, 15–20 per cent from clearing bushland, 15 per cent through direct purchase, and the remainder either through a combination of rent and/or borrowing from other villagers, from Sukuma households, or granted through village institutions. The most concerning trend in the data is the large number of months (between four and six) that

Table 5.2a Household characteristics compared across years: continuous variables. Coefficient of variation (CV) is calculated as Std. dev./Mean, providing a standardized measure of inequality. A between group linearity coefficient in an ANOVA model is significant for total sacks ($F_{1, 1440}$=79.99, p<0.001), livestock in TLU ($F_{1, 1439}$=16.25, p<0.001), and household assets ($F_{1, 1440}$=27.19, p<0.001), as shown in Figure 5.1

1995	Total sacks	Months without maize	Livestock in TLU	Acres	Household assets
N	154	137	154	154	154
Mean	6.1087	4.7737	1.6740	3.5146	38.2818
Std dev.	5.21737	2.18280	2.53351	2.78553	68.34731
CV	0.8541	0.4573	1.5134	0.7926	1.7854
Range	25	10.00	14.40	15.00	306.15
Min.	0	0.00	0.00	0.00	0.00
Max.	25	10.00	14.40	15.00	306.15
1998	**Total sacks**	**Months without maize**	**Livestock in TLU**	**Acres**	**Household assets**
N	183	na	182	176	183
Mean	4.1151	na	1.5258	3.7858	41.5017
Std dev.	5.24074	na	2.46586	2.35094	61.61767
CV	1.2735	na	1.6161	0.6210	1.4847
Range	36.00	na	14.80	13.50	276.92
Min.	0.00	na	0.00	0.50	0.00
Max.	36.00	na	14.80	14.00	276.92
2000	**Total sacks**	**Months without maize**	**Livestock in TLU**	**Acres**	**Household assets**
N	193	171	193	189	193
Mean	5.3498	3.9825	1.2782	2.6730	35.8011
Std dev.	6.30353	2.73641	2.26448	1.78670	66.06115
CV	1.1783	0.6871	1.7716	0.6684	1.8452
Range	48.00	10.00	15.90	12.00	454.84
Min.	0.00	0.00	0.00	0.00	0.00
Max.	48.00	10.00	15.90	12.00	454.84
2002	**Total sacks**	**Months without maize**	**Livestock in TLU**	**Acres**	**Household assets**
N	207	181	207	191	207
Mean	6.6928	6.4254	0.8077	2.1531	38.7244
Std dev.	7.44025	2.83847	1.38957	1.76547	61.14074
CV	1.1117	0.4418	1.7203	0.8200	1.5789
Range	49.00	12.00	7.60	13.00	330.84

Min.	0.00	0.00	0.00	0.00	0.00
Max.	49.00	12.00	7.60	13.00	330.84

2004	Total sacks	Months without maize	Livestock in TLU	Acres	Household assets
N	219	182	219	219	219
Mean	9.3816	6.7473	1.0982	2.0553	50.5002
Std dev.	12.91663	3.02327	2.21175	1.87112	68.45379
CV	1.3768	0.4481	2.0140	0.9104	1.3555
Range	95.00	12.00	21.00	12.00	354.03
Min.	0.00	0.00	0.00	0.00	0.00
Max.	95.00	12.00	21.00	12.00	354.03

2006	Total sacks	Months without maize	Livestock in TLU	Acres	Household assets
N	224	202	224	224	224
Mean	11.7854	6.1089	1.6094	2.3969	92.0740
Std dev.	12.33836	2.99884	3.23097	1.96650	279.47930
CV	1.0469	0.4909	2.0076	0.8204	3.0354
Range	66.00	12.00	21.00	13.00	3089.93
Min.	0.00	0.00	0.00	0.00	0.00
Max.	66.00	12.00	21.00	13.00	3089.93

2010	Total sacks	Months without maize	Livestock in TLU	Acres	Household assets
N	267	235	267	267	267
Mean	11.2137	4.4809	2.5764	2.8236	118.9566
Std dev.	14.70482	3.32991	4.23682	2.14937	390.62051
CV	1.3113	0.7431	1.6445	0.7612	3.2837
Range	132.00	12.00	24.50	15.00	5193.72
Min.	0.00	0.00	0.00	0.00	0.00
Max.	132.00	12.00	24.50	15.00	5193.72

households have no maize in their store prior to the next harvest season (Figure 5.1c). This probably reflects temptation to sell food crops directly after harvest for much-needed cash, although note that there is no statistically linear trend in this measure. There is also weak evidence of greater inequality in farm production (total sacks show increased ranges and coefficients of variation across years, Table 5.2a).

Turning to off-farm activities, the proportion of households with one or more member doing piecework labour for Sukuma and in brewing varies greatly between years (particularly high in 1998 with El Nino and 2004 with heavy

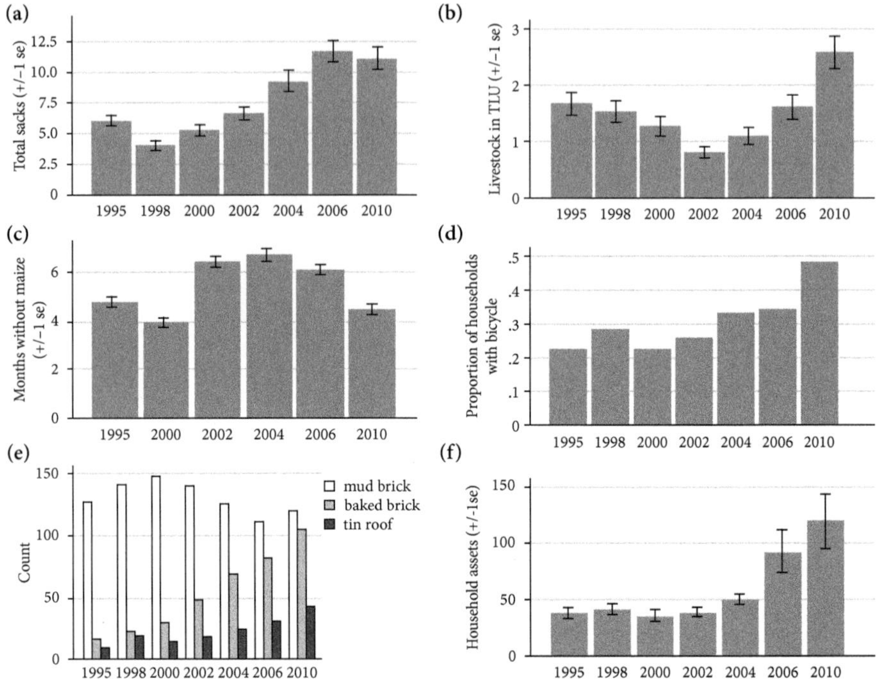

Figure 5.1 Changes across years in (a) number of sacks harvested by the household, (b) number of livestock per household, (c) number of months without maize in the store (no data for 1998), (d) proportion of households with one or more bicycles, (e) building material quality of the primary residence, and (f) cash value of household assets (in thousand TZ shillings). Mean and standard errors (a–c, f), proportions (d) and counts (e) are shown. Statistics in Tables 5.2a and 5.2b.

floods), but shows no overall secular trend (Table 5.2b). Similarly, the proportion of households supplementing farming with off-farm crafts and trade stays relatively stable over time (Table 5.2b). Households engaging in business increase from 10 per cent to 25 per cent of the village (Table 5.2b), wage labour from 13 per cent to 30 per cent (Table 5.2b), bike ownership from 23 per cent to 48 per cent (Table 5.2b, Figure 5.1d), drum ownership from 12 to 20 per cent, ownership of a primary dwelling with baked bricks from 17 per cent to 55 per cent (Table 5.1b, Figure 5.1e), and with a metal roof from 6 per cent to 16 per cent of the village (Table 5.2b).

In short, these descriptive cross-sectional data suggest farm productivity and the number of livestock owned have increased, with implications for housing quality, and the ownership of assets. This has not changed the proportion of households engaged in crafts and trade, but has increased the more capital-intensive business activities. These changes most likely reflect improved opportunities to market crop surpluses, and the availability of labour and ancillary

Table 5.2b Household characteristics compared across years: binary variables. A significant increasing linear patterning (Pearson's Chi-square linear-by-linear association) is found over time for having one or more household member involved in business (Chi-square=78.75, $n=1455$, $p<0.001$), wage labour (Chi-square=123.69, $n=1455$, $p<0.001$), for the household owning one or more bicycles (Chi-square=51.36, $n=1455$, $p<0.001$), drums for beer-making (Chi-square=20.09, $n=1455$, $p<0.01$), and for the household being constructed of baked bricks and/or tin roof (Chi-square=20.09, $n=1455$, $p<0.01$). Households engaged in traditional trades and crafts have declined somewhat (Chi-square=78.75, $n=1455$, $p<0.001$)

	1995											
	Farming household	<1 acre farmed	Crafts/trade	Business	Piecework	Brewing	Wage labour	Salaried	Bicycle	Drum	Baked brick	Tin roof
N	154	154	154	154		154	154	154	154	154	153	153
Proportion	0.93	0.08	0.55	0.10		0.65	0.13	0.07	0.23	0.12	0.17	0.06
	1998											
	Farming household	<1 acre farmed	Crafts/trade	Business	Piecework	Brewing	Wage labour	Salaried	Bicycle	Drum	Baked brick	Tin roof
N	183	176	183	183	183	183	183	183	183	183	183	183
Proportion	0.96	0.01	0.40	0.05	0.58	0.28	0.07	0.05	0.28	0.10	0.22	0.10
	2000											
	Farming household	<1 acre farmed	Crafts/trade	Business	Piecework	Brewing	Wage labour	Salaried	Bicycle	Drum	Baked brick	Tin roof
N	193	189	200	200	200	200	200	200	193	193	193	193
Proportion	0.94	0.07	0.34	0.06	0.28	0.57	0.29	0.04	0.23	0.08	0.23	0.07

Continued

Table 5.2b Continued

	2002											
	Farming household	**<1 acre farmed**	**Crafts/trade**	**Business**	**Piecework**	**Brewing**	**Wage labour**	**Salaried**	**Bicycle**	**Drum**	**Baked brick**	**Tin roof**
N	207	191	208	208	208	208	208	208	207	207	207	207
Proportion	0.88	0.12	0.34	0.03	0.00	0.38	0.03	0.05	0.26	0.09	0.32	0.09
	2004											
	Farming household	**<1 acre farmed**	**Crafts/trade**	**Business**	**Piecework**	**Brewing**	**Wage labour**	**Salaried**	**Bicycle**	**Drum**	**Baked brick**	**Tin roof**
N	219	219	219	219	219	219	219	219	219	219	219	219
Proportion	0.91	0.21	0.42	0.16	0.50	0.66	0.37	0.07	0.33	0.13	0.42	0.11
	2006											
	Farming household	**<1 acre farmed**	**Crafts/trade**	**Business**	**Piecework**	**Brewing**	**Wage labour**	**Salaried**	**Bicycle**	**Drum**	**Baked brick**	**Tin roof**
N	224	224	224	224	224	224	224	224	224	224	224	224
Proportion	0.96	0.17	0.31	0.17	0.40	0.59	0.23	0.08	0.34	0.14	0.50	0.14
	2010											
	Farming household	**<1 acre farmed**	**Crafts/trade**	**Business**	**Piecework**	**Brewing**	**Wage labour**	**Salaried**	**Bicycle**	**Drum**	**Baked brick**	**Tin roof**
N	267	267	267	267	267	267	267	267	267	267	267	267
Proportion	0.95	0.10	0.36	0.25	0.21	0.64	0.30	0.04	0.48	0.20	0.55	0.16

business on the new road. Nevertheless the large number of months in which households are without maize is concerning, piecework for Sukuma continues, and inequalities in asset-holding and crop production are increasing.

Changes in Household Wealth Rankings over Time

Studies of economic change in the developing world commonly rely on wealth indices as an easy way (famously 'without tears', Filmer and Pritchett 2001) to assess wealth differences between households. Typically, these are based on principal components analysis, with the first components being converted into a wealth rank whereby economic differences are identified. In most rural communities these days however it may be ill-advised as an analyst to assume that there is a single dimension along which economic capacity varies (e.g., Randall and Coast 2015). Heterogeneity among livestock herding, farming, wage earning, and business households renders economic indices based on PCA (e.g., Filmer and Pritchett 2001, Howe et al. 2012) problematic, since rarer household types that are doing well (or badly) may not load informatively on the first principal component (Bingenheimer 2007, Kaiser et al. 2017). For example in a comparison of fifty-six villages across northern Tanzania a generic wealth ranking revealed minimal differences between monogamous and polygynous households, yet livelihood-specific measures of wealth (land in cultivation, livestock) showed polygynous households to cultivate more land and own more livestock (Lawson et al. 2015). Furthermore, wealth rankings are often poorly predictive of expenditures (Howe et al. 2009), and are also effectively impossible to compare across sites without a normalizing procedure that combines household wealth rankings with mean wealth per capita nationally, and national Gini coefficients (Hruschka et al. 2015).

Here I adopt a different approach, supplementing the raw data reported above with the use of indigenous wealth category rankings that aim to capture a constellation of factors (assets, productivity, use of labour, coping mechanisms, etc., see Table 5.1) that impact a household's well-being. Examining the cross-sectional distribution of indigenous wealth categories for households over censuses, there is corroborative evidence of economic improvement (Figure 5.2). The 'destitute' and 'very poor' (*IWC_cat*), the 'dropping out' or 'marginally dropping out' (*IWC_Dorward*) and the 'extremely poor' (*IWC_Loiske*) are all declining in frequency. On the other hand, the 'rich' and 'very productive' (*IWC_cat*), the 'stepping up', the 'stepping up and out', and the 'comfortable' (*IWC_Dorward*), and the 'rich' and 'very rich' (*IWC_Loiske*) have stayed quite stable. Where we see most expansion is among households I call 'struggling' (*IWC_cat*), Dorward calls 'hanging in', and Loiske call the 'average farmer'. This likely reflects increasing economic opportunities in the village, particularly more wage labour and perhaps more clients for business activities.

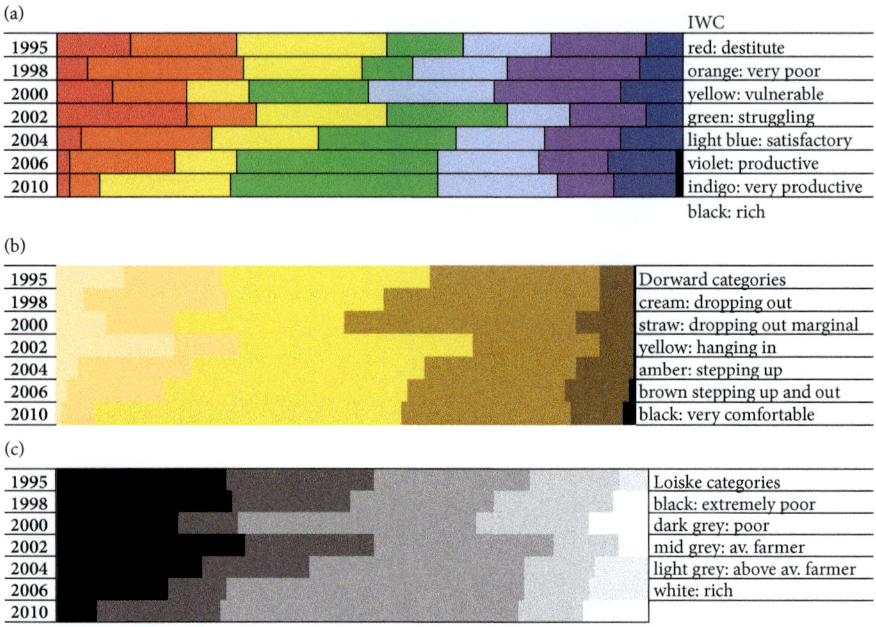

Figure 5.2 The distribution of indigenous wealth categories across years: (a) categories created for this study; (b) data recoded to align with Dorward's categories; (c) data recoded to align with Loiske's categories.

In short, not everyone is on the rising ship, but the new economy is increasingly sheltering more people from total destitution. There was nevertheless little evidence (in 2010) of great riches extending beyond one or two families, notably those with political office.

Is Economic Improvement Caused by Selective Emigration?

Improvement in economic conditions could reflect differential outmigration from the village if, for example, relatively poor households are more likely to leave. Similarly very poor households may dissolve, and therefore not be present at a subsequent census. This selection dynamic is unlikely to mar inferences drawn from this study, since at each census all households (including new ones) were included. It is nevertheless of interest to determine whether household persistence (effectively the subsequent fate of the household within the next census (an interval of two, three, or four years)) is influenced by household wealth (in assets). This requires not cross-sectional but longitudinal analysis.

Households that persist with the same paired household heads across censuses tend to be wealthier than households that have disappeared at the next censuses

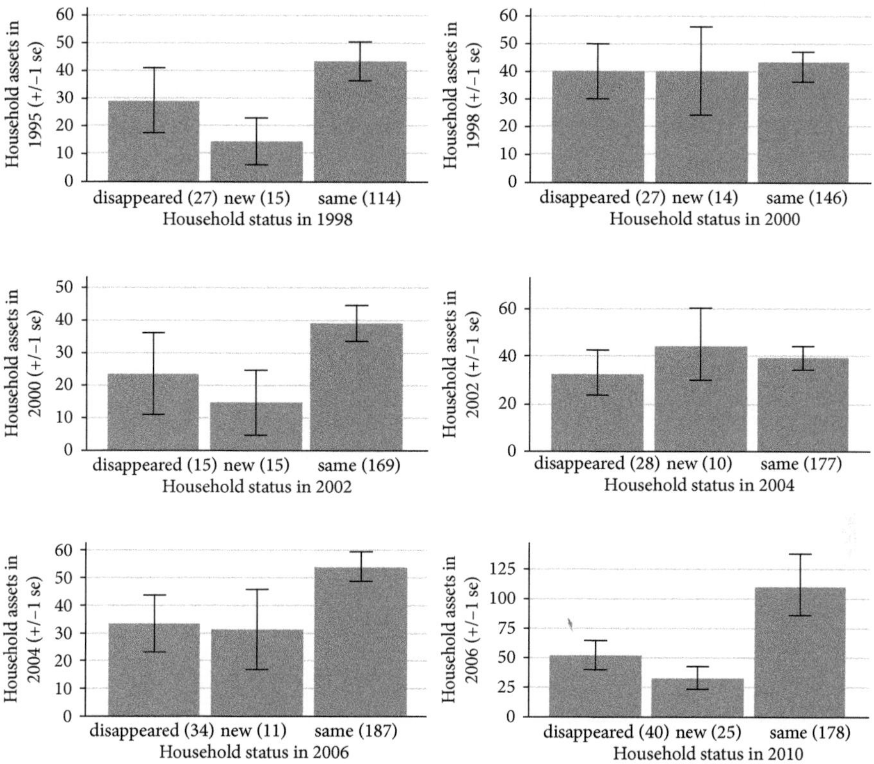

Figure 5.3 Plots showing the association between household wealth and persistence at subsequent census for transitions between (a) 1995 to 1998, (b) 1998 to 2000, (c) 2000 to 2002, (d) 2002 to 2004, (e) 2004 to 2006, and (f) 2006 to 2010. Households in the subsequent census are classified as 'disappeared' (the household is not found in the village at subsequent census), 'new' (the household is headed by a new pairing of individuals from within or outside of the village) or 'same' (the household is headed by the same individual(s) at both censuses). Number of households in parentheses. None of the differences in household assets between households of different status are statistically significant, although the pattern is quite consistent. (a) F=1.49, ns; (b) F=0.01, ns; (c) F=1.48, ns; (d) F=1.76, ns; (e) F=1.56, ns; (f) F=1.26, ns.

(e.g., 1995–8, 2004–6, and 2006–10). Also, households that re-form as new households between censuses, for example as a result of first marriages, of divorces, and/or remarriages, are typically somewhat poorer than more persistent households. Note however that the differences are not significant in any transition (Figure 5.3) resulting from the very large standard errors.

Briefly, differential household attrition cannot account for the increasing wealth of households over the 1995–2010 census because of the use of full censuses in this study.

Wealth Transitions of Individuals

Given that households are somewhat ephemeral phenomena (as apparent from the sample sizes in Figure 5.3), it is perhaps more informative to focus on individuals as linked to their household wealth to see what wealth transitions look like at the personal level. Here, again using longitudinal data, I present transition matrices between indigenous wealth categories (Table 5.3; *IWC_Loiske* is shown, but the patterning is highly comparable across the other categorizations). To read the table, of the twenty-four individuals ranked as extremely poor in 1995, twelve advanced to being ranked as poor, eleven to average farmers, and five to above average farmers. In some years almost twice as many individuals moved up in status rather than down (these totals are shown in the table); only between 2000 and 2002 was there a general decline in status reflecting reductions in economic activity contingent on a marked collapse in piecework, wage labour, and business in 2002 (Table 5.2b) that may be associated, in part, with a poor harvest and with livestock disease prompting the departure (temporarily) of many Sukuma households from the valley.

In short, focusing on individuals does not temper the general finding of improved economic circumstances for most people. Note however that future analyses will incorporate additional individual-level variables, in particular age, gender, marital status, and number of dependents as well as individual economic activities, to identify more precisely the factors influencing changing wealth status over an individual's lifetime. The finding that individuals typically improved with respect to their household wealth between 1995 and 2010 may prove to be considerably more nuanced than portrayed here.

Gender and Wealth Transitions

Household, or domestic unit, level data obscure intra-household inequalities. This is a problem because there can be marked differences in bargaining and decision-making power within households, patterned typically by gender and age (e.g., Quisumbing and Maluccio 2003, Doss et al. 2008, Bevis and Barrett 2013); this can be particularly acute in polygynous households (Barr et al. 2019).

The data from Mpimbwe allow two insights into such gender inequities: the first relies on individual economic activities (still to be analysed), and the second on the wealth rank transitions individuals make between two sequential censuses in which they are present in the village. This latter measure is inevitably somewhat constrained. This is because *to the extent individuals remain in the same household paired to the same household head* the improvements/declines in wealth ranking between years will be the same for males and females. However given the

Table 5.3 Transition matrices for indigenous wealth categories (following Loiske).

		1995					
		Extremely poor	**Poor**	**Average farmer**	**Above average farmer**	**Rich**	
1998	Extremely poor	24	17	10	2	0	**59 down**
	Poor	12	15	13	0	0	
	Average farmer	11	16	27	6	0	
	Above average farmer	5	3	14	19	11	
	Rich	0	2	2	10	6	
Total						**75 up**	**225**
		1998					**Total**
		Extremely poor	**Poor**	**Average farmer**	**Above average farmer**	**Rich**	
2000	Extremely poor	23	8	17	2	0	**56 down**
	Poor	0	9	8	3	0	
	Average farmer	40	33	22	6	2	
	Above average farmer	5	5	19	32	10	
	Rich	2	3	2	17	10	
Total						**126 up**	**278**
		2000					**Total**
		Extremely poor	**Poor**	**Average farmer**	**Above average farmer**	**Rich**	
2002	Extremely poor	25	14	47	3	2	**164 down**
	Poor	17	7	32	13	1	
	Average farmer	12	5	32	30	14	
	Above average farmer	2	2	8	18	8	
	Rich	0	0	2	10	12	
Total						**58 up**	**316**

Continued

Table 5.3 Continued

		2002					Total
		Extremely poor	Poor	Average farmer	Above average farmer	Rich	
2004	Extremely poor	30	13	6	2	0	47 down
	Poor	32	15	4	2	2	
	Average farmer	19	27	60	6	0	
	Above average farmer	1	6	9	18	12	
	Rich	3	2	8	13	12	
Total						120 up	302

		2004					Total
		Extremely poor	Poor	Average farmer	Above average farmer	Rich	
2006	Extremely poor	18	11	14	2	1	67 down
	Poor	8	16	4	2	0	
	Average farmer	31	28	79	15	6	
	Above average farmer	0	0	14	12	12	
	Rich	0	2	7	10	20	
	Very rich	0	0	0	0	2	
Total						102 up	314

		2006						
		Extremely poor	Poor	Average farmer	Above average farmer	Rich	Very rich	Total
2010	Extremely poor	5	2	15	1	0	0	80 down
	Poor	13	9	21	2	1	0	
	Average farmer	22	11	89	24	8	0	
	Above average farmer	5	0	17	6	6	0	
	Rich	0	0	15	4	23	0	
	Very rich	0	0	0	1	2	4	
Total						90 up		306

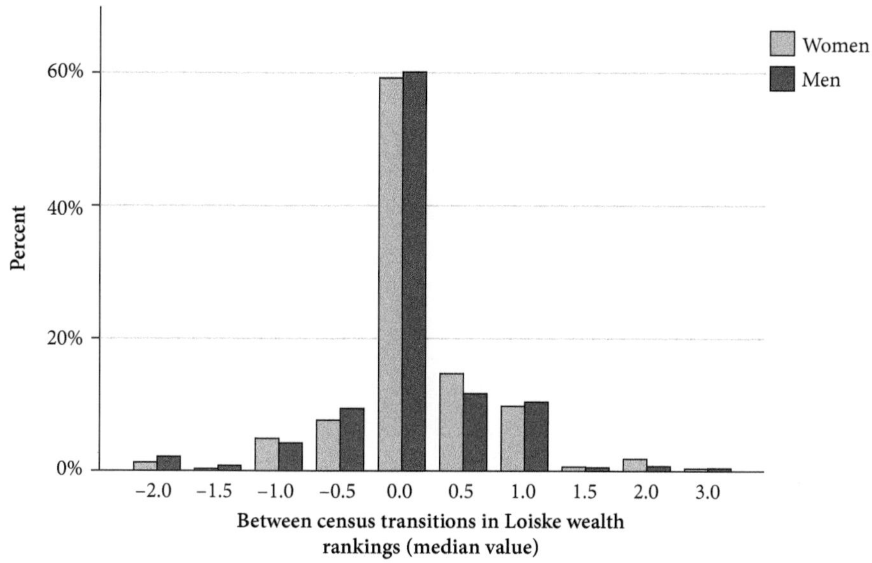

Figure 5.4 The distribution of between-census transitions in wealth rankings for all individuals for women and men separately.

considerable instability of domestic units (with instability captured by any change in the paired household heads between two sequential censuses, as shown in Figure 5.3) there is some scope for analysing the different economic careers of women and men using these longitudinal data.

The distribution of all between-census transitions in wealth rankings for all individuals identified as household heads across years are shown in Figure 5.4 (*IWC_loiske* is shown, but again the patterning is indistinguishable across the alternative indigenous wealth category rankings). Perhaps unsurprisingly this distribution clusters around no change, or a small trend towards positive change as averaged across transitions, as suggested in Table 5.3. The figure shows the indigenous wealth category transitions for gender. There is no obvious difference among men and women with respect to showing a declining, or indeed increasing, economic status. Again, caution is needed in interpreting this result of no sex differences in economic status because of the constrained nature of the measure of household wealth. Furthermore, as noted above, more nuanced analyses incorporating a fuller range of individual-level measures are needed to determine whether there are really no within-household inequities in changing economic well-being over time.

Assets as Indicators of Well-Being

Asset holdings are increasingly becoming a widely used measure of wealth (see Chapter 3). Here I examine the relationship between asset holdings and productivity, indicators of household stress, and measures of the education and health of household members.

Assets and Farm Productivity

The relationship between productive assets and economic productivity is bidirectional. With a bicycle a man can sell a fish in town, thereby enhancing the motivation to catch a surplus. With the extra cash, the gleam of a motorcycle can be seen in the eye of the fisherman, or more likely the farmer who will then diversify from maize and cassava to sunflower, a sack of which can be strapped on the back of the motorcycle and driven to town. Even more obviously, a farmer with oxen can bring more land into production than one without, and use her cash income to enter into a partnership over a tractor, thereby further increasing productivity, if land is available. Notably, items typically thought of as luxuries in some nations, such as a camera, a television, or a small solar panel can provide the basis for a business in a village—services for copying official documents, viewing sports events, or a mobile barber service respectively.

Recognizing then that causality is not easily specified, if assets are an important component to a household's economic portfolio we would expect to see associations between a household's assets and their productivity. Here we look at household assets [*household assets*] in relation to a key measure of productivity—the total number of sacks produced [*total sacks*] as well as the household's ownership of livestock [*TLU*]. Bivariate correlations across years are shown in Table 5.4. Associations between household assets and economic productivity are positive and significant across all years, as are the associations between assets and livestock. An example of one such bivariate association, between total household assets and the total number of sacks produced is shown for the first census in Figure 5.5.

Table 5.4 Bivariate correlations within years of household assets with the total number of sacks produced and livestock owned. Pearson's correlation coefficients and significance levels are shown

Year	Total sacks	Livestock in TLU
1995	.439 (154) **	.314 (154) **
1998	.507 (183) **	.268 (182) **
2000	.560 (193) **	.386 (193) **
2002	.545 (207) *	.358 (207) **
2004	.607 (219) **	.464 (219) **
2006	.294 (224) **	.395 (224) **
2010	.608 (267) **	.602 (267) **

** $P<0.01$, * $P<0.05$.

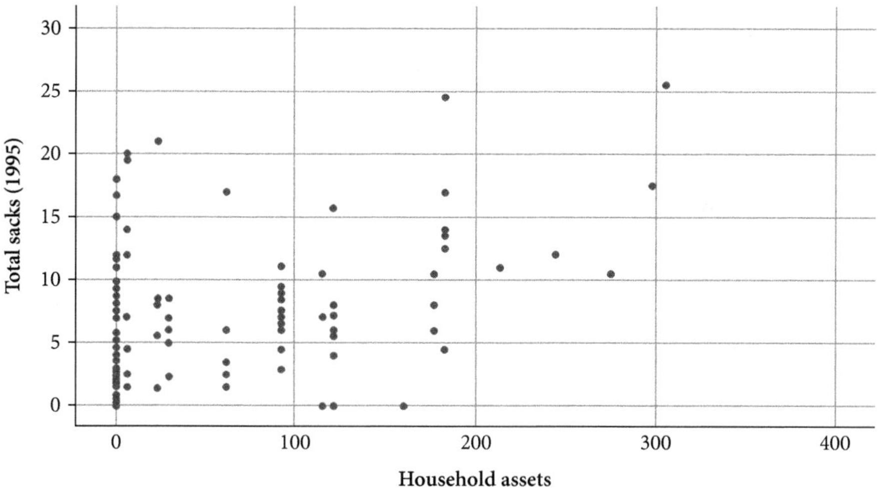

Figure 5.5 Bivariate plot of total sacks harvested and total household assets (in thousand TZ shillings). Data shown for 1995 only. For Pearson's correlations, see Table 5.4.

In short, household assets and livestock ownership are strong indicators of farm productivity, although the causality is likely bidirectional.

Assets and Stress

If household assets protect against stress we would expect to see negative associations with both food insecurity and least preferred economic activities, in this context conducting piecework (kuhemea) for Sukuma neighbours. The measure of food insecurity (*months without maize*) is based on the number of months without maize in the store, and shows strong and consistent negative associations with total household assets across years (Table 5.5, illustrated for 1995 only in Figure 5.6). Similarly, the engagement of one or more household members on Sukuma farms (*piecework*) is associated with low household wealth as measured by assets (Figure 5.7).

In sum, households with fewer assets experience longer periods with no grain in their store, placing their subsistence at the whim of the market prices, and they are more likely to resort to disfavoured option of working on Sukuma farms.

Assets, Education, and Health

Ultimately as scholars we need to cast a much broader net around the concept of well-being, security, and satisfaction. Specifically we should combine measures of material wealth (Kaiser et al. 2017), relational wealth (Guyer 1993) (conceived as

Table 5.5 Bivariate correlations within years of household assets with food insecurity. Pearson's correlation coefficients and significance levels are shown

Year	Number of months without maize
1995	–.536 (137) **
1998	no data
2000	–.345 (171) **
2002	–.319 (181) **
2004	–.210 (182) **
2006	–.316 (202) **
2010	–.306 (235) **

** P<0.01.

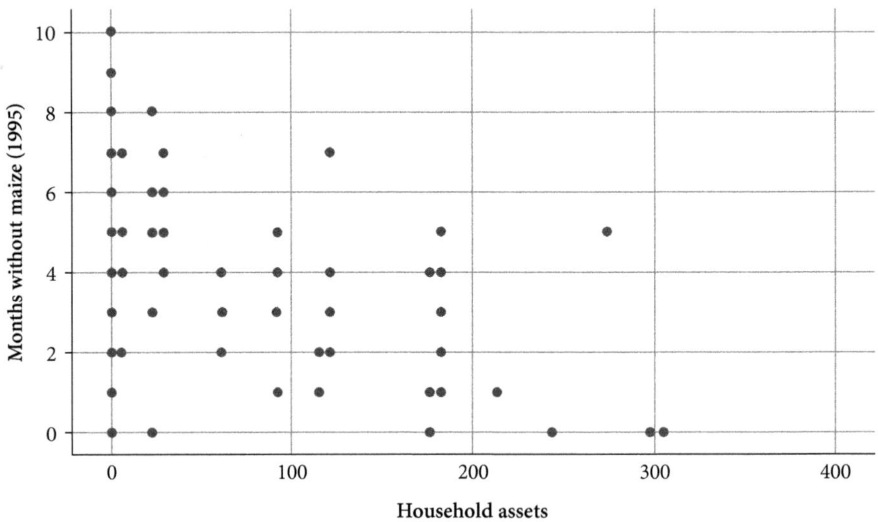

Figure 5.6 Bivariate plot of number of months without maize and total household assets (in thousand TZ shillings). Data shown for 1995 only. For Pearson's correlations, see Table 5.5.

both between and within households relationships, Koster 2018), and somatic wealth (individual endowments and capacities in health and education, Kaplan 1996). For example, we know that low perceived social support in Mpimbwe contributes both to maternal depression and food insecurity (Hadley and Patil 2006, Hadley et al. 2007). With data on material, relational, and somatic wealth (or capital) we can begin to determine how and why successes (and failures) in each domain interact over time (Borgerhoff Mulder et al. 2009, Bowles et al. 2010). Here, as a first step, we explore whether household assets are associated with more distal (and perhaps more emically salient) indicators of well-being—education and growth of young household members, and BMI of adult household members. Again directionality cannot be

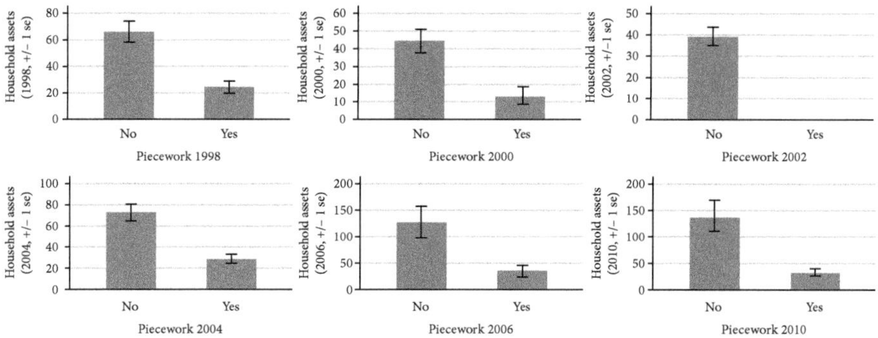

Figure 5.7 Plots showing the association between the presence or absence of a household member doing piecework (kuhemea) and household wealth for censuses in (a) 1998, (b) 2000, (c) 2002, (d) 2004, (e) 2006, and (f) 2010. T-test comparisons are significant or marginally significant across all years (1998: T=4.79, df=181, p<0.001; 2000: T=2.97, df=191, p<0.001; 2002: n/a; 2004: T=5.09, df=217, p<0.001; 2006: T=2.42, df=228, p<0.001; 2010: T=1.77, df=265, p=0.076).

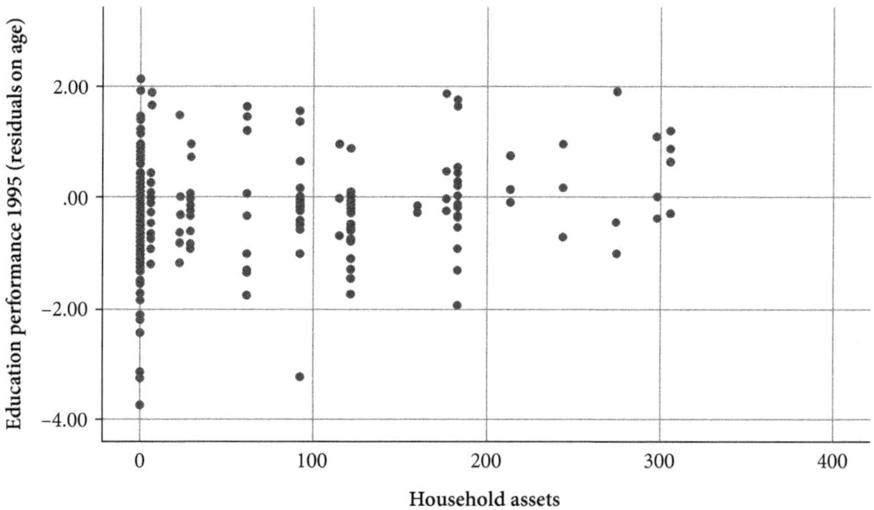

Figure 5.8 Education of school-aged household members plotted on household assets (in thousand TZ shillings). Data shown for 1995 only. An ordinary least squares regression that combines data across all years, with repeated measures for subjects (n=1194) across censuses (<7), shows a significant positive association between assets and educational performance ($F_{1,174}$=1.312, p=0.005).

securely identified, since healthy adults (and healthy and educated children) are more likely to be able to accumulate assets.

Looking first at schooling, there is a strong relationship between household assets in any one year and the age-specific education (*educational performance*) of school-aged children living in the household that year (Figure 5.8).

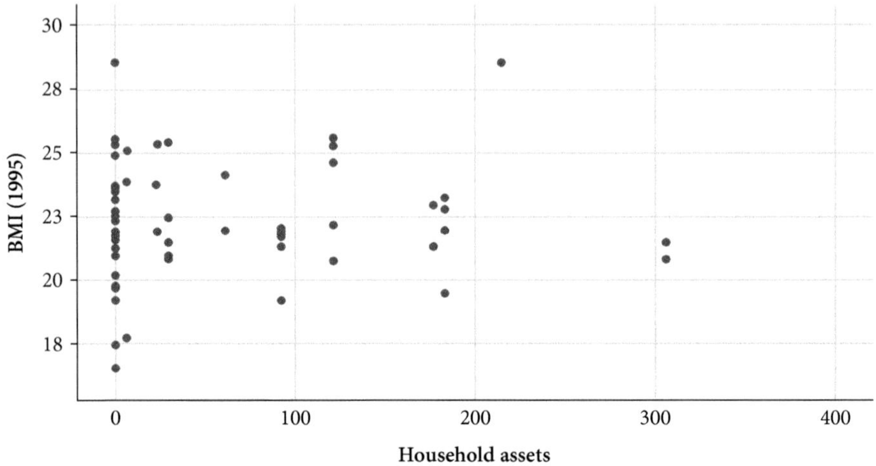

Figure 5.9 The Body Mass Index (BMI) of adult household members (who have reached their twentieth birthday) plotted on household assets (in thousand TZ shillings). Data shown for 1995 only. Combining data across surveys ordinary least squares regression, with repeated measures of subjects (n=1,110) across anthropometric surveys (<7), shows a marginally significant positive association between assets and BMI ($F_{1,159}$=1.173, p=0.082).

Turning to the health of household members, I use anthropometric data to look first at adults (those who have passed their twentieth birthday), whose growth is no longer positively associated with age. Body Mass Index (BMI) shows a small positive association with household assets (Figure 5.9). Finally, for individuals under 20 years, age- and sex-specific measures of heights and weights (*Z-height*) and weight (*Z-weight*) are more appropriate indicators of well-being. Again child heights and weights for age are positively associated with household assets (Figure 5.10).

In short, household assets are linked to good educational outcomes for school-aged household members, to adult BMI, and to the heights and weights of household members under 20 years of age.

Discussion

Changes in Economic Livelihoods over Time

With respect to my first question, it is clear that economic livelihoods have generally improved in Mpimbwe. Families produced and sold more crops in 2010 than in 1995. Agricultural profits are invested in assets, including better houses, business enterprises, and livestock (primarily smallstock, but a few ambitious

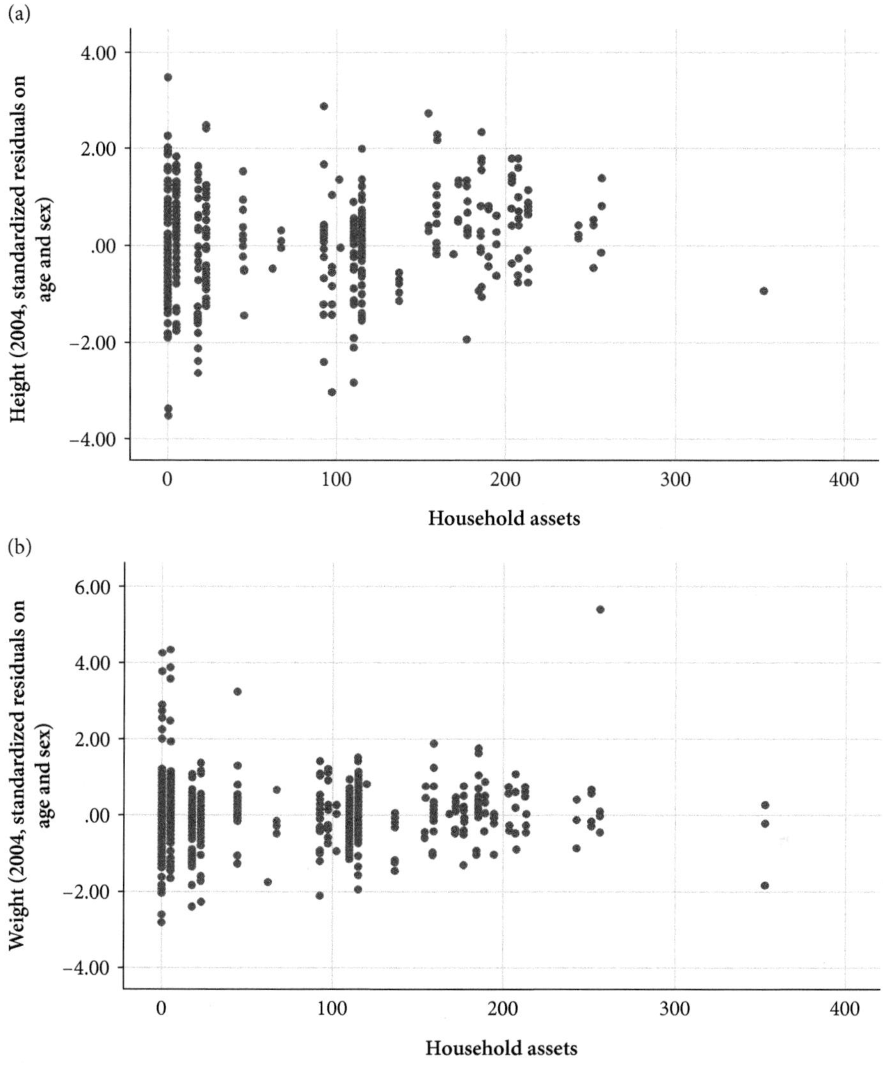

Figure 5.10 The growth of household members prior to their twentieth birthday plotted on household assets. Plots show standardized residuals of (a) height and (b) weight on age, standardized for each sex. Data shown for 2004 only. Ordinary least squares regression with repeated measures of subjects (n=754, n=936) across anthropometric surveys (<7) shows a significant positive association between assets and height, and assets and weight ($F_{1,128}=1.365$, $p=0.008$, $F_{1,134}=1.729$, $p<0.001$) respectively.

men and women buy oxen). Furthermore the indigenous wealth categories clearly show that the poorest are getting less poor (and/or less numerous), rather than the rich getting richer (with a few exceptions). Interesting this was not my subjective impression, but may reflect the fact that the few really poor households now stand out as being particularly deprived.[1] These positive changes largely reflect the growth in commercial farming which is no doubt contingent on improved policies and better marketing opportunities, including the new roads connecting Sumbawanga to Mbeya, and the northern Rukwa Valley to the Fipa Plateau. Other improvements in public services—a partially staffed dispensary in Mirumba since the early 2000s and a ward secondary school—are also likely important contributors.

A worrying concern is the large number of months families are without grain in their barns, reflecting a tendency for households to sell maize after the harvest for much-needed cash, or to convert it into beer (again for cash). Similarly, it is worth stressing that many households still resort to piecework farm labour, paid with a bowl (bakuli in Swahili) of grain for a day's work, and that they question whether the arrival of the Sukuma is a net positive or negative development for the people of the Rukwa Valley (Seel et al. 2014). In addition in a community where inequalities are quite marked (Pimbwe household wealth shows a Gini coefficient of 0.56, see Gurven et al. 2010) increasing inequalities in crop production and assets ownership is an unwelcome trend.

McMillan and Harttgen (2014) find that much of Africa's recent growth and poverty reduction can be traced to declines in the share of the labour force engaged in agriculture. These authors attribute poverty reduction to an increase in the productivity of labour as it moves from low productivity agriculture to higher productivity manufacturing and services (see also Dercon and Gollin 2014, who find little evidence that investments in agriculture generate improvements in social welfare in sub-Saharan Africa). While this may be true at the national level, at the local level economic advances are being made primarily through agriculture, as seen in Mpimbwe and other sites in Tanzania. More broadly, studies of social change in agrarian contexts suggest that rural labour markets fuel differentiation within villages that favour only a minority (Mueller 2011, Greco 2014). While this had evidently not occurred in Mpimbwe by 2010, there are indications that such changes might be underway, with the emergence of one or two very rich and politically connected families (pers. obs. 2014, 2016).

The developments in Mirumba are quite similar to those at other sites in Tanzania covered in this volume. Most notably, concepts of wealth and well-being in Mpimbwe are largely congruent with those found elsewhere (but cf. Chapter 3). This is perhaps unsurprising given the considerable homogeneity among many of Tanzania's ethnic groups, given linguistic integration under Swahili and the relatively strong market incursions in much of the country. For example, as in Howland and colleagues' chapter, uwezo (Swahili for 'power, ability') is commonly mentioned as an indicator of economic security and well-being.

[1] I have discussed this discrepancy elsewhere http://livelihoodchangeta.wixsite.com/tanzania/blog.

Pimbwe stress the importance of household independence and autonomy, again consistent with Howland and colleague's observation that 'dependence on others' is an indicator of poverty. Indeed, even at the individual level, to set up one's own household (kujipikia in Swahili, literally 'to cook for oneself') marks a major rite of passage and success in attaining independence. A quantitative study of sharing between households revealed surprisingly few ties among households (particularly the richer households) compared to other sites globally (Kasper and Borgerhoff Mulder 2015) and in Tanzania (De Weerdt and Dercon 2006) where, in contrast to Mpimbwe, the rich are more strongly networked than the poor (De Weerdt 2004). Yet despite this prized striving for independence, perceived social support networks prove to be important for child health outcomes (particularly among poorer families, Hadley 2004). Clearly there is a tension between the much-coveted autonomy and having to rely on the help of kin networks.

I did notice, however, some nuance to the discussion around the possession of material assets among the people of Mpimbwe, insofar as the ownership of visible material wealth attracts accusations of witchcraft (Borgerhoff Mulder and Beheim 2011, Kasper and Borgerhoff Mulder 2015). Assets can be seen as dangerous liabilities, because they lure envy. In their day-to-day conversations, the Pimbwe appear to place more value on the *means* of production (access to land, livestock, and labour) and on the *products* of their labour (sacks of grain to store/ sell, and cash) than on consumer items per se, perhaps because of their fears of jealousy. There is less evidence of this at other sites reported in this collection. Furthermore, access to cash is the subject of much daily discussion in village life, particularly among women, again diverging somewhat from the site reports in Howland et al. (2021). Variation in the extent to which Tanzanian communities value productive capital as opposed to goods that signal status might be an interesting question to explore across the sites represented in this collection of chapters.

Finally, and consistent with other sites, education is considered an important aspect of wealth, although there is acute awareness that the costs invested in educating children (substantial, despite the recent availability of free secondary schooling at the ward level) are rarely compensated for, given the rarity with which secondary-educated students obtain paid employment. Education is clearly a gambit—it places individuals in a better position to start and successfully run small business ventures at the village level, but it also puts them at high risk of frustration, despair, and depression often because unemployed ex-students feel they are letting their family down.

Ultimately in Mpimbwe the path out of poverty still lies in farming (including livestock production), with people converting their profits into improved housing quality and assets, although there has also been an increase in capital-intensive business activities and opportunities for wage labour. However, as noted above, not everyone is on the rising ship.

Assets as an Indicator of Well-Being

Turning to my second question, household assets are a useful indicator of well-being. Assets show consistent associations with productivity, with absence of measures of stress, and with education and health outcomes. As such, the general increase in assets over the period between 1995 and 2010 reveals a broader positive trend for peoples' lives.

The direction of causality between assets, productivity, education, and health (as measured through anthropometrics) is nevertheless not necessarily one way. In some cases, asset are clearly causal. For example, children living in houses with concrete floors are more likely to avoid infections than those in mud houses, and therefore to grow better. The associations of assets with education and piecework however are less direct. Most likely, families with the cash to buy lamps, bicycles, and even a mobile phone are more likely to be able to purchase uniforms and shoes for their children's schooling, and to avoid the food shortages that drive household members into daily piecework. Here the assets are not a direct cause of positive well-being outcomes, but rather an indicator of ability or uwezo (Howland et al., this volume); indeed assets likely function as important stores of value, particularly in rural areas where agricultural production is seasonal. Furthermore, assets may provide the additional benefit of protecting families from requests for cash loans—when earnings are tied up in bricks they can't easily be solicited by needy relatives. Finally assets, or rather the lack thereof, act as clear signals of poverty or want. For all these reasons assets may be implicated in positive well-being outcomes for families, but through diverse pathways.

Before leaving the association between assets and well-being two caveats are required. First, despite the predictive value of assets in this study, it is important to emphasize that how poverty or wealth is best measured necessarily depends on the researchers' goal. If the objective is to determine how to reduce poverty, my view is that it is best to take an emically informed stance on what constitutes 'poverty' or 'wealth' in a community. In this regard my fifteen-plus years of ethnography in Mpimbwe would suggest that food security, child health, and education are the principal goals (or targets) of most Pimbwe adults (male and female). Households that secure these goals are not 'poor'. Accordingly, the appropriate analytical strategy would be to *identify the strongest economic predictors of these targeted outcomes*. As such, we should not be focusing, necessarily somewhat arbitrarily, on any preferred measure (e.g., assets, income, consumption, etc.). Rather we should combine multiple dimensions of 'wealth' through the use of shadow pricing (e.g., Borgerhoff

Mulder et al. 2009). This procedure first calculates the regression coefficient of, for example, livestock ownership, agricultural land, and house quality on, say, child survival. It then uses these estimated parameters to weight these predictors (livestock, land, house type) as indicators of poverty (or the absence thereof). In this way the predictors of emic wealth are empirically recoverable.

Second, households are aggregations of individuals whose interests do not necessarily coincide. Their boundaries are highly permeable, and their persistence over time is variable. Accordingly, further analysis of these data should incorporate individual-level variables, in particular age, gender, birth order, marital status, and number of dependents, as well as individual economic activities, to identify more precisely the factors influencing changing well-being over an individual's lifetime. The inferences that can be drawn from household level studies are therefore limited (see also Doss et al. 2008, Randall and Coast 2015, Madhavan et al. 2017).

The Value of Village-Level Studies

Are longitudinal village level studies, such as reported here, worth the effort? And, a related question, can we generalize from case studies such as this? There are three points to make. First, village-level data have considerable importance in pointing to the paths whereby national developments affect the lives of citizens. Second, spatial heterogeneity in prosperity within nations is increasing, making locally based studies increasingly relevant for policy. Third, such studies are unusual.

Who benefits from national level changes in prosperity? The literature on African economic performance focuses on aggregate average growth rates, and pays little attention to the quality of that growth, the distribution of such growth, and the significance for the individual actors (Jerven 2010 and 2013). Furthermore we now know from using multilevel modelling across Demographic Health Survey sites in Tanzania that aggregate level statistics can both conceal and exaggerate associations observed at the level of individuals and villages (Lawson et al. 2015). In addition, national level studies typically ignore emic views on well-being (Tucker et al. 2011). Against this background anthropologists, geographers, rural sociologists, and some economists are motivated to collect and analyse individual-level economic data at the village level (for a pioneering example, see Bliss and Stern 1982), to operationalize their variables in ways that make sense locally, to capitalize on the quality rather than the quantity of data, and where possible to conduct long-term studies. With individual data taken at the village level we can begin to determine who benefits from national level changes in the economy, and (ultimately) how. In short village studies provide insights into the specific pathways and mechanisms whereby developments at the national (and global) level impact peoples' lives.

Specificity nevertheless trades off against generality. Is this a problem? If nations were relatively homogenous the answer might be no. The global patterning of inequality is nevertheless changing, with levels declining between nations and increasing within nations (Atkinson et al. 2011, Lakner and Milanovic 2013). Indeed, recent use of high resolution spatially patterned data reveals that despite national-level improvements in children's growth and education between 2000 and 2015, striking subnational heterogeneity persists, differences that are even widening in sub-Saharan countries (Graetz et al. 2018, Osgood-Zimmerman et al. 2018). To the extent that this is general, attention must shift from national to local patterning of inequality, if we are to address the causes, dynamics, and potential solutions to poverty. Here again village-level studies are particularly valuable.

Finally, as noted in the introduction to this collection, village-level economic studies are surprisingly rare, particularly those that track poverty dynamics using panel analyses. The present study is unusual in that it provides an immensely detailed longitudinal account of the fate of all villagers using repeat censuses across years. Censuses are preferable to samples, insofar as marginal individuals are less likely to be missed. Furthermore the economic circumstances of households that disappear, and that arrive, are detected. With additional analysis of the present data, the dynamics whereby individuals both manage and fail to prosper can be determined. Whether or not the effort is worthwhile will depend on further insights that can be gleaned from these data, although the experience of sharing so many of these adventures with different families has definitely been valuable for both the researcher and (at least hopefully some of) the community.[2]

Conclusion

What can we conclude more generally from case studies such as this for the debate over the 'African Growth Miracle'?

Certainly this result is surprising. Rukwa, as noted above, has been peripheral to development consistently over the last one hundred years. It lay between Belgium, German, French, and British areas during the 'Scramble for Africa' period, and then served as a 'labour reserve' (Tambila 1981, Mgawe et al. 2013,

[2] On a personal note, this long-term economic research helped galvanized a campaign to improve social, economic, and ecological conditions in Mpimbwe, an initiative that has now become growing as a grassroots community programme http://www.lcmo.or.tz/.

Seel et al. 2014). Even with significant development initiatives (such as 'Rukwa Ruka' ('Rukwa Fly' in Swahili), Jerve and Ntemi 2009), it lagged behind into the 2000s in terms of education, food security, and productivity, especially in the Rukwa Valley (Wandel and Homboe-Ottesen 1992).

More generally, what do findings like this imply for the debate over the 'African Growth Miracle'? Some will find vindication of their views, and others will see this as a localized exception that cannot be taken as representative. In reality, this study neither endorses nor refutes either narrative. It does not make a claim of that order. Rather it reveals the value of detailed data of this sort, and of measures with which we can understand better the dynamics of social change. Furthermore, with such data across sites that enjoy different levels of state investment in public goods, it would be possible to investigate the interactions between private wealth and public goods—dynamics that are critical to understand if Tanzania is to reduce its substantive, and in some instances increasing, regional inequalities (Maliti 2016).

References

Adam, C. S., P. Collier, and B. Ndulu (eds) (2017). *Tanzania: The Path to Prosperity*. Oxford: Oxford University Press.

Arndt C., A. McKay, and F. Tarp (eds) (2016). 'Growth and Poverty in Sub-Saharan Africa.' UNU-WIDER studies in Development Economics.

Atkinson A. B., T. Piketty, and E. Saez. (2011). 'Top Incomes in the Long Run of History.' *Journal of Economic Literature* 49(1): 3–71.

Barr, A., M. Dekker, W. Janssens, B. Kebede, and B. Kramer. (2019). 'Cooperation in Polygynous Households.' *American Economic Journal: Applied Economics* 11(2): 266–83.

Barrett, C. B. (2011). 'Assisting the Escape from Persistent Ultra-poverty in Rural Africa.' Center on Food Security and the Environment: Stanford Symposium Series on Global Food Policy and Food Security in the 21st Century.

Barrett, C. B. and M. R. Carter. (2013). 'The Economics of Poverty Traps and Persistent Poverty: Empirical and Policy Implications.' *The Journal of Development Studies* 49(7): 976–90.

Benjaminsen, T. A. and I. Bryceson (2012). 'Conservation, Green/Blue Grabbing and Accumulation by Dispossession in Tanzania.' *Journal of Peasant Studies* 39: 335–55.

Bevis, L. and C. B. Barrett (2013). 'Decomposing Intergenerational Income Elasticity: The Gender-Differentiated Contribution of Capital Transmission in Rural Philippines.' *World Development* 74: 233–52.

Bingenheimer, J. B. (2007). 'Wealth, Wealth Indices and HIV Risk in East Africa.' *International Perspectives on Sexual and Reproductive Health* 33(2): 83.

Bliss, C. J. and N. H. Stern (1982). *Palanpur: The Economy of an Indian Village*. Oxford: Oxford University Press.

Bluwstein, J., J. F. Lund, K. Askew, H. Stein, C. Noe, R. Odgaard, F. Maganga, and L. Engström (2018). 'Between Dependence and Deprivation: The Interlocking Nature of Land Alienation in Tanzania.' *Journal of Agrarian Change* 18(4): 806–30.

Borgerhoff Mulder, M. (2009). 'Serial Monogamy as Polygyny or Polyandry? Marriage in the Tanzanian Pimbwe.' *Human Nature* 20(2): 130–50.

Borgerhoff Mulder, M. and B. A. Beheim (2011). 'Understanding the Nature of Wealth and Its Effects on Human Fitness.' *Philosophical Transactions of the Royal Society B* 366: 344–56.

Borgerhoff Mulder, M., S. Bowles, T. Hertz, A. Bell, J. Beise, G. Clark, I. Fazzio, M. Gurven, K. Hill, P. Hooper, et al. (2009). 'Intergenerational Wealth Transmission and the Dynamics of Inequality in Small-Scale Societies.' *Science* 326: 682–8.

Borgerhoff Mulder, M., T. M. Caro, and A. O. Msago (2007). 'The Role of Research in Evaluating Conservation Strategies in Tanzania: The Case of the Katavi-Rukwa Ecosystem.' *Conservation Biology* 21(3): 647–58.

Bowles, S., E. A. Smith, and M. Borgerhoff Mulder (2010). 'The Emergence and Persistence of Inequality in Pre-modern Societies: Introduction.' *Current Anthropology* 50(1): 7–17.

Brockington, D. (2001). 'Communal Property and Degradation Narratives: Debating the Sukuma Immigration into Rukwa Region, Tanzania.' *Cahiers d'Afrique* 20: 1–22.

Brockington, D., O. Howland, V. M. Loiske, M. Mnzava, and C. Noe. (2018). 'Economic Growth, Rural Assets and Prosperity: Exploring the Implications of a 20 Year Record of Asset Growth in Tanzania.' *Journal of Modern African Studies* 56(2): 1–27.

Carter, M. R. and T. J. Lybbert (2012). 'Consumption versus Asset Smoothing: Testing the Implications of Poverty Trap Theory in Burkina Faso.' *Journal of Development Economics* 99(2): 255–64.

Chuhan-Pole, P. M. A. (2011). 'Yes Africa Can: Success Stories from a Dynamic Continent.' Washington DC, The World Bank.

De Weerdt, J. (2004). 'Risk-Sharing and Endogenous Network Formation.' *Insurance against Poverty*. S. Dercon. Oxford, Oxford University Press: 197–216.

De Weerdt, J. and S. Dercon (2006). 'Risk-Sharing Networks and Insurance against Illness.' *Journal of Development Economics* 81(2): 337–56.

Dercon, S. (2006). 'Economic Reform, Growth and the Poor: Evidence from Rural Ethiopia.' *Journal of Development Economics* 81: 1–24.

Dercon, S. and D. Gollin (2014). 'Agriculture in African Development: Theories and Strategies.' *Annual Review of Resource Economics* 6(1): 471–92.

Dorward, A. (2009). 'Integrating Contested Aspirations, Processes and Policy: Development as Hanging In, Stepping Up and Stepping Out.' *Development Policy Review* 27(2): 131–46.

Doss, C., J. McPeak, and C. B. Barrett (2008). 'Interpersonal, Intertemporal and Spatial Variation in Risk Perceptions: Evidence from East Africa.' *World Development* 36(8): 1453–68.

Evans, D., S. Hausladen, K. Kosec, and N. Reese (2014). 'Community-Based Conditional Cash Transfers in Tanzania: Results from a Randomized Trial.' Washington DC, The World Bank.

Filmer, D. and L. H. Pritchett (2001). 'Estimating Wealth Effects without Expenditure Data—or Tears.' *Demography* 38(1): 115–32.

Graetz, N., J. Friedman, A. Osgood-Zimmerman, R. Burstein, M. H. Biehl, C. Shields, J. F. Mosser, D. C. Casey, A. Deshpande, and L. Earl (2018). 'Mapping Local Variation in Educational Attainment across Africa.' *Nature* 555(7694): 48.

Greco, E. (2014). 'Landlords in the Making: Class Dynamics of the Land Grab in Mbarali, Tanzania.' *Review of African Political Economy* 42: 225–44. DOI: 10.1080/03056244.2014.992403.

Gurven, M., M. Borgerhoff Mulder, P. Hooper, H. Kaplan, R. Quinlan, R. Sear, E. Schniter, C. von Rueden, S. Bowles, T. Hertz et al. (2010). 'Domestication Alone Does Not Lead to Inequality: Intergenerational Wealth Transmission among Horticulturalists.' *Current Anthropology* 51(1): 49–64.

Guyer, J. I. (1993). 'Wealth in People and Self-Realization in Equatorial Africa.' *Man* 28(2): 243–65.

Hadley, C. (2004). 'The Costs and Benefits of Kin: Kin Networks and Children's Health among the Pimbwe of Tanzania.' *Human Nature* 15(4): 377–95.

Hadley, C., M. Borgerhoff Mulder, and E. Fitzherbert (2007). 'Seasonal Food Insecurity and Perceived Social Support in Rural Tanzania.' *Public Health Nutrition* 10(6): 544–51.

Hadley, C. and C. L. Patil (2006). 'Food Insecurity in Rural Tanzania Is Associated with Maternal Anxiety and Depression.' *American Journal of Human Biology* 18: 359–68.

Hadley, C. A. (2005). 'Ethnic Expansions and Between-Group Differences in Children's Health: A Case Study from the Rukwa Valley, Tanzania.' *American Journal of Physical Anthropology* 128: 682–92.

Harttgen, K., S. Klasen, and S. Vollmer (2013). 'An African Growth Miracle? Or: What Do Asset Indices Tell Us about Trends in Economic Performance.' *Review of Income and Wealth* 59: S37–61.

Hassine, N. B. and A. Zeufack (2015). 'Inequality of Outcomes and Inequality of Opportunity in Tanzania.' World Bank Policy Research Working Paper 7260. Washington DC, The World Bank.

Howe, L. D., B. Galobardes, A. Matijasevich, D. Gordon, D. Johnston, O. Onwujekwe, R. Patel, E. A. Webb, D. A. Lawlor, and J. R. Hargreaves (2012). 'Measuring Socio-Economic Position for Epidemiological Studies in Low- and Middle-Income Countries: A Method of Measurement in Epidemiology Paper.' *International Journal of Epidemiology* 41(3): 871–86.

Howe, L. D., J. R. Hargreaves, S. Gabrysch, and S. R. Huttly (2009). 'Is the Wealth Index a Proxy for Consumption Expenditure? A Systematic Review.' *Journal of Epidemiology & Community Health* 63: 871–7.

Howland, O., D. Brockington, and C. Noe (2021). 'The Multiple Meanings of Prosperity and Poverty: A Cross-Site Comparison from Tanzania.' *Journal of Peasant Studies* 48: 180–200.

Hruschka, D. J., D. Gerkey, and C. Hadley (2015). 'Estimating the Absolute Wealth of Households.' *Bulletin of the World Health Organization* 93(7): 483–90.

Jahnke, H. E., G. Tacher, P. Keil, and D. Rojat (1988). 'Livestock Production in Tropical Africa, with Special Reference to the Tsetse-Affected Zone.' Proceedings of a meeting of the African Trypanotolerant Livestock Network, Nairobi, 23–27 November. Nairobi, International Livestock Centre for Africa and the International Laboratory for Research on Animal Diseases: 3–21.

Jerve, A. M. and E. J. K. Ntemi (2009). 'Rukwa Ruka: The Attempt of a Foreign Donor to Uplift a Neglected Region: A Study of the Impact of Norwegian Aid to Rukwa Region, Tanzania.' CHR Michelsen Institute (CMI).

Jerven, M. (2010). 'Accounting for the African Growth Miracle: The Official Evidence—Botswana 1965–1995.' *Journal of Southern African Studies* 36(1): 73–94.

Jerven, M. (2013). *Poor Numbers: How We Are Misled by African Development Statistics and What to Do about It.* Ithaca, Cornell University Press.

Johnston, D. and A. Abreu (2016). 'The Asset Debates: How (Not) to Use Asset Indices to Measure Well-Being and the Middle Class in Africa.' *African Affairs* 115(460): 399–418.

Kaiser, B. N., D. Hruschka, and C. Hadley (2017). 'Measuring Material Wealth in Low-Income Settings: A Conceptual and How-To Guide.' *American Journal of Human Biology* 29(4): e22987.

Kaplan, H. (1996). 'A Theory of Fertility and Parental Investment in Traditional and Modern Human Societies.' *Yearbook of Physical Anthropology* 39: 91–135.

Kasper, C. and M. Borgerhoff Mulder (2015). 'Who Helps and Why? Cooperative Networks in Mpimbwe.' *Current Anthropology* 56: 701–32.

Koster, J. (2018). 'Family Ties: The Multilevel Effects of Households and Kinship on the Networks of Individuals.' *Royal Society Open Science* 5: 172159.

Lakner, C. and B. Milanovic (2013). 'Global Income Distribution: From the Fall of the Berlin Wall to the Great Recession.' Washington DC, The World Bank.

Lawson, D. W., S. James, E. Ngadaya, B. Ngowi, S. G. M. Mfinanga, K. Hartwig, and M. Borgerhoff Mulder (2015). 'No Evidence that Polygynous Marriage is a Harmful Cultural Practice in Northern Tanzania.' *Proceedings of the National Academies of Sciences* 112(45): 13827–32.

Madhavan, S., S. Clark, D. Beguy, C. W. Kabiru, and M. Gross (2017). 'Moving beyond the Household: Innovations in Data Collection on Kinship.' *Population Studies* 71(1): 117–32.

Maliti, E. (2016). 'Horizontal Inequality in Education and Wealth in Tanzania: A 20-Year Perspective.' WIDER Working Paper 2016/114s.

Maliti, E. (2018). 'Dimensions of Inequality in Tanzania: Status, Trends and Policies.' REPOA Tanzania.

Mashindano, O., K. Kayunze, L. Da Corta, and F. Maro (2013). 'Growth without Poverty Reduction in Tanzania: Reasons for the Mismatch.' *Translating Growth into Poverty Reduction: Beyond the Numbers*. F. Kessy, O. Mashindano, A. Shepherd, and L. Scott. Dar es Salaam: Mkuki na Nyota: 121–41.

McMillan, M. S. and K. Harttgen (2014). 'What Is Driving the "African Growth Miracle"?' NBER Working Paper No. 20077, April 2014.

Mgawe, P., M. Borgerhoff Mulder, T. Caro, and S. J. Seel (2013). *Historia ya Kabila la Wapimbwe*. Dar es Salaam, Mkuki na Nyota Publishers.

Mueller, B. E. T. (2011). 'The Agrarian Question in Tanzania: Using New Evidence to Reconcile an Old Debate.' *Review of African Political Economy* 38: 23–42.

Mushongah, J. and I. Scoones (2012). 'Livelihood Change in Rural Zimbabwe over 20 Years.' *Journal of Development Studies* 48(9): 1241–57.

Osgood-Zimmerman, A., A. I. Millear, R. W. Stubbs, C. Shields, B. V. Pickering, L. Earl, N. Graetz, D. K. Kinyoki, S. E. Ray, and S. Bhatt (2018). 'Mapping Child Growth Failure in Africa between 2000 and 2015.' *Nature* 555(7694): 41.

Quisumbing, A. R. and J. A. Maluccio (2003). 'Resources at Marriage and Intrahousehold Allocation: Evidence from Bangladesh, Ethiopia, Indonesia, and South Africa.' *Oxford Bulletin of Economics and Statistics* 65(3): 283–328.

Radelet, S. (2010). *Emerging Africa: How 17 Countries Are Leading the Way*. Washington DC, Centre for Global Development.

Randall, S. and E. Coast (2015). 'Poverty in African Households: The Limits of Survey and Census Representations.' *The Journal of Development Studies* 51(2): 162–77.

Ravallion, M. (2014). 'Income Inequality in the Developing World.' *Science* 344(6186): 851–5.

Salerno, J., J. Mwalyoyo, T. Caro, E. Fitzherbert, and M. Borgerhoff Mulder (2017). 'The Consequences of Internal Migration in Sub-Saharan Africa: A Case Study.' *Bioscience* 67(7): 664–71.

Seel, S.-J., P. Mgawe, and M. Borgerhoff Mulder (2014). *The History and Traditions of the Pimbwe*. Dar es Salaam, Mkuki na Nyota Publishers.

Tambila, A. (1981). *A History of Rukwa Region (Tanzania) ca 1870–1940: Aspects of Economic and Social Change from Precolonial to Colonial Times*. Hamburg University. PhD.

Tucker, B., A. Huff, Tombo J Tsiazonera, P. Hajasoa, and C. Nagnisaha (2011). 'When the Wealthy Are Poor: Poverty Explanations and Local Perspectives in Southwestern Madagascar.' *American Anthropologist* 113(2): 291–305.

Wandel, M. and G. Homboe-Ottesen (1992). 'Food Availability and Nutrition in a Seasonal Perspective: A Study from the Rukwa Region in Tanzania.' *Human Ecology* 20(1): 89–107.

Willis, R. G. (1966). 'The Fipa and Related Peoples of South-West Tanzania and North-East Zambia.' London, International African Institute.

Young, A. (2012). 'The African Growth Miracle.' *Journal of Political Economy* 120(4): 696–739.

6
'Modern' Farming and the Transformation of Livelihoods in Rural Tanzania

Katherine A. Snyder, Emmanuel Sulle, Deodatus A. Massay, Anselmi Petro, Paschal Qamara, and Dan Brockington

Epilogue pages 401–406

Economic Growth, Agriculture, and Intensification

There has been considerable attention and debate, at a macro-level, on the changes taking place in agriculture across the African continent and whether these changes are or can result in poverty reduction and significant economic transformation (Collier and Dercon 2014, Barrett et al. 2017, Christiaenensen et al. 2011, Davis et al. 2017). Generally in Africa, economic growth has increased significantly particularly from 2000 onwards (Jayne et al. 2010, 2018, Binswanger-Mhkize et al. 2010, 2017, Andersson Djurfeld et al. 2018). GDP in the region has grown by nearly 35 per cent between 2000 and 2014 (Jayne et al. 2018: 777). The drivers of growth vary but signs point to urbanization, infrastructural development, and tourism (Barrett et al. 2017). Annual agricultural growth, by comparison, has been smaller, with a growth of just 4.6 per cent between 2000 and 2016 (Jayne et al. 2018: 777, figures adjusted for inflation). Nevertheless, there are changes in this sector, with changing diets and growing urban populations demanding more food. Liberalized policies have led to an influx of new varieties of improved seeds and other agricultural inputs (Jayne et al. 2018, Reardon 2015). Barrett et al. (2017) suggest there is a wider structural transformation of rural economies taking place with traditional forms of agriculture becoming more productive.

These differing portrayals of rural affairs have quite different implications for our understanding of change in rural communities. The sober view of African agriculture portrays rural communities that are, economically, changing little compared to the other sectors. The more optimistic view suggests more dynamism. This chapter provides a different perspective on these debates. Here we focus on the micro-level to explore how changes in the wider national economy

Katherine A. Snyder, Emmanuel Sulle, Deodatus A. Massay, Anselmi Petro, Paschal Qamara, and Dan Brockington, *'Modern' Farming and the Transformation of Livelihoods in Rural Tanzania* In: *Prosperity in Rural Africa? Insights into Wealth, Assets, and Poverty from Longitudinal Studies in Tanzania.* Edited by: Dan Brockington and Christine Noe, Oxford University Press. DOI: 10.1093/oso/9780198865872.003.0006

have affected the lives and livelihoods of a rural community in Tanzania. This attention to the local level expands our understanding of the impact of change but complicates the picture constructed by macro accounts (Mashindano et al. 2011) that have described stasis, if not growing poverty, in the agricultural sector, because the forms of growth are not benefitting the rural poor. Östberg et al. (2018) and Brockington et al. (2018) provide similar accounts of changes in livelihoods in rural communities elsewhere in Tanzania.

We focus on the local level because, at the heart of the debate about change to rural economies in Africa and the agricultural sector is the question of intensification. In what circumstances have smallholders increased their productivity—and how readily have they done so? Yet, specifically with respect to intensification there is a particular deficiency of detailed studies that track communities and families over time. As Brockington et al. (2018) observe, the studies and data that inform these analyses draw upon data sets that do not provide adequate illustration of what is actually happening in rural communities. Drilling down to community level shows how varied and differentiated economic growth, agricultural productivity, and changes in livelihoods can be (Andersson Djurfeldt et al. 2018). So, local level studies, to contextualize growth as Andersson Djurfeldt et al. (2018) argue, are important for assessing some of the conclusions that arise from the national and regional-level data. This research aimed to understand growth and changes in livelihoods and agricultural production in a rural community in Tanzania over a thirty-year period. We investigated the relationship between national trends, policy, and local farming practices and outcomes at the local level in Mbulu District.

Tanzanian Policies: Smallholder Farming and Intensification

In Tanzania, as a result of economic liberalization policies in the 1980s and onwards, basic consumer goods became more available in the 1990s and the monopoly of state trading companies and co-operatives ended. Liberalization of input and output markets has had an impact, particularly on maize production which Cooksey states 'has been one of the success stories of agricultural liberalisation in Tanzania' (2011: 561). In the '90s, overall macro-economic growth, as measured by GDP, was very slow. But, as Andersson Djurfeldt et al. (2018) note, growth picked up dramatically in the 2000s. This pattern in Tanzania matches change across the continent (Jayne et al. 2018).

More than 70 per cent of Tanzanians depend on agriculture for their livelihoods (Msuya et al. 2018). While agriculture is critical to Tanzania's national economy, its share of GDP declined from 50 per cent in 2000 to less than 24.7 per cent in 2014 (Msuya et al. 2018: 139). This decline reflects growth in other sectors of the Tanzanian economy such as construction, mining, and services. Within agriculture, growth can be traced to an increase in production of products like tomatoes, onions, and potatoes and an increase in the staples of maize and rice (Coulson 2015). Various national policies from 2000 onwards have attempted to spur agricultural growth. The Agriculture Sector Development Programme (ASDP) which came out in 2001 had, as its goal, a 5 per cent per annum increase in agricultural growth and to reach 10 per cent by 2010 (Coulson 2015: 56). The focus of the ASDP was on production, rather than on marketing, which Coulson argues would have given more significant benefits to farmers.

In 2009, the Tanzanian government launched Kilimo Kwanza (Agriculture First) which highlighted public-private partnerships and emphasized investment in large-scale agriculture and outgrower schemes that smallholders would join. In parallel to Kilimo Kwanza was the launching of the Southern Agricultural Growth Corridor of Tanzania (SAGCOT). SAGCOT targets roughly one-third of the land area of Tanzania for large-scale agricultural investment, encouraging foreign direct investment and partnerships with smallholder producers who would produce on contracts (Coulson 2015: 60).

These policy responses are the latest in a long search across many African countries for ways of improving growth in the agriculture sector. As is evident from the shift in national policy in Tanzania, large-scale agriculture and significant investment, often from foreign investors, is seen to be a key strategy to achieve growth. Others have argued that the smallholder sector in particular, because it supports most of Tanzania's rural population, deserves more investment and support. In his review of smallholder and large-scale farming in Tanzania, Coulson concludes:

> [O]verall, as it was for the Germans more than 100 years ago and for the British 60 years ago, the cheapest and quickest means to increase agricultural production in Tanzania is to support and trust small farmers by ensuring that marketing arrangements are in place that will give them fair prices for the crops they sell. (2015: 66)

There have been several reviews of the contributions of small farms to overall development and poverty reduction in developing countries, and Africa in particular (Wiggins et al. 2010, Graeub et al. 2016, Lowder et al. 2016). Proponents of investing in large farms claim they have greater efficiency (in terms of output per person) and benefit from economies of scale. Those in favour of small farms argue to the contrary, suggesting that small farms have higher productivity per hectare. There is some consensus that, depending on agro-ecological conditions and access to inputs and other support, extremely small holdings are unlikely to secure livelihoods or reduce poverty (Wiggins et al. 2010, Harris and Orr 2014). Indeed, there is literature which suggests that for the very poor, off-farm income generating activities are more critical for their livelihoods and survival (Bryceson 2002). In terms of reducing poverty, Wiggins et al. indicate that there are still 'few studies that directly compare the impact on poverty of agricultural growth from large farms to that from small' (2010: 1344). Arguments against the 'unproductive' small farm are used to justify the promotion of large farms through foreign or national investment.

At the heart of the question of whether smallholders can sustain a transformation in productivity is the issue of intensification. There are two components to this—can more food be produced (to meet future needs and sustain growth) and can it be produced sustainably, without environmental degradation. Through 'Sustainable Intensification', it is hoped that 'yields are increased without adverse environmental impact and without the cultivation of more land' (Royal Society 2009, cited in Garnett and Godfrey 2012: 8). Development agencies and international agricultural research centres such as the Consultative Group on International Agricultural Research (CGIAR), increasingly focus on promoting an African Green Revolution involving increased inputs in the form of improved seeds, chemical fertilizer, irrigation, and mechanized agriculture. The approach of these programs is primarily technical and quantitative in the form of higher yields (Scoones and Thompson 2011, Davidson 2012, Ollenburger et al. 2019). While experts see intensification as the way forward for African agriculture, adoption of some of the recommended practices by smallholder farmers remains low. In part, low adoption rates reflect farmers' real concerns with the increased risks that come along with dependence on the market, with growing cash crops, with using inorganic fertilizer, and with shifting cropping patterns. Diversification is more often the strategy that farmers follow as a response to the highly unpredictable environment in which they live.

Part of the problem in advancing this debate is the poor quality of data that are available. Measuring agricultural productivity is challenging in most global south contexts as the data can be unavailable or unreliable. While Tanzania puts considerable effort into gathering credible statistics, farmer recall and estimates can be very challenging. Additionally, agricultural officers may feel pressed to report positive figures of growth (Coulson 2015). National-level figures also mask the significant differences at the regional and local level. However, the lack of data does not stop the proliferation of truth claims. As Christiaensen observes of African agriculture 'stylized facts drive research agendas and policy debates. They provide a sense of importance, help frame the inquiry and are used to galvanize resources' (2017: 1).

The Setting and Research Method

To explore these various themes on poverty, agricultural development and smallholder intensification, this chapter will focus on one farming community from 1990 to the present. It traces the factors influencing farmers' decisions and their assessment of the changes in their livelihoods.

Its focus is the Iraqw people who are an agro-pastoral, southern Cushitic-language speaking people who live throughout Arusha and Manyara Regions in northern Tanzania. This research focuses primarily on Kainam and Murray wards in Mbulu District, which the Iraqw refer to as their 'homeland'. The district sits between Lake Manyara and Lake Eyasi and has a population, as of the 2012 census, of 320,279 people, up from 237,280 in 2002. Both Kainam and Murray wards were sub-divided more recently to create two new wards, Nambis and Nahhasey. With the sub-division of the original two wards come further resources from district government, in the form of schools and health facilities. This research includes these new wards.

The highland homeland of the Iraqw people ranges in elevation from 1,500 to 2,300m and is densely populated at over 240 per sq km. The total population of this area is 36,362, up from 19,048 in the 1988 census. The Iraqw name for this area is Irqwa Da'aw or Mama Issara in Swahili. Migration out of the homeland has been taking place since the colonial era and now Iraqw are found throughout Arusha and Manyara Regions and, more recently, are moving as far away as Kilindi and Handeni near the coast, a distance of over 500km.

This chapter focuses on smallholder agriculture yet has to be taken in the context of what broader purpose and livelihood these activities sustain. Iraqw definitions of poverty are bound up with wider national and global narratives around development (Swahili: maendeleo). Most Iraqw define wealth as a combination of material assets, together with the ability to educate your children, take care of your family's health, and the ability to withstand shocks. Of course, the assets that count as valuable change over time (Green and Hulme 2005). Indeed, particularly when assets are considered, the measurements of wealth are constantly changing (Brockington et al 2019). For example, assets that people mention now as desirable and important to acquire include electricity (often solar), cell phones, sheet metal for roofing, bricks for building, and motorcycles. Most of these were unattainable or unavailable in the 1990s. What enables them to acquire these assets varies from household to household but includes wage labour, selling crops, livestock, and, significantly, tree products. Many respondents suggested that if you work hard, use improved seeds, apply manure to your field, and take care of your livestock, you will achieve maendeleo.

Mama Issara is well watered with springs and streams running year-round. Rainfall is bimodal and averages 1,000mm a year. In the cold dry season, mist accumulates in this highland area making cultivation of wheat and other crops possible on the hillsides. Dry-season cultivation also takes place in the valley bottoms where irrigation, primarily by buckets or furrows, is often used.

In the homeland, farmers cultivate small plots of land (average is 2 acres) by hand hoe. Cultivation with ox plough is impossible as the slopes are too steep and the valley-bottom soils too dense and often waterlogged. Agricultural production focuses on maize and beans (which are both staples and sold for cash), sweet potatoes, Irish potatoes, wheat, sorghum, millet, leafy greens, bananas, onions, and tomatoes. Some crops grown in the 1990s, such as finger millet, appear not to be grown today. Crops grown specifically for cash include tobacco, pyrethrum, and coffee. For a brief period in the early 2000s, farmers planted artemisia when a foreign investor came with seeds and agreed to buy the harvest. This project went well for a couple of years (though some farmers complained the plants, which are used to cure malaria, brought mosquitoes) but then the investor disappeared and farmers uprooted the plants. Coffee has gone through many vicissitudes according to global prices and local marketing issues, but is now on the upsurge again with farmers planting new varieties.

Colonial-era agricultural officers held up the Iraqw as model farmers, extolling their sophisticated soil management practices (Snyder 1996). Archival documents reported on labour-intensive bench terraces, cut-off drains, contour planting, mulching, crop rotation, and intercropping. The Iraqw farming system in the homeland has attracted much attention over time, both from colonial agricultural extension officers and from scholars interested in intensive agriculture (Börjeson 2007). From the colonial era to the present, there has been considerable change in land-use practices as farmers respond to national and global markets and as population pressure changes how they use their limited land resources. According to oral history and colonial reports, Iraqw farmers in the homeland produced enough food to meet their needs in the colonial era and, in times of drought, were able to supply neighbouring, drier areas with food.

Of the authors, Snyder has been carrying out research for nearly three decades, for long and short periods, in this area. Sulle, Massay, Petro, and Qamara have grown up in the homeland and the latter two still reside there. Brockington has long-term research experience in Tanzania in neighbouring zones, including with the Iraqw. The study combined qualitative (focus groups and interviews) and quantitative methods and compared data across two household surveys, one carried out in 1995 (n=150), the other in 2017 (n=180). Over twenty individuals were interviewed, including farmers, extension officers, government officials, timber sellers, maize traders, and input sellers. Six focus groups were held with women, men, and youth (separately). Long-term experience in one farming community allows for a unique perspective not only on specific indicators of change, such as production or the increase in assets, but also affords insight into the meanings attached to these changes and the social dynamics that such changes affect.

Findings

Changes to Agriculture

In the 1990s, some of soil management techniques were on the decline and youth complained they were old-fashioned practices from colonialism (Snyder 1996: 327).

Today, fewer people have terraces and they have instead adopted less intensive soil conservation practices as indicated in Table 6.1 below. Intercropping and crop rotation are still widely practiced. Tree planting is widespread but, according to our sources, is carried out less for soil erosion control than for income generation.

In the 1990s, surplus production had declined considerably and many (90 per cent) relied on buying food, or exchanges with relatives and friends (kuhemea) to meet their needs (the majority of farmers reported only meeting 62 per cent of their needs). In the 2017 survey, production appears to have increased and 90 per cent of farmers surveyed reported that they were able to meet their food needs through their production (Tables 6.2 and 6.3). Today, farmers still seek maize elsewhere, but most purchase (92 per cent) the needed maize rather than exchange within social networks (44 per cent). A large proportion also 'beg' for food from neighbours (67 per cent). Respondents indicated that purchasing food through social networks is usually cheaper than on the market and can have added benefits in the present and future (such as information or help with school placement for children, loans, market price information, etc.). It may involve costs later as reciprocity of some kind will be expected.

Table 6.1 Land management practices from household survey for 2017

Practice	% households
Terraces	15
Ridging	10
Cut-off drains	14
Grass strips	31
Tree planting	99

N=180. Unfortunately, the 1995 survey did not include data on soil conservation practices.

Table 6.2 Household farm size and cropping patterns

	1995	2017
Mean farm size	2.5 acres	2 acres
% households selling crops	47	71
% Hhs with food deficit	47	10
% Hhs growing maize	100	100
% Hhs growing beans	78	91
% Hhs growing sorghum	57	8
% Hhs growing millet	57	12
% Hhs growing sweet potato	66	78
% Hhs growing Irish potato	26	35
% Hhs growing wheat	66	22

N=150 (1995), N=180 (2017).

Table 6.3 Average annual harvest data of principal crops across households

Crop	Harvest (kg) 1995	Harvest (kg) 2017	% Selling 1995	% Selling 2017
Maize	748	1621	5	39
Beans	76	164	10	54
Irish potatoes	124	306	17	90
Sweet potato	802	761	na	na
Wheat	401	134	na	na

N=150 (1995), N=180 (2017).

While staple crops grown have remained constant over time, cash crops shift according to the market. As is evident from the table above, productivity of maize, beans, and Irish potatoes has increased significantly at the household level. According to farmers, this increase reflects both the use of improved seeds, pesticides, and practices, but also market demand. Maize, beans, and potatoes are sold frequently, with potatoes, in high demand from urban markets, sold by almost all families growing them. Wheat is no longer a favoured crop and is now mostly consumed in the household, as are sweet potatoes.

The type of seeds that farmers choose to plant has changed dramatically since the 1990s. Then, elders were sceptical of improved hybrid seeds believing them to be less resistant to pests and weather conditions. Additionally, they indicated the taste of the food from improved seeds was not as good. In the 1990s, farmers also planted up to fifteen seeds in one hole and had spacing of about two feet between each hole. They used this technique to foil cutworms that were a serious problem in the area in drier years (Snyder 1993). Extension agents regularly admonished farmers to let go of these 'traditional' practices and adopt 'modern' ones of two seeds per hole and spacing of about a foot between holes.

In 2017, in focus groups and interviews, farmers all claimed to have adopted improved seeds (mbegu bora) as well as 'modern' planting practices. They attributed their greater maize production to these changes. The reservations that elders expressed in the '90s about being overly dependent, and thus vulnerable to markets (and the rise and fall of prices), have largely been abandoned by this next generation of farmers. While farmers have embraced improved seeds, some still plant local varieties as well. One woman noted that local varieties are important for pregnant women who like to chew on the stalk of young maize plants as they would sugar cane. She said 'you can't do this with improved varieties'. They also continue with local varieties to reduce risk as they think these varieties better adapted to local conditions. In sum, production has shifted notably to improved maize seeds. In addition, farmers now regularly apply pesticides to their crops to combat cutworm and stalk borers, which has helped them maintain their harvests.

Most respondents said that when market prices are good, they are able to make some small profits. However, if crop prices drop on the market, even breaking even can be a challenge, given the cost of labour and input purchases. While farmers have adopted the new and 'modern' farming practices of improved seeds and planting practices (Table 6.4), they have not been so keen on adopting chemical fertilizers. Most farmers who we encountered on this survey, and indeed, in many years of working and living in this region, believe that chemical fertilizers ruin the soils and if you start using them, you will be dependent on applying them forever. As one man commented, 'If you use chemical fertilizers the soil dries out and is ruined. You will then have to use fertilizer all the time to get any harvest.' They link the application of chemical fertilizer with causing further soil fertility decline. As noted in Snyder (1996), farmers continue to apply and rely on livestock manure to enhance their soils. As manure can be scarce, they usually apply it only in the planting hole.

From Table 6.5 below, we can see some interesting shifts in labour patterns. Reliance on paid labour has increased significantly, even in labour exchanges with neighbours. When discussing cooperative labour, many respondents spoke about the past when you could just brew beer, cook some food, and people would come. These days, as one man emphasized, 'You have to pay cash'.

In the '90s, there was a certain scorn about working as a day labourer. So, farmers often imported labour from neighbouring communities like the Ihanzu or Wanyiramba. Today disdain for day labour has gone and young men and women,

Table 6.4 Input use

Input	1995	2017
Improved seeds	0	83 %
Pesticides	71 %	83 %
Inorganic fertilizer	0	0

N=150 (1995) N=180 (2017).

Table 6.5 Labour patterns

Labour	% households 1995	% households 2017
Day labour (vibarua)	23	48
Help from neighbours	71	88
Exchange with neighbours	2	61
Payment to neighbours	0	45
Provide beer	77	10
Provide food	71	1

N=150 (1995), N=180 (2017).

who have no plots of their own or other ways of making money, regularly take up day labour on local farms. One middle-aged woman explained that, while young men work as day labourers, they rarely save their money, 'Young men will work as vibarua in the morning till around midday, get paid and then head out to kijiwe[1] to drink for the afternoon. The next day, they do it over again. They don't ever manage to save any money though.' Young people may hire out their labour as individuals but, as some respondents suggested, they also form labour groups.

The division of labour has been a topic of discussion for some time in Mama Issara. In the past, as many respondents observed, men and women had clearly defined responsibilities. Men were responsible for clearing the land and then men and women shared the work of planting and weeding. Women apply manure to the fields and harvest the crops. From the '90s onwards, women have complained that men do less and less labour on the farm and more falls to them. Government officials have raised the issue in local village meetings and have admonished men to spend more time on the farm (Snyder 1996). The term vijiwe was not in use in the '90s and there were far fewer shops and cafes around.

Livestock

Livestock have always been central to the Iraqw economy and culture. In the pre-colonial era and after independence until the mid-1990s, livestock were the major indicator of wealth for Iraqw. Their rituals, to honour the dead or to appease the earth spirits, involve sacrificing animals. The Iraqw have a complex system of livestock loans that establish and strengthen networks and bonds between individuals and households across the landscape and beyond to other agro-ecological zones (Snyder 2002 and 2005).

How community members in Mama Issara view livestock and its importance has changed significantly. According to respondents in interviews and focus groups, cattle are far less important today and many claimed that their numbers have dramatically declined. They noted lack of pasture as the main reason for the reduction in numbers. As one older man said: 'There is no pasture today. People are cultivating everywhere.' Some farmers have decided to keep fewer cattle and stall feed them. Decreasing pasture has given rise to the practice of planting grass for fodder. Farmers can also sell grass to other livestock keepers. This shift is noticeable across the landscape. Planted grass strips are evident along the hillsides (31 per cent of households reported having them) where they were rare in the '90s, when pasture was still more available.

The decline in pasture has increased in the last few years as grazing land is converted to farmland. Local government has encouraged these shifts by urging

[1] A kijiwe (vijiwe plural) is a gathering place with a small shop or a collection of shops and small tea stalls where people hang out, play cards, and drink tea, coffee, or beer.

farmers to produce more agricultural crops (Snyder 1996). Livestock keeping was often talked about as 'the ways of the past' and 'not modern'. Projects to introduce, promote, and expand the use of stall-fed 'modern cows' began in Mama Issara in the '90s and have re-surfaced in recent years.

Given local narratives about the decline in cattle numbers, it was surprising to find the 2017 survey results in Table 6.6 below showing little change in average 'traditional' (local breeds) cattle holdings. Collecting accurate information about livestock numbers is always challenging as farmers are reluctant to give this information and, for the Iraqw, they loan cattle out and receive loans as well. Thus, one's cattle may be spread out over the district and beyond depending on the loan and the individual's social network (Snyder 2002).

Goats are not well suited to the cold temperatures of Mama Issara and do better in the lowlands. Pigs are very popular because there is a reliable market for them and they reach maturity quickly and eat a wider variety of food. Most households keep chickens (82 per cent).

Farmers still participate in livestock loans of traditional breeds of cattle, though they are not as prevalent as they were in the past. In the 1995 survey, 56 per cent had cows on loan. From the 2017 survey, only 7 per cent had cows on loan but 27 per cent had cows loaned out to others. The social implications of this decline in the livestock loaning system are hard to interpret. Livestock were important for bride wealth, and cementing social relationships across the region. Loans allowed farmers to manage the risk of disease wiping out their herds by distributing their stock across a wider landscape. Additionally, reducing the number of stock on your compound helps ease the demand on household labour and resources for feeding.

Agroforestry

A notable change across the landscape of Mama Issara is the increase in tree cover. Tree planting was on the increase in the '90s, but at that time, the strategy

Table 6.6 Livestock holdings

Livestock type	Mean no. 1995	% households (1995)	Mean no. 2017	% households 2017
Traditional cattle breed	5.4	84	5	77
'Modern' cattle breed	n/a	n/a	2	9
Goats	5	52	5	36
Sheep	4	48	5	59
Pigs	2	73	3	87
Donkeys	2	4	2	2

N=150 (1995), N=180 (2017).

was to plant and harvest after fifteen years or so to meet cash needs, often for school fees. Farmers referred to trees as a 'bank account' (Snyder 1996). Continuous planting and planting after harvesting was less a pattern then. Now however, travelling through the homeland, trees cover many of the hillsides. In focus groups and conversations with farmers, they explained that, in some cases, the soils on the hillside plots are so exhausted from continuous use that they are more suitable to growing trees than food crops.

Fuelling the interest in tree planting is the growing demand for timber and other tree products, particularly with a rise in construction in Mbulu, the district capital some 15–30km away. Farmers can sell planks of grevillea and eucalyptus for about TZS 3,000 per plank and the price for pines and cypress species is 3,500 per plank (roughly \$1.30 and \$1.50 at 2017 exchange rates). This demand has led farmers to prioritize fast growing timber species like eucalyptus, pines, grevillea, and cypress. Tree holdings from both the 1995 and 2017 surveys are in Table 6.7 below.

A total of 99 per cent of survey respondents claimed they had trees on their farms and the average was 227 trees. The changes in species composition primarily reflects changes in local markets and in the costs of producing products (fruit trees like orange, lemon, and pear require more pesticide purchase). The demand for avocado has grown significantly along with its price over the last several years. Several respondents remarked, when asked why so many people are planting trees, 'Today, trees are our cows'. While trees may have replaced cattle as a form of wealth, they do not serve the same social function as livestock. As described in Snyder (2002) exotic species such as those in the list above are considered private

Table 6.7 Percentage of households with specific tree species

Species	1995 per cent of households	2017 per cent of households
Have trees on farm	83	99
Pinus sp	22	49
Grevillea robusta	94	88
Eucalyptus sp	12	93
Cupressus sp	48	30
Black wattle (Acacia mearnsii)	80	50
Banana	82	38
Orange	71	41
Avocado	28	71
Lemon	82	56
Guava	71	56
Pear	70	14
Coffee	25	5

N=150 (1995), N=180 (2017).

resources in ways that indigenous species are not (or were not in 1995). Farmers purchase seedlings and trees are considered an investment, so they are not freely given for firewood, help with building materials, or for other household uses. Additionally, timber species tend to be the property of men and harvesting them is often the work of young men, who pursue this as a day labour job. Women are more in control of produce from fruit trees that they sell in local markets. In focus groups and the household surveys, respondents assert that farm resources are for the entire family. However, in practice, each household has its own system of access, use, and control that tends to run along gender and generational lines. Trees are also very useful ways to mark farm boundaries, which is increasingly important in times of land scarcity and competition (Snyder 1996).

Farmers consider trees an excellent investment, enough so that land that would otherwise be farmed is being turned into woodlots, particularly on plots where the soil fertility is perceived to be low. Households reported several uses for their on-farm trees including firewood (44 per cent of households), timber sales (32 per cent), own construction purposes (7 per cent), fruit sales (25 per cent), and charcoal production (8 per cent). Black wattle, introduced in the colonial era, is the favoured species for charcoal. It has declined significantly since the '90s largely because of heavy exploitation for charcoal production and the expansion of timber species. Turning land over to tree production is made possible only by expansion into new areas or by intensifying production on other plots. Thus, each household possibly pursues intensification, de-intensification, extensification, altogether on their farm.

Assets

While trees and livestock are certainly valuable assets that can be turned into cash, Iraqw households now own assets that were not present during the 1990s (Table 6.8). Indeed, the 1995 survey did not even ask about ownership of many of the assets currently counted today.

In the '90s, Snyder knew of only one house that had a motorbike and no one owned a television, solar panel, or a cell phone and very few houses had sheet metal roofs. Electricity came to Mbulu town in 2000 and has only more recently made its way to Mama Issara through the government's rural electrification program and through the spread of solar panels, many of which are leased from companies. When looking at assets such as these, it is interesting to remember a remark by a respondent back in the 1990s who said, 'During Nyerere's time, there was nothing in the shops. Today, there are many things in the shops but we do not have the money to buy them.' It appears that more people are able to obtain the cash to buy commodities today. Several of those in the survey who have purchased solar panels, televisions, or motor bikes have access to off-farm income in

Table 6.8 Asset ownership from household survey for 2017

Asset	% households
TV	6
Motor bike	8
Solar panels	17
Bicycles	28
Radio	59
Sheet-metal roofing	71
Cell phones	76

N=180. Data on assets such as these in this table were not collected in the 1995 survey because they were not evident at all or they were so few.

the form of salaried wages. Others may be receiving remittances from children who have migrated out but in the household survey, no household reported receiving remittances. Household members may be brewing beer, selling handicrafts, have a small shop, or engage in some other informal income generation to meet cash needs. However, there are certainly households that appear to earn cash to purchase these assets from their on-farm activities, through either the sale of maize, beans, and potatoes, livestock sales, or the sale of tree products. These assets indicate a household's success, but unlike cows and trees, they do not reproduce themselves and create more resources. Disease and climate-related challenges pose risks to livestock and trees so they are by no means an easy and certain investment.

Wealth and Poverty

In Mama Issara, social differentiation, while present, is not extreme. In focus groups, respondents used the criteria in Table 6.9 below to define wealth categories and measure their community's status.

Aligning the household survey data on farm size and cattle ownership with the wealth categories from the criteria in the focus groups proved difficult. For example, of the nineteen households who had ten or more cows, only nine of them had 3 acres of land or more. The household with the most cattle (eighteen) had 4.75 acres of land. As is evident in Table 6.10 below, by using these two criteria, the majority of households would be classified as poor.

The meaning of wealth has changed over time as various resources have become available. Sheet metal roofs were expensive and out of reach for most households in the 1990s. Small businesses were few and secondary schools came into Mama Issara in the mid-'90s, one in each ward at that time. Now, there are

Table 6.9 Local definitions of wealth in Mama Issara

Wealth category	Land	Cropping patterns	Education	Livestock	Other
Wealthy (10 per cent)	3–4 acres of farm land	Planted both cash and food crops; many trees on farm	Education level of household head (HH) is high; has one or more educated (i.e. secondary school) children and/or employed children	At least ten head of cattle plus pigs and or chicken	Can provide for needs of family; educate children; pay for necessities; have small businesses; and a good house with iron-sheet roofing and bricks
Average (60 per cent)	2 acres	Some trees	Education level of HH head is normal; at least one child in school or employed	At least 5–6 cattle plus pigs	Good house with iron-sheet roofing sometimes with trees or bricks
Poor (30 per cent)	1 or less than 1 acre		Education level of HH head is low	One or no cow at all and nothing else	Cannot provide for family; thatch roof on house

Data from focus groups held separately with men, women, and youth in Mama Issara wards in 2017.

four operating secondary schools and one in the final stage of construction in the homeland so significantly more students are going beyond primary level. Most of the households that fall in the wealthy category have sources of off-farm income, either through salaries from employment as civil servants, teachers, health officers, or through off-farm businesses. The very poor are often widows, those with physical disabilities or female-headed households.

The Wider Context

The availability of transport and inputs makes agricultural activities more profitable and attractive to many today. In the '90s, bicycles and foot travel were the main means to reach Mbulu town. Transporting maize in and out of Mama Issara was challenging and relied almost entirely on donkeys. There was no public transportation until after 2002.

In the last five to six years, the availability of transportation has increased dramatically. Today, Landcruisers and mini-buses ply the route daily from Mama Issara and back and people use public transportation to carry out their business in Mbulu and to transport their produce. Women, who regularly sell charcoal, particularly appreciate this change: 'We used to carry it on our backs all the way

Table 6.10 Wealth information from household survey for 2017

Farm size	No of HHs	% of HHs	Cattle	No. of HHs	% of HHs
3 acres or more	39	22	ten head or more	19	11
2 acres	57	32	five to nine head	40	22
Under 2 acres	84	46	Under five	121	67

N=180.

to Mbulu. Now we can put it in a vehicle and get to Mbulu, sell the charcoal, run our errands and return quickly.'

Transportation and improved roads have also made stocking shops and small businesses easier. There are a number of shops in Mama Issara and in Mbulu town that sell hybrid seeds and other agricultural inputs. In addition to small shops, there are many more small restaurants selling coffee, beer, and tea than there were in the '90s. These developments suggest there is more cash in circulation today. These developments are not exclusive to Mbulu District but instead reflect patterns throughout Tanzania. As Green (2015) observes for Ulanga District in southern Tanzania, improvements in infrastructure and increased demand for agricultural products from urban areas have spurred economic transformations. She describes the rise of a middle class, based primarily in urban centres, who increase demand for food crops and milk, pork, and chickens resulting in 'innovation in the local agricultural economy' (Green 2015: 304). In addition to infrastructural and market changes, Tanzania's decentralization policy has resulted in an expansion of government offices and staff to accommodate new administrative units (villages, wards). As a result, as Green (2015) notes, there is an increase in government officers in rural areas. There are more people now with salaries living and working in these rural areas which has also influenced improvements in agriculture and led to an increase in local businesses.

Electricity has come to Mama Issara and continues to expand, resulting in more lights in people's homes and less reliance on kerosene. It has also allowed some small businesses to start up, providing access to television in particular. Watching football matches and foreign soap operas are popular at the *vijiwe.* Other small businesses like maize grinding mills and welding have also sprung up in Mama Issara.

Discussion

Contrary to reports of stagnation in the agricultural sector for the continent as a whole (Diao et al. 2006), in assessing longitudinal change in Mama Issara, it is evident, comparing household farm production from 1995 to that of 2017, that agricultural productivity has increased, due to the use of hybrid seeds, pesticides, more standardized planting practices and the expansion of farming into what was formally grazing land sides. Additionally, in the northern part of the homeland, farmers, ignoring the restrictions on cultivating up the mountain, have expanded fields to the top of the slopes. While expansion of agriculture into areas previously uncultivated such as mountains may increase production, it is less clear whether, over the longer term, it is sustainable as natural resources are being degraded in the process. In focus groups, respondents expressed concern about these patterns, claiming, 'People do not listen to elders today.' Many said this generation of elders has less knowledge concerning land-use restrictions of the past and that they have little authority over the youth. One main concern was that water sources, primarily springs that used to run all year round, have dried up. Respondents further linked the drying up of water sources to land use changes including planting of water thirsty trees such as eucalyptus in water catchments. Many farmers are cultivating close to water sources in an effort to obtain every inch of available soil. The expansion onto the steep slopes in the north has not been accompanied by the 'traditional' soil and water management practices that were in place in the colonial era, in part because these fields are not considered secure as they were not granted to farmers by local government or through inheritance.

While respondents stated that the shift to hybrid seeds has led to a considerable improvement in their livelihoods, this change is not without its risks. In 2018, the government, in an effort to ensure national food security, banned the sale of maize outside of the country and farmers in Mama Issara were already feeling the effects. Prices for their maize dropped significantly making it difficult to cover the costs of labour and inputs. One farmer remarked, 'With the prices of maize being so low on the market because the border to Kenya is closed, I will not be able to cover all the cost of labour and inputs from selling my maize'. Maize traders also were suffering. With the price of maize so low on the market and the inability to export, particularly to Kenya, traders struggled to cover their costs and faced significant risks of pest damage while storing maize to wait for prices to rise.

In addition to maize seed hybrids, we also see a shift away from some 'traditional' crops like millet and sorghum. In part, this reflects the greater market demand for maize but also the difficulty in finding enough labour for crops like millet, that require constant vigilance to scare birds away.[2] The demand for Irish potato, due in part to changing tastes and the proliferation of small restaurants in Mbulu, has increased. Chips, once a special treat, have become far more common in local restaurants. Finally, beans have also become an important cash crop and prices on the market have been consistently attractive to farmers. Interviews and

[2] Labour that used to be provided by children who are now at school.

focus group participants frequently mentioned the rise in production and sale of horticultural crops like tomatoes, leafy greens, and onions (this is not captured in the surveys). With improved transport, these crops have become far easier to sell in Mbulu, specifically for women. As one Mbulu market vendor said, 'all our produce comes from Mama Issara'.

Trees are a critical component of rural livelihoods in Mama Issara. Farmers earn cash from charcoal, timber, and fruit. Trees on farms are often overlooked in research and assessments of farm productivity. National policies concerning trees tend to focus on forest reserves and forestry and agricultural departments often do not collaborate. Tree products can be crucial to rural livelihoods as they serve as important sources of cash in times of need (Place and Garrity 2015). Miller et al. (2018), in their review of national household survey data, found that 54 per cent of rural smallholders have trees on farms in Tanzania, with 18 per cent having timber species and 25 per cent with fruit trees. In Mama Issara, the demand for timber, first documented by Snyder (1996) in the mid-'90s, has continued and expanded. Timber buyers in Mbulu explained that demand from Mbulu town but also Babati, the regional capital, and even Arusha is stimulating the market. They also said 'In Mbulu, most of the timber we buy comes from Mama Issara'. Snyder (1996) observed that tree planting represented a less intensive land-use practice as, after the initial investment, labour and capital needs decrease substantially. More recently, farmers are taking whole hillsides, which they see as too degraded for successful crop production, and turning them into woodlots.

In the '90s, farmers relied more on exchanges, livestock sales, and cash purchase to meet their food needs. Today, the adoption of hybrid seeds and other inputs and practices, such as greater investments in hired labour, marks a process of intensification on agricultural fields that has resulted in both greater food security and in greater participation in the market. When farmers convert degraded land to tree production, they must either expand their crop production into areas previously used for grazing, or they must intensify production on other remaining plots in usually highly productive, valley-bottom land. Valleys, over the past several decades, have increasingly been converted to agricultural plots, where they used to be reserved for thatch grass and for grazing.

Pig production has held steady since the '90s and the number of households keeping pigs has increased. The market for pork ties farmers in Mama Issara not only to consumption in Mbulu but as far away as Moshi town in the north and Dar es Salaam in the south. Pig production has both a fairly high and rapid rate of return, if compared to other livestock. Farmers rely on pigs, timber, staple crops, horticultural crops, and fruit sales for cash to purchase any food deficits.

Off-farm income generating activities, either through salaried work as a schoolteacher or health worker, or through day labour, or owning and running small businesses are also quite common in Mama Issara and underline the importance of off-farm work. However, while de-agrarianization may be occurring in other parts of Tanzania and the continent (Bryceson 2002), the evidence from Mama Issara suggests a continued reliance on agriculture for local livelihoods and an increased investment in intensification on specific farm plots. This pattern is similar to that found in Andersson Djurfeld et al. (2018) work on re-agrarianization. As in many rural systems, diversification of livelihoods appears to be essential to make a living and weather the risks of any economic activity (Ollenburger et al. 2019).

In the mid-'90s, maintaining social networks, through food exchanges and through livestock loans were important for sustaining livelihoods and getting access to resources. Today, with market improvements, farmers rely more on cash, for purchasing food, hiring labour, and obtaining livestock. Indeed, as one man said, 'You can't get someone to help you carry a bucket of water 100 meters if you don't pay them today'. However, social networks are still maintained through food exchanges and livestock loans, though they almost always involve cash. Neighbourhood groups have become an important feature of the local landscape today and manage a variety of social needs, such as providing help for medical care (transport of sick person, hospital costs), weddings and other events through pooling of cash contributions. In the '90s, young men from a neighbourhood carried sick people to Mbulu town. Today, neighbours simply hire a vehicle for transport. These neighbourhood groups address conflicts, mediate disputes, and sometimes serve as revolving loan groups.

Returning to the debate on smallholder versus large-scale farms, the long history of farming in Mama Issara shows where and how small farms can be successful through diversification and responding to markets. It also points to the potential limitations of small farms, particularly the constraints presented by their overall size and resource base. Overall, farmers state that their livelihoods have improved in Mama Issara, largely through farming. However, this improvement has been dependent on wider economic changes in the economy. As Davis et al.' (2017) study of agriculture across twenty-two countries in sub-Saharan Africa shows, farming is still the sector where most households make a living. In Mbulu District, farming is the main livelihood of most of the population. Agricultural productivity is in part stimulated by the growth of off-farm economic activities, most of which, as Davis et al. (2017) have also found, are linked to agriculture and natural resources. Small restaurants rely on local produce, youth become agricultural traders or woodcutters to make a living when the lack of farmland pushes them to seek other opportunities, timber traders stimulate land-users to plant more timber, which also results in the growth of small-scale tree nurseries. Finally, road improvements, the expansion of the transportation sector and the arrival of electrification have also supported greater investment in agriculture.

Because of limited farm size and topography, agricultural production in Mama Issara may not result in an economic transformation that ensures greater long-term security or a significant increase in income and assets from what is seen today. However, it is clear that over the last twenty-eight years significant improvements in people's lives have occurred. More children are going to and completing school, there are more opportunities in the informal sector for trade and small businesses, the timber trade continues to expand and demand remains high. These positive trends are also evident elsewhere in Tanzania (Brockington et al. 2018, Östberg et al. 2018) and in some other countries in the continent such as Ghana (Houssou et al. 2018). Overall, however, throughout Tanzania, off-farm income-earning activities still remain few and lack of capital a considerable constraint, both for starting businesses and for further on-farm investment. In focus groups and interviews, respondents often mentioned the lack of access to capital as a major constraint to their livelihoods.

While the changes in livelihoods in Mama Issara indicate signs of some aspects of poverty reduction, we would qualify what is perceived to be poverty in the local imagination. Residents of Mama Issara may not recognize a decline in poverty because they did not think themselves to be poor originally. Snyder was conducting research in Mama Issara in the 1990s, when the results of a World Bank report on global poverty (and Tanzania's low ranking globally) were announced on Tanzanian national radio. A group of young men with whom she was talking, when hearing of Tanzania's poor ranking, looked puzzled and said 'We can't be that poor. We feed ourselves, send our children to school and have decent houses. Why are we thought to be poor?' At that time, many of the assets available today were not available then and the availability of transport or electricity was low or non-existent. A thatched roof house was considered perfectly decent housing and sending your children to primary school was viewed as sufficient.

With wider shifts in development and exposure to a globally interconnected world, the goals and aspirations of Mama Issara residents have changed. It is a common perception that young people today appear to have little desire to pursue farming. Their parents claim that now that they have had an education, their children no longer want to farm but only want office jobs. Indeed, that, they suggest, is what drives them to waste time at the local vijiwe. However, in focus groups with youth, they asserted that they do want to farm but that their parents do not give them land to cultivate and the work they do on the land contributes to the household but does not help them build up independent resources, ones they could use to marry and start life on their own. Thus, they pursue farm labour jobs, odd jobs for shopkeepers, transport, and a variety of other small jobs.

Iraqw have a long history of migrating out to search for other employment opportunities or for land on which to farm and raise livestock. This pattern continues today but it is unclear, given population growth in Tanzania more broadly, if these strategies will be sustainable in the future. Today, young people are moving to areas far more distant than they did in the '90s and the many decades before that when migration focused on contiguous zones. In Mama Issara, given the size of household land holdings that will no doubt continue to decrease if out-migration declines, it is unlikely that intensification alone can meet consumptions demands. Iraqw farmers in the homeland are quick to respond to market opportunities, either in new cash crops, the revival of old cash crops (pyrethrum, tobacco, coffee), or demand for pork or for tree products. These diversified land-use strategies have served farmers well and have enabled them to invest in assets and their children's educations. As prices on the market for food crops such as maize and beans rise and fall, this diversification strategy is important for weathering these sometimes steep ups and downs of the market that are affected by national and regional trade policies.

Conclusion

As this and other studies of local farming systems demonstrate in this volume and elsewhere (Whitfield 2017, Brockington et al. 2018, Houssou et al. 2018, Östberg et al. 2018), it is important to ground truth national and international narratives that underscore the stagnation of rural smallholder farming systems and rural poverty. Local-level studies often provide a very different picture which is clear in Whitfield's (2017) review of Netting's (1993) seminal work on smallholder farmers in Nigeria and its relevance for studies of rural farming in sub-Saharan Africa today. Understanding the complexity and diversity of small-scale agricultural systems is of continued relevance. He concludes that:

> The values of smallholdings as laid out by Netting—that they are adaptive, flexible and innovative—similarly encourage a rethink of dominant policy and research and innovation models that have sought to intervene, in a topdown way, within smallholder systems. (2017: 262)

This assertion is particularly important today as national policies and international agencies increasingly turn away from smallholder agriculture in favour of large-scale investment. Additionally, agricultural research centres such as the Consultative Group on International Agricultural Development (CGIAR) and the Alliance for a Green Revolution in Africa (AGRA) focus on a technocratic 'impact-at-scale philosophy' (Whitfield 2017: 260) that may not fit well with the diversity of small-scale farming systems across the continent (Ollenburger et al. 2019).

While the Comprehensive Africa Agriculture Development Programme (CAADP) of the African Union, which calls for a commitment of 10 per cent of national annual budgets to agriculture, is an important step in increasing investment, its implementation has been inconsistent across the continent. Tanzania has signed up to the CAADP agreement but funds allocated to the Ministry of Agriculture are often only sufficient for paying salaries and administrative costs.

At the level of the districts, agricultural staff have few funds available for operational costs. Furthermore, district budgets tend to prioritize education, health, and infrastructure over agriculture.[3]

Regardless of these challenges, the myth that Christiaensen (2017) exposes, that smallholder farmers are slow to respond to 'modern' farming methods, is obviously a myth in Mama Issara. This study has shown that farmers there and undoubtedly throughout the country have done an impressive job at improving their farms, raising agricultural productivity and their households' livelihoods with little support from the government especially after implementation of Structural Adjustment Programmes. Before shifting investment to focus on large-scale farming, more direct investment in smallholder agriculture and the markets that support it, might have a bigger impact on more people.

References

Andersson Djurfeldt, A., F. M. Dzanku, and A. C. Isinika (2018). Agriculture, Diversification and Gender in Rural Africa: Longitudinal Perspectives from Six Countries. Oxford, Oxford University Press.

Barrett, C. B., L. Christiaensen, M. Sheahan, and A. Shimeles (2017). 'On the Structural Transformation of Rural Africa.' *Journal of African Economies* 26, AERC Supplement 1: i11–35.

Binswanger-Mkhize, H. P. and S. Savastano (2017). 'Agricultural Intensification: The Status in Six African Countries.' *Food Policy* 67: 26–40.

Binswanger-Mkhize, H. P., A. F. McCalla, and P. Patel (2010). 'Structural Transformation and African Agriculture.' *Global Journal of Emerging Market Economies* 2(2): 113–52.

Börjeson, L. (2007). 'Boserup Backwards? Agricultural Intensification as "Its Own Driving Force" in the Mbulu Highlands, Tanzania.' *Geografiska Annaler: Series B, Human Geography* 89(3): 249–67.

Brockington, D., O. Howland, V.-M. Loiske, M. Mnzava, and C. Noe (2018). 'Economic Growth, Rural Assets and Prosperity: Exploring the Implications of a 20-Year Record of Asset Growth in Tanzania.' *The Journal of Modern African Studies* 56(2): 217–43.

Brockington, D., O. Howland, V.-M. Loiske, M. Mnzava, and C. Noe (2019). 'Assets and Poverty Dynamics: The Methodological Challenges of Constructing Longitudinal Surveys in Tanzania.' *Tanzanian Development: A Comparative Perspective* D. Potts, Boydell and Brewer, Witney: 95-115.

[3] Interviews with district staff in multiple districts in Tanzania.

Bryceson, D. F. (2002). 'The Scramble in Africa: Reorienting Rural Livelihoods.' *World Development* 30(5): 725–39.

Christiaensen, L. (2017). 'Agriculture in Africa—Telling Myths from Facts: A Synthesis.' *Food Policy* 67: 1–11.

Christiaensen, L., L. Demery, and J. Kuhl (2011). 'The (Evolving) Role of Agriculture in Poverty Reduction—An Empirical Perspective.' *Journal of Development Economics* 96(2): 239–54.

Collier, P. and S. Dercon (2014). 'African Agriculture in 50 years: Smallholders in a Rapidly Changing World?' *World Development* 63: 92–101.

Cooksey, B. (2011). 'Marketing Reform? The Rise and Fall of Agricultural Liberalisation in Tanzania.' *Development Policy Review* 29: 57–81.

Coulson, A. (2015). 'Small-Scale and Large-Scale Agriculture: Tanzanian Experiences.' *Looking Back, Looking Ahead—Land, Agriculture and Society in East Africa, A Festschrift for Kjell Havnevik*. M. Ståhl. Uppsala, The Nordic Afrika Institute: 44–73.

Davidson, J. (2012). 'Basket Cases and Breadbaskets: Sacred Rice and Agricultural Development in Postcolonial Africa.' *Culture, Agriculture, Food and Environment* 34(1): 15–32.

Davis, B., S. Di Giuseppe, and A. Zezza (2017). 'Are African Households (Not) Leaving Agriculture? Patterns of Households' Income Sources in Rural Sub-Saharan Africa.' *Food Policy* 67: 153–74.

Diao, X., P. Hazell, P. D. Resnick, and J. Thurlow (2006). 'The Role of Agriculture in Development: Implications for Sub-Saharan Africa.' *International Food Policy Research Institute (IFPRI) Discussion Paper*. Washington DC, IFPRI.

Garnett, T. and H. C. J. Godfray (2012). *Sustainable Intensification in Agriculture: Navigating a Course through Competing Food System Priorities*. Food Climate Research Network and the Oxford Martin Programme on the Future of Food. Oxford, Oxford University Press.

Graeub, B. E., M. J. Chappell, H. Wittman, S. Ledermann, R. B. Kerr, and B. Gemmill-Herren (2016). 'The State of Family Farms in the World.' *World Development* 87: 1–15.

Green, M. (2015). 'Making Africa Middle Class: From Poverty Reduction to the Production of Inequality in Tanzania.' *Economic Anthropology* 2(2): 295–309.

Green, M. and D. Hulme (2005). 'From Correlates and Characteristics to Causes: Thinking about Poverty from a Chronic Poverty Perspective.' *World Development* 33(6): 867–79.

Houssou, N., M. Johnson, S. Kolavalli, and C. Asante-Addo (2018). 'Changes in Ghanaian Farming Systems: Stagnation or a Quiet Transformation?' *Agriculture and Human Values* 35(1): 41–66.

Harris, D. and A. Orr (2014). 'Is Rainfed Agriculture Really a Pathway from Poverty?' *Agricultural Systems* 123: 84–96.

Jayne, T. S., J. Chamberlin, and R. Benfca (2018). 'Africa's Unfolding Economic Transformation.' *The Journal of Development Studies* 54(5): 777–87.

Jayne, T. S., D. Mather, and E. Mghenyi (2010). 'Principal challenges Confronting Smallholder Agriculture in Sub-Saharan Africa.' *World Development* 38(10): 1384–98.

Lowder, S. K., J. Skoet, and T. Raney (2016). 'The Number, Size, and Distribution of Farms, Smallholder Farms, and Family Farms Worldwide.' *World Development* 87: 16–29.

Mashindano, O., K. Kayunze, L. Da Corta, and F. Maro (2011). 'Growth without Poverty Reduction in Tanzania—Reasons for the Mismatch.' *Translating Growth into Poverty Reduction: Beyond the Numbers*. F. Kessy, O. Mashindano, A. Shepherd, and L. Scott. Dar es Salaam, Mkuki na Nyota: 121–42.

Miller, D., J. C. Muñoz-Mora, and L. Christiaensen (2018). 'Do Trees on Farms Matter in African Agriculture?' *Agriculture in Africa: Telling Myths from Facts: Directions in Development*. L. Christiaensen and Lionel Demery. Washington DC, The World Bank: 115–22. DOI:10.1596/978-1-4648-1134-0.

Msuya, E. E., A. C. Isinika, and F. M. Dzanku (2018). 'Agricultural Intensification Response to Agricultural Input Subsidies in Tanzania: A Spatial-Temporal and Gender Perspective, 2002–15.' *Agriculture, Diversification, and Gender in Rural Africa: Longitudinal Perspectives from Six Countries*. A. A. Djurfeldt, F. M. Dzanku, and A. C. Isinika. Oxford, Oxford University Press.

Netting, R. M. 1993. *Smallholders, Householders: Farm Families and the Ecology of Intensive, Sustainable Agriculture*. Stanford, Stanford University Press.

Ollenburger, M., T. Crane, K. Descheemaeker, and K. E. Giller (2019). 'Are Farmers Searching for an African Green Revolution? Exploring the Solution Space for Agricultural Intensification in Southern Mali.' *Experimental Agriculture* 55(2): 288–310.

Östberg, W., O. Howland, J. Mduma, and D. Brockington (2018). 'Tracing improving Livelihoods in Rural Africa Using Local Measures of Wealth: A Case Study from Central Tanzania, 1991–2016.' *Land* 7(44): 1–26.

Place, F. and D. Garrity (2015). *Tree-Based Systems in Africa's Drylands*. Washington DC, The World Bank.

Reardon, T. (2015). 'The Hidden Middle: The Quiet Revolution in the Midstream of Agrifood Value Chains in Developing Countries.' *Oxford Review of Economic Policy* 31(1): 45–63.

Royal Society (2009). *Reaping the Benefits: Science and the Sustainable Intensification of Global Agriculture*. London, The Royal Society.

Scoones, I. and J. Thompson (2011). 'The Politics of Seed in Africa's Green Revolution: Alternative Narratives and Competing Pathways.' *IDS Bulletin* 42(4): 1–23.

Snyder, K. A. (1993). *'Like Water and Honey': Moral Ideology and the Construction of Community among the Iraqw of Northern Tanzania*. PhD dissertation, Department of Anthropology. New Haven, Yale University.

Snyder, K. A. (1996). 'Agrarian Change and Land-Use Strategies among Iraqw Farmers in Northern Tanzania.' *Human Ecology* 24(3): 315–40.

Snyder, K. A. (2002). 'Modern Cows and Exotic Trees: Identity, Personhood and Exchange among the Iraqw of Tanzania.' *Ethnology* 41(2): 155–73.

Snyder, K. A. (2005). *The Iraqw of Tanzania: Negotiating Rural Development*. Boulder, Westview Press.

Whitfield, S. (2017). '"More Vital to Our Future Than We Realize?" Learning from Netting's Thesis on Smallholder Farming, 25 Years On.' *Outlook on Agriculture* 46(4): 258–64.

Wiggins, S., J. Kirsten, and L. Llambí (2010). 'The Future of Small Farms.' *World Development* 38(10): 1341–8.

7

Women's Tears or Coffee Blight?

Gender Dynamics and Livelihood Strategies in Contexts of Agricultural Transformation in Tanzania

Christine Noe, Olivia Howland, and Dan Brockington

Epilogue pages 384–387

We are doing drive through villages in Arumeru, and stop to talk to a group of elders and local leaders. I get out of the car and three little girls, all aged about three, come to say hello to me. They have been studying at their teacher's house, 'learning to read!' they tell me:

(one of the girls, staring at the car) 'Do you drive that?!'

OH: Yes! Of course. When you're older, you can also drive a car if you want.

'No! Me, I'm going to be a pikipiki driver, with a bodaboda business.'

OH: Wow! (turning to one of the other little girls) What about you? Will you drive a car, or a piki?

'No. I will have my own bajaji and my own business, driving to Tengeru market to sell vegetables and bananas. I've already helped my uncle to drive his bajaji so I know what I'm doing!'

pikipiki—motorbike; bodaboda—motorbike taxi; bajaji—a three-wheeled motorbike taxi used for carrying goods

Extract from Olivia Howland's field notes, 18 October 2017

Introduction

What happens to rural societies when the economic basis of their existence is suddenly transformed for the worse? When crops on which they had relied for income and livelihoods suddenly become worthless, or smitten by diseases whose treatment is just too expensive to bear? And, most particularly, how are the impacts of these misfortunes mediated by gender relations within the societies they afflict, and how do they themselves alter gender relations?

Christine Noe, Olivia Howland, and Dan Brockington, *Women's Tears or Coffee Blight? Gender Dynamics and Livelihood Strategies in Contexts of Agricultural Transformation in Tanzania* In: *Prosperity in Rural Africa? Insights into Wealth, Assets, and Poverty from Longitudinal Studies in Tanzania*. Edited by: Dan Brockington and Christine Noe, Oxford University Press.
 DOI: 10.1093/oso/9780198865872.003.0007

One of the most well-known instances of declining fortunes of rural producers is the collapse of farm gate coffee prices which reflects a mixture of over-supply and marketing structures. It has been particularly exasperating for development activists and campaigners who have seen coffee farmers' incomes collapse and this juxtaposed to the rise of consumer prices in rich countries. All of this creates the uncomfortable contradiction of rich companies in the value chain profiting from northern drinking habits while southern farmers go hungry. Ponte neatly captured the contradictions observing that:

> the global coffee chain has gone through a 'latte revolution', where consumers can choose from (and pay dearly for) hundreds of combinations of coffee variety, origin, brewing and grinding methods, flavoring, packaging, social 'content', and ambience. At the same time, international prices for the raw product... are the lowest in decades. Coffee industries in developing countries are in disarray. Coffee farmers are losing a source of livelihood. (Ponte 2002b: 1099)

We do not dispute the enormous challenges, and injustice, that this transformation of the coffee industry has entailed. But we need properly to understand the complexity of the dynamics resulting. In particular before we can assume that the effects of these changes are necessarily negative for all rural families, and all members of them, we have to understand better how such dynamics play out in different contexts. Specifically we contend that changes in the external economic, political, and social environments are fought over and contested within households. Gender relations will determine what a coffee revolution looks like on the ground. If we are to understand well the impacts of the changing coffee economy then we have to understand how they intersect with intra-household dynamics. Exploring these changes allows us to make contributions to debates about the different dimensions of poverty and prosperity, and the importance of considering how these are contested within families (Orr et al. 2014, Ossome 2014, Brockington et al. 2021).

In this chapter we address this need for a better understanding of the gendered impacts of decline. We use a unique longitudinal data set that allowed us to revisit families surveyed in 1996 after a twenty-year interval. We show that for women in Meru in north-eastern Tanzania, the demise of coffee is not mourned as much as one might expect. This is partly because the gendered division of labour that produced the coffee was oppressive for women. It is also because new livelihood opportunities are emerging from the nearby expanding city of Arusha, which are more liberating in terms of opportunities for women. Accordingly many women in Meru welcome the demise of coffee, and the pests and diseases which have contributed to it.

Yet we show also that moves away from coffee to other livelihood strategies are still strongly gendered. Men contest the loss of power they experience with the declining coffee economy as much as women celebrate it. Women still feel oppressed despite these changes, and this paper will examine these changes in the context of post-coffee Meru society. The types of crops and businesses controlled by men and women have changed, but this has resulted in new struggles for women, and not always, as they hoped, greater financial or social freedoms. Welcome progress in some areas has come with regression in others.

We proceed as follows. First, we discuss some of the literature on gendered divisions of labour and contests over social and economic change particularly as it pertains to East Africa. We then focus on the changes that have afflicted Meru showing how coffee once sustained growing prosperity for much of the twentieth century but has since declined. We argue that studies which explicitly explore the gendered impact of these changes are few. Next, we describe our methods in which we are fortunate to draw on two different intimate accounts of Meru rural society—the late Rolf Larsson's detailed PhD thesis and its data written in the mid-1990s (2001), and the formative years of Christine Noe, the corresponding author on this paper. To develop our argument we next explore gender ideologies in Meru and consider how they are changed by the decline of the coffee sector and rise of new economic opportunities. Finally we conclude by considering the implications of these findings for work on measuring progress using economic indicators.

Women, Agriculture, and Coffee

Women's rights and freedoms matter for rural livelihoods. Over 60 per cent of women are employed in agriculture (Raney et al. 2011). Women are at the forefront of rural livelihoods in African contexts, caring for livestock and tending crops (Guèye 2000, Wangui 2008, Kristjanson et al. 2017). Estimates of women's share of agricultural labour on the continent vary between 24 per cent (Niger) and 56 per cent (Uganda), with a general average of close to 50 per cent (Raney et al. 2011, Palacios-Lopez et al. 2017). Yet women's work in agriculture continues to be neglected. Women are recognized to have less access to farming inputs, technologies, and, importantly, decision-making power (Kristjanson et al. 2017). This is in addition to the fact that structural shifts in global and local economies continue to alter rural women's strategies for survival. Carolyn Sachs argues in a recent study that:

> rural women continue to work harder, suffer greater material deprivation (sometimes oppressed and exploited) and have less access to income-earning opportunities but they have continued to create and shape rural lives.
>
> (Sachs 2018: 3)

This global issue is important in Tanzania, where most people, and most women, are employed in agriculture. Here 70 per cent of economically active women work in agriculture (Mbilinyi 2016). Agriculture remains the mainstay of most Tanzanians. Just under 70 per cent of the population lives in rural areas, and most are smallholders. Consumption poverty (captured by poverty lines) is disproportionately concentrated there just over 80 per cent of the poor live in rural areas (URT 2019). This gives the impression that rural areas are concentrations of stasis and inactivity and government policies (SAGCOT, Kilimo Kwanza) seek to transform apparently rural communities dominated by 'subsistence' agriculture (World Bank 2015). But this impression is misleading. Poverty-line data exclude peasant investment in assets and so conceal new forms of rural prosperity (Brockington 2021, Brockington et al. 2021). New cash crops in the form of sesame, sunflowers, and irrigated crops are providing new sources of income (Corbera et al. 2017, Woodhouse et al. 2017, Östberg et al. 2018). Rural areas in Tanzania are sites of dynamism and change.

Yet this economic change is not necessarily socially progressive for women. Women's status is still marginal and precarious particularly in more patriarchal contexts (Madaha 2014). In some instances women in Tanzania, who have in recent years gained rights to land and access to assets due to local change in cultures and norms, report an improvement in their general position in society as well as empowerment and political strength (Goldman et al. 2016). But this not driven by national level pushes or policy initiatives. Rather, as Ossome shows, social practices and the customary laws which accompany them are arenas of contestation (Ossome 2014). Tanzanian societies can appear to resist social change as men and women are continually contesting opportunities and change. Rural women's rights and needs in some societies are not on the sort of upward trajectory which measures such as the Sustainable Development Goals (SDGs) like to envision. Instead the situation may be better characterized by flux rather than progressive change.

For this reason it is particularly important to understand how women fare when sweeping changes brought about through shifts in value chains (or land grabbing) occur. Ossome has argued that:

> Understanding the customary systems that mediate women's relationship with the state, capital, and community is critical for shaping the nature of interventions by feminist activists. (2014: 172)

She recognizes that much of this custom derives from patriarchal societies' encounters with patriarchal capitalism and colonialism, and that its pedigree is poor in that respect. But she also insists that this 'should not blind us to the democratic and transformative possibilities inherent in the contestations taking place in these arenas' (ibid.).

The dynamics between cash crops and food crops provide useful insights with which to understand gender dynamics in rural African societies, and the contestation and formation of custom and tradition (Ranger 1993). There is evidence that women's share of agricultural labour increases with female education and land ownership—enhancing the possibilities of contestation (Palacios-Lopez et al. 2017). In particular, the cash crop–food crop dynamic can cross often traditionally female realms of food provisioning, and realms that men seek to control by providing cash incomes. Orr and colleagues (2014), studied the case of Zambia where groundnuts are largely regarded as a women's crop and cotton as a men's crop. They suggest that women rights to control the income from certain crops does not matter as much as women's share of the workload. As such, men may neglect women's crops as long as theirs' are fetching good prices, but take on decisions for marketing and spending of the sales in different ways (including neglecting some household cash needs). Women have greater control over food crops but only as long as these crops do not gain greater commercial value than other crops that a household produces. Or to put this differently, what counts as a food or cash crop, or women's or men's crop, can vary considerably contingent on whether it is sold or consumed. The shift of produce from 'subsistence' to 'commercial' will be the very substance of gender disputes in many rural households.

Brockington observed similar processes in rather different circumstances in pastoral societies in northern Tanzania (Brockington 2001). Here men in families who had suffered eviction from a game reserve and lost livestock sought to use women's income (from sales of milk or medicines) to provide for needs they had once paid for. Women resisted these moves.

In some contexts control over crops is not just about financial issues but is closely intertwined with the construction of gender identities that hinge on determining who undertakes what labour, how that labour is performed and at whose behest (Mbataru 2007, Razavi 2016). When women challenge the ownership of income from high-value crops such as coffee, they challenge also male identity, which, in most patriarchal societies, is strongly linked to household property ownership and control over family affairs (Orr et al. 2014).

Coffee makes a particularly interesting lens through which to explore the gender dynamics of agriculture and agriculture change. The sector is fascinating and important because farmers' incomes have declined, but at the same time demand has continued to grow. Yet it is remarkable that, amid all the attention paid to coffee economies, a remarkably small proportion of the literature or research explores the gendered dynamics of coffee production and the gendered consequences of its decline.

Coffee was once the mainstay of Meru agriculture. It grew from the early decades of the twentieth century supporting a vibrant economy and much progressive change (Spear 1997). Coffee sustained strong co-operative societies which focused on marketing of local agricultural crops while also supporting the provision of subsidized farm inputs. More importantly, cooperative societies organized farmer's coffee incomes to facilitate long-term investments in educational infrastructure such as secondary schools. Meru Social Development and Education Trust was established in 1980s and over three secondary schools were built through contributions made from coffee farmers. School fees were subsidized for Meru children.

The importance of coffee is clearly visible in Rolf Larsson's extensive survey of over 750 households that was conducted in the mid-'90s. Larson showed that the vast majority of families depended on selling bananas and coffee and milk (Table 7.1). Every single household he spoke to had cattle and many also sold milk; all had smallstock which were kept in the lowlands (Table 7.2). There was considerable inequality within Meru society, as the amounts of land actually farmed could vary considerably (Table 7.3). But the main point to note is that despite the inequalities of amount of land worked and goods sold, there was remarkable uniformity in the nature of the local economy—coffee was pre-eminent.

Since the 1990s there has been a dramatic and considerable decline in production and coffee trade in Tanzania as it faced a series of compounding challenges. Coffee co-operatives which had provided important support for quality coffee production and marketing, and helped to subsidize inputs, began to fail (Hillbom 2012). This reflected price fluctuations. Maghimbi (2010) reports that low coffee prices in the global market caused cooperatives in mainland Tanzania to accumulate huge bank debts. With the lack of support from co-operatives, poor quality control common to individual or small-scale producers made much

Table 7.1 The rural coffee economy of 1996

Farm produce	Households producing on mountain (%)	Households selling (%)	Main farm income source (household/ in % of column total)
Bananas	92.1	83.5	11.3
Coffee	84.4	83.3	40.8
Milk	77.8	64.6	35.7
Maize	54.7	12.1	2.2
Fodder grass	56.5	1.4	0
Beans	39.3	5.6	0.1
Sweet potatoes	27.8	15.7	0.5
Vegetables	30.4	24.5	5.8
Cassava	9.2	0	0
Irish potatoes	4.1	0.7	0
Other farm produce	3.2	3	0.3
No farm produce	0.5	3.2	3.2
Total	—	—	100

Total no. of households 753; Source: Larsson, 2001: 71–94.

Table 7.2 Livestock ownership 1996

Livestock	1	2	3	4	5	6	7	9	10	11	14	18	Total
Cattle	3	141	179	150	48	17	2	1	2	1	1		545
Smallstock		15	13	745								2	775

Source: Larsson original data.

of the coffee produced suitable only for the local or regional market, where prices are lower and demand is less vigorous (Ponte 2002a: 25). Furthermore, the withdrawal of government subsidies had a significant impact on living standards for farmers (Ponte 2002a: 22) and their ability to continue to grow coffee commercially. This largely wiped out the benefits of higher prices in coffee in the mid-1990s (Larsson 2001: 220–1). By 2001 these cooperatives had lost their traditional role in protecting coffee farmers (Maghimbi 2010). Pests and diseases invaded coffee as farmers could not afford direct purchase for pesticides.

In Meru two afflictions were particularly important. Leaf rust (emelea in Kiswahili), or hemileia vastatrix, is a type of fungus which originated in East African coffee plantations, but spread globally. It causes greatly reduced yields and poor-quality beans. Unfortunately, the only way to either prevent or cure leaf rust is the application of expensive fungicides or the removal of plants. As well as leaf rust, borer beetles (known locally in Meru as sambembe) are prolific pests, and many Meru farmers are affected by either, or both, of these issues. After emelea, sambembe, and the dramatic drop in coffee prices, many Meru men were forced to give up cultivation of coffee as their main source of income (Dancer 2015: 30). The treatment for emelea and sambembe is more expensive than the price achieved at market[1] and coffee became financially unviable for many Meru families, especially when government subsidies ceased.

The impact of lower prices, combined with higher prices for inputs to deal with pests and diseases, have been complicated in Tanzania. Maghimbi notes that price declines have seen production fall in the Kilimanjaro area, but increase in the south of the country (Maghimbi 2007). This he attributed (in a paper which barely mentioned gender) to improving economic opportunities in other sectors. In Meru, as public intervention in coffee markets had decreased, and many of the coffee cooperative societies and boards had either closed or were significantly reduced in power and size by the mid-1990s, diseases caused a decrease in production and stock generally. Prices became more volatile due to deregulation. As Ponte reports, before deregulation, prices would fluctuate by 15 per cent a month. Post-deregulation brought price fluctuations of 43 per cent from 1998–2000

[1] From focus group discussions, this was the main reason why people removed coffee from their farms, or ceased to harvest their coffee.

Table 7.3 Differences in wealth and farming activity 1996

Wealth group	a. Mean of total land cultivated (acres)	b. Mean of land owned on the mountain (acres)	c. Mean no. of coffee trees	d. Mean no. of dairy cows	e. Education (mean years in school)	f. 'Capital goods' (mean rank 1–753)	g. 'Income security' (mean rank 1–753)	h. Mean scores on wealth index (1–100)
Poorest	0.8	0.5	59	0.3	3.3	308	213	27
Poor middle	1.4	0.9	156	0.9	4.1	330	298	38
Middle	2.9	1.5	287	1.3	4.3	343	343	50
Wealthy middle	5.5	2.2	532	1.8	5.7	378	485	62
Wealthiest	10	4.2	830	2.7	8.8	538	600	79
Wealthiest 3 per cent	13.7	6.1	1059	3.6	11.8	683	627	86
Total mean	3.5	1.6	327	1.3	4.8	361	367	49

a. Land on both mountain and lowlands. b. Resident and additional plots on the mountain. c. The 'Standard' no. of trees per acre is 400. d. Including heifers. e. Mean years in school, primary education is seven years. f. Capital goods and asserts. g. Ability to save or need to borrow money. h. Index running from 1–200 based in mean rank of indicators a–g. All between group differences are statistically significant at <0.001 level (ANOVA).

Reproduced from: Larsson 2001.

Table 7.4 Proportion of families growing different crops 1996 to 2017

Crop	1996: All villages	2017: Three villages
Bananas	92	84
Coffee	84	28
Maize	55	83
Fodder	57	1
Beans	39	54
Vegetables	30	28
Sweet potatoes	28	2
Cassava	9	0
Irish potatoes	4	24
Sunflower	0	6
Trees	0	4

Table 7.5 Livestock ownership 2017

Village	0	1	2	3	4	5	6	8	9	15	Total
Cattle	58	41	30	17	8	4	2	0	1	0	161
Smallstock	118	12	11	10	6	0	0	1	1	2	161

(Ponte 2002a: 20). Such variability in prices led to loss of confidence for farmers and unreliability of the market, leading to many farmers increasingly giving up coffee in favour of vegetables, with a stronger local market and more reliable prices.

The results of this decline are clearly visible in the farms that the Meru now cultivate when we conducted our surveys in 2017 (see methods below). Coffee is only grown by a minority of families. New crops like potatoes and trees have become more important (Table 7.4). In some villages only half of the families own cattle and smallstock are infrequent (Table 7.5). In terms of occupations of adults in our survey who were not in education, only 50 per cent said that they were only farmers, 42 per cent said that they were not farmers at all but engaged in various sorts of business (n=367).

The contours of this story are well known, but it is remarkable how rarely gender relations feature in its telling. Indeed we have been able to find only isolated papers which examine this explicitly.[2] Bacon's work on coffee co-operatives in Nicaragua has shown that these became vehicles for (contested and uneven) female empowerment in different contexts (Bacon 2010). This became visible in the leadership of some co-operatives.

[2] And others which discuss farmers or smallholders but barely use (and sometimes do not mention at all) the words 'gender', 'women', or 'men' (Coady et al. 2003, Christiaensen et al. 2006, Eakin et al. 2006, Pirotte et al. 2006).

Closer to our own study Patrick Mbataru offers a long-term perspective on the gendered consequences of the collapse of coffee among the Kikuyu people in Nyeri in Kenya (Mbataru 2007). He describes how, before the coffee economy women had traded grain and other goods for income which they controlled, and how men's coffee income had curtailed that activity. With the collapse of coffee these female trading networks and opportunities have revived. Women have found new sources of income, and there is some evidence that control over milk supplies is contested by men as a replacement for coffee income. But Kikuyu women see this as their money. Since they provide the cattle feed, Mbataru claims that men who won the battle for the money, could lose the war for the cow. As he observes:

> The control of the milk production therefore becomes one of the most contested areas of family production, which leads to frequent domestic conflicts.
> (Mbataru 2007: 112)

Indeed men appear to be doing rather little, and suffer 'psychological torment' as a result. They have lost the 'symbolic authority' of being the provider and 'their power was severely dented on the home front' (ibid.: 110). While women are earning money and organizing women groups, men are doing little and, according to one informant, suffer an 'inherent incapability to organise anything collectively' (! ibid.).

Hillbom's work stands in stark contrast to Mbaratu's, and our own. She has researched agricultural change in Meru since the mid-'90s, although has not focused so much on the gendered relations of agricultural production (Hillbom 2011 and 2014). She takes a different view as to the gendered consequences of the new cash crops to the work we present here. Her observations are worth quoting in full:

> Few men adopt individual strategies which combine petty trading of food cash crops with farming. They may still be part of a household strategy where the husband stays at home farming, while his wife goes to the market to sell the household produce as well as engage in petty trading. This division of labour within the household makes the husband concentrate on the local community, while the wife has more connections to the world outside the village. It also strengthens the economic position of women within households, as they are in control of a large part, or even all, of the household's cash income. Some husbands even confess to having no insight into the incomes brought in by their wives, and relying completely on their budgeting for the family's economic strategies.
>
> The explanation for female dominance in trading with food crops lies in the local historical division of labour and incomes. Traditionally, women were responsible for feeding the family, especially the children. As farming food crops

> was primarily for subsistence purposes, this was the responsibility of the wife, while the husband controlled the cash crop, such as coffee. The negligible surplus production, particularly of bananas and milk, could be sold by the wife and generated some minor income from trading. Women of today have maintained their position as the petty traders in the family. What has changed drastically is the context. Farm intensification, with the introduction of new high-value food crops such as vegetables, and increasing urban demand, including demand for traditional staple crops such as maize and bananas, has significantly expanded both supply and demand for the trading sector controlled by women.
>
> (Hillbom 2012: 676–7)

These statements differ substantially from our own view and we will return to them in the discussion of this paper. Suffice to show here that it may not be appropriate to see food cash crops as simply the domain of women. Rather different sources of family income are contested.

If we anticipate contest then we can expect the change of coffee economy to have a significant consequence on gender relations. In Meru, much like Nyeri, men traditionally controlled both the cultivation of, and the finances associated with, coffee (Dancer 2015). Women would be expected to do much of the labour. They would weed, pick, wash, dry, and clean the beans. Noe has described this in detail (see the Epilogue). When sold, men would retain the money from coffee without having to inform wives of how that money was being used. Women tended to exert more control over income from milk and bananas. It is precisely the dynamics of this division of labour, controls, and crops that we have to explore in order to understand what the coffee crisis has done to rural societies.

Methods

We have been revisiting the field sites and interviewees of the late Rolf Larsson. He was tragically killed while travelling back to Meru to conduct his own re-study. Fortunately we have been granted access to his data and, more fortunately, one of the authors, Christine Noe was herself raised and brought up on Meru—and was in fact in senior school at the time that Larsson was conducting his research in the villages which bordered hers.

Larsson's extensive research looked at Meru agricultural practices, and his research was conducted at a household, or domestic unit level, as well as at the village level. He interviewed an astonishing 753 families drawn from six villages along an altitudinal gradient. The value of his comprehensive work cannot be overstated—we are able, using his data, to go back and trace families from his original sample, to understand what has happened to them in the past twenty years. Further, his ethnographic detail at a village level has meant that we can understand changes in ideologies and social concepts, vital to a longitudinal study like ours.

We have chosen three of these villages at the top, middle, and bottom of the gradient for the revisits. In addition to revisiting the families he went to (we were able to meet with 75 per cent of them) we have also undertaken focus group discussions (of around fifteen women and men conducted separately), participant observations, and key informant interviews, during October of 2016 and a later, follow-up visit in March 2017 and June 2018.

We also draw considerably on Noe's intimate knowledge of the region and its dynamics. Noe grew up tending coffee on her family farm and at home like many other Meru girls. Her childhood (and young adulthood) in Meru is indelibly inscribed by the long hours of labour undertaken tending coffee bushes and washing coffee beans in cold Meru mountain streams before dawn.

Our methods reflect the two purposes which enervate our research. On the one hand we feel that, empirically, it is important to document the stories that we tell in this chapter. They are missing in the literature and their relative absence is troubling. And, ideologically we feel it is important for women's voices to be heard and that 'it is women's experiences and the way women themselves frame their claims that should form the starting point for research' (Dancer 2015: 19).

Nevertheless it has been a struggle. Our presence in the villages was very much controlled and facilitated by the male elders and village leaders. It was from them we gained permission to conduct our research and fieldwork, and so they assisted with the visiting of individual householders, and any group meetings we required. They explicitly told us that there was no point in having a women's focus group, as women had nothing interesting to tell us and did not understand the workings of local Meru society: only they, the men, could provide us with reliable information especially because this was about coffee, which is known to be a men's crop (regardless of where it draws labour from).

Gender Ideologies in Meru Society

The rural economy of Meru therefore has been transformed by the collapse of coffee—what effect has this had on gender relations within households? The Meru people are well known as being a patriarchal society. This means that men strongly influence women's access to resources, finances, and their social and business interactions (Meinzen-Dick et al. 2011). The change in livelihoods is likely to have a significant impact on the status and day-to-day difficulties faced by women in Meru because of the ideals to which women are subject.

Meru men have a number of expectations about themselves that they had to fulfil to remain respectable. First, men control family wealth. Family wealth has in the past and at present (to some extent) been dependent on land. The control of land gives men the power to determine the land use, how family labour is used on that land and the distribution of income generated from it. As such, men are expected to keep the behaviour of their wives and children in check, and to make sure that everyone behaves in a way considered right and proper for Meru families. This would include that women are disciplined to work mostly on family farms, take care of zero-grazed livestock and keep up the homes as opposed to doing 'loose' jobs such as business and casual labour.

Men must earn more than women, but they are not expected to have to collate many different projects to earn this money. It is normal for a Meru man to have one or two major projects and his wife will take care of many smaller roles with less perceived significance. Men are the primary decision-makers: any important decisions will be made by the man. Smaller and less important decisions can be made by the woman, but the final say is always for the man.

Men must never help the wife in the kitchen. Men who help their wives in the kitchen or who get involved in any 'women-only' tasks will be a laughing stock. Mothers will shoo their male children out of the kitchen, in case he gets a 'reputation'. Men who help their wives with 'women-only' tasks will be shamed by their peers and socially outcast. Women's behaviour must always be regulated by their fathers or husbands. They are, as one man described to us, the chairman, and the wife is considered the deputy chairperson. A woman who is unlike this is known to be 'sitting on' her husband.

There are also strong expectations with respect to women's social behaviour which affect her economic opportunities. Haram (2001) explains that two different types of women are identified in Meru social narratives: the clean woman, and the dirty woman. The clean woman is the woman who stays at home and does not go out much. She works very hard on her domestic or farming duties, and wears unfashionable, or traditional clothing. She is obedient and does not talk to men. The dirty woman is the woman who travels outside of her home village. She might work in town, and it could be rumoured that she is a prostitute. As soon as a Meru woman travels, or is out of sight of a Meru man, she is thought to be out of control.

These normative ways in which Meru understand and conceptualize gender ideology are important for understanding gender in relation to the decline in the coffee economy. As Haram has observed:

> ...men have experienced a dramatic reduction in income due mainly to the fall of coffee prices in both the local and the world markets. Thus, changing social and economic conditions have generated new strategies in the household economy.... (Haram 2001)

As we have seen many of these new strategies are off farm incomes, including small businesses, trading, and non-agricultural strategies. As income generation moves increasingly to off-farm incomes, women are involved in income generation activities which often involve being out of their homes for periods of time: it is then that women need to be even more controlled. They are out of sight of their men, and crossing geographical (and therefore also moral) boundaries. Their economic independence makes them a threat, and it is at these times that gender ideology is most powerful. It reinforces social stratifications in order that social norms can be maintained in times of economic change or social upheaval.

How Have Gender Norms Changed because of Emelea and Sambembe?

> It is because of our tears, the tears of women, that coffee got this disease, emelea. Many crop researchers have come to Meru to try and find a cure for emelea, but they cannot, because this is not caused by sickness, it is caused by women's tears.
>
> Women's focus group discussion, Meru, 19 October 2016[3]

With the collapse of coffee, household economies revolve around different goods and activities. Today, bananas are the most widely cultivated crop. Even if a family has no farm, they will have a banana tree in their compound. Bananas were traditionally a women's crop. This means that a woman is able to make money from it without having to reveal to her husband exactly how that money is spent although women explained that they mostly invest this money in the education of their children, and this is known by their husbands. She is still required to give a proportion of this to her husband, which she will not deny, as the consequence may involve limited freedom for activities such as attendance to the market.

But without coffee, men were left with no primary source of income. They would have to ask their wives for money from the sale of bananas. To rely on their wives for money would be considered shameful. Women could not deny their husbands money even though they knew it was mostly used for drinking alcohol. Doing so would cause conflicts which extend as far being denied permission go to the market to sell more bananas. If they disobeyed and went to market, we were told, 'she might as well stay there!' They would be beaten if they returned home after such behaviour. We continually heard 'Meru men must be real men!' and allowing your wife to financially support you is not what a 'real Meru man' would concede.

[3] Interestingly Mbataru also refers to the grain trading of Kikuyu women as being originally financed by the 'tears' of coffee money (2010). The reference is somewhat obscure but perhaps refers to the practice of discontinuing and devaluing women's food production, and instead importing grain, during the golden age of coffee

So in order to have a source of income for which they did not have to account to their wives, Meru men have begun to claim a species of banana for themselves. This species, mshare, is a highly commercial breed of banana, fetching higher prices than other types compared to kisasa/uganda and ndizi ng'ombe. The former is closely related to matoke, the Ugandan origin species of bananas that is mainly used for family food while the latter—as its name suggests—was in the past food for cows and raw material for local brew (mbege). Because mshare fetches higher prices, men seek to make it a men's crop.

Women described the situation with bananas as 'trying to turn bananas into Tanzanite', They see men imagining that women get lots of money when they sell bananas at the market, likening bananas to Tanzanite (a high value extremely rare gem that is found nearby). Hence they are forced, by male expectations, to finance many household activities—education, health, food, and asset acquisition. This gives women mixed feelings about these developments. They are happy that there is some income coming their way but concerned that men have left everything to them (including provision of money for their alcohol). They complained that if they sell their species of banana, their husbands demand money from them. They will take this money and 'convert it into piss' because they are spending their wives' hard-earned cash on alcohol.

The women lamented all the wasted opportunities that could have been created with this money, which they saw as especially painful since now bananas are not exclusively a woman's crop. These views were the same across all three women's focus groups, and women said that these changes in gendered control of certain crops have led to increased power struggles between men and women.

It is still primarily the woman's job to sell the bananas in the market. A man can only do so if he is bringing so many bananas to market that he must (and can afford to) carry them in a pickup. If the bananas are only enough to carry on the head, then these must be sold (and carried) by a woman. Men cannot carry bananas on their heads, only in a pickup or on a motorcycle. The division of labour here is determined by the amount of income likely to be achieved by the quantity of bananas. More money means it is a man's job.

Furthermore milk, we were told[4] (formerly exclusively for women), has become divided: the milk produced in the evening is for the women. This is used at home for making evening and morning tea. The milk produced in the morning is only for the men, and it is sold. Women do not have control of this source of income.

Men only used to go to the farm to check on their coffee plots. This has changed after the loss of coffee for most families. Men, as we have discussed, control high-value commercial crops, and so men are increasingly going to banana farms. As

[4] Both men and women explained this to us across focus groups, interviews, and informal conversations.

other crops gain commercial value (as it is with maize, potatoes, and carrots), men have taken responsibility for marketing.

One positive aspect of this change, say women, is that 'you cannot eat coffee', but at least you can eat potatoes and carrots. They say diets have improved, and despite these crops being controlled by their husbands, the women see this aspect as a positive change. This contributes to their belief that 'God brought coffee disease', because of their tears.

Since the coffee market became unviable, women have diversified away from farming. They do not like being 'unpaid labourers on the husband's plots',[5] and so many have gone into business. SACCOs (savings and cooperative groups), and microfinance loans, have in recent years facilitated women's business opportunities, but in all of our focus groups, women reported that men do not like them doing business. Indeed, men told us that women often misuse money from loans.[6] Women said that they have greater ability to make an income for themselves these days, and much more time for business, as they no longer have to work on the coffee farms. This is seen by men as women trying to take over from them as the head of the family, with control of finances, which might explain why men see women as misusing money. However, it is clear that men acknowledge women now have greater power, which comes with ownership of assets: 'they have a place in decision making because they own their own capital'.[7]

Discussion: Contesting Change in Meru

The coffee farmers of Meru are popularly known as one Tanzania's early success stories. These were, in the words of one observer, 'the Freemen of Meru' (Nelson 1967). They fought violent imperial oppression and extensive land alienation to launch the celebrated Meru Land Case against the British rulers which foreshadowed and hastened the Independence struggle. They formed co-operative unions which were wealthy and co-ordinated enough to buy back farms settlers sold, and pay for educational trusts that subsidised the education of thousands of their children (Spear 1997, Neumann 1998).

Perhaps 'free<u>men</u>', however, is the apposite term. For the untold story that underpinned this success was female labour—and hard female labour at that. As Noe describes preparing coffee required washing beans early in the morning in cold mountain streams before school, picking every berry from the bushes, and retrieving and piling the beans appropriately before sale—and all this to produce the revenues that men alone controlled.

[5] This was reported by women whenever coffee was mentioned.
[6] Men's FG, 21 April 2017.
[7] Men's FG, 21 April 2017.

This explains the bitter voices that we encountered in our fieldwork. Many female informants were pleased that there is no coffee any more as the work was very hard, labour intensive, and unpleasant, and they had no way of knowing how the money was spent from all their hard work. One woman commented, 'I hope bananas too acquire diseases'. Some women have also come to hate the banana business, as they feel that men have taken it from them.

It may seem strange that women could be so opposed to a source of revenue which had driven so much 'progress' for their community as a whole. But communities are differentiated. We have to be attentive to the misfortunes that this success generated and who experienced them. Indeed some women celebrate the demise of coffee because of the financial freedoms new economic activities now make possible:

> ...better these vegetables than coffee. Let coffee get lost. Men would sell the coffee we toiled over, eat, spend the money with other women...he would not even bring home a piece of kanga[8] It is better now that we have somewhere to grow vegetables.[9]

But we cannot see the demise of coffee as ushering in a new era of relative female freedom. Rather it brings in a new period of contest over the ownership and control of revenue streams and the proper domains of male and female activity. These disputes are a constant part of everyday life (Box 7.1). The gendered contests over commercial crops are central aspects of daily life and filter people's interpretation of change.

Women see some progressive change amidst these economic shifts. This includes women having their voices heard, women accessing loans, women

Box 7.1 Contestation of gender roles in Meru

'Women have become kings!'—Meru man, 19/10/16

Husband: Men do cook!

Wife: Well, we've been married for more than 40 years and I don't even know if you can make tea!!

Husband: I can make a cooking fire.

Wife: I have never seen that happen!

—Meru husband and wife, 19/10/16

Source: Authors' fieldwork.

[8] A cloth wrap worn by women.

[9] A Meru woman, speaking at a women's focus group, March 2017.

starting businesses, and no longer working on the coffee plots: these are all seen as considerable steps forward. On the other hand some women feel that life is worse than twenty years ago, because men have taken over what were once small businesses for women. However, most of them agree that despite all the struggles in the control of family income after the cessation of coffee cultivation, they are more empowered today. They have more opportunity to be heard and to take control of the family.

Older women believe that the younger generation of women is even more independent and are able to 'speak' without the traditional consequence of violence. Younger couples are more likely to work together on tasks. However, for many women, the strict gender roles and control of finances remain. The cessation of coffee has not made as dramatic a change to women's equity as men might believe as in their saying, 'women have become kings'.

Our point here is not that these new income-earning possibilities for which Meru women are fighting provide security. As Ossome observed, growing female participation in informal labour markets can simply entail more vulnerability and exclusion (Ossome 2015). But in the context of patriarchal Meru societies, and small formal sectors which exclude most people anyway, they provide resources for which women want to fight.

In this light it is instructive to return to Hillbom's account of gender relations (pages 163–4) because it is so different from our own. What could explain it? In between the first version of this paper being published (in *Agrarian South*) and this chapter going to press we have been able to exchange ideas with Hillbom (pers. comm. 21/4/20) and have updated our discussion to reflect them.[10] First we must recognize that the sorts of gender relations she describes can and do exist. Hillbom is reporting her findings from the field. They come from a slightly different part of Meru, and from a slightly earlier period. Some of the differences therefore may be geographical and historical.

But there are differences in the conceptual frameworks we have used. Perhaps the most important is that we disagree with Hillbom's suggestion that if food crops were 'traditionally' subsistence and under female control then, when they acquire more commercial value, they will remain under female control. The literature (Orr et al 2014) we have considered above suggests otherwise. Andersson Djurfeldt has also recently published a similar assessment of this literature which draws the same conclusion:

> numerous studies, both contemporary and historical, concern the male dominance over cash crop production and sales and the growing male control over women's crops as they become commercialized. (2018: 83)

[10] We are grateful to Ellen for the constructive and collegiate exchange our different ideas have prompted.

When women's crops become commercially valuable men seek to control them. Indeed in Hillbom's other work (2011) she points to increasing competition within household over income from milk. This unsurprising if, following Ossome (2014), we should expect this sort of change in control over commercial crops because we need to see the gendered domains of control over land, labour, and their products as *contested*. Male and female realms are not given by tradition, rather these traditions are forged and re-made through myriad interactions every single day.

Conclusion

Sadly, it seems that these three outspoken and determined little girls in the extract at the beginning of the paper will face a number of challenges to their dreams. Female bajaji or pikipiki drivers simply do not exist in Meru society at the moment. If they did, their peers, parents, and fellow Meru would see them as 'loose' women, with poor morals. They would be unlikely to marry, as their husbands would be shamed for not adequately 'controlling' them, or for allowing themselves to be dominated by their wives. Meru women are not allowed to be in a more senior role than their husbands and they are not facilitated to earn more money than men. It would be highly unusual if these girls did manage to achieve their dream jobs as bodaboda drivers or bajaji drivers.

As women find new, entrepreneurial ways of making money, men seek ways to take them over. High-value bananas, once a women-only crop, are now controlled by men. Chicken businesses, also originally only seen as fit for women, are taken over by men, as men lose their coffee business, and search for more commercial ventures. We are not arguing that the men are doing this in a particularly malicious way, but that this strongly patriarchal society expects men to take over from women, and assumes that men will control any significantly commercial, income-generating activities. Men used to control finances from the coffee business, but now that coffee has become unproductive due to a slump in the market, pests, and diseases, men have sought to control other commercial ventures. The transference of control by men from coffee to bananas, to chickens, to high-value vegetable growing, is a seemingly 'natural' order which women struggle to avert.

Men see women as usurping their control of finances. They believe that women have achieved greater freedoms and financial control during the past twenty years. Women see this very differently; they feel that whatever small progress they make is rapidly followed by men taking over this control. They are happy to be rid of the hard physical labour coffee crops require from them, but are angry that many small businesses, formerly the preserve of women only, have been usurped by their husbands, allowing women even less financial autonomy.

In an era of the Sustainable Development Goals we are accustomed to talking about progress towards those goals and setting targets and indicators of welcome change. Yet the case of change in the context of Meru coffee suggests this may well not be the best way of conceiving of these dynamics. The targets and these indicators matter. But the linear thinking in terms of progress does not allow for regress. From the perspective of the women in Meru, any movements towards development goals have to be viewed through a lens of contested gender dynamics which could reverse hard-won gains.

It may be tempting, when reading some of the other chapters in this collection to conclude that assets provide a good proxy of measuring rural well-being. We hope that this chapter discourages that conclusion. There are indeed cases where assets do correlate well with some measures of well-being (as Borgerhoff Mulder shows in Chapter 5). But as Borgerhoff Mulder emphasizes, these are local relationships, that may not be replicated elsewhere. In Meru the growth of assets that coffee farming enabled brought unevenly distributed costs and benefits for men and women. A focus only on that growth in assets and not the labour which produced them will miss those vital dynamics. The light that a focus on assets sheds on some aspects of rural dynamics cannot blind us to the limits of their insights.

References

Andersson Djurfeldt, A. (2018). 'Gender and Rural Livelihoods: Agricultural Commercialisation and Farm/Non Farm Diversification.' *Agriculture, Diversification, and Gender in Rural Africa. Longitudinal Perspectives from Six Countries.* A. Andersson Djurfeldt, F. M. Dzanku, and A. C. Isinika. Oxford, Oxford University Press: 81–112.

Bacon, C. M. (2010). 'A Spot of Coffee in Crisis: Nicaraguan Smallholder Cooperatives, Fair Trade Networks, and Gendered Empowerment.' *Latin American Perspectives* 37(2): 50–71.

Brockington, D. (2001). 'Women's Income and Livelihood Strategies of Dispossessed Pastoralists: The Case of Mkomazi Game Reserve.' *Human Ecology* 29: 307–38.

Brockington, D. (2021). 'Persistent Peasant Poverty and Assets. Exploring Dynamics of New Forms of Wealth and Poverty in Tanzania 1999–2018.' *Journal of Peasant Studies* 48(1): 201–20.

Brockington, D., E. Coast, O. Howland, A. Mdee, and S. Randall (2021). 'Assets and Domestic Units: Methodological Challenges for Longitudinal Studies of Poverty Dynamics.' *Journal of Peasant Studies* 48(1): 159–79.

Christiaensen, L., V. Hoffmann, and A. Sarris (2006). 'Coffee Price Risk in Perspective—Household Vulnerability among Rural Coffee Growing Smallholders in Rural Tanzania.' Paper presented at the CSAE Conference 2006: Reducing Poverty and Inequality: How Can Africa Be Included? Held on 19–21 March 2006, at St Catherine's College, Oxford.

Coady, D., P. Olinto, and N. Caldes (2003). 'Coping with the Coffee Crisis in Central America: The Role of Social Safety Nets in Honduras.' Washington DC, IFPRI.

Corbera, E., A. Martin, O. Springate-Baginski, and A. Villaseñor (2017). 'Sowing the Seeds of Sustainable Rural Livelihoods? An Assessment of Participatory Forest Management through REDD+ in Tanzania.' *Land Use Policy*. DOI: 10.1016/j.landusepol.2017.09.037.

Dancer, H. (2015). *Women, Land and Justice in Tanzania*. Woodbridge, Boydell & Brewer Ltd.

Eakin, H., C. Tucker, and E. Castellanos (2006). 'Responding to the coffee Crisis: A Pilot Study of Farmers' Adaptations in Mexico, Guatemala and Honduras.' *The Geographical Journal* 172(2): 156–71.

Goldman, M., A. Davis, and J. Little (2016). 'Controlling Land They Call Their Own: Access and Women's Empowerment in Northern Tanzania.' *The Journal of Peasant Studies* 43(4): 777–97.

Guèye, F. (2000). 'Women and Family Poultry Production in Rural Africa.' *Development in Practice* 10(1): 98–102.

Haram, L. (2001). '"In Sexual Life Women Are Hunters": AIDS and women Who Drain Men's Bodies. The Case of the Meru of Northern Tanzania.' *Society in Transition* 32(1): 47–55.

Hillbom, E. (2011). 'Farm Intensification and Milk Market Expansion in Meru, Tanzania.' *African Studies Review* 54(1): 145–65.

Hillbom, E. (2012). 'Market Institutions Benefiting Smallholders in Contemporary Meru, Tanzania.' *Journal of Modern African Studies* 50(4): 657–70.

Hillbom, E. (2014). 'From Millet to Tomatoes: Incremental Intensification with High-Value Crops in Contemporary Meru, Tanzania.' *Journal of Eastern African Studies* 8(3): 400–19.

Kristjanson, P., E. Bryan, Q. Bernier, J. Twyman, R. Meinzen-Dick, C. Kieran, C. Ringler, C. Jost, and C. Doss (2017). 'Addressing Gender in Agricultural Research for Development in the Face of a Changing Climate: Where Are We and where Should We Be Going?' *International Journal of Agricultural Sustainability* 15(5): 482–500.

Larsson, R. (2001). 'Between Crisis and Opportunity. Livelihoods, Diversification and Inequality among the Meru of Tanzania.' Lund, PhD Thesis, Lund University.

Madaha, R. (2014). 'Organized and Gendered Media Advocacy at the Centre of the Feminist Movement in a Patriarchal Tanzania.' *Africa Review* 6(1): 18–29.

Maghimbi, S. (2007). 'Recent Changes in Crop Patterns in the Kilimanjaro Region of Tanzania: The Decline of Coffee and the Rise of Maize and Rice.' *African Study Monographs* Suppl. 35(March): 73–83.

Maghimbi, S. (2010). 'Cooperatives in Tanzania Mainland: Revival and Growth.' Rome, ILO.

Mbataru, P. (2007). 'Women in the Coffee Society: The Case of Nyeri, Kenya.' *Études Rurales* 108: 101–16.

Mbilinyi, M. (2016). 'Analysing the History of Agrarian Struggles in Tanzania from a Feminist Perspective.' *Review of African Political Economy* 43 (supl.): 115–29.

Meinzen-Dick, R., N. Johnson, A. Quisumbing, J. Njuki, J. Behrman, D. Rubin, A. Peterman, and E. Waithanji (2011). 'Gender, Assets, and Agricultural Development Programs. A Conceptual Framework.' CAPRi Working Paper No. 99. Washington DC, IFPRI.

Nelson, A. (1967). *The Freemen of Meru*. London and New York, Oxford University Press.

Neumann, R. P. (1998). *Imposing Wilderness: Struggles over Livelihood and Nature Preservation in Africa*. Berkeley, University of California Press.

Orr, A., T. Tsusaka, S. Homann-KeeTui, and W. Msere (2014). 'What Do We Mean by "Women's Crops"? A Mixed Methods Approach.' *ICRISAT SocioEconomics Discussion Paper Series*. Nairobi, International Crops Research Institute for the Semi-Arid Tropics.

Ossome, L. (2014). 'Can the Law Secure Women's Rights to Land in Africa? Revisiting Tensions between Culture and Land Commercialization.' *Feminist Economics* 20(1): 155–77.

Ossome, L. (2015). 'In Search of the State? Neoliberalism and the Labour Question for Pan-African Feminism.' *Feminist Africa* 20: 6–24.

Östberg, W., O. Howland, J. Mduma, and D. Brockington (2018). 'Tracing Improving Livelihoods in Rural Africa Using Local Measures of Wealth: A Case Study from Central Tanzania, 1991–2016.' *Land* 7(44): 1–26.

Palacios-Lopez, A., L. Christiaensen, and T. Kilic (2017). 'How Much of the Labor in African Agriculture Is Provided by Women?' *Food Policy* 67: 52–63.

Pirotte, G., G. Pleyers, and M. Poncelet (2006). 'Fair-Trade Coffee in Nicaragua and Tanzania: A Comparison.' *Development in Practice* 16(5): 441–51.

Ponte, S. (2002a). *Farmers and Markets in Tanzania: how Policy Reforms Affect Rural Livelihoods in Africa*. Oxford, James Currey.

Ponte, S. (2002b). 'The "Latte Revolution"? Regulation, Markets and Consumption in the Global Coffee Chain.' *World Development* 30(7): 1099–122.

Raney, T., G. Anríquez, A. Croppenstedt, S. Gerosa, S. Lowder, I. Matuscke, J. Skoet, and C. Doss (2011). *The Role of Women in Agriculture*. Rome, FAO.

Ranger, T. (1993). 'The Invention of Tradition Revisited: The Case of Colonial Africa.' *Legitimacy and the State in Twentieth-Century Africa: Essays in Honour of A. H. M. Kirk-Greene*. T. Ranger and O. Vaughan. Basingstoke, Palgrave: 62–111.

Razavi, S. (2016). 'The 2030 Agenda: Challenges of Implementation to Attain Gender Equality and Women's Rights.' *Gender & Development* 24(1): 25–41.

Sachs, C. (2018). *Gendered Fields: Rural Women, Agriculture, and Environment.* London, Routledge.

Spear, T. (1997). *Mountain Farmers*. Dar es Salaam, Berkeley and Los Angeles, Oxford, Mkuki na Nyota, University of California Press, James Currey.

United Republic of Tanzania (URT) (2019). 'Tanzania Mainland. Key Indicators Report. 2017–18 Household Budget Survey.' Dodoma, National Bureau of Statistics, Ministry of Finance and Planning.

Wangui, E. (2008). 'Development Interventions, Changing Livelihoods, and the Making of Female Maasai Pastoralists.' *Agriculture and Human Values* 25(3): 365–78.

Woodhouse, P., G.-J. Veldwisch, J.-P. Venot, D. Brockington, H. Komakech, and A. Manjichi (2017). 'African farmer-Led Irrigation Development: Reframing Agricultural Policy and Investment?' *Journal of Peasant Studies* 44(1): 213–33.

World Bank (2015). 'Tanzania Mainland Poverty Assessment.' Washington DC, The World Bank.

8

The Sesame Seed Cash Injection

Commodity-Fuelled Asset Booms in Remote Rural Tanzania

Dan Brockington

Epilogue pages 390–393

Introduction

At the time of writing the most recent household budget survey data for Tanzania have been released from the 2017/8 round of the Household Budget Survey. On the face of it poverty rates in Tanzania appear to have declined substantially, with poverty declining from 34.4 per cent to 26.4 per cent nationally between 2007 and 2018, and extreme poverty (food poverty) declining from 11.3 per cent to 8 per cent in the same period (URT 2019).

However, for rural researchers, this report makes depressing reading because these changes are driven primarily by decreases in urban poverty, far more than rural poverty. The proportion of people living in urban areas who were poor has declined from 24.1 per cent in 2007 (16.4 per cent in Dar es Salaam) to 15.8 per cent in 2017/8 (8 per cent in Dar es Salaam). Whereas the decline in rural areas is smaller in absolute and proportional terms: 37.6 per cent to 31.3 per cent. The respective declines in extreme poverty are 12.9 per cent to 4.4 per cent for urban areas (Dar es Salaam 7.4 per cent to 2.3 per cent) and 18.4 per cent to 9.7 per cent for rural areas. Economic growth seems disproportionately to benefit urban areas. Distance from the metropolis makes you poor.

As if to emphasize that point further, some of the most rural and remote regions of Tanzania are reported to have the highest incidences of poverty. And the starkest case is Rukwa Region, in which 45 per cent of the population experiences basic-needs poverty—which is higher than the incidence of rural poverty for all of Tanzania in 1991/2 (URT 2009). Rukwa seems not only just forgotten by the progress that the rest of the country enjoys. It seems, according to these standards, to have gone backwards.

Dan Brockington, *The Sesame Seed Cash Injection: Commodity-Fuelled Asset Booms in Remote Rural Tanzania* In: *Prosperity in Rural Africa? Insights into Wealth, Assets, and Poverty from Longitudinal Studies in Tanzania.* Edited by: Dan Brockington and Christine Noe, Oxford University Press. © Dan Brockington 2021. DOI: 10.1093/oso/9780198865872.003.0008

Rukwa then provides an excellent site to examine more carefully the fundamental premise of this research project. As we saw in Chapter 2 poverty-line data must omit investment in productive assets. Yet those assets are precisely the sort of thing that rural Tanzanians seek to invest in. As we saw from Chapter 3, accruing those assets is fundamental to local definitions of poverty, prosperity, and well-being. This begs the question, are the measurements of consumption that constitute poverty lines measuring the right things? Are they counting the things that matter to rural Tanzanians?

We have already seen in Chapter 5 that, for one remote village near Rukwa, there are signs of increases in well-being, both in terms of assets, and in terms of the relationship of those assets with other aspects of prosperity. Here we explore a different case, that of Mtowisa in the District of Sumbawanga (Rural).

I argue in this chapter that the answer is equivocal. On the one hand it is plain that measurement of daily consumption will fail to capture the important investments in productive assets, and large purchase items like metal roofing. We can document clearly, by taking asset histories, how people have been able to invest in new assets as a result of a substantial increase in cash crop prices and a reduction in transport costs and improvement in transport infrastructure in the region. At the same time it is clear that, in the context of population growth and migration into the village, there are also many new families and residents who have not been able to join in these transformations. The majority of residents in this village remain poor. Moreover the land frontier has now closed, accessing new land is now much harder. The nature and meaning of poverty that people experience now will change from that they endured when I first worked in this area.

Methods

I had lived in Mtowisa, then a remote village in the Rukwa Valley, for a year in 1999–2000 as part of a post-doctoral research fellowship in which I studied the consequences of the immigration of large numbers of wealthy Sukuma agro-pastoralists, who brought with them large herds, improved cattle, and new crops and farming methods and who had been integrating into the area for over twenty years (Brockington 2001, 2006, 2007, and 2008).

I made two return trips to Mtowisa in August 2016 and April 2018. The first to conduct the resurvey, the second to follow up and present findings to villagers. I revisited, with assistants, sixty-four families, and interviewed local shopkeepers, district government officials, and business leaders based in Dar who purchase crops there. I also travelled to neighbouring villages and fishing camps with friends, visited new irrigation schemes, held three village meetings (for women and men in 2016 and a collective feedback meeting in 2018) as well as meetings with local leaders. I now remain in touch by phone with friends who live there.

The advantage of the original survey that I conducted in Mtowisa is that it was not a sample. I surveyed the entire central village, covering just over four hundred families. The central village means that it excludes outlying farmsteads that were predominantly the domain of wealthy Sukuma agro-pastoral households who lived out beyond the margins of the village with large cattle herds. This re-study has therefore not been able to track the changing fortunes of the families who were the wealthiest in this area in 1999–2000 and who appeared, anecdotally, to have remained wealthy in 2016. However given the focus of this paper on the impact of economic growth on the rural poor this gap in the survey does not vitiate the findings.

But having a complete original survey meant that I could conduct a much more thorough re-visit. In the first instance I could sample families from that original survey, stratifying the population into groups according to key aspects of wealth relevant in 2000. In the second it was easier for me to deal with the problem of attrition because, if I was unable to visit a particular family, I could then re-select a different representative of that group from the original population. The nature and targets for each group, and the actual numbers achieved, are shown in Table 8.1.

Since I was able to replace missing families the problem of attrition recedes, but note the patterns in it. First there are older families whose heads had died, and had dispersed by the time of the revisit. A second group were those who had been younger, and who had moved away by the time of the revisit. These two groups had opposite tendencies with respect to ownership of herds and ploughs, with the younger groups tending to be poorer, and the older groups richer.

A key assumption of our methods is that domestic units (aka families) were sufficiently stable to make a re-survey of assets owned by families worthwhile. This proved to be the case as there were only four incidences of divorce. The sample however contains a larger than normal group of domestic units headed by single women (eighteen out of sixty-four or 28 per cent), whereas only 14 per cent had this characteristic in 2000. This is because we interviewed a relatively large number of widows whose husbands had died; we also interviewed three widowers.

There is also a crucial difference between the sample taken in 2016 and the survey of 2000: all the domestic units heads I re-visited are now sixteen years

Table 8.1 Sampling of different social groups

Characteristics in 2000	Count in 2000	Visited 2016	Moved 2016	Died 2016
Owned livestock or a plough	157	24	5	8
No livestock or plough ownership	245	40	18	8
Total	**402**	**64**	**23**	**16**

Source: Author's data.

Table 8.2 Characteristics of surveyed, deceased, moved, and unsurveyed families from 2000 data

Group	Average of age of DU head in 2000	Plough ownership in 2000 (ppn of families)	Cattle ownership in 2000 (ppn of families)
Died	54	31	25
Moved	36.3	4	9
Surveyed	40.6	14	20
Not surveyed	40.5	14	21

Source: Author's data. Kruskal-Wallis tests find no significance difference in the number of cattle (p=0.32) or ploughs (p=0.07) owned by families that were surveyed, that were missed, or that died, but the difference in mean of household head's age is significant (p=0.03).

older. None was under 35 years old. The findings that I report below are therefore not representative of younger families in the village (we will return to this point later). To control for this difference all the comparisons of asset ownership reported below compare domestic unit heads who are over 35 now with domestic unit heads who were over 35 in 2000. If I simply compared the sample of 2016 with the entire village in 2000 I would not be comparing like with like. I would be comparing the condition of an older sample in 2016, with that of a much younger population from 2000. The latter would appear poorer because if its relative youth, the former wealthier due its seniority (as Table 8.2 implies). This could lead to a false impression of improving prosperity.

There are therefore two caveats which have to be remembered when we explore the findings. First, this survey excludes the very wealthy Sukuma agro-pastoralists, who were missed in the original survey. Second, I cannot talk about the contemporary experience of younger domestic units.

Findings

Initial Poverty and Subsequent Transformation

If ever there was an archetypal place to examine persistent peasant poverty, then it would be Mtowisa. The village is not far, as the crow flies, from the regional capital of Mtowisa, which is barely 15km away. But the flying crow has an easier route than humans, as it can soar over the 1200m escarpment that separated the town from the village. In 2000, residents had to walk between the two. This was a village that felt far from anywhere.

Its residents felt they were poor. It was expensive to transport crops and so prices were low. Productivity was also low, with most people being only small-scale farmers, cultivating 2 acres or so. Despite abundant unused lands, farming activity increased only marginally with the age of the domestic unit head, or with family size. It was difficult to sell surplus and some feared 'bad jealousy' i.e. retribution from neighbours that success might occasion (cf. Foster 1965). Visible signs of wealth were few. Most lived in simple grass-roofed houses. Only 20 per cent of families owned cattle and then but small herds; there were few ploughs.

I must not paint a picture of abject poverty. Just over half of residents' adult men (54 per cent) had owned cattle at some point in their lifetimes. The place was blessed by fertile soils, plentiful lands, reasonably reliable rains, a lake full of fish, grasslands with low tick burdens, and a game reserve that was not well guarded on the other side of the lake. Mtowisa may have been hard to get to, but it was still only a (long) day's walk there and back, and it was possible to headload up a basket of dried fish or chickens and earn enough in a day to pay the various government taxes required at the time for a whole year. Some farmers cultivated rice as a cash crop when the rivers flooded in the wet season, and one or two had constructed their own irrigation ditches to channel river water to their farms more reliably. Moreover there was a particularly wealthy group of farmers in the region, Sukuma immigrants from Tabora, Shinyanga, and Mwanza, who managed huge herds of cattle (numbering into the thousands) and large areas of land (Brockington 2001). Their arrival had brought changes to farming practices (encouraging ploughing) as well as changes to the crops grown: maize had recently replaced finger millet as the main staple, sunflowers and rice were being grown more frequently. It had also brought tensions and greater risks for smaller farmers as their farms were vulnerable to livestock damage for which there was rarely compensation.

But the main point remains. Most people were poor. They did not have the means to cultivate much land, and could not earn good prices for their produce. It was possible to accumulate livestock, land, and other assets, but this required time—and good luck. I had many records of people who would spend a year or more of their youth as herd boys for Sukuma cattle owners, and receive in return one cow or ox in payment (an annual salary of about $50), only then to lose the animal to disease or overworking it. Many people remained orientated to subsistence rather than commercial production.

What happened to such poverty in the sixteen years between my visits? This was a period of strong economic growth nationally, and, as we have seen, the benefits of that growth are thought not to have filtered down to rural areas. Does Mtowisa exemplify these trends or defy them?

The village was much less isolated. There is a large phone tower in the village (since 2008). The road between Mbeya and Sumbawanga had just been metalled (completed in 2014), there was also now an improved road between Sumbawanga and Mtowisa with good bridges across the rivers that could be used all year round (this was completed in 2007). There was a regular bus service in the dry season along the length of the valley, and a daily bus service to Sumbawanga (which had started in 2013) as well as smaller hiaces throughout the day (since 2015).

The village centre was transformed. I had known it as a sleepy place with one shop and a small hospital, where cars came infrequently (barely once a month), and motorbikes were rare. Now there were numerous shops, nearly twenty motorbike taxis, gas and electric welding (the latter run on a powerful generator), several phone shops, and a well-equipped hardware store. The hospital had an operating theatre and there were lots of solar-powered lights (and stereos, making the place a much louder one at night).

There was an abundance of metal-roofed homes, and many single rooms being rented. Numerous pigs roamed the streets or were kept in small compounds near people's houses (these had also been unusual in 2000). The small irrigation furrows I had left behind were still present, and indeed had expanded in number. In the dry season they were used (since about 2012) to cultivate tomatoes, cabbage, and onions and there were around ten petrol powered pumps which withdrew river water to pump to nearby farms.

But these first impressions can be potentially misleading. We cannot be sure if the people enjoying these trappings of wealth were poor or not without a more detailed revisit. And it is easy not reasonable to assume that the wealth so conspicuously in the town centres is shared by all residents. This is precisely the sort of road-based bias against which Chambers warned so many years ago (Chambers 1981). Twenty motorbike taxis would not indicate that Mtowisa's peasants have become richer. It just indicates that twenty people now own (or rent) motorbikes.

The Sesame Seed Cash Injection

The survey data I collected in 2016 suggest two crucial differences between the wealth, in assets, of the residents of Mtowisa now compared to what it had been. On the one hand the older families in Mtowisa enjoy higher levels of prosperity, as measured in assets, than they did sixteen years ago. They enjoy higher levels of prosperity than their counterparts of an equivalent age expected to achieve in 2000. They are wealthier because of their farming, and, in particular because they are selling more cash crops, specifically sunflower seeds and sesame, with the latter providing the most substantial change.

The evidence for this change is as follows. First, with respect to key measures of herd and plough ownership the sample visited is wealthier than it was in the past, and compared to the group of similar-aged domestic unit heads in 2000 (Table 8.3). Oxen ownership has increased by half (and if we include oxen borrowed from wealthy patrons it doubles to 41 per cent). Pig ownership has increased dramatically, and ownership of ploughs has more than doubled.

Table 8.3 Key asset ownership, 2000 and 2016 (percentage)

Group	Oxen	Goats	Pigs	Ploughs	N
Sample in 2016	41	38	16	38	64
Population in 2000	20	35	0	17	219

Source: Author's data. Note the population in 2000 excludes family heads less than 35 years old and cattle include oxen borrowed from wealthy land owners. Differences in cattle, pigs, and ploughs are statistically significant: cattle χ^2=11.84, p=0.001; pigs χ^2=35.47, p<0.001; ploughs χ^2=16.04, p<0.001; df=2 in all cases.

Table 8.4 Land put to different crops in 2000 and 2016 (acres)

Crop	2000	2016
Maize	329.3	112.75
Rice	38.5	25
Sunflower	0.25	21.25
Sesame	0	57.75
Farmers	219	64

Source: Author's data. Differences are statistically significant; χ^2=15870.5, df=3, p=0.001. With area measured in acres the contingency table has too many low value cells, so the test was conducted on different units of area.

Second, with respect to farming activity, people are simply farming more. Farming activity increases more with family size than it did previously (Figure 8.1). All families are farming more cash crops, with proportionally less maize is grown than before (Table 8.4).

Third, housing quality has improved, particularly with the spread of metal roofing.[1] Improved roofing material matters because, with the increased presence of cattle in the region (and loss of grassland over several decades to forest regrowth and farms) good, long-lasting thatching grass (lasting 5–10 years) is hard to get. People instead are reliant on rice straw (which lasts one year) or lake reeds (lasting two). Moreover thatched houses are more likely to catch fire (making it riskier to go away), and they harbour vermin. They are also, perforce, smaller than metal-roofed houses, to reduce the effort of collecting the thatch required for large houses. Houses with metal roofs can be subdivided into a family home and rentable rooms (providing a useful extra income of 8,000–12,000/= per month). Finally a metal roof is a status symbol, a visible sign of prosperity.

[1] On Google Earth I counted the appearance of metal roofs from 8/10/2003 (the first image available) to 7/10/13 (the last image). In Mtowisa in 2003 there were ninety-one metal-roofed structures. A further 442 new metal-roofed structures were built by October 2013.

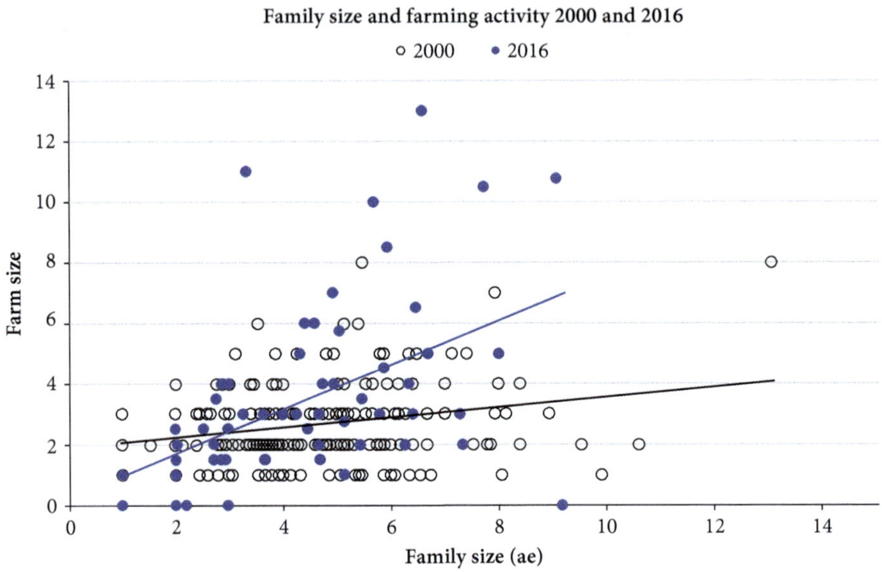

Figure 8.1 Family size and farming activity 2000 and 2016.

There were increasing numbers of rather grand houses also being constructed—distinguished by their complicated roof structures.[2]

The other source of evidence on housing change are the narratives that I was told repeatedly by many people: that they had been able to invest in their houses because of their farming activity, and this had taken off since about 2010 (Table 8.5). The main reason for that growth in investment, as Figure 8.2 shows, is the increased sales of sesame and sunflower seeds. But, from focus group discussions, it was plain that sesame seed prices were the main driving force of change. Sesame appeared in small quantities in 2007 and 2008 in Figure 8.2, but takes off significantly from 2010 onwards, at the same time as decisions to invest also increase substantially.

These price rises were driven by international demand and global rises in these commodity prices, not by changes in the marketing system (Figure 8.3). Similar dynamics have driven prosperous sesame seed farming in other parts of Tanzania (Corbera et al. 2017). Other studies have shown that sesame seed marketing arrangements in Lindi and Mtwara Region which use respectively the District

[2] In Swahili these are called 'migongo minne' (four-backed houses), i.e. not a simple 'A'-frame roof structure. The presence of these houses was particularly noticeable because in 2000 I had been part of the communal work parties that were detailed to reconstruct the local secondary school that the parents in the village had built and that the government had recently taken over. As part of the take-over the government ordered that the teacher's accommodation (which had been locally designed) be knocked down and re-built according to government standards. Then, in 2000, there was a great deal of complaint that these new houses were far too big. And they were nothing compared to the fine houses being constructed by locally wealthy residents.

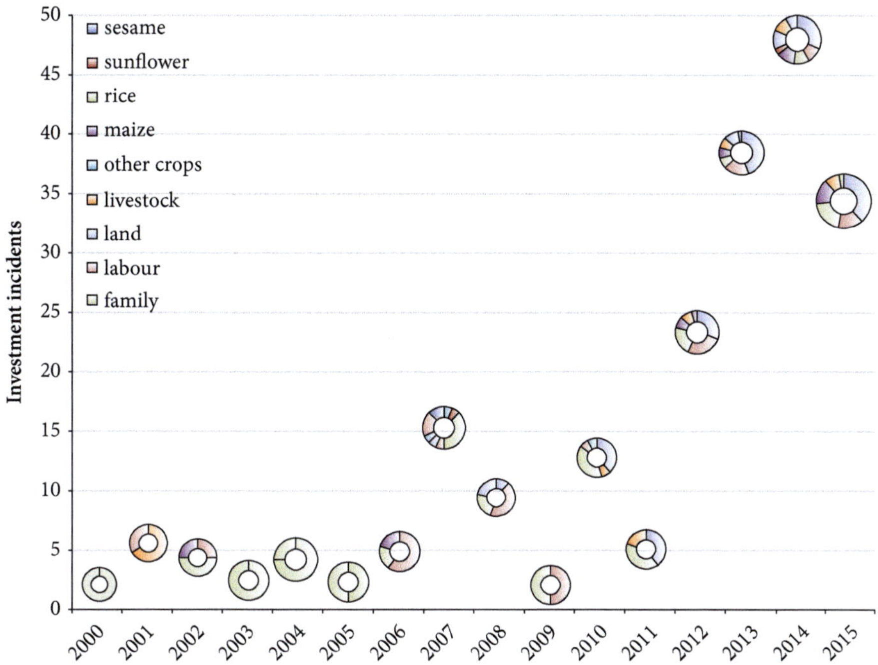

Figure 8.2 Sources of investment in assets.

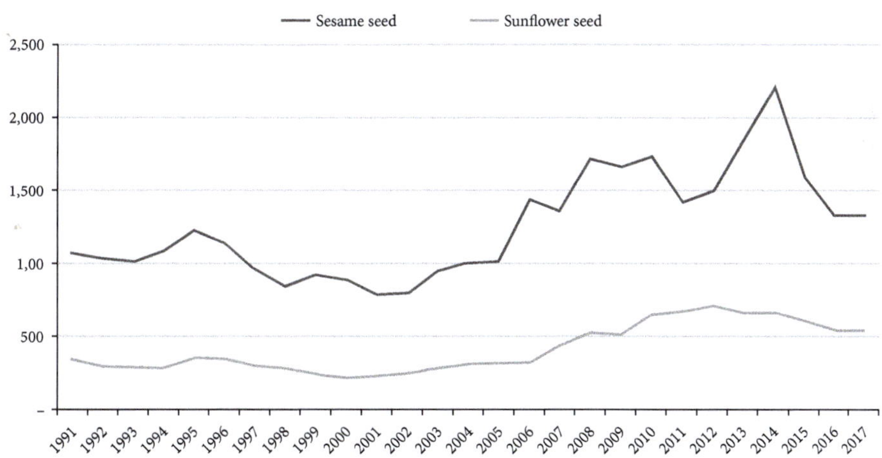

Figure 8.3 Global producer prices for sesame and sunflowers ($US/tonne).

Stakeholders' Price Setting Forum and the Warehouse Receipt System have been instrumental in fostering demand (Mashindano and Kihenzile 2013). However in the case of Rukwa, there was no organization of the marketing arrangements by government officials. There has been no organization of producers into Agricultural Marketing Co-operatives (they were first established in 2018). There

Table 8.5 Net asset investment

Asset Acquisition	2001–5	2006–10	2011–15
House construction	8	13	34
Metal roof	4	12	33
Oxen	–1	3	8
Pigs/Goats	2	2	12
Land	0	7	4
Plough/Cart	0	4	15
Milling machine/Motorbike	–1	0	2

Source: Author's data.

was merely a willing buyer in the form of a major agricultural exporter (the Export Trading Company).

I was able to interview the pioneer farmer of modern varieties of sesame. He described a situation of gradual prices rises in the 2000s with demand kicking off in 2009 when many sesame seed buyers appeared in the village. From that point on prices sky-rocketed reaching as much as 2,000/– (nearly US$1.00) per kilo. Farmers were able to yield fantastic returns, of, I was told, between 250,000/= and 300,000/= per sack. This is more than enough for a roll of metal roofing, and only two rolls would be required to roof a standard sized house.

One story illustrates well the joy and surprise that these returns caused to farmers in Mtowisa. I was told that one farmer (we will call him Darius), whom I met in the survey work and who had not been particularly industrious or wealthy in 2000, went up to Sumbawanga to sell his sesame in 2011. This was a collective enterprise, with many farmers loading their harvest onto the lorry of the local shop owner to take it to the depot in Sumbawanga where better prices can be realized. On receiving his payment for two sacks of sesame (500,000/=) Darius was simply left in shock.[3] He sat down in a corner of the weighing room, still full of the hustle and bustle of heavy sacks being moved, weighed, and paid for, because he had never in his life expected to have so much money. His friends had to guide him to a guest house where he could safely spend the night. The next day he had recovered sufficiently to buy metal sheets for a new house (which are also much less easily stolen than money). He built a new house that year and extended it the year after following further sales.

It is because of repeated stories like Darius's that the appearance of Mtowisa, and the daily lives of so many of its residents have been so thoroughly changed. Higher sesame seed prices have given a substantial cash injection to many people's livelihoods. Moreover regional production data suggest that this was not

[3] Expressed by my respondent as 'Amekaa bubuwazi'. This is a local version of 'amepigwa mbumbuwazi'.

Table 8.6 Sesame seed sales in Rukwa Region

Year	Tons	Tz sh/kg	Tz sh	$US
2013–14	5528	1950	10,779,600,000	6,610,000
2014–15	4472	2000	8,944,000,000	4,710,000
2015–16	11,218	1277	14,325,386,000	6,570,000
2016–17	3705	1625	6,020,625,000	2,740,000

Source: Regional production figures.

merely a local phenomenon. This crop was scarcely grown when I was working there in 1999–2000. Yet, if these figures are to be believed then, in the last four years, it has injected more than $US20 million into the local economy (Table 8.6).

Patterns in Improvement

Altogether 66 per cent of the sample had experienced an increase in assets in some way over the previous sixteen years—but what subtler changes does this bald statistic conceal? There are two general trends to note. First, the improvement in assets is general across most wealth groups, but richer, more productive families have tended to be able to benefit from the cash crop returns more than families who were poorer and farming less in 2000.

The evidence for that is visible in the slightly different performance of the different categories of farmers I identified in 2000. Those who did not engage in kibarua work (casual labour), or who only performed kibarua work for other people, are least likely to have improved their asset base. Those with more assets, and more engagement in kibarua work (as sellers or buyers) are most likely to have improved their assets (Table 8.7).[4] There are some qualifications to this pattern. The richest group did not increase their assets the most, reflecting the fact that they were also older and more likely to retire and withdraw from farming. Also these differences are only tendencies, and do not denote contours of disadvantage. At least 50 per cent of any group improved their assets.

The second trend is that female-headed domestic units, and smaller families tended to improve their asset base less than male-headed larger units (Table 8.8). This trend reflects changes in the lifecycle of domestic units where older people

[4] Casual labour is a contested aspect of peasant studies. Performing such labour can be associated with demeaning work and be an aspect of class formation (Mueller 2011). I found that in Rukwa in 2000 performing kibarua work was not necessarily associated with low status—it merged with reciprocal labour relations. It was possible to perform kibarua for one person, and employ kibarua yourself at a later date. Kibarua can also be undertaken in order to save and invest in a particular project. These days kibarua can be a sign of poverty—if it is the only means of support—and a means of accumulation.

Table 8.7 Asset growth performance by 2000 wealth group.

Wealth group in 2000	% of families improving asset base
Owns cows and a plough	63
Owns cows only	83
Owns either pigs, goats, or a plough	82
None of assets above, pays for and performs kibarua	80
None of assets above, only pays for kibarua work	62
None of assets, neither pays for or performs kibarua	56
None of assets above, only performs kibarua work	50

Table 8.8 Differences between families gaining assets and losing/showing no change in assets 2000–6

Asset change	Mean family size 2000 (average)	No. of female-headed households (av. age)	No. of dual-headed households (av. age)
Static/Decline	3.7	16 (57)	14 (56)
Growth	4.1	4(47)	30 (51)

Source: Author's data.

farm less, where widows also farm less, and where both tend to support fewer dependents.

In addition, across the sample, in the midst of all this prosperity there were repeated, if infrequent, incidents of continued poverty or impoverishment. Some families seem to have been unable to benefit from the changes transforming their neighbours. My friends and informants explained this as an inability to plan affairs (kupanga maisha) such that their expenditure matched their means. Conversely those who had been able to improve their assets spoke also of restricting expenditure (bana matumizi, literally clamp down on uses) to do so.

Others, although they had gained in assets, had lost in other ways, suffering from divorce or death of partners, or simply the travails of old age, such that life now was decidedly unhappier. A couple of families had lost assets with which they began (land and/or livestock) because they had been forced to sell because of various hardships. There are also some incidents of apparent investment in assets more accurately being a case of releasing liquidity or altering asset portfolio. This applied to older families who sold land, or parts of their plots, to fund house-building. We also visited families who had invested in oxen and land, but had lost their herds and been forced to sell their land because of diverse misfortunes. Building an asset base requires good luck as well as wise decision-making.

But if the general perspective across domestic units has been positive, what about within them? What changes within families does the rising prosperity documented above conceal? Within domestic units the changes experienced because of the investment in assets seem to be reasonably well shared by men and women. Fipa society is one where both men and women can own and dispose of land and livestock. Weeding workloads, I was told (and saw), are equally shared. The move to cash crops did not appear to have increased men's income, but women's work.

Women have been disadvantaged, however, by the growing population of the village, and the failure of water supplies to keep pace with people's needs. Women, not men, collect water, and there were repeated complaints about the length of time required, and the restrictions on allowances per home. Cooking (also women's work) now requires charcoal, as there are fewer trees on farms. There were also three cases of female-headed households who had lost access to land through family or neighbour disputes, or because their husbands had died leaving them childless, and therefore with no access to their husband's family land. Older female headed households were particularly unlikely to see an improvement in their assets (Table 8.8).

Finally, it bears repeating that assets are but one aspect of prosperity. The families I visited, in the main, had enjoyed a recent cash injection from which they had invested in assets. But there are many other dimensions of poverty that remain untouched by this welcome change. The standards and ease of accessing health and educational services, expenditure, care for the long term sick and elderly, basic measures of dignity, and so on are all ignored by this survey. Our methods and sources do not allow us to make the long-term comparisons required to document the changes (or lack thereof) that have occurred here. But that does not make them any less important.

The restrictions of looking at assets is best illustrated by our question 'has life improved for you now compared to 2000?' In response some 43 per cent of respondents felt that life was improving, 40 per cent felt that it had got worse, and 15 per cent of people felt it was as hard as ever. When 55 per cent of a sample insist that life is worse now, or as bad, as it was sixteen years ago, and when life was indeed hard sixteen years ago, then that majority is a significant finding. Particularly because, when answering that question, even those who felt life had got better usually qualified that by insisting that the improvement was marginal at best.

Growing Poverty and Inequality

However the other crucial difference between the state of the village now and earlier is that there are trends towards class formation and inequality that indicate that the fortunes of new cash crops are not universally enjoyed. The primary evidence for this is that there is now a substantial group of households—around 44 per cent of the village—who are characterized as not having their own lands and

Table 8.9 Wealth groups and their distribution in the study site

Group	Typical Characteristics	Number of domestic units	Proportion
1	Has a good house with a tiled floor and electricity (solar), and water inside the house A 20-acre farm, a shop and cars; has goats, pigs, and 100 cows; has a huge store of crops—100 sacks; does not do casual labour	4	<1
2	Has a good home with cement walls/floor and solar and water at the home; has a 10-acre farm; a pikipiki and a bicycle; has around 5 cows, goats, and pigs; does not do casual labour	44	4
3	Has a metal roof and solar; has a 5-acre farm and a bicycle; owns 2 cows, 5 goats, and a plough; pays for kibarua work and does some kibarua work (ploughing with family oxen)	116	11
4	Burnt-brick house roofed with grass not metal roof; no electricity; no water at home; has chickens, goats, and pigs but no cows; has a bicycle but not a plough; does kibarua work	369	34
5	Rented house; no solar; dependent on casual labour; some do not rent a farm; some rent a 0.5–2-acre farm	472	44
6	Homeless and destitute	6	1
Unknown		71	7
Total		1082	

Source: Author's data.

working for other people (Table 8.9). This is not a category of people that existed in large numbers in 2000. Rather almost everyone farmed, and those who did not have their own, but rented, were so few that we were able to organize a second survey in 2000 examine why they did not have their own plot.

Casual labourers earn relatively low sums. With board and lodging included it can be just 2,000/– per day, less than one dollar. Otherwise labourers are paid by the area, which means that weeding an acre of rice for 50,000 shillings can be five days work, or ten days, depending on the weed load. These are not sums that will make people wealthy quickly.

This group exists partly because Mtowisa has a relatively large collection of housing stock to rent rooms in. There is often casual work to be had, and the recent boom in sesame seed created a good deal of work. It has attracted immigrants who rent rooms in the new houses sesame seed farmers have built. There are also migrants who are drawn to the lake—and the sometimes wealthy fishermen are not well captured in the wealth rankings the focus groups created. Nevertheless it is plain that the sesame seed boom is not a universally experienced blessing. Those farmers with the land and means to farm it have profited. But it is creating new forms of differentiation.

The sesame seed cash injection is therefore concomitant with an incipient process of class formation in the village which has seen the differentiation of families into those who own their own land and those who can subsist by renting out their labour. The complete survey taken in 2000 is no longer a good characterization of the village. As inevitably happens in longitudinal and panel surveys, a new baseline is required.

Ironically, however, at the same time as inequality appears to be increasing, local tolerance of it also appears to be growing. Focus groups at the feedback meeting in 2018 suggested that the increased wealth reflected immigration and mixing of different tribes and that this reduced the 'bad jealousy' that used to hold people back. The same was discussed more informally in bars and during casual conversation. Commentators noted that the elders used to have the power to control where and when rain fell, which was advantageous, but that these same elders would curse, and thus kill, people who became too successful. Now both powers are gone. Wealth accumulation that was once controlled by curses, death threats, and fears now faces fewer impediments.[5]

Conclusion

The changes we have recorded here—both the increased wealth and the attendant rise in inequality—derive in part because this village has become more closely integrated into the global capitalist system. The improved roads and communications infrastructure have seen crop prices rise at the farm gate.

The developments at Mtowisa thus fit with the fifth element of Hall's typology of forms of land grabbing, that of 'commercialisation in situ'. She describes this as small-scale producers being incorporated into commercial value changes (Hall 2011). The attendant consequences, in the context of a closed land frontier, is a new prevalence of landlessness that is the obverse of the local forms of accumulation that we have documented here. As Hall and colleagues later observed,

[5] The specific advantages mentioned during these discussions were that when road building contractors had been working on roads in the rainy season they were then able to go to the weather controllers and persuade them to keep the rains of specific parts of their construction sites at sensitive times. Whether or not this is actually true, it is a social fact, people believed it and that belief constrained their own personal improvement plans.

the important issue for understanding poverty dynamics in such developments is not whether this shows that small or large farms are better but rather 'how different farming models co-exist and the ways in which poor people can navigate opportunities among them' (Hall et al. 2017: 532). Accordingly as these forms of commercialization and in situ accumulation spread throughout Tanzania we need to understand how the opportunities and the misfortunes they present are negotiated.

In this instance we must note that the driving forces of change are also fickle. Sesame seed has been hit by a disease which did not respond to treatment and which has made the crop too unreliable to be farmed any more. The crop price fluctuates considerably and there is no government support mechanism to tide farmers over the vicissitudes of global demand. Cash hungry farmers are now turning to more reliable cash crops (sunflower) as well as irrigated vegetables for their money. The mechanisms which allowed some farmers to become less poor, indeed prosperous with respect to their assets, have not allowed sustained reduction in poverty.

Notwithstanding the mechanisms the point is that assets matter. They matter both as a means of external observers to record change, and to local determinations of a good life. Understandings of poverty dynamics in peasant populations have to take account of the local definitions and meanings of wealth and the things that peasants themselves count as important. They are not well-served by measures of prosperity which preclude the possibility of counting investment which matters to rural people—which is clearly the case with commonly used consumption-based surveys. These are not well placed to track the 'mores of consumption and the utilities of wealth' in Tanzanian contexts.[6]

Many of the families with whom I spoke place considerable significance on the major purchases that they will need to make in order to have a good life and provide for their children. They will need to buy a plot (150,000/=), build a good house (300,000–500,000/=), buy land (400,000/= an acre for un-irrigated land), buy oxen (200,000/= a head), and a plough (150,000/=). And most of the families in this sample were taking significant steps in building that asset base. These purchases, so vital in local notions of progress, are not captured in poverty-line data.

Or to put this more generally, understanding investment in productive assets and houses will be central to answering three of the four questions of Bernstein's haiku—'Who owns what? Who does what? Who gets what? And, what do they do with it?' (Bernstein 2010: 22). This will require more longitudinal studies which track and explain change in asset portfolios. Doing so will help us to understand what forms of poverty persist amongst whom.

[6] The phrase is Steve Wiggins pers. comm. 14 March 2019. Consumption surveys are useful if they track the economic utility (or benefits) of expenditure, but less useful if they miss such expenditure.

References

Bernstein, H. (2010). *Class Dynamics of Agrarian Change*. Halifx and Winnipeg, Fernwood Publishing.

Brockington, D. (2001). 'Communal Property and Degradation Narratives: Debating the Sukuma Immigration into Rukwa Region, Tanzania.' *Cahiers d'Afrique* 20: 1–22.

Brockington, D. (2006). 'The Politics and Ethnography of Environmentalisms in Tanzania.' *African Affairs* 105(418): 97–116.

Brockington, D. (2007). 'Devolution, Community Conservation and Forests: On Local Government Performance and Village Forest Reserves in Tanzania.' *Society and Natural Resources* 20: 835–48.

Brockington, D. (2008). 'Corruption, Taxation, Democracy and Natural Resource Management in Tanzania.' *Journal of Development Studies* 44(1): 103–26.

Chambers, R. (1981). 'Rural Poverty Unperceived: Problems and Remedies.' *World Development* 9(1): 1–19.

Corbera, E., A. Martin, O. Springate-Baginski, and A. Villaseñor (2017). 'Sowing the Seeds of Sustainable Rural Livelihoods? An Assessment of Participatory Forest Management through REDD+ in Tanzania.' *Land Use Policy*. DOI: 10.1016/j.landusepol.2017.09.037.

Foster, G. M. (1965). 'Peasant Society and the Image of Limited Good.' *American Anthropologist* 67(2): 293–315.

Hall, R. (2011). 'Land Grabbing in Southern Africa: The Many Faces of the Investor Rush.' *Review of African Political Economy* 38(128): 193–214.

Hall, R., I. Scoones, and D. Tsikata (2017). 'Forum: Land and Agricultural Commercialisation in Africa. Plantations, Outgrowers and Commercial Farming in Africa: Agricultural Commercialisation and Implications for Agrarian Change.' *Journal of Peasant Studies* 44(3): 515–37.

Mashindano, O. and P. Kihenzile (2013). 'Assessment of Practices of Agricultural Production, Marketing and Domestic Trade Policies in Tanzania.' ESRF Discussion Paper 45. Dar es Salaam, Economic and Social Research Foundation.

Mueller, B. E. T. (2011). 'The Agrarian Question in Tanzania: Using New Evidence to Reconcile an Old Debate.' *Review of African Political Economy* 38(127): 23–42.

United Republic of Tanzania (URT) (2009). 'Household Budget Survey 2007 Main Report.' Dodoma, National Bureau of Statistics.

United Republic of Tanzania (URT) (2019). 'Tanzania Mainland. Key Indicators Report. 2017–18 Household Budget Survey.' Dodoma, National Bureau of Statistics.

9

Self-Made Farmers and Sustainable Change?

Entrepreneurs and Development in Goima and Mirambu

Wilhelm Östberg, Joseph Mduma, and Dan Brockington

Epilogue pages 406–409

Introduction: Environmentalism in Tanzania

Tanzania's commitment to environmentalism and conservation is essential to the country's identity, politics, and economy. It defines it geographically, in that an extraordinarily high percentage of its land area (close to 40 per cent) is protected and denied to human use and habitation. The only other African country which comes close is Botswana, and that nation has a population approximately one-thirtieth the size of Tanzania's. It matters historically in that the Arusha Manifesto, ghost-written for President Nyerere by the WWF, stated a commitment to maintain conservation policies begun in the colonial and mandate eras. It is vital politically, as Tanzania's determination to pursue strong conservation policies, including violent anti-poaching measures and expanding its conservation estate reflects the enduring influence, ideological and financial, of what Brockington has called an 'environmental-conservation complex' (Brockington 2006).

But Tanzania is not merely an environmental state, it is an environmental nation. Belief in and support for environmental protection emanates from the most basic levels of Tanzanian society. There is widespread belief that tree cover and rainfall are causally linked, with the former causing the later, even at the smallest scales. This does not mean that people do not cut down trees, they do so abundantly (McNicol et al. 2018). Tanzania loses 400,000 ha forest annually, and is among the ten countries in the world that has the largest net loss of forest area (Kideghesho 2015). There is also pressure on water and grazing resources which is driven by smallholder use, as well as by large-scale land alienations impacts on smallholders (Bluwstein et al. 2018). But rural Tanzanians are vocal and

Wilhelm Östberg, Joseph Mduma, and Dan Brockington, *Self-Made Farmers and Sustainable Change? Entrepreneurs and Development in Goima and Mirambu* In: *Prosperity in Rural Africa? Insights into Wealth, Assets, and Poverty from Longitudinal Studies in Tanzania*. Edited by: Dan Brockington and Christine Noe, Oxford University Press. DOI: 10.1093/oso/9780198865872.003.0009

concerned about the collective consequences of these changes. It is part of everyday discussion (Brockington 2006). Contests over village resources are also contests over contrasting understandings and interpretations of environmental change.

Environmental pressures and environmental concerns are surprisingly muted in many of the chapters in this collection. These were villages where land frontiers had closed. The stories are of intensification and changing crops or social relations. However, in the area discussed here, environmental change, and anxiety about environmental change, are themes that are uppermost on many people's minds.

As in many other chapters we describe remarkable change in the fortunes of once poor rural farmers (as measured in assets). As in other villages this is a qualified success, and, as in other villages, it is driven by smallholder efforts. However in this area the role of intensification (reduced fallow time) and extensification (increased farm area) is clearer than anywhere else. Villagers have been reaping nature's subsidy—the fertile soils that freshly cut forest provides. As we shall see this raises important questions about the sustainability of the transformations we describe.

Methods and Context: Studying and Re-studying Goima and Mirambu

The case study reported in the present chapter originates from environmental concerns. The study site is close to the Kondoa Irangi Highlands in Central Tanzania, infamous for its devastating problems of land degradation (Tanzania 1977, Mung'ong'o 1995). Already the colonial government initiated ambitious rehabilitation interventions, which from the mid-1970s were further intensified, leading among many other things to the radical measure to evict in 1979 all livestock from the 125,600 ha so-called Kondoa Eroded Area. The interventions met with considerable local resistance (Östberg 1986 and 2000, Mung'ong'o 1995), but they had effect; notable landscape changes were registered (Östberg 1986, Backéus et al. 1994 and 1996, Mbegu 1996). In the early 1990s a comprehensive research project studied both landscape changes and the effects of the rehabilitation efforts.[1]

The Burunge Hills border on the Kondoa Eroded Area (Figure 9.1). In the early 1990s, the starting point for this study, the Burunge Hills were notably much better preserved than the Kondoa Highlands. At the time, this appeared something of an enigma. The two areas shared many characteristics: types of soils and bedrock, rainfall patterns, crops grown, livestock kept. Why had the Burunge Hills fared so

[1] The 'Man-Land Interrelations in Central Tanzania' project, jointly run by The Institute of Resource Assessment, University of Dar es Salaam, and the School of Geography, Stockholm University (Christiansson et al. 1991, Christiansson and Kikula 1996).

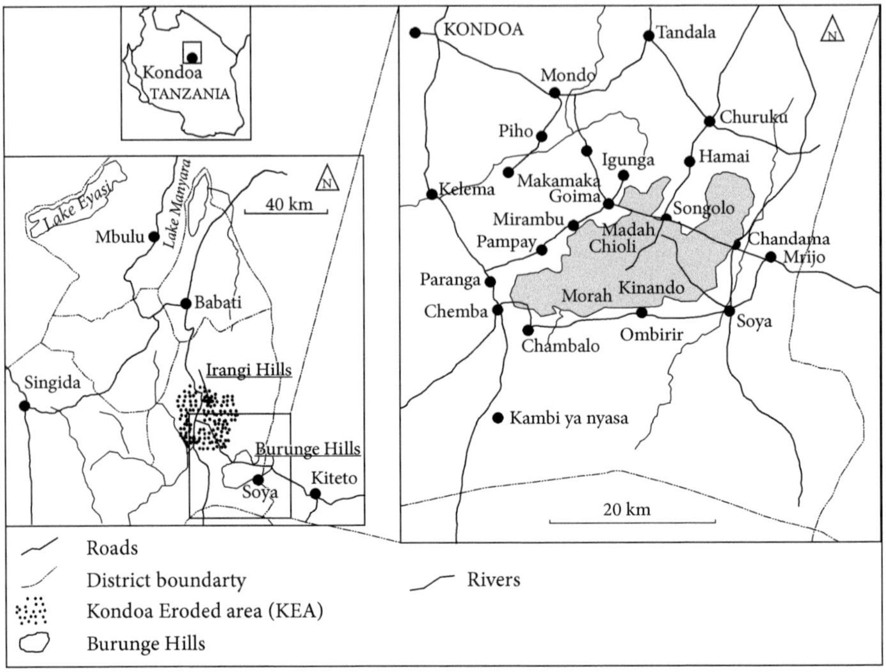

Figure 9.1 Goima and Mirambu villages on foot slopes of the Burunge Hills, south-east of Kondoa town, and the Kondoa Eroded Area.

much better than the Kondoa Highlands? It fell on Östberg, as a member of the research project studying 'man-land' (sic) interactions in Kondoa, to find this out.

Joseph Mduma, of the Tanzanian Forestry Department, which was the organization responsible for the extensive land rehabilitation project in the Kondoa Eroded area, teamed up with Östberg. They worked in two villages, Goima and Mirambu, on the western slopes of the Burunge Hills, situated in the Chemba District, as well as in the hills. Between 1991 and 1994 they lived in the area for periods of two to three months at a time, interrupted by periods of three to four months for analysis and writing-up. In 1991–3 they carried out a comprehensive survey among 10 per cent of the households in the two villages during different times of the cultivation year (farm sizes, crops, household composition, livestock, etc.). The data collected formed the basis for the re-study in 2016 of the area.

Follow-up visits were made in 1997, 2006, and 2007. In 2005 the area was visited by a Dutch sociologist Monique Slegers, and we could draw on her findings (Slegers and Östberg 2008, Östberg and Slegers 2010). When the two villages were restudied for the 'Long-term Livelihood Change in Tanzania' research project, Mduma and Östberg were joined by the project's team members Olivia Howland, Cathbert Mwanyika, and Einhard Mwanyika.

Table 9.1 Success rates in recontacting original families

Characteristic	Goima	Mirambu
Wealth group 1	100%	100%
Wealth group 2	69%	81%
Wealth group 3	63%	92%
Male-headed	65%	91%
Female-headed	71%	77%

In 2016 (two visits, with an additional follow-up visit in 2018) we tried to locate all the households interviewed in 1991–3. The levels of attrition are relatively low (Table 9.1). Moreover, there is no tendency in the data for the attrition to affect particular groups. In particular, given that the villages appear to have got richer (as we shall see) we have to be clear that this is not due to poorer families who were once present having now just disappeared, through death or migration. Table 9.1 shows that there is no trend for higher attrition rates in the poorest groups across both villages: attrition is slightly higher among the poorest in Goima (37 per cent missing as compared to 31 per cent from wealth group 2), but lower in Mirambu (only 8 per cent missing when compared to 19 per cent in wealth group 2).

Nor could we spot any consistent trend in terms of attrition of dual- and female-headed households across both of the villages, with attrition in female-headed households being lower than the dual-headed households in Goima (29 per cent as compared to 35 per cent) and higher in Mirambu (23 per cent compared to 9 per cent).

We have grouped the 1991/3 categories 2 and 3 into category 2 and categories 4–6 into category 3. The 100 per cent re-contact rate for the richest families is misleading because there are only three families in those cells.

The changing composition of households over time has made some changes to the presence of female-headed households in the follow up in Mirambu alone. In the original survey 50 per cent of households in Goima, and 38 per cent in Mirambu, were female-headed. In the revisited group the proportion changes to 47 per cent and 20 per cent.

However we can get a deeper picture of the forms of bias that might be at work if we look beneath headline wealth categories to the construction of family units. There is a sadly long history of talking about societies using terms like family or household in unreflective ways. These can obscure gender or generational dynamics, or simply fail to mention how a household unit was defined (Randall et al. 2011, Randall and Coast 2015). As explored in Chapter 4 of this volume, family units are often essential to understand the changes in assets which we explore, but they have to be examined carefully.

For the work of the 1991 survey, Östberg and Mduma used village rosters from Goima and Mirambu to construct the sample frame. The basic unit, in the view of the village offices, was a 'kaya' (household) which they more specifically defined as a 'house'. This was made up of people sharing a roof. This definition meant that an aged and/or sickly person sleeping in his/her own dwelling would count as a separate domestic unit, even if he/she on a daily basis was provided with food from relatives, or neighbours. They typically would have only a small piece of land, an aged house of low quality, and they did not own much more than the clothes they wore. In the wealth rankings, people in this category were usually described as 'helpless'. The advantage with following the local practice of registering them as a separate domestic unit was, from the point of view of our survey, that these cases of poverty were not concealed (they constituted 7 per cent of the sample). However, for the 2016 re-survey these units have largely disappeared—they had died. Ours is a record therefore of what happened to the people who have survived long enough to talk to returning researchers.

Nevertheless it appears that Goima and Mirambu villages are rather stable social entities. Moreover, the households provided a useful unit to record changes of assets, which we use as one dimension to capture the transformation the area has gone through over a period of twenty-five years. Still, we must note that there are aspects of this story which are not told here. We do not, for instance, have data on the contests over what sorts of assets (cows, land, farms, houses, education) to invest in. Such issues must form the subject of other investigations.

Goima and Mirambu Villages in the Early 1990s

At the time of the original study, Goima was the headquarters of Goima division, then in Kondoa District, and should have been in a position to attract development interventions. It did not. Goima was being bypassed by other lowland villages like Chandama, Jangalo, Mrijo, Songolo, Soya, and the then recently established settlements in the Burunge Hills, like Madah. Those were the places that traders from Arusha and Dodoma visited to buy crops. There immigrants cleared in the forests and sure enough got bumper harvests from the virgin lands. Small shops and canteens were opened, new schools started, nascent churches and mosques appeared while Goima remained dormant.

Our original study also included Mirambu village, situated along a poor road heading southwest from Goima, difficult to pass during rains. Mirambu was to represent an 'ordinary' village where the administration was less obviously present, and also because its economy was said to be more based on livestock than was the case in Goima.

In the early 1990s, people in both Goima and Mirambu villages were poor. Half of the households could not support themselves on their land (Östberg 1995: 40–4) but had to take on day labour for others to make ends meet. Admittedly 1991–4 were dry years, which of course worsened the situation, but the Burunge in fact had a long history of doing casual work in neighbouring areas, and memories of famines when large parts of the population had left the area were still present.

This notwithstanding, the Burunge of the early 1990s perceived their land to be vast and resourceful. They envisaged their country as an almost endless expanse of land. This attitude rhymed with their mode of production. A field was cultivated for one to three years, and then fallowed for at least three years. During clearing, tree stumps and roots were left in the field so that vegetation would regenerate fast. The basic principle of farming was to capture the strength of newly cleared land. Soil fertility was continuously replenished by the forest.

Many Burunge felt assured that as long as the forest remains, life would return even if droughts bring suffering. The forest also provided meat, honey, berries, green leaves, and wood products (Östberg 1995: 56, 118–27). The paradox was that while the living conditions of many Burunge were poor by modern standards, they still felt that their forests and their land were abundant. Immigrants could count on a permissive attitude to land: Oaymo da hida sliimaa, 'a field is for everyone'.[2]

The men cleared the forest, while both men and women cultivated the land. Hand hoes were the common agricultural implement, although some ploughed with oxen, or, fewer, with tractors (Table 9.2). Immigrants invariably used ploughs and cultivated permanent fields. The early 1990s saw the beginning of a transition from rotational bush fallow to permanent fields.

Drought-tolerant bulrush millet and sorghum were cultivated, as was finger millet. Both local demand and the beer industry at Arusha made growing finger millet profitable (Kawa 1993: 77, Östberg 1995: 192–4). Maize was appreciated as a food and was easier to market than bulrush millet, and was therefore grown

Table 9.2 Mode of cultivation (%) in Goima and Mirambu villages, 1991/3 (farmers) and 2016 (plots)

	Goima 1991/3	Goima 2016	Mirambu 1991/3	Mirambu 2016
Hand hoes	64	17	66	31
Ox plough	18	18	27	25
Tractor	18	65	7	44
n	50	54	45	127

Goima: χ^2=29.84, df=2, p<0.001; Mirambu: χ^2=13.07, df=2, p<0.002.

[2] This key phrase is reproduced in the Burunge language, while other terms are Swahili words, which was the language used in the field studies.

although its water requirements made it a less well-suited crop in this semi-arid area.[3] Yields were generally low, as was true of Dodoma region as a whole.

The Burunge traditionally lived in the hills, and on the flats surrounding the Burunge Hills. During Tanzania's villagization process in the 1970s people were moved off the hills and settled in villages. By the mid-1980s this policy was no longer as strictly enforced as before, and some families returned to their old settlements and fields. They were soon followed by immigrants from other areas, notably the Kondoa Eroded Area, who wanted to benefit from the restored soils in the hills. Immigrants also arrived in Goima and Mirambu villages, and in the early 1990s a quarter of the population in Goima identified with other ethnic groups. In Mirambu village the corresponding figure was 16 per cent. In most neighbouring communities, the immigrants were in majority and the proportion of immigrants have continued to grow.

Goima and Mirambu Some Twenty-Five Years Later, First Impressions

The road! It is wide and with a gravel surface. In the early 1990s an old, battered, and erratic bus passed through Goima in the morning on its way to Kiteto, returning in the afternoon. Now, frequent buses link Goima to Kondoa, Babati, Dodoma, Singida, Iringa, Dar es Salaam, Tanga, and beyond.

Goima village has a new skyline. There is electricity, and a communication tower. A new spacious mosque, a newly built, sizeable church for Kanisa la Mungu (God's church), a secondary school. The Catholic church is there as before. There are many new permanent buildings with high-raised roofs covered with metal sheets. One can buy stationary, photocopies, cosmetics, spare parts for motorcycles, cement, and diesel. Such goods were not on sale in Goima in the early 1990s.

Mobile phones are everywhere; buses, tractors, lorries, motorcycles travel the roads. Goima has become connected. It is not that there were no motorcycles twenty-five years ago. The Executive Officer of Goima Division had one at his disposal, as did the Ward Forest Officer, and the Agricultural Officer. But by 2016 there were more than thirty-five motorcycles in the village, privately owned, and the number is increasing by the day.

The transformation has coincided with population growth. The number of households in Goima grew more than 2.5 times from 1991 to 2016, from 507 to 1350, and in Mirambu, it almost doubled, from 350 to 672. The increase is faster

[3] Goima area has a semi-arid climate with an average annual precipitation of below 550mm. The rain falls between November and May with the rest of the year being very dry. Rainfall is both scarce and unpredictable.

than the annual population increase in the Dodoma Region, which was 2.1 per cent during the last inter-censal period (2002–12).

Mirambu village does not look that different from how it was twenty-five years ago, although there now are more houses, and the farming areas have been expanded considerably. The primary school has been extended and it is well maintained. The village office looks just as it did twenty-five years ago. The truly modern houses in Mirambu are few.

In both villages, commercial life has expanded dramatically. In Goima, shops are almost four times as many as they were twenty-five years ago, and they are much better stocked. The number of grinding mills and oil presses have more than doubled. There are now seven tractors based in Goima as compared to just one in the early 1990s and 128 ploughs. Likewise, Mirambu is today better endowed with facilities when compared to the early 1990s. There are three tractors, three power tillers, and three grinding mills in the village, twenty-eight motorcycles, no less than 106 ploughs (in a village of 672 households), and twenty-five solar panels.[4]

The Crucial Water Issue

One of the biggest changes to the area is the improved water supply. In the early 1990s, the water situation was desperate. At least one member of most households, often a child, spent hours every day during the long dry season drawing water for household needs from wells that were dug deep into dry riverbeds situated kilometres away from home. Any discussion about farming and livelihoods started and ended with the comment 'if only it rains' (Östberg 1995: 31). What can you do when there is not enough water for people, crops, or livestock?

Today, there is a large water body at Adia in a valley that is just west of Goima. In 2016, a large earth wall was constructed leading seasonal water from a gully into the valley and a shallow lake developed. In November 2016, just before the rainy season, it still contained water. Livestock could be watered closer to home instead of having to be taken to distant watering points at Kelema River. People could also get water from wells in the sand fans immediately below the new water reservoir. The changes that access to water has brought to the village cannot be overestimated. Apart from making life so much easier, and improving people's chances to enjoy better hygiene, it has also made it possible to expand livestock herds and to undertake new building projects. Water for consumption is furthermore ferried into Goima village, at cut cost, by two of the new entrepreneurs in

[4] Details are provided in Östberg et al. (2018, table 2), available on open access at https://www.mdpi.com/2073-445X/7/2/44/htm

the village because they, as they say, see the need and want to contribute to the area's well-being.

The water situation has improved also in Mirambu when compared to the early 1990s. A Christian NGO, Compassion, has drilled a borehole for a children's support centre that they have run in the village since 2014. They offer water for households for 100 Tz sh a jerry can (about US$0.04 at the time of writing). The new lake at Adia similarly eases life for the Mirambu livestock keepers.

Both villages have a long history of failed water projects. In the early 1990s, we documented all water projects we could find evidence of from the colonial period up to the time of our stay in the area. It became a catalogue of good intentions, plans, attempts, and failures. We learned about dams, boreholes, wells, rain ceremonies, prayers. It seemed everything had been tried. Yet there still was not water in Goima and Mirambu. And now there is this large water expanse surrounded by low hills. What had happened was that one of the entrepreneurs/grain traders in Goima had hired a grader from the Roads Department, working on the new road in Goima, and had an embankment built which forced water to move towards the natural depression in the landscape. Infrastructural development initiatives are no longer in the hands of the authorities but happens at private initiatives.

After more than half a century's attempts to get water in Goima, it is now there. The lake is shallow and two or three consecutive dry years will, people fear, make it dry up again. The wall leading water into the depression is anything but permanent and will need to be reinforced at some time. But for the moment there is water reasonably close to Goima, and after all these years it seems a miracle. The way it happened, however, is no miracle but tells how the transformation of the area now happens.

The Farming Boom

Briefly put, it appears that most households in Goima and Mirambu have prospered, and this is because they are able to farm more. In the early 1990s, farming in Goima and Mirambu was largely undertaken with hand hoes with 64 per cent and 66 per cent respectively of land cultivated thus. Tractors were used by 18 per cent in Goima[5] and 7 in Mirambu. By 2016, 65 per cent in Goima and 44 in Mirambu used tractor (Table 9.2). The farmed areas grew correspondingly.

In both Goima and Mirambu, the median size of cultivated land had been three acres (1.2ha) while the mean land owned was 6.7 acres (2.7ha) and eight acres (3.2ha) respectively. By 2016, the mean cultivated area (not the area owned) had increased, in Goima to 6.5 acres (2.6 ha) and in Mirambu to 7.4 acres (3ha—Table 9.3).

[5] A survey carried out by extension agents showed that by 1997, 24 per cent of Goima farmers used tractors (Dejene et al. 1997: 31).

Table 9.3 Land farmed (acres) in Goima and Mirambu villages 1991/3–2016

	Goima	Mirambu
Average land farmed 1991/2	4	3.7
Average land farmed 2016	6.5	7.4
n	14	26

This table only uses paired families from the original visit and subsequent revisit; excludes 5 outlier families from 1993. Pair Sample test for both villages: $t = -2.279$, $df = 39$, $p < 0.029$.

The expanded land use has been made possible by improved farming technology. The dominance of hand hoes has been replaced by the dominance of tractors in Goima. Levels of ox ploughing remain unchanged. Now, only minorities (17 per cent in Goima and 31 per cent in Mirambu) cultivate land with hand hoes. This growth of farms is clearly visible in the landscape with much more land, on the plains and in the hills, put to use.

The expansion of land used is particularly important because the local definitions of poverty associate it not so much with landlessness as with an inability to use land owned properly because the families lack the capital or labour to do so. Working the land well requires money for ploughing, good seeds, manure, and/or chemical inputs. Poverty is expressed by not being able to use land as well as one might—by not being able to generate an income from assets. Thus, the expansion in land cultivated, made possible by greater access to tractors, is both likely to be a driver of wealth increase (it increases production and returns) and an expression of that greater wealth.

The farming boom in Goima and Mirambu is not associated with intensified production. In the early 1990s no Goima or Mirambu farmers in our sample used any farm inputs. The picture had not changed by 2016. Only 4 per cent of the farmers in the Goima and Mirambu samples for the early 1990s used manure in their fields, and quite sparsely at that. In 2016, 5 per cent of the Goima farmers used manure, while none in the Mirambu sample did. A district by-law stipulates that manure must be removed from the cattle enclosures and used in the fields. This was rarely enforced at the time of our visit. Villagers cited lack of transport and fear that manure increased pest incidence.

Five per cent of the Goima farmers used improved seeds, but other farm inputs were not used. Neither in Goima, nor in Mirambu, do any shops stock improved seeds. In this respect, Goima and Mirambu are still, in 2016, relatively remote outposts.

Although no farm inputs are used, yields of maize are much higher now than in the original survey (Table 9.4). The comparison is, however, unreliable as the original yield data were collected during a particularly dry period when

Table 9.4 Yield per acre (kg) of different stable crops in the two study sites

Crop	1991/3		2016	
	Goima	Mirambu	Goima	Mirambu
Bullrush millet	146	NA	420	NA
Maize	258	147	556	875
Sorghum	170	133	480	238

Goima: x^2=7.85, df=2, p<0.02; Mirambu: x^2=78.1, df=1, p<0.001.

respondents were bemoaning their unproductive farms. Our hypothesis is that there has in fact been little real change in the productivity per unit area. The current yield figures reflect, we hypothesize, the fact that many new or recently opened fields are used, with their good natural fertility, and also that tractor ploughing can be more thorough than hand hoes (but will have more profound long-term impacts on soil fertility).

Cash crops have grown in importance, as has trading. In addition to maize, bulrush millet, finger millet, and sorghum, people also grow sunflower, pigeon peas, green grams, cow peas, pumpkins, watermelon, and other 'small crops'. Cash crops became important in the late 1990s, and particularly sunflower has a stable and good market. Village focus groups discussing our findings insisted that the most important cash crop that was driving the new-found wealth was sunflowers.

Increased wealth in land is matched by the trends in livestock ownership (Table 9.5). In the early 1990s, 18 per cent of families owned livestock in both Goima and Mirambu. By 2016, 32 per cent of the households in Goima owned cows, and 38 per cent in Mirambu. Mean herd size for cattle owners has risen substantially to 10.5 in both of the villages, from 2.7 in Goima and 0.6 in Mirambu. More cattle also means more livestock-powered goods, such as carts and ploughs, which have increased almost five times.

There has also been a growth in the incidence of smallstock ownership. In the early 1990s, 23 per cent of families in Goima had smallstock. This had risen to 39 per cent in 2016. In Mirambu, smallstock ownership has more than doubled from 23 per cent of families to 49 per cent. There are signs that the increased wealth in Mirambu has in particular strengthened the cattle economy, while the increased resources in Goima have been used for improved housing, farm expansion, and education.

We have registered how the profits from farming have led to increased number of tractors and motorcycles, improved housing, more consumer goods, investment in livestock, and so on. What we do not have figures for are the sizeable sums that leave the area to be invested in business and real estate in Kondoa, Dodoma, and other towns.

Table 9.5 Percentage of families owning cattle and shoats, Goima and Mirambu villages

	Goima 1991/3	Goima 2016	Mirambu 1991/3	Mirambu 2016
Cattle	18	32	18	34
Shoats	24	39	18	49
n	51	34	45	41

Goima: x^2=4.57, df=2, $p<0.1$; Mirambu: x^2=12.4, df=2, $p<0.005$.

Improved Livelihoods

Asked about what the main changes during the last decades have been, people commonly emphasized that they now live in better houses and that all children attend school. Housing quality was not recorded in the original survey, simply because virtually all the people at that time lived in tembe houses (wattle and daub houses with mud roofs). In 2016, 76 per cent of people in Goima lived in houses with galvanized metal sheet roofs, which was mentioned in focus groups in both Goima and Mirambu as a key signifier of wealth. In Mirambu, 67 per cent of interviewees lived in houses with roofs covered by metal sheets. This is a clear, and much appreciated, change to the early 1990s when only the very richest families lived in houses of this type.

The fact that all children now attend school is likewise a widely appreciated change. The fact that girls attend to the same extent as boys was highlighted in our focus group meetings. Admittedly this happened in a public arena where equality between genders is an expected attitude, but our understanding is that this is a widely shared sentiment, and an irrefutable change compared to twenty-five years ago.

In both villages, casual work (kibarua in Swahili), which was the affliction and economic mainstay of the early 1990s, had by 2016 been drastically reduced. Indeed, the proportion of people that are undertaking it has generally halved (Table 9.6). This major turn is, in our opinion, the most significant change over the last twenty-five years despite the profound material changes that anyone can observe in Goima village centre. That no longer half the number of households must rely on casual labour to be able to provide for themselves changes everything. Interestingly, many in Goima and Mirambu, are not as impressed as we are, as we shall see below.

Moreover, the meaning of casual labour has changed. In the early 1990s, being dependent on kibarua was what defined poverty. Payment was low, often the load of grains that you could carry home after a couple of days' or a week's work. Attendance to the home fields suffered, meaning reduced harvests, in addition to the strain on family life with one or more adults being away from home for long

Table 9.6 Casual work in Goima and Mirambu villages (proportion of sample)

	Goima 1991/3	Goima 2016	Mirambu 1991/3	Mirambu 2016
Employing casual labour	22	21	15	15
Performing casual labour	76	44	73	39
N	42	34	40	41

Goima: x^2=5.8, df=1, $p<0.02$; Mirambu: x^2=16.0, df=1, $p<0.001$.

periods. In 2016, the situation was different. Now some, particularly young people, took on casual work 'to better their lives', for instance to be able to buy a goat, or metal sheets for roofing, and not to 'hunt for food'.

Changing Perceptions of Wealth and Quality of Life

In the 1990s, in both of the villages, well-off families were those who could feed themselves. The catch-all term that villagers used to rank the households was uwezo (strength, ability), or their nafasi (literally 'space', but here, rather 'possibilities'). Those who were poor were described as people who lack strength (hana uwezo). The guiding principle was a household's ability to cultivate the land, rather than the size of the land holding itself. Capacity to plough with oxen or tractors and to hire farm labour meant that a household was regarded as well-off.

Note that wealth was not necessarily about owning the oxen (or tractors) per se, rather it focussed on the potential to produce food and to solve problems. The poorest families were those who had to work as farm labourers to meet their daily needs, and in there was also a category of people who were dependent on others to survive (Östberg 1995: 40–3).

Wealth rankings in 2005 provided findings that were rather similar to the 1990s. More than half of the households could not support themselves from their own farms. Day labouring continued to be an important aspect of life in the villages. Farm size had now become more important as a criterion of wealth (Slegers and Östberg 2008: 141–2).

When focus groups defined wealth groups in 2016, two major changes were obvious. First, a significant majority of the families were classified by villagers as being of medium wealth. Poverty (locally defined) was no longer a dominant experience. The middle groups had expanded, while the poorest categories had contracted (Table 9.7). In Mirambu, our informants said that the big change is that many poor households have moved to the category 'ordinary people'.

Table 9.7 Changing wealth profiles—proportion of families in different wealth classes

Wealth group	Goima			Mirambu		
	1993	2005	2016	1993	2005	2016
1	2	4	0.5	2	8	6
2	45	41	64	48	37	71
3	53	55	35	50	55	23

Goima 2005–16: x^2=76.6, df=2, $p<0.001$; Mirambu 2005–16: x^2=43.4, df=2, $p<0.001$. Wealth group 3 follows the Mirambu classification which combines categories 3 and 4 of the 2016 categories. We have grouped categories 2 and 3 of the 1991/3 survey into category 2 of the 2016 survey. We have grouped categories 4–6 of the 1991/3 survey into category 3 of the 2016 survey. We have grouped categories 4–6 of the 2005 survey into category 3 of the 2016 survey. Note that in 2016 Goima is based on the complete village lists and Mirambu from some vitongoji (sub-villages).

By 2016 there was a considerable shift in the meaning and definition of wealth.[6] Uwezo remained the factor upon which wealth is determined, but this now means new things. Now it was no longer a matter of being able to work one's land but included being able to afford health care, and to pay for educating one's children, as well as quality of housing. Investments, like owning a tractor or a milling machine, were points of reference for the wealthiest. Trading now also appeared as a means for people to better their lives. These all indicate a more diversified economy and improved livelihoods.

Also in Mirambu, the meaning of poverty had changed: the poor are now defined as those who have 'only' a few cattle, and these are put in the same group as those who have none and have to do casual work to keep going. In other words people who are currently counted as poor are designated as such because they do not have things that were once the property of a privileged few. So, not only are there more wealthy families, but the standards of what it means to be wealthy have risen.

Interestingly, while records of assets and farming activity show notable increases, people's own perceptions of their lives are not as positive (Table 9.8). In Goima and Mirambu, a majority of people (56 per cent and 61 per cent respectively) thought that life was better before—and this particularly reflects the views of the female-headed households who tended to prefer their earlier lives. In some respects, this should not be surprising as many people were recalling the times of their youth when they were healthier and more vigorous. Some people also feel strongly about how the forests in the hills now are gone, and they worry that there is less land that is available for the next generation. Assets provide only a partial insight into the nature of social change in these localities.

[6] Details are available in Östberg et al. 2018, table 11, available on open access at https://www.mdpi.com/2073-445X/7/2/44/htm

Table 9.8 Is life better or worse now than at the last survey, by village and gender of the domestic unit head

Village	Women			Men		
	Better now	No difference	Better before	Better now	No difference	Better before
Goima	4	1	11	9	1	8
Mirambu	1	2	5	11	2	20

Migration and Change

The population of Goima and Mirambu has more than doubled since the original survey was made, ahead of natural population growth. The immigrant households are thus under-represented in our restudy based on a sample of the village composition in the early 1990s.

The substantial growth of land farmed (Table 9.3) took place on the plains surrounding Goima and Mirambu villages but particularly in the Burunge Hills. Neither the village councils of the communities surrounding the hills nor the district administration were actively managing the colonization of the hills. It was just happening. For example, the settlement Madah in the hills had 111 households in late 1989, 142 households by May 1992, 169 by the end of that year, and 234 by 1994, much ahead of any natural population increase. Today Madah is a registered village with a Full Primary School, a village government, mosque, shopping centre, tractors. It has far more inhabitants than the population of the entire hills area in 1994.

Already in the early 1990s the area experienced a steady influx of immigrants, particularly of 'environmental refugees' from the neighbouring Kondoa Eroded Area. In the villages bordering on Goima and Mirambu—Jenjeluse, Igunga, Songolo—the Burunge were already in minority, and this was also the case in the hills, which at the time were rapidly being settled. Some Burunge families returned to their old lands. But more than that immigrants arrived. In 1994, we estimated the population of the hills to 443 households, living in ten communities. The biggest group were Rangi with 187 households, followed by the Burunge with 165, and the Barabaig with sixty-eight households (Östberg 1995: 168).

This increase derived from several sources. Often the strategy of newly arrived immigrants was to plant maize and sorghum in the Burunge Hills, using as little labour as possible, while also retaining fields in the home area. To expand into new areas had for a very long time been the preferred Rangi mode of dealing with problems of land availability and quality (Östberg 1986: 29–31 and 2000: 249, Mung'ong'o 1995: 85–7). When new land now became available in the fairly nearby Burunge Hills, this became a favourite expansion area. In years with fair rains there would be something to gain at both ends. Eventually, as roads were improved and rudimentary schools established, families were keener to move from the exhausted soils in the Irangi Highlands and settle in the emerging communities in the Burunge Hills. A further influx came from Barabaig, Iraqw, and Maasai livestock keepers who seasonally arrived with their herds to graze in the hills. An increasing number of them also settled. Moreover, resourceful people made money by large-scale tractor cultivation, using hired labour for the farm operations.

We had originally arrived in Goima and Mirambu to find out why the Burunge area was less affected by land degradation than the Kondoa Eroded Area. Our report documented a movable mode of production, distinctly different from the permanent, de-stumped fields of the Irangi Highlands. Burunge of the early 1990s favoured temporary clearings in the forest (Östberg 1995: ch. 2, ch. 6). That, however, was a life that was. Now it is commercially oriented, mechanized farming that reigns.

Drivers of Change

The restudy of Goima and Mirambu villages brought out remarkable changes in a comparatively short time. We apply a twenty-five years perspective, but in fact the major changes date only some ten years back. During the revisits in 1997, 2006, and 2007, developments were registered. Goima had become connected to the national electricity grid, a communication tower was there. Housing was gradually improving. Medicines were available at the Goima dispensary, which in the early 1990s would have been a rare strike of luck. The supply of school books had improved. A secondary school was being built. But ten years later, in 2016, we still met a totally different scenario.

Discussing the causes of the pervasive changes in Goima and Mirambu, our informants were eager to discuss also another dimension of change than the improved infrastructure. They dwelt on changed mindsets and attitudes. One such change that was emphasized was the reduced alcohol consumption. In the early 1990s, people used to be away for days, 'following pombe (alcohol)', we were told, and we could also recall this. 'However, they have now come to their senses' (while) 'those who continue with pombe remain poor .... Less money is being spent on local brews than previously' (interview, 10 November 2016). We have no data to test whether this change has happened or not, but if drinking has declined drastically there seem to be two factors responsible: one is a revivalism within the Christian community and the expansion of Islam. The other factor is that incomes have increased so much that people can afford to improve their houses, pay secondary school fees, buy better clothes, and invest in solar panels, motorcycles, televisions, and other consumer durables. 'Some drink less because there are other things to do with their money', we were told.

Another prominent driver of the changes in local eyes is changing attitudes towards farm work. This came up in discussions about rain. In the 1990s, people said that if only it rains everything would be fine. But now, some informants objected to that view, as one put it:

> What matters is that you work. Not the rains. That you all the time think that you can do better. People used to be content with cultivating two acres (0.8ha) growing bulrush millet. Yes, they got food enough to feed the family. But what is that? It was when people turned to commercial crops that things started to change. When they grasped that they could earn money, they also started to work, and not just roam around.

Some observers suggested that the greater desire for money reflected more social diversity, and specifically immigration. Immigrants, we were told, stimulate the community: 'they came and they worked'. They start new activities, and they make use of the land and earn money from farming, in turn motivating others. When money is available, traders arrive, and people are stimulated to grow commercial crops, and the economy grows.

Another factor has been the role of wealthy entrepreneurs who dominate the booming grain trade in Goima and Mirambu. They have played decisive roles in bringing about the transformation, particularly in Goima village. Their modus operandi involves a mixture of good business knowledge and practices that allow for them to make money out of their neighbours' poverty and poor bargaining position, combined with instances of more philanthropic activity. For example, as many farmers cannot afford to hire a tractor, they ask the entrepreneurs to plough for them and as payment for the service the tractor owner will get access to half the ploughed land for the cultivation season. In this way, the entrepreneurs get access to farmland at a low cost.

They also act as an informal bank. People in need of cash ask for a loan, which after the harvest will be repaid in grains at a predetermined price below the market value (up to as much as a third of the price), and the trader increases his margins considerably. The entrepreneurs have also invested in village infrastructure, and with it have built up their social capital.

Sustainable Growth?

Members of the local elite, the village officials, teachers, and entrepreneurs, are all optimistic about the future. More and more land is put under the plough and the demands for agricultural products is strong. Goima and Mirambu are booming. However, the entrepreneurs' optimism contrasts with many farmers' fears that their children will face difficulties in accessing land, and that the fertility of the land is reducing. Signs of soil erosion were evident in many fields. This is in marked contrast to the situation in the early 1990s, when farmers described the Burunge Hills as an endless expanse of land, waiting to be cultivated whenever needs arose. There was a belief that soil would regenerate itself faster than it could be eroded.

Fifteen years later, by 2005/6, local perceptions of natural resources had notably changed. Many farmers worried about increased drought, which was perceived to be driven by local reductions in forest cover. The opinion was shared by rich and poor farmers, men and women. However, the notion was particularly strong among female-headed and younger households, reflecting that female-headed households were less endowed with resources, and therefore, particularly vulnerable, while young farmers had a shorter memory of droughts (Östberg and Slegers 2010: 258). Rainfall records did not tally with the perceived increased severity of drought, but rather reflected a local interpretation of the diminishing resource base (ibid.: 255).

Ten years further on, in 2016, and the extent of transformation of the local environment is plain. The expansion of farming has come at a clear cost—forest cover and trees are drastically reduced. Two maps tell the story. In the early 1990s the Burunge Hills were a well-vegetated area (Figure 9.2). Now the situation has totally changed. By 2016 the forest is largely gone, and the hills covered by farms (Figure 9.3).

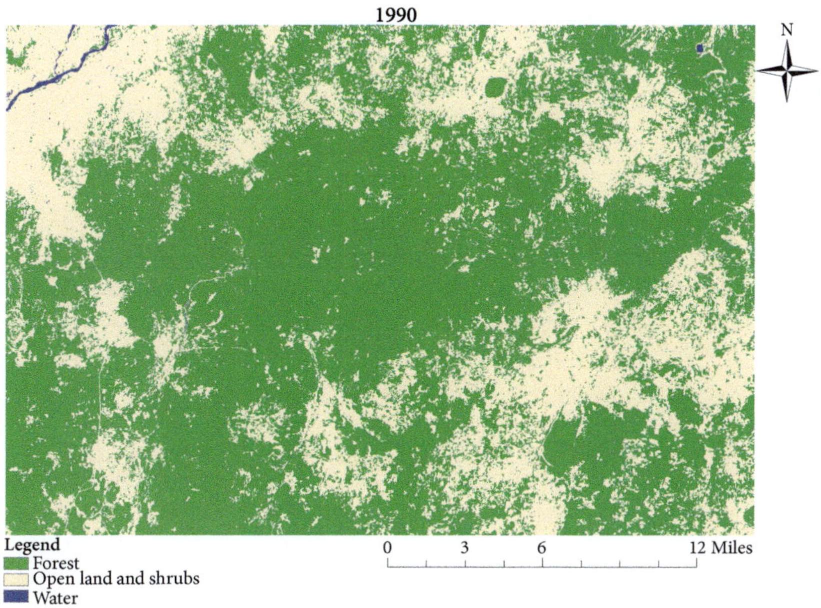

Figure 9.2 The Burunge Hills, 1990. The forest dominates. Map by Jeppe Schou.

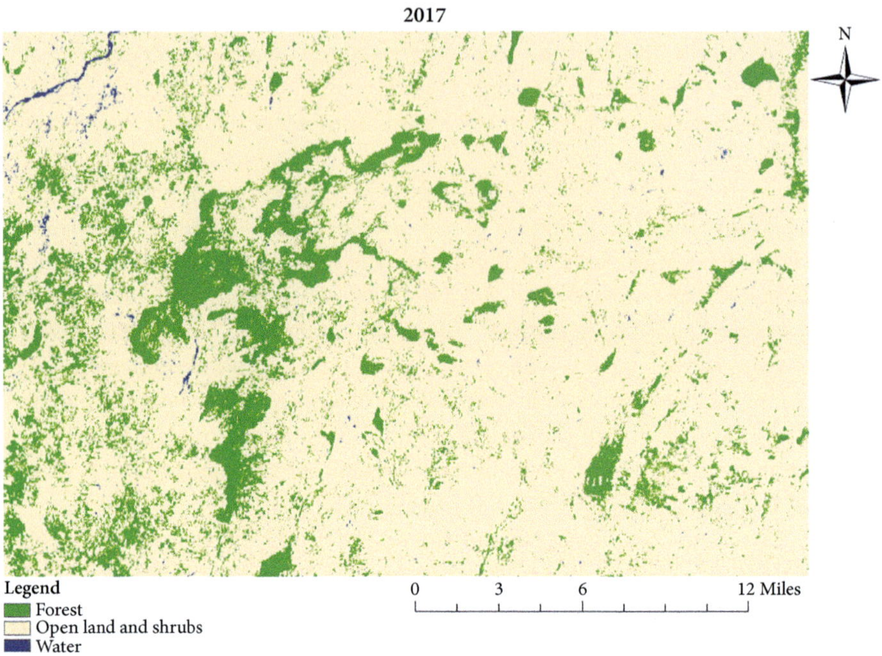

Figure 9.3 The Burunge Hills, 2017. The forest has been decimated to about 5 per cent of the area, and only remains on steep mountain sides. Map by Jeppe Schou.

To monitor land cover changes in the Burunge Hills during the period under study, five maps covering the years 1990–2017, were prepared. The first and the last of the maps are reproduced here. Landsat images taken during July, August, and September were used. These months provided best visibility, and also sorted out forest cover best. 'ISO cluster unsupervised classification' proved to best discriminate between different land types. Originally five classes were identified, forest, forest hillside, shrubs, open land, and water. The first two land classes were merged into one, as were the following two, in order to better bring out the contrast between forested areas and non-forested areas. This also reduced the problem of variation in vegetation caused by wetter and drier years. The images from the ISO cluster unsupervised classification were compared with Google Earth images to check if they matched, which they did.

It is not surprising therefore that in 2016, the worry that clearings would result in diminishing rains persists. People argued that rain clouds gather over forests, and with the forests largely gone, the area will no longer attract rains. They felt that they were now facing a changed environment. Over twenty-five years, the attitudes had moved from trusting that nature will provide, to a concern that the area's current farming bonanza may soon be over. The Burunge used to talk of good land as being 'cold', which when over-exploited turns 'hot', describing an environment where rains could be expected to a new situation where rain clouds pass without delivering. They describe the 'hot' land as 'pushing' the rains away.

The changes that we have documented are in accordance with country-wide patterns, indeed with Africa-wide experiences. Current agricultural growth is in particular characterized by increasing the farmed area (Fuglie and Rada 2013). Only 17 per cent of increased agricultural productivity can be attributed to increased use of inputs and technical change (IFAD, 2016: 138). One assessment is that in Tanzania 'agricultural productivity has remained stubbornly low' and that the use of agricultural inputs is quite low (ESRF 2015: 64). Another way of putting this is that the improved livelihoods that we documented in Goima and Mirambu are based on resource extraction and extensification. This situation is unlikely to be sustainable under current forms of land management.

Conclusion: Challenging a Dominant Discourse on Rural Change in Tanzania

Our findings run contrary to widespread views that the agricultural sector is relatively stagnant and unresponsive to change. They likewise contradict pessimistic interpretations that argue that Tanzania's 7 per cent growth in GDP in recent years bring little return to rural people. Using local measures of wealth and measures of assets, however, it is obvious that Goima and Mirambu people have become substantially wealthier.

We reiterate that a most striking change since the early 1990s is that most households can now support themselves on their land, and many do this on a substantially improved living standard, while twenty-five years ago, half the number of households survived only with the help of underpaid day labour.

Living standards were very low in the early 1990s. By 2005/6 the pattern of social stratification remained similar, as noted above, while by 2016 many people had moved up the local ladder of progress. If this is sustainable or not will depend on the extent to which farming productivity can be raised, how off-farm income possibilities develop, and how farmers manage their environment. This notwithstanding, the experiences from Goima and Mirambu suggest that the critics may be overlooking important forms of local economic dynamism in their arguments.

Rural societies in Tanzania, even in its poorest regions, are more varied than the theories of persistent poverty suggest. Our work suggests that by using local measures of wealth, far more dynamism becomes visible. Moreover our informants insisted that it was precisely the local dynamism and initiative that was ultimately responsible for the change their villages experienced. They emphasized that the local initiatives had mattered. Many pointed to the driving role of locally based entrepreneurs, and they emphasized a new local ethos of hard work, in a way that reverberated with sentiments from the socialist post-independence era. Infrastructural change (new roads and transport facilities), as well as the abundance of land, provided enabling conditions. Similarly, the growth of the Tanzanian economy, with its greater demand for agricultural goods, and its cheaper provision of things, like motorbikes and metal roofing, stimulate growth. But, they are merely that: stimulants. They are not, in themselves, responsible for the improvements we have documented.

We do not have the data to test the power of this interpretation, but it is important to note it. Further research to distinguish between exogenous factors such as infrastructure and marketing arrangements, and endogenous factors, such as attitudes to wealth and work, are required.

In a twenty-five-year perspective, the changes are dramatic, as we have reiterated throughout this article. However, when comparing the village to other Tanzania villages, Goima and Mirambu look ordinary. What is so special with a good range of shops, a communication tower, buses, a secondary school, and a new spacious mosque? Well, perhaps little. But, this is our point. For it is precisely this mundane but widespread change that might tell a wider story of improved livelihood conditions in other peripheral parts of rural Tanzania. Goima and Mirambu are, as Tanzanians would put it, 'catching up', and becoming ordinary, whereas just twenty-five years ago the story was quite different. If Goima and Mirambu are just like any Tanzanian villages, then we need to look at the stories that their mundane asset growth portray in order to get a richer picture of the nature of social and economic change in the country as a whole.

References

Backéus, I., Z. K. Rulangaranga, and J. Skoglund. (1994). 'Vegetation Changes on Formerly Overgrazed Hill Slopes in Semi-Arid Central Tanzania.' *Journal of Vegetation Science* 5: 327–36.

Backéus, I., Z. K. Rulangaranga, and J. Skoglund (1996). 'The Dynamic Interrelationship between Vegetation and the Environment on the Formerly Eroded Kondoa Irangi Hills.' *Changing Environments: Research on Man-Land Interrelations in Semi-Arid Tanzania*. C. Christiansson and I. S. Kikula. Report No. 13. Nairobi, Sida, Regional Soil Conservation Unit: 54–63.

Bluwstein, J., J. F. Lund, K. Askew, H. Stein, C. Noe, R. Odgaard, F. Maganga, and L. Engström (2018). 'Between Dependence and Deprivation: The Interlocking Nature of Land Alienation in Tanzania.' *Journal of Agrarian Change* 18: 806–30.

Brockington, D. (2006). 'The Politics and Ethnography of Environmentalisms in Tanzania.' *African Affairs* 105(418): 97–116.

Christiansson, C. and I. S. Kikula (eds) (1996). 'Changing Environments: Research on Man-Land Interrelations in Semi-Arid Tanzania.' Report No. 13. Nairobi, SIDA, Regional Soil Conservation Unit.

Christiansson, C., I. S. Kikula, and W. Östberg (1991). 'Man-Land Interrelations in Semi-Arid Tanzania.' *Ambio* 17(2): 144–52.

Dejene A., E. K. Shishira, P. Z. Yanda, and F. H. Johnsen (1997). 'Land Degradation in Tanzania. Perceptions from the Village.' Technical Paper No. 370. Washington DC, The World Bank.

ESRF (2015). '*Tanzania Human Development Report 2014. Economic Transformation for Human Development.*' Dar es Salaam, Economic and Social Research Foundation. United Nations Development Programme, Tanzania Office.

Fuglie, K. O. and N. E. Rada (2013). 'Resources, Policies, and Agricultural Productivity in Sub-Saharan Africa.' United States Department of Agriculture, Economic Research Report Number 145.

IFAD (2016). 'Rural Development Report 2016. Fostering Inclusive Rural Transformation.' Rome, International Fund for Agricultural Development, Rome.

Kawa, I. H. (1993). 'The Dodoma Region Soil Conservation Project (HADO), Tanzania: Is It Institutionally Sustainable?' PhD thesis, School of Development Studies, University of East Anglia.

Kideghesho, J. R. (2015). 'Realities on Deforestation in Tanzania—Trends, Drivers, Implications and the Way Forward.' *Precious Forests*. M. Zlatic. IntechOpen: 21–47. https://wwww.intechopen.com.

Mbegu, A. (1996). 'The Problems of Soil Conservation and Rehabilitation Lessons from the HADO Project.' *Changing Environments: Research on Man-Land Interrelations in Semi-Arid Tanzania*. C. Christiansson and I. S. Kikula. Nairobi, SIDA, Regional Soil Conservation Unit, Report No. 13: 147–57.

McNicol, I. M., C. M. Ryan, and E. T. A. Mitchard (2018). 'Carbon Losses from Deforestation and Widespread Degradation Offset by Extensive Growth in African Woodlands.' *Nature Communications* 9(3045): DOI: 10.1038/s41467-41018-05386-z.

Mung'ong'o, C. G. (1995). '*Social Processes and Ecology in the Kondoa Irangi Hills, Central Tanzania.*' Stockholm, Department of Human Geography, Stockholm University, Meddelanden series B93.

Östberg, W. (1986). '*The Kondoa Transformation. Coming to Grips with Soil Erosion in Central Tanzania.*' Uppsala, Scandinavian Institute of African Studies.

Östberg, W. (1995). *Land Is Coming Up: The Burunge of Central Tanzania and Their Environments.* Stockholm University, Stockholm Studies in Social Anthropology 34.

Östberg, W. (2000). 'Eroded Consensus: Donors and the Dilemmas of Degradation in Kondoa, Central Tanzania.' *Producing Nature and Poverty in Africa*. V. Broch-Due and R.A. Schroeder. Uppsala, Scandinavian Institute of African Studies: 243–66.

Östberg, W. and M. F. W Slegers (2010). 'Losing Faith in the Land: Changing Environmental Perceptions in Burunge Country, Tanzania'. *Journal of Eastern African Studies* 4: 247–65.

Östberg, W., O. Howland, J. Mduma, and D. Brockington (2018). 'Tracing Improving Livelihoods in Rural Africa Using Local Measures of Wealth: A Case Study from Central Tanzania, 1991–2016.' *Land* 7(2), 44: 1–26. https://www.mdpi.com/2073-445X/7/2/44/htm.

Randall, S. and E. Coast (2015). 'Poverty in African Households: The Limits of Survey and Census Representations.' *Journal of Development Studies* 51(2): 162–77.

Randall, S., E. Coast, and T. Leone (2011). 'Cultural Constructions of the Concept of Household in Sample Surveys.' *Population Studies* 65(2): 217–29.

Slegers, M. F. W. and W. Östberg (2008). 'The Strength of the Land and the Missing Rains. Environmental Change in Goima, Tanzania, and Farmers' Growing Concerns.' *Exploring Farmers' Perceptions of Drought in Tanzania and Ethiopia*. M. F. W. Slegers. Wageningen University, Erosion and Soil & Water Conservation Group: 129–50.

United Republic of Tanzania (URT) (1977). 'The Threat of Desertification in Central Tanzania.' A Technical Paper prepared for the United Nation's Conference on Desertification, 29 August–9 September 1977. Dar es Salaam.

10

Prosperity, Equality, and Power

Perspectives from Gitting and Gocho, Manyara Region

Vesa-Matti Loiske and Dan Brockington

Epilogue pages 409–412

Introduction

Reading *The Village That Vanished* was a strange experience. The book was based on three years of research by Vesa-Matti Loiske in the early 1990s and describes the village of Gitting, in Hanang District in Manyara Region. One of the most prominent facts about Gitting then was its poverty. Loiske found high levels of destitution and dependence on day-labouring (32 per cent of families). A further 27 per cent of families were poor, living in inadequate houses, with few assets, no livestock, and dependent on daily labour.

Reading the book was strange because the reader (Dan Brockington) was then studying the book twenty years after Loiske's work, while living in the village of Sagong, a few miles away from Gitting. Brockington was perplexed because he simply could not recognize such high levels of poverty. He was then surveying residents of Sagong and knew from that work, and the previous thirteen years of visits, that the levels of deprivation that Loiske reported were rare. Nor could his in-laws, all lifelong Sagong residents, relate to the picture that the book described.

Brockington contacted Loiske to discuss his confusion. Our conversation then led to a series of visits to Gitting and Gocho (which split from the original village) by Brockington in 2013 and later re-visits of the families in Loiske's original 1993 survey in 2016. This was in fact the pilot study, from which the broader project that has led to this book was conceived. This entire collection stems from that exchange.

We found in Gitting remarkable improvements in prosperity, as locally measured. Families which had been poor were now richer (and families which had been wealthy had dissipated somewhat). But the really interesting thing about this study is why that should be the case. Gitting experienced no substantial improvement in road infrastructure between Loiske's study and Brockington's

Vesa-Matti Loiske and Dan Brockington, *Prosperity, Equality, and Power: Perspectives from Gitting and Gocho, Manyara Region* In: *Prosperity in Rural Africa? Insights into Wealth, Assets, and Poverty from Longitudinal Studies in Tanzania.* Edited by: Dan Brockington and Christine Noe, Oxford University Press.
DOI: 10.1093/oso/9780198865872.003.0010

revisit. Local technologies improved (more ploughs, tractors, and lorries), and provision of some services also got better (water points, clinics, and schools). But much of the change in Gitting seems to have been endogenously driven. If external factors have made a difference then they have done so because of a reorganization of Gitting society that made it possible to benefit from these changes.

Our work in Gitting and Gocho is also interesting in that we have been discussing the differences we have found and our findings with villagers for some time. Dan Brockington circulated summaries of the early findings that were written in Swahili, as well as holding public meetings to discuss these findings in 2013. Loiske returned two years later, and subsequently, to talk through the same changes. There are signs that public discussion in Gitting and Gocho of this research has got richer over the years, in that the focus groups Loiske held has provided a more thorough set of insights and reflections than those Brockington encountered. We will return to this issue at the end of this chapter.

We proceed first by explaining our methods, then we examine what changes in assets we found in Gitting. Finally we try and explain the changes we found, drawing up on the findings of Loiske's focus groups to do so.

Methods

To undertake this work we have taken a one-off survey conducted in the early 1990s and turned it into a longitudinal survey by re-surveying the same households. Gitting was surveyed by Loiske between 1991 and 1994 as part of his PhD (Loiske 1995).[1] Loiske's first step was to explore the distribution of wealth in his study area. His unit of analysis was the 'household', which was defined as any homestead registered on the village lists.[2] The categorization system of wealth that he used, and its accuracy, is fundamental to the argument of this paper and it is important to dwell upon it.

Loiske's informants divided households into seven groups—two poor, two average, and three varieties of wealthy farmer. The criteria they used are shown in Table 10.1. From this table it should be instantly apparent that the local classification of wealth was fundamentally a measure of use and ownership of *assets*, as has been observed elsewhere. Lest this ranking scheme should now appear dated, we have included for comparison the criteria used in the work of Higgins and da Corta, for research in the same country (Higgins and da Corta 2013). With some

[1] Gitting was subsequently split, for administrative purposes, into two contiguous villages named Gitting and Gocho. For simplicity's sake we shall simply refer to 'Gitting' in the text.

[2] This household list included all families in the village but omitted itinerant agricultural labourers from the neighbouring region of Singida who were given temporary accommodation on farms. The omission is important because it means that this survey and its long-term findings are no guide to the changing fortune of itinerant labourers. It is a guide to the fortunes of land-owning farmers.

Table 10.1 Wealth stratification systems for Tanzania

Wealth group	Wealth group characteristics Loiske	Wealth group characteristics Higgins and Da Corta
1	Immensely rich; knows no barriers; has cars, lorries, etc.	Rich (tajiri); significant assets and local power; involved in large-scale or employment of labour
2	Very rich; many cattle and much land; owns a tractor but not a lorry; has businesses and land in towns	Owns large-scale non-farm assets; may lend money
3	Rich; employs many vibarua; has many cattle; has businesses	
4	Above average farmer; some cattle; farms their own land and uses vibarua work occasionally	Resilient (tajiri kiasi, mwenye uwezo); sufficient capacity (e.g. assets, social networks) to prevent significant downward mobility relative to overall productive wealth; may employ small amounts of labour on the farm or be involved in small-scale trade
5	Average farmer; a few cattle; farms their own land without using vibarua work	Vulnerable but not poor (tete ila siyo maskini); more productive assets which take the family through the year; during good times can save; during bad times will reduce family consumption; vulnerable to downward mobility with a significant shock
		Poor (maskini); access to limited productive assets (land and livestock); cannot earn enough from farming or trade to take family provisioning through the whole year so will reduce family food consumption; cannot save much in good years; must sell assets in order to cope in a crisis; vulnerable to downward mobility to 'very poor' category but not to 'destitute' category
6	Poor; rents land out to others; depends on casual vibarua work for daily needs; few if any livestock	Very poor (maskini sana); no clear livelihood source; no significant productive assets; dependent on selling labour and/or scavenging; erratic income and food access; very vulnerable to becoming destitute with shock
7	Extremely poor; unable to get work easily; hard to rent their land out to others; suffering from alcoholism and/or illness	Destitute (maskini hohehahe); depends on others for basic needs; cannot work; tends to be socially excluded

Vibarua work refers to casual labour. *Source*: Loiske 1995; Higgins and Da Corta 2013: page 17.

differences they match reasonably well. The importance of assets in local measure of prosperity in rural Tanzania is enduring.

Loiske established these wealth categories, and the distribution of households within them, with some rigour. He began by taking a list of all households in the village which had been allocated land in the villagization operation. He then arranged for eighteen separate key informants to rank these households in order of wealth. All the key informants were men, and were aged between 25 and 45, and were mostly themselves middle-ranking farmers; 609 households were ranked in this way. From this ranking exercise emerged the seven categories of wealth which are shown in Table 10.1. Loiske then randomly selected 20 per cent of the households of each wealth group (122), of which he was able to interview and/or visit ninety-four for his research.

Brockington revisited the original families in 2013 to explore how livelihoods had changed, and what might explain these changes. Of the ninety-four households Loiske surveyed we were able to identify eighty-six, of which Brockington visited seventy-seven. This was part of a year of sabbatical research during which he was based in the neighbouring village of Measkron. He conducted his work in part with one of Loiske's former research assistants, and with the assistance of a former village executive officer, who was identified by the village leadership as a useful assistant, and who was old enough to remember the condition of families when Loiske was conducting the research. Interviews were conducted in a mixture of Swahili and Iraqw, which sometimes required translation into Swahili.

'Household' surveys should ring alarm bells among Africanist researchers who are familiar with longstanding critiques of all that households can conceal (Guyer 1981, Moock 1986). Our reasons for using this social unit are complex, and covered in paper length elsewhere (Brockington et al. 2021 and see Chapter 4 of this volume). Suffice to say here that we hope we do not use 'households' in the cavalier way that has too often characterized social surveys (Randall et al. 2011, Randall and Coast 2015). Rather we explore the changing fortunes of families because these are the appropriate unit of analysis with which to explore trends in assets. Land, livestock, and homes in Gitting are not individually owned, but the collective wealth of families. Decisions to sell or rent out any assets are discussed and fought over. Children's education is generally supported by a larger network of relations. It is because we are exploring trends in assets that we need to talk about households and families. For the same reason, we do not attempt to explore changes in fortunes per capita—this would not be socially meaningful in this context. We realize that this method is limited because it risks obscuring changing gender dynamics and intergenerational dynamics.

When meeting with villagers we used a mixture of quantitative and qualitative methods, building on our own experience, and others (Lawson et al. 2003, Adato et al. 2007, Howe and McKay 2007, de Weerdt 2010, Shaffer 2012). The quantitative element re-surveyed households visited earlier, and individuals who have left original households to set up their own homes. The qualitative included a discussion of any changes with household members that become apparent in the re-survey as soon as that survey was completed. In addition we took more detailed oral histories from a representative sub-sample of households to explore important events and changes that have taken place in the intervening years. We took village, crop, and economic histories (including crop prices) from key informants and district and regional records to build up a picture of the general changes in the area. There were two community-level methods that complemented these tasks. First we undertook a participatory wealth ranking of all households in the village (conducted with the village executive officers, village chairs, and sub-village chairs) in order to compare how wealth distributions now compare with the past, and to see whether the households we have re-surveyed are still representative of their broader communities. Finally we shared summaries of findings and changes in public village meetings so that community members can discuss our findings and offer improvements or correction to them.

Results

Gitting should be a good place to be a farmer; it is well-endowed for agriculture. The village is close to Mt Hanang, a large extinct volcano. Soils are generally fertile, and Gitting sits on the wetter side of the mountain. It is predominantly composed of the Iraqw ethnic group whose proclivities for agriculture were commended by British colonists (Snyder 2005). Gitting has a slightly unusual history, in that the British supported a select few families in the village to purchase tractors and other implements in an attempt to create an agricultural yeomanry (Raikes 1978). This led to some fabulously wealthy families in the village, farming hundreds of hectares annually (Loiske 1995). All this land was redistributed in the villagization operation of the early 1970s, with every household receiving four acres each.

The most significant finding from Loiske's research, however, despite these endowments, were the very high levels of poverty that he reported (Table 10.2). This table makes for depressing reading: it shows that over 56 per cent of households were poor in some way (shaded in dark grey), meaning that they were either destitute (the single largest category), or dependent on uncertain and variable day labour for their livelihood. Indeed it is possible that these levels of poverty are higher than those found in the HBS nationally in 1991/2, for this found less than 40 per cent of people were below the basic needs poverty line.

The most important difference our re-survey found from past conditions is that most people seem to be much richer. 85 per cent of families are in the average wealth categories (shaded in light grey in Table 10.2). The destitute are now as rare as the rich, and the poor as a whole constitute just 10 per cent of people.

Table 10.2 Social stratification in Gitting in the 1990s

Wealth group	1990s		2013	
	No. of H'hlds	% of H'hlds	No. of H'hlds	% of H'hlds
1: Immensely rich	5	1.0	4	0.4
2: Very rich	6	1.0	15	1.3
3: Rich	18	3.0	20	1.8
4: Above average	106	17.4	678	59.4
5: Average	116	19.0	297	26.0
6: Poor	163	26.8	101	8.8
7: Very poor	195	32.0	27	2.4
Total	**609**		**1142**	

Source: (Loiske 1995) and Participatory ranking exercise with village leaders and executive officers 2013. This table compares all residents in 1990s with all residents in 2013. The difference is highly significant: χ^2=529.21; df=6.

There are three possible scenarios that could explain this change. First, it is possible that the poor people of twenty years ago have simply left the village. Alternatively the poor families could have got richer. Or there may be a mixture of both factors.

When Brockington revisited the families surveyed by Loiske, he found that few people had left the village. Those that had gone tended to belong to richer families whose wealth lay in livestock. They moved to areas where there was more space for grazing. Instead, the reason why there are more wealthy families is because people who were poor have now become richer. This can be seen in Table 10.3, this shows the same general movement of households out of the poorest categories (in dark grey), and into the middle categories (in light grey).

But this is not a simple story of greater prosperity for all. The actual dynamics are more complicated, and these are shown in Table 10.4. Here the two columns on the left show where the families were in the early 1990s, and the columns on the right show where they were at the time of resurvey. Notice two things about this table. First it shows that most families from the poorer families category have become richer. Those who started off in the poorest categories (5, 6, or 7) have tended to move up to richer groups. But notice that the families which started off in richer categories 2, 3, and 4, have tended to get poorer, or stay the same. There are therefore two sets of changes to explain—why have the richer families gotten poorer, and why the poorer families richer? Both issues were discussed in interviews with families and two village discussion groups.

Focus groups and oral histories suggested several driving forces behind the demise of the wealthy. Rich families have become poorer because of illness, because of family troubles (divorce, or the expense of seeking or maintaining a

Table 10.3 Change to visited households 1990s–2013 part 1

Wealth group	1990	2013
2	2	0
3	5	12
4	18	29
5	12	24
6	21	7
7	19	5
Total	77	77

Source: Loiske 1995 and Brockington's fieldwork 2013. This table compares the status of households visited in the 1990s with their status in 2013.

second wife), through taking to drink or simply because they are older and have lost their powers. Rich families appear poorer simply because they are moving through the later stages of life cycles which sees them allocate assets to their children. Some once richer families are headed by elderly couples who are simply less able to manage large farms than they were before.

In other cases the demise merely reflects the inadequacy of the categorization system. Investments in education did not appear in Loiske's original scheme. Yet some of the wealthy families in the village have done just that, investing returns from agriculture, and selling agricultural assets (livestock, tractors), in order to fund their children's training. This means that they appear to be less wealthy than before, but they are compensated by their children being employed as teachers or government officers and benefitting from the regular salaries resulting.

With respect to the move out of poverty, four explanations were offered in focus groups and interviews. The most frequently voiced was that people have got richer because they have worked hard at their farming. They have been able to invest in cattle, modern seeds, and farm implements. This work has been more rewarding because local terms of trade for farm produce has improved. Table 10.5 shows that crops have generally increased their farm gate prices by between 160 per cent and 300 per cent in the last twenty years. Moreover, as Table 10.6 shows, some cash crops are now yielding considerably greater returns, relative to maize, than they were in previous years. Thus whereas two sacks of beans used to be able to purchase three of maize, now they can purchase almost five.[3] Thus families who farm cash crops have been able to secure their subsistence needs more easily

[3] These prices and terms of trade have not been altered by reduced transportation costs due to road improvements. Road links to the main towns of Babati and Arusha have been generally unchanged for the period under study, half being paved, and the other half unmetalled. The tarmac road between Arusha and Singida (which passes near Gitting) was only completed in 2012.

Table 10.4 Change to visited households 1990s–2013 part 2

Households in 1990s		Wealth distribution in 2013				
Original wealth group	Number of households in each group	3	4	5	6	7
2	2	2				
3	5	1	2	1	1	
4	18	5	4	6	1	2
5	12	2	5	4	1	
6	21	2	12	6	1	
7	19		6	7	3	3
Total	77	12	29	24	7	5

Source: Loiske 1995 and Brockington's fieldwork 2013. This table compares the status of households visited in the 1990s with their status in 2013.

and, possibly, generate a surplus. Another way of putting this point is that the villagers we surveyed demonstrated substantial improvements in prosperity, founded upon retention of assets, and improved returns to them (due to crop price increases), as well as growth of assets (herds) and investment in homes and education.

A second cause of poverty that many families reported was alcoholism. Accordingly poverty has declined as some have been able to stop drinking, or, in other cases, children have taken over the farm from alcoholic parents (generally fathers) who merely rented their land out each year for enough money to keep them in drink. Loiske's work shows that this was a serious problem in the 1990s. Conversely those poor families who stayed poor during the years of our survey were often unreformed alcoholics.

We cannot tell whether alcoholism was the cause or consequence of poverty. It was probably a mixture of both. We should also note that alcohol sales are often a means by which women (who make and sell alcohol) gain access to money which is controlled by men (who are the main consumers of the drink). Our data do not allow us to comment on the social dynamics of the relative demise of alcoholism. The point is simply that fewer families in this survey now suffer as a result of it than was the case before.

A third possibility that could explain greater prosperity is that local exploitation of poor families by rich families in the village has decreased. Loiske's work and local history makes clear that some of the wealthy farmers in the 1990s (the yeomanry families the British supported) were able to rent much land while paying poor families little money for it. They controlled the tractors required to plough up large areas of land, and particularly some of the heavier clay soils which dominated some families' farms. Now, however, as more people have ploughs, oxen and tractor ownership has broadened, it is harder for the richer

Table 10.5 Average farm gate price in Hanang

Deflation by	Years averaged	Maize	Beans	Wheat	Potatoes	Sunflowers	Pigeon peas
Purchasing power parity	1990–3	34.70	56.21	35.18	40.86	28.23	29.35
	2009–12	70.74	169.69	114.62	136.84	58.46	105.10
	Increase	204%	302%	326%	335%	207%	358%
Consumer price index	1990–3	14,135	22,958	14,340	16,683	11,538	11,997
	2009–12	22,605	54,300	36,039	42,228	19,139	35,026
	Increase	160%	237%	251%	253%	166%	292%

Source: Hanang District Council Records

Table 10.6 Relative price of 100kg of maize to 100kg of other crops in Hanang

Years averaged	Beans	Wheat	Potatoes	Sunflower	Pigeon peas
1990–3	162%	101%	118%	82%	85%
2009–12	240%	159%	187%	85%	155%

Source: Hanang District Council Records. Prices have been deflated by the Consumer Price Index.

families to dictate terms. Investment in assets has broadened the productive base of the village as a whole.

Fourthly, in a number of ways, some of the tasks that women have undertaken have become, relatively speaking, easier. There are now readily accessible diesel-powered mills to grind corn (as opposed to grinding by hand using stones) and water is more easily available at village stand pipes. There are more clinics, which was reported in the focus groups to have improved maternal health. All these measures will have enabled women to put more of their time into more remunerative work. Infrastructural improvements in their lives may have led to more productive use of agricultural assets.

Relating These Findings with the Literature

Our data do not allow us to determine which of the causes of change described here is most important. Our sample size is not large enough, nor the measurement of assets precise enough, for that sort of modelling and correlation. However the value of this sort of research is to suggest hypotheses for testing in larger studies, and useful avenues of enquiry that may be pursued further, as well as suggesting methodological insights. In that spirit we discuss four challenges that this research poses.

The first challenge is the relationship between rural economies and national level GDP. What are we to make of the fact that rural prosperity in Gitting has risen alongside national GDP growth? Does this suggest that rural economies are well tied to national economic growth? Could counting assets reveal unrecognized growth?

We feel such speculation is premature. We believe that exploring assets makes it possible to tell more stories about the nature of economic and social dynamics in rural areas. But we do not think that the findings from Gitting necessarily prove that a rising national GDP has reduced poverty in this village. That assumes that national GDP figures and local incidences of rural prosperity or poverty are well connected in the first place.

It is, however, possible that GDP figures are only weakly related to livelihoods in remote rural areas. We know that GDP has risen as a result mainly of growth in the manufacturing, mining and service sectors. Agriculture contributes only 30 per cent of GDP (World Bank 2015). Thus, depending on the composition of GDP growth, it could be misleading to expect a good relationship between GDP growth and rural livelihoods if the change in GDP does not derive from agriculture.

We must also recall that the statistics used to estimate agricultural contributions may well be weak and unreliable (cf. Jerven 2011). They simply do not capture much of the activity in the informal sector which dominates life in rural Tanzania. Edwards reports the well-known case of the drought of late 2005 in Tanzania, the worst for twenty years, in which food crop production is estimated to have declined by between 10 and 15 per cent in 2006. Nevertheless government statistics show that agricultural GDP grew by 4.1 per cent in that year (Edwards 2014: 244–5). Official figures for the agricultural component of GDP may not be accurate enough to explain village-level growth.

Thus it might be possible for the agricultural sector to thrive, and for the broader economy not to and vice versa. If, in fact, most farmers contribute relatively little to the crop sales measured in GDP calculations then it is likely that their own livelihood dynamics could be quite separate from the changes suggested by GDP. As Dercon and Gollin have observed, poor spatial connectivity can increase the heterogeneity of countries' agricultural sectors and render some areas effectively closed economies (Dercon and Gollin 2014: 483).

Viewed thus we should not be surprised that GDP increases seems poorly reflected in the consumption patterns of the rural poor, as we discussed in Chapter 2. Nor in fact should we read too much into the fortunes of Gitting (as measured in assets) appearing to match those of the nation. Rather than trying to explore the connections between the two scales of activity (village and nation), we would require separate sets of explanation for change in each.

The second surprising result from this work is the proposition that people could have become more prosperous as a result of greater agricultural activity and higher crop prices (shown in Tables 10.5 and 10.6). This is surprising because most accounts of Tanzanian agriculture emphasize its low productivity and stasis (Gollin and Goyal 2017). Investigations suggest that most rural households are net consumers, not producers, of food and therefore any increase in crop prices should make most rural people poorer. Jayne and colleagues have shown that for numerous countries in the region, most agricultural surplus is produced by a small minority of relatively large farms and prosperous farmers (Jayne et al. 2010). We have reproduced their findings in Table 10.7 and supplemented it with Tanzanian data from the LSMS. The Tanzanian data show the same levels of inequality as other countries, and suggest the same basic point. Because most rural households in Tanzania buy more food than they sell, increasing crop prices should make most families poorer not richer.

Table 10.7 Distribution of farming activity in selected African countries

Country and year of survey	Attribute: Mean	Quartiles of land ownership per capita			
		Lowest quartile	Second quartile	Third quartile	Highest quartile
Kenya 2003/4	Farm size	0.58	1.25	2.12	5.91
	Crop sales ($)	261	672	979	1500
Ethiopia 1996	Farm size	0.2	0.67	1.15	2.58
	Crop sales ($)	48.3	118	173	380
Rwanda 2001	Farm size	0.32	0.63	1	1.82
	Crop sales ($)	56.3	74.5	120	280
Mozambique 2002	Farm size	0.53	1.2	1.76	3.14
	Crop sales ($)	11.8	26.1	34.1	61.4
Zambia 2000	Farm size	0.71	1.6	2.75	5.81
	Crop sales ($)	42.7	77.3	109	148
Tanzania 2010/11	Farm size	1.05	2.39	3.96	10.46
	Crop sales ($)	24	64	113	239
	Livestock sales ($)	64	58	42	76

Source: Jayne et al (Table 10.7) and LSMS 2011 data (for Tanzania). Tanzanian data includes all households, urban or rural, who farmed land. All sales figures have been converted to 2011 US, using the CPI deflator available on at http://www.measuringworth.com.

Similarly Bryngelsson and colleagues have expanded Jayne and colleagues' analysis using the 2004 KDHS and by including all foods, and not just the main staples (Bryngelsson et al. 2012). They found that 87 per cent of the rural population are net buyers of food. Smaller farmers both produce less, and are often required to sell any surplus when the price is particularly low. Therefore, if this was the case in Gitting, then the increased prosperity we record in assets will have happened despite food price increases, not because of them. Higher food prices would not make the rural poor richer, it would add to their troubles.

But we must be careful with such national-scale generalizations of rural economies. Analyses of their dynamics must allow for more complexity, as Dercon and Gollin put it '[t]he central fact of agriculture in sub-Saharan Africa is enormous heterogeneity' (Dercon and Gollin 2014: 483), and this includes within country heterogeneity (ibid.: 485). Kagera, from where Bryngelsson and colleagues' data came, is a major coffee-growing area, which has a particular dynamic reflecting changes in the coffee economy, and a long-term decline in coffee prices. In Hanang, which depends on cultivating wheat, potatoes, maize, and beans, there will be a different history.

We also have to factor in livestock whose economic contributions have been consistently under-estimated (Behnke and Metaferia 2011, Behnke and Muthami 2011, Behnke and Nakirya 2012, Behnke and Osman 2012). In

Tanzania, livestock sales are more important than crop sales for households with smaller farms (Table 10.7, bottom row). This reflects the fact that many pastoral families may not cultivate much land. Their poor crop sales are not a good indication of the returns they experience from participating in the rural economy. They participate through selling livestock and milk (Brockington 2001).

In addition to the complex geography of rural economies, the dynamics of economies over time will have variable impacts upon poorer households. Bryngelsson and colleagues argue that while food price rises in the short term may be harmful to households who spend most of their money on food, and who are net purchasers of food, in the longer term the consequences are more complicated. Higher food prices can lead to higher rural wages and to increased agricultural productivity, such that more families become net producers not net consumers.

Finally it is important to consider what variety of foods households produce and the extent of their dependence on purchased produce. This variety, the diverse changes in costs of each food relative to others, and the multiple margins on which consumption can be adjusted lead Dercon and Gollin to conclude that the welfare implications of food prices changes are very complicated (Dercon and Gollin 2014: 481). Bryngelsson and colleagues emphasize that households which produce a significant proportion of their own food can benefit from both increasing *and* decreasing food prices. They explain this as follows:

> by altering their consumption basket they can…increase their welfare ….If food prices go down, they can shift towards better quality food or more food consumption at the expense of a relatively small decrease in non-food consumption. If food prices go up, on the other hand, they can similarly shift towards more non-food consumption at the cost of a relatively small decrease in food quality or quantity. These new options should increase their total welfare.'
>
> (Bryngelsson et al. 2012: 131)

This point matters because LSMS data for Tanzania shows that, with respect to staples, most families, most of the time, are net producers, not net buyers of their staple food (Table 10.8).[4] 66 per cent of rural residents in this survey enjoy surpluses almost all year round. They could belong to those households who produce significant proportions of their own food and thus benefit from all food price changes, both increases and decreases.

It is therefore possible to explain how smallholders could prosper from small farms and rising food prices. Nevertheless, given the starkness of Jayne and colleagues' findings, the prosperity we have recorded in Gitting remains surprising.

[4] The consumption data in the LSMS survey are collected for only one week. We have taken that weekly consumption to be typical of the month from which it was collected.

Table 10.8 Net production and purchase of staple through the year

Land quartile	J	F	M	A	M	J	J	A	S	O	N	D	% of rural ppn
No land	−6.8	−9.8	−7.7	−8.3	−8.7	−8.8	−6.8	−5.6	−2.5	−8.8	−7.2	−6.5	16
Lowest	−2.4	−4.2	−5.2	−3.0	7.9	2.0	2.5	1.9	11.0	−1.5	−3.8	4.1	17
Second	−0.1	4.0	6.3	21.5	13.1	16.5	12.6	3.5	12.3	6.0	2.9	6.0	18
Third	1.4	2.6	8.0	20.7	16.3	12.4	9.5	9.2	12.8	13.1	7.3	8.2	22
Richest	5.3	9.6	16.0	17.6	17.4	15.9	9.1	10.0	9.2	7.6	7.8	4.2	26
Households visited	216	210	177	179	241	192	229	275	126	186	307	245	

Source: LSMS 2011. Table includes all rural households and shows net weight of staple produced (+) or purchased (–) in the week sampled. Grey cells indicate net deficit of staple food.

But comparative data that would allow us to compare our finding with others are few. Our suggestions do not fly in the face of hundreds of studies because adequate survey data simply do not exist, beyond this collection. We venture it therefore as a possibility which requires more investigation.

The third surprise is that asset accumulation seems to have reversed processes of rural differentiation. Studies from elsewhere in Tanzania show that wealthy rural families are able to maintain their wealth through exploitative labour practices, or through using their wealth to provide political influence to facilitate land acquisition (Mueller 2011, Greco 2015). Gitting complicates this picture. Exploitative land hiring arrangements have declined, as has the extremes of inequality that British support had fostered. In part this may be due to the fact that we considered a broader bundle of assets other than just land. In part it may be because land was still relatively plentiful and so it was harder for inequalities to grow and deepen. Unworked land was still cheaply available during Brockington's fieldwork within a day's bicycle ride of Gitting. Hardworking, but poor, families could thus accumulate assets through agricultural activity. The class dynamics of Tanzanian villages are complex. The form and level of inequality that are found will vary according the measurements used to determine prosperity and poverty, the distribution of the means of production, and the accessibility of the different engines of productivity (land, labour, credit, productive assets).

Finally there is the question of the gender dynamics of the increasing prosperity we have recorded. Our study has focused on families and domestic units, which necessarily obscures the gendered distribution of benefits within them. Given that most of these domestic units in this area are led by men, who will ostensibly own many of the assets, in some respects we have documented most clearly improving male fortunes rather than general fortunes. As one anonymous reviewer of the submitted MS put it 'some households may have acquired more assets and improved on them *because* of the labor and investment of female members who are not entitled to dispose of them or use them for collateral.' This recalls processes described in Meru in Chapter 7.

There is much truth in that observation, and, at the same time, we must recognize (as in Chapter 7) that male control over these assets is not a given. It is contested, and husbands and fathers can lose those fights. In some instances families were able to prosper because (male) children and their mothers conspired against their fathers to stop them renting out family land in order to feed a drinking habit. In other instances family disputes are played out in competing attempts to control assets. Women for example will own and breed pigs, whose sale they control. Their husbands will try and usurp control of the animals, and, on occasion fail to do so.

Nevertheless the point remains that if our study has shown the importance of studying change in assets, then it has also highlighted the need to explore how rural men and women separately use farm and off-farm income to invest in assets. The way in which women invest it in land, improved equipment, livestock, and the education of children is not well described in the literature. This will explain, in part, why the changing fortunes of some rural families are still hidden to some researchers, economists and government planners.

Discussing Changes in Gitting and Gocho

Following Brockington's research, Loiske, with Olivia Howland, conducted further work in Gitting and Gocho to discuss changes, and the earlier findings in more depth. This consisted of two focus groups, with four women in one group, four men in one group, who were all selected for being knowledgeable of the history of the villages. They were between 60–75 years of age and had all had political posts during the early 1990s and after. The findings were then discussed with two key informants, one from Gocho village and one from Gitting. This work was conducted in October 2018.

These accounts are interesting because they are much more detailed and comprehensive than those that emerged from Brockington's focus groups that were undertaken when the research was first concluded. They bring up a mixture of endogenous, specific to these villages, and exogenous change which has been happening across Tanzania.

With respect to exogenous changes, the most important change, is the deregulation of the market for crops. Markets now functioning much better, the prices are generally much higher, market availability is not a problem and not monopolized by the elite in the village as many actors comes to the village and offer transport of products, buy products straight from the farmers and pay market prices as prices can be checked through cell-phones and the Internet. In this respect the improvement in communications from cell-phones is also important because it makes market knowledge available in the villages. Similarly transport facilities are improved (there are more lorries to transport goods) so that market availability for goods is improved as is travel in general.

These informants also noted that farmers have better inputs leading to more outputs for sale. Specifically the introduction of modern seeds and pigs increased productivity and income, for pigs mainly for women that are empowered economically and got higher status in the village. This, they claimed, more than compensates for the economic consequences of land fragmentation due to population growth and heritage. The importance of pigs is illustrated by the decline of the African pig virus which had disrupted the production of pigs that was so important for women's income. The outbreak of the virus was generally over by the early 2010s and the pig production has recovered as has the economy of women.

Other infrastructural changes informants mentioned was that electricity in the villages had improved many things: communication, studies, electrically powered machines, fridges, and freezers. The improvement of the schooling system has had effects on the general education level in the village but has also given young people hope for the future. Finally they noted that health care has also improved and the villagers have better health conditions than before; this also makes it possible for people to work harder.

But note of this list that many of these changes (the improvement in transport infrastructure and secondary schools) are relatively recent—they cannot account for the longer-term changes. Also recall Östberg and colleagues' Chapter 9—the external changes count for nothing unless people have the mindset, social skills, and network to effect these opportunities in their own lives. The external changes provide an enabling environment that require more local changes to bring into being.

In this respect, on endogenous changes informants noted that awareness of the structures of exploitation of the poor by the elite grew. This became possible because of political change in which the old leaders, linked to those elites, lost power. As a result the behaviour of the poorer farmers changed. Instead of allowing the elite to use the poor farmers land the poor farmers started to cooperate. Women were crucial in this process of raising awareness, especially when it came to cooperation between farmers.

Loiske's informants, all of whom had held public office in these villages at the time that the changes began to come in, also noted that the change in leadership was instrumental in re-forging social relations within the villages. They observed that the new village leadership was more professional, better educated, more democratic, and supports the efforts of the poor villagers as well as the tee-total movement among women. The leaders managed to attract various projects to the villages, introducing better seeds and other harvest improving technologies. They encouraged private investments in shops, restaurants, and all kinds of entrepreneurship especially transport businesses. The strength of the new leadership elites also coincided with a moment of weakness in the old elites as these groups tried to transfer their economic activities from the exploitation of land and labour in the village to external economic activities where they largely failed.

Perhaps most interesting of all was the fact that in the focus groups, and with the key informants, there were long discussions as to how these changes have affected people's minds. People (both men and women) feel more self-reliant, are more self-confident, they are prepared to cooperate to become free from the elite's patriarchal bonds that dominated before and there is a belief that the future is bright. People do work harder and agree with the late President Magufuli that 'Hapa Kazi Tu' is the way forward. The final comment from one of the key informants (who was a strong supporter of Nyerere's policies in 1991) was that 'during Nyerere we had Ujamaa, but now we have the real Ujamaa'.

Conclusion

It is premature enthusiastically to welcome Tanzania's recent decades of economic growth if that growth has not included the poor. It is difficult to see what purpose growth serves if it is not inclusive. Equally, before condemning its lack of connection to the rural poor, we have to know how to measure the benefits (or otherwise) that economic growth might have. Current misgivings about Tanzanian economic growth excluding the poor have been based primarily on measures of consumption. This is an important aspect of poverty, as it shows in a basic material sense that the economic growth the rest of the country enjoys is not well shared. But nevertheless this measure overlooks change in assets. We cannot conclude from the stasis in poverty lines that economic growth is not assisting households to move out of poverty (more broadly defined).

The findings from this paper suggest that it is important to explore change in assets, as well as change in consumption, if we are to understand how inclusive economic growth is for the rural poor. The families described in this village have experienced a remarkable change of fortunes in the last twenty years, as measured by their assets. Measures of household prosperity which ignore assets will be unable to capture the sorts of dynamics described in this survey.

The data presented here suggest that determining the inclusivity, or otherwise, of economic growth in the absence of understanding trends in assets is premature. Current poverty lines rely solely on consumption indices of a restricted range of goods. They exclude productive assets, as we have seen in Chapter 2. But understanding poverty dynamics during times of economic growth requires incorporating a notion of the dynamics of asset use and ownership. Rather than asking why growth is not inclusive, it is important first to ask what patterns in inclusivity and exclusivity are visible according to different definitions of wealth and poverty and different sources of data.

References

Adato, M., F. Lund, and P. Mhlongo (2007). 'Methodological Innovations in Research on the Dynamics of Poverty: A Longitudinal Study in KwaZulu-Natal, South Africa.' *World Development* 35(2): 247–63.

Behnke, R. H. and F. Metaferia (2011). 'The Contribution of Livestock to the Ethiopian Economy—Part II.' IGAD LPI Working Paper No. 02–11. Addis Ababa, IGAD LPI.

Behnke, R. H. and D. Muthami (2011). 'The Contribution of Livestock to the Kenyan Economy.' IGAD LPI Working Paper No. 03–11. Addis Ababa, IGAD LPI.

Behnke, R. H. and M. Nakirya (2012). 'The Contribution of Livestock to the Ugandan Economy.' IGAD LPI Working Paper No. 02–12. Addis Ababa, IGAD LPI.

Behnke, R. H. and H. M. Osman (2012). 'The Contribution of Livestock to the Sudan Economy.' IGAD LPI Working Paper No. 01–12. Addis Ababa, IGAD LPI.

Brockington, D. (2001). 'Women's Income and Livelihood Strategies of Dispossessed Pastoralists. The Case of Mkomazi Game Reserve.' *Human Ecology* 29: 307–38.

Brockington, D., E. Coast, O. Howland, A. Mdee, and S. Randall (2021). 'Assets and Domestic Units: Methodological Challenges for Longitudinal Studies of Poverty Dynamics.' *Journal of Peasant Studies* 48: 159–79.

Bryngelsson, D. K., A. Åhlén, C. Azar, and U. M. Persson (2012). 'The Effect of Food-Price Movements on African Households.' *International Journal of Agricultural Resources, Governance and Ecology* 9(3/4): 121–46.

de Weerdt, J. (2010). 'Moving out of Poverty in Tanzania: Evidence from Kagera.' *The Journal of Development Studies* 46(2): 331–49.

Dercon, S. and D. Gollin (2014). 'Agriculture in African Development: Theories and Strategies.' *Annual Review of Resource Economics* 6: 471–92.

Edwards, S. (2014). *Toxic Aid: Economic Collapse and Recovery in Tanzania*. Oxford, Oxford University Press.

Gollin, D. and R. Goyal (2017). 'Agricultural Transformation in Tanzania: Linking Rural to Urban through Domestic Value Chains.' *Tanzania: The Path to Prosperity*. C. S. Adam, P. Collier, and B. Ndulu. Oxford, Oxford University Press: 685–709.

Greco, E. (2015). 'Landlords in the Making: Class Dynamics of the Land Grab in Mbarali, Tanzania.' *Review of African Political Economy* 42(144): 225–44.

Guyer, J. I. (1981). 'Household and Community in African Studies.' *African Studies Review* 24(2/3): 81–137.

Higgins, K. and L. da Corta (2013). 'Understanding Structural Influences on Poverty Dynamics in Tanzania—Using a Relational Life History Q-Squared Approach.' *Translating Growth into Poverty Reduction: Beyond the Numbers*. F. Kessy, O. Mashindano, A. Shepherd, and L. Scott. Dar es Salaam, Mkuki na Nyota: 11–26.

Howe, G. and A. McKay (2007). 'Combining Quantitative and Qualitative Methods in Assessing Chronic Poverty: The Case of Rwanda.' *World Development* 35(2): 197–211.

Jayne, T. S., D. Mather, and E. Mghenyi (2010). 'Principal Challenges Confronting Smallholder Agriculture in Sub-Saharan Africa.' *World Development* 38(10): 1384–98.

Jerven, M. (2011). 'Growth, Stagnation or Retrogression? On the Accuracy of Economic Observations, Tanzania, 1961–2001.' *Journal of African Economies* 20(3): 377–94.

Lawson, D., A. McKay, and J. Okidi (2003). 'Poverty Persistence and Transitions in Uganda: A Combined Qualitative and Quantitative Analysis.' Working Paper 38. Manchester, University of Manchester, Chronic Poverty Research Centre.

Loiske, V.-M. (1995). *The Village That Vanished: The Roots of Erosion in a Tanzanian Village*. Stockholm, Stockholm University.

Moock, J. L. (1986). *Understanding Africa's Rural Households and Farming Systems.* Boulder, Westview Press.

Mueller, B. E. T. (2011). 'The Agrarian Question in Tanzania: Using New Evidence to Reconcile an Old Debate.' *Review of African Political Economy* 38(127): 23–42.

Raikes, P. (1978). 'Rural Differentiation and Class Formation in Tanzania.' *Journal of Peasant Studies* 5(3): 285–325.

Randall, S. and E. Coast (2015). 'Poverty in African Households: The Limits of Survey and Census Representations.' *Journal of Development Studies* 51(2): 162–77.

Randall, S., E. Coast, and T. Leone (2011). 'Cultural Constructions of the Concept of Household in Sample Surveys.' *Population Studies* 65(2): 217–29.

Shaffer, P. (2012). 'Ten Years of "Q-Squared": Implications for Understanding and Explaining Poverty.' *World Development* 45: 269–85.

Snyder, K. (2005). *The Iraqw of Tanzania: Negotiating Rural Development.* Boulder, Westview Press.

World Bank (2015). 'Tanzania Mainland Poverty Assessment.' Washington DC, The World Bank.

11

Ricing Fortunes

Agricultural Growth, Farm Intensification, and Paddy Specialization in Two Tanzanian Villages

Agnes Andersson Djurfeldt, Ellen Hillbom, and Elibariki Msuya

Epilogue pages 414–417

Introduction

Smallholder-based rice-led agricultural growth through farm intensification and paddy specialization is a development path that has commonly been associated with the South East Asian Green Revolution experience of the 1970s (Hayami and Ruttan 1985). In sub-Saharan Africa, only Madagascar and West Africa have been traditional paddy-producing areas, but over recent decades, rice has gained increasing popularity throughout the region and is gradually taking over from alternative grain staples such as maize and millet. With growing consumer demand, new income earning opportunities are opening up for domestic paddy producers (Balasubramanian et al. 2007). With both rice consumption and paddy production increasing substantially, Tanzania provides an example of this relatively recent trend and the country is now the fourth largest rice producer in Africa, in terms of tons harvested (FAOSTAT 2018).

In this chapter, we provide an in-depth study of two villages in Kilombero District in south-central Tanzania, one of the rice baskets of Tanzania. Here, agricultural growth and farm-intensification dynamics are based on the expansion of the production of paddy rice over the past decade and a half. Relying on a mixed-methods approach we show that over the time period from 2002 to the present, smallholder farmers have significantly increased the area under paddy, total rice production, and land productivity. Similar to the South East Asian examples, the intensification dynamics in the two villages are based on a combination of technological change through new rice varieties and farm in-puts as well as mechanization, and improved producer incentives transmitted through expanding markets. Experience suggests that the possibilities for enhancing agricultural productivity

Agnes Andersson Djurfeldt, Ellen Hillbom, and Elibariki Msuya, *Ricing Fortunes: Agricultural Growth, Farm Intensification, and Paddy Specialization in Two Tanzanian Villages* In: *Prosperity in Rural Africa? Insights into Wealth, Assets, and Poverty from Longitudinal Studies in Tanzania.* Edited by: Dan Brockington and Christine Noe, Oxford University Press. © Agnes Andersson Djurfeldt, Ellen Hillbom, and Elibariki Msuya 2021. DOI: 10.1093/oso/9780198865872.003.0011

in an African smallholder context are not quite as bleak as is sometimes assumed (see e.g. Collier and Dercon 2014).

Meanwhile, the two villages offer a couple of unique twists to this conventional pattern of technology and market-induced intensification, related to the development of the broader Tanzanian spatial economy and the evolution of gender-based land control patterns. The traditional theoretical literature on intensification pathways has commonly focused on agrarian transformation and linkages to the non-farm economy. Such perspectives posit an evolutionary path away from agrarian livelihoods in rural areas to non-farm occupations among an increasingly urbanized population (see Timmer 2009). However, in Tanzania as well as in other sub-Saharan countries, we currently see the unfolding of a multifaceted rural development path wherein different economic activities, e.g. agriculture and services, mix in the same locations. Further, we need to add an analysis of the gendered patterns of this transition as these aspects have commonly been omitted in models that seek to explain structural transformation as a gradual macro-level movement of economic activities and people from the rural to the urban, initiated by an intensification in staple crop production.

Our aims in the following are therefore several. At an overarching level we demonstrate and quantify the increases in agricultural productivity in paddy production specifically and link these to changes in technology as well as commercial incentives to illustrate the potential for a rice-based intensification process in a Tanzanian context. Moreover, we elucidate the features of this process in the two villages in question qualitatively to reflect on the pre-conditions and broader context for intensification provided by shifts in rural-urban economic opportunities and gender-based changes in access to land. A final, theoretical aim therefore is to further the understanding of rural transformation, and intensification processes, from the vantage point of these dynamics. Here we link to recent bodies of literature that acknowledge rural-urban linkages in a more general sense and normatively point to the importance of gender inclusivity in reducing poverty and enhancing growth, but do not offer either as explanations of rural transformation dynamics.

The following section contains a description of the trends of rice production in the larger Tanzanian context. It is followed by a theoretical framework and thereafter the methodology, data sources, and sites are described. The analysis of the data is presented in four theoretically motivated themes, before we conclude.

Rice-Led Agricultural Growth in Tanzania

Arab traders first introduced rice to the coastal areas of Tanzania and during the nineteenth century the crop spread along the caravan routes to the inland. It was

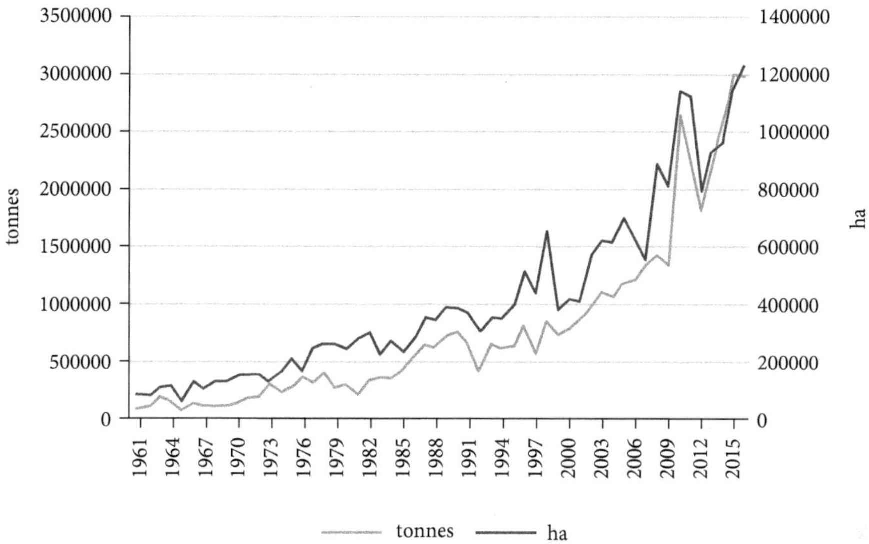

Figure 11.1 Rice paddy—production (tonnes) and area (ha) in Tanzania, 1961–2016.

considered more productive although less reliable compared to millet and sorghum, and from the 1960s it grew in importance as a subsistence staple crop (Iliffe 1979: ch. 3). Production did not, however, really take off until after Structural Adjustment Programmes were introduced in the mid-1980s (see Figure 11.1). Following the policies of economic liberalization the depreciation of the exchange rate made imported rice more expensive and opened up trade in domestic production. Rice went from being a subsistence crop to becoming a food cash crop characterized by increasing commercialization. From 1985 to the turn of the millennium it was the fastest growing food crop in the country with an annual production increase of almost 11 per cent making it the second most important food and commercial crop after maize (Amani 2006: 8). An indication of the importance the Tanzanian government attaches to the rice sector was the launching of the National Rice Development Strategy in 2008. The vision was to transform the existing sector, thought to be focused too much on 'subsistence' production, into something deemed more commercially orientated. The production target was set at a doubling of rice production by 2018 (RLDC 2009: 23), a goal that appears to have been reached already in 2016 (see Figure 11.1).

Initially rice was primarily consumed in rice producing areas and urban centres, but with changing consumption patterns and increasing incomes, demand has spread throughout the country (Amani 2006: 8, RLDC 2009). Market expansion has led to additional land being put under rice cultivation and increasing commercial specialization amongst producers.

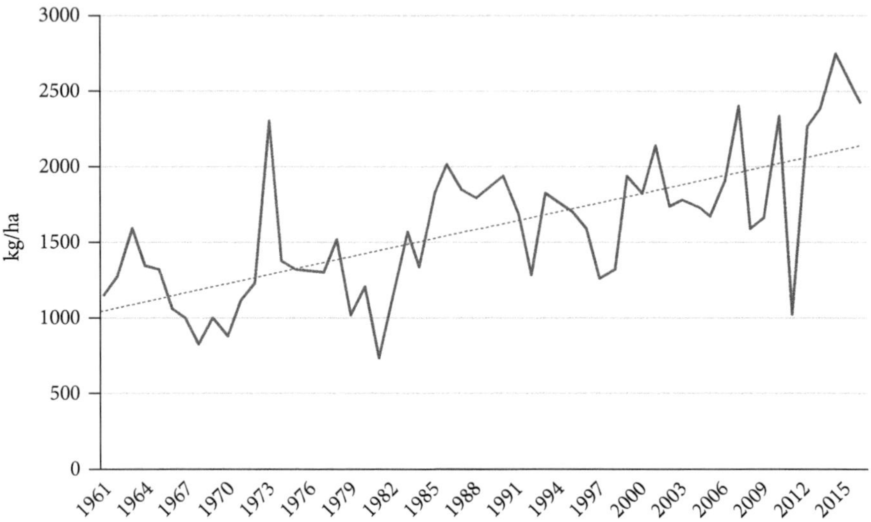

Figure 11.2 Land productivity in rice cultivation (kg/ha) in Tanzania, 1961–2016.

This is a fast-moving sector with substantial increases in both large-scale farms controlled by overseas investors (see e.g. Sulle 2017), commercial Tanzanian farmers (see e.g. Greco 2015), and a growing number of smallholders. The latter likely constituting the vast majority of rice producers. Some reports suggest that around 70 per cent of all rice grown in Tanzania is produced relying on rain-fed farming systems, while 30 per cent takes place within small village-level traditional irrigation systems (RLDC 2009: 6). Census data suggest that between 3 per cent of farmers growing rice in the Living Standards Measurement Survey of 2012/13 used irrigation, and 6 per cent of rice farmed in the 2007/8 agricultural census was irrigated (Woodhouse et al. 2017). However, using new radar data Bowers et al. (2018) suggest that FAO data on irrigation activity in rice growing areas in central Tanzania may be underestimated by up to two orders of magnitude. This shows that data on informal and unrecognized irrigation is unreliable and that accurate figures are difficult to obtain.

Women participate in all aspects of the rice value chain, particularly planting, weeding, harvesting, and threshing although to a lesser degree in trading which is traditionally considered to be men's domain in many Tanzanian societies. Nevertheless, since men in Tanzania generally have better opportunities for accessing and controlling key inputs such as land, water, credit, and technology, they are commonly understood to constitute the core group of producers (RLDC 2009: 13).

As we can see in Figure 11.2 the expansion of the rice sector is not only taking place in terms of increasing production and area under cultivation, but yields have also improved, although fluctuations have been significant. Explanations for improvements in land productivity lie in technological change, e.g. mechanization, irrigation, improved crop varieties, and fertilizers, as well as better farming methods introduced by extension services.

Rice cultivation is particularly successful in the Central Corridor consisting of Tabora, Shinyanga, and Morogoro Regions. Half of all land under rice cultivation is found here (RLDC 2009: 6). Rice paddy cultivation in Kilombero Valley in Morogoro Region goes back to the mid-nineteenth century. Initially, it was centred along the Kilombero River, depended on run-off water, and was primarily farmed for subsistence purposes. Since the turn of the millennium, however, technological change in the form of the introduction of new machinery has made it possible to expand the areas under cultivation and increase production. Agricultural growth has been further encouraged by market expansion and rice has been turned into an increasingly commercialized crop (Kato 2007).

Farmers either sell their produce as paddy or take it to the local mill to be hulled and sold as rice. The buyers are usually local agents and prices fluctuate depending on season, location and market channels. Milling, i.e. the de-stoning, husking, polishing, and grading involved in turning paddy into rice, is growing as a processing industry in the rice-producing areas. The industry is largely dominated by small and medium scale enterprises (RLDC 2009: 14–15).

Theoretical Perspectives on Agricultural Transformation

Agricultural transformation contains a great variety of different development pathways. To understand their specifics and to typologize and draw generalizing conclusions about their mechanisms and drivers, we look inside the processes themselves and conduct in-depth investigations at the micro level (Timmer 2009). In the present study we examine two villages that could be potential examples of an ongoing national trend of rice-led agricultural growth characterized by increasing production, expansion of land area under rice production, and land productivity improvements. The process appears to contain both extensive and intensive growth at the same time.

The Green Revolution in South East Asia in the 1970s was a classic case where high population density drove a process of rice-led agricultural intensification primarily based on the use of abundant labour resources, the introduction of biological technological change, and subsequent improvements in land productivity. Meanwhile, sub-Saharan Africa has been characterized by land abundance and labour scarcity; agricultural growth has primarily taken place in the form of extensive growth (Austin 2008). The exception has been pockets of so called 'islands of intensification', which to a higher degree have resembled Asian land-labour ratios (Widgren and Sutton 2004, Hillbom 2014). With population increase and changing land-labour ratios in sub-Saharan Africa generally, the land frontier has been reached, or is about to be reached in a growing number of regions (Djurfeldt et al. 2005). This transition phase means that the old gap between the typically Asian and African agricultural growth experiences is slowly eroding.

The classic theory for understanding how land-labour ratios shape and drive agricultural growth is found in the induced innovation literature represented by Binswanger, Hayami, Ruttan, and others (see e.g. Binswanger and Ruttan 1978, Ruttan and Hayami 1984, Hayami and Ruttan 1985). The fundamental hypothesis is that change in factor endowments, particularly the relative price of land and/or labour, determines the way that farmers participate in processes of technological and institutional change. The assumption is that actors within a system of production use technology to substitute the scarce production factor. When the scarce factor is labour, mechanization is a rational technological solution to raise labour productivity. When it is land, technological change aims to increase land productivity through e.g. irrigation, bio-chemical technology, and introduction of high-value crops. The primary empirical dichotomy used to illustrate the theory is land-abundant USA and labour-abundant Japan (Hayami and Ruttan 1985).

The development of the rice sector in Tanzania appears not to lend itself to either one of these two extremes, but rather consists of a mix of them. The area under rice cultivation is expanding and increasing mechanization plays an important role as an enabler. Commonly capital has been the truly scarce factor of production for African smallholders, a circumstance that has prevented the large majority from investing in machinery. The rising profitability of rice farming, however, allows for increasing use of tractors and other machinery leading to extensive growth and improving labour productivity.[1] Meanwhile, improving yields are partly explained by access to new machinery, but also to biological innovation in the form of e.g. fertilizer schemes and access to new crop varieties.

Notwithstanding the induced innovation theory's focus on technological change, it recognizes that the use of technology is conditioned by institutions and that the two are intertwined (Ruttan 1978). While the Tanzanian state has set up national rice strategies, its farm in-put subsidy programs and local extension services have more direct effects on smallholders' production (Msuya, Isinika, and Dzanku 2018).

Despite significant increase in domestic rice production, Tanzania is far from being self-sufficient (FAOSTAT 2018). Consequently there is scope for further marketable surplus production, commercialization, and specialization. Matching demand with supply requires well-functioning markets providing incentives for further productivity increase and technological change. In sub-Saharan Africa,

[1] This can be illustrated by the work of Woodhouse and others who surveyed hundreds of irrigating farmers in Tanzania in 2017. They found that power tillers were increasingly reported by respondents as a means of land preparation (Woodhouse pers. comm.).

market expansion and the integration of smallholders have encountered numerous difficulties and hindrances, particularly high transaction costs due to e.g. poor information and inadequate market infrastructure. Such market failure in turn cements low agricultural productivity (Barrett 2008, Shiferaw et al. 2008). However, there are also studies showing that African smallholders, given the right incentives and resources, will commercialize and deliver surplus production for agricultural markets (see e.g. World Bank 2007, Hillbom 2012).

Increased knowledge and better understanding of development challenges adds new perspectives to the existing theoretical discussion. While the induced innovations theory with its concern for bottom-up change and local stakeholders address the issues of inclusion in agricultural growth processes, it lacks a gender perspective. In rural Africa, men access and control agricultural resources to a substantially higher degree than women. What explains the unequal formal control is debated, if there are generalizable gender gaps that regularly favour men over women (FAO 2011, Quisumbing and Pandolfelli 2010), or if such outcomes rather depend on the local context (Andersson Djurfeldt et al. 2013). Notwithstanding, studies have proposed that improved female control over agricultural resources would be positively related to both securing agricultural livelihoods and initiating broad-based pro-poor growth (FAO 2011). Enhancing women's control over agricultural resources is associated with efficiency gains such as greater possibilities for securing credit and access to technologies that require capital (Agarwal 2003), managing shocks such as natural disasters or economic crises (Duflo and Udry 2004), and enabling households to surface from poverty traps (Doss 2006).

Finally, in induced innovation theory, processes of farm intensification are understood to be endogenous rather than exogenous to the economic system and each region's pathway is different as it is dependent on local factor endowments. This does not mean that we hypothesize that these systems are isolated or without exogenous influx (Binswanger 1978). In the broader transformation process urban areas have for instance been important as nodes of knowledge transfer and providers of input- and output markets to raise agricultural productivity (See Hazell, Haggblade, and Reardon 2007). Recently, a growing literature on rural transformation at a general level recognizes the importance of rural-urban linkages to agricultural growth, but the shifts in economic opportunities between the two sectors and its effects on capital flows and technology transfers has not been recognized.

A better understanding of the interplay between local-level factor endowments, institutional dynamics, and broader commercial opportunities both within and outside agriculture contextualizes the process of structural transformation in our case study. We will now move on to see how these factors—changing land-labour ratios, mechanization, biological innovation, state-led skill training, market expansion, and changing gender roles—play out in the two case villages.

To what extent have these factors been influencing trends in rice production over the years 2002–17? Can changing gender relations—especially related to control over land explain intensification patterns? How do endogenous and exogenous forces intersect and explain the nature of intensification processes in the two villages?

Data Sources, Site Selection, and Description

The point of departure for this study is a quantitative dataset—the Afrint database, which has been collected in fifty-six villages in six African countries in three rounds since 2002. Site selection for the qualitative fieldwork that constitutes the qualitative segment of the data, was carried out on the basis of trends identified in the quantitative dataset. The analysis draws on both sources of data, however.

Quantitative Data

The larger Afrint database contains data from six countries, Ghana, Kenya, Malawi, Mozambique, Tanzania, and Zambia, collected in fifty-six villages in fifteen regions. Data were collected in three rounds, 2002, 2008, and finally in 2013 (Ghana, Kenya, Malawi, and Zambia) and 2015 (Tanzania and Mozambique). The cross-sectional data cover 2544 households for the final round of data collected, and the full panel for the period as a whole (rounds I to III) comprises of 1566 households. Our focus in this chapter is the final data collection round 2008 to 2015, since the data suggest that entry into paddy production has occurred rapidly in the past decade.

The research design was based on multiple stage purposive sampling, with the original aim being to select countries, regions, and villages that held the potential for agricultural intensification at the start of the project (see Djurfeldt, Holmén, et al. 2005 for a discussion of the original principles for site selection). Within the broad context of this criterion, one dynamic and one less dynamic region was purposively selected in each country. In the case of Tanzania, Morogoro and Iringa Regions were selected, with Morogoro being the more dynamic region. Households within the villages were sampled on the basis of a random stratified sample, with the data being statistically representative at the village level. A balanced panel design has been used to maintain the representativeness of the dataset between the rounds of data collection, making up for attrition and changes in village populations by sampling additional respondents.

The focus of the project, and thus the contents of the survey, have shifted somewhat since the first phase of the project. The first round of data collection focused on production and technology related to the major grain staples (maize, rice, sorghum) and cassava, the second round added more detailed information on commercialization and also for the first time included cash income data. Finally, the third round captured some intra-household aspects of income generation not covered in the first two rounds. While one general challenge in capturing change over time relates to the addition of variables along the way, in the case of production dynamics related to rice specifically, longitudinal data is available throughout the project cycle. Interviews were carried out with the farm manager.

A couple of general caveats relates to the survey methodology used: interviewing the farm manager is problematic for a couple of reasons—on the one hand it presumes perfect information on the part of the respondent and on the other (especially important from a gender perspective) this approach may hide intra-household inequalities related to food security and income distribution for instance. The survey samples at the village level, are small and it is therefore not generally possible to compare the data for male- and female-managed households at the village level since the limited sample size raises the risk for type 2 errors (false negatives). The chapter uses the village data from the two villages for the years 2008 and 2015, predominantly using data for the rice farmers covered by the dataset. The total number of rice farmers in 2008, was thirty-six for Idete and forty-three for Katurukila. For 2015, the number of rice producers was thirty-six for Idete and forty-one for Katurukila. While the dataset can tell us something about production trends and technology use, it cannot therefore provide sufficient explanations for these changes. For this purpose we need qualitative data.

Site Selection

As mentioned above, the two study villages were selected based on trends in the quantitative dataset. This is described in more detail in another publication (Andersson Djurfeldt 2017), but briefly, site selection was based on an interest in understanding and unravelling the gender-based patterns of what in the literature is described as 'pro-poor agricultural growth'—that is an inclusive, commercially driven process of agricultural expansion. In the dataset as a whole eighteen villages were selected, where household livelihoods had improved on the basis of increased agricultural commercialization between the last two rounds of data collection (short-term growth) or between the first and the last (long-term growth). Five of these villages were found in Tanzania, with three selected for qualitative fieldwork, Idete and Katurukila in Morogoro (Kilombero District) and Kitelewasi in Iringa District. During the course of fieldwork it became clear that Kitelewasi was a case of urbanization gradually enfolding a rural hinterland rather than an example of dynamic agricultural growth. The chapter therefore focuses on Idete—a village whose growth has occurred between the second and third round of data collection, and Katurukila, a village that has seen an uninterrupted growth trend since 2002.

Qualitative Data Collection

Qualitative data were collected between 17 and 27 of November 2017 by a team of researchers consisting of the three authors of this chapter and five research assistants who were trained in a workshop before the start of data collection. The research assistants did separate interviews with both spouses in twenty-five households in each village to gain an understanding of intra-household dynamics related to control and decision-making in agriculture and income generation. In addition, women heading their own households were sampled and interviewed. Households were selected among the surveyed households and stratified by income per adult equivalent.

A set of key informant interviews and focus group discussions were also carried out in the villages. The purpose of these were to gain an understanding of the broader dynamics of change that had occurred since data collection in 2015 and to elucidate the reasons behind the trends in the quantitative data. These interviews were carried out by the authors. For the qualitative analysis, this chapter focuses strongly on the data from the key informant interviews and focus group discussions.

Site Description

Idete village is located about 21km from Ifakara town and is one of the four villages in Idete ward. It is serviced by public transport and thus easily accessible. The population is estimated to 2,802 individuals staying in 682 households. The main grown crop is paddy, which is used as both a cash and a food crop. The main rice varieties are local varieties (Zambia, Super India, Kalimata, Mbawa mbili) although there is an increase of farmers opting for the hybrid variety SARO. Maize, bananas, sweet potatoes, and some vegetables are also grown for subsistence. Chickens are the most popular livestock. Teak-tree farming is starting to gain popularity among villagers although it is an activity mostly pursued by outsiders (i.e. people not living in the village). Kilombero Valley Teak Company is the biggest buyer and supporter of teak-tree farming.

Katurukila village has an estimated population of 2,786 individuals and is found between Kilombero town and Ifakara town in Mkula ward. It is located 60km from Ifakara town and does not have regular public transport. Villagers relies on motorbikes (known as bodaboda) for transport to the Kilombero-Ifakara main road. Agriculture is the main economic activity. Being close to

Kilombero Sugar Company means that farmers in the village participate in the out-grower contract farming scheme, growing sugarcane (cf. Sulle 2017, West and Haug 2017). Sugarcane is however available as an option only for a minority of farmers as the initial capital requirements are high. Rice is cultivated by nearly all households in the village and is the main food and cash crop. Due to the surrounding sugarcane plantations, available land area for farm expansion is limited.

Like most of Kilombero area Idete and Katurukila have a tropical climate with bi-annual rainy seasons. The short rainy season falls between December and March and the long rains (known as Masika) fall between April and June. In total, the area receives an annual rainfall ranging from 1,200mm to 1,400mm. Most farmers primarily rely on rain, but in Katurukila there are also small-scale, farmer constructed, water-control devices for irrigation.

The dominant marketing systems in the two villages is an open free market for agriculture and livestock whereby prices are determined by supply and demand. Farmers in the two villages have access both to the internal market and the export market. Harvested paddy is either stored at home or at warehouses adjacent to nearby milling machines, at a cost. In addition, farmers in Katurukila have an option of selling paddy through the warehouse receipt system. This system increases farmers bargaining power and thus the price they receive.

Empirical Analysis

Production and Land Use for Paddy

As a first observation, we note that the trends of both extensive (increasing area under production) and intensive (improved yields) agricultural growth found at the national and regional levels are mirrored in the development of rice paddy cultivation in the two villages, as such data from the study sites confirm broader national trends. In some respect they also show the potential of yield improvements through a classical grain-intensification-based trajectory also in the case of sub-Saharan Africa.

All households except one grew rice in 2008, by 2015, all households except three (two in Idete and one in Katurukila) grew rice. The importance of rice as a driver of intensification dynamics is confirmed by the quantitative data, but there are differences between the two villages. First, while in Idete the mean cultivated area under rice has increased by 70 per cent, in Katurukila the area under paddy remained unchanged (see Table 11.1). Second, production volumes also increased dramatically in Idete. The change in Katurukila is more modest (see Table 11.2), but still sizeable in relative terms.

A closer look at the yield data (Table 11.3) reveals that intensification has occurred primarily in Idete since 2006–8, which has caught up with and outpaced

Table 11.1 Mean cultivated area under rice (ha), three-year average, by village

	2006–8	N	2013–15	N	Difference	Sig.
Idete	0.74	36	1.26	35	0.52	***
Katurukila	1.07	42	1.04	41		

Total number of cases 2006–8: Idete 36, Katurukila 43; total number of cases 2013–15: Idete 36, Katurukila 41. One extreme case was removed in Katurukila for 2006–8 and one extreme case in Idete for 2013–15.

Table 11.2 Mean production of paddy (kg) per household, three-year average, by village

	2006–8	N	2013–15	N	Difference	Sig.
Idete	1127	36	3186	36	2059	***
Katurukila	1708	42	2422	41	714	**

One extreme case was removed in Katurukila for 2006–8.

Table 11.3 Yields (kg/ha) 2006–8, 2013–15

	2006–8	N	2013–15	N	Diff.	Sig.
Idete	1433	36	2464	36	1031	***
Katurukila	1529	42	2222	41	693	***

One extreme case was removed for Katurkila for 2006–8.

the yields in Katurukila since the previous round of data collection. Nonetheless, also in Katurukila yield increases have been pronounced.

The increases in rice production is a general feature, not driven by outliers. It was reported by respondents in the qualitative interviews in both villages. The share of the median as a proportion of the mean increased slightly in both villages meaning that median production rose faster than average production, pointing to slightly improved prospects for the bottom half of the sample (see Table 11.4).

The point that commercialization was one of the main drivers of production increases was repeatedly stressed in focus group discussions and by key informants. In Idete, for instance, the participants in the male focus-group discussion argued that not only had market access improved in general, but also that the production of several varieties of paddy was a competitive advantage in attracting wholesalers to the village.

Table 11.4 Median three-year average household production (kg) and three-year average cultivated area (ha), paddy, by village 2006–8 and 2013–15

	Production		Area	
	2006–8	**2013–15**	**2006–8**	**2013–15**
Idete	840	2693	0.62	1.01
Katurukila	1400	2080	0.93	0.81

Table 11.5 Share of households who sold paddy (market participation) and average amount sold by household, by village, 2008 and 2015

	Market participation (%)			
	2008	**2015**		
Idete	0.83	0.94		
Katurukila	0.86	0.93		
	Average amount of paddy sold per household (kg)			
	2008	**2015**	**Difference**	**Sig.**
Idete	559	1947	1388	***
Katurukila	755	1569	814	**

The role of commercialization is confirmed also by the quantitative data—the share of households participating in the paddy market is near universal, and sale volumes have on average increased dramatically as suggested by the data in Table 11.5. A marketable surplus has emerged between the two rounds of data collection. The qualitative interviews also mentioned the importance of rising prices. The quantitative data suggest that price improvements are part of a long-term trend: the data on price perceptions shows that already in 2008, twenty-two out of twenty-eight respondents in Idete perceived prices to have improved since 2002 and thirty-one out of thirty-eight households in Katurukila agreed. By 2015, nineteen out of thirty-four, and thirty-one out of thirty-eight respondents in Idete and Katurukila respectively were of the opinion that prices had improved since 2008. Steadily improving prices and better market access may therefore offer part of the explanation for what appears to be an agrarian-based process of livelihood improvements, generated by increases in production and yields.

Technology Use and Modes of Technology Transfer

Improved technologies as an explanation for production increases and rising yields was a cross-cutting theme in all interviews—the institutional mechanisms behind this are based on a combination of group dynamics, extension services, immigration, and extension services provided by local level government officials, NGOs, and other organizations. In both villages, the formation of groups for purposes of technology transfers was actively encouraged.

The use of extension services has been largely unchanged in both villages—in the case of Idete 55 per cent of the households in 2015, reported receiving extension, either from government services or private organizations, such as NGOs, during the past year. The corresponding share for Katurukila was 52 per cent. While, there were no statistically significant changes in the extent to which farmers received extension, the increasing formation of groups is reflected in the data for Idete: 10 per cent of the sampled farmers belonged to a local farmer's group in 2008, compared with 29 per cent in 2015 (a difference that was statistically significant at the 1 per cent level).

Indeed, in the rice-growing areas where we have worked especially, the method of working through farmers groups had been propagated by a local government-employed female extension agent. In the past, there had been accusations of laziness and inactivity directed at her by the male farmers. In response, she had sensitized farmers into forming groups, while others had been mobilized by the government through the distribution of subsidized fertilizer, which was based on the formalization of groups. At the time of the interviews in November 2017 there were forty-eight active groups involved in livestock and farming in one village. These groups are self-organized but assisted in drafting constitutions and finally formalized through the approval of the extension agent. The main purpose of the groups in both villages, apart from accessing fertilizer, was to farm collectively on demonstration plots, where the visual effect of production improvements could be exhibited, inspiring change in the village.

Despite the emphasis on improved technologies, as a starting point it can be noted that seed varieties grown are mainly traditional types used for dry rice production. In both villages farmers primarily rely on rain, although in Katurukila rain is complemented with a low-technology farm-led irrigation system. In Idete, in 2008, a handful (six) of households reported that the main variety of rice that was grown was an improved variety, a number that actually dropped by 2015. In Katurukila, by contrast, nine households out of forty-one planted improved varieties as their main variety in 2015, compared with one in 2008. The qualitative data, however, contains detailed information on the types of varieties (SARO and Iyara64) being disseminated by the extension services also in Idete. The mismatch between the quantitative data in this case, therefore may suggest a misinterpretation of the question or the term 'improved seed'.

The use of inorganic fertilizer varies between the villages, largely a result of differences in soil conditions. In 2015, less than a third (ten) out of thirty-six respondents in Idete used chemical fertilizer. For the remainder, the majority stated that their soils were fertile and therefore they did not need fertilizer, while the rest could not afford to buy fertilizer. In Katurukila, by contrast three-quarters of the households used chemical fertilizer and only one household did not do so because of high soil fertility. Here, also the use of fertilizer has increased since 2008: only seven households used fertilizer on rice in 2008, compared with thirty in 2015. The use of pesticides varied between the villages—in Idete 14 per cent of the households used pesticides on rice, whereas in Katurukila 46 per cent did in 2015 (sig. at the 5 per cent level). Data for herbicide use was not collected during 2008, but it should be noted that farmers in both villages, and Idete especially make use of herbicides—81 per cent of the households in Idete, and 46 per cent of those in Katurukila used herbicides on paddy in 2015. Increased use of herbicides was also put forth as an explanation for rising yields in the case of Idete.

Shifting Rural-Urban Economic Opportunities as Explanations of Technology Transfer

An important, if not the main, driver of intensification may come from beyond the villages. The proliferation of relatively inexpensive agricultural machinery is clear in both villages, and also along the roads leading into the villages. The growing availability of tractors and combine harvesters are mentioned as an explanation both for increasing farm sizes as well as higher productivity in both villages. This could be a result of the government Kilimo Kwanza (which translates to 'Agriculture First') initiative in which Pillar No. 7 aims at industrialization to promote agriculture by addressing the needs of agricultural producers. Backward linkages through supply of agricultural machinery and implements was a government priority in this context. Moreover, through the agriculture window of the Tanzania Investment Bank, individual farmers and farmer groups could access finance for machinery and implements to enhance mechanization.

Investing in tractors and agricultural machines that can be rented to small-scale farmers has become a business opportunity in Morogoro and other smaller urban centres. Informants in Katurukila argued, that opportunities for making money in the urban economy have gradually dwindled as part of the government's clamp-down on corruption and tendering procedures and this has led to investments in the agricultural sector.

Changes in land preparation are striking, especially in Idete, where less than a quarter of the households used tractors for land preparation in 2008, compared with 83 per cent in 2015. In Katurukila, tractor ploughing was more frequent in 2008, but also increased during the period, with 70 per cent of the farmers preparing their land by using a tractor in 2015. Labour shortage in the villages could also explain this shift. The secondary education system from 2004 to 2009 through the Secondary Education Development Program (SEDP) phase 1 tripled the number of secondary schools in the country. This meant that more youth in the villages could now attend secondary school, thus withdrawing them from engaging in farm activities. The second phase of SEDP with assistance of the World Bank started in 2010 and further increased the access of many youth to secondary education. The farming population is thus ageing, and replacement is minimal. Mechanization and productivity improvements are a response to demographic change that is driven partly by the expansion of education.

Land Use Changes—Growing Demand, Formalization, and Individualization

Further explanation for broader livelihood changes and the dynamics between productivity increase are related to two aspects noted in the qualitative data: on the one hand the growing commercial prospects in paddy raise the value of land and enable poorer households to rent out land to urbanites or farmers from other villages keen to explore such prospects. In turn, it was suggested that this raises incomes and living standards among the landholders.

A second change that was noted was the individualization of farming, especially for women, either through renting land or through land rights that were being individualized through the titling schemes being rolled out in the villages. At the time of the quantitative data collection the latter had not been completed, nor is it possible to trace intra-household control and access to land through this dataset. The argument was nonetheless made in focus group discussions with both men and women as well as in the interviews with extension staff, that the possibilities for women individually to cultivate land, especially through renting land, was improving productivity. The incentives for women's production on such land were higher than on family land, given the general understanding that the income generated from sale of produce from land that women themselves were renting would be kept by the wife. The re-investment of incomes into improved housing by women and the general demonstration effect of women engaging successfully in agriculture were also noted as sources of rising productivity in discussions with male respondents. Husbands would gradually be convinced by the improvements being made, overcoming their hesitation to adopt new technology.

While the growing value of land cannot be captured in increases in productivity among the sampled households, for 2015, we have nonetheless documented the existence of a rental land market. In both villages, renting out land was less frequent than renting in land: in Idete, 32 per cent of the households rented land, while 26 per cent rented out land, compared with Katurukila, where 40 per cent of households rented in land and 19 per cent rented out land. The average total cultivated area is the same in both village, 2.1 hectares. The share of rented land of total farm size (which includes both cultivated area as well as land under fallow) points to a strong reliance on the rental market: 55 per cent and 57 per cent respectively of total farm size consisted of land rented in for the twelve households in Idete and the seventeen in Katurukila who stated that they rented land. There is a strong negative correlation (–0.39 significant at the 5 per cent level), between the share of rented land and total farm size, raising concerns about the vulnerability of small-scale households in the rental market. Losses of land were also frequent in Idete, where 26 per cent of the respondents stated that they had lost land that they considered they had the right to cultivate. Unlike the qualitative data, the quantitative data, do not suggest that land is being rented out by the poorer households for the benefit of both parties, but rather that the poorer households are reliant on the rental market for the bulk of their cultivated area.

Concluding Remarks

This case study from two Tanzanian villages in Kilombero District shows the potential of a rice-led, smallholder based agricultural transformation process in an African context. Rice production on average had increased more than area under cultivation in both villages pointing to processes of both intensification and expansion. They demonstrate that remarkable increases in productivity are possible in small-holder farming systems. Some interventions recently have insisted that only step changes which move labour out of unproductive agricultural sectors can bring about the growth poor countries need (Collier and Dercon 2014). This may be the case in the long term, over the decades those authors were considering. But the productivity gap between agriculture and other sectors may be over-estimated (McCullough 2017). The transformations possible we have documented in smallholder farming suggest that routes to higher productivity can be built on this sector.

We identify four factors that have been of importance as main drivers of these growth processes. First, commercialization and market expansion due to diversification of paddy varieties and improved prices have provided economic incentives for farmers to specialize in paddy and increase production. Second, technological change in the form of mechanization and new farm in-puts, e.g. up-graded rice varieties has increased land productivity. Thirdly, improved access to extension services and the introduction of new farming practices has also contributed to these dynamics. Finally, an individualization of production, where family members work on their private fields rather than on jointly owned land, has motivated intensified efforts to increase production.

While technological change and the diffusion of innovations was a pivotal aspect also of the Asian Green Revolution, in the case of Idete and Katurukila, this rests on the uptake and transfer of technology through group dynamics and immigration, which may be unique to the villages. A key question in this context is whether such processes are replicable to other geographical and institutional settings?

Linkages to the outside economy have been a mixed blessing: on the one hand the relative benefits of investing in rural areas have enhanced or even sparked mechanization in the areas, on the other hand, growing pressure and demand for land could cause stratification as already vulnerable segments of the population become even more vulnerable (Greco 2015).

Meanwhile, the growing pressure on land and the government push for formalizing land titling has had the unintended consequence that farming is becoming increasingly individualized, which has had a positive effect on women farmers especially. Individualized tenure is also prompted by the will to benefit from improved prices among both women and men. In the event, the ability to engage in individual farming on rented land is put forth as an explanation of the rising productivity among women.

References

Agarwal, B. (2003). 'Gender and Land Rights Revisited: Exploring New Prospects via the State, Family and Market.' *Journal of Agrarian Change* 3(1–2): 184–224.

Amani, H. K. R. (2006). 'Agricultural Development and Food Security in Sub-Saharan Africa (SSA). Building a Case for More Public Support. The Case of Tanzania.' Working Paper No. 06. Rome, Policy Assistance Unit for the FAO Subregional office for East and Southern Africa.

Andersson Djurfeldt, A. (2017). 'Pro-Poor Agricultural Growth – Village Dynamics and Commercialisation Pathways, APRA Working Paper 3.' Brighton, Agricultural Policy Research in Africa, Institute of Development Studies.

Andersson Djurfeldt, A., G. Djurfeldt, and J. Bergman Lodin (2013). 'Geography and Gender Gaps: Regional Patterns of Income and Farm-Nonfarm Interaction among Male- and Female-Headed Households in Eight African Countries.' *World Development* 48: 32–47.

Austin, G. (2008). 'Resources, Techniques, and Strategies South of the Sahara: Revising the Factor Endowments Perspective on African Economic Development, 1500–2000.' *The Economic History Review* 61(3): 587–624.

Balasubramanian, V., M. Sie, R. J. Hijmans, and K. Otsuka (2007). 'Increasing Rice Production in Sub-Saharan Africa: Challenges and Opportunities.' *Advances in Agronomy* 94: 55–133.

Barrett, C. B. (2008). 'Smallholder Market Participation: Concepts and Evidence from Eastern and Southern Africa.' *Food Policy* 33: 299–317.

Bowers, S., D. Brockington, H. Komakech, C. M. Ryan, G.-J. Veldwisch, J.-P. Venot, and P. Woodhouse (2018). 'Under the Radar. Remote Sensing of Irrigation in Africa and the Implications for the (In)Visibility of Irrigation Practices.' Forthcoming in *Water Alternatives*.

Collier, P. and S. Dercon (2014). 'African Agriculture in 50 Years: Smallholders in a Rapidly Changing World?' *World Development* 63: 92–101.

Djurfeldt, G., H. Holmén, M. Jirström, and R. Larsson (2005). *The African Food Crisis – Lessons from the Asian Green Revolution*. Wallingford, CABI Publishers.

Doss, C.(2006). 'The Effects of Intrahousehold Property Ownership on Expenditure Patterns in Ghana.' *Journal of African Economies* 15(1): 149–80.

Duflo, E. and C. Udry (2004). 'Intrahousehold Resource Allocation in Cote d'Ivoire: Social Norms, Separate Accounts and Consumption Choices.' Cambridge, MA, National Bureau of Economic Research.

FAO (2011). 'Women in Agriculture: Closing the Gender Gap for Development.' Rome, Food and Agriculture Organization. http://www.fao.org/docrep/013/i2050e/i2050e.pdf [accessed April 2016].

FAOSTAT (2018). http://www.fao.org/faostat/en/#data/QC [accessed April 2018].

GAIN Report (2017). 'Tanzania: Grain and Feed Annual: 2017 Tanzania Corn, Wheat and Rice Report.' Global Agricultural Information network, USDA Foreign Agricultural Service. https://gain.fas.usda.gov/Recent%20GAIN%20Publications/Grain%20and%20Feed%20Annual_Dar%20es%20Salaam_Tanzania_3-29-2017.pdf [accessed April 2018].

Greco, E. (2015). 'Landlords in the Making: Class Dynamics of the Land Grab in Mbarali, Tanzania.' *Review of African Political Economy* 42(144): 225–44.

Hayamin, Y. and V. W. Ruttan (1985) (revised and expanded edition). *Agricultural Development: An International Perspective*. Baltimore and London, Johns Hopkins University Press.

Hazell, P., S. Haggblade, and T. Reardon (2007). 'Structural Transformation of the Rural Nonfarm Economy.' *Transforming the Rural Nonfarm Economy: Opportunities and Threats in the Developing World*. S. Haggblade, P. Hazell, and T. Reardon. Baltimore, Johns Hopkins University Press: 83–98.

Hillbom, E. (2012). 'Market Institutions Benefiting Smallholders in Contemporary Meru, Tanzania.' *Journal of Modern African Studies* 50(4): 657–79.

Hillbom, E. (2014). 'From Millet to Tomatoes: Incremental Intensification with High Value Crops in Contemporary Meru, Tanzania.' *Journal of Eastern Africa Studies* 8(3): 400–19.

Iliffe, J. (1979). *A Modern History of Tanganyika*. Cambridge, Cambridge University Press.

Isinika, A. C., G. C. Ashimogo, and J. E. D. Mlangwa (2003). 'Africa in Transition: Macro Study Tanzania (Final Research Report).' Lund, Lund University Macro Reports, Country Case Studies, Lund University.

Kato, F. (2007). 'Development of a Major Rice Cultivation Area in the Kilombero Valley, Tanzania.' African Study Monographs, suppl. 36: 3–18. Kyoto, Graduate Schools of Asian and African Area Studies, Kyoto University.

McCullough, E. B. (2017). 'Labor Productivity and Employment Gaps in Sub-Saharan Africa.' *Food Policy* 67: 133–52.

Meertens, H. C. C., L. J. Ndege, and P. M. Lupeja (1999). 'The Cultivation of Rainfed, Lowland Rice in Sukumaland, Tanzania.' *Agriculture, Ecosystems & Environment* 76(1): 31–45.

Mghase, J. J., H. Shiwachi, K. Nakasone, and H. Takahashi (2010). 'Agronomic and Socio-Economic Constraints to High Yield of Upland Rice in Tanzania.' *African Journal of Agricultural Research* 5(2): 150–8.

Quisumbing, A. R. and L. Pandolfelli (2010). 'Promising Approaches to Address Needs of Poor Female Farmers: Resources, Constraints, and Interventions.' *World Development* 38(4): 581–92.

RLDC (2009). 'Rice Sector Strategy: Improving Rice Profitability through Increased Productivity and Better Marketing Focusing on Tanzania's Central Corridor.' Rural Livelihood Development Company, Dodoma. http://www.rldp.org/downloads/rice_strategy.pdf [accessed April 2018].

Ruttan, V., H. Binswanger, Y. Hayami, W. Wade, and A. Weber (1978). 'Factor Productivity and Growth: A Historical Interpretation.' *Induced Innovation: Technology, Institutions, and Development*. H. Binswanger and V. Ruttan. Baltimore and London, Johns Hopkins University Press: 44–87.

Ruttan, V. and Y. Hayami (1984). 'Toward a Theory of Induced Institutional Innovation.' *Journal of Development Studies* 20(4): 203–24.

Shiferaw, B., G. Obare, and G. Muricho (2008). 'Rural Market Imperfection and the Role of Institutions in Collective Action to Improve Markets for the Poor.' *Natural Resource Forum* 32: 25–38.

Sulle, E. (2017). 'Social Differentiation and the Politics of Land: Sugar Cane Outgrowing in Kilombero, Tanzania.' *Journal of Southern African Studies* 43(3): 517–33. DOI: 10.1080/03057070.2016.1215171. Tanzania: Grain and Feed Annual. https://gain.fas.usda.gov/Recent%20GAIN%20Publications/Grain%20and%20Feed%20Annual_Dar%20es%20Salaam_Tanzania_3-29-2017.pdf [accessed April 2018].

Towards Implementation of National Rice Development Strategies in Tanzania. https://riceforafrica.net/downloads/Countries/tanzania/Tanzania_Promo_Word.pdf [accessed April 2018].

Timmer, P. (2009). *A World without Agriculture: The Structural Transformation in Historical Perspective*. Washington DC, AEI Press.

West, J. J. and R. Haug (2017). 'The Vulnerability and Resilience of Smallholder-Inclusive Agricultural Investments in Tanzania.' *Journal of Eastern African Studies* 11(4): 670–91.

Widgren, M. and J. Sutton (2004). *Islands of Intensive Agriculture in Eastern Africa*. Oxford, James Currey.

Woodhouse, P. et al. (2017). 'African farmer-Led Irrigation Development: Reframing Agricultural Policy and Investment?' *Journal of Peasant Studies* 44(1): 213–33.

World Bank (2007). 'World Development Report 2008: Agriculture for Development.' Washington DC, The World Bank.

12

Involution and Enterprise in Rural Areas

A Twenty-Year Perspective on Rural and Agricultural Change in Morogoro

Stefano Ponte and Dan Brockington

Epilogue pages 387–390

Introduction

The character and prospects of market-driven agrarian change in Tanzania has provoked considerable foreboding. Issa Shivji's predictions are probably the most wide ranging and depressing (Shivji 1992). As we have seen in Chapter 2, he envisaged that the inroads of capital and advent of more industrial agriculture would produce 'starving middle and poorer peasantry' (Shivji 1992: 129) and even a 'landless peasantry' (Shivji 1992: 128). He made these predictions in the late 1980s, and, revisiting them in 2017, felt he had been sadly vindicated (Shivji 2017).

As should be clear in this collection, we do not share this assessment of change in rural Tanzania. The middle and poorer peasantry are not starving. Levels of food poverty are in fact declining (albeit too slowly). There is greater differentiation between the middle and poorer peasantry, with the middle peasantry accruing assets. We do not see a merging of rural groups united in their want.

Shivji's prediction not only flattened social difference between rural groups in particular societies, lumping middle and poor together. It also erases geographical difference. It tells one story across a whole nation (indeed nations). This is also something we find hard to recognise. The stories in this collection speak of diversity and variation.

However, if Shivji's account is mistaken because it is too totalizing, it may still be true in particular places and specific locales. Indeed the misfortunes that Shivji feels are widespread have been recorded in places. Some of Brockington's early work documented disadvantage and vulnerability that arises from land loss to conservation and large-scale farms in pastoral areas (Igoe and Brockington 1999,

Stefano Ponte and Dan Brockington, *Involution and Enterprise in Rural Areas: A Twenty-Year Perspective on Rural and Agricultural Change in Morogoro* In: *Prosperity in Rural Africa? Insights into Wealth, Assets, and Poverty from Longitudinal Studies in Tanzania.* Edited by: Dan Brockington and Christine Noe, Oxford University Press. © Stefano Ponte and Dan Brockington 2021. DOI: 10.1093/oso/9780198865872.003.0012

Brockington 2002). More recent moves to alienate lands for capital threaten the livelihoods of thousands of farmers (Maganga et al. 2016, Bluwstein et al. 2018). Even if the scale of the threat may have been exaggerated (Locher and Sulle 2013 and 2014), the dangers are still plain and real for many families.

It is therefore important to take seriously detailed case studies from particular places, particularly when the nature of change and its local consequences, are disputed. Studies of change in the Uluguru Mountains in Morogoro region provide an excellent opportunity to do so. Here we revisit a series of debates in the late 1990s and early 2000s which have examined the long-term prospects of peasants in this region.[1]

In the first instance there were two rather gloomy predictions for farmers in these mountains. Hadjivayannis conceived of market penetration, the subordination of Uluguru society to the external world, and commoditization as the factors shaping agrarian change, making farmers passive recipients of structural change (Hadjivayannis 1993). He envisaged a vicious cycle of subordination to market forces which undermines the reproduction of the peasantry.

Van Donge in contrast emphasized social and actor-oriented determinants of agrarian change to explain an area where agriculture, and indeed the broader social fabric, was 'in decline' (van Donge 1992). Yields were static or declining, with soils exhausted, or suffering from erosion (cf. Jones 1996) and fertilizer use limited. But people in the area 'refuse[d] to contemplate switching to crops other than maize and using the cash earned from such crops to buy more food' (Jones 1996: 90). Agriculture was a risk-minimizing activity, not profit orientated. A disproportionate number of young men migrated to find work while women stayed at home looking after (unproductive) farms. Van Donge even suggested that the Luguru may have become demoralized, or somehow have lost belief in their own lifestyle. Decline such as this arose not from outside forces, but endogenously, from internal dynamics (van Donge 2002).

The processes these observers envisaged operating are different in their detail and structures. The one is driven by external forces, the other by internal dynamics. But they have in common the notion that population pressure and land scarcity combined to produce a crisis of agriculture looming dauntingly over the future of rural livelihoods.

In contrast Ponte's doctoral research clashed with the predominant depictions of the Uluguru Mountains being in a 'multiform crisis' (Hadjivayannis) and to farmers being 'trapped in decline' (van Donge). On the basis of fieldwork carried out in 1996/7, Ponte argued that the impact of market liberalization on rural livelihoods had been relatively positive in the area—where the rise in non-farm

[1] Morogoro Region has aroused much interest because of large-scale land alienations in Kilombero District and associated large-scale capital investment. Here however we are concerned with longer term trends within small-scale farming societies.

incomes has compensated for the general fall in farm incomes (Ponte 2001). The involuted mindsets van Donge had found seemed not to have persisted.

The progress farmers made still had to overcome multiple challenges. In Mgeta in the late 1990s, although agriculture was not going through an easy transition—especially for poorer farmers—new possibilities were being skilfully utilized (Ponte 2001). Land scarcity (especially for horticulture) were the main feature of agriculture. Deforestation and soil erosion were problems, and inputs had become increasingly expensive. In these circumstances, the main ways households could improve their quality of life—short of leaving the area altogether and in addition to relying on remittances from outside—were to expand land cultivated in other locations, to experiment with alternative farming systems, and to increase non-farm incomes.

Some of the changes observed at that time suggested an ongoing process of commercialization of agriculture—such as the increasing importance of vegetable cultivation, the growth of pig rearing, the substitution of hired labour for exchange labour, and an emerging market for land. Food security however was still a key factor influencing planting decisions and input allocation. Farming households showed a remarkable degree of flexibility and innovation—demonstrated, for example, by the emerging transition from cabbage to Irish potato cultivation. Wealthier farmers were benefiting from these changes, as increasing amounts of capital were needed to ensure food security, get access to land, hire labourers, and engage in commercialized pig rearing. Poorer farmers, especially those relying exclusively on agriculture for their livelihoods, were becoming more marginalized. The inhabitants of Mgeta were doing all the above, with a certain measure of success. Instead of being helplessly caught in a poverty trap, rural dwellers were reacting to marketing changes, demographic pressure, and land degradation in multiple and innovative ways, and in a majority of cases managed to improve their quality of life.

Importantly for the argument of this chapter, these changes were not general to Tanzania. Rather they stood out as different from other locations Ponte had researched 'since farmers' adaptations to changing markets had not led to higher incomes in other areas that [he] had researched in Tanzania' (Ponte 2002b: 313). In this respect his account accords with van Donge who deliberately tried to explore how the specific internal dynamics of a particular place could account for stasis and decline.

The case of the Uluguru Mountains therefore provides an excellent opportunity to provide a longer-term place-specific study, and a counterpoint to the generalizations with which we began. Our work is based on revisits to Mlali (first surveyed by Ponte in 1996 and by Ellis and Mdoe in 1999), a lowland village with relatively good land and favourable conditions for tomato cultivation. We re-surveyed thirty-two households from this village (out of fifty from the original samples) in 2016. Nyandira and Langali are neighbouring mountain villages in

Mgeta ward, a ninety-minute drive up the road from Mlali. The former was surveyed by Ellis and Mdoe in 1999, the latter by Ponte in 1996. Cumulatively, we revisited forty-three households in Mgeta (out of fifty from the original sample), also in 2016. We also undertook six focus groups in three villages as well as a number of key informant interviews.

Findings

Change in the Uluguru Mountains

The general trends we found in Langali and Nyandira are of continued efforts to engage in commercially orientated agriculture. There are some changes to the manner in which they are doing so. While cabbage was the top cash crop in Mgeta in the past, it has now been almost entirely replaced by Irish potatoes. A variety of other vegetables (from carrots to cucumbers) are still cultivated. Due to different altitude and climatic conditions, tomatoes ripen later in Mgeta than in Mlali, so they do not compete in the same seasonal market, making them profitable even in the smaller plots and harder terrain of the highlands. Root diseases are affecting cabbage cultivation, and fertilizer needs to be applied to any crop (even maize) to obtain decent yields. In other words, reliance on farm inputs, although not new, has increased. Relatives who have moved down to the plains or in urban areas are key sources of cash or loans to purchase inputs. The other source is small livestock (pigs, goats, chicken, farmed fish) that can be sold according to need. If all else fails, households rent out their plots to those who have funds to prepare the land and buy inputs, and work as farm labourers. Land preparation, given the terrain, is exclusively done by hand. Other researchers have found that, when combined with techniques of sustainable intensification, agricultural-based strategies can yield substantial improvements (Mdee et al. 2018).

Elders and focus groups participants did not report a massive outmigration flow, as portrayed in the 1990s literature, although they highlighted the lack of inward migration. In 2016, they also reported, surprisingly, that most households had access to land through inheritance and use-rights from their clan, although plots have become increasingly fragmented in time. Also surprising (but supported by field observations) was their claim that land per se was actually available, but mostly in locations far away from the village and where transport costs may not justify the effort after all. Focus group participants and interviews with elders suggested that the apparent availability of land can be explained as follows:

- plots may lack enough natural fertility and need to be left fallow for a few years;
- they may be too far away to be cultivated;

- the household may not have the resources to prepare and tend for the land, including farm input purchases; and
- even in this case, they may not want to rent it out for fear of not being paid at the end of the season.

Revisits to interview the original households that were originally surveyed in 1996 suggest a more complex picture of livelihood trajectories than in Mlali. While there are examples of upper mobility that emerged in the past twenty years, they are related to inheritance and a mixture of good management and good luck (lack of disease outbreaks in vegetable cultivation and favourable prices), at least in the first few years of cultivation after inheritance. These are accompanied by numerous instances of relative stagnation or decline, which are related to disease outbreaks, lack of resources to buy inputs, and only limited support from migrated household members. Housing conditions, even in these instances, have improved, and some of the children who have left and migrated elsewhere have found permanent employment or opened a business, thus sending remittances back to Mgeta. It is not easy to make a living on the Uluguru Mountains, but the people living here were not, and still are not 'trapped in decline'.

Transformations on the Plains

In previous work on rural livelihood change under market liberalization in Tanzania, Ponte argued that to understand rural transformation and processes of accumulation it is important to pay attention to the nature of the crops farmers grow (Ponte 1998). In particular, it is important to look at farmers' choices of 'fast' versus 'slow' growing crops because they use different marketing strategies for each. Most of the major fast crops grown in Tanzania (for example tomatoes, cabbage, or carrots) are susceptible to quicker deterioration; therefore, they have to be sold right after harvest at whatever price the market allows. Slow crops (most export crops, but also staples like maize and rice) can be sold before the next harvesting season arrives, if the household can wait that long, but the time interval is shorter than for slow crops.

In 1996, people talked about maisha magumu to refer to the problems encountered in post-liberalization rural life in Tanzania. The literal translation is 'hard life', but the meaning went beyond a mere sense of hardship and combines rising levels of contractual vis-à-vis 'traditional' social negotiations over access to resources such as land, labour, markets, and food (Ponte 2002a). Maisha magumu also reflected higher cash requirements for farming households because of:

- higher school fees and higher health expenditures;
- incentives and copying effects which make people buy, or feel they need to buy, more consumer goods;

- the establishment or the changing demands of an increasing number of off-farm enterprises;
- higher prices for agricultural inputs;
- increased use of hired labour; and
- the need for cash to ensure services which in the past were provided through social negotiations and the exchange of favours and labour (Ponte 2001).

Because cash requirements had become higher and spread throughout the entire year, farmers opted to grow crops with faster returns and/or with multiple or continuous selling seasons. In this way, they could get faster returns for their efforts and/or a continuous flow of cash. If farmers cultivated slow crops, they had to wait longer from land preparation to sale. They might distribute sales throughout the year, but then they had to deal with storage problems, social demands on their food stocks, and theft.

The 'fast crop' phenomenon was particularly distinctive in Mlali in the mid-1990s, a village located about 45km from Morogoro town, on the plains below the Uluguru Mountains. Mlali was, and still is, easily reachable via tarmac road as far as Mzumbe University, and then a short well-graded dirt road. The village is now served by many minibuses trawling back and forth from Morogoro town, while it was served by a few minibus lines in the mid-1990s. The centre of the village has literally boomed. There is a new market area and over fifty shops of all kinds, including two dedicated shops for agricultural inputs and various food joints. In 1996, there were fewer than ten, much smaller, shops. One of the most obvious changes we observed is the ubiquitous presence of young men on their pikipiki (motorbikes), a swarm going back and forth along the main road and larger footpaths, or hanging around waiting for their next client. Many of the pikipiki in the village are owned by well-off farmers. They are operated by young men, who pay a daily rate until they can buy it from the owner (a form of lease). Twenty years ago, only the very rich usually government employees had a motorbike—totalling less than five in Mlali. We counted eight out of thirty-two households who owned motorbikes in our sample. There are now also several private cars, parked in front of well-built houses with porches and electricity, and even a private truck. There were no private cars in the village in 1996.

Mlali was not a place where collective action was particularly strong even in 1996—by then the local primary cooperative society had already gone under, and the village farm had already been divided up and distributed to residents. The local economy at that time was driven by tomato cultivation, which had been introduced already in the early 1980s. Twenty years later, tomato cultivation is an even stronger driver of rural livelihoods in Mlali (with over 11 acres cultivated by the households we revisited), at least for those who have enough resources to buy farm inputs, own land or can rent it, and can draw household labour, hire farm workers, or use tractor services for this intensively cultivated crop. This also includes labour to carry water for irrigating tomato plants (a few wealthy farmers have installed drip irrigation). While paddy and maize are still farmed in the village, sorghum (the traditional food crop in this area) is less so. Sorghum grows more slowly than maize, and is not ready to harvest early enough to free up plots for the main tomato cultivation season. Therefore, farmers prefer to plant maize and then tomatoes after the maize harvest. There is a vibrant land rental market in Mlali, with plots being rented twice a year, depending on the planting season and with rental prices linked to the type of crop planted (premium prices are charged for the main tomato season).

Focus groups in Mlali, said that a key indicator of wealth is the amount of land put under tomato cultivation, not merely the amount of owned land. Ownership is not as important as the ability to use land—in our recent survey 30 per cent of land farmed to grow vegetables was rented. The key issue is thus access to capital or credit to rent land, buy inputs, and employ workers or, occasionally, use tractor services for cultivating tomatoes. The current use of tractors for land preparation (reported in 11 per cent of plots in the survey) is particularly interesting, as there was no sign of this service twenty years earlier.

Households in the top two wealth layers, as defined in focus groups, seem to be able to use tractor services for all their cultivated land, with at least five tractors available in a radius of a few kilometres. But even those in the middle wealth ranks, who prepare land by hand, seem to fare relatively well (as indicated by the quality of housing), as long as they have either accumulated funds, can sell an asset or borrow from relatives or from their social network to buy inputs, and on occasion hire labour. Without fertilizer and agrochemicals, tomato yields are much lower, and those who cannot afford them tend to rent out their plots to others. These tend to inhabit the lower wealth ranks, followed by those who, for health or other reasons, cannot take care of themselves.

A Rising 'Rural Middle' and Inequality

One of the challenges in tracking changes in poverty and prosperity using locally determined measures of wealth is that the meaning of wealth changes over time. People who were rich by the standards of twenty years ago might be considered poor now (cf. Mushongah and Scoones 2012). The good and assets that people aspire to (education, phones, financial services) are all different. It is thus difficult to compare like with like.

Houses however have long been a marker of social difference.[2] It is useful to explore changes in house condition over time. This shows that mud walls and

[2] Van Donge reported, based on fieldwork from 1985–7 that 'housing is the most notable indicator of wealth' (van Donge 1993: 83).

Table 12.1 House improvement in the three study villages

Roof	2016/17		
1996	Organic	Metal	
Organic	5	25	
Metal	4	38	
Total	9	63	
Walls	**2016/17**		
1996	**mud**	**brick**	**cement**
mud	9	14	1
brick	5	38	6
cement		1	
Total	14	53	7

Note the bricks can improve in quality if burned rather than sundried bricks are used, however the type of brick used in the earlier surveys was not always recorded. Grey cells indicate improved housing condition. So fourteen homes which had mud walls in 1996 now have brick walls in 2016/17. Twenty-five houses which had organic roofing material (commonly thatch) in 1996 had metal roofs in 2016/17. Most houses have maintained their condition (57 per cent with respect to roofing, 63 per cent with respect to walls), but 34 per cent have improved their roofs, and 28 per cent their walls. A smaller minority have declined in quality, thus four houses had metal roofs in 1996 but organic roofing material in the revisit.

sunburned bricks were quite common then, while now baked bricks are the norm. Cement floors, plastered walls, and indoor sanitation were only for the very rich then; they now have spread to the upper-middle ranks as well. As Table 12.1 shows, the clearest change is in roofing material, but also in the quality of walls (indicated in the highlighted cells).

In both Mlali and Mgeta housing condition suggests a rising group of middle wealth villagers, generally suggesting a movement from a pyramidal wealth structure in 1996 to more of a pointed egg structure nowadays (Ponte and Brockington 2020 and see Noe and Brockington this volume).[3] Inequality between the top and bottom categories seems to have increased in the past two decades. At the same time, the size of the 'middle ranks' (in local terms) seems to have increased substantially.

These changes have considerable implications for levels of inequality in the villages we have worked in. The range of wealth has increased. The poor and

[3] Note that in one site, Nyandira, Ellis and Mdoe found a larger middle group in their research in this village in 2001. Nyandira was also reported to be relatively commercialized by van Donge (1992).

destitute of today will share many of the characteristics of the poor and destitute of twenty years ago. The forms of poverty from which they suffer (no assets, poor houses, clothing, diets, and health) remain the same. However, at the upper end, the wealthy can now be much more wealthy, and in more ways, than they previously could. Their homes can be larger, with more amenities and finer finishing than what was common twenty years ago. Their means of transport are more modern, they can have more forms of power (solar and mains electricity), their children can go to private schools, and they can earn more money from more diverse sources than a generation ago.

Livelihood Trajectories

In both Mlali and Mgeta, many more non-farm activities, businesses, and transport services are available than two decades ago. And infrastructure (roads, marketplaces, and electricity provision) has improved markedly. Does that imply a general improvement of all livelihoods? Our re-visits to the original households in these Morogoro sites suggest four trajectories, the first of which is the most common.

- Trajectories of *agriculture-based improvement* based on expansion and intensification of tomato/vegetable cultivation—translating into much improved housing quality, more assets (including means of transport), diversification into other economic activities, ready availability of funds to solve health problems, and some of the children having gone through secondary education (or even tertiary) and formal employment in urban areas. This trajectory characterized 44 per cent of households we re-visited in the two Morogoro sites.
- trajectories of *marginal improvement or 'getting by'* in tomato/vegetable cultivation (less land, lower use of inputs) that suffices to: improve living conditions and types of assets; sometimes diversify in small business; access health services when needed (even if it entailed the sale of livestock or other small assets); and invest in some of the children's education (secondary school). In some cases at least one child landed a government job or set up a profitable business, sending remittances that further improved access to working capital for farming. This trajectory characterized 27 per cent of households we re-visited.
- Trajectories of *stagnation and decline*, where households could not get access to enough capital to purchase inputs, and thus limit their farming activities to food for partial self-sufficiency; members of these households tend to work in other people's fields as daily labourers; while their housing conditions may not have become worse, these households tend to send their children to primary school only, and to have little or no diversification into

non-farm activities; they also tend to struggle to find resources to take care of health problems. This trajectory described about 14 per cent of households we re-visited.

- Trajectories of *pauperism*, where people are not able or willing to take care of themselves, are not able to work for others, and rely on their household's help or other people's handouts. This is typical of ageing households and affected around 10 per cent of households we re-visited.[4]

With all the provisos we highlighted earlier, what seems to be emerging is a process of rural transformation based on smallholder agriculture. This is more clearly the case in Mlali, where the mainstay cash crop has remained the same, but the intensity of its cultivation has increased. This seems to have provided enough resources for further investment in retail activities and transport services—at least for a substantial proportion of the population. In Mgeta, rural transformation is less clearly rooted in smallholder agriculture, although it is happening for a minority of households. Farming systems are fairly similar to those observed twenty years ago, but with a different mix of cash crops. Input use is increasing and now necessary to obtain sufficient yields even for food crops, thus increasing risk and vulnerability in view of recent crop disease outbreaks. On the Uluguru Mountains, rural transformation seems to be stemming from a more complex combination of economic diversification, remittances, and marginal productivity gains for farmers who have enough access to capital to buy inputs. These processes are of course not universal, even within villages, but in general it seems fairly reasonable to suggest that wealth segmentation has switched from a pyramid structure to a 'pointed egg', with Mgeta having a larger base than Mlali. We explore this further in Chapter 17.

Conclusion

Research into the long-term dynamics of rural transformation in Africa is handicapped by a lack of good longitudinal and panel data which can reveal some of the poverty and prosperity dynamics. This deficiency is particularly glaring in countries like Tanzania, which has enjoyed substantial economic growth in the past two decades or so. It is difficult to specify what consequences this growth has had in rural areas, particularly when data about rural economies are poor and these rural spaces and resources are heavily contested.

On the basis of a diverse set of case studies from different parts of the country, a unique database and some in-depth examples we have shown that a diversity of processes and outcomes characterize different instances of rural transformation

[4] For the remaining 6 per cent of households we could not determine a clear trajectory.

in Tanzania. At the same time, when improvement occurs it seems to be fuelled by small-scale agriculture. These economic 'success stories' defy the predictions of the champions of large-scale agriculture and externally induced 'green revolutions'. They also challenge the more gloomy predictions that held Tanzanian small-holders as helpless prisoners of larger structural problems.

We cannot refute claims that land alienation is affecting poverty dynamics in some locations of Tanzania. None of the sites we have revisited suffered recent land loss due to agricultural investment, conservation, or mining. But, if anything, this reinforces the arguments that land loss will be harmful, because losing land removes the driver of relative prosperity—small-scale agriculture.

It is important to recall the limits of our methods. They have allowed us to cope with an important feature of rural life that is excluded by common measures such as poverty-line data. But looking for change in assets is a poor way of understanding the changing fortunes of migrant or itinerant labour. It can make it hard to see changes within domestic units, or between socio-economic groups and thus class dynamics. For that, the insights of the ethnographer which accompany the survey work, and the oral histories of change, are required.

With these provisos in mind, the main policy implication of our observations is that while there may be a role for large-scale commercial agriculture for rural transformation in Tanzania, it is not necessarily the only or best option in terms of poverty reduction at the village level. Even if there is land for it, it is not at all clear that large-scale commercial agriculture yields more benefits to rural households than those based on smallholder accumulation we reported here. The current focus on 'corridor investments' and large-scale commercial agriculture, such as that visible in Tanzania, with its deliberate renunciation of small-scale agriculture, may thus be misplaced.

References

Bluwstein, J., J. F. Lund, K. Askew, H. Stein, C. Noe, R. Odgaard, F. Maganga, and L. Engström (2018). 'Between Dependence and Deprivation: The Interlocking Nature of Land Alienation in Tanzania.' *Journal of Agrarian Change* 18: 806–30.

Brockington, D. (2002). *Fortress Conservation: The Preservation of the Mkomazi Game Reserve, Tanzania*. Oxford, James Currey.

Hadjivayannis, G. G. (1993). 'Stratégies paysannes face à la crise: adoption des innovations, diversification des activités et differenciations sociales dans un village tanzanien: Mgeta, Morogoro.' Thesis. Paros, Université de Paris I.

Igoe, J. and D. Brockington (1999). 'Pastoral Land Tenure and Community Conservation: A Case Study from North-East Tanzania.' Pastoral Land Tenure Series 11. London, IIED.

Jones, S. (1996). 'Discourses on Land Degradation in the Uluguru Mountains, Tanzania: Evolution and Influences.' *Journal of Rural Studies* 12(2): 187–99.

Locher, M. and E. Sulle (2013). 'Foreign Land Deals in Tanzania. An Update and Critical Review on the Challenges of Data (Re)Production Land Deal Politics Initiative.' LDPI Working Paper 31, The Land Deal Politics Initiative (LDPI), University of Zurich, http://dx.doi.org/10.5167/uzh-79407.

Locher, M. and E. Sulle (2014). 'Challenges and Methodological Flaws in Reporting the Global Land Rush: Observations from Tanzania.' *Journal of Peasant Studies* 41(4): 569–92.

Maganga, F. P., K. Askew, R. Odgaard, and H. Stein (2016). 'Dispossession through Formalization: Tanzania and the G8 Land Agenda in Africa.' *Asian Journal of African Studies* 40: 3–49.

Mdee, A., A. Wostry, A. Coulson, and J. Maro (2018). 'A Pathway to Inclusive Sustainable Intensification in Agriculture? Assessing Evidence on the Application of Agroecology in Tanzania.' *Agroecology and Sustainable Food Systems* 43(2): 201–27.

Mushongah, J. and I. Scoones (2012). 'Livelihood Change in Rural Zimbabwe over 20 Years.' *The Journal of Development Studies* 48(9): 1241–57.

Ponte, S. (1998). 'Fast Crops, Fast Cash: Market Liberalization and Rural Livelihoods in Songea and Morogoro Rural Districts, Tanzania.' *Canadian Journal of African Studies* 33(2): 316–48.

Ponte, S. (2001). 'Trapped in Decline? Reassessing Agrarian Change and Economic Diversification on the Uluguru Mountains, Tanzania.' *Journal of Modern African Studies* 39(1): 81–100.

Ponte, S. (2002a). *Farmers and Markets in Tanzania: How Policy Reforms Affect Rural Livelihoods in Africa.* Oxford, James Currey.

Ponte, S. (2002b). 'Reply to van Donge.' *Journal of Modern African Studies* 40(2): 313–20.

Ponte, S. and D. Brockington (2020). 'From Pyramid to Pointed Egg? A Twenty-Year Perspective on Poverty, Prosperity and Rural Transformation in Tanzania.' *African Affairs*. 119: 203–23.

Shivji, I. G. (1992). 'The Roots of an Agrarian Crisis in Tanzania: A Theoretical Perspective.' *The Tanzanian Peasantry: Economy in Crisis*. P. G. Forster and S. Maghimbi. Aldershot, Avebury: 124–50.

Shivji, I. G. (2017). 'The Concept of 'Working People'.' *Agrarian South: Journal of Political Economy* 6(1): 1–13.

van Donge, J. K. (1992). 'Agricultural Decline in Tanzania: The Case of the Uluguru Mountains.' *African Affairs* 91: 73–94.

van Donge, J. K. (1993). 'Trapped in Decline: A Sociological Analysis of Economic Life in Mgeta, Uluguru Mountains Tanzania.' PhD Thesis, Wageningen University.

van Donge, J. K. (2002). 'Trading Images? A Comment on Ponte's Reassessment of Agrarian Change in the Uluguru Mountains.' *Journal of Modern African Studies* 40(2): 303–11.

13

Rural and Agrarian Transformation 1984–2018 in Three Marginal Villages in Njombe Region, Tanzania

Esbern Friis-Hansen

Epilogue pages 398–399

Introduction

This chapter tells the past thirty-five years of the histories of Maliwa, Mammongolo, and Ngamanga villages, located in Njombe Region in the Southern Highlands of Tanzania. It is based on a longitudinal study revisiting the sixty-six domestic units that participated in the original study undertaken in 1983–5. The aim of the original research was to understand changes in land tenure and land use since Tanzania's nationwide 'villagization' programme that took place in 1974, ten years previously (Friis-Hansen 1987).

An important feature of these three villages was that they were marginal in relation to the rest of Njombe Region. At the time of the original study Njombe was the centre of a green revolution in the 1980s based on maize production and using subsidized and loan-based technology packages containing hybrid seeds, fertilizer, and pesticides, turning the region into the country's food basket (Rasmussen 1986). The three villages in this study were marginal in four respects. Physically, poorly constructed and maintained roads left them relatively isolated from interaction with the outside world. Developmentally, they had little influence over the allocation of state resources and were largely out of reach of development policies and institutions. Technologically, they had very little access to inputs and advice for improving agricultural enterprises. Finally, two villages were disadvantaged environmentally, Maliwa being too cold for maize, the main crop in Njombe, because of its location at 2,100m altitude, and Ngamanga being too dry for maize, being located in semi-arid zone that only received 600mm of rainfall annually.

Esbern Friis-Hansen, *Rural and Agrarian Transformation 1984–2018 in Three Marginal Villages in Njombe Region, Tanzania*
In: *Prosperity in Rural Africa? Insights into Wealth, Assets, and Poverty from Longitudinal Studies in Tanzania*.
Edited by: Dan Brockington and Christine Noe, Oxford University Press.
DOI: 10.1093/oso/9780198865872.003.0013

When I revisited the three villages three decades later, they were no longer marginal. It was clear that major socio-economic developments had taken place. The first part of this chapter will therefore examine the agrarian and rural transformation of the three villages and the pace in which they took place in relation to three overall historical periods. The second half of the chapter examines the extent to which these agrarian and rural transformations have proved socially inclusive by analysing changes in well-being among the participants (primary units) in the original study and their descendants (secondary units). Using farmers' own perceptions of well-being, combining assets and entitlements/relationships, changes in the ranking criteria of well-being are discussed. However, first the section will recapture and summarize the prior situation at the time of the original study and discuss the research and fieldwork methodologies used during the follow-up study.

Fieldwork Methodology

I revisited the three villages several times. In 2011 group interviews and qualitative interviews with key informants and participants in the original study were carried out in all three villages using a semi-structured questionnaire. The focus was on agricultural and rural change during the 1980s, 1990s and 2000s.

Re-interviews with the original domestic units (households) using quantitative survey tools were undertaken in 2017/18. The original study sample comprised a total of sixty-six households in the three villages. The re-interviews only managed to identify and re-interview thirty-four of the original domestic units and secondary units. This amount to ten to twelve cases in each village which I judged to be too low to generate meaningful data. I therefore decided to analyse the questionnaires qualitatively and to follow them up with additional interviews when required. Following up qualitative in-depth interviews was carried out with village officials, key informants, and selected domestic households in 2018.

In 2017 I carried out focus-group discussions with key stakeholders and with separate groups of men and women in all three villages to explore local perceptions of well-being and changes in well-being over time. Asset-based indicators as a measure of relative well-being have been shown to be more relevant than the consumption-based indicators used by the World Bank and many national statistical departments in the Global South (Abraham and Kumar 2008, IFAD 2016, Chapter 2 this volume). Kumar used ranking indicators of asset-based well-being to compare how rural people fall into and out of poverty across countries. Recently asset-based indicators have used to compare livelihood changes over time (Mushongah and Scoones 2012). However, using asset-based indicators alone to assess levels of well-being has been criticized (Sen 1993, Ravnborg et al. 2004).

This suggests that aspects of social relations and entitlements to indicators of well-being should be taken into account as well.

Over the past two decades, DIIS researchers have used well-being ranking, methodology-based perceptions of well-being among groups of local key informants (Friis-Hansen and Duveskog 2005). This methodology was first developed by Ravnborg (1999) and later adapted for use in East Africa (Ravnborg et al. 2004). The resulting well-being ranking was developed with the aim of making it generally valid over the whole region. Therefore, outlying context-specific indicators were removed, leaving only the generic well-being ranking indicators that proved to have general validity.

The outcome of the 2017 focus-group discussions was thirteen well-being ranking indicators, of which six are asset-based indicators (land, animals, house, food security, quality of food, and quality of clothing), three are social relations-based indicators (working as casual labour, hire casual labour, and non-agricultural enterprises), two relate to access to social services (health and education), while the final two are social indicators (gender status of household and age). The qualitative interviews with key informants resulted in three current well-being indicators that include context-specific indicators for each of the three villages.

Prior Situation

Villagization, or the nationwide compulsory resettlement of the rural population of Tanzania into nuclear settlements, was implemented in the Southern Highlands during the dry season of 1974 as part of President Nyerere's Ujamaa policy. In the southern highlands the original study identified three main types of village settlements, two of which are represented by the original study villages. In the first settlement type, represented by Maliwa and Mamongolo villages, two or more smaller settlements have been amalgamated into a village with a minimum of 150 households. In both villages, farmers lived scattered in the valley bottom before villagization, with easy access to natural resources, such as the three types of fields located on the hillside, valley bottom and wetland, water and forest resources, and hilltop grazing land. In the case of Maliwa village farmers who lived in the smaller Unege Valley, located three and a half hours walking distance from Maliwa Valley, were forcefully resettled in Maliwa, where they were allocated half an acre each to build a new house. The farmers from Unege were all resettled in a nuclear settlement on a hillside, while the original inhabitants of Maliwa were allowed to continue to live in their scattered houses. In the case of Mamongolo village, three settlements, each with fewer than 150 households, were amalgamated into two villages. The resettlement pattern was similar to that of Maliwa village. Farmers from Makoo Valley were forced to resettle on small plots located close to each other, while the native people of Mamongolo were not resettled. In the second settlement type, represented by Ngamanga village, people living scattered were all resettled in a nuclear settlement, in houses organized in rows. Ngamanga is located in flat semi-arid area, and before villagization farmers lived scattered with relative large distances between households because of the extensive character of their agropastoral farming systems. In the third type of settlement, not represented by any of the three original study villages, farmers living scattered in a valley along a ridge were all resettled in houses organized in rows along a road on top of the ridge (Rasmussen 1986, Friis-Hansen 1987).

The original study found that while villagization had forced some families to be resettled long distances from their original homes, others had been affected less or not at all. While villagization changed rural settlement patterns, it was only accompanied by reforms to land tenure to a limited extent. Land located in the centre of the new village settlements was appropriated by village governments from their owners and allocated as small plots for those who had been resettled so they could build a house and cultivate for their own subsistence. However, those who had been resettled over long distances and therefore were no longer able to cultivate their fields located back in mahami (the areas they originally inhabited) were not given sufficient new land to cultivate close to their new homes.

The original study was carried out a decade after villagization and showed how those who had been moved long distances had become marginalized, as compared with those who were moved shorter distances or not moved at all. 'Newcomers' either had to spend hours walking back to their old fields or had to rent land from those who were 'native' in the village settlement, either of which limited their levels of agricultural production. More frequently they worked for other farmers and became politically marginalized. Available household labour time for productive work in the fields was not only constrained by the increased walking distances to agricultural fields, water sources, and firewood, but also by the withdrawal of child labour into education and the large amount of time spent on compulsory communal village projects and village meetings (Friis-Hansen 1987).

The original study analysed the impact of villagization on changes in land use and agricultural production. The study concluded that in general fields close to the village settlements were cultivated more intensively, especially by farmers who had been resettled by villagization, with inadequate use of fertilizer resulting in the already low yields declining even further. Agricultural intensification took different forms in the three study villages, including reductions in fallow periods (Mamongolo), more crops being grown through intercropping (Maliwa) and shifts in cropping patterns (Ngamanga).

Poverty was abundant in the three villages at the time of the original study in the early 1980s, with up to 85 per cent of households being poor (the concept of poverty is discussed later). Agricultural production in the study village was primarily focused on subsistence, with sales of surplus production when available to pay for social reproduction, including school fees and clothing (Friis-Hansen 1987). The traditional food system, comprising three overlapping subsistence food bridges, as described by Branner Jespersen (1971), was still being practised at the time of the study. The three subsistence food bridges were: (1) crops and vegetables planted in August (early dry season) in fields located adjacent to streams in the valley bottom using residual moisture (vinyungu), and harvested green little by little in March–April and mature/dry in May; (2) rain-fed crops (beans, peas, sorghum, and maize) planted at the start of the rainy season in December and picked little by little green from the fields in May–June; and (3) harvesting mature, dry, rain-fed crops in July and consuming them in July–February. The total harvest of dry rain-fed crops was very low and recorded by the original study in debe (twenty-litre tins) rather than bags. The poor, who were numerous, frequently experienced food deficits during the third food bridge. During the four months from November to February many poor only had food for one meal a day and had to access food through social networks.

At the time of the original study, major agricultural labour tasks were carried out by means of an informal collaboration between farmers (called migoe in the local Kibena language) and the traditional farming system, which ensured that labour requirements were equally distributed throughout the year, was still in place (Branner Jespersen 1971). During the main rainy season from November to May, farmers worked in the fields located on the slopes and ridges. The key labour input was for clearing fallow, while labour requirements for planting, weeding, and harvesting were limited. Harvests took place at the start of the dry season (June–July), while after August to October farmers cultivated the valley bottom (vinyungu) taking advantage of the residual moisture in the soil along the streams. These valleys were highly fertile and yields were higher than elsewhere.

Farmers in the three villages had very limited access to services or manufactured products. Mamongolo and Maliwa villages had a small, poorly stocked government-owned village shop with basic items such as tea, sugar, soap, and a limited selection of clothing, while agricultural inputs and implements, such as hoes and ploughs, were unavailable. Ngamanga village had no shop.

The original study found that in all three villages 'Ujamaa' fields were cultivated collectively, all households in the village being obliged to participate. Political leaders decided what should be grown, often reflecting national campaigns urging farmers to work harder and cultivate specific crops (Raikes 1987). Communal production was directed by village managers appointed by the ruling Chama cha Mapinduzi party. Households who failed to show up during the bi-weekly cultivation of the Ujamaa field were subject to stiff fines or sometimes even imprisonment. With some notable exceptions, the productivity of most Ujamaa fields in Njombe was low. In part this was because of low work morale and passive resistance, as part of the surplus was appropriated by the village officials, and in part because of mismanagement by village managers, who were politically rather than agriculturally motivated (Friis-Hansen 1987).

Agrarian and Rural Transformation: Spatial and Social Differentiation

In the past decade the African continent has experienced agrarian and rural transformation. There are, however, large spatial and social variations in the intensity and pace of these changes, both between and within countries (Haggblade et al. 2010, Berdegué et al. 2013, IFAD 2016, Agergaard et al. 2019). Agricultural transformation, including 'rising agricultural productivity, increasing commercialization and marketable surpluses, and diversification of production patterns and livelihoods' (IFAD 2016: 23), is included in a broad socio-economic process of change embodied in the wider concept of rural transformation. Rural transformation 'involves expanding decent off-farm employment and entrepreneurial opportunities, better rural coverage and access to services and infrastructure, and greater access to, and capacity to influence, relevant policy processes' (ibid.). Furthermore, rural transformation involves diversifying rural livelihoods, with reliance on agriculture gradually being replaced by reliance on off- and non-agricultural activities associated with a decrease in rural poverty (Ellis 2005).

In economic history one of the dominant debates of the past decade has been whether long-term economic change is driven primarily by institutional change or changes in factor endowments (such as land or labour availability). National economic and agricultural policies are influencing the socio-economic and institutional situations in rural areas and may be important drivers for either economic growth or stagnation (Hillbom and Svensson 2013). On the other hand, the changes in endowments of natural resource factors, such as population growth and pressure on natural resources, may stimulate local technological innovation and long-term productivity growth (Fischer-Kowalski et al. 2014).

Analysis of fieldwork data from the three villages in Njombe suggests that both agrarian and rural transformations have taken place during the thirty-five-year period (1983–2018). In terms of agrarian transformation, many but not all farmers in the three villages have shifted from subsistence farming to being engaged in commercial agricultural enterprises, for example, potatoes in Mamongolo and Maliwa, pine trees in Mamongolo and Maliwa, and tomatoes in Ngamanga. Similarly, evidence from the three villages indicates that a rural transformation has taken place, including an increase in commercial non-agricultural enterprises, a shift towards a formal labour rural market and improved access to social services and infrastructure.

Historically in industrial countries agrarian transformation has resulted in rural and structural transformations, with the emergence of a highly productive agricultural sector employing a small share of the total labour force. The rural population otherwise rendered surplus by these changes was absorbed by industrialization in urban centres (Hillbom and Svensson 2013). Evidence from the three villages indicates that rural transformation has largely been financed by government and development partners, rather than increased agricultural productivity. Moreover, the timing and sequence of agrarian and rural transformation differ, evidence from the three villages indicating that rural transformation preceded agrarian transformation.

Based on group discussions with key informants in the three villages and literature on the political history of Tanzania (Boesen et al. 1986, Friis-Hansen 2000, Coulson 2013) three very broad historical periods can be identified, each with a distinct set of economic and agricultural policies and associated socio-economic and institutional contexts: (1) 1984–9, characterized by economic crisis, adjustment, and state-sponsored agricultural modernization; (2) 1990–9, characterized by privatization, liberalization, and market failure; (3) 2000–18, characterized by economic growth and the emergence of private-sector institutions. In the following sections we will analyse agrarian and rural transformation in the three villages during each of these historic periods.

Economic Crisis, Adjustment, and State-Sponsored Agricultural Modernization (1984–9)

Tanzania experienced an economic crisis in the early 1980s with significant macro-economic imbalances and, as a consequence, shortages and the erratic supply of most basic commodities (Boesen et al. 1986). In 1982 the country received emergency loans and was placed under an Economic Structural Adjustment programme by the World Bank. However, in spite of the economic crisis, the government continued to promote 'state-sponsored agricultural modernization' through its parastatal institutions, which enjoyed monopoly status (Coulson 2013). Villages in the Southern Highlands that were located in high-potential areas and with access to the main roads benefitted from pan-territorial minimum crop prices, subsidized loan packages containing hybrid maize seed, fertilizer and pesticides, and general subsidies for input prices. The Southern Highlands shifted from being an area that was self-sufficient in food and marketed production of 2000 tonnes per year in the 1970s to becoming the nation's food basket in the 1980s, with annual marketed maize production of 250,000 tonnes (Rasmussen 1986). However, because of the economic crises, subsidized inputs only reached about one-third of the farmers in the Southern Highlands (Friis-Hansen 1987). Qualitative group interviews during the revisits indicate that, because of their marginal status, the three study villages did not receive state support and were excluded from the green revolution in the rest of Njombe.

The socialist Ujamaa policy gradually weakened during the 1980s, as was reflected in the three study villages. The forced collective cultivation of Ujamaa fields, which was still practised during the original study, was abolished in 1985 and the former Ujamaa fields subdivided into private bega-kwa-bega (shoulder-by-shoulder) plots, where farmers were forced to cultivate the same crop, as directed by political campaigns. Although farmers were now able to keep the proceeds, the system of bega-kwa-bega production quickly became equally unpopular, as farmers were forced to grow cash crops for which there was no market. According to group interviews in the three villages, the bega-kwa-bega system was also abolished at the end of the 1980s.

As another indication that the Ujamaa era was coming to an end, restrictions on village settlements were quietly lifted in 1986, and farmers were allowed to move back to their former homes if they wanted to. However, none of the domestic and secondary units interviewed in the three villages had moved back to their former homes. Farmers explained that, after living in nucleus settlements for twelve years, they had become accustomed to having access to social services, such as schools, water supplies, and health clinics, and to living in close proximity to others. Primary education for the children and access to a dispensary were given as reasons for people choosing to remain in the village settlement during the follow-up survey. However, group interviews indicate that some farmers moved back to their old homes (Mahami), in particular in Ngamanga village, as the consequences of inadequate access to land were most severe in this village.

Privatization, Liberalization, and Market Failure (1990–9)

By the end of the 1980s, the Tanzanian state was bankrupt and had no choice but to accept a structural adjustment loan from the World Bank. The formulation of the adjustment policy was based on the report 'Sub-Saharan Africa: From Crisis to Sustainable Growth' (World Bank 1989). The report argues that to push agriculture on to an upward path, it was necessary to 'get prices right' by making exchange rates more competitive and by reducing public marketing margins in order to allow producers a higher share of the world market price. The focus in these arguments was on export crops. In terms of food-crop marketing the reform argued for liberalization by eliminating 'distortions' such as pan-territorial pricing, subsidies on inputs and restrictions on private trade (Friis-Hansen 2000: 25–6).

A review of the performance of agricultural policy in Africa after adjustment (Friis-Hansen 2000) concludes that, while the elimination of state and parastatal intermediary organizations to some extent increased cost effectiveness, it left a number of areas uncovered, as private entrepreneurs found the returns too low or the risk too high in the absence of institutional or infrastructural support. Friis-Hansen (2000) argues that in Tanzania structural adjustment has been socially and geographically skewed, favouring the better-off farmers and those living in areas where there is good market access. While in part this has been a deliberate attempt to let market forces determine where it is most profitable to produce, these policies have had serious costs, in particular for farmers living in areas with high transport costs to market who previously cultivated food crops using subsidized inputs.

This is exactly the situation for green revolution farmers in the Southern Highlands of Tanzania. Structural adjustment reforms envisaged diversification of production in such areas. However, this did not take place in the 1990s. The abolition of fertilizer subsidies and the cancelling of pan-territorial pricing meant that it was no longer economically viable for farmers in the Southern Highlands to cultivate hybrid maize using bio-chemicals. From maize yields above three tonnes per ha using bio-chemical inputs, yields were reduced to half a tonne per ha without the use of inputs. Market production of maize from the Southern Highlands collapsed from one year to the next, while maize production shifted to Morogoro and other areas closer to the Dar es Salaam market.

Maliwa village experienced an unexpected change in the 1990s. The village was a net buyer of maize, as no one grew maize in Maliwa because of overnight frost in the growing season. However, because of the collapse in maize production in Njombe Region as a whole, there was no longer any commercial maize available to purchase. In 1998 some farmers therefore decided to cultivate maize using small amounts of fertilizer bought from remittances send back by family members working outside the village. Farmers explained during a group interview that it had become possible to cultivate maize as it had become warmer (perhaps due to climate change) and that it was cost effective for them to grow maize using small amounts of fertilizer, compared with buying maize at high prices from Njombe town.

During this decade many donor-financed development programme experimented with new approaches to agricultural development such as tree planting. Several agricultural and environmental development programmes were introduced in the Southern Highlands, in particular the Hifadhi ya Mazingira (Protect the Environment) Natural Resources Conservation and Management Programme in Tanzania (HIMA) that promoted sustainable agricultural production, natural resource management, and forestry production among farmers, by utilizing participatory approaches that involved the local population and relevant 'indigenous knowledge' (Danida 2007).

During this decade, farmers from Mamongolo and Maliwa villages engaged in planting pine and cypress trees on mountain tops and steep slopes. Farmers learned about tree planting from the Danida-supported HIMA project implemented in parts of Southern Highlands. In Ngamanga farmers started combining cow manure with limited amounts of fertilizer to grow sunflowers intercropped with cowpeas for marketing.

The biggest change for the three study villages during the 1990s was a dramatic increase in migration to urban centres in search of work. A group of young men moved from Mamongolo village to Tunduma, a town on the border between Tanzania and Zambia, in the late 1990s. They started out as migrant labourers and thereafter settled permanently and became engaged in business activities such as small shops and money-changing. Later they attracted many others to join them (interview with secretary Mamongolo village 2011).

This migration to Tunduma has been accompanied by other out-migration such that the pressure of population and production on resources in the three study villages indicates that population-land ratios have not increased significantly. The number of permanent residents in the villages has remained more or less constant over the three decades, as the surplus population has migrated to urban centres. During an interview in 2017, the village chairman stated: 'The number of people living in Maliwa should have doubled during the past thirty years, but instead it has stayed at the same level as in the 1980s.'

However, other demographic changes have taken place: most importantly, the fertility rate has fallen by 50 per cent from around 7 to 3.5 children per woman. The secretary of Maliwa village estimated that more people from Maliwa now live outside the village than in the village, with consequences for both remittances and investments. While many resident households in Maliwa have relatives outside the village, only some receive remittances to the extent that it changes their livelihood.

Economic Growth and the Emergence of Private-Sector Institutions (2000–18)

All three villages have since the turn of the century initiated a process towards an agrarian transformation by engaging in commercial agricultural and silvicultural enterprises. This change has predominantly been market driven under liberal trade policies with limited influence or support from the state. Four factors seem to have stimulated this change. Firstly, a consistent strong urban demand for agricultural and silvicultural products spurred by high economic growth, averaging 6–7 per cent increase in GDP a year (World Bank 2019). Secondly, that the three previous marginal villages became much better physically linked to the market. This is illustrated in Table 13.1 below. For Ngamanga and Maliwa the construction of improved roads made a huge difference in terms of connecting to the outside world. In all three villages private traders now accessed the villages with trucks and competed to buy farmers products.

Table 13.1 Rural transformation of Maliwa, Mamongolo, and Ngamanga villages

	1970s	1980s	1990s	2000s	2010s
Primary school	X 0 #				
Community shop		X 0			
Community milling machine		X 0			
Dispensary		X	0 #		
Community water supply			X 0 #		
Secondary school in next village			X 0 #		
Iron sheets on houses			X 0 #		
Private shops			X 0 #		
All season road		0		X #	
Solar electricity in houses				X 0 #	
Mobile phones				X 0 #	
PVC irrigation pipes				X 0 #	
HIV dispensary unit				X 0 #	
Specialized shops and services				X 0 #	
Competing traders in village				X 0 #	
Private mobile saw mill				X 0	
Motorbikes				X 0 #	
Daily bus service				#	X 0
Improved market place				#	X

Note: X=Maliwa, 0=Mamongolo, and #=Ngamanga.

Thirdly, the availability of industrial goods from China in Njombe Region from 2005, including PVC irrigation pipes (for potatoes and tomatoes) and mobile saw mills (for pine trees), motorbikes, and solar electricity systems, made another huge impact that stimulated agricultural and silvicultural enterprises and as well as general rural development. Specialized private shops, daily bus service and mobile phones further revolutionized farmers' access to agricultural inputs and market information.

Fourthly, the net emigration of young people out of the three villages during the 1990s has during the 2000s turned into a net immigration of people and/or resources. In the past five to ten years, there has been an increasing tendency for young people to stay in the village. Furthermore, an increasing number of those who emigrated are returning to villages and bring with them resources to invest in improved houses and high-cost agricultural enterprises such as irrigated potatoes, tomatoes, or pine trees, or invest in non-agricultural enterprises such as guesthouses, specialized shops, or restaurants. Ngamanga village, in particular, has experienced population growth after the construction of a new road connecting it directly to Makambako town. Maliwa and Mamongolo villages have experienced a considerable increase in investments in establishing woodlots of pine trees by emigrants from the villages who now live in urban centres.

The three main agricultural and silvicultural enterprises are: (1) irrigated potato green revolution in Mamongolo and Maliwa, (2) rush to establish woodlots of pine trees in Maliwa and Mamongolo; and (3) irrigated tomato production in Ngamanga. Together they are the main drivers of an agrarian transformation in the three villages.

The Potato Green Revolution

Njombe Region has experienced a second green revolution since the turn of the century (Koizumi 2007, Njombe Regional Commissioners Office 2016). The first green revolution in Njombe was based on subsidized packages of hybrid maize seed, fertilizer, and pesticides during the 1980s, as described by Rasmussen (1986). The potato green revolution is based on the use of fertilizer, pesticides, and to some extent irrigation. However, 99 per cent of farmers continue to use locally retained potato seed varieties, given the limited availability of planting material for the improved potato variety (kikondo) because of the absence of an effective seed industry. Nevertheless, the potato green revolution has been one of the main forces driving agrarian transformation, in particular over the past decade. The follow-up study found clear evidence of this in Maliwa and Mamongolo villages. Potato cultivation is not new in the Southern Highlands, having been introduced by German missionaries as early as the 1920s (Macha et al. 1982) and have good growing conditions there because of the high elevations (1,700 to 2,800 meters above the sea level) and high rainfall.

The potato green revolution in the Southern Highlands has been driven by the private market, with limited direct state support. Over the past decade annual production of potatoes has varied between 500 and 900 thousand tonnes (Njombe Regional Commissioners Office 2016). A recent PhD thesis on the potato value chain in Njombe (Daniel et al. 2018) shows that Njombe farmers grow an average of 1.6 acres of potatoes per household, with a harvest of 6–10 tonnes per year. With post-harvest producer prices for potatoes similar to those of maize, and yields twice those of maize, potatoes have become a highly attractive enterprise for farmers in Njombe, in particular in villages that are marginal for growing maize (see Box 13.1).

Forestry Driven by Private-Sector Investments sk944

Many pine trees were planted in Maliwa and Mamongolo villages with the dual aim to protect the environment and as a cash crop during the 1990s, with support from donor agencies, such as Danida. However, because of difficulties with physical access to markets, the planting of woodlots progressed slowly until the mid-2000s. To access the market, small-scale tree growers had to fell their trees using manual saws, manually transport the four-metre-long tree trunks to the

Box 13.1 Case study: Charles's potato production in Mamongolo village

In Mamongolo village potatoes are mainly grown by young men. One example is Mr Charles Sanga, the son of Tobias Sanga, who participated in the original study. He inherited land from his father and planted 1.5 acres located in the valley with potatoes in 2005. He used his savings (350,000 TZS) from work as a migrant in Dar es Salaam to buy local potato seeds, fertilizer, pesticides, a fifty-metre PVC water pipe, and two sprinklers. Connecting the PVC pipe from a small stream to sprinklers has enabled Charles to produce a second potato crop during the dry season. The potatoes are sold to traders, who collect the crop in trucks. In 2017 the farm-gate price for rain-fed potatoes in Mamongolo village was 30,000 TZS per bag, while the price for irrigated potatoes was 55,000 TZS per bag. Charles's total income from the sale of potatoes was approximately 4 million TZS, of which he spent around half a million on inputs. Selling potatoes has been the main income for Charles's household, paying for school fees, building a new modern house and acquiring a motorbike. (Interview, December 2017)

road, and hire a private truck to transport them to sawmills, which were located some 300km away adjacent to Sao Hill state forest. The availability of cheap mobile sawmills and chainsaws from China in Njombe from 2005 allowed timber traders to buy trees from farmers while still in the field and process them into timber in situ. During the late 2000s many farmers sold the trees they planted in the early 1990s and earned much higher income than from crop production. This spurred a timber rush among farmers. On the one hand many farmers planted pine trees on part of their land and on the other land village governments in both Mamongolo and Maliwa reclassified common grazing areas into land for tree planting. This land was either allocated to villagers or sold to outside investors who were interested in establishing wood plantations in the village. One example is in Maliwa village, where the village government in 2012 sold 100 acres grazing land to a group of six shop keepers from Njombe town. The income was used to build a new village government office (see Box 13.2).

Tomato Production in Ngamanga

The construction of a direct road from Ngamanga village to Makambako in 2000 cut down travelling time from four hours on a difficult road to fifteen minutes

Box 13.2 Case study: William, remittances and investments in Mamongolo village

In 1983 William, one of the farmers who participated in the original study in Mamongolo village, lived in a poorly constructed mud hut with his family, his children being in primary school. Today he is old and lives alone in a new modern house with solar electricity, a fridge, a satellite TV, and a water tap inside the house. The house was built by one of his sons Joseph, who left the village, but is supporting him financially. Joseph emigrated in 1993 to Tunduma, a town on the Zambian border, where he worked for ten years as a black-market currency trader. In 2003 Joseph moved with his family to Dar es Salaam, where he built a business that imports used cars from Dubai. With the help from his farther, Joseph bought 50 acres of grazing land in 2010, on which he has planted pine trees. (Qualitative interview 2017)

Box 13.3 Case study: Richard, once poor now a well-off tomato farmer in Ngamanga village

Richard was 17 years old in 1983 and the son of one of the domestic units in the original study. He also worked for the original study as a research assistant. He was in his early thirties when the tomato boom started in Ngamanga village. He did not own land himself at the time and for some years he cultivated tomatoes on fields that he rented for a year at a time in the vinyungu. Eventually he has accumulated sufficient surplus to buy land of his own. He also managed to buy six oxen and a plough that he uses to cultivate rainfed sunflowers. Income from irrigated tomatoes has also paid for building a new modern house with solar electricity and paying school fees for his children. His tomato production is intensive and he used expensive F1 hybrid tomato seeds, fertilizers, and pesticides that produced high yields.

on tarmac. By cultivating tomatoes in the wetland areas (vinyungu) farmers in Ngamanga are able to supply Makambako with tomatoes during the off season where prices are much better than when rainfed tomatoes are in season. In 2017, when the study team revisited Ngamanga, tomato production had become the main commercial enterprise in the village and a tomato market had developed in the village, where traders came in trucks from Makambako to buy tomatoes (see Box 13.3).

Main Social Changes

This section discusses the extent to which agrarian and social transformations have been socially inclusive by undertaking a comparative analysis of well-being and well-being ranking criteria in 1983 and 2017 based on farmers own relative perception of well-being then and now. Overall, the analysis finds a significant reduction in poverty in all three villages. As for the change in people's perception of poverty, the analysis indicates minor changes in *type of ranking criteria* that farmers identify as important for well-being, with significant changes in each *individual criterion's value/content*. Through group discussions the study identified fourteen unique well-being ranking criteria based on farmers' perception of well-being. Six of these criteria are based on assets, two are based on relationships, while four are social, i.e. food security, food quality, gender, and age. After identifying the well-being criteria, the groups were asked to assess the what proportion of people in the village belonged to each of the three wealth categories. The results were triangulated and inconsistencies between different assessment were questioned and adjusted accordingly. The result was three sets of well-being assessments to which there was agreement among villagers. The analysis uses Maliwa village as an example.

Table 13.2 indicates a very high level of poverty during the time of the original study, which is consistent with the author's observations at the time. The table further indicates that the poverty level has been reduced to less than a third, while the average well-being category has grown most. The present study does not have information about social mobility between the three categories, which is likely to be considerable given length of the period (thirty-three years). Qualitative observations indicate that the main source of income for upwards social mobility are whether the household are engaged in commercial agricultural enterprises or high-entry non-agricultural enterprises. As shown earlier, the growth in these enterprises has mainly taken place over the past ten to fifteen years, predominantly driven by younger farmers.

Meanwhile the study observed a clear downward social mobility for old farmers, as reflected in age being identified as a well-being ranking criteria. I further observed in the revisits that many farmers above 60 years old in the three villages were poor, as they were no longer able to work sufficiently in the fields and did not receive adequate support from their children. One example from a domestic

Table 13.2 Well-being change in Maliwa village, 1984–2017

	Well-off	Average	Poor
1984	10%	5%	85%
2017	25%	50%	25%

unit in the original study is Mr Edward. In 1983 he was in his forties, chairman of Maliwa village and well-off in terms of land and livestock. During the revisit in 2017 the study team interviewed him, now in his late seventies and still living in his old traditional house. He was poor and food insecure, being too old to grow his own food and with no relatives to support him. Mrs Rozina is another example from a domestic unit in the original study in Maliwa village. She is now 90 years old and the study team met her busy weeding in a field with beans. Also she was alone, outliving her husband and children. She survives by selling pine trees which were planted by her late husband in the 1990s and uses the money to pay for casual labour in fields. She told the team that she had only ten trees left to sell to support her as a pension.

Farmers' perceptions of well-being have changed from 1983 to 2017, as indicated in Table 13.3. Overall, the biggest changes have happened in the substance of the well-off well-being category, however it is nevertheless also correct that those who were poor in 2017 were better off that those who were poor in 1983. We will discuss this in detail below.

The six asset-based criteria for well-being ranking used are: 'land', 'agricultural enterprises', 'livestock', 'non-agricultural enterprises', 'housing', and 'clothing'. Land for cultivation as an important well-being criterion has not changed. However, land for tree planting, the main economic enterprise in Maliwa village, has become a new important well-being criterion. Trees are in part planted on former village grazing land that is allocated to 'capable farmers' (interview with village secretary Maliwa village 2017). Secondly, some farmers who own more land than they cultivate convert some of their land to woodlots with pine trees. For this reason it has become more difficult for poor farmers to rent land for cultivation. The importance of ownership of livestock as a well-being criteria has decreased, in part because of the non-commercial character of livestock keeping, a decrease in access to grazing land, and also due to the expansion of tree planting.

The well-being ranking criteria for housing have changed dramatically. In 1983 there were no houses with roofs made of corrugated iron sheets. In 2017, such roofs were common among all households. Housing well-being values have shifted to appliances within the house, such as water taps, toilets, and solar-based electricity. Similarly the content of well-being criteria for clothing has improved for all.

The two relational well-being criteria, 'work as day labourer' and 'hire labour', are the criteria that have changed most during the period. At the time of the original study in 1983 both well-off, average, and poor were equally involved with reciprocal labour arrangements (called migoe), although well-off farmers tended to arrange more migoe than others (as they had more land under cultivation), and poor tended to attend more migoe to eat the food and drink the beer served after the work. In 2017 a fully commercial labour market existed where well-off

Table 13.3 Well-being ranking criteria in Maliwa village

	Maliwa WBR	Well-off		Middle		Poor	
		1983	2017	1983	2017	1983	2017
A	Land	5–10 acres	5–10 acres	2–5 acres	2–5 acres	Less than 2 acres	Less than 2 acres. Renting land
A	Animals	30–50 cows	<20 cows, 30–50 goats	5–6 cows	2–3 cows, 5–10 goats	None	No cows or goats
A	Non-agricultural enterprise	Brewing local beer	High-entry enterprises (13 shops, motorbikes, 4 milling machines, 3 guest houses, 1 restaurant)	Brewing local beer	Informal food stand, brewing local beer, burning charcoal	None	None
A	Agricultural enterprise	NA	5–10 acres pine trees planted	NA	1–5 acres pine trees planted	NA	No trees planted
A	House	Most unburned bricks, thatched roof; few burned bricks, few iron roof, few grass windows	Burned bricks, iron roof, plastered, solar, glass windows, satellite TV, water tap	Unburned bricks or mud walls, thatched roof, no glass windows	Burned bricks, iron roof, not plastered, some glass windows, some solar, no private water tap	Mud walls, thatched roof, no glass windows	Mud or unburned bricks, some iron roof, no plastering, no glass windows, no solar
A	Clothing	More than one set of clothes; wear out clothes before buying new; own shoes	Buy new clothes frequently; follow fashion	Few items of clothes only; some own shoes	Buy new or second hand clothes when needed	Own one worn out kanga only; no shoes	Buy new clothes when old worn out; do not own shoes; no formal clothes for church

	Maliwa WBR	Well-off		Middle		Poor	
		1983	2017	1983	2017	1983	2017
R	Work as day labourers	Contribute to reciprocal labour arrangements	No work for others	Contribute to reciprocal labour arrangements	Only work for others during years with crop failure	Contribute to reciprocal labour arrangements; food for work	Work year-round for others or whenever they need money or food
R	Hire labour	Call for reciprocal labour arrangements	Hire day labour for all tasks year-round	Call for reciprocal labour arrangements	Hire day labour for specific tasks	Sometimes call for reciprocal labour arrangements	Not hiring day labour; participate in reciprocal labour arrangements
S	Food security	Self-sufficient through three food seasons	Food secure year-round; net sale of maize	Food insecure in some years	Food secure if no crop failure	Food-insecure during rainy season December–April	Income from day labour used to buy food during periods of food insecurity
S	Food quality	Eat meat during special occasions e.g. weddings or funerals	Eat meat year-round once a every week or when available	Eat meat during special occasions, such as weddings or funerals	Occasionally eat meat, when access to cash income	Never eat meat	Eat meat during special occasions, such as weddings or funerals
S	Access to health	Travel to outside public health centre when needed	Use private hospital outside village if required; buy medicine when needed	Travel to outside public health centre when needed if money is available	Use public hospital outside village if required, others village health centre; buy medicine when needed	No access to health services in village, cannot afford to travel outside village	Use village health centre only; cannot always afford medicine when needed

Continued

Table 13.3 Continued

	Maliwa WBR	Well-off		Middle		Poor	
		1983	2017	1983	2017	1983	2017
S	Access to education for children	Public primary school only; few public secondary outside village	Private secondary school, tertiary education if sufficient grades	Public primary school only	Public secondary school, tertiary education if sufficient grades	Some not in public primary school only	Some not in primary school; some public secondary school; few tertiary education if very talented and community sponsored
S	Gender	Male-headed households	NA	Male-headed households	NA	Female-headed households	NA
S	Age	Below 55 years old	Below 60 years old	Below 55 years old	Below 60 years old	Above 55 years old	Above 60 years old

Note: A=asset-based WBR criteria, R=relational WBR criteria, S=social WBR criteria. Land for cultivation has not changed as a well-being criterion.

farmers can hire day workers year-round for all agricultural tasks and poor may work as day labourers year-round or whenever they need cash income.

The social well-being categories 'food security' and 'food quality' have improved for all three categories of farmers. In 1983 poor farmers were food insecure for five months every year, while poor farmers in 2017 have the opportunity to work as day labourers and earn sufficient income to buy 20kg of maize. 'Gender' as a social well-being category played a more dominant role in 1983 compared with 2017. During a focus-group meeting it was mentioned that female-headed households can today engage in economic enterprises on equal terms with male-headed households. That was not the case in 1983, when female-headed households were an indicator of poverty. Finally, two social well-being categories are concerned with access to public health and educational services. There has been a clear improvement in access to health and educational service between 1983 and 2017. However, the well-being criteria reveal a remarkable social differentiation in access to social services.

Conclusion

Because of the marginality in terms of physical access and political and institutional relationships with the state through which development was mediated, the three villages were excluded from taking part in the green revolution that occurred elsewhere in Njombe during in the 1980s. Most farmers within these three villages were at the time not able to provide for their own subsistence and were food insecure during large parts of the year. This was in part because of the failed Ujamaa policy that placed restrictions on where they could settle and what they could do. While structural adjustment during the 1990s had dramatic consequence for the green revolution farmers in the Southern Highlands, the consequences for agricultural development were less dramatic for farmers in these three study villages and characterized by continued stagnation. Seen through the eyes of these farmers, the major change in the 1990s was that they became less controlled by the state. A large part of the youth in the three villages, and Southern Highlands as a whole, emigrated to urban centres to find work and send remittances back to their families. These first two decades were characterized by an emerging rural transformation in terms of improved access to social services financed by the state and development partners but no agrarian transformation.

Major changes occurred at the turn of the century in all three villages. Within a period of a few years they shifted from being marginal to being in the centre of agrarian transformation driven by potato and tomato green revolutions and a timber rush. The study explains this remarkable market-driven shift away from marginality as a combination of different but related events, including:

construction of roads combined with better means of transport and communication; growth in urban demand for agricultural and silvicultural products; and the availability of a few essential agricultural equipment, in this case cheap PVC water pipes and mobile saw mills. The past two decades in these three villages were characterized by a combination of mutually interlinked rural and agrarian transformation.

The study finally shows that these rural and agrarian transformations have been largely inclusive through a combined reduction in the proportion of people who are poor and a higher threshold for what it means to be well-off, average, or poor. The study reveals that changes in people's perception of well-being is not just about changes to the criteria used, but about the content of the individual criteria. However, the improvements in what it means to be well-off are much greater than the improvements in what it means to be poor. An example of the changes in the content of an *asset-based well-being ranking criteria* is 'housing', where the 'well-off' category is no longer about whether the house is built with burned bricks, but availability of amenities such as glass windows, private water tap, solar electricity, and satellite TV. Meanwhile the content of the 'poor' category has only changed slightly, from mud walls and thatched roof to walls of mud or unburned bricks and some iron roofs. Changes to *relational well-being criteria* have been dramatic for both the 'well-off' and 'poor' categories, as the system has totally transformed from an informal reciprocal labour exchange relationship towards a formal rural labour market. One consequence of this change is that able-bodied poor people are more food secure, as they now have the opportunity to work as day labourers and earn sufficiently to buy food for their family. Finally an example on changes in a *social well-being criteria* is access to health services where people in the 'poor' well-being category now have access to village health centres and HIV units, but cannot afford expensive medicine, while people within the 'well-off' well-being category use private hospitals outside the village and can afford medicine if required.

References

Abraham, R. A. and K. S. Kavi Kumar (2008). 'Multidimensional Poverty and Vulnerability.' *Economic and Political Weekly* 43(20): 77, 79–87.

Agergaard, J., C. Tacoli, G. Steel, and S. B. Ørtenblad (2019). *Revisiting Rural–Urban Transformations and Small Town Development in Sub-Saharan Africa*. New York, Springer Press.

Anderson, P. K. (2008). 'A Global Perspective of Potato Production in Emerging Markets.' http://www.scri.ac.uk/scri/files/IIPP%20presentations/PamelaAnderson.pdf.

Berdegué, J. A., R. Tomás, and A. J. Bebbington (2013). *Rural Transformation*. Ottawa, IDRC.

Boesen, J., K. Havnevig, J. Koponen, and R. Odgard (1986). *Tanzania: Crisis and Struggle for Survival*. Uppsala, Scandinavian Institute for Africa Studies.

Coulson, A. (2013). *Tanzania: Apolitical Economy*. Oxford, Oxford University Press.

Danida (2007). 'Impact Evaluation of HIMA, Iringa Region Tanzania.' https://www.oecd.org/countries/tanzania/40567752.pdf.

Ellis, F. (2005). *Small Farms, Livelihood Diversification, and Rural-Urban Transitions: Strategic Issues in Sub-Saharan Africa*, in The Future of Small Farms. Proceedings of a Research Workshop, Wye, UK June 26–29, 2005.

FAOSTAT (2014). 'Potato World: Production and Consumption.' http://faostat.fao.org/default.aspx.

Fischer-Kowalski, M., A. Reenberg, A. Schaffartzik, and A. Mayer (eds) (2014). *Ester Boserup's Legacy on Sustainability Orientations for Contemporary Research*. New York, Springer.

Friis-Hansen, E. (1987). 'Changes in Land Tenure and Land Use Since Villagization and their Impact on Peasant Agricultural Production in Tanzania—The Case of the Southern Highlands.' CDR Research Report no. 11 and IRA Research Paper no. 16. Copenhagen and Dar es Salaam, Centre for Development Research & Institute of Resource Assessment.

Friis-Hansen, E. (eds) (2000). *Agricultural Policy in Africa after Adjustment*. Copenhagen, Centre for Development Research.

Friis-Hansen, E. and D. Duveskog (2005). 'The Empowerment Route to Well-Being.' *World Development* 40(2): 414–27, 2011.

Haggblade, S., P. Hazell, and T. Reardon (2010). 'The Rural Non-Farm Economy: Prospects for Growth and Poverty Reduction.' *World Development* 38(10): 1429–41.

Hillbom, E. and P. Svensson (eds) (2013). '*Agricultural Transformation in a Global History Perspective*.' London, Routledge.

IFAD (2016). 'Rural Development Report 2016. Fostering Inclusive Rural Transformation.' Rome, International Fund for Agricultural Development.

Jespersen, C. B. (1971). 'Southern Highlands Socio-Economic Study.' Mbeya, Uyole Agricultural Research Centre.

Josphat M. and I. Scoones (2012). 'Livelihood Change in Rural Zimbabwe over 20 Years.' *The Journal of Development Studies* 48(9): 1241–57.

Koizumi, M. (2007). 'Comparative Study of Farming Systems in Southwestern Tanzania: Agrarian Adaptation in a Sociohistorical Perspective'. Kyoto University Research Information Repository. Center for African Area Studies. African Study Monographs.

Macha, A., G. Semuguka, and R. Mwambene (1982). 'Potato Improvement in Tanzania.' Paper presented at the Regional Workshop on Potato Development and Transfer of Technology in Tropical Africa. 22 August to 1 September, Addis Ababa.

Mishili, D. B. F. and E. Lazaro (2018). 'Farmer's Participation in Irish Potato Marketing in Njombe Urban and Wanging'ombe District, in Tanzania: Value Determinants.' *Journal of Agricultural Economics and Rural Development* 4(1): 335–43.

Njombe Regional Commissioner Office (2016). 'A Brief Report on Potato Production in Njombe Region.' Njombe, Njombe Regional Offices.

Raikes, P. (1987). 'Eating the Carrot and Wielding the Stick: The Agricultural Sector in Tanzania.' *Tanzania: Crisis and Struggle for Survival*. J. Boesen, K. Havnevig, J. Koponen, and R. Odgard. Uppsala, Scandinavian Institute for Africa Studies: 105–41.

Rasmussen, T. (1986). 'The Green Revolution in Southern Highlands.' *Tanzania: Crisis and Struggle for Survival*. J. Boesen, K. Havnevig, J. Koponen, and R. Odgard. Uppsala, Scandinavian Institute for Africa Studies: 191–205.

Ravnborg, H. M. (1999). 'Developing Regional Poverty Profiles Based on Local Perceptions.' Cali, Colombia, CIAT.

Ravnborg, H. M., J. Boesen, A. Sørensen, Z. Akello, B. Bashaasha, S. Kasozi, M. Kidoido, and V. Wabukawo. (2004). 'Gendered District Poverty Profiles and Poverty Monitoring Kabarole, Masaka, Pallisa, Rakai and Tororo Districts, Uganda.' DIIS Working Paper 2004: 1.

Sen, A. (1993). 'Capability and Well-Being.' *The Quality of Life*. M. C. Nussbaum and A. Sen. Oxford, Oxford University Press: 30–53.

World Bank. (1989). 'Sub-Saharan Africa: From Crisis to Sustainable Growth.' Washington, DC, The World Bank.

World Bank. (2019). 'The World Bank in Tanzania.' https://www.worldbank.org/en/country/tanzania/overview.

14

Exploring Long-Term Changes in People's Welfare on the Uporoto Highlands, Mbeya District, Tanzania

Cosmas Sokoni and Verdiana Tilumanywa

Epilogue pages 397–398 and 399–400

Introduction

The debates over the consequences of economic growth, upon which this volume is founded, have a long history. In the late 1990s Tibaijuka and Cormack argued that despite the achievements in economic growth indicators of poverty in Africa continued to rise both in incidence, depth, and severity (Tibaijuka and Cormack 1998: 7). Economic reforms of the 1990s had led to impressive economic growth rates, but the social sectors that provide for the basic needs have deteriorated. Their arguments found support from a later World Bank report (2000) which found that the number of poor people in sub-Saharan Africa increased from 217 million in 1987 to 219 million in 1998, leaving almost half of the residents of the continent poor (World Bank 2000). This has necessitated a call for redistributive policies and welfare programmes.

Tanzania seems to provide a test case for this debate. The Tanzanian economy and the agricultural sector grew in the 1990s, but little benefit was, apparently, felt by the rural poor (URT 2011). Adjustment policies seem to have led to a widening gap between the rich and poor. Chachage (1993: 242) argued that the majority of the people who were poor before Structural Adjustment Programmes have become poorer. This is likely to be so in rural areas where the agricultural sector has been exploited to support the formation and growth of a small group of private capitalists outside the sector itself. National reforms and related economic achievements may leave out the majority poor especially those living in rural areas. As Sokoni (2001) observed, for example, the marketing reforms of the 1990s constrained agricultural intensification by smallholder farmers.

Cosmas Sokoni and Verdiana Tilumanywa, *Exploring Long-Term Changes in People's Welfare on the Uporoto Highlands, Mbeya District, Tanzania* In: *Prosperity in Rural Africa? Insights into Wealth, Assets, and Poverty from Longitudinal Studies in Tanzania.* Edited by: Dan Brockington and Christine Noe, Oxford University Press. DOI: 10.1093/oso/9780198865872.003.0014

Table 14.1 Annual growth rates of gross domestic product mainland Tanzania, 2006–15

Year	2006	2007	2008	2009	2010	2011	2012	2013	2014	2015
Rate	6.7	7.1	7.4	6.0	7.0	7.9	5.2	7.3	7.0	7.0

Rutasitara (2002: 1) noted that some socio-economic groups or sectors gained while others lost as evidenced through persisting poverty. This necessitated a shift of development policy and strategies towards more inclusive growth and broad-based growth.

The tension between a growing economy and the uneven distribution of its benefits has continued in recent years. Tanzania has recorded impressive economic growth, with a Gross Domestic Product (GDP) annual growth rate of 7 per cent over the past decade (Table 14.1) in contrast to an average annual GDP growth rate of 3.3 per cent between 1960 and 2005 (Wuyts 2008: 5). For example, the per capita income grew from Tsh 628,259 in 2008 to 693,185 in 2009 (URT 2011). A review of the Five Year Development Plan 1 (FYDP1) (2016/17–2020/21) notes that while other sectors of the Tanzanian economy registered impressive growth, the agricultural sector grew at 3.4 per cent in 2014 in comparison to 2.7 per cent in 2010. Although the National Five Year Development Plan 2016/17–2020/21 reported that poverty is becoming more responsive to economic growth, there is still a concern that economic growth is not inclusive.

The mismatch between growth and poverty reduction in Tanzania has been a subject of research interest. On one hand research has focused on explaining the reasons for limited trickle-down (Mashindano et al. 2013). On the other hand, researchers question the adequacy of the methodology of using nation-wide statistics for capturing what actually transpires at the village level. For example Wiggins (2000) contested the conventional wisdom that Africa has been experiencing agrarian crisis as presented in national statistics by using village-level statistics that showed little evidence of decline, and concluded that the crisis was exaggerated as national statistics underestimate farm output. Moreover, other ways of depicting people's welfare, apart from national statistics, can shed more light on the change in livelihoods and welfare of rural families. As other contributors to this volume have argued (Brockington and Noe in Chapter 2) measures of poverty which are derived from measures of consumption, may only capture some of the dynamics of rural poverty.

This paper identifies long term changes in rural families' welfare basing on change in family assets in context of the cropping systems of the Uporoto Highlands in southern Tanzania. It is based on a longitudinal study of households studied in 1997 (Sokoni 2001) and a revisit to the same households in 2016 and 2018. Family assets can show the wealth status of a family as they are a manifestation of savings and accumulation of wealth among families. Where data on income are not readily available, tracing family asset change serves as an alternative means of understanding wealth dynamics of rural households. It further seeks to explain the changes and establish the extent to which they are related to broad/nationwide policy changes. Lastly the paper intends to draw out the implications of the changes in asset to the general welfare of rural communities.

The chapter presents interesting paradoxes. In terms of actual assets people own, most families have experienced a decline, or relatively little change, with the possible exception of Shibolya village. However, in terms of qualitative narratives, most families appear to have improved their asset base. Here we present the findings and try to explain the patterns.

Description of the Study Area and Methods

The Uporoto Highlands extend into three districts of Mbeya Rural, Rungwe in Mbeya Region, and Makete in Njombe Region (Figure 14.1). The Uporoto Highlands are endowed with a wide range of natural resources including fertile volcanic soils and natural forests. Most of the remaining forests are reserved. These forest reserves include: Poroto Ridge, Ikhoho, Bange, Sawago, Ilungu, and Livingstone Mountains. The establishment of the Kiwira Forest Plantation (2,784 hectares for sawn timber) in 1960s (Ngaga 2011) and the extension of pine tree plantations near Igoma village affected the availability of rangelands for livestock keeping.

The recent enforcement of restrictions to access and use the forest reserves on the Uporoto Highlands has again limited local people's access to land resources. Some villagers on the Uporoto Highlands did access land for crop cultivation on the former Kitulo Dairy Farm. However the Kitulo National Park established in 2005 covering an area of 413km^2 has engulfed the Kitulo Dairy Farm which further limited access to arable land on the Uporoto Highlands.

An earlier study (Sokoni 2001) covered six villages that were representative of the ecological zones of the Uporoto Highlands (Figure 14.2). This follow-up study revisited three villages out of the six, namely Shibolya, Igoma, and Ulenje.

Shibolya village is located on the middle zone, on the plateau, with altitude of 2,100–2,300m above sea level. The dominant farming systems in the village have been wheat and maize on the lower parts and Irish potato, maize, and cabbage on the upper part. The village is close to the Mbeya–Kyela–Malawi highway.

Igoma village is also on the middle zone, on a dissected plateau, with altitude of 2,200–2,300 metres above sea level. The cool climate in the village has been favourable to farming system dominated by Irish potato, maize, and cabbage. The village is a rural market centre that serves other villages on the highlands. It has regular transport service to the urban centres of Mbeya, Tukuyu, and Makete.

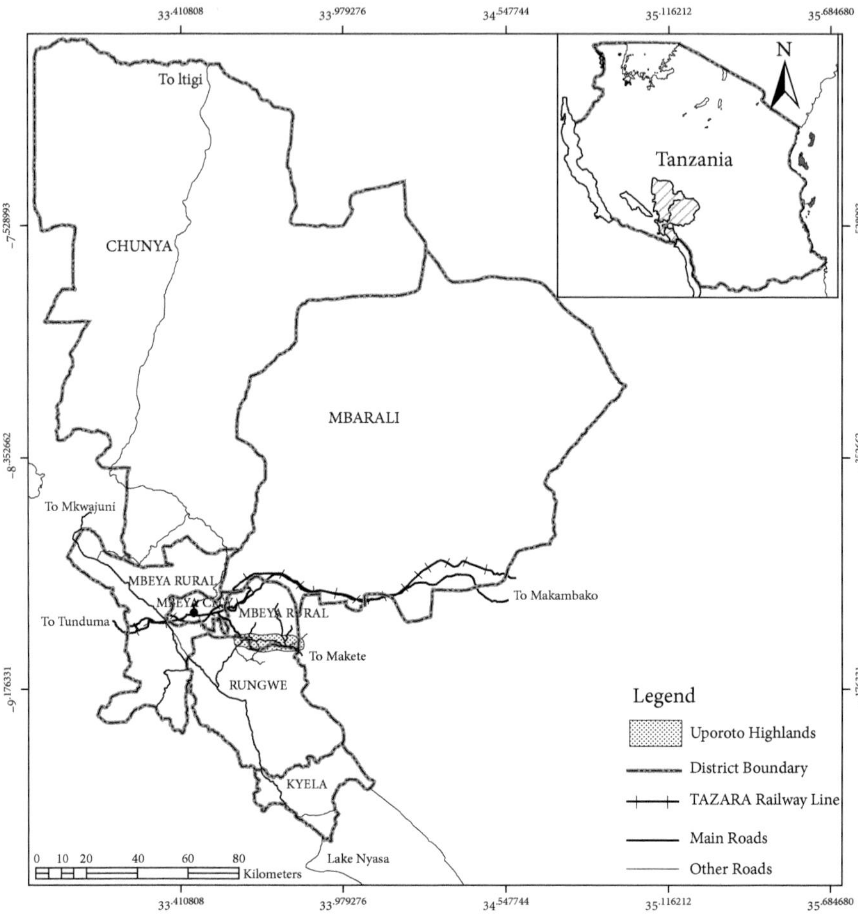

Figure 14.1 Location of the Uporoto Highlands, Tanzania.

Ulenje village is on the lowland, below the escarpment that separates the Uporoto Highlands and the Usangu Plains on the rift valley. It is warmer than other villages, with an altitude of 1,900–2,100m above sea level. Two main farming systems of wheat and maize; and coffee and bananas were traditionally practised.

This study explores changes in cropping systems and asset such as houses, land, and livestock as these matter to the local definition of wealth. The research was undertaken in 2016, giving a span of nearly twenty years from 1997 when the earlier study was conducted. Methods used in data collection include separate group discussions with men and women in each of the villages and interviews with key informants. Also a household survey using a questionnaire was conducted to actual families of the selected villages that were covered by the earlier study in 1997. A revisit to the study villages was undertaken in 2018 with the

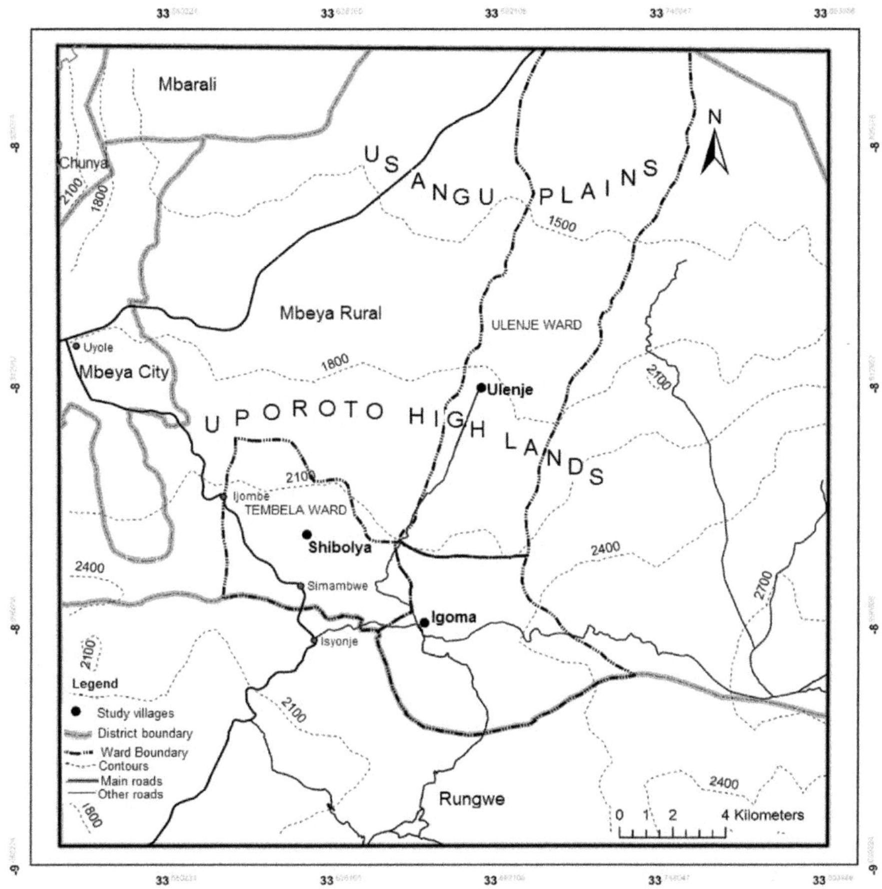

Figure 14.2 Location of the study villages.

intention of probing reasons for the observed patterns of change from the data collected in 2016. This involved conducting group discussions at each of the three study villages, interviewing key informants, and revisit to some families. As with the other surveys we focused particularly on family assets because these are often used to categorize rural families into wealth groups, for example housing (Sokoni and Shechambo 2005).

Changes in Cropping Systems and Household Assets on the Uporoto Highlands

Agriculture is the mainstay of the villages visited for this survey with families relying on crop farming and livestock keeping. Changes in crops grown reflect variations among families in their response to emerging opportunities arising from nationwide development initiatives and policy. The Uporoto Highlands have witnessed change in key crops that drive change in family asset accumulation and decline.

There has been considerable change in the farming system in this area. There are notable declines in Irish potatoes, wheat, and coffee. In 1997 Irish potatoes were grown nearly by all families, and now are grown by 60 per cent of families. Other crops including wheat, green peas, and beans are grown by fewer families while coffee is no longer grown by any of the surveyed families. While the above crops are grown by fewer families now, some other crops have gained importance. Pyrethrum for example, was grown by only 6 per cent of the families in 1997 but in 2016 the number has increased to 30 per cent. Trees were not grown in 1997; however 6 per cent of the families are growing trees now. Food crops such as onions, finger millet, tomatoes, sunflower, and millet are no longer grown by any of the surveyed families. Growing of cabbage has remained stable (Table 14.2).

Patterns vary across different villages. In Ulenje and Shibolya villages, growing of Irish potatoes has increased at the expense of declining cultivation of wheat and green peas. In 1997, wheat was a key cash crop in these villages. Sokoni (2001) noted the importance of wheat crop, especially with the adoption of a wheat variety known as juhudi that replaced traditional varieties that were not demanded in urban markets. Decline in wheat growing in Ulenje and Shibolya villages is attributed to lack of markets. Furthermore, in Shibolya village wheat has been taken over by pyrethrum.

Although Irish potato is a dominant crop, there is a notable decline in the proportion of families growing it. Reports from group discussions in the three villages acknowledge that Irish potato is a key cash crop, however it is highly demanding in use of external inputs and in terms of capital. Wealthy families are

Table 14.2 Change in proportion of families growing different crops, 1997 to 2016

Crop	% of households growing 1997	% of households growing 2016
Maize	96	99
Irish potatoes	91	60
Wheat	61	12
Green peas	30	15
Beans	28	13
Onions	26	0
Cabbage/Spinach	23	22
Coffee	12	0
Pyrethrum	6	30
Tomatoes	1	0
Finger millet	1	0
Millet	1	0
Sunflower	1	0
Trees	0	6

likely to engage in Irish potato cultivation while poor families find it difficult to afford. Whereas Sokoni (2001) reported a decline in pyrethrum cultivation, twenty years later, it is apparent that pyrethrum is grown by more households. This is due to improvement in the marketing and prices of the pyrethrum flowers. For example the price for 1kg of dried pyrethrum flowers increased from Tz shs 1,500/= in 2014 to 2,500/= in 2018. Private agents procure pyrethrum flowers from farmers and there were no problems reported on payments. Pyrethrum flowers are taken to Mafinga, Iringa, where a processing factory is located. In addition to better marketing services and good prices, growing of pyrethrum does not require use of external inputs. Pyrethrum is re-emerging as a key cash crop by replacing other crops. It was reported in group discussions that that pyrethrum replaces maize fields at Igoma and wheat fields at Ulenje and Shibolya villages.

Sokoni (2001) reported a coffee banana farming system in Ulenje village. However, coffee cultivation appears to have declined tremendously among the households studied (cf. Chapter 7 of this volume). Coffee is a perennial crop that requires a long period to yield output and is capital intensive. Farmers at Ulenje reported that coffee marketing and prices have not been attractive. Coffee farms are being replaced by Irish potato fields.

Another crop that has experienced decline among households is onions. Sokoni (2001) did report garlic as an emerging cash crop on the Uporoto Highlands. However, it seems its cultivation has not been sustained and it is no longer grown by any of the revisited households. Farmers at Igoma reported that although garlic is high value crop, its market was not certain. There was no local market as it is not commonly used by the local people of Uporoto Highlands. Lack of reliable external markets may have been due to the very small scale of its cultivation that might have not been able to attract traders from urban markets.

Another change on the Uporoto Highlands is an emerging conversion of agricultural land into woodlots. This is apparent from the current landscape of the Uporoto Highlands depicting crop fields interspaced with woodlots (Figure 14.3). This increase in the conversion of farmland into woodlots is not solely found on the Uporoto Highlands. Tilumanywa (2013) observed the same practice on the Rungwe Mountain Ecosystem. During group discussions in the three revisited villages, farmers explained that in 1990s sale of pine trees for timber was paying well following a growing demand for timber from rapidly growing urban centres. Key informants explained that this development was influenced by the harvesting of trees from the nearby Kiwira Forest Plantation that proved to be a lucrative business for private traders. The Kiwira Forest Plantation undertook large-scale planting of pine trees in the 1970s which matured for harvest in the 1990s. Private traders were allowed to procure woodlots and harvest timber for transportation and sale in urban markets. It was reported by key informants from Igoma village that some farmers who were engaged as labourers in the tree-planting exercise of

Figure 14.3 Woodlots on farm land in Shibolya village.

the Kiwira Forest Plantation the 1970s managed to take some seedlings for planting in their own farm land. At this time trees were planted on marginal lands including areas adjacent to streams and river valleys. As marginal lands became scarce with time, tree planting was extended into pyrethrum fields because the crop had declined in its importance. These farmers who planted pine trees in the 1970s also benefited from harvesting and sale of timber to urban markets.

Pine tree planting as practiced on the Uporoto Highlands appears not to be well integrated with the prevailing farming system. Pine trees take ten to fifteen years to mature. Farmers did not report any significant direct benefit of pine trees on other crops grown. Instead, pine tree woodlots are reported to force other farmers to plant trees because shade effects from woodlots lowers crop productivity of adjacent crop fields. A farmer at Shibolya reported that he was compelled to plant trees on his farm because two fields on either side of his farm were planted with trees and shaded his fields. Tilumanywa (2013: 137) observes the same phenomenon in the Rungwe Mountain ecosystem. Group discussions acknowledged that this phenomenon has contributed to the increasing conversion of farmland into woodlots in the revisited villages.

Other reasons for converting fields into woodlots include: exhaustion of a field's fertility, fields being located too far for the household to grow crops, inability of a household to use all its land for growing crops, unsuitability of land for growing crops, as an investment for future income, and as means of hoarding land. Furthermore, tree planting is attractive because it does not require external inputs. Many of the villages on the Uporoto Highlands were affected by villagization of the early 1970s and which resulted in people living a long distance from their farms when they were moved to new village locations. Such distant fields are often targeted in pine tree planting exercises.

However, over the years, as shown by the households revisited in 2016/17 farmers seem to have realized that the returns to woodlots are less than use of the land for crop cultivation. Informants at Igoma reported that a decline of the market for timber has encouraged farmers to consider clearing woodlots and replace them with other crops. Reverting from woodlots to use of the fields for crop cultivation reflects Ponte's view (1998, and Chapter 12 in this volume) that farmers abandon slow crops and adopt farm enterprises that yield cash quickly. It was further reported in the group discussions that the high demand for timber from urban markets led to a higher rate of tree harvesting than planting among smallholder farmers. To meet the demand some farmers harvested immature trees. Immature trees are no longer demanded in the market as they produce wood products of poor quality. This has led to enforcement of regulation that requires farmers to harvest trees of the age of at least ten years. While farmers who are better-off can afford to wait until tree mature as required by the regulation, poor farmers opt to remove immature trees and replace them with crops. At Ulenje and Igoma villages it was reported that now farmers are removing trees, and woodlots are replaced with potato fields. At Shibolya village, it was reported that the pace of planting trees has gone down. As Ngaga (2011: 37) observes for Mufindi District, often woodlots are established without adequate consideration of profitability of timber growing per unit area and in comparison with other crops. Group discussions with small-scale farmers in the study villages reported that pine trees are not paying.

The importance of green peas had already shown a declining trend in the 1990s as indicated in Sokoni (2001). Green peas were grown in ridges and terraces. This had dominated the landscape of the Uporoto Highlands. Sokoni (2001) reports that on the Uporoto Highlands terracing disappeared with the decline of cultivation of green peas. This is yet another feature of the Uporoto Highlands where apparently land management practice are tied to a crop grown rather than to a land conservation practice for conservation's sake alone. Sokoni (2008) relates the dominance of Irish potato cultivation and its land management practices and its replacement of other crops to increasing land degradation on the Uporoto Highlands. This implies that as farmers change crops and cropping systems in search of better incomes from farm produce land conservation practices may have to be re-learned.

Hired Labour

A well-recognized form of wealth is the ability of a farmer to employ others. Wealthy families are those with the liquidity to employ others, poorer families are those who have to work for others (cf. Chapter 3 in this volume). The study villages in 1997 demonstrated a wide variety of employment patterns—with one village hardly employing other people and another with many employers—but as a whole was relatively balanced in favour of employing people. Currently, in the revisited villages a common system is to hire labour for a piece of daily work or on daily basis where payment is Tsh 5,000 per person per day. Sokoni (2001) noted this as a sign of increasing commercialization of labour on the Uporoto Highlands. It is also noted elsewhere in rural areas of Tanzania that with increasing agricultural commercialization, hired labour has substituted exchange labour (Ponte 1998).

However, data collected from households revisited in 2016 show that balance noted earlier in household use of hired labour has now shifted. A clear majority of people are no longer hiring farm labour (Table 14.3). If we compare individual families we can see that the picture is not all negative—a small number of families who were not hiring labour now are (Table 14.4). But these tend to be the wealthier families; most families rarely employ others.

Sokoni (2001) noted increasing commercialization of labour replacing traditional ways of soliciting farm labour through a reciprocal labour system. Irish

Table 14.3 Change in hiring labour on farms, 1997 to 2016

Village	1997		2016	
	Hired labour	No hiring	Hired labour	No hiring
Iwalanje	16	14	–	–
Nyalwela	26	4	–	–
Kikondo	2	28	–	–
Shibolya	13	17	7	16
Ulenje	16	14	7	13
Igoma	19	11	8	13
Total	**92**	**88**	**22**	**42**

Table 14.4 Number of families who began and ceased to hire labour, 1997–2016

Village	Ceasing hiring labour	No change	Began hiring labour	Total
Shibolya	7	13	3	23
Ulenje	5	13	2	20
Igoma	7	12	2	21
Total	19	38	7	64

potato growing is the major crop that requires labour in all of its stages of production of field preparation, planting, weeding, putting fertilizer, harvesting, and packing for transportation. As noted that production of Irish potato demands high capital investment, it is grown by a few well-to-do rural families. The decline in potato farming may explain why there seems to be a drop in the use of hired labour among the households. A further reason may be that as families get older they become less vigorous in their farming activity and so have less cause to hire in labour.

It was further noted through focus group discussions that there has been a shift from use of hired labour from outside the villages to greater use of local labour. In-migrant labour that was commonly used in the 1990s is considered now too expensive and not suited for the kind of labour required in the different stages of growing Irish potatoes. In-migrant labour requires accommodation and food, even for days they are not engaged in paid labour.

Assets

The first notable change in the study area is that farmers are cultivating less land than they were in 1997. It is important to note that the variables compared are not exactly the same. The 1997 study recorded plots *owned* while the 2016 study recorded plots *farmed*. It is thus possible that people were not farming all the

Table 14.5 Land farmed (acres) in 1997 and 2016

Village	Land owned and farmed 1997	All land farmed 2016	Change in %
Shibolya	2.6	1.0	−61.5
Ulenje	5.1	2.8	−45.0
Igoma	4.1	1.4	−65.8

plots they owned in 1997 (thus land owned in 1997 is larger than land farmed). We have excluded this possibility by not counting fallowed land. Or that they were renting other plots and farming them (thus land owned in 1997 is smaller than land farmed).

The differences between land owned and farmed in 1997 and land farmed in 2016 are substantial, with reductions in land farmed of between 45 per cent and 66 per cent, as shown in the Table 14.5 above.

During the follow up visit in 2018, in all the three villages, it was confirmed that reduction of land cultivated was real. This was attributed to land scarcity on the Uporoto Highlands whereby as families grew in size part of the same land owned by a family was given to sons/daughters. A respondent at Igoma village reported: 'I used to have 3 acres of farmland long time ago, but now I only have 1.5 acres, the rest has been given to my children.' Generally it was reported during group discussions that there was no new virgin land for expanding farms. Sokoni (2001) did report increasing use of land along rivers/valleys in the study area due to increasing population pressure of land resources. The Uporoto Highlands are a dissected plateau with numerous river and streams which used to be covered by natural vegetation but are now cleared. Farm families in Ulenje and Igoma reported that use of land along river/stream valleys for agricultural production has become more restricted as regulations pertaining to environmental management are enforced. The Kitulo Dairy Farm and the numerous forest reserves that were in the 1970s to 1990s used for cultivating crops were no longer accessible due to more strict enforcement of the regulation on their use. A greater part of the formerly Kitulo Farm that was used for farming is now part of the new Kitulo National Park where farming is prohibited.

At Igoma village farmers reported loss of agricultural land by converting it into woodlots. The landscape of the Uporoto Highlands is currently dominated by woodlots mainly of pine trees grown for timber. This holds land that would have been used for agricultural production for too long and yet the returns from woodlots are not impressive. Group discussions held in the three villages reported that in most cases the decision to convert farmland into woodlots was not well conceived and already some farmers consider removing trees to make the land on woodlots available for crop cultivation.

It was also reported that some households have lost part of their land assets by selling in order to earn some income required to access basic services such as health, education, and household groceries. This was reported in a group discussion at Igoma, Ulenje, and Shibolya. It is evident that transaction of land is still in practice as Sokoni (2001) reported.

Poorer households sell land when they need to raise money to address social problems they encounter (sickness) or needs they develop (education). Some poor households are likely to lose land while those well-off have the opportunity of accumulating land through such transactions. A respondent in Igoma village, for example, had to sell half an acre of his farm in order to pay for hospital costs after his wife had a motorcycle road accident. Another respondent in Ulenje village sold half an acre of his land in order to raise money for taking his mother to hospital as she suffered from heart disease.

Among richer households, investment on land assets is considered of great importance. Land values appreciate and having more land gives opportunities for diversification of crops cultivated. In some cases richer households procure more land and plant trees as a means of keeping land for future use.

Communal village farm land that used to be a source of land assets for families in the 1960s to 1990s has disappeared. None of the villages, except Shibolya, had village-governed agricultural land that could be given freely to its people. Shibolya village has some agricultural land that is hired out to villagers per season. This enables families that can afford it to hire land from the village for crop cultivation. However, the small amount of land available to the village government and cost of hiring does not guarantee access to the land by poorer families.

Like land, livestock is an important matter for understanding change in rural welfare and livelihoods. Trends in livestock ownership from 1990s to 2010s are mixed. Smallstock ownership has declined in all villages. But in Shibolya and Ulenje cattle and pigs have increased. Cattle ownership includes two trends. First average herd size has increased marginally in Shibolya and more substantially in Ulenje. Second, it has decreased in Igoma (Table 14.6). In a group discussion at Igoma village it was explained that cattle keeping has declined from 1990s because areas that were used for free-range grazing are no longer available. The extension of the area planted with pine trees by the Kiwira Forest Plantation in the 1970s took a significant portion of land that was used by villagers for open grazing. Sokoni (2001) describes the traditional livestock-keeping system that involved movement of large herds of livestock from villages to areas far away (mainly to the open areas of Kiwira Forest Plantation and of various natural forest reserves) where livestock was kept for some months to allow crops on fields to grow and mature. During the dry season herds of livestock were allowed back to the villages to feed into crop fields after crops had been harvested.

This system of livestock keeping is no longer viable after Kiwira Forest Plantation extended its area planted with trees. In addition, access to the numerous forest reserves has become more restricted by the Forest Department.

Table 14.6 Change in average cattle ownership in 1997 and 2016

Village	1997	2016
Shibolya	0.6	0.8
Ulenje	1.1	1.8
Igoma	1.4	0.6

Furthermore, the establishment of the Kitulo National Park in 2005 has also reduced land accessible for free grazing. Villagers were of the opinion that open grazed livestock will be liable to poor health and susceptible to diseases. This means that the only viable livestock-keeping system is keeping a few livestock that are stall-fed. But farmers considered this system of livestock keeping very costly. Poor families are not likely to afford zero grazing, and often if they do they encounter conflicts with other farmers when livestock trespass into other persons' farmland and residences.

Shibolya village appears to be an exception with a recorded increase in cattle ownership. In a follow up visit in 2018, villagers in Shibolya indicated that on average a household has four to five cows. Proximity of the village to Mbeya city is likely to be an added advantage. This village is located about 15km from Mbeya City and is accessible through a tarmac road that connects Mbeya City to Tukuyu town and the Malawi border to the south. Recently there has been a more organized collection of milk from the small-scale farmers for supply to the Mbeya city market. Also farmers indicated that extension services to farmers had improved. Proximity to Mbeya City is therefore an opportunity to the families of Shibolya villages. Furthermore, upcoming young families use income from Irish potatoes, cabbages, and motorcycles commonly known as 'bodaboda' to invest in livestock.

If we trace herd ownership among actual herd owners, rather than an average village herd, we can see that cattle owners have increased in Shibolya, stayed constant (but with clearly larger herds) in Ulenje, and declined substantially in Igoma as indicated in Table 14.7.

Average smallstock herd size has decreased in all villages as shown in Table 14.8. This reflects the fact that more families have seen their herds decline than increase (Table 14.9) except for Ulenje, which shows an increase in smallstock.

Pig ownership has increased in the villages of Shibolya and Ulenje (Table 14.10). It is not certain that this was influenced by growing demand from towns for pork. It was noted however, there was significant local consumption of pork within the villages. With the decline in cattle herds, pork has become a substitute for beef. The relatively greater decrease in pig ownership at Igoma village is partly associated with the development of the village settlement to a large centre with some

Table 14.7 Change in incidence of cattle ownership

Village	Decrease	Same	Increase
Shibolya	3	12	8
Ulenje	5	10	5
Igoma	9	11	1

Table 14.8 Change in average smallstock size

Village	1997	2016
Shibolya	1.1	0.6
Ulenje	3.5	3.0
Igoma	1.1	0.7

Table 14.9 Change in incidence of smallstock ownership

Village	Decrease	Same	Increase
Shibolya	7	12	4
Ulenje	9	5	6
Igoma	4	14	3

Table 14.10 Change in incidence of pig ownership

Village	Decrease	Same	Increase
Shibolya	0	17	6
Ulenje	3	13	7
Igoma	7	11	3

urban characteristics. Households keeping pigs have often encountered conflicts with neighbours and often have been required to pay dearly where pigs have trespassed to neighbours' premises. A respondent in Igoma village sold three pigs in 2014 because they kept getting sick and the individual could not afford to treat them.

House ownership is an important indicator of wealth status of rural households. A number of studies have used types of rural houses (based on building materials for walls, floor, and roof) to identify wealth groups (see for example Sokoni and Shechambo 2005). This study examined the changes in quality of houses as a means of identifying welfare of households. One of the reported achievements that had made livelihoods better is the improvement in housing.

Figure 14.4 Typical bamboo-roofed house of the Uporoto Highlands of 1990s.

Narratives of respondents depict a high proportion of households that improved housing. Typical houses made of bamboo walls (with mud) and bamboo or grass roof that were common in the villages in the 1990s have been replaced with houses with brick walls and corrugated iron sheet roof (Figure14.4). Many respondents attributed the better lives that they feel they enjoy now to living in a modern and spacious house. Sources of money for improving houses included sale of livestock, land, and key cash crops. In quite a number of cases support from family members living in town helped households to build new houses. Recently access to electricity is likely to make housing even better. None of the villages had electricity in 1990s, but all the study villages were connected to the national grid of electricity by 2016. However, many of the poorer families do not have connection to electricity in their houses as they cannot afford the fees for connection.

In probing the disappearance of bamboo and grass houses, group discussions at Igoma and Shibolya informed that these building materials are not available any more. The diminishing of forests and grassland accessible by farmers, mentioned earlier, contributed to this situation. This means use of the house roofed with corrugated iron sheets for distinguishing wealth categories of farmers is no longer valid as this is almost the only means of roofing houses that almost all families use.

Other Notable Changes

Through discussion groups, villagers acknowledge change in access to services. There is a significant development in health infrastructure in the study villages from 1997 and 2016. In 1997 only Ulenje had a dispensary. By 2016, health facilities had been established including a public health centre and a private dispensary a run by the Roman Catholic Church at Igoma, and a dispensary at Shibolya.

Access to secondary education has also improved. In 1997 there was only one private secondary school among the three villages. In 2016 each village had a secondary school. However, for the rural households this has meant greater demand for cash in order to access education and health services. As mentioned earlier some poor households have been compelled to part with some of their assets in order to access health and education services. The government of Tanzania has from 2016 offered free primary and secondary education. However, this does not mean there are no costs to families pertaining to provision of education to their children.

Improvement in transportation has contributed to a better life on the Uporoto Highlands. All three villages are now served with regular transport service to the nearby urban centres of Mbeya, Kiwira, and Tukuyu. In 1990s, Ulenje village was disadvantaged because of lack of transportation services to the nearby towns. However, in the 2010s a regular bus transport connecting the village to Igoma and Mbeya City has been maintained.

The introduction of bodaboda for commercial transport has greatly facilitated movement of people and goods in rural areas of Uporoto Highlands. Being a mountainous region, the use of bicycles had not developed as in other flat areas. Motorcycles serve in the collection of produce from farm to homes or collection points for delivery to urban markets. Sokoni (2001) identified long distances from homesteads to farm as one of the constraints of the farming systems of the Uporoto Highlands. In this context the use of motorcycles to transport produce from farm to homes and markets is a great improvement in rural transportation. It was reported that there were about one hundred motorcycles in Igoma village alone and around ten each in Ulenje and Shibolya villages. However, poorer farmers are disadvantaged because they often cannot afford the cost of transportation through bodaboda.

Another major change in rural livelihoods on the Uporoto Highlands is in communications. Most families do own, access, and use mobile phones for communication. This has facilitated interactions among family members within and outside the village and has enhanced the ability of rural families to overcome distance constraints. Local administration work has also been eased through mobile phones. Improvement in communication is likely to have enhanced production and marketing of agricultural produce.

Restricted access to forest reserves in the study area has to a great extent influenced villagers' livelihoods. At Shibolya village, informants reported more strict restriction on access and use of Ikhoho Natural Forest Reserve. Similar observations of restricted access to Livingstone Mountain Forest Reserve and Bange Forest Reserve were reported at Igoma village and Ulenje village. The establishment of the Kitulo National Park has in particular been reported to have brought encounters between small-scale farmers with the park officials as they enforce the restriction of access and use of resources within the national park and forest reserves. In addition to restriction of access to the remaining natural forests in the Uporoto Highlands, it was reported in a group discussion at Ulenje village that there is greater enforcement of the requirement not to cultivate 60 metres on either side of rivers or streams.

Change in Wealth Status

With respect to people's perceptions of how life has changed there are some surprising differences (Table 14.11). Shibolya, with its increased herd sizes contains more people who think that life is better now than before. Igoma, despite its decreasing herd sizes, has a roughly equal split, and in Ulenje most people think life was better in the past, at the time of the original survey, compared to now.

The final data we have derived from qualitative accounts of changes in assets and important events in people's lives. We used these histories to determine whether peoples' assets were increasing or decreasing. The summary of that work is presented in Table 14.12. In terms of the asset histories we were able to collect, the majority of families in all villages appear to be improving their lives a lot.

Table 14.11 Is life better now or at the time of the first survey?

Village	Before	Now	Same	Total
Shibolya	9	14	2	25
Ulenje	12	7	2	21
Igoma	9	8	4	21
Total	**30**	**29**	**8**	**67**

Table 14.12 Change in assets of households (excluding land)

Village	Better	Same	Unclear
Shibolya	13	5	4
Ulenje	17	2	2
Igoma	12	7	2

It is difficult to reconcile these different perspectives. But they are not completely incompatible. It is possible for people to become richer despite farming less land if farming large areas is no longer the mainstay of their livelihood. Likewise it is possible that people may be recovering status to what they used to have in 1997—thus they are on an upward trajectory now, having declined in intervening years. During the follow-up visit to the villages in 2018, attempts were made to probe further on the findings of these narratives.

Having a better house was considered a reason for greater prosperity. Certainly, a good quality house opens up more opportunities in health and hygiene, and with access to electricity benefits are even greater. Many respondents felt prosperous by living in decent house. Declining prosperity was linked to the increasing burden of taking care of families where resources were limited. Incidences of illness, disability, loss of household bread winner though death, or out migration overburdened some households to the extent that prosperity was hard to realize. From the narrative about a quarter of the households had lost parents due to death. Such households had often to sell the few assets they had in order to survive. This unfortunately compelled them to more misery. Such disadvantaged groups are not likely to realize benefits of economic growth.

Drivers of Prosperity

Assets are not only indicators of prosperity but also drivers for prosperity. Land is an important asset for wealth creation among rural households. It is clear from the study villages that land is scarce due to increasing population density. The typical landscape of the Uporoto Highlands is of farmland fragmented into small fields with no or little indication of untouched land for agricultural production.

The key crops that drive change to prosperity in the study villages are Irish potatoes for all villages and cabbages for Shibolya. Ulenje village is trying to catch up with Irish potato production after losing coffee and wheat as important cash-earning crops. However, Ulenje is constrained by scarcity of land and a more disadvantaged location in relation to accessing urban markets. Unfortunately, growing Irish potatoes is capital-demanding and not easily affordable by poor families. Such families find it difficult to realize prosperity through cultivation of Irish potatoes.

The Uporoto Highlands are experiencing rapid population growth amidst land scarcity for expansion of agricultural activities. In theory this scenario is expected to encourage agricultural intensification. However, this has not been realized. While poor families find it difficult to adopt agricultural intensification technologies, better-off families find it easy to rely on acquisition of more land for increasing agricultural production rather than intensifying use of agricultural inputs and technology. This explains what Sokoni (2001) called partial agricultural intensification on the Uporoto Highlands.

Availability and access to urban markets is an important driver of change in welfare of rural families on the Uporoto Highlands. With improvement in transport and communication infrastructure and services, rural families have more opportunities for reaching urban markets. Demand for agricultural produce influences what farmers choose to grow and accumulate as asset. Changes in market conditions do influence change in the farming system and crop composition. Farmers' response to opportunities arising from this improved access to markets varies with their economic status. The process of integration to the market however marginalizes poorer families who are compelled to lose rather accumulate assets such as land and livestock.

The Uporoto Highlands are rich in natural resources that have been under forest reserves. Some of the development in livestock and crop farming in the 1990s were influenced by access to and use these natural resources for agricultural production. Recent developments and the national emphasis on conservation of the natural forest including the establishment of the nearby Kitulo National Park have brought greater restrictions on use of reserved land for agriculture. This has seriously affected the livestock-keeping system of open grazing. The option of zero-grazing system, though desirable, is difficult for poor households as it requires more capital and energy for livestock management. All in all further restrictions on use of natural forest reserves has contributed to the increase in zero grazing of cattle and smallstock.

Conclusion

In general terms some aspects of life are better now than in 1997. However, according to the qualitative information gathered the status of welfare varies remarkably among families. While well-off families on one hand have benefitted much from changes in the socio-economic environment by accumulating more wealth and assets that enhance their welfare; poor families on the other hand seem to have been disadvantaged by being compelled to sell their assets in order to meet the increasing cost of accessing social services. Consequently some of the latter have lost land and turned to selling labour to other farmers.

Between 1990s and 2010s, there have been improvements in availability and access by families to social services including education, health facilities, transportation, and communication. However, this has meant increasing need for cash. Improvement in rural infrastructure for transportation and communication has meant greater opportunities for rural families to interact with urban markets that have encouraged greater production of crops and animal products needed in urban markets. Increased access to electricity from 1995 in Igoma and Ulenje villages and from 2015 in Shibolya village has opened up opportunities for better life and means of earning a living for the well-off families. Access to water has improved in the villages except for Shibolya village, whose villagers are still fetching water from rivers and streams.

Changes in household assets such as land, livestock, and housing do show long-term changes for better welfare among rural communities. However, poorer families appear to have not fared well in saving and building an asset base for improving their well-being. Improvement in conditions of housing is one of the indications of change to a better welfare among rural households.

The observed changes in families' welfare are driven by a number of factors. Fast cash-earning crops (Irish potatoes, cabbages, carrots) have played a major role. This has been facilitated by a better access to urban markets and the prevailing liberal market that gives families flexibility to decide what to grow. Better transportation and communication has been instrumental towards this development. However, cultivation of most of these crops requires more energy and external inputs. Many poor families have been disadvantaged.

The improvement in access to electricity is a driver to farmers' engagement in non-farm occupations for earning extra incomes outside agriculture and building their asset base. The socio-economic environment has opened up more opportunities for women to engage in production and own assets including land.

It is worth noting that drivers to prosperity are not static. In the 1990s the importance of pyrethrum had declined but appears to have re-emerged in the 2010s, particularly for the poorer families that cannot afford the expensive production of Irish potatoes. Once a driver to prosperity, tree planting seem to have lost its importance in recent years. It is apparent that conversion of crop fields into woodlots is in the long run not cost effective.

References

Chachage, C. S. L. (1993). 'Forms of Accumulation, Agriculture and Structural Adjustment in Tanzania.' *Social Change and Economic Reform in Africa*. P. Gibbon. Uppsala, The Scandinavian Institute of African Studies: 215–43.

Mashindano, O., K. Kayunze, L. da Corta, and F. Maro (2013). 'Growth without Poverty Reduction in Tanzania—Reasons for Mismatch.' *Translating Growth into Poverty Reduction: Beyond the Numbers*. F. Kessy, O. Mashindano, A. Shepherd, and L. Scott. Dar es Salaam, Mkuki na Nyota: 133–56.

Ngaga, Y. (2011). 'Forest Plantations and Woodlots in Tanzania.' African Forest Forum Working Paper vol. 1 issue 16. Nairobi, Africa Forest Forum.

Ponte, S. (1998). 'Fast Crops, Fast Cash: Market Liberalisation and Rural Livelihoods in Songea and Morogoro Districts, Tanzania.' *Canadian Journal of African Studies* 32(2): 316–48.

Rutasitara, L. (2002). 'Economic Policy and Rural Poverty in Tanzania: A Survey of Three Regions.' Research Report No. 02.1, Dar es Salaam, REPOA.

Sokoni, C. H. and T. C. Shechambo (2005). 'Changes in an Upland Irrigation System and Implications to Rural Poverty Alleviation: A Case of Ndiwa Irrigation System, West Usambara Mts., Tanzania.' Research Report 05.1, Dar es Salaam, REPOA.

Sokoni, C. H. (2001). 'The Influence of Agricultural Marketing Reforms on Highland Farming Systems in Tanzania: The Case of the Uporoto Highlands, Mbeya Region.' PhD Thesis, University of Dar es Salaam.

Sokoni, C. H. (2008). 'Commercialisation of Smallholder Production in Tanzania: Implications for Sustainable Resources Management.' *The Geographical Journal* 174(2): 158–61.

Tibaijuka A. K. and A. Cormack (1998). 'Financing the Social Sectors in Sub Saharan Africa: A Review of Literature.' *The Social Services Crisis of the 1990's: Strategies for Sustainable Systems in Tanzania*. A. K. Tibaijuka. Aldershot, Ashgate: 5–46.

Tilumanywa, V. T. (2013). 'Land Use and Livelihood Changes in the Mount Rungwe Ecosystem, Tanzania.' PhD Thesis, Stellenbosch University.

United Republic of Tanzania (URT) (2011). 'The Demographic and Health Survey 2010.' Dodoma, National Bureau of Statistics.

Wiggins, S. (2000). 'Interpreting Changes from the 1970s to the 1990s in African Agriculture Through Village Studies.' *World Development* 28(4): 631–62.

World Bank (2000). 'African Poverty at the Millenium: Causes, Complexities and Challenges.' Washington DC, The World Bank.

Wuyts, M. (2008). 'The Growth–Poverty Nexus in Tanzania from a Development Perspective.' Special Paper No. 08.27. Dar es Salaam, Mkuki na Nyota Publishers.

15

Improved Livelihoods on Less Land

The Case of Ilambilole and Ikuwala Villages in Iringa Region, 1996–2017

Torben Birch-Thomsen and Esbern Friis-Hansen

Epilogue pages 417–420

'Origin of the Story'

This chapter takes its point of departure in an interdisciplinary strategic environmental research programme Centre for Research on Sustainable Agriculture in Semi-Arid Africa (SASA), financed from 1994–9 by the Danish Environmental Research Programme (Ministry of Environment). The collaborative venture involved researchers from the Centre for Development Research, the Royal Veterinary and Agricultural University and Roskilde University (Department of Geography and International Development Studies, RUC). The research referred to in this chapter is linked to the two sub-projects entitled 'Changing resource utilization and livelihood strategies' and 'Sustainable management of natural resources through local institutions', undertaken between 1996–8 in two villages (Ikuwala and Ilambilole) within the semi-arid parts of Iringa Region in Tanzania (see Figure 15.1). Ikuwala is located in Mazombe Ward close to the local centre of Ilula, a ward headquarters in 1997 and proclaimed a township in 2002 (Lazaro et al. 2019) with relatively easy access along a dirt road. Ilambilole, on the other hand, is located in Ismani Ward, and in 1997 was only accessible over rough dirt roads with limited access (4WD) during the rainy season. This was changed with the upgrading of the Iringa–Dodoma highway in 2013 and the connection between Kising'a and Ilambilole (see later for further details).

The original results of this research, reported in SASA (1999), Birch-Thomsen et al. (2001), McDonagh et al. (2001), and Birch-Thomsen et al. (2007), were based on data collected in a two-stage process of fieldwork in the two villages. The first stage focused on land use and cover, settlement patterns, and environmental change through a combination of remotely sensed data (aerial photography and satellite images), field observation and group and individual interviews.

Torben Birch-Thomsen and Esbern Friis-Hansen, *Improved Livelihoods on Less Land: The Case of Ilambilole and Ikuwala Villages in Iringa Region, 1996–2017* In: *Prosperity in Rural Africa? Insights into Wealth, Assets, and Poverty from Longitudinal Studies in Tanzania*. Edited by: Dan Brockington and Christine Noe, Oxford University Press. © Torben Birch-Thomsen and Esbern Friis-Hansen 2021. DOI: 10.1093/oso/9780198865872.003.0015

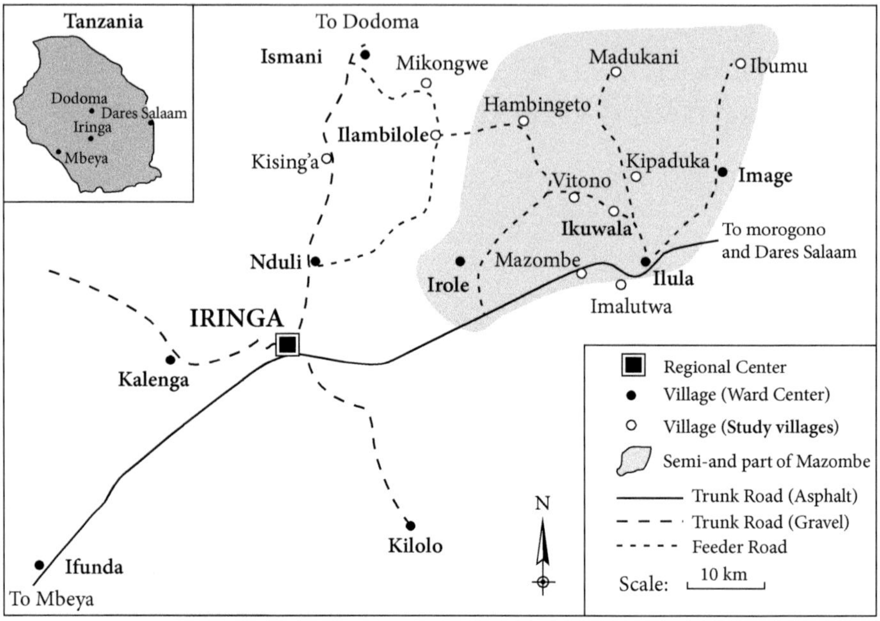

Figure 15.1 Location of study villages.

The second stage concentrated on a socioeconomic baseline survey with a random sample of thirty-four households in each village (including data on sources of income, agricultural production, and marketing) and qualitative information on the diversification of sources of income and the nature of decision-making within ten households (for more details see Birch-Thomsen et al. 2001). In 2016–17, the original research was followed up with a revisit to the two communities and households included in the first research with the aim of reporting and analysing changes in livelihoods and well-being within the past twenty years.

Methods of the Revisit

During the revisit to and restudy of the two villages, several methods were used. First, focus-group discussions were held with men and women respectively, also representing different age groups, to explore local definitions of wealth, wealth categories, and development progress in the villages. Second, a restudy of the original domestic units (households) using the ODK quantitative survey was undertaken (see Box 15.1). Third, a separate wealth-ranking exercise of the current households was conducted using the current wealth criteria. Fourth, qualitative interviews were conducted to collect information on the history of the domestic households, their internal dynamics, history of land use, mobility of household members, etc. Fifth, the expansion and densification of settlements in the study villages were analysed using Google Earth time series of satellite images—2005–14.

Box 15.1 Success of identifying the original domestic units in the two villages

Ikuwala

- Revisit to twenty-six households out of thirty-four, of which three households had moved from Ikuwala to Ding'inayo (4km), close to the urban centre of Ilula, and in one case the head of HH had passed away; now headed by the old wife.
- Of the eight missing households, three no longer exist (passed away, age above 55 at the time of the original survey—all classified as 'poor' in 1997), and five could not be located (two 'poor', two 'medium', one 'wealthy').

Ilambilole

- Revisit to twenty-one HH (+ one secondary domestic unit—son, Charles) of thirty-four.
- Of the twelve missing households five no longer exist (passed away, age above 60 at the time of the original survey—one 'wealthy' and four 'medium'), and seven could not be located (two 'poor', four 'medium', one 'wealthy').

Prior Status and Conditions

Findings of the Original Study (1996–8)

As part of the SASA project, a wealth-ranking exercise was undertaken in all study sites, including Ikuwala and Ilambilole villages, as part of the baseline survey based on locally identified indicators of inequality (for further discussion of the wealth-ranking criteria, see below). Based on the argument that livelihood divisions say more about resource management than socioeconomic divisions (the wealth ranking), the sub-project developed a livelihood classification focusing on 'changing resource utilization and livelihood strategies' (see Box 15.2). One of the results was that households that were otherwise classified as part of the intermediate wealth group were actually following more enterprising strategies more closely related to the well-to-do households (for more details, see Birch-Thomsen et al. 2001).

An important aspect of the research findings was the significance of agriculture as the resource base for households within all the strategy groups. This was to some extent contrary to the deagrarianization process reported in other studies (Bryceson 1999: 174). Although income diversification was taking place, agriculture remained the most important sector to which other income-earning opportunities related. The study identified four factors as important in explaining patterns of resource utilization and degradation:

Box 15.2 Characteristics of identified livelihood strategy groups in Ikuwala sub-village

Peasant-labour coping strategy (n=10)

- Low agricultural income
- Piecework (within farming)
- Income from sale of fuelwood, grass, baskets
- Beer-brewing

Peasant strategy (n=11)

- Some agricultural income (tomatoes, sunflower)
- Additional income from piecework, natural resources, crafts, and petty commerce

Accumulating farmer strategy (n=13)

- Substantial agricultural income (tomatoes, maize)
- Additional income from business, craft, and rent
- Employers; predominantly for weeding

- The dominant resource management practices, in place since the mid-1950s, were still influenced by *opportunities of farm expansion*, reinforced by opportunities for *accumulating farmers* with access to technology (oxen and plough) and local, regional, and national markets for their commercial crops (tomatoes, sunflowers, and maize, particularly in Ikuwala, located close to the local market in Ilula; see Figure 15.1), potentially generating substantial incomes.
- *Poverty on a massive scale* (extremely low land productivity, food insecurity, and reliance on piecework) influenced resource management among both the poorest and the lower middle households (approximately one-third of all households; dominated by peasant-labourers). Their management capabilities and their efforts to introduce intensification were reduced. The strategies embarked upon indicate that these *households struggled to remain farmers*.
- The fact that the areas of Mazombe and Ismani were scarcely populated in the late 1950s and early 1960s indicate that *population growth (natural increase plus in-migration) and intensified land use (shortening of fallow length) occurred over one generation*. Knowledge and capacity still had to catch up with the process of intensification—intensified land use with low-level use of chemical fertilizers and improved seeds.

- Political and institutional changes were observed to be important in explaining *unequal access to land* and forest resources, often *explained by institutional ambiguity* and lack of enforcement of rules at both village, ward, and district levels.

Historically, economic growth in the study area has been achieved by moving the agricultural frontier. The expansion of agriculture from the 1950s to the late 1990s was documented through analyses of remote sensing data and interviews with key informants in both sites and villages (Birch-Thomsen et al. 2001, Birch-Thomsen et al. 2007; see also Figure 15.2). Land use changed from approximately 5 per cent of land under cultivation in the mid-1950s around the few early settlements (between ten and fifteen households) to 55 per cent by 1966. This dramatic expansion of agriculture and the clearing of forest was a common trend in the area (including Ikuwala) and created an agricultural frontier during the 1950s. Through interviews with the daughter of one of the early commercial farmers, we learned how the newcomers (people of the Wabena ethnic group from Njombe District/Region) employed kinsmen to assist in the land-clearing and cultivation, leading many to decide to settle and start farming themselves. An example was given where 'three hundred acres was cultivated and two hundred workers employed'. Settlement continued to be dispersed. The reduced area of land under cultivation towards 1978 was explained by villagization, that is, the forced

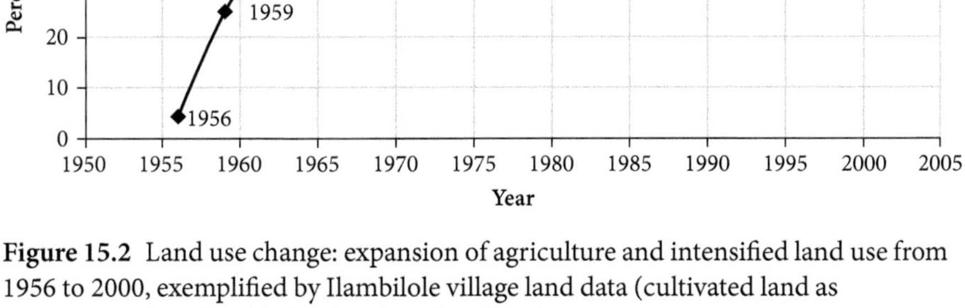

Figure 15.2 Land use change: expansion of agriculture and intensified land use from 1956 to 2000, exemplified by Ilambilole village land data (cultivated land as percentage of total arable land within the village).

Source: Birch-Thomsen et al. 2007, based on land use classifications of aerial photographs (1956, -59 and -78); USGS-declassified satellite photography (1966); and Landsat satellite images (1986, -96, and 2000).

movement of people into villages, and government-driven intensification. Land was abandoned or left fallow for a long time, either because it was claimed by the new village government (some disputes were still ongoing in 2017) or because of distance the new settlements were from the fields. The slower increase observed after 1978 included re-cultivation of some of the fallow fields from the 1950s and 1960s, but also through the inclusion of land in the hills and border areas in the seasonally flooded lowlands (Mbuga). The intensity of land use observed in 2000 showed that hardly any more land could be transferred to cultivation.

Accessing land by renting or buying it became increasingly common as land became scarcer within the village. As shown in Figure 15.3 this practice extended beyond the village administrative boundaries (often related to more fertile land on the edge of the seasonal flooded areas), but another conclusion was that there was limited scope for the continuation of this process (SASA 1999). The expansion of agriculture and conversion of grassland into farming increased conflicts between farmers and agro-pastoralists (from the Maasai group).

In summary, the SASA study in the 1990s of livelihoods and resource management showed the following:

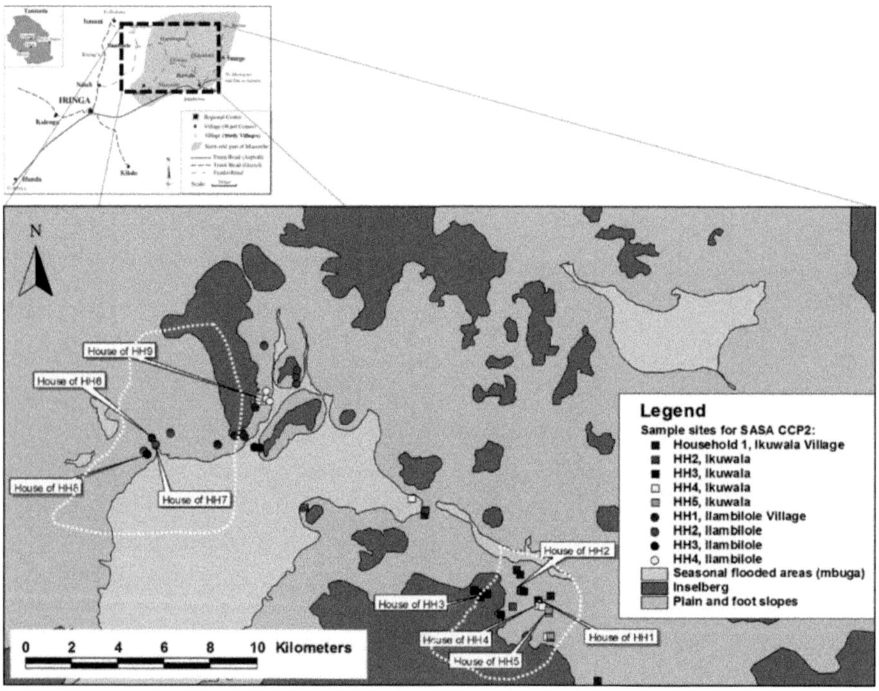

Figure 15.3 Location of houses and fields of nine households selected for in-depth interviews and field visits during the 1996–8 research. In addition to the landscape units of the study area, the dotted white lines indicate approximated village borders.

- a case of more people, more erosion (and loss of productivity) countering small-scale farmers' potential for intensification and the underlying forces driving this development (the so-called Neo-Boserupian school, as argued by Tiffen et al. 1994);
- a case of *land degradation (the neo-Malthusian school of thought)*, which on the community level was more related to the livelihood strategies of the poor (coping) than to the better off farmers who had the ability to pursue *expansive* and *accumulating* strategies.

These two 'schools of thinking' might fruitfully relate to each other, especially in marginal semi-arid areas, where the dynamics of population increase and environmental change are often factors to consider in relation to changes in farming practice.

Overall Changes

When the SASA study ended in 1998, Ilambilole and Ikuwala were sleepy dusty villages located in semi-arid areas. While Ikuwala was located relatively close to the main road, Ilambilole was only reachable on a poorly maintained unpaved road. Social services were limited to rudimentary primary schools, health dispensaries, and a few small shops. Public water taps existed in Ilambilole, but in Ikuwala village water had to be collected in buckets from nearby Ilula village.

In the mid-1990s crop cultivation had recently been mechanized as a result of an NGO operating an ox-training centre in the area. The SASA household survey shows that 71 per cent of households in Ikuwala and 91 per cent in Ilambilole used ox-ploughing, of whom 63 per cent and 35 per cent respectively owned their own ox-ploughs. Yields were very low, and maize was the main crop that was grown for subsistence, with surplus production being sold. The SASA household survey showed that 47 per cent of households in Ikuwala and 65 per cent in Ilambilole sold maize. Forty per cent of those who had surplus production for sale sold fewer than five bags. Seasonal household food insecurity was common, and it was common that the young left for the city in the hope of a better future. Besides selling maize, both tomatoes (by 68 per cent of households) and sunflower (by 50 per cent of households) were sold by households in Ikuwala, and for Ilambilole only sunflower was sold (by 71 per cent of households)—no tomatoes.

These agricultural activities however took place in the midst of considerable poverty. They were relatively spartan and generally small scale and were associated with land degradation. Opportunities for accumulation and wealth creation were limited. The two authors were therefore surprised when they returned two decades later to find both villages in the midst of dynamic socio-economic change. A new tarmac road between Iringa and Ilambilole had reduced the travel time from half a day to less than an hour. There are now eight scheduled trips with a minibus everyday between Ilambilole and Iringa and numerous motorbikes for hire. The improved road has also greatly improved market access. Today Ilambilole village has numerous trucks for hire and a newly established guesthouse where external traders can stay during the marketing season. Social services have improved considerably, with the building of a new secondary school, upgrading of the dispensary to a hospital, and not least access to electricity in 2015. In 2017 more than a third (231) of households had an electricity connection, and one out of every ten (fifty-six) had a private water tap.

Population Increase, Change in Direction of Migration, Change in Importance of Remittances

According to a population census from 2017 (village office), Ilambilole village has a population of 3,928 persons (1,868 men and 2,058 women). Mr Muhanji (chairman of Ilambilole village during the time of the original study in 1990s) estimates that the population of Ilambilole has doubled over the past two decades. Fifty per cent of this increase happened over the past five years (the 2012 population census recoded 2026 people in Ilambilole village). According to Mr Muhanji, migration of young people to urban centres has declined since the turn of the century and young people today see a future for themselves by staying in the village. In addition, because of the good public transport, every month new houses are constructed by people living in nearby Iringa town, who stay in the village during weekends and holidays—cheap access to land and potential to grow food crops for the family were mentioned as some of the reasons.

This immigration is in sharp contrast to the net emigration that characterized Ilambilole during the SASA study decades ago (Interview with former chairman, Mr Muhanji in 2017). In the 1990s Tanzania was experiencing the consequences of structural adjustment programmes that had eliminated subsidized markets and inputs for agricultural products. The consequences in Ilambilole and Ikuwala were the disruption of maize production and widespread household food insecurity that fuelled emigration to urban centres (Friis-Hansen 2000).

The shift from emigration to immigration has also affected the importance of remittances. While 27 per cent of households in Ikuwala received remittances in 1996, this had fallen to 17 per cent in 2016. The reduced importance of remittances was even greater in Ilambilole village, where 22 per cent of households received remittances in 1996 and only 4 per cent in 2016.

The case below illustrates the importance of migration and remittances during the late 1990s and early 2000:

> Andreas is thirty-three years old and the son of Moses who was interviewed in 1996 for the SASA study. Moses died in 1998 and left 7 acres (plus a 1-acre plot

with the house) to the three children. Andreas, being the only boy and the oldest child (16 years old at that point), had a meeting with his sisters regarding what to do with the land. Normally, in 1998, the son would inherit all land, but he wanted to change this, so he negotiated with his two sisters that he should get 3 acres and the sisters 2 acres each. This is a change from the traditional way of dividing land when parents leave land to their children (normally only to the sons). This practice was also observed in another case of a 'secondary domestic household' in the village and seems to be an important gender-related change in land inheritance!

Soon afterwards (in 1999) one of his sisters migrated to Dar es Salaam to find a job and earn an income to give her a living. She was lucky to get a job and a few years later got married—she still lives in Dar and keeps in regular contact over telephone. He and another sister, who is married and lives in the village, cultivate the 7 acres (including the fields of the sister in Dar). Because of the hardships in Ilambilole he decided to move to Dar to stay with his sister in 2011, leaving his wife and two small children behind in the village; the wife's family supported them and looked after them. His brother-in-law is a fundi, a handyman and builder, and Andreas worked with him for a year through which he learned construction skills and earned and saved some money, sending some of it back to his wife as a remittance.

Increased Pressure on Land Resources and Intensification of Agriculture

Population increase has contributed to increasing the pressure on land resources, especially for the poorer farmers. Dramatic increases in livestock numbers in Ilambilole have further contributed to the pressure on land. The increase in livestock occurred after the establishment of a cattle dip in 2006 that reduced livestock mortality. According to statistics on the wall of the village office, the number of cattle was about 8,000 in 2017, largely owned by Masaai agro-pastoralists, who are settled in their own part of the village south of the village centre and separated from most of the cultivated land. All attempts by the village government to impose bylaws to limit the number of livestock have failed due to resistance from these herders. The large wetlands (mbuga) that extend to neighbouring Ikuwala and Vitono villages provide grazing for this increased number of cattle. However, according to the village chairman, the overstocking of cattle in the sub-village populated with Maasai households has caused a high pressure on access to grazing and fodder. During the dry season this pressure spills over into conflicts with farmers in the rest of the villages, as Maasai-owned cattle will graze on crop residues in post-harvest maize fields without permission from the owner (interview with village chairman 2017). The study did, however, not focus on this conflict.

As a result, cultivated land is used more intensively and with reduced use of fallow. Since around 2010, many more farmers have been following the advice of agricultural extension officers to apply improved seeds, mineral fertilizers, pesticides, and recently also herbicides increasingly for maize cultivation. This has increased yields and allowed some well-off and emerging farmers to produce the same or more using less land—average land cultivated per household has declined from 6.2 acres (1997) to 4.5 (–27 per cent), and a similar trend is seen in Ikuwala, with a change from 9.2 acres to 6.9 (–25 per cent). Meanwhile others have continued using traditional methods of farming, though with low and stagnant yields. Another response to decreasing soil fertility has been a change in cropping patterns, with a decline in the cultivation of beans and an increase in the cultivation of sunflowers (group interview 2017).

Whereas land for agriculture in Ilambilole and Ikuwala villages in the 1990s was mostly prepared by ox-ploughing, two decades later, during the follow-up study in Ilambilole, no farmers were using hand hoes for cultivation, ownership of ploughs and oxen was common, and more than one hundred ox teams and twenty-six tractors were operating.

Enterprise Innovation and Access to Competitive Markets

The increased production capacity among the well-off farmers who used seasonal inputs and enhanced access to competitive markets—in particular the new all-weather road connecting Ilambilole with Kising'a village at the Iringa–Dodoma highway (see Figures 15.1 and 15.4)—through increased transport opportunities (buses, lorries, cars, motorbikes) have led to increased sales of crops, especially for traditional crops, e.g. maize and sunflowers, as well as new crops, e.g. tomatoes in Ilambilole.

Maize has remained the main stable crop that almost all farmers are cultivating. While production and prices for maize have always varied both within and between seasons, according to farmers these variations have become stronger. In farmers' perceptions, the rainy season has become more unpredictable, and the maize crop is frequently affected by drought. Even though market institutions have matured (i.e. more competition between crop traders in the village as their number has increased), the large inter-seasonal variations in price that existed in the mid-1990s are still present today. Farmers' needs for cash incomes are high immediately after the harvest, and most farmers sell to middlemen and hawkers at low prices. In addition, maize prices varied considerably from season to season. Because of the combination of high vulnerability of production and low prices post-harvest, cases were observed where the farmers who have stuck to growing maize as their main commercial enterprise have been unable to accumulate or improve their well-being.

Figure 15.4 Construction of the metalled surface of the all-weather road between Ilambilole and Kising'a, November 2017.

The most important new commercial enterprise in Ilambilole village is tomatoes. Tomatoes were already being cultivated in the area in the mid-1990s, in particular in Ikuwala village, located near Ilula along the Iringa–Dar es Salaam road. What is new is the innovative way in which early-season tomatoes have been grown in Ilambilole since 2014. The rainy season starts three to four weeks earlier in Ilambilole village compared with Ilula village, where most tomatoes are grown. Tomato farmers in Ilambilole produce tomato seedlings in small nurseries ahead of the rainy season (see Figure 15.5). These nurseries are irrigated with buckets of water collected from public domestic water taps. To mitigate the risk associated with the uncertainty of when the rainy season starts, farmers produce a sequence of two sets of tomato seedlings, one week apart. This allows them to replant tomatoes if the first set of seedlings fail because of early-season drought. Early-season tomatoes fetch up to 35,000 TSh per tenga (the basket used to carry tomatoes in, equivalent to about 60 kilos), compared with prices as low as 2000 TSh per tenga during the peak season. Successful tomato farmers cultivate up to 6 acres of early-season tomatoes, from which they can earn several million TzSh (several thousand $US) each season.

Diversification and Upgrading of Non-agricultural Activities

Diversifying from agriculture to non-agriculture enterprises is a key socio-economic change that has occurred over the past two decades. In the mid-1990s

Figure 15.5 Home garden tomato nursery in Ilambilole.

agriculture dominated along with low threshold non-agricultural activities such as brewing and selling a drum of millet or maize beer (pombe), charcoal burning, traditional handicrafts, and petty trade. Today non-agricultural activities play a much more important role and comprise four different types of high-threshold enterprises, namely shops and bars, processing of agricultural products, hiring of tractor and transport services, and trading in crops. While non-agricultural activities were an occupation of the poor in the 1990s, it is today an occupation of the wealthiest. Table 15.1 below shows the extent of non-agricultural enterprises in Ilambilole village today.

Two forms of enterprise, tractors and shops, are dominant. In 1996 there were no tractors in Ilambilole and only one in Ikuwala. Today there are twenty-six tractors in Ilambilole (Table 15.1). In 1996 there were only a few poorly equipped shops and a small teahouse in Ikuwala and Ilambilole villages. Today there are not only more shops, twenty-eight in Ilambilole village as shown in the table, but also a range of different shops offering specialized services, such as household items, furniture, bicycle repair, mobile phone and electronics, mechanic and not least agricultural input supply and tools.

Another large-scale non-agricultural activity that a small group of well-off farmers have become engaged in is trading in crops. These crop traders rely on the historical intra-seasonal variations in the price of maize. They buy maize at low prices immediately after the harvest, store the maize safely for three to six

Table 15.1 Private shops and business in Ilambilole village 2017

Enterprises and services	Number
Tractors	26
Sunflower oil mill	2
Maize-milling machine	6
Shops	28
Supermarkets	3
Guesthouse	1
Bars	4

Source: Interview with chairman and secretary of Ilambilole village.

months and sell it to urban customers when prices are higher during the rainy season. Historically they have been able to double their capital over a six-month period. To be successful, crop traders need start-up capital to buy crops, have safe storage and access to the hire or ownership of a truck, and be trustworthy and respected in the community. Successful crop traders often combine this activity with the cultivation of early-season tomatoes, as the timing of these htwo activities are complementary (tomatoes in February–May, crop trade in July–December).

Towards a Commercial Rural Labour Market

In the mid-1990s, the labour markets in Ilambilole and Ikuwala villages were in transition, with a decline in traditional reciprocal labour arrangements—in Kibena/Kihehe called migoe or 'beer party'—towards increased use of casual labour. In the traditional migoe system, a farmer can call on her friends and neighbours to help carry out a specific task that can be done by a group of farmers in one day, such as weeding a field. Locally brewed opaque finger millet or maize beer is served after the work. In return, you are expected to send a family member to participate if or when someone who had worked on your field previously organizes their own beer party. At the time of the SASA study, well-off farmers had abandoned the migoe system and were using casual labour paid in cash or kind (food or ploughing services) during periods of labour peaks (land preparation and weeding). Poor farmers had begun to work as casual labourers during these periods, with negative effects in respect of delaying land preparation and weeding on their own cultivated fields.

Today, two decades later, the labour system has undergone yet another transition. Increase in casual labour use was observed in a study of the rural hinterlands of Njombe town (Ørtenblad et al. 2019). The traditional migoe system is no longer practised and has been replaced by hiring casual labour paid with cash. Use of casual labour instead of relying of family labour has also become much more widespread among the wealthiest farmers. Well-off farmers hire casual labour for all tasks all year round, while some poor farmers rely on casual labour work as their main occupation all year round. For early-season tomato farming, the labour market has been even more formalized. Tomato farmers hire labour from outside the village on contract for the duration of the tomato-cropping season. These contract labourers usually stay and eat with their host family. For a more detailed discussion of the emerging rural labour market in Iringa, see (Mshote 2012).

Trajectories

Ikuwala and in particular Ilambilole have experienced considerable socio-economic development over the past two decades. A good indicator of this economic growth is the construction of new houses and improvements to existing houses. In what follows we discuss this using the case of Ilambilole, the map below, which covers the central settlement, showing a dramatic increase in the number of new houses between 1995 and 2008 (sixty-four houses, or 5.3 houses per year) and even higher growth rate of houses from 2008 to 2014 (forty houses, or 6.7 houses per year; see Figure 15.6 and 15.7 below). One should note that the newly constructed houses are considerably bigger than the houses that existed in 1996 and that a number of larger houses with communal functions (guesthouse, bars, shops) have been constructed along the main street.

Qualitative group interviews, moreover, indicate that the quality of houses has improved considerably across all three well-being categories (see Table 15.2). In 1996 the main difference between the houses of the well-off farmers and those of the poorer farmers were whether they had burned bricks and corrugated iron roofs (see Figure 15.7). In 2017 many of the houses of the poor have iron-sheet roofs, while the houses of the well-off and middle group have improvements such as electricity, television, piped water, windows with glass, etc.

Change in Rural People's Perceptions of Well-Being

In 1996, well-being was assessed using three asset-based indicators (ownership of land, ownership of livestock, and crop production) combined with three social indicators (household food security, work for others, hire of labour).

In addition to these six indicators, another six indicators were added in 2017, namely three more asset-based indicators (ownership of implements, access to electricity, and quality of house) and three more social indicators (use of seasonal agricultural inputs, access to education, and access to health services). Adding new indicators of well-being is in part the result of methodological differences

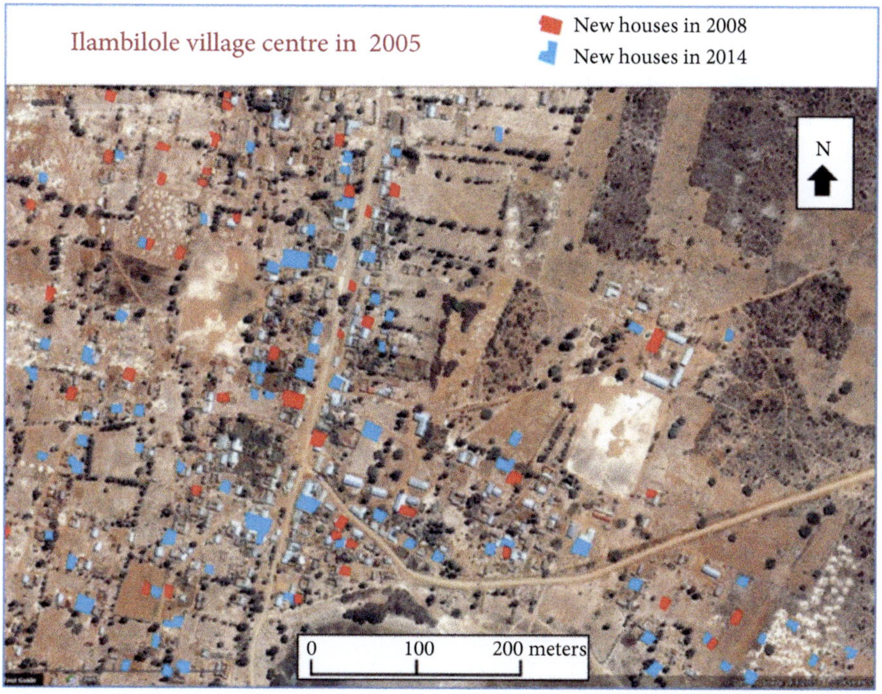

Figure 15.6 Expansion and densification of settlement in Ilambilole village, 2005–14.
Source: Google Earth time series of satellite images: 2005, 2008, and 2014.

(number indicators were deliberately kept low during the 1996 survey, as they were based on quantitative data) and in part because farmers perceive some indicators as becoming more important for well-being. Examples of indicators added by farmers because of their increased importance to well-being are access to health and educational services, where service levels have increased considerably (e.g. upgrading of health clinic to hospital and building of secondary school in Ilambilole village) and where access to these services to a large extent depends on the well-being status of the household. See Table 15.2 below summarizing farmer's perceptions of well-being in Ilambilole in 2017.

Qualitative individual and group interviews with farmers indicate, moreover, that for some indicators the content has remained constant, while the gap between the poor and well-off has increased for others. Examples of this increase in social differentiation are the two indicators relating to labour relations. In 1996 one or a few casual labours was used by the well-off during agricultural labour peaks, e.g. for land preparation and weeding. According to SASA data (1996) twelve households out of thirty-four (35 per cent) worked as casual labour. In 2017, the well-off hired ten to twenty casual labours all year round for all agricultural tasks, and as a new development, average farmers also now hire casual labours. Moreover, a new labour arrangement has developed whereby workers from outside the village

Figure 15.7 Housing standard in (A) 1996 and (B) in 2017.

are employed by the well-off or average farmers for two to three months during the tomato season. The content of the 'work as casual labour' well-being indicator has also changed. In 1996, poor farmers typically worked as casual labourers for well-off farmers for short periods a few times yearly. In 2017 casual labour had become the main occupation for some poor farmers.

Change in Well-Being, 1996–2017

Table 15.3 below show the change in well-being over a twenty-year period, based on re-interviews of the participants of the 1996 SASA household survey (or their

Table 15.2 Farmers' perceptions of well-being in Ilambilole village 2017

Well-being criteria	Wealthy	Average	Poor
Land	>20 acres	5–20 acres	<5 acres
Agriculture production	25 MT maize/>3 tonne/acre; large-scale tomato production	12 MT maize/<2 tonne/acre; some engaged in tomato production	1.5 MT maize/1/3 tonne/acre; not involved in tomato production
Use of inputs	Improved inputs on all of the fields every year; use herbicide	Partial use of inputs; combined use of fertilizer and rotation of fields	Use local seed; rotate fields and occasional fertilizer of manure
Livestock	>300 cows, 150 goats, 100 pigs, and 50 improved chickens	10 cows, 10 pigs, 10 goats, and 15 local chickens	5 goats, 1 pig, and 5 local chickens
Hire casual labour	Hire 10–15 workers for all tasks; seasonal labour for tomato production	May hire workers for some tasks; hire seasonal labour for tomato production	Never hire causal workers
Work as casual labour	Never work as casual labourer	Occasional work as casual labourer, when in need of cash to pay of expenditure	Shift between working as casual labourer and working in own farm
Implements	Own tractor, oxen/plough, donkey-cart, car/lorry, and/or motorbike	Some own oxen/plough, donkey-cart others hire; own motorbike	Hire tractor or oxen for land preparation; some own bicycles
Electricity	All have solar/electricity; electric light, satellite TV, and fridge	Solar and some access to electricity; electric light and some satellite TV	No solar or electricity
House	Burned bricks, tile, or iron roof; some have inside water tap, toilets, glass windows	Unburned bricks, iron roof; not plastered; some have glass windows	Unburned bricks/mud wall, iron/thatched roof; no glass windows

Source: group interview with key informants and individual follow-up interviews.

secondary units). Both villages have experienced a significant decline in the number of poor (an approximately 30 per cent decline in both Ikuwala and Ilambilole villages; see Table 15.3). In Ikuwala, the decline in poverty has translated into a corresponding increase in the middle well-being ranking category, while in Ilambilole village the number of well-off has almost doubled.

These changes in the relative numbers belonging to the three well-being categories hide a more complex picture of both upward and downward social mobility (1) between the well-off and the middle, and (2) between the middle and the poor. The evidence also shows that no one who was a well-off farmer then is poor today and no one who was poor then is well-off today.

Table 15.3 Changes in well-being, 1996 to 2017, in Ilambilole and Ikuwala villages

Village	Well-being category	1996	2017
Ilambilole	Well-off	16%	29%
	Middle	38%	33%
	Poor	47%	38%
Ikuwala	Well-off	21%	19%
	Middle	46%	57%
	Poor	33%	23%

Source: SASA household survey 1996 and follow-up survey of primary and secondary households 2017.

The 1996 SASA study found that farmers' perceptions of well-being categories based on criteria relating to assets and social relationships and entitlements did not provide a clear picture of the types of resources from which wealth was derived or how resources were allocated. In particular, among the middle well-being category one finds different patterns of resource use and allocation, where some resemble the well-off business-oriented farmers, while others are more defensive in their strategies, like the poor well-being category.

Changes in Livelihood Strategies

As discussed in the introduction, the SASA study identified three livelihood strategies, the accumulating strategy, the peasant strategy, and the peasant-labour coping strategy. During the follow-up study, through qualitative case-study interviews with selected households we explored how these three livelihood strategies have evolved over two decades.

The *original accumulating strategy* comprised a diverse group of both young and established households with high incomes from both agriculture and sources based on business, crafts, and rents. They sought to invest incomes derived from agriculture in expanding the cultivated area and in non-agricultural income-generating activities such as running kiosks, masonry, the maize trade, or investments in housing (Birch-Thomsen et al. 2001). Through discussions with farmers in 2017, we found that this had been further developed and transformed into an *integrated market and agriculture strategy* with two key characteristics. First, these households view agriculture as a business and base their decisions and focus their activities on what is demanded by the market and is profitable to produce. Secondly, these households are able to combine and create synergies between agricultural activities during the rainy season with the crop trade and other business activities in the dry season. The follow-up study identified two groups of people following this livelihood strategy: first, farmers who were accumulating two decades ago and who gradually used their resources to build synergies between agriculture and business, as in the case of Augustini discussed below; and secondly, a group of young male graduates from secondary-school with limited capital, but wide social networks (using mobile phones) and the ability to exploit business opportunities.

Augustini, who lives in Ilambilole village, is an example of a well-established and innovative farmer who has successfully integrated her business and farming activities. Augustini explained that she had managed to build a reputation as a shrewd crop trader to organize farmers to deliver their maize harvest to her warehouse, where she stored the crops for three months before reselling it to urban wholesalers or resident tomato farmers. She has twelve children, and the whole extended family helped each other with trading. One of her daughters owned a four-tonne lorry, which she used to transport the maize. There are today clear synergies between the trade in crops and agriculture. She started growing tomatoes as a cash crop in 1998, but the poor road made it a high-risk enterprise, and prices were as low as 1000 TZs per tenga. The opening of a new and improved road in 2015 provided an opportunity to introduce tomato production in Ilambilole village. By preparing tomato seedlings before the first rains (using water from the public domestic water supply), Augustini has been able to harvest tomatoes three to four weeks before the main tomato season and earn premium prices. In 2016 she sold 200 tenga of tomatoes for 30,000 TSh each, giving her an income of six million TSh. She used this income to buy maize from other farmers at 70,000 TSh per bag, which she sold on to wholesalers at 100,000 to 130,000 TSh per bag three months later. Some of this income is used for home consumption and inputs for tomato production, while the remainder is used to support secondary and university education for her children.

Charles's father practised a peasant-labour coping strategy in 1996 and is today engaged in an integrated market and agriculture livelihood strategy. When Charles (see Box 15.1) returned from Dar es Salaam to Ilambilole village in 2012, he used his savings to invest in cultivating tomatoes as a high-input enterprise. He stated, 'tomatoes have changed our living, it is the reason for our development'. Similar to established sell-off farmers, he is able to grow an early-season tomato crop. He prepares irrigated tomato seedlings using expensive improved seeds ready for planting with the first rains and applies fertilizer and pesticides. In the 2016/17 season he produced 145 tenga of tomatoes from 1 acre, from which he earned 3.6 million TSh. Some of this he transported on a hired truck and sold in Ilula wholesale market, and some was sold to local middlemen.

The *original peasant strategy* was associated with neither taking too much risk nor engaging strongly in the market economy. This group combined intermediate agricultural incomes with making craft items from natural resources and petty business. This peasant strategy has today been replaced by a *conservative production-oriented livelihood strategy* in which households focus on agricultural production, e.g. cultivating maize, sunflowers, and other traditional crops. The follow-up study found that farmers who adhered to this livelihood strategy were less interested in marketing or linking up with outside traders, but simply sold their surplus production to local traders in the village.

Mr Justin Wilson in Ikuwala village is a farmer who twenty years ago was one of the wealthiest in the village, engaged in a strategy to accumulate as much land as possible and cultivate maize using a tractor bought with a bank loan. When he was revisited in 2017, Mr Wilson gave the impression of being a conservative middle-aged farmer with a stagnant farm. He had persisted with a production focus, e.g. the extensive cultivation of maize, and had not been able to successfully respond to dry season market opportunities such as growing tomatoes or trading crops. The risks associated with cultivating maize have increased significantly over the past two decades. On the one hand, climate change has increased the variability of the rainfall pattern and maize production, leading to crop loss in early or mid-season droughts, as was the case in 2016/17, when Mr Wilson harvested only twenty bags of maize from 14 acres. On the other hand, maize may also be loss-generating during good rainfall seasons, when all the farmers have good harvests, resulting in low market prices. This was the case during the 2017/18 season, when the prices paid by local crop traders was less than 10 $US per 90kg bag, insufficient to cover the seasonal input costs. While Justin Wilson was clearly still well-off, he was perceived as stagnant compared with younger and more dynamic farmers/traders in the village.

Finally, the *original peasant-labour coping strategy* was associated largely with poor farmers pursuing subsistence farming and occasional casual work for others, as well as earning an income from the collection of natural resources, e.g. thatching grass and fuelwood. During the follow-up study in 2017 we found that this strategy had been replaced with what we identified as a *poverty-trapped livelihood strategy*. These farmers are for a variety of reasons poor and unable to produce a significant surplus for marketing. An important element in this strategy is taking work as casual labourers. Some are trapped in poverty because of the poor yields of the field crops (predominantly maize), poor crop husbandry and insufficient money to buy mineral fertilizer or cow manure. Others are engaged in working as casual labourers for other farmers as their main occupation. Today work as day labourers is available year-round, and the pay has increased to 3 $US per day, which allows workers to be food secure. However, others are too old or sick to cultivate their fields properly or to work as casual labourers.

Luben from Ikuwala village was poor when the SASA project interviewed him in 1996 at the age of 33 and was in spite of some progress still perceived as poor today twenty years later. He is still cultivating the same 4 acres he owns along with also renting a field in the wetlands. He grows a mixture of maize, sunflowers, and cowpeas. During the 2017 season he harvested 3.5 bags of maize, which was insufficient to feed his family. The explanation for the low yields was poor rain and poor crop husbandry. He also grew tomatoes on his rented wetland fields and in 2017 harvested 15 tenga in the first week, which he sold for 13,000–15,000 TSh per tenga at the main market in Ilula Township. After the first week, prices were so low that he gave up selling any more. Other sources of cash income come from selling ten bags of sunflower at 50,000 TSh per bag and looking after other people's livestock. Luben has experienced two major improvements to his livelihood over the past twenty years. First he managed to build a new house with burned bricks and iron roofing. Secondly, he has managed to buy or otherwise accumulate twelve cows and fifteen goats, which he keeps in a boma next to his house, assisted by a young boy who lives with his family. The income he receives for looking after an additional twenty cows includes keeping the milk and manure produced by the animals. Access to grazing is a major challenge, and he was fined 100,000 TSh by the village government in 2016 because his cows were grazing on other people's land. He had to sell three loads of cow manure at 50,000 TSh per load to pay the fine, even though he needed it for his own fields. Even though ownership to assets in terms of twelve cows and fifteen goats place him in the average well-being category (see Table 15.2), he is nevertheless perceived by himself and others as poor because of low scores in other well-being categories. For example, he told us during the re-interview in 2017 that he had no money to buy inputs for improved crop production, including fertilizer and hybrid tomato seeds.

Conclusion

Change in the Role of Land

At the time of the SASA project (1994–9), access to land was seen as the most important asset across all household categories. For the well-to-do households the focus was on expanding their land holdings by either buying or renting land outside the village area. This strategy of land accumulation was seen as an investment in improving overall livelihoods. For the medium-wealth group, farming was important as a strategy sustaining their livelihoods. This included renting land, which allowed the household flexibility according to its needs and availability. For the poorer households land was constrained to small and low fertility plots, which was compensated through working as casual labour for other farmers.

In 2017 land was no longer seen as the only or most important source of accumulation. As entrepreneurial households stated in particular, it was now seen as more important to use land efficiently based on better land management through the use of external inputs (improved seeds, fertilizers, and pesticides/herbicides). The accumulation strategy had shifted from extensive land to intensive land-use practices (using less land with increased yields). Furthermore, strategies combining farming with other business activities (e.g. crop trading, shop-keeping, and other income-generating activities) were seen as a way of improving livelihoods.

Changes in Well-Being

Based on the follow-up study, we find indications of a general improvement in well-being across all categories. However, at the same time social differentiation has increased within communities, as illustrated in Figure 15.8 below. One should note that, while all have become better off, the rate of improvement in well-being has been higher for the well-off than for the poor.

While the overall trend is increased well-being, there are variations between the two villages. In both villages the percentage belonging to the poor has declined. In Ilambilole the percentage who belong to the well-off well-being category has increased, while it is the middle well-being category that has increased in Ikuwala village. Moreover, qualitative fieldwork revealed considerable upward and downward social mobility between well-being categories, in particular between the middle and well-off well-being category and the middle and poor well-being category. Qualitative interviews indicate that downward social mobility is experienced when two or more major expenses (e.g. sickness in the family, secondary education, investments in improvements to the house) and/or temporary reductions in income (e.g. drought, failure in business and trade) occur at the same time. Upward social mobility seems increasingly to be associated with education.

Change in Livelihood Portfolio

The 1990s study concluded that the dominant overall strategy was related to farm production and that investments (when possible) went back into farming.

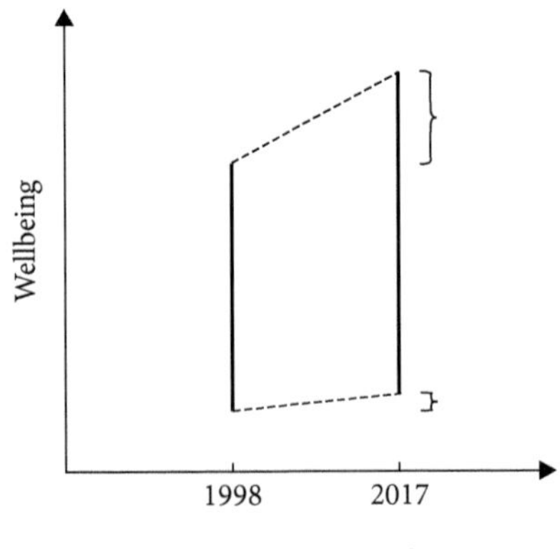

Figure 15.8 Relative overall changes in well-being from 1998 to 2017.

In contrast to the livelihood strategies identified in the original study (see Box 15.2), the follow-up study revealed much more diversified livelihood strategies. The revisit study indicates that some farmers have become much more business-oriented and engaged with what the follow-up study called an *integrated market and agriculture strategy*. Farmers who have managed to establish synergies between agricultural, non-agricultural enterprises and trade are among those who have experienced the highest increases in well-being. Farmers who are engaged in a *conservative production-oriented livelihood strategy* have not experienced any upward social mobility. This group includes some of the farmers who were following the 'accumulating farmers' strategy' in the 1990s and have continued their extensive farming practices. Farmers who follow a *poverty-trapped livelihood strategy* are fewer today compared with the 1990s, even though many of the mechanisms are the same. Working as casual labour for other farmers or businesses has become much more important for this group.

Part of the change in livelihood compositions has been enabled through increased rural-urban linkages spurred by the transformation of Ilula over the past two decades, from 'village' to 'township' status (Agergaard et al. 2021). These changes includes improved infrastructure (roads, public transport, communications), access to profitable tomato markets (local traders, lorry rental, TASAF market in Ilula Township), and improved access to education and health services (see Lazaro et al. 2019).

References

Agergaard, J., S. H. Kirkegaard, and T. Birch-Thomsen (2021). Between Village and Town: Small-Town Urbanism in Sub-Saharan Africa. *Sustainability* 13(3) 1417. https://doi.org/10.3390/su13031417.

Birch-Thomsen, T., P. Frederiksen, and H.-O. Sano (2001). 'A Livelihood Perspective On Natural Resource Management and Environmental Change in Semi-arid Tanzania.' *Economic Geography* 77(1): 48–66.

Birch-Thomsen, T., B. Elberling, B. Fog, and J. Magid (2007). 'Temporal and Spatial Trends in Soil Organic Carbon Stocks Following Maize Cultivation in Semi-arid Tanzania, East Africa.' *Nutrient Cycling in Agroecosystems* 79(3): 291–302.

Bryceson, D. F. (1999). 'African Rural Labour, Income Diversification and Livelihood Approaches: A Longterm Development Perspective.' *Review of African Political Economy* 80: 171–89.

Friis-Hansen, E. (2000). 'Agricultural Policy after Adjustment.' Copenhagen, Center for Development Research.

McDonagh, J., T. Birch-Thomsen, and J. Magid (2001). 'Soil Organic Matter Decline and Compositional Change Associated with Cereal Cropping in Southern Tanzania.' *Land Degradation and Development* 12: 13–26.

Lazaro, E., J. Agergaard, M. N. Larsen, J. Makindara, and T. Birch-Thomsen (2019). 'Urbanisation in Rural Regions: The Emergence of Urban Centres in Tanzania.' *European Journal of Development Research* (*EJDR*) 31(1): 72–94.

Mshote, E. (2012). 'Rural-Urban Migration.' Paper presented at the RUCROP Stakeholder Workshop, Mikumi, Morogoro, August 20, 2012.

SASA (1999). 'Completion Report—Centre for Research on Sustainable Agriculture in Semi-Arid Africa (SASA), 1994–1999.' Report submitted to 'The Danish Environmental Research Programme', Danish Ministry of Environment and Danida.

Tiffen, M., M. Mortimore, and F. Gichuki (1994). *More People Less Erosion: Environmental Recovery in Kenya*. Chichester, John Wiley.

Ørtenblad, S. B., T. Birch-Thomsen, and L. Msese (2019). 'Rural Transformation and Changing Rural–Urban Connections in a Dynamic Region in Tanzania: Perspectives on Processes of Inclusive Development.' *European Journal of Development Research* 31(1): 118–38.

16
The Urbanizing Frontier, Change and Continuity
Uchira 1996–2018

Anna Mdee

Epilogue pages 394–397

Introduction

Stepping out of the bus in Uchira in 1996 the first thing that you noticed was the dust. The highway stretching from Nairobi to Dar-es-Salaam, unpaved at this point, split the village in two. Clouds of red dust hurled into the air by the lumbering lorries, crowded *dala-dala*, and the occasional DFP-plated[1] Landcruisers and tourist vehicles created a thick blanket that shrouded the village during daylight hours. Despite (or because of) the dust, the economy of Uchira grew as a market and transport town. I arrived there, with two friends, in the summer of our second year at the University of Cambridge as undergraduates. A chance meeting in Cambridge, of a Tanzanian doctor, had drawn us there for a six-week period. Working with the village council, we produced the 'Uchira Village Report', based on an archaeology of aid-funded projects and public infrastructure. We lived with a farmer and part-time Pentecostal pastor and his family, in the neighbouring village of Kirua, a further 6km up the hills that rose beyond Uchira. Our energetic and wily guide, village councillor Ernest Msuya, escorted us, naïve students, in the politics and rhythms of the place. These are the roots of this chapter: a first attempt to delineate a narrative of change and continuity in Uchira over a period of twenty-two years.

I explore here two broad brush aspects of Uchira during this period: livelihoods patterns and public and private infrastructure. Part of the basis for these

[1] *Dala-dala* is Swahili for the small minibuses that provide most short-range transport. DFP is an acronym for 'donor-funded project' and is the official licencing designation for vehicles imported through aid projects.

Anna Mdee, *The Urbanizing Frontier, Change and Continuity: Uchira 1996–2018* In: *Prosperity in Rural Africa? Insights into Wealth, Assets, and Poverty from Longitudinal Studies in Tanzania.* Edited by: Dan Brockington and Christine Noe, Oxford University Press. DOI: 10.1093/oso/9780198865872.003.0016

observations is several discrete anthropological interactions generating data from multiple methods (my PhD field work and a DFID funded project 2004–6, work with a local NGO from 2002–11, research for a Bill and Melinda Gates funded study in 2016). But Uchira is not just a research site, it is a place that is indelibly woven into my life, personally and professionally. There are two accounts of change woven into this chapter—change to Uchira, and change in the way I *see* Uchira. I have seen it as a student of anthropology in the 1990s, as a young mother and new academic in the 2000s, and in the last decade as maturing academic, aid critic, wife, in-law, and mother of a village Chairman's grandchildren.

Uchira defies a single narrative of change, and all this chapter attempts to do is to comb out one or two of the threads. The Nigerian novelist, Chimamanda Ngozi Adichie, argued in her influential TED talk 2009 that there is danger in trying to tell a single story: it necessarily reduces and simplifies.[2] Yet, some development academics and the aid industry tend to want a simple narrative, and it is inevitable that this book, a collection of diverse stories will be read and interpreted by some who are looking for 'evidence' to support their preferred narrative and assumptions. The careful and thoughtful analyst will always be cautious in making conclusions, but the claim-making simplification monster of the aid business will not (Hickel 2016, Chambers 2017, Yanguas 2018).

I take inspiration in this chapter from anthropologists in political ecology, and the work of Tania Murray Li (2014) and Paige West (2016) in their explorations of conjunctures: the factors and forces that shape social relations, lives, and livelihoods, but that do not determine them. Maia Green's (2014) longitudinal anthropological exploration of civil society in southern Tanzania also gave me confidence that my own observations on the cultural force of the concept of maendeleo (development) were justified. This chapter is a first attempt to give form to some of the ways Uchira has changed since 1996.

To some degree, Uchira can be read as a story of a frontier, in the sense that Li (2014) uses it. It grew as a settlement (1950s) when land was easily available to those who would settle there. By 1996 there was no more spare land, it was all claimed, and owned in one way or another. This structured relations between people: between the generations, and between incomers and the settlers. Since that time, water infrastructure and availability intersect with urban spread and rapid population growth. Climate dynamics, new technologies, the patterns of Tanzanian economic growth, the evolution of the CCM state, fervent religiosity, aid, and development interventions all influence Uchiran lives. Yet there is also considerable consistency here. For many life and livelihoods are not significantly different in the period from 1996 to the present time. Livelihood characteristics remain remarkably similar, even if there is some change in the assets that people

[2] https://www.ted.com/talks/chimamanda_adichie_the_danger_of_a_single_story?language=en.

hold. The provision of health and education services is recognizably consistent (with changes in access, but not in quality), and surely supports a narrative that the economic growth seen in recent decades has not translated into transformation in public service provision, except in quite ad hoc and aid-dependent fashion (see Kessy et al. 2013).

The chapter is divided into three sections: the first maps how Uchira has changed physically through comparing observations on infrastructure and institutions from points in 1996, 2004, and 2016 using maps which detail institutions and noteworthy features of 'development' (as defined by the village council). The second part explores the nature of services provision in more detail, based on detailed observations and interviews throughout the period of 1996 to the present time. Finally, the nature of dynamics of livelihoods patterns in Uchira are reviewed through comparative analysis of life history and livelihoods interviews in 2004 and 2016, supplemented with interview and observation data from across the entire period. Finally, the chapter concludes by highlighting key observations of change, but also of continuity and decline.

A Village on a Frontier

Uchira is a village settlement, 15km east from Moshi on the Dar-es-Salaam main highway. A village (kijiji) in Tanzania refers to the lowest level of the local government system, and is a geographical unit comprising a number of smaller hamlets (kitongoji). Hence the village area of Uchira covers the area of settlement around the highway (comprised of small shops, public institutions, and bars), but also extends some 6km upland to border the next village of Kirua and 6km into the flat plains to Miwaleni Springs, covering a total area of around 100 km^2.

Uchira evolved as a settlement in the 1950s–60s as land shortages on the slopes of Kilimanjaro and the Pare Mountains encouraged migration (of younger sons) from both Chagga and Pare ethnic groups. These plains were frontier land for those willing to settle. Originally land allocations were presided over by elders from these areas, but with the abolition of 'traditional' authority under Nyerere control of lands came under the control of the village council. Land ownership patterns dating back to the original settlers are still present, and an active market for land leasing was evident in the 1990s.

By the 1990s, Uchira was an active market town around the highway—small grocery shops, hardware stores, carpenters, mechanics, and barbers lined the roadside (Figure 16.1). The weekly livestock and vegetable markets attracted Maasai cattle traders from a wide area and contributed to the local economy, and particularly the establishment of pubs and bars to serve the market-day trade. Away from the roadside trading activities, Uchira's agricultural economy was

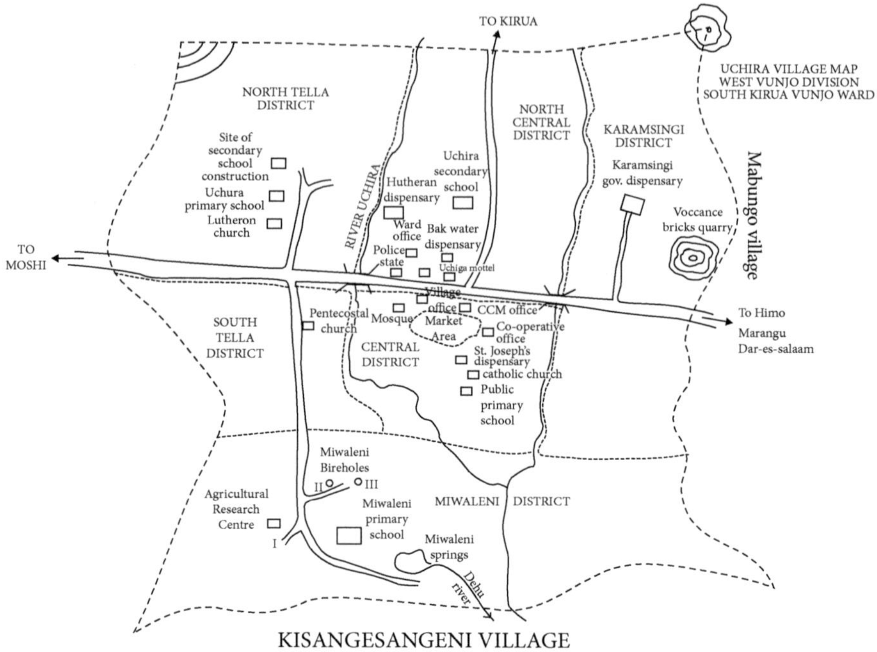

Figure 16.1 Uchira village map, 1996.

based on the rain-fed cultivation of maize and beans primarily for food, with some additional cultivation of ground nuts and sunflowers as cash crops for those with the capital to invest in agricultural inputs. The 1996 study identified various attempts were made over the decades to tap local water sources for irrigation. In the 1970s FAO built a series of irrigation reservoirs with boreholes (labelled on Figure 16.1 as boreholes 1, 2, and 3), but they were never fully operational as designed (see De Bont 2018). At this time, the diesel pumps and boreholes attached to these sites were being used on a small scale, but this was highly limited due to the cost of fuel. The village council of Uchira had a plan to dam the seasonal Uchira River for irrigation and was actively seeking funds for the project.

The other significant livelihood activity in Uchira was quarrying stone and gravel for building—local people say that 'Uchira grows stones', and there was one significant large quarry site (run as a co-operative) where the volcanic rock was cut by hand tools into bricks. The large blocks were also broken up for sale as aggregate, with this activity being done by individuals and family groups.

By 1996, Uchira was a heterogenous settlement in terms of wealth. Its setting in Kilimanjaro Region makes it part of one of the most socially and educationally mobile areas of Tanzania. Early missionary activity in education led many Chagga and Pare to important positions in newly independent Tanzania. Hence in Uchira, in 1996 there were several very large and luxurious dwellings constructed by successful migrants, eager to demonstrate their success in their home village. Uchira is further heterogenous in terms of ethnicity (primarily a mix of Pare and Chagga, but with small numbers of other groups) and religion (various Islamic and Christian denominations). Religious identity appeared to be quite fluid and people changed religion/affiliation and intermarried. In 1996, the Catholic and Lutheran churches were significant providers of health services.

The village council were active in pursuing local development projects. Market activities generated local revenue through taxation and fees, and the council mobilized villager's contributions and labour to begin the construction of a secondary school. Three primary schools served different areas of the village, and the government-operated Karamsingii dispensary offered health services. The biggest problem for Uchira, according to the village council, was domestic water. Uchira did have the remnants of a piped water system, constructed in the late 1960s, but this had ceased to function. In the rainy season, irrigation channels, rainwater collection, and the seasonal rivers served domestic water needs. However, in the dry season women and children had to walk significant distances to the hills, or down to Miwaleni Springs to fetch water. Private tankers also brought water to the village for purchase.

Uchira in 2004

I did not return to Uchira in the years between 1996 and 2002; however, Ernest Msuya, my first guide, wrote regular letters to me concerning village council projects. They were seeking assistance to build a hospital ward at the Karamsingii dispensary. GtZ (now part of GiZ) had come with a project to rehabilitate the water supply through community-based management, and the villagers had completed the building of Mashingia Secondary School. They were just awaiting the adoption of the school by the district council, and for the Ministry of Education to supply teachers. The main highway had been paved by the central government using loan finance from the World Bank. The red dust no longer choked the village during daylight hours.

My PhD research (Cleaver and Toner 2006; Mdee 2008, Toner 2008) forms the basis of my observations in 2004–5. My focus was on the community-based management of the water supply but sought to embed this in an analysis of participation and power in the collective life of the village. I spent extended periods living in the village in 2004 and 2005 working with Ernest Msuya. Figure 16.2 maps the village infrastructure in 2004.

The most significant physical changes in the village between 1996 and 2004 were increases in the number of religious institutions, particularly Pentecostal churches (see Mdee 2013); and an expansion in quarrying activity, with five large-scale sites. The completion of the water project led to the construction of the

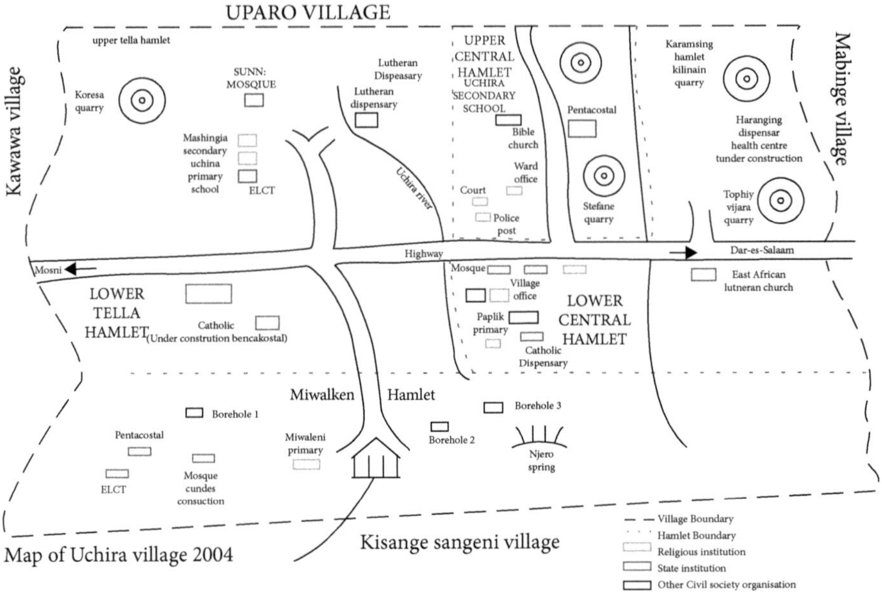

Figure 16.2 Map of Uchira village, 2004.

Uchira Water Users' Association (UWUA) office, and this organization had become a significant political force in the village. The village council had become noticeably weaker. The village chairman in 1996, was now the chairman of UWUA and remains so to the present time. Twenty-four public water points were operational, selling water to villagers. Many of the wealthier families had private metered water connections. However, the water supply could still not meet demand throughout the year, and was rationed in the dry season.

The livestock market was closed suddenly, by the district government, in 2004 due to an anthrax outbreak and this had a significant impact on Uchira's roadside trading economy. It has never re-opened. The decline of several of the bars since the early 2000s followed. 2004 and 2005 were drought years, agricultural production was severely affected, and hunger was visible in Uchira. Some families were receiving food aid, particularly those caring for large numbers of dependents driven by the HIV/AIDS pandemic which impacted, to some degree, on most families.

Uchira in 2016

I returned many times to Uchira between 2004 and 2016, having married the son of the village chairman, and being actively involved with Ernest Msuya in a local NGO working on rights to services for people living with HIV/AIDS (See Mdee and Thorley 2016), and other projects. However, I did not map changes in the village until 2016, when I revisited livelihoods interviewees from my 2004 PhD fieldwork. Figure 16.3 was drawn by Yusuph Mfinanga (one of the original research assistants from the 2004/5 fieldwork, and who led the 2016 fieldwork).

The expansion of religious building and quarrying appeared to have stabilized. A new private girls' Islamic secondary school has opened, and the Angel's Gate Children's Village for children with special needs is operating on the road to Kirua. The new dynamics of change in the physical nature of the village were now through private farmer-led irrigation, with local investors irrigating plots from bore-holes and the Miwaleni Springs. There is also an increasing population of urban incomers buying up village plots. These immigrants are relatively wealthy. Uchira is an attractive location for urban commuters from Moshi, as it is on the main road, has mains-grid electricity connection, and a reliable water supply. They find a ready market of affordable (for wealthy urbanites) land in the older generations of Uchirans who are eager to sell their plots to meet the cash demands of a 'modern' life. With the recent in-migration the number of 'modern' houses—larger dwellings in their own compounds—has increased. Even in the 1990s the numbers of unimproved so-called 'traditional' houses were relatively low and numbers of these dwellings have further declined since 2004. They are more likely to be found in the remoter areas of the village.

Figure 16.3 Map of Uchira and Koresa villages, 2016.

In 2015 Uchira was split into two villages—Uchira and Koresa due to the population growth. Koresa is the western portion of former Uchira and incorporates the Miwaleni Springs settlement. It is in the process of the developing the infrastructure and institutions required of a village—a village council, assembly, and village office. The village chairman of Koresa, my father-in-law, is still seeking funds to dam the river for irrigation.

Dynamics of Service Provision

The nature of my first interactions in Uchira has enabled me to present a detailed longitudinal assessment of public and social service provision. My academic focus in the years since 1996 has been on a holistic and integrated view of local governance and collection action on these aspects of village life. Table 16.1 attempts to capture the nature of service provision at data points of 1996, 2004, and 2016, although my regular interactions in intervening years also allow me to comment on the dynamics of the changes that are observed.

In 1996, the village council was firmly in control of collective village life. The council collected the national development levy and head taxes in the livestock market, and mobilized villagers to make additional financial and labour contributions. It had resources and power. It was able to build a secondary school (Mashingia) and had begun work on the ward building (with the primary aim of providing maternity services, and response to the health demands of HIV/AIDS) at the dispensary site in the Karamsingii hamlet. Uchira was already a highly differentiated settlement in terms of wealth in 1996. The wealthy village residents did not use local services, as they could purchase better health and education in the urban areas.

The three primary schools were full to bursting in 2004. Fees had been abolished and enrolment had surged. Although parents complain about the contributions that are still required for school: uniforms, food, water, and firewood. New classrooms were constructed through a nationally funded programme. There are not enough teachers to meet the government requirements for pupil-teacher ratios—Miwaleni primary revealed three teachers attempting to manage 510 pupils. In 2016 the primary schools still look the same as in 1996 and 2004, but with some new classrooms built by NGO funds. There are more teachers, but the population now necessitates running two schools from the same buildings—they operate in shifts.

Mashingia Secondary School was adopted by the district council and began operations in the early 2000s. In 2016 it had more female pupils than male (330 to 180), with hostels for girls built with Australian NGO funds. Secondary school fees were abolished in 2015 but girls have to pay to stay in the hostel. Like many

Table 16.1 Overview of public and social services provision.

	1996	2004–6	2016
Health, Government	Public dispensary; few medicines; all fever recorded as malaria; no water or electricity connection; medical assistant (MA) present	Ward building funded by V2V at request of village council; promise of staff from DC; gas-powered fridge donated from Japan; all fever still recorded as malaria; no doctor/MA present	Rapid test for malaria available; ward building still not finished or staffed; still no water or electricity connection; basic medicine availability; no doctor/MA present
Education	Secondary school being constructed by VC with contributions; 3 primary schools; 1 private secondary	Mashingia sec. operational; little change observed in classrooms format but more kids in school and classroom building under PADEP	Mashingia sec., girls outnumber boys; very high failure rates; girls' dorm built; few teaching resources; new Islamic girls' secondary established
Water	Rehabilitation of old system desired; plan for dam on Uchira River	UWUA established; cost recovery (see Toner 2008)	UWUA still functioning; demand increasing; supply challenge Funds still being sought for dam; new boreholes sunk privately and increased pumped irrigation
Social welfare and NGO inputs	Religious institutions; HIV pandemic impacting through migration	Religious institutions; increasing economic and care burden from HIV pandemic; KIWAKKUKI, women's HIV org. (implicated in corruption over food aid)	Angel's Gate Children village, https://www.youtube.com/watch?v=KYUbTyR45as; Miwaleni classrooms; Mashingia girls' hostel; religious institutions
Religion + attached services	Lutheran, health centre; very dilapidated Catholic; new health centre and borehole, high cost; Bakwata Islam; popular Dr Lyimo and good service	Lutheran, minor improvement (painted); Catholic, as previous—considered better quality but high charge; large Catholic Cathedral being built; Dr Lyimo moved on to another place; all RIs have attached *chekechea* (Kindergarten); several new churches, Pentecostal	Lutheran, same as previous; doctor unimpressed; new church being built; Catholic, as previous; large Cathedral established; Dr Lyimo returned, operating independently; new mosques; 'boko haram'

Tanzania government secondary schools, Mashingia has a high failure rate in the national examinations. Eighty out of 134 students failed completely at form 4 in 2014/15, and forty-one scored division 4- also regarded as failure in terms of progression to later stages of education. Division 1, 2, or 3 is required to progress to A-levels. The teachers at Mashingia are disillusioned. The school is struggling, it has to pay very high bills for water to UWUA, the pregnancy rates for female pupils are high, and there are few good prospects for employment for pupils who fail.

In 1996 the private Uchira secondary school already catered for education demand amongst the more financially able village residents, who could not afford more expensive urban schools, and whose children had failed to win access to government schools. In 2016 it continues to operate, but it is a low-priced school with poor infrastructure and also struggles to get students to pass at form 4. The new private Islamic girls' secondary is popular and attracting day pupils from surrounding areas.

In 2004 numbers of boys and girls were not significantly different in primary school. But in 2016 both primary and secondary schools reported better performance by girls. Boys are seen as lazier and only interested in quick money.

Different health providers, from local healers to sophisticated, and expensive facilities owned by the Catholic Church, catered to different financial abilities in the village. We found that, in 2016, health service provision has not changed significantly since 2004. The government-funded Karamsingii dispensary is still not connected to the water supply or to mains electricity, and staffing levels are similar to those in 1996. A hospital ward constructed by the village government has never been fully completed or operational. The Lutheran dispensary is almost identical in 2016 as it was in 1996, one medical assistant, a small collection of dilapidated buildings, and a medicine cupboard featuring little more than packets of Panadol. Most people just buy what drugs they can through at the small pharmacies on the main highway. Those with the means to pay look beyond the village for services.

By 2004, the power over the collective life of the village was shifting and fracturing. The village council was weakened in 2004. With the livestock market gone, and the development levy abolished, it had few resources. This remained the case in 2016, when it could only collect some revenues from land registration and sales.

Religious identity was intensifying, but also diversifying. Pentecostal churches of various natures and foundation were springing up, some as individual projects, some supported through overseas patronage. The struggling farmer, who hosted me in 1996, became a successful pastor living in a nearby town with children at a private secondary school. The Catholic Diocese of Moshi was demanding labour and contributions from villagers to build a huge church at the junction to Miwaleni Springs, and the foundations had already begun to take shape. Most of the religious facilities offer Kindergarten services on a fee-paying basis.

The new community-based water management organization (UWUA) was commanding control of village labour and financial contributions. With GtZ funds, it had a new office, meeting hall, and transport. It generated revenue through payments for water at public and private taps and demanded that the village council ensure that villagers give two days labour per week in communal labour (an obligation which fell on the poorest, see Cleaver and Toner 2006). In 2016 UWUA is still in operation, but has to some degree been absorbed by a more strategic district-wide approach to water provision. The system of water collection at the public taps has changed. More people have private water connections and sell water to those without their own connection.

Livelihoods Patterns in Uchira 2004–16

Finally, I examine changes in livelihoods patterns and wealth ranking in Uchira. During my 2004/5 fieldwork we mapped wealth and livelihoods patterns in Uchira, through sixty-seven detailed life history interviews, and a further 150 livelihoods interviews (see Table 16.2). The local research team designed a three-category wealth ranking for 2004—they argued that the three categories (the have-nots, those getting-by, and the big shots) captured essential differences in assets and livelihoods in the village population. Life history interviewees were purposively selected to cover the three locally identified wealth categories, and taking into consideration differences in gender, religion, and ethnic origin.

The 'have-nots' (estimated at around 30 per cent of total population in the village) were those households with small land holdings (an average of 1.7 acres) that were dependent on their own labour to process natural resources, e.g. through

Table 16.2 Wealth ranking for Uchira, 2004–5.

Category	Attributes
Poor / 'have nots'	Only one meal per day; house with thatched roof and in state of disrepair; torn and dirty clothes; poor health; malnourished children; poor and intermittent education; hires/owns less than 2 acres for farming; uses public dispensary/herbs for medicine
Middle / 'getting by'	2 meals per day; buys second hand clothes; owns 2–5 acres; gives children primary education and secondary if possible; has reasonable house (iron sheets, volcanic block walls); can afford to go to hospital if necessary; has chickens, goats, and 2–3 cows; has business activities/some employment (teachers/nurses); most use public taps, some private taps
Wealthy / 'big shots'	Farms 5–50 acres; good houses; dresses smartly; children at expensive secondary schools; uses private hospitals; owns bars, minibuses, tractors, and cars; well-paid employment (regional government/private companies/ development activities)

the crushing of aggregate, weaving baskets, or gathering grass from cows, or through selling their labour for low-waged agricultural activities. Their agricultural activities depended on low input production of maize, which formed the bulk of their food, but was also sold to meet cash demands such as paying for water and village contributions. These were households with high levels of dependents, such as grandparents caring for children orphaned by HIV/ AIDS. These households struggled and could suffer from shortages of both food and water. They frequently tried to alleviate their needs through seeking assistance from kin and wider social networks.

The majority of the village (an estimated 60 per cent) were viewed as 'getting by', and had the resources to feed, clothe, and educate themselves within their networks. This category covers considerable differentiation in terms of assets, income, and expenditure. Landholdings for this group were slightly larger, and agricultural activities more diversified. Off-farm activities were also highly significant for this group and included a wide range of skills-based small enterprise such as tailoring, carpentry, and bicycle repairs, as well as trading and retailing activities within local markets. Employment in this group could also include primary school teachers, bus drivers, and conductors. This group was highly heterogenous in terms of income and expenditure, and wealth could be precarious. The loss of employment, an illness requiring expensive treatment, alcoholism, or the theft of critical productive assets could all cause rapid declines in wealth and well-being.

The most powerful group in collective village life were the 'big shots', comprising perhaps 10 per cent of households/kin networks. These tended to be families of the original frontier pioneers who had relatively large landholdings (up to 50 acres). They had the capital to invest in large business ventures such as building bars and hotels, running transport businesses, or practising capital-intensive agriculture such as irrigated horticulture. Such households also benefitted from remittances from family members for whom early investments in education had yielded well-paid employment in the cities or overseas.

2016—What Has Changed?

In 2016, members of the original 2004 research re-visited the residential locations of thirty of the sixty-seven life-history interviews. This was combined with key informant interviews on livelihood characteristics and dynamics in Uchira. The 2004 wealth-ranking categories were still viable. The three categories and profiles developed in 2004 remain as a useful explanatory typology (see Table 16.3). There are still those who struggle, have little land, and depend on their own labour for survival.

Table 16.3 Livelihoods patterns from life history interviews, 2004–5.

Total interviews n=67/ Category	Agricultural production	Diversification/Income-generating activities	Expenditure	Shortages/Assistance
Poor/'have-nots' (n=24)	Maize only (22); mixed maize/ beans (2) Average acreage: 1.7	Basket-making (2); fetch firewood (1); make aggregate/gathers stones (4); carry volcanic blocks (8); day labour (5); selling sugar cane (1); sells herbs (1); makes *mbege* (1); repairs utensils (1); sells fodder grass (3)	Primary school contributions (cash + food); water, public taps (5–10 Tsh per bucket); food (250–1000 Tsh per day if money available); village contributions	Miss food (11); miss water (13); no medical treatment (5); assistance from family (11); assistance from neighbours (5); assist family (3); school fees paid by government for children of disabled parent (1)
Middle (n=27)	Mixed farming (maize, beans, sunflower, groundnuts) (16); maize only (11) Average acreage: 2.0	Employment (2); tailoring (1); selling livestock (2); making *mbege* (3); selling secondhand clothes (2); horticulture (2); milk production (2); sign-writing (1); bicycle repairs (1); electrical repairs (1); selling kerosene in Kenya (1); wood business (1); selling vegetables (1); crop dealing (1); day labour (6); mason (1); selling food (1)	Primary school contributions; Kindergarten; village contributions; food (1000 Tsh per day); water, public tap/ private tap (5–10 Tsh per bucket); secondhand clothes; private health costs	Miss food (11); miss water (13); no medical treatment (5); assistance from family (11); assistance from neighbours (5); assist family (3); school fees paid by government for children of disabled parent (1)
Wealthy ('big shots') n=6	Mixed farming (maize, beans, groundnut, sunflower)	Own bar (2); salaried employment (1); transport business (2); wholesale shop (1); selling herbal medicine (1); horticulture (2)	School fees; village contributions; supporting relatives; health expenses; water, private taps; electricity; vehicles/consumer goods; food, 3000 Tsh per day	School fees (HE & FE); capital

Nobody in Uchira/Koresa will tell you that the area is getting richer, or that poverty is reducing. Life is still hard is a familiar refrain, as it was in 1996 and 2004. Certainly, livelihoods patterns look remarkably similar to those mapped in 2004, for those who are resident in Uchira. The new dynamic is an influx of 'outsiders' coming to build residential houses, but these people remain largely as connected to the urban area.

An overview of livelihood patterns in Uchira in 2016 is summarized in a key informant interview as follows:

> People depend on small-scale agriculture and small business, agricultural crops are maize, beans, groundnut, tomatoes, onions, and watermelons, and residents in most cases cultivate 1 to 2 acres, those who cultivate more than 2 acres most of them are people from outside the village. In small business people are engaging in activities like shops, selling of vegetables especially for women, transportation i.e. bodaboda (motorbike taxis). Some are involved in bricks cutting, stone digging, and aggregate crushing and these people who are engaging in these activities most of them are poor (low-income earners) who also depend on manual labour to make their daily earning. (Village executive officer: Koresa)

Table 16.4 shows an overview of livelihoods in 2016 and captures key areas of expenditure.

There is a universal view (in every interview and focus group) that agriculture is getting harder due to declining rainfall and declining productivity due to crop and livestock diseases. In addition, sales of land for residential build have decreased the availability of grazing land for livestock. Whilst overall cropping patterns are largely unchanged since 1996, there is some visible increase in irrigated production in the Miwaleni area, which began around 2008.

> Not enough rains, not enough crops and livestock keeping has decreased due to drought caused environmental destruction and other human activities, this problem started more in the year 2006. In the past, almost the land in Uchira was covered by trees but now there are few trees—almost all are destroyed due to human activities. (Women aged 54)

> Agriculture these days has become so costly, it needs a lot of money to invest as diseases have increased and you cannot get enough crops if not using modern seeds and fertilizers, while the cost of inputs is high. There are some people leave agriculture but there are a few who invest a lot of money in farming activities and end up with no harvest. A successful farmer is the one who is doing an irrigation farming. (Man aged 28)

> The agriculture situation is not good, productivity has declined, the rain it rains, and it is heavy but it rains for a short period of time. Animal diseases have

Table 16.4 Livelihoods and expenditure, 2016.

Local status	Livelihoods activities	Land holdings and yield	Indicative prices	Contributions and expenses
Poorest 'Uchira still grows stones'	Digging toilets; cutting stone and crushing gravel; day labour; making *mbege*; trading vegetables	1 acre (9 bags in a good year, 1 in 2016) 1 acre (2 bags in 2016, 1 for food and 1 for school)	80,000–95,000 for Kokoto lorry (7 weeks)	Non-western medicine or local dispensary; primary school, 8,000 Tsh, 1 bucket maize and 4kg beans per year; water, public tap 20 Tsh per bucket; no phone
Getting by (covering a large range)	Selling land; farming, maize and beans; trading cattle; public employment; border trade; pikipiki driving; hairdressing; remittances	2 acres (can be 40 bags, 2016: 1 bag); 2.5 acres (15 bags good year, 2016: 5); 2 acres (2016: 6 bags maize, in past 20 bags)	Ag. inputs subsidy 130,000 Tsh for 100kg fertilizer/10kg maize seed 1,000–8,000 per customer (hairdressing)	Loans and savings groups (1,500–5,000 Tsh per week); food per day 7,000–8,000 Tsh; has a phone, from entry level to basic smart phone; primary/sec. school contributions: books, exams, boarding; local dispensaries; private tap, 50 Tsh per bucket (20L)
Big shots	Mixed farming: maize, groundnuts, beans irrigated, onions/tomatoes; livestock: zero-grazing; wholesale shop; bars; capital investment: motorbikes, *dala-dalas*; remittances	5+ acres (mix of ownership/rental 50,000 Tsh per acre 2016); some irrigation (1 acre of tomatoes can yield 60 bags twice per year)		School fees: 2 million Tsh+ per year for good secondary; local development projects; religious contributions; family support; capital investment: motorbikes; medical: urban facilities; food expenditure; 10,000 Tsh+
Incomers	Employment in town; business in town	Residential plots	Plot price: 7 million for 1/4 acre (20 million for 1.5 acre by road side)	Education; capital investment; all urban-focused

> increased and the area for grazing has now decreased—the reasons for these changes are due to the impact of climate change including deforestation and air pollution. (Man aged 67)

In both 1996 and 2004 farmers viewed agricultural production profits as being in decline. In 2016 only those who can irrigate are thought to be guaranteed good production, producing tomatoes, onions, and other horticultural crops. Certainly, there is some increase in farmer-led irrigated agriculture in proximity to Miwaleni Springs. This has been increasing since 2008 (See De Bont 2018, Mdee and Harrison 2019). Individual capitalist farmer-investors lease the land from the original settler residents. These investors require significant capital to invest in pipes, pump, diesel and seeds, pesticides, fertilizer, and labour and many take loans to establish this production.

However, the returns from this agriculture are also uncertain. In late November 2016 all of this irrigation activity was shut down by government officials; as it turns out farmers were drawing water without a permit and their activity was illegal. A national news story was featured on ITV, with farmers complaining that they were now in a terrible position as their fields had already dried up and they still had loan liabilities.

Whilst those who are not cultivating crops such as tomatoes see such production as easy in comparison with rain-fed maize and beans, those who do cultivate tomatoes suggest it is more difficult to get a good return.

> If you decide to cultivate lets say tomatoes with irrigation, at the end of the day tomato is ready for harvest but there is no market due to inflation, do you think this person will be back again in the farm for this situation? Because all the capital has already evaporated. (Young man in focus group)

As in 1996 and 2004, in 2016 Uchira had a mixed agricultural/non-farm economy. A large range of other activities contribute to local livelihoods. Interviewees mentioned: fattening and selling cattle, digging toilets, making local brew, buying and selling vegetables, operating small grocery shops, importing and selling soap from Kenya, hairdressing, cutting bricks, and cutting aggregate. Some households also have members who are employed as teachers, and police officers. All these activities were present in livelihoods in 2004. One significant new activity is driving motorbike taxis, although this is available to a small proportion of young men and competition is high. The motorbikes are owned by those with more capital and leased to drivers for a daily fee.

Inflation and the escalating costs of services are cited as reasons why life does not feel any easier. Mobile phone purchase and airtime are also significant new costs since 2004. Ownership of a smart phone, and the capacity of the user to access new mobile-based and internet services is a new axis of differentiation, as is education. Education is a major family investment and the costs of private schooling are racing ahead of inflation. This is not just an expense for the wealthy, but many of those who are 'getting by' will sacrifice expenditure and take loans to put their children into private secondary school, but the rewards of this investment are a lottery. There are few formal employment opportunities, and many of the educated youth and their parents are disillusioned with the outcomes.

There are two trends in Uchira in 2016 that draw further attention for their impact on the dynamics of the local economy and social relations: the thriving and active land market, and the nature of residence and remittance through kin networks.

The rehabilitated water supply, and increasing expansion of urban Moshi, has made Uchira an attractive place to purchase land. Land leasing was also common in the 1996 and 2004 interviews so extends over the twenty-year period. However, land sales and transfers are now intensifying. Currently there is a pattern of land sales by original residents. These sales are often executed by older men with original land allocations selling family land for daily consumption needs, such as medical treatment, or to build housing and pay school fees. This can lead to family disputes, as the next generation see their anticipated inheritance disappearing. The market prices for this land are rapidly increasing. My husband bought a small plot adjacent to his parent's home in 2008 for 1 million shillings. Similar plots at the road side in 2016 might reach 7 million shillings.

Remittances from family members who have migrated to other parts of Tanzania are a significant component of livelihoods in Uchira, but Uchira is also a place of refuge and retreat when required. This was certainly the case in 1996 and 2004, although wider economic, political, and social forces change how these dependencies shift. The life history interviews in 2016 suggest a picture that echoes that presented by Ferguson (2013) or Neves and Du Toit (2013) in South Africa, where land distribution is highly differentiated, and the rural economy is dependent on the urban, and local livelihoods provide little more than a means of getting by for most. Dependence on kin relations to negotiate and manage the challenges of existence extend to those who are at 'home' and those who now live elsewhere.

This demonstrates a critical shortcoming of the methodological approach of longitudinal household surveys as it can miss how these networks operate and change (see Chapter 3 this volume). The majority of interviewees mentioned remittances from absent kin as an important source of income, and this extends to all groups: for the struggling it is how they meet their basic needs, for those who are getting by, it is the source of capital for business, for meeting health expenses and school fees; and it is also the same for the big shots whose expenses for health, education, and capital investment are much higher. However, family networks may also encompass members who could fit into each of these categories. Family remittance networks are now intensified through ease of communications (mobile phones, Whatsapp) and mobile banking. Expenditure claims can be rapidly and easily shared, contributions sought, and monies remitted. The form and pattern of family decision-making and disbursement varies, remitting members may come and go depending on their means, as may recipients. Typically, those with the most income will make the greatest contributions, but this will also depend on their own personal inclinations and the extent of their connectedness to home.

These examples from the data show the diversity of remitting arrangements:

> Among these children two have permanent government jobs, one employed as a lawyer in Lushoto and one as a soldier in Dar es Salaam, the others are self-employed in small businesses like shops, and some in farming activities. They send some money to support family expenses and health services. There is no limit to contribution, everyone contributes the amount of money he/she has. If we have a problem then we sit together as family members and sort it out.
>
> (Man aged 45)

> In 2008 I stopped doing small business activities in the market due to a health problem. After my children got jobs in 2010 they opened a shop around home for me and I am involved in the shop selling up to this moment, as well as doing farming activities. I get assistance from children for home expenses. I receive 50000tsh per month. I then also aid the son of my sister: food, clothing, and shelter and school food contribution 82000tsh per year My sister cannot pay for her son due to low income—her husband is drunkard and careless.
>
> (Female age 54)

Family members who establish themselves in the urban areas or overseas, who have progressed in education are expected to contribute to wider family activities. The boundaries of these networks are dynamic and shifting, obligations are almost continually in negotiation.

Yet, at the same time, the rural home can also be a place of refuge from the harsh urban economy. It is common for younger migrants to return home after the completion of studies, whilst waiting to find work or further opportunities. Girls who have become pregnant will often remain at home and be expected to contribute to agriculture and family business activities—such as serving in shops. Equally, they can also leave their children behind with grandparents and other family members and migrate if opportunities for employment or business arise.

The following examples illustrate these patterns:

> In 2011–2013 I joined the College of Agriculture at Himo In Moshi Rural District. After completing the college I didn't get a job and I am now at home doing private work, providing animal treatment services to the villagers when

> their cattle get sick as well as advising them on how to take care of their cattle and other advice. I am also engaging in farming activities, seasonal farming. I am working hard but have very little achieved. I have studied, but there is no vacancy for employment. (Young man aged 28)

> I came to live with my mother and joined secondary education in 2011 at Uchira girls' Islamic secondary school and completed in 2014. The performance was not good and at the same time I got pregnant and have a son. I still live with my mother and she is the one who supports with my kid. The father of the kid is still in school therefore cannot support him. I expect that I will go back to my studies but for now I am just assisting at home. (Young woman aged 20)

Conclusion

Uchira tells many stories. It tells of a frontier settlement where livelihoods became increasingly differentiated by the 1990s as land ownership patterns were locked down. Where increasing population intensify the market price for the land, favouring those who own and control it, and disadvantaging those who rely on their own labour.

It tells of a village government in charge of collective village life in the 1990s, actively collecting taxes and mobilizing around village projects. Yet this capacity appears to be eroded, and village government in 2018 is rent seeking from property taxes. 'Development' since the 2000s is increasingly NGO and religious led. Is this a fracturing of local governance? Why was it easier to mobilize funds to construct an enormous Catholic church, rather than to finish the ward building at the government dispensary? This governance deficit is not an Uchira problem, this is ironically a result of shambolic decentralization policies (see Mdee and Mushi 2020).

It tells of agricultural struggle, to subsist and persist; of livelihoods freed to struggle in the winds of neoliberal markets, after the collapse of co-operatives; of the overexploitation and degradation of land and water resources. The new agricultural boom for those who can produce with irrigation is possible for a handful, but they must also be lucky with the markets, and be able to access capital. Life does not feel as though it is easier—the environment is worse, needs for expenditure intensified.

It tells of kin networks and connections that have to support, care, build, and invest. This is not a romantic tale; these networks are only as strong as their members—and their resources have limits. Life in the urban areas is also harsh and expensive. Educational success is no guarantee to well-paid employment or income. Perhaps Uchira tells a story for other places, where economic and social differentiation on frontiers is still in process.

References

Boesten, J., A. Mdee, and F. Cleaver (2011). 'Service Delivery on the Cheap? Community-Based Workers in Tanzania and South Africa.' *Development in Practice* 21: 41–58.

Chambers, R. (2017). *Can We Know Better? Reflections for Development*. Rugby, Practical Action Publishing.

Cleaver, F. and A. Toner (2006). 'The Evolution of Community Water Governance in Uchira, Tanzania: The Implications for Equality of Access, Sustainability and Effectiveness.' *Natural Resources Forum* 30(3): 207–18.

de Bont, C. (2018). 'Modernisation and Farmer-Led Irrigation Development in Africa: A Study of State-Farmer Interactions in Tanzania.' PhD dissertation, Department of Human Geography, Stockholm University.

Ferguson, J. (2013). 'Declarations of Dependence: Labour, Personhood, and Welfare in Southern Africa.' *Journal of the Royal Anthropological Institute* 19(2): 223–42.

Green, M. (2014). *The Development State: Aid, Culture & Civil Society in Tanzania*. Suffolk, Boydell & Brewer Ltd.

Hickel, J. (2016). 'The True Extent of Global Poverty and Hunger: Questioning the Good News Narrative of the Millennium Development Goals.' *Third World Quarterly* 37(5): 749–67.

Kessy, F. L., O. Mashindano, and A. Shepherd (eds) (2013). *Translating Growth into Poverty Reduction: Beyond the Numbers*. Dar-es-Salaam, Mkuki na Nyota Publishers.

Li, T. M. (2014). *Land's End: Capitalist Relations on an Indigenous Frontier*. Durham, Duke University Press.

Mdee, A. (2008). 'Towards a Dynamic Structure-Agency Framework: Understanding Individual Participation in Collective Development Activities in Uchira, Tanzania.' *International Development and Planning Review* 30(4): 399–421.

Mdee, A. (2013). '"I Prayed and God Gave Me This Car": The Role of Religious Institutions in Shaping Change in Tanzania.' *A Holistic Approach to Human Existence and Development*. K. Olu-Owolabi and A. Ekanola. Ibadan, Nigeria, Hope Publications: 000–000.

Mdee, A., and L. Thorley (2016). 'Knowing Your Rights is Something, but Not Enough: Exploring Collective Advocacy and Rights to Treatment and Services for People Living with HIV in Tanzania.' *Africanus* 46(2): 40–56.

Mdee, A. and A. Mushi (2020). 'Untangling Blame and Responsibility for Service Delivery and Local Governance Performance: Testing a Grounded Social Accountability Approach in Tanzania.' *Local Government Studies*. DOI: 10.1080/03003930.2020.1842735.

Neves, D. and A. Du Toit (2013). 'Rural Livelihoods in South Africa: Complexity, Vulnerability and Differentiation.' *Journal of Agrarian Change* 13(1): 93–115.

Toner, A. (2008). 'Who Shapes Development? An Ethnography of Collective Village Life in Uchira, Tanzania.' PhD thesis, University of Bradford.

West, P. (2016). *Dispossession and the Environment: Rhetoric and Inequality in Papua New Guinea*. New York, Columbia University Press.

Yanguas, P. (2018). *Why We Lie about Aid: Development and the Messy Politics of Change*. London and New York, Zed Books.

PART III
CONCLUSIONS

17
Telling the Stories of Asset Accumulation

Christine Noe and Dan Brockington

Explaining Change and Observing Its Consequences

The repeated tendencies of the chapters in this book are of growth in assets and increasing prosperity according to local definitions. This is not the universal story. It is not true for all groups or in all places. But it is the general trend. The trend is replicated in other recent research from the country (Keane et al. 2020).

The strength of this tendency is plain in the way that so many of the researchers who have conducted these revisits have been surprised by what they found. They were expecting persistent poverty, they found unexpected instances of particular forms of prosperity. This was the case not just with our own case-studies but also those of Vesa-Matti Loiske, Willie Östberg, Monique Borgerhoff Mulder, Esbern Friis-Hansen, Torben Birch-Thomsen, and Stefano Ponte. These are all seasoned researchers, and they were not expecting the trends they found.

Lest it not be obvious already, we do *not* conclude from these findings that Tanzanian peasants have been portrayed as poor but are 'really' wealthy. That would be wrong. Wealth, and poverty, are multi-facetted. Wealth cannot be equated with assets, or somehow reduced to it. Rather, as we explained in Chapter 2, the methods used to measure poverty based on consumption surveys omit important dimensions of rural prosperity. Poverty derived from consumption data must, of necessity, exclude investment in the productive assets that are so important for rural people's own definitions of prosperity. We cannot have a complete understanding of change in rural poverty and prosperity without attention to assets.

Attention *only* to assets will not give us a complete understanding of rural poverty and prosperity dynamics because change in assets can be poorly correlated with other measures of well-being. Indeed it is conceivable that the savings required to invest in assets means that other measures of well-being may diminish as assets grow. When peasants tighten their belts to build assets bases they may have to do so literally, not metaphorically. Moreover where assets do track other measures of well-being in particular places (as Monique Borgerhoff Mulder found in Chapter 5) then that relationship may be specific to those places and those people. It is unwise to extrapolate too broadly.

Christine Noe and Dan Brockington, *Telling the Stories of Asset Accumulation* In: *Prosperity in Rural Africa? Insights into Wealth, Assets, and Poverty from Longitudinal Studies in Tanzania.* Edited by: Dan Brockington and Christine Noe, Oxford University Press. DOI: 10.1093/oso/9780198865872.003.0017

Is there a general pattern or explanation that can be gleaned from these diverse case studies? At one level it is clear that the different case studies that cut across Tanzania have demonstrated how these farmers have made investments on agricultural and non-agricultural assets that have driven significant changes in rural livelihoods over the past twenty years. But in another respect one of the most salient points across these different case studies is their diversity. The proximate driver of rural transformation, and its timing, has varied in *every* single location. In some instances it arises from changes in sesame seed prices combined with infrastructural improvements (Chapter 8). In others it links to rising prices of potatoes and wheat relative to maize, without infrastructural change, and with decreasing inequality (Chapter 10). In another the cash crop is sunflower seeds, and the growth in farming activity has been hastened by growing inequality in the form of entrepreneurs bringing in tractors (Chapter 9). In yet more instances the changes derive from tree plantations (Chapter 13), or there may be too many such plantations (Chapter 14) or prosperity is found in swapping coffee cultivation for vegetables and market gardens (Chapter 7). Diversity reigns. If there is a story to tell in all of this, it is only, perhaps, that there is no one story.

Farmers' investments have ranged from new seeds and fertilizers to replacing hand hoes with oxen and tractor services. This has also meant letting go some traditional crops and farming practices to adopt new crops which have high market value and which require investing in fertilizers and pesticides. Decisions to do so and to replace low-return traditional crops (such as coffee in Meru) with seasonal crops such as carrots and Irish potatoes lead to higher returns, with small plots of land providing two harvests per year. Investments in new cash crops such as sunflowers, tomatoes, and sesame have involved risk-taking due to their requirements for modern farming practices and market instabilities. Other cases such as in Njombe and Mbeya where crops are replaced with pine trees have meant putting labour on non-farm activities while the trees continue to grow. Across the study villages, we have seen farmers navigating the change to increase their farm outputs mostly by investing in better practices, farm inputs, and more labour.

Children's education has increasingly gained importance in the definition of wealth. While the government policy of no fees for secondary schools and the availability of secondary schools in every ward have certainly driven changes in the sector, farmers are full of aspirations for their children to go beyond basic education. This has meant trading crops, livestock, and even working as kibarua (casual labour) for school fees which are expensive in private schools. The sites in Meru have demonstrated exceptional trends. Even with the shrinking of land sizes for most households and loss of coffee as a cash crop, parents have invested heavily in education. Almost one in five children (19 per cent) have gone to university, against a national average of just 1 per cent.

The data for our different sites suggest that rural people have invested a great deal in education and off-farm business (Bryceson 1999). They are no longer just farmers but also business women and men. The role of remittances may be shifting in some areas from assisting families to feed and improve housing conditions to investing in high-value crops, trees, shops, and guest houses, as Friis-Hansen's work in Chapter 13 shows. The rural has become a site where emigrants of the 1990s look back to for expansion of their investment portfolio.

There are other interesting trends too with significant impacts on our understanding of livelihood changes. For example, money for kibarua work can be directed towards investment in people's own farms and businesses, rather than basic provisions and just getting by. People find motivations to work and produce from their own land because harvests can also generate the needed cash. In Meru, for example, through kibarua work, the landless of 1990s have acquired land, milk cows, and have educated children. They are no longer poor by their own definitions. We know this is not normally the case; the dictates of poverty drive people to sell labour (Homewood et al. 2020). But aspirations of prosperity can also be an aspect of this behaviour.

However it is unsatisfactory simply to assert that diversity reigns, that there are no patterns or tendencies which we can derive across these case studies. It is possible to derive a generalized model of how growth in assets has occurred in diverse sites across rural Tanzania. Figure 17.1 shows the variety of causes of investment in rural assets, in the form of growing rural incomes which derived from improved returns to farms. Investment is also possible because of reduced

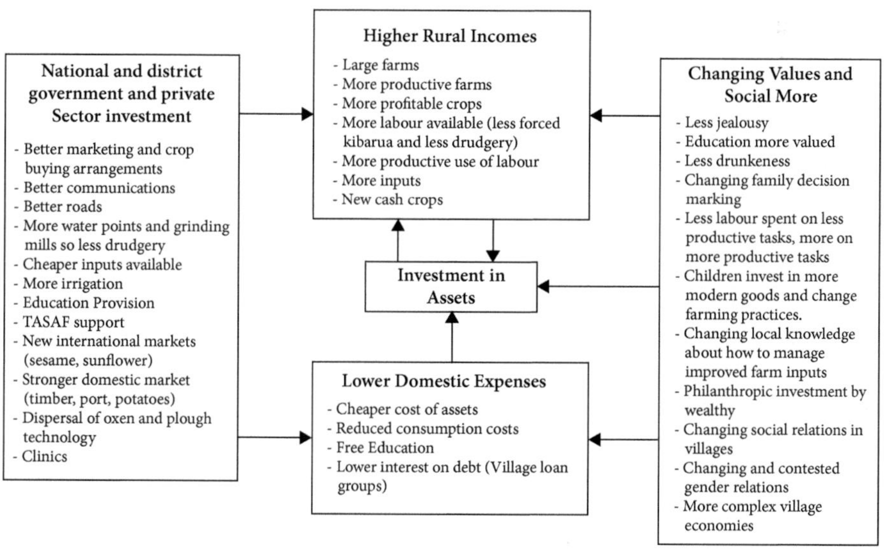

Figure 17.1 Explaining asset investment.

costs of some of the assets people wish to purchase (such as education and cheaper motorbikes). However underlying these changes are a series of developments in the public sphere, following investment by local and national governments and by the private sector (in phones for example). There are also changes in the way that people have responded to these opportunities—the changing outlook with respect to more commercial practices, the readiness to risk the opprobrium of their neighbours should they get richer (Chapter 8), the willingness to wrest farms from the hands of elders whose drinking habits made it harder to put them to productive use (Chapter 10).

We recognize that this model may recall one of Julius Nyerere's more passionate speeches about the need for agricultural, rural, and social modernization. It may appear to advocate the whole-sale transformation of rural society to a more modernist form. But our point is not that this is what rural Tanzanians need to do, or should be doing. Nor is it a description of what has happened to rural Tanzanians generally. It is simply a compilation of the factors and reasons that we have been told by our informants have brought change.

Our data do not allow us to determine which of these factors are most important nationally—neither the survey design nor the granularity of the data (the number of data points from each location) make that possible. But the diversity of the studies suggests that placing single weightings on individual variables across the country would have limited worth. We have sites where road infrastructure has changed very little, and social relations within the village become more equal (Gitting and Gocho), to sites where infrastructure has been transformed and relations are less equal (Mtowisa), to sites where greater inequality in the form of wealthy philanthropists is transforming village infrastructure. A single story in such circumstances is difficult.

Instead we recommend that it would make more sense for future researchers to focus on the circumstances by which different individual cash crops have brought prosperity to different sorts of villagers in the long durée. By focusing on particular commodities (rice, sesame, carrots, potatoes) it will be possible to see what mixture of physical infrastructure, marketing, commodity chain developments, and social and cultural change has been necessary to produce these productivity gains.

If it is hard to generalize about the anatomy of the causes of the changes we have observed it may be easier to point to one common consequence that is emerging in some (again not all) of our study sites. In many of the communities we carried out research in the 1990s and early 2000s, wealth was characterized by a pyramid distribution in rural villages. Most people were, by local measures, poor. The rich were few and rare.

This was, we believe, a general characteristic. Poverty distributions in many communities in low-income African countries have long been skewed: the wealthy were few, there is only a small middle group, and most people were poor.

Most land holdings are small (2 hectares or less). Most people are young—children or young adults. Most people have no herds, and of those that do, most herd sizes are small (fewer than five animals). Most people live in poor quality houses, few in fine dwellings. Most people only complete primary school, not secondary school; formal employment is rare, and so on. The importance of explaining these distributions is one of the most persistent challenges of economic and social research.

One of the more striking patterns to emerge from this collection of studies is that the prevalent domination of the poorest farmers that characterized Tanzanian villages for so many decades is beginning to shift. In just over half of the locations (eleven out of eighteen) where we could assess asset distribution during our re-visits in 2016–18 the predominance of the poor in a classic pyramid distribution has changed.[1] It has been replaced by a 'pointed egg' distribution, with the largest segment constituted by 'middle' or 'average' farming households. This pattern is shown in the black graphs in Figure 17.2.

We have to be careful about generalizing this claim. First, a substantial minority (39 per cent) of sites for which we have data do not conform to this pattern. There poverty predominates. Second, our sites are not drawn from a representative sample, and so we cannot be certain which of these distributions, the pyramid or the pointed egg, is more generally representative of the country. Third, even if there are fewer people in the poorest groups, this does not necessarily mean that a new era of prosperity has been unleashed in these villages. Not being poor does not raise the bar very high. The poorest people are characterized by their basic dwellings, their lack of basic daily provisions, the fact that they have to work for other people whenever they need money, and cannot rely on their own farms. Access to slightly better housing, less dependence on daily wage labour, and more reliable access to daily provisions hardly denotes wealth. Nonetheless the tendency of these data does suggest the hypothesis that in diverse communities in rural Tanzania, village communities feel that they are getting wealthier by their own standards. We would like to see this proposition explored in further studies.

The Surprises of This Work

Despite all the qualifications the appearance of relative prosperity is clear. It is also likely to be surprising, in different ways, for three rather different groups.

In the first instance, where we have observed prosperity it seems to have been driven from different forms of small-scale agricultural activity. But the very

[1] The predominantly poor distributions are evident in Loiske's thesis (1995) and Ostberg's first studies. It is also clear in the more extensive work of Ellis and Mdoe (2003).

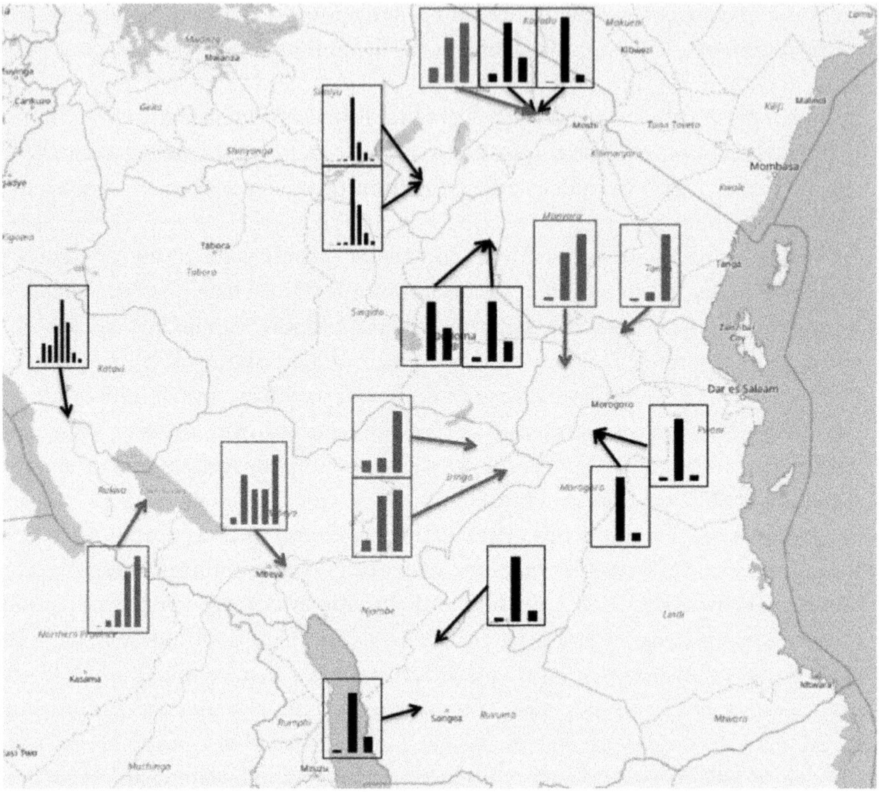

Figure 17.2 Different distributions of wealth and poverty by local definitions across Tanzania. This figure originally appeared in Ponte and Brockington 2020.

possibility of rural prosperity in Tanzania from small-scale agriculture will be surprising to some observers. It does not fit well with the general trends in the Tanzanian government's development goals, visions, policies, and strategies for growth and alleviation of poverty. These are based on the understanding that the country seems to have made slow progress in attaining the level of economic growth envisioned. The agricultural sector has especially appeared in official publications to have failed to contribute meaningfully to the national development despite its potentials for doing so.

In the minds of policy-makers, a robust agricultural sector would produce food and cash crops for local and external markets. It would also generate employment for the large proportion of rural population. This would then increase the sector's contribution to GDP. Smallholder agriculture is not thought to do this work. It has to be transformed. This envisaged transformation has, repeatedly, not happened in Tanzania according to official narratives. Most of the initially declared enemies—poverty, diseases, and ignorance—have persisted in rural areas. They dominate the past and present discussions about rural development and poverty alleviation. Agriculture is thought not to have raised its economic share to balance with the amount of labour force in the rural areas. This is to say that small farmers have not contributed enough to, nor benefitted from, their national economic development.

One of the problems, as we shall see below, is that this view holds that it is hard for rural areas to prosper because smallholders practice 'subsistence agriculture'. This is a particularly unhelpful misrecognition of their activities. It implies that farmers consume all that they produce, sell little (if anything), and purchase little food too. But this simply does not describe what we have seen, or what decades of scholarship reports (Bernstein and Woodhouse 2001, Bernstein 2010). There are very few rural households who eschew markets entirely. Where farmers do consume their own produce, and sell little, such activity is unstable. 'Subsistence' agriculture is but a paved road, or price fluctuation, away from becoming commercial agriculture. Alternatively, market incentives and infrastructure can remain unchanged, but families can begin to sell more produce because of changing norms and desires among their members. Subsistence-orientated farming can become much more commercial when ambitious children inherit land from tired parents. The need to send children to school, invest in mobile phones, or simply the desire to control the proceeds of their labour may encourage more sales.

The dynamism, innovation and potentiality in smallholder agriculture contains within it the seeds of its own transformation. We have found that farmers have seized opportunities that have come with road improvements and rural electrification, and improved telecommunication and means of transport. Access to markets, supply of seeds, pesticides, and fertilizers have all become less costly and strenuous. These changes motivate better farming practices and investments on non-farm assets. This requires thinking about rural economies and productivity differently from previous policy documents. We will return to this issue below.

The second audience who may be surprised are those who rely on consumption surveys and poverty-line data for their understanding of change in rural areas. As we saw in Chapter 8 persistence of poverty in rural agricultural areas is plain in the latest statistics. The most recent Household Budget Surveys released at the time of writing indicate that both incidence of poverty (the share of the population whose income or consumption is below the poverty line) and extreme poverty are higher in rural compared to urban areas at a rate of 31.3 per cent and 15.8 per cent respectively (NBS 2019). So too, extreme poverty is more pronounced in rural areas (at 9.7 per cent) than in urban areas (at 4.4 per cent). Comparatively, the most rural area—Rukwa Region—has the highest rate of poverty compared to other regions, at 45 per cent for incidence poverty and 19.8 per cent for extreme poverty (NBS 2019). Moreover, as we saw in Chapter 8, the decline of poverty is slower in rural areas than in urban areas.[2]

[2] We should note that levels of urban poverty may themselves be under-reported in part because the costs of urban living are not properly appreciated (Mitlin and Satterthwaite 2013).

We do not doubt the validity of these statistics in their own terms. As measures of consumption go there are few better. But we do question whether it is appropriate to read off facts about poverty from these statistics. Daily consumption levels are important, but they will, of necessity, be a poor way of measuring change in societies which save daily and continually in order to invest in productive assets.

One of the important lessons that emerges from this book is that we need measures of poverty which can capture both consumption and asset investment (cf. Piketty 2014). The repeated picture that has been presented in this book suggests that rural Tanzania is, after all, not *only* poor in the way that is captured in official narratives. These statistics misread—they miss entirely—small farmers' diverse means of enjoying their wealth. This also means that these statistics are likely to *underestimate these farmers' contributions to national change and development, both in terms of how they create that wealth, and the forms of consumption that it allows.*

It is clear from the case studies in this book that an important aspect of rural life that we have been able to document has escaped the attention of most political and economic analysts in the country. Without necessarily increasing the levels of consumption, many households have significantly improved their wellbeing according to locally defined measures.

This calls for the need to rethink what measures of poverty are used, how prosperity is defined, and how Tanzania's policies and strategies alleviate the former and promote the latter. To repeat, we have not found, in this research, that Tanzanian rural areas have been mistakenly labelled as 'poor' when they should be considered to be relatively wealthy. Rather, perhaps in keeping with our varied disciplinary backgrounds, we have found there are forms of locally valuable prosperity which have thrived in a variety of circumstances.

But if there is more wealth, in ways that matter to rural farmers, and if this has come from small-scale agriculture, then the third group who will be surprised by these results are the critics of neoliberal economic policies and reforms which have swept through Tanzania in recent decades. The present authors have themselves been critics of neoliberalism, particularly as it pertains to environmentalism and conservation. Nevertheless the reforms to the government and economy of Tanzania under the influence of neoliberal institutions (the World Bank and IMF) have coincided with the growing asset base of rural Tanzanians.

This general association, however, requires nuance. Neoliberal reforms cover a broad swathe of activity, from privatizing parastatals, to liberalizing market controls, and reducing government expenditure on key services. Any general association such as we have observed needs much more specific claims about changes deriving from particular policies to be meaningful. As we show in the next section neoliberal policies have not always been sensitive to smallholder productivity.

Joining up Rural and Agricultural Development Policies

The seventeen Sustainable Development Goals (SDGs) seek a converging agenda that will eradicate poverty and achieve sustainable development. In signing up to this agenda, Tanzania committed to end poverty and hunger, and achieve good health, well-being, and quality education, among other things, by 2030. This coincides with the country's development agenda which is articulated in 'Vision 2025' in which Tanzania envisions graduating from a least-developed country to a middle-income country with a high level of human development. In particular, the low productivity agricultural economy will have been transformed to a semi-industrialized one led by modernized and highly productive agricultural activities.

This is a common thread that has run through much agricultural and rural policy in Tanzania for some time. The National Strategy for Growth and Reduction of Poverty I (NSGRP, which ran from 2005–10), stated that the country will have an agricultural sector that is modernized, commercialized, and profitable and utilizes natural resources in a sustainable manner (URT 2005). Similarly when the mid-review of Vision 2025 was performed in 2009/10, annual agricultural growth was 4.2 per cent (which is below the expected average of 6.7 per cent) and some of this slow progress was attributed to the fact that:

> agricultural development did not live up to the expectations of the rural, agricultural-dependent households who were still using ancestral techniques, depending on increasingly unpredictable weather conditions, and with limited access to credit and extension services.' (URT 2011b: 4)

In brief these statements and policies indicate that the dynamic and industrious smallholder sector in Tanzania which is producing so much *unrecognized* wealth is, by virtue of the invisibility of its productivity, demanded to change. The Tanzanian state has been vigorous in its ambitions and policy directives to achieve this already existing change.

Dissatisfaction as to the perceived state of the rural economy has led to many plans, policies, and strategies that focus on rural development generally and on agricultural transformations in particular. The National Strategy for Growth and Reduction of Poverty (NSGRP) I (2005–10) and II (2010–15) provides a framework for harmonized rural development but drawing heavily from the agricultural sector development strategy (URT 2016a). When Tanzania signed the NEPAD's Comprehensive African Agriculture Development Program (CAADP) in 2010, it also agreed to develop a national framework of implementation of regional objectives. This included achieving 6 per cent annual growth in the agricultural sector in order to reduce poverty and achieve food security (URT 2011a).

Tanzania's Agricultural and Food Security Investment Plan (TAFSIP) was launched in November 2011 as a ten-year comprehensive investment plan for agricultural and rural development. TAFSIP mapped the investment needed for the agricultural sector to achieve both regional and national targets. First, the plan attributed the disconnect between agriculture and its contribution to economic growth with, among others, the fact that the sector is driven by small-scale farmers who produce for subsistence, low use of improved inputs, market constraints, under-nutrition, and malnutrition in the population, all of which constrained productivity.

TAFSIP called upon the private sector as a catalyst to the sector's growth (URT 2011a). The Kilimo Kwanza policy and the Southern Agricultural Growth Corridor of Tanzania (SAGCOT) Catalytic Fund as its first invention were promoted as measures to stimulate private sector investments. Opportunities for large-scale investments in agriculture were promoted and plans for small farmers to participate in these sectoral transformations focused on outgrowing, block, and contract farming (URT 2016a). In addition there is the commercial farm component of Agricultural Big Results Now (a special programme designed to have aggregate impacts on various strategic areas of agricultural transformations).

These policies can only be understood as part of an international agenda for agricultural modernization that has gained local support from policy-makers and some local academics who equate peasants with backwardness (Forster and Maghimbi 1992, Maghimbi et al. 2011) and large-scale farming with modernity. National policies qualify this modernity as constituting farm sizes of over 20 hectares (combined with outgrower and contract farming), a particular number of livestock, and with continuous commercial activities throughout the year (URT 2016b). Through the stimulation of such policies policy-makers hope that small-scale farming will 'change beyond recognition' (Kweka and Ouma 2019).

But the problem with such ambitions is that they do not recognize the changes that are already taking place. The smallholder sector that these policies see is not the one that we have explored. Furthermore critics observe that to achieve the transformations envisaged these interventions will lead to a new and more serious set of problems arising from the change of land rights and lack of purchasing power along the agricultural value chain (Sulle 2015, Kuzilwa and Mpeta 2017). These policies support capitalist penetration through contracts that have hindered the social reproduction of the peasantry (Moyo and Patnaik 2011). Instead smallholder farmers require sustainable solutions to the recurring problems of land tenure insecurity, quality and affordable seeds and fertilizers, good prices and reliable markets for produces, agricultural infrastructures, subsidies, affordable loans, and areas for pasture.

This book has documented various creative ways that farmers have used to move out of poverty. The nature of their activities and especially investments in assets are imbedded in everyday life experience of the rural environment. In some cases, choices of investments start as a cultural issue before commercial opportunities emerge. In other cases, only a small shift in farming practice triggers transformation from old practices to those compliant with new market opportunities. Without donor funds, farmers have moved from growing traditional maize for food to carrots and potatoes or using fertilizers that have not been used in the past.

The kind of changes in smallholder farming we are excited about in this book do not feature prominently in the policy discussions about smallholder farming. Yet, we have found powerful locally driven transformations which are free from loans and conditional contracts for accessing modern inputs and selling of harvests. Local transformations emerge from a social fabric in which the rural economy is embedded. Farmers have different skills, ambitions, and strategies to move from one wealth rank to another. It is for this reason that understanding local perceptions of change and how that change happens is an important step towards policy support for small-scale farming and rural development.

For the changes we have observed to feature more prominently, then current data available to policy-makers in the country will need to be used differently. According to Kilama and colleagues (2016), the current requirements for the assessment of SDGs are likely to be sponsored by donors who may simply want national-level data for comparative purposes.

In February 2019, the National Bureau of Statistics (NBS) organized a statistics stakeholder's workshop to discuss the controversy that had emerged after the release of the country's new statistics law (2018). The controversy revolved around the new legal restrictions for the use and change of 'official statistics'.[3] The opening statement of NBS's Director—Dr Albin Chuwa—emphasized the importance of the country's control of its statistics. In her words 'nchi hazipinduliwi na majeshi bali ni takwimu'. Literally meaning that government revolutions are not caused by army forces but statistics.

In the light of the history of agricultural development policy in Tanzania that we have summarized here, a change in direction in agricultural policy which recognized the vigour of the smallholder sector would indeed be radical. But it would not be revolutionary. Taking change in assets seriously does not replace using poverty lines based on consumption. Each measure is useful. Moreover asset data are collected by diverse government surveys. Taking assets more seriously is eminently compatible with existing government statistical work.

[3] This law forbade the publication of statistics which were deemed to be contradictory of official government statistics.

Exploring Asset Dynamics in Longitudinal Research

As we observed in the introduction to this collection, these chapters are a contribution to the surprisingly niche field of longitudinal research. Here we reflect on the value of these studies, and their surprising paucity.

Done well longitudinal research can offer exceptional insights, as two rather different studies illustrate. Li's (2014) *Land's End* is based on nine visits, of up to several months, over a nineteen-year period to the same set of communities in central Sulawesi. Her detailed and highly praised ethnography shows how exploitative capitalist relations and deprivation emerge from within. They are driven by local residents and endogenous desires for progress and change. The second example comes from revisits to Palanpur, in India, every ten years for over fifty years, which has been led by mainstream economists (Bliss and Stern 1982, Lanjouw and Stern 1998, Himanshu et al. 2018). These works are full of facts about income, assets, inequality, livelihoods, and changing caste dynamics. The latest volume allows development economists the chance to reflect on how wrong theories were that had envisaged a shift of labour from rural economies to formal industrial employment. Contemporary livelihoods are much more precarious than economic theories had originally predicted.

However reviews of longitudinal studies highlight an unfortunate fact: it appears to be relatively rare in African research. White's summary contains works from Asia, South East Asia, and Central America; Wolford adds examples from South America (White 2014, Wolford 2016).[4] There are edited collections which compile longitudinal studies for South Asia (Breman et al. 1997, Himanshu and Rodgers 2016) and South East Asia (Rigg and Vandergeest 2012), but not Africa. The method has not been as well used in African contexts as it could be.

There are obvious exceptions. Caplan's work in Mafia provides over three decades of insight built on strong persistent friendships, observation, and conversation (Caplan 1992, Caplan 1997). Guyer's (1997) *An African Niche Economy* studied change in the hinterland of Ibadan, Nigeria, to understand how farmers pursued careers within the constraints and opportunities that unfolded in the face of growing urban demand but restrictive national economic change. Mortimore's seminal contribution to understanding adaptation to drought entailed a thirteen-year study of a village in northern Nigeria (Mortimore 1989). The 'AFRINT' database has tracked four thousand farmers across nine countries with three visits since 2002 (Djurfeldt et al. 2011, Andersson Djurfeldt et al. 2018). Bill Kinsey and colleagues' long-term study of re-settlement in Zimbabwe provides unique insights into the consequences of land reform that stretch back over four decades

[4] White, reviewing Rigg and Vandergeest's edited collection (2012), invoked several other studies (Redfield 1950, Epstein 1973, Castañeda 1995, Pincus 1996, Epstein, Suryanarayana, and Thimmegowda 1998, Eder 2000). Wolford, reviewing Li's work (2014) mentioned (Stolcke 1988, Ortiz 1999).

(Hoogeveen and Kinsey 1999, Dekker and Kinsey 2011). The Gwembe Tonga Research Project has provided a wealth of insights on change in Southern Zambia since 1956.[5] Wade Pendelton's research in Windhoek provides valuable insights into how people cope with life before and after apartheid (Pendleton 1996). Richard Lee, Megan Biesele, and Robert Hitchcock have enjoyed decades of work among Basarwa in Botswana (Lee et al. 1996, Lee 2012). Camilla Toulmin has recently published a study of over thirty years of change in a rural Malian village (Toulmin 2020).

Other studies provide landscape-scale studies of decades of changing prosperity. Tiffen, Mortimore, and Gichuki's *More People Less Erosion* (1994) adopted a landscape-scale approach documenting a rise in investment in the landscape—at the same time missing the exclusions and disadvantage that this change visited upon poorer domestic units within that landscape (Murton 1999). Moore and Vaughan's remarkable re-study of Audrey Richards work in northern Zambia provides insights into one hundred years of change across a large area, deliberately eschewing a village-based approach—partly because of the lack of precision that Richards herself provided on where she had worked (Moore and Vaughan 1994).

Shorter studies include Whitehead's work (2006) on persistent poverty in Ghana, Murton's work (Murton 1999) exploring and questioning the beneficiaries of landscape change in Machakos, and Mushonagh and Scoones who examined changed meanings of wealth in one Zimbabwean village between 1986–7 and 2006–7 (Mushongah and Scoones 2012). The latter found, inter alia that in 2006–7 cash had become less important for determining wealth, and health more important. A host of assets (house quality, solar panels, mobile phones) had become elements of a wealthy lifestyle in the later survey that were absent in the 1980s. The Kagera restudy (Tanzania) provides remarkably detailed information in a region for which there is otherwise little historical data (de Weerdt 2010, Beegle et al. 2011). There are also some useful panel datasets from Ethiopia (Dercon 2006, Dercon et al. 2009, Liverpool-Tasie and Winter-Nelson 2011, Dercon et al. 2012). These are characterized by their tendency to focus on the qualities of domestic units and individuals, and quantitative analyses of the same (e.g. Borgerhoff Mulder 1995), and pay less attention to the politics of poverty creation and reduction (Harris 2009).

Longitudinal studies, then, are used in African contexts, but those we have listed are fewer than the studies reported in the edited collections we mentioned in Asian contexts. They have not, until this book was published, been numerous enough to collate for any particular region or country. This in turn reflects that fact that, more generally, longitudinal studies are surprisingly rarely used to understand social change. This is a niche research field. One indication of their

[5] http://www.uky.edu/~cligget/gwembe.htm.

rarity is that recent edited collections to this genre use the method in their title. Their authors know it will distinguish them. Examples include *The Changing Village in India, Insights from Longitudinal Research* (Himanshu and Rodgers 2016) and *Revisiting Rural Places* (Rigg and Vandergeest 2012).

One of the reasons that such studies are niche is that they are hard to do. Setting aside the methodological challenges, not many people are able to return to former study sites. It is hard enough undertaking one study, let alone finding the time and funding to return. Most of the best cases are from anthropology, which has been founded on deep commitments to particular places (Kloos 1997, Kemper and Royce 2002).

The availability of longitudinal data is changing. The Living Standards Measurements Surveys have been instituted since the late 2000s in a number of African countries precisely to tackle the lack of panel data that make it possible to document change. These are already beginning to yield insights (Christiaensen 2017). But these tend to be national-scale samples intended to afford national-level generalizations. They cannot provide detailed insights into particular places and the nuts and bolts of local change.

We submit that, despite the methodological difficulties, longitudinal studies could usefully become more normal in social science. It is, after all, routine for well-resourced countries to set up large panel data sets precisely in order to trace change accurately over time among their citizens. Imagine the wealth of resources and insights that would become possible if, on getting tenure, established academics were expected to return to their original field sites and discuss their first findings, and future research directions, with the communities with which they had worked.

And what change would it make if more Tanzanian scholars who are part of the change described in this book revisited their old research sites? There are possibilities that the change could be taken for granted given the challenges of studying familiar environments, possible research fatigue and subjectivity. Yet, as captured in Christine Noe's experience in Meru, Cosmas Sokoni and Verdiana Tilumanywa's in Uporoto Highlands, and Emmanuel Sulle's in Mama Issara, taking part in the analysis of change to one's own region could provide a unique opportunity for bringing new insights into rural livelihood changes.

Our point is not that all researchers must do this sort of study. But they need to find a good reason why they should not. When well-written works come out that do provide long-term perspectives then the insights make for some of the best possible research—robust, insightful, rigorous, and predicated on a deep understanding of how and why places and their residents change.

Conclusion

Tanzanian farmers are richer in assets than we have previously realized. They have been able to accrue these assets by savings, tightening expenditure, and by growing their income from smallholder farming. They have responded to market incentives, infrastructural development, and social change.

These achievements are not widely recognized. Critics on the left maintain that Tanzanian farmers endure persistent poverty. Critics on the right insist that farming must be transformed. The one argue that rural development policies are misguided, the other that they are not being fulfilled. Both miss the mark. Tanzanian smallholders have been better able to prosper, according to their own measures, than either side admits.

Policies which empower smallholders, ensure their secure access to land, which make farm inputs more accessible, and farm gate prices more rewarding will generate locally valued prosperity. Responding to change on the ground means that the data used in national and international measurements of poverty and prosperity need to fit closely with local aspirations. This requires considerable flexibility, and ways of accommodating diversity in the statistics collected.

If this volume proves useful then, in some respects it emphasizes the benefits of keeping an open mind, and being ready to admit early mistakes in this sort of research project. We ourselves had little idea what this project would lead to when we embarked upon it. We had conducted one study in central Tanzania in which we found that villagers were unexpectedly wealthy (Brockington et al. 2018). But we had no grasp of how widespread, or not, that pattern would be. We sought to scale-up that study, to find more case studies where we could revisit families and households over time. We did not anticipate finding the general patterns of growing assets that we have reported in this volume. Nor did we anticipate that there would be such variety in the timing and causes of the change.

Indeed we must also confess that we did not even properly understand the limitations of poverty-line data when we first embarked on this research. That insight came from our collaborations with the NBS. It was through our exchanges with them that it became clear that poverty-line data must systematically exclude the forms of prosperity that we were examining.[6] In our presentations of this work internationally we have found that this lesson needs to be more broadly learned. For economists it is obvious. But for most other social scientists this has come as a surprise.[7]

Our ability to tell a bigger story, to bring together insights from different cases and researchers has fundamentally depended upon the broad-minded and generous contribution of a large number of other researchers. This has not been a single project. It was a federation. In some respects this has, in fact, been more than just a research group, it has been the gathering, and formation, of a small

[6] Our first paper we published on this topic even demonstrates that missed understanding (Brockington et al. 2018). We had to correct ourselves in later works (Brockington 2021).

[7] We have presented this work at several invited research seminars and talks in a number of different countries in Europe as well as Tanzania. Of the approximately two hundred people who have attended these seminars, who tend to be well-qualified researchers, barely ten were aware of the exclusions of poverty-line data.

epistemic community, of people who first began to meet each other over twenty years ago as they worked on PhD projects. It has been one of its joys and privileges to bring together so much experience and insight into change in rural Tanzania. The Epilogue to this book captures, we hope, some of the energy and honesty that flowed in these gatherings.

Even now, writing as the COVID-19 pandemic has just begun and its implications remain uncertain, our hope is that other researchers will seek to emulate the same methods that we have used, in other places. We recognize that they may be able to do this differently. We have been reliant on old survey data, which we revisited with tablet-based surveys. But many rural people in Tanzania have lives on-line, they frequent Facebook and other social media. Access to these is riven with exclusions, but nonetheless they provide insights into change, issues, and concerns on a much more frequent basis. The tried and trusted methods, which hinge on continuity in the researcher presence, will remain important. And they will do well to incorporate the new methods and data that new social practices allow. This will mean the formation of other, different epistemic communities.

We would welcome that warmly. We have had the privilege of listening to the stories of hundreds of rural Tanzanians. It is an important and vital task. There will be new ways of listening to and communicating these stories in the future from which we look forward to learning.

References

Andersson Djurfeldt, A., F. M. Dzanku, and A. C. Isinika (2018). *Agriculture, Diversification and Gender in Rural Africa: Longitudinal Perspectives from Six Countries*. Oxford, Oxford University Press.

Beegle, K., J. De Weerdt, and S. Dercon (2011). 'Migration and Economic Mobility in Tanzania: Evidence from a Tracking Survey.' *The Review of Economics and Statistics* 93(3): 1010–33.

Bernstein, H. (2010). *Class Dynamics of Agrarian Change*. Halifx and Winnipeg, Fernwood Publishing.

Bernstein, H. and P. Woodhouse (2001). 'Telling Environmental Change Like It Is? Reflections on a Study in Sub-Saharan Africa.' *Journal of Agrarian Change* 1(2): 283–324.

Bliss, C. J. and N. H. Stern (1982). *Palanpur: The Economy of an Indian Village*. Oxford, Clarendon Press.

Borgerhoff Mulder, M. (1995). 'Bridewealth and Its Correlates: Quantifying Changes over Time.' *Current Anthropology* 36(4): 573–603.

Breman, J., P. Kloos, and A. Saith (1997). *The Village in Asia Revisited*. Delhi, Oxford University Press.

Brockington, D. (2021). 'Persistent Peasant Poverty and Assets: Exploring Dynamics of New Forms of Wealth and Poverty in Tanzania 1999–2018.' *Journal of Peasant Studies* 48(1): 201–20. DOI: 10.1080/03066150.2019.1658081.

Brockington, D., O. Howland, V.-M. Loiske, M. Mnzava, and C. Noe (2018). 'Economic Growth, Rural Assets and Prosperity: Exploring the Implications of a Twenty Year Record of Asset Growth in Tanzania.' *Journal of Modern African Studies* 56(2): 217–43.

Bryceson, D. F. (1999). *African Rural Labour, Income Diversification and Livelihood Approaches: A Long-term Development Perspective*. Leiden, African Studies Center.

Caplan, P. (1992). 'Socialism from Above: The View from Below.' *The Tanzanian Peasantry: Economy in Crisis*. P. G. Forster and S. Maghimbi. Aldershot, Avebury: 103–23.

Caplan, P. (1997). *African Voices, African Lives: Personal Narratives from a Swahili Village*. Abingdon, Routledge.

Christiaensen, L. (2017). 'Agriculture in Africa—Telling Myths from Facts: A Synthesis.' *Food Policy* 67: 1–11.

de Weerdt, J. (2010). 'Moving out of Poverty in Tanzania: Evidence from Kagera.' *The Journal of Development Studies* 46(2): 331–49.

Dekker, M. and B. Kinsey (2011). 'Contextualizing Zimbabwe's land Reform: Long-Term Observations from the First Generation.' *The Journal of Peasant Studies* 38(5): 995–1019.

Dercon, S. (2006). 'Economic Reform, Growth and the Poor: Evidence from Rural Ethiopia.' *Journal of Development Economics* 81: 1–24.

Dercon, S., D. O. Gilligan, J. Hoddinott, and T. Woldehanna (2009). 'The Impact of Agricultural Extension and Roads on Poverty and Consumption Growth in Fifteen Ethiopian Villages.' *American Journal of Agricultural Economics* 91(4): 1007–21.

Dercon, S., J. Hoddinott, and T. Woldehanna (2012). 'Growth and Chronic Poverty: Evidence from Rural Communities in Ethiopia.' *The Journal of Development Studies* 48(2): 238–53.

Djurfeldt, G., E. Aryeetey, and A. C. Isinika (2011). *African Smallholders: Food Crops, Markets and Policy*. Wallingford, CABI.

Ellis, F. and N. Mdoe (2003). 'Livelihoods and Rural Poverty Reduction in Tanzania.' *World Development* 31(8): 1367–84.

Forster, G. and S. Maghimbi (1992). *The Tanzanian Peasantry: Economy in Crisis*. Aldershot, Avebury.

Guyer, J. I. (1997). *An African Niche Economy: Farming to Feed Ibadan 1968–88* Edinburgh, Edinburgh University Press.

Harris, J. (2009). 'Bringing Politics Back into Poverty Analysis: Why Understandings of Social Relations Matters More for Policy on Chronic Poverty than Measurement.' *Poverty Dynamics: Interdisciplinary Perspectives*. T. Addison, D. Hulme, and R. Kanbur. Oxford, Oxford University Press: 205–24.

Himanshu, P. Jha and G. Rodgers (2016). *The Changing Village in India: Insights from Longitudinal Research*. Oxford, Oxford University Press.

Himanshu, P. Lanjouw, and N. H. Stern (2018). *How Lives Change: Palanpur, India and Development Economics*. Oxford, Oxford University Press.

Homewood, K., M. R. Nielsen, and A. Keane (2020). 'Women, Wellbeing and Wildlife Management Areas in Tanzania.' *The Journal of Peasant Studies*. DOI: 10.1080/03066150.2020.1726323.

Hoogeveen, J. G. and B. Kinsey (1999). 'Land Reform, Growth and Equity: Emerging Evidence from Zimbabwe's Resettlement Programme—A Sequel.' *Journal of Southern African Studies* 27(1): 127–36.

Keane, A., J. F. Lund, J. Bluwstein, N. D. Burgess, M. R. Nielsen, and K. Homewood (2020). 'Impact of Tanzania's Wildlife Management Areas on Household Wealth.' *Nature Sustainability* 3: 226–33.

Kemper, R. V. and A. P. Royce (2002). *Chronicling Cultures: Long-Term Field Research in Anthropology*. Walnut Creek, CA, Altamira.

Kilama, B., C. George, L. Katera, and N. Rutatina (2016). *Assessing Data for the Sustainable Development Goals in Tanzania*. Dar es Salaam, REPOA.

Kloos, P. (1997). 'Restudies in Anthropology: Modalities, Limitations and Alternatives.' *The Village in Asia Revisited*. J. Breman, P. Kloos, and A. Saith. New Delhi, Oxford University Press: 429–50.

Kuzilwa, A. and D. Mpeta (2017). 'Strategies and Policies for Agricultural Development in Tanzania.' *Contract Farming and the Development of Smallholder Agricultural Businesses: Improving Markets and Value Chains in Tanzania*. A. Kuzilwa, N. Fold, A. Henningsen, and N. Larsen. London, Routledge: 48–62.

Kweka, O. and S. Ouma (2019). '"Changing beyond Recognition"? Reimagining the Future of Smallholder Farming Systems in the Context of Climate Change.' *Geoforum* Pre-publication. DOI: 10.1016/j.geoforum.2019.1005.1029.

Lanjouw, P. and N. H. Stern (1998). *Economic Development in Palanpur over Five Decades*. Oxford, Clarendon Press.

Lee, R. B. (2012). 'The !Kung and I: Reflections on My Life and Times with the Ju/Hoansi.' *General Anthropology* 19(1): 1–4.

Lee, R. B., M. Biesele, and R. K. Hitchcock (1996). 'Three Decades of Ethnographic Research among the Ju/'Hoansi of Northwestern Botswana: 1963–1996.' *Botswana Notes and Records* 28: 107–20.

Li, T. M. (2014). *Land's End: Capitalist Relations on an Indigenous Frontier*. Durham, Duke University Press.

Liverpool-Tasie, L. S. O. and A. Winter-Nelson (2011). 'Asset versus Consumption Poverty and Poverty Dynamics in Rural Ethiopia.' *Agricultural Economics* 42: 221–33.

Loiske, V.-M. (1995). *The Village That Vanished: The Roots of Erosion in a Tanzanian Village*. Stockholm, University of Stockholm.

Maghimbi, S., R. Lokina, and M. Senga (2011). 'The Agrarian Question in Tanzania?' A state of the art paper. Nordiska Afrikainstitutet, University of Dar Es Salaam.

Mitlin, D. and D. Satterthwaite (2013). *Urban Poverty in the Global South: Scale and Nature*. London, Routledge.

Moore, H. L. and M. Vaughan (1994). *Cutting Down Trees: Gender Nutrition and Agricultural Change in the Northern Province of Zambia, 1890–1990*. Portsmouth, NH, Heinemann.

Mortimore, M. (1989). *Adapting to Drought: Farmers, Famines and Desertification in West Africa*. Cambridge, Cambridge University Press.

Moyo, S. and U. Patnaik (2011). *The Agrarian Question in the Neoliberal Era: Primitive Accumulation and the Peasantry*. Dar es Salaam, Pambazuka Press.

Murton, J. (1999). 'Population Growth and Poverty in Machakos District, Kenya.' *Geographical Journal* 165(1): 37–46.

Mushongah, J. and I. Scoones (2012). 'Livelihood Change in Rural Zimbabwe over 20 Years.' *The Journal of Development Studies* 48(9): 1241–57.

NBS (2019). 'Tanzania Mainland Household Budget Survey: Key Indicators Report 2017–18.' Dar es Salaam, Ministry of Finance and Planning.

Pendleton, W. (1996). *Katutura: A Place Where We Stay—Life in a Post-apartheid Township in Namibia*. Athens, Ohio University Press.

Piketty, T. (2014). *Capital in the Twenty-First Century*. Cambridge, MA, The Belknap Press of Harvard University Press.

Ponte, S. and D. Brockington (2020). 'From Pyramid to Pointed Egg? A Twenty-Year Perspective on Poverty, Prosperity and Rural Transformation in Tanzania.' African Affairs 119(475): 203–23. DOI:10.1093/afraf/adaa002.

Rigg, J. and P. Vandergeest (2012). *Revisiting Rural Places: Pathways to Poverty and Prosperity in Southeast Asia*. Singapore, NUS Press.

Sulle, E. (2015). 'Land Grabbing and Agricultural Commercialization Duality: Insights from Tanzania's Transformation Agenda.' *Afriche e Orienti* 17(3): 109–28.

Tiffen, M., M. Mortimore, and F. Gichuki (1994). *More People, Less Erosion: Environmental Recovery in Kenya*. Chichester, John Wiley.

Toulmin, C. (2020). *Land, Investment, and Migration. Thirty-Five Years of Village Life in Mali*. Oxford, Oxford University Press.

United Republic of Tanzania (URT) (2005). 'National Strategy for Growth and Reduction of Poverty (NSGRP).' Dar es Salaam, Vice President's Office.

United Republic of Tanzania (URT) (2011a). 'Tanzania Agriculture and Food Security Investment Plan (2011/2012–2020/2021).' Dar es Salaam, Ministry of Agriculture, Livestock and Fisheries.

United Republic of Tanzania (URT) (2011b). 'The Tanzania Five Year Development Plan (2011/2012–2015/2016): Unleashing Tanzania's Latent Growth Potentials.' Dar es Salaam, President's Office, Planning Commission.

United Republic of Tanzania (URT) (2016a). 'Agricultural Sector Development Strategy—II 2015/2016–2024/2025.' Dar es Salaam, Ministry of Agriculture, Livestock and Fisheries Development.

United Republic of Tanzania (URT) (2016b). 'Large Scale Farms Survey Report, 2012–2013.' Dar es Salaam, Ministry of Finance and Planning.

White, B. (2014). 'Revisiting Rural Places: Pathways to Poverty and Prosperity in Southeast Asia.' *Journal of Peasant Studies* 41(4): 635–8.

Whitehead, A. (2006). 'Persistent Poverty in North East Ghana.' *Journal of Development Studies* 42(2): 278–300.

Wolford, W. (2016). 'Land's End: Review by Wendy Wolford.' *Journal of Peasant Studies* 43(4): 950–4.

Epilogue

Doing Longitudinal Research

Christine Noe, Stefano Ponte, Dan Brockington, Anna Mdee, Cosmas Sokoni, Esbern Friis-Hansen, Verdiana Tilumanywa, Katherine A. Snyder, Emmanuel Sulle, Willie Östberg, Vesa-Matti Loiske, Monique Borgerhoff Mulder, Agnes Andersson Djurfeldt, and Torben Birch-Thomsen

The research that has been presented in this book is the product of decades of learning, individually and collectively of multiple researchers, research teams and research assistants. The chapters presented in this collection have been shared in two separate writing workshops, one in Copenhagen, the other in Arusha. On each occasion we listened to the work presented, offered observations and criticisms and then went back to work again on the papers we had shared.

But the process of doing research is always much more complicated, more intimate and intricate than any academic paper or book chapter can reveal. On the evening of the last day of the last workshop in Arusha we sat down to share some of the more personal stories, motivations and tribulations that lie behind the formally presented findings of the previous pages. This Epilogue is a smoothed transcription of that discussion—with some of the reactions of the other researchers listening also included. Two people (Stefano and Agnes) could not be present in Arusha, and we have added transcripts of further conversations with them recorded after they had seen a draft of the first account.

We do not wish provide much additional narrative to this discussion. You will read here how researchers from different disciplines, personal backgrounds, biases and academic and national traditions have approached the same problem (as nationals or expatriates) of trying to understand communities and places in this one country we call 'Tanzania'. And how the communities in which we have worked have come to manage, shape, divert, influence, or curtail researchers' interests in them. You will read how we have struggled to understand our research questions, how we have sought belonging and community, how we have negotiated positions as insiders and outsiders and even found love. The methodological purist may detect the odd mistake in the techniques we have used to do our work. But it is important to give some insight into how we muddled through, and what these joys and tribulations have meant to us and some of the people with whom we have worked.

Christine (Chapter 7)

Unlike most of the researchers here, it was not me who did the original research but Rolf Larsson. At the time of his research, I was still doing my secondary education at Makumira Secondary School, which is in my village Ndatu, right in the middle of his study sites. I was grateful for the opportunity to work on a livelihood change project and very happy to have come across Rolf's work about 'Livelihoods, diversification and inequality among the Meru of Tanzania'.

When the opportunity of doing a re-study came up I had this drive to go and do something and to write about the bitterness of coffee (laughter). My personal experience was bitter yet some people are enjoying the coffee (more laughter). I did not grow up drinking coffee. As in most other households, coffee was rarely available for drinking. The owners of coffee plants and beans they produced (almost always the men in Meru) would guard coffee strictly from the beginning of the process (picking) until it was sold. There was so much to do to get to the last point—the sale. But as a girl, in common with most women, I had to participate in the labour but never the sales.

What I remember most is the common saying that 'if the coffee bean goes down, make sure you go with it!' This was to stress the point that no single bean should be wasted. This would be at the picking point, which was usually around the rainy and coldest months (May–August), followed by piling, washing and sorting the harvested beans. Most of these activities depended on family labour. It meant going through the farm after school to pick up coffee loads and help with piling before dinner. It also meant waking up early to take coffee to the river for washing before going to school. Piled coffee could not stay for more than one day without washing with running water otherwise the grade is affected. Waking up early in the coldest months to wash coffee in the river before going to school was simply bitter! No wonder that when coffee disappeared (due to diseases and price cuts), women celebrated and associated this disappearance with their tears, caused by all this work and so little return. This is why we have focussed on that in my chapter—about 'women tears' and how these women have managed to navigate the change.

As you can see I have grown up here and I know things and this was home. But I have not always wanted to come here as a researcher. I wanted to come here as home. So there was that combination. And when I came, there was also a very confusing feeling for me because you kind of know things but you have to ask about them (laughter). But you don't really get surprised about things. You [the other researchers in the room] you go to new places you get to know new culture and this and that. For me I'm here, I know this place and I almost expect people to say something I know. So this excitement of learning new things has not been there. And I think it has been preventing me from learning because I don't go further to ask more and probe. Because when you are in a group discussion almost everyone knows that you are part of them. So at some point you get involved in answering questions as well because people will ask you 'what happened to your mother' if you are with a group of women and you actually become a source of information for the rest of the group. You are no longer the researcher, but the researched.

There were good things about being culturally attached to this place and being a researcher because there is easy access to information; with the issue of language you know it—even if people want to hide something you know it. People also have confidence in you and they give even more than you would want to ask. And there is an opportunity to cross-check with people who are not even your targets. On getting back home in the evenings, my father kept asking me and Olivia 'So you went to Malala today what did you find out there?' And then he would disagree and say 'No that is not the case here'. So you get to know the case of the village that is not even part of this study. In terms of learning I learned the process of really being a researcher, and being a subject and how to distance yourself from things that you are studying. I find it interesting because of that experience. I think I am also better placed than you who are coming and going. I can speak with more authority.

Just before this final workshop, Dan joined me for fieldwork in Mulala village. He kept picking up stories of selling cows and buying land or paying school fees, which I did not really pay much attention to. I told him 'that's always what my father did to expand his land inheritance and get school fees for eight of us'. The stories reminded me of a common saying among the Meru parents who had children in secondary schools. That is 'I have finished my cows'. This was especially pronounced by parents whose children underperformed (temporarily or long-term). The connection was drawn such that if the family had many children and one or two of them underperformed, there would be double stress for the underperforming one—from parents and the other children—because the entire family is involved in raising the cows.

Zero-grazing is especially a difficult activity in Meru highlands. Not just because you have to go up and down with loads of grasses or banana leaves to feed the animals but because sourcing the grasses is hard. For most families, land is too small to grow fodder. Searching for grasses further down the mountain was the order of the day for my family. If you are downhill already on other errands, you would want to combine that with fodder at the end of the day. This involved going to fenced settler farms within and beyond the village. I remember many instances of sneaking into highly guarded settler farms and the risks involved in meeting the guards and dogs, sometimes in school uniform (because one had to cut down the time to go home and back). All of you here know this place [the 'Danish Centre' where the workshop was held] as a pleasant place to work and meet, but I first encountered it as a young child because it is full of sweet grass and if we got up really early we could walk here and creep through the fence and harvest the grass before it was light. Do not call this stealing. It is not a sin if the cow is hungry (laughter). Moreover there is, just behind this Danish Centre, a National Development Cooperation's livestock artificial insemination farm. The farm keeps high-grade cows and bulls which are fed with first-class fodder. If you manage to feed your cow with some of that fodder, you were assured of doubling the amount of milk in just a day. It was so attractive for villagers to sneak in. The importance of cows for the general family economy and milk for daily use made everyone responsible for trying to get some. These memories enrich my reflections about being a researcher in the place I grew up.

Family investments in education meant foregoing good meals (accompanied with meat) and better housing (block houses with electricity). Parents would take the risk, especially given the lack of employment after school. The risk was especially high for parents who took girl children to school. Two bad things were expected by the community generally; pregnancy at school or marriage after school. Taking a girl child to school seemed a riskier investment. Those who did (like my parents who had seven girls and only one boy) would be under immense pressure to ensure that they didn't become bad examples of failed investments. This is almost typical of Meru families then and now. The difference is that more and more girls have done well in school hence motivating others.

In our first visit to Mulala village, Olivia and I were a bit unsure of the meaning of what one of our respondents—Paulo Akyoo—told us. We met him at the village centre before taking us to his home. Along the way to his house he told us how 'there were no longer poor people in the village'. People had quit drinking because they 'met Jesus' and that everyone was a born again. Knowing God gave people the right direction, he said to us. We passed his parent's home—Nndosa Akyoo—which was the first that shocked us because of the story that we had just heard. An old mud house with rusty iron sheets and two small thatched roofed huts as kitchen and for two goats gave Olivia and me mixed feelings. Then we arrived at Paulo's two-room house made of mabanzi [wooden] walls. After a long prayer from him, he went straight to his story which made our confusion of 'no more poor people' fade away. He had taken four children to school. He had a university graduate, a school teacher, one still at college, and the last in a private secondary school. All his energy had gone into paying school fees even though he wanted to build a better house.

After this household I told Olivia my father could say exactly the same thing to Rolf Larsson but with a twist. Rolf's time here was when there was still coffee and the cooperative society built, maintained, and serviced a coffee farmer's school. My school—Makumira—was connected to both the Lutheran church and Meru coffee farmer's cooperative society. Through coffee sales, individual members could contribute in building and maintaining the school and in turn school fees for Meru children would be subsidized. With the good relations my father had with the school administration, fees could wait for coffee sales. In case of a poor coffee harvest or late payments, it was possible for parents to exchange maize and bean harvests straight from the farm to the school store. Although with some pain (due to low prices at the time of harvest) my parents could keep us in school (sometimes four of us at the same time). But, nonetheless, coffee, maize, and beans could not be enough. A sale of one or two male calves would be required to finish school fees. Little if any could be saved to expand land holdings or improve the family house.

Like many other farmers today, Paulo replaced coffee with other seasonal crops—potatoes and carrots. The difference is in the marketing arrangements and some risk mitigation strategies that coffee farmers enjoyed. After visits to other households, Olivia and I changed our understanding of poverty and wealth. We started paying a lot more attention to the stories about how households had invested in different kinds of assets.

Coming back to Dan's questions about cows and land, the new stories corrected an earlier conclusion I had drawn in this study that land had become less important as a measure of wealth in the case of Meru. The fact that people trade cows for farm plots (whenever a land sale opportunity arises) and for children's education makes land an important family asset. One of the surprises that emerged during the recent visit with Dan was that we heard from two formerly landless women who had worked as kibarua and managed to buy land, pay school fees, and even give an inheritance of land to their children. Land was therefore an important starting point for uplifting of social and economic statuses of their households and those of their children. After these stories, I recently went back to test my earlier ideas with my father—that I didn't think land is so important now for the Meru people. He simply joked, 'I didn't know I finished my cows to get you stupid'.

Stefano (Chapter 12)

The first thing that I thought, was that reflecting on longitudinal work was really difficult because rural Tanzania had changed, but so had I. So I spent a lot of time trying to dissect what about Tanzania was changing and what was about me and my perception, experience, age, or academic status having changed that could explain what I thought I was observing.

I think the key question for me after the two trips I did in 2016 and 2017 and during the process of looking at the data, sifting through all the interview and focus group material and writing was 'What does it mean to be objective in this context where twenty years have passed?' I want to explore some ideas about this. In essence these are personal reflections but they are meant to stimulate further reflection on what it means to do interpretive work—especially on long-term longitudinal studies and in particular in my case when I did not go back to these places for a long time. My experience was not like the more common anthropological approach of going back every year or two, and there are challenges in that approach as well. It was about going back after twenty years, a very big gap. The before and after are very different situations essentially.

In 1996/7 I was a young PhD student. I had very little funding, so little that I could not afford a translator. I had to spend my first period there perfecting the language and being comfortable enough to start doing research. That was in a context when PhD schools in the United Kingdom were quite relaxed about students spending a long time in the field. As a matter of fact it was a badge of honour to stay longer. So I planned to stay six to nine months but I ended up staying eighteen, which was totally fine. It was not seen as a failure like now, even though it was riddled with failures (laughter).

But even though it was long-term fieldwork, it was divided into various locations. I did not spend eighteen months in the same place. I stayed in six different locations in two districts plus a lot of time in Dar sorting out the national-level stuff on policy. These were the days pre-mobile phones when the landlines did not work and so you had essentially to take the daladala [small bus] and get there. You wait for the person to show up and when they did not you went back and your day was gone. So in terms of efficiency and time to think about the little that you had gathered we had loads of time—there was nothing else to do. Every other day the electricity was off so one day I was gathering data and the other day with electricity I would be typing up my notes. Essentially the timeframe was so much more stretched out.

And then there was this extra complication as my partner was also doing her PhD at that time in the same locations on a totally different set of issues. So I was really trying to focus on my own work and then I would go to a household for an interview and somebody off the cuff would say 'Who is that other skinny mzungu going around—that woman—she must have a really bad husband, look how skinny she is' (laughter). And other people were asking what sort of man was I, after all where were our children?! (prolonged laughter).

And I had come in with a clear focus. I wanted to see what impact structural adjustment and market liberalization had on farming households and farming systems. Exactly twenty years later, in 2016/17, I was older, more established. People liked to call me 'Profesa' which added a whole new layer of authority that I did not have in the first visit. By then I'd been working in Tanzania twenty years, it was like a third home to me. And then going back with a project is different because on a PhD you are all on your own, it is everything or nothing, the risks are very high. This other project was with a group of great people run by this crazy guy from Sheffield, whom I have also known for twenty years. I stayed maybe a total eighteen days instead of eighteen months which means a lot. I am more experienced, but also you can do a lot more now in a shorter time, it is easier to travel around, you have mobile phones and our focus was more narrow.

So I came into the field for the re-study with a lot of worries and fears, despite the fact that it was a fun project, quite removed from my main current agenda. The main fear was 'What am I going to find about the people I interviewed?' I remember some of the households very well, I had gone through some of the transcripts and all these memories were coming back. What if we could not find them or if they had died or bad things had happened to them or their kids? It was tense for me coming back, especially the first time when we were in Morogoro which is the place where I spent most time during my PhD research.

But I decided in any case I'm going to go with all the pictures I have from the time before twenty years ago. I found all the focus groups pictures, I printed them out and brought them with me. And then it was so great to find so many of the people. In general the fact that we could find so many was very surprising for me. This is something we experienced across a project. And not only that, but I would remember them. It is easier perhaps for them to remember me, because I was the stranger coming in, but I also remembered them.

And then there are the funny things people say after twenty years. I had brought pictures of me and three children, so I was finally at almost the age of 50 considered a real man (laughter). But I was not quite prepared for the very first household that we found the guy comes to me and says umezeeka—'you have become old' (laughter). What do you do about that? You know, time has passed. And the second time it was umenenepa—'you have become fat' (laughter), and the third one was 'Your Swahili has really gone downhill' (laughter), and the fourth one was 'Where is your wife?' (laughter), and the fifth one was 'Where you been all this time?' (prolonged laughter). So it was not an easy ride, I started feeling uncomfortable (laughter). I did not know how I should react. My Swahili was good enough to understand, but I could not respond well, so I just blurted my way through.

Anyway the main thing in terms of the observations was the amazing changes that I've seen. The roads, solar panels, the quality of the houses, the pikipikis all around, all the shops. Then you think 'Maybe I'm being naïve'. This is all just because I'm not staying for long enough to find the hidden poverty and the problems and all that. And to some extent that is all true, but I could not ignore all the things that were objectively there.

Whether these things have the same 'value' to people than in the past is something we have discussed in the group and is a different story indeed. Some things are taken for granted now but at that time they were much more important.

Part of my reaction was like 'Wow!, this is really great', but part of it was 'I do not have time to dig deeper', I'm going to have a superficial, naïve perception. So when we had the first research meeting in Copenhagen with the larger group of researchers I was very nervous. We were twelve people, many of them critical of markets generally, a certain ilk of researcher. I was going to say 'Wow, whatever happened with respect to markets it looks not too bad' and I was totally nervous.

But I was not the first person to speak, I think I was the third talking from the top of our heads about what our first impressions were. But I remember, on hearing the first account, that my shoulders completely relaxed because I thought 'Phew, I don't have to say that first' because other people had seen the same changes too. Many of us, perhaps with one exception, came with variations of a generally common narrative.

So it was really weird to reflect upon how important it was for me what other people thought. We had been going to Tanzania for a long time, and seen many changes. Everyone knew that in urban areas there had been a lot of change. But I personally thought that these changes would not have affected the most remote regions. But then I went to the most remote area I've been to [Ligunga in Ruvuma Region] which is really far off and I just thought 'Wow'. But at first I felt vulnerable reporting things that were so different to my expectations and intellectual orientation.

Intellectually, my first reaction was 'Were the arguments from my PhD right? Do they still hold?' It took me a while to get over that. Eventually I realized it was not about my arguments, it was about understanding change. And in the paper I have written with Dan I have had to concentrate hard to make it not about me and my intellectual standing, but about understanding change itself. So the issue for me shifted. It was not 'Have the changes been positive?', but 'Where and why and how are they positive?', and that became much more liberating.

That's a problem we face. You can change in general but you are so attached to what you had before. It is really difficult to be detached from it and to take a backseat and try to be 'objective'. A lot of the work I do is qualitative. The interviews and focus groups shape our impressions more strongly than the survey work we do. I was concerned that I may not have been able to see well in only a short visit. For example, is this argument that we make about a pointed egg really accurate, or have we changed our definitions or not understood dynamics in the village. After all a lot of what matters about assets is not their monetary terms, but their implications for social status in a situation. Accruing an asset does not really create socially recognized wealth if everyone else has the same asset. So what is the meaning of having a metal roof now compared to twenty years ago?

The last thing that stayed with me after we finished this work was this lingering question: now what? Do we wait another twenty years and go back when I'm really, really old, and really, really fat (laughter), and my Swahili is completely gone? (laughter). So now what—help me out!

Dan (Chapter 8)

To understand how and why I went to Rukwa and what it was like you have to know a little bit more about what I did during my PhD. That was with Kathy

Homewood at UCL. Kathy has worked a lot with pastoral societies and is a biological anthropologist. A lot of the techniques there involved counting things really well, enumerating things, which provided fantastic lenses into changes which are going on in different societies. So I was measuring milk yields, I was recording diet, I was weighing children and calculating their height as well. And I was doing this for samples in two different villages and then repeating it every two months. It was really really hard. I'd be in one place for three weeks and then would not go back there for another two months, but then I wouldn't be in any other place for longer than three weeks. I was incredibly footloose, incredibly mobile, and could not put down roots. It took a long time for people to get used to me. My sample was too large because I made the classic mistake of trying to take on too much, which meant I was rushed all the time. At the end of each round I would write my data, realize there are loads of holes, and have to go back and there was constant pressure because I also knew that without these data I would not really be able to do the PhD that I set out to do well.

Plus, I was working around the Mkomazi Game Reserve which was a political nightmare.[1] Because pastoralists had been evicted from it in the late 1980s and it was specifically our remit to look at the consequence of the eviction on those pastoralists. So I was working with the group who were also taking the government to the court. And very early on my PhD it appeared as if I was collaborating with pastoralists in disobeying Game Reserve rules. This almost meant that my PhD got stopped for understandable reasons. But when my project was almost thrown out by the government it did then mean that the pastoralists, who themselves had decided not to co-operate meet with me because they suspected I was a government stooge, decided that maybe I was not so bad anymore, maybe we could work with this guy. But with a start like that there were just continual tensions all the way through. The experience of that, especially when I met other anthropologists working in the field like Jim Igoe, made me realize that I wanted to find another place in Tanzania where I didn't actually have to travel anywhere else at all. I wanted to hang out in one village and it had to be a hugely long way away from any conservation area whatsoever (laughter). And I needed to spend time with people on their own terms. As I'm sure you will recognize, when you are collecting biological anthropological data it is to very particular agendas and sometimes people don't get it. And on this occasion I wanted a project that people could understand more easily. And that is partly why I ended up in Mtowisa in Rukwa.

The other factor shaping that choice was that I was collaborating with the Ministry of Water and Livestock and they were interested in changes arising from the migration of people to the south and that's why they said 'Go to Rukwa. We

[1] This is described in *Fortress Conservation* (Brockington 2002).

have not got many reports on what is going on there and we would like to know more about it.' So it is a mixture of my desire to do better fieldwork, basically, because there were all sorts of problems with my PhD fieldwork when I look back on it and this was a chance as my mentor (Bill Adams) recognized at the time 'to have another bite of the cherry', to do rural fieldwork again, but do it better. And this was my chance.

And that aspect of it worked with bells on. When I was in Mtowisa in 1999–2000 I was able to 'hang out', to spend time informally people. I went to learn much more about how the Sukuma and Fipa people were interacting and working together. I was able to do that but the process meant working with people in the fields. It meant learning how to plough, weeding with them, herding with them, being invited out to people's houses and having meals and talking about life histories. I had friends there with whom I could talk and just chew the fat. I spent a lot of time in the bar in the evenings with the chairman and his friends learning to drink wanzuki which was a lovely honey beer. You just learned so much and observed so much all the time.

The irony was that I was coming to look at change in natural resource management. I asked people 'how do you decide who gets to graze in particular areas?' and they said 'What do you mean? There is a grassland we just put our cows on it. We don't need to ask anyone' (laughter). So that didn't work. So I said OK, I'll look at irrigation, there's loads of rice irrigation so I asked 'When you decide who gets to water the rice what you do?' and they said 'We'll be having a meeting next Tuesday and you can come along' and I thought 'Yes! I can see indigenous water management practices.' And then they said 'It's rained, there's loads of water, the meeting is cancelled' (laughter). But I spent a lot of time working with mechanisms of village and district government who had huge power in resource allocation and learned a lot about that. I joined the football team and learned to play football. I used to be quite fast and they put me on the wing when you could run up and down fast and it did not make much difference if you could not actually kick. I was also volunteering at the secondary school because they did not have a maths teacher at the time so I helped out. I felt thoroughly embedded and it was just an absolutely wonderful experience.

There was some political activism at the time, this being still the early days of multi-party elections and younger men in particular were beginning to look to other political parties to express their desires. I was anxious to avoid any involvement in politics—it could easily go badly wrong. I even left the village to work elsewhere when the hustings for CCM candidate for the district council came through. But villagers wanted to recruit me for various campaigns. I was asked to intervene in the struggle that they had with the district council to have a road built down the escarpment, allowing a more direct route to Sumbawanga. And one particularly active young man interviewed me about my findings towards the end of my time there. I told him about the problems of governance and government that I was working on, and would later write up. He was not impressed. 'Yes we know all that,' was his basic response. 'But dealing with that is our problem. We deal with it every day. You need to recommend in your research that we need more agricultural inputs so that we can improve our farming. That will make a difference here.' And so I was sent up the escarpment again to negotiate with a German business man who was buying up large quantities of crops across the region and persuade him to come and buy produce in Mtowisa.

And that was 2000 and coming back in 2016 I was quite nervous. I was thinking 'what was I going to find?' This is in a place which had been incredibly poor. There was so little there, at the same time as there was so much. There was a lake that was full of fish, the soil is incredibly fertile too, it is well positioned in between ecological zones where you can grow wheat on the escarpment and oranges in the valley. Coming back I did not know what to expect. Then I realized that unlike 1999 when you had to walk between the village and the regional town which took six to seven hours, now there was a bus service. And it turned out that the bus driver had been one of my pupils at the secondary school. He told me about this mzungu (white person) who had used to live in Mtowisa (laughter), and then reminded me of all the ways in which I had failed to control the secondary school class which I had conveniently forgotten. And then there was arriving and the bus being surrounded by bodabodas (motorbike taxi—which were completely new to me in Rukwa), and then the telephone mast and the other changes which so many of us have seen.

But the joy of the return was when you were recognized—because I had not been back for sixteen years because I'd lost touch with people. And I met again the children whom I had taught to play frisbee and each of them insisting that each was my favourite frisbee thrower. And then, during the survey, people coming up to you and insisting that 'When you have interviewed that person you need to come and talk to me next'. And I said 'It's a random sample' or words to that effect and they said 'I'm not having that you're coming to me next'. And that experience was remarkably enjoyable. Plus of course what I was finding was that the people who had generally speaking been worse off had had this pulse of resources being injected into their family incomes and homes.

And when I went back a couple of months ago again in April (and conducted the participatory wealth ranking of the whole village), I realized that the people I had surveyed were effectively part of a different community. The village had changed. My sample was no longer a means of providing a representative sample of what was going on in the village. And that was quite sobering but hugely important to learn.

Anna (Chapter 16)

We all have such embedded stories. It would be really interesting to forget about our research and think about ourselves as an individual in the place. I know lots of us have been getting involved in side projects. That human interaction with the community is really interesting and often tells us so much more of complexity and nuance than our research does. For me that sort of interaction with Uchira came before going there as a researcher.

I came to Uchira in a random way. I was an undergraduate at Cambridge, I had started studying natural sciences. I had found this growing sense of dissatisfaction with natural sciences as a way of understanding the world. I became very interested in ideas of poverty, development, and Africa. I had been to Tanzania in a gap year collecting data on the marine park efforts around Mafia Island. The bit I enjoyed most had been working in the local communities and particularly going out on boats with the fishermen, looking at what they were catching, but just interacting with them, understanding what they did every day and the types of challenges they faced.

My dissatisfaction with science did not have an outlet until I discovered anthropology and particularly social anthropology. I will always be grateful to the Cambridge system that allowed me to change in my second year to study anthropology. Making the switch from natural sciences to anthropology was not easy. There was a whole new set of philosophical debates to catch up on and a whole language that others who had done first year in anthropology already had and were equipped with. And of course essay writing skills is not something that natural scientists are necessarily blessed with.

Having changed to anthropology I was getting involved in groups like Survival International. I was going to a meeting of Survival International one evening when my friends and I noticed a small African woman walking down the street. She was also looking for the meeting, which was in a café nearby. This woman was a Tanzania doctor who was staying with friends in Cambridge and she told us this story in a very articulate and passionate way of how she had worked for years to build a health centre in this village called Uchira, in northern Tanzania, and how the Catholic Church had come in and wrestled it away from her and were accusing her of scandals and embezzlement.

Being excited 20-year-olds full of activist verve we said we would come and investigate the story. So we put together a little project and I ended up going with a couple of people including other social anthropologists. Our contact's story and association with the village were complicated, and she told us that we cannot be associated with her in the village. So she arranged for us to work with a village councillor, called Ernest Msuya.

Ernest became my very long-term collaborator. He was then in his 30s and a member of the village council. He was passionate and enthusiastic about the village and what could be done and how he was going to change things. And he was our guide. We were naïve. We had barely travelled and did not know much at all. He took us around the village and told us about the village in his own words. We interviewed a lot of people in all corners of the village, we went to every local institution—the schools, the churches, the village office, the health centres. This became the basis of my longitudinal data from 1996.

My research became, through Ernest, an archaeology of development projects in the village and also an assessment of village infrastructure and institutions. But we did not know what we were doing. We were making this up as we went along. We had done some reading on PRA and interview techniques but it was very much 'research by feel'. That became my undergraduate dissertation which studied aid and institutions through gift theory.

We also wrote a report called the Uchira Village Report which the village council told us they had found really useful when they tried to lobby for later village projects. From this lobbying they ended up with a big water project funded by GTZ. That water project later became the subject of my PhD when I returned to Uchira in 2002.

The link with Uchira between 1996 and 2002 was maintained by Ernest. He wrote me long letters and would send pictures about what was going on and he asked me to help raise funds for building a small health centre. In this sense, I cannot be a neutral objective academic about Uchira at all. In this period I was a young activist, raising money for building a health centre and supporting Ernest in his mission.

Coming back later to Uchira and doing my PhD was also a serendipitous affair. I never set out to do a PhD, that was the last thing I wanted to do on leaving university. I was going to go and work in development and 'save the world'. After university I had travelled, teaching English in Nepal. When I came back I had wanted to stay in Yorkshire (and not in London) and do something impactful. I got a job that involved mentoring disadvantaged youth in North Yorkshire. I was then also doing a Master's degree with the Open University and I was also fundraising for the village clinic for Ernest. I had not thought of an academic career and was just seeing where things took me.

Then, in 2001, I saw a job advertised at Bradford University for a ten-month part-time research assistant. This was on a DFID-funded project on sustainable livelihoods, and was going to cover Tanzania, Uganda, and South Africa. I thought it was my dream job and I applied for it even though I'd not finished my Master's degree. I was offered the job and Bradford shaped the next thirteen years of my life. I was able to do the PhD alongside that project and by 2007 was a permanently employed Senior Lecturer. So much for avoiding academia!

That first project for Bradford took me back to Uchira. Back in Uchira, I stayed in the Uchira Village Inn, and spent the evenings talking to the manager, Samuel Mdee and Ernest. From our evening conversations on the politics of the water project, I realized that the topic would make a good PhD. I talked about this with Frances Cleaver [Anna's supervisor then at Bradford] and we raised funds for it from the ESRC. We looked at village collective life, but using water project as a focus, and as a lens for understanding the politics of 'community-driven development'.

My research is rooted in a determination to be open about where you are in the research process and being open about how the research is being constructed. I suppose what I'm trying to say is that I realize I've always been part of the story and not simply recording it or observing it. I've always been very engaged and embedded different ways as a naïve undergraduate or then as a slightly more mature academic. I've always been conscious of not being the expert too. I am always continually surprised now after twenty years of engagement about how much I have to learn and still learn.

While I was doing my PhD, Samuel introduced me to his son, who was a young nervous-looking 24-year-old who wanted to work for me as a research assistant. I agreed to work with him; he could conduct a study of how young people in the village saw collective village life. Ernest was not too pleased about this. This young man Christopher duly came back to work with me and, well, now Chris and I have since been together for fifteen years and married for twelve. That meant a whole new level of intricacy opened up in terms of learning how families function, how expectations are managed, getting my head around remittances, and understanding how people are linked within the villages by kinship and friendship. I found that the more embedded you become, the more complex things are and the more interconnected. The less you know about a place the easier it is to research set simple parameters. You can go and count things that you think you recognize.

And this is what I found very hard about resurveying the same households, because how I saw the household had changed in that time. For example, when I was there in 2004 and doing my tap survey (as part of the PhD) and there was one particular tap, outside the house of the family that I married into. When I didn't know them, it looked as though there were three different households living around it. Two of them were female-headed households, and one of them was a male-headed household with a smarter house. When I married into that family, I realized that they actually all functioned as one household. Then thinking back through the life-history interviews from 2004–5 I realized that other interviewees were also part of the same extended family. So I have really struggled with that, the more I know about the village the more I find that the interconnections are so strong that I find it hard to differentiate between individual households because still the networks of sharing and reciprocity and expectations are so strong.

Rather, I think that one of the most valuable things to come out of this long-term engagement is actually being able to see social mobility dynamics now when

I look at the generations and how they change. As an example I think of my husband's younger brother who has gone from being a village boy at the local secondary school to now being a very successful consultant in the aid business in Dar es Salaam with many projects on the go. I saw how that happened, and how it was enabled partly through family networks and linkages, and our remittances from the United Kingdom that assisted to get him into university. He is hugely successful but now faces barriers of wealth and class in Dar es Salaam as he doesn't have the same family wealth as his social circle. Seeing his everyday experiences and those of other younger Tanzanians has helped me see how social differentiation is changing rapidly in Tanzania.

You do not see that so much at the village level. There are differences in the housing. But that interconnection with the urban and the opportunities you give your children are really influencing differentiation. This sort of longitudinal research can be the only type of research that can give us some of those insights.

Cosmas (Chapter 14)

I also went in an area where I was born and there are a couple of things that I remember that would be good to share. One of them is related to recruitment of research assistants who were from the area. These people were engaged in some other activities within the village. Apparently one of them was a secretary in the local court (we call it 'baraza'). And during his work I think he interacted with a lot of people, some in a good way and some in a bad way. And it did happen when we were as a team in different villages we went to a village where some members of that particular village had a case in court and it seems my research assistant had not treated them well (laughter). This was very bad for the team because they wanted to beat him but we were lucky because the chairman of the village rescued us; but it is an experience that I remember. We were lucky the research proceeded well.

And related to that the organization when we had village meetings or focus group discussions, oftentimes we could not do this without the assistance of the local authority like the village chairman or the village executive officer. But in one village, the village chairman had authority over villagers and he could choose who to speak and make some people not to say anything. In this one village that particular discussion was really controlled by the village chairman and we had to use other means to try and see these people and get further information rather than relying on this method of focus group discussion.

When I was working in my own village I really decided not to do any interviews (myself) because many of these people were related to me (my assistants undertook the interviews). And later on when I was looking at the papers after the interviews by the research assistants I noticed that a brother of mine who was a head of a household had given false information (laughter). It really disturbed me. The people did not know I was doing the research, my assistants were doing it. I did not do the interview. So I decided to call my brother and ask him 'You said this and this. Why did you say so because this is wrong, and you know it. Why did you want to spoil my research?' (laughter). He also felt very bad. He had to apologize but I am not sure of the answers I was even getting from my own village, whether these were really correct or not.

But a good thing also was that these people appreciated that they had someone in the university. By then in the 1990s there were only three of us from the locality in the universities. So seeing that there was someone from the locality who was in the university they did really appreciate it. It was a positive thing so they were ready to provide some information and assist me.

Esbern (Chapters 13 and 15)

I would like to say something about a study that goes all the way back to Ujamaa. As a student, before I finished my Master's, I got a student job and ended up spending six months in Iringa, Songea, and Mbeya working for the Water Master Plan Project that was planning domestic water supply for 1800 villages. I spent six months driving around from village to village with domestic engineers. This was before the tarmac road down to Songea was built and farmers were greeting me by slaughtering a chicken or even a goat. And it was a bit of a culture shock for me because for the first time when I came, in 1980, I was only 22.

During that period I realized that villagization, implemented six years earlier, was having a major impact on people's lives. I realized then that the villagization happened in the dry season of 1974 and the government moved people, from where they had lived on the foot-slopes of the mountains, with easy access to natural resources including water, to the roads to be accessible by bureaucrats and the influence of modernity. This meant most people in villages were now settled in higher altitude than the water sources and the Water Master Plan had to plan gravity water schemes that got water supplies from as far as 50km away. So I wrote my Master's project about the water scheme. And then after my Master's, I immediately got this research grant to go to Tanzania and do further work on this topic. Back then, when I did not have a family, I could spend a long time in Tanzania where everything was slow. I went for nine months for the first trip, I spent three weeks out in the field and then one week with colleagues from the University of Dar es Salaam, and then three weeks back in the field again. It was a time when there was poverty. I mean real poverty. Some people in Maliwa village had never seen a small car. There was not a single wheel in the whole village, there was no machine. The only cloth poor women had was one kanga. There were no new hoes in the community shop and people used worn-out hoes. I took a hoe from the Chinese factory in Dar es Salaam for each of the families that I interviewed and I should never have done that because then I was like Santa Claus and everybody wanted things from me and I totally spoiled my reputation as a researcher (laughter). But there was real poverty, dire poverty.

And for some reason I had this drive towards seeing people far away, so I ended up with villagers in very marginal areas that you had to drive a whole day to reach. Today I do not know why I chose those villages so far away (laughter). Because it took me a long time to drive out there. You would have to drive around with 120 litres of petrol on the back seat, two of those green 60 litres plastic containers, because you would have to be able to drive all the way from Dar es Salaam and back again, as the petrol stations up-country were often empty.

In Maliwa village they had a very low productive local bean variety and so I went to talk to the national bean breeder at Uyole agricultural research station and she gave me an appropriate modern variety that I brought back to the farmers. Farmers were still cultivating this bean variety when I revisited the village and they had named it after me, the bean is called mzungu.

It has been a great experience to revisit these villages and I really appreciate having this opportunity to mentally travel back in time. Quite a few recognized me, and I gradually could recognize some of the farmers.

Verdiana (Chapter 14)

In 2007 I was completing my Master's and that was my first time to engage in research activities. I was looking at the Impact of Mining Activities on Forest Resources and I took a case study of one of the mines in Mara Region (Nyamongo Gold Mine). I had prepared all my research tools for focus group discussions and key informant interviews and questionnaires to the households. I had all the permits for the research activity. I was set for the field. I went to the villages. I selected two villages in that area. Remember in these villages the ethnic group is the Kuria. You have probably read about them, they are such a harsh people. If you are a woman or a girl you are nothing in that society, women are not valued as per their culture.

So when I went to the villages then the village chairman said 'It is so difficult for you to interview the people in this village or to talk to them with your questionnaire. So give me all the questionnaires and I will distribute them to the people in the village and give me one week (laughter) and you will collect the questionnaires from me.' And there was no other alternative. So I handed all my questionnaires to him and went back home with the expectation that I would get my filled in questionnaires after a week. And after a week I went back to collect the questionnaires as planned and he said 'You know I was sick. I have not distributed the questionnaires. Give me another week.' So I gave him another week, yet he managed to collect only five filled questionnaires out of one hundred questionnaires that I handed to him. I was confused and disappointed.

And then time was not on my side, I was under pressure because the university has its deadlines on submitting the dissertation for examination, you have to do the field work at a particular time and you have to come back to the university and write. I was thinking 'What am I going to do now?' So I asked him if he could give me somebody to guide me in the village and do the interviews myself. He agreed to give me someone to guide me to the households. So I stayed in the villages for about seven days and I got cooperation from the people and about fifty questionnaires were completed. And from that day I said 'Why am I doing all this if the people who I'm interacting with are not ready to give me the information?' I did not want to do more research after my Master's because the fieldwork was so hard.

But I was able to meet the deadlines and my dissertation was passed. Since I was an employee of the University of Dar es Salaam since November 2006 and one of the requirements was I to do a PhD, I was thinking 'Now I have to go back to the field!' (laughter). And writing a proposal was really a challenge for me, what should I write about? Which place should I go to in Tanzania? Will I go back to the same place as last time? Luckily enough I was involved in a project that was looking at small and medium-sized towns in Tanzania around mountains. For Tanzania Mt Rungwe was selected for the project and I thought I should try the southern part of the country and that is why I went to Rungwe. Although I was not an indigenous person, surprisingly, the people there were very co-operative, they were very welcoming, they asked me questions and I did not get any difficulties. So even this time when Cosmas asked me to assist with his research I was very comfortable in Mbeya. So I realized in Tanzania, we are much divided societies where you go to fieldwork and it becomes so difficult to get the information. It is only recently that women are valued in some of these societies. Indeed it was difficult for a woman to do her research work in such societies.

Christine

And in Maasai communities too, I did my fieldwork on the other side of Meru—dry rangelands. I just had to become the daughter of the chairman (laughter). I was walking around with him and he was saying 'Look, this is my daughter as you can see she looks like that [Christine is tall]'. Having the support of the big man in the village allowed me easy access to my respondents. I could also hold a public meeting, which I did not know I could given that I was just a young woman then and the fact that only men could show up or speak at such meetings. Often, I was taken out of the subject area to answer some questions about if I really believed that men and women could get equal rights and how the world would be if that happened. These discussions extended to the chairman's compound in the evenings after work. I was asked my opinions about genital mutilation (about which I knew little), marriage, and children (with a lot of concerns that I did not have any of these at the age of 26). I gained confidence progressively as a young woman in such a patriarchal society.

I came to learn that I inspired some of these Maasai parents without realizing it. I did my Master's research when I had just been employed as a tutorial assistant at the University of Dar es Salaam. I could therefore convince the parents that it was worth educating girl children the same way they did their boys. Two years down the line, I hosted the chairman's children in Dar es Salaam—Moses and Paulina—who had come for their university matriculation examinations. After the first degree, Moses went back to look after his herd of cattle. Paulina (having no cattle of her own), studied a Master's degree and got employed at Sokoine University of Agriculture. These are important reflections as I work on my next paper about 'Mountain Students'. In this paper I discuss how Meru parents (especially those in the middle wealth and poor group) have used farm returns to invest in their children's education.

Katherine (Chapter 6)

I did not go into the field intending to do a classic ethnography but I felt compelled to do so after living there. At this time in anthropology, more traditional topics of ethnography were considered very colonial and passé so the ethnography I eventually wrote was an unconventional path to choose at the time.

I found my way to the Iraqw homeland of Mama Issara through the advice of two people; one, Garry Thomas, was an anthropologist friend of my brother who had done some work for the American Friends Service as a volunteer and worked in Karatu (then Mbulu District). The other was my advisor, John Middleton, who had two bits of advice for me; one was 'don't go live in a swamp' and the other was 'why not go to Mbulu where Ed Winter has done some work'. So, off I went. It was a bit like throwing a dart on a map. Garry put me in touch with his former research assistant, Patrick Qorro, who in 1990 was the member of Parliament for Karatu. He was the MP for twenty years. I met Patrick, his wife Martha, and their children in Dar es Salaam and he very generously set everything up for me. I was young and impressionable and also extremely grateful for all the help that he and his wife Martha (who is still at the university) gave me. He passed me on to one of his friends in Arusha who then put me on a bus. Patrick's driver then picked me up on the escarpment and took me to Mbulumbulu, where I spent a few days with the family. I was then deposited with one of Patrick's friends in Karatu and I spent my Christmas holidays with that family who remain friends today. Patrick was also friends with the district commissioner of Mbulu with whom I stayed after leaving Karatu. After a week or so of staying in the DC's guesthouse, I was taken to Kainam and deposited in a house of a primary school teacher who was away on a teacher training programme. In the end, I had very little choice where I was going, but I was enormously grateful for the help and hospitality I got along the way.

The house in the primary school was a bit of a disaster and the teachers were really nervous about putting this mzungu there. So instead, they put me in a shed (laughter)! This was a temporary measure until they figured out what to do with me. They were very worried about me because clearly I had no idea what I was doing or how to live in a rural community in Tanzania. I think they were thinking 'she doesn't know how to cook, she doesn't know how to carry water on her head, what we can do with this lady, how are we going to care for her, she's going to die and they're going to come after us (laughter)'. So for two weeks they cooked all my meals and delivered my bathwater for me and after that I said 'This cannot go on, you can't keep looking after me, I do know how to live—I live on my own in America, I can handle this.' And so I moved into my own house, learned how to carry water on my head, which was a source of enormous hilarity, and got on with figuring out what I was doing out there.

Soon after I arrived, there was a village meeting with officials visiting from the district. I sat in the crowd but was quickly ushered to the 'special visitors' dais. I protested but one woman, herself a Chagga outsider, said 'they will be worried about you anyway because of metimani so you should sit with the officials'. I had no idea what she was talking about and little interest in sitting with the government officials but obeyed. Later, I came to learn what she meant. Because I was woman alone, I was quite suspicious. Among the Iraqw, women who become pregnant out of wedlock or who have suffered miscarriages or stillborn or other deaths are quarantined [this is called metimani]. In the past, unwed pregnant girls were cast out in the bush. So, as my Chagga friend seemed to be implying, my Iraqw hosts might be wondering 'Is that's what happened to her, has she got cast out, is that why she's here?' (laughter). Clearly, the explanation I gave about wanting to learn about life in their community made absolutely no sense. Who goes around the world and does that kind of thing?

In the literature, the Iraqw had always been held up as excellent farmers which led me to propose a study on agrarian change and drivers of change. But, after a couple of months of talking about farming, I got bored doing that, so I started letting people guide me about what they wanted me to learn about. And what I ended up coming up with was something that looked very much like a salvage ethnography, in that it captured everything they wanted to tell me and made sure I took down. Older men and women were particularly keen for me to hang out with them, attend their rituals, and to write down their stories because their own children had very little interest in these topics. Young people thought I was a crazy. Why did I hang out with all these old people all the time and listen to them?

Some told me people were asking 'Has this person really come all the way from America to listen to this? These people really have money to throw away' (laughter). Living among Iraqw was easy in many respects and challenging in others. Iraqw learned in the colonial era to appear to agree to colonial administrators' demands, but then secretively pursue their own agendas. While extremely welcoming, it took a good year for people to be comfortable enough with me to begin inviting me to their rituals and elder council (men's and women's) meetings and so on.

Two years of living in that village totally transformed my life; I don't see the world in the same way and I never will again. For example, the Iraqw have beliefs about numbers. There are good numbers and bad numbers. Good numbers are even numbers that can be divided easily among people. So, today, I cannot give someone an odd-numbered thing now. I cannot hand them something which is only in one or three, which would be shocking. When I had a post-doc, I went back for a year and for the first time had a vehicle. I had a little Suzuki Samurai. Now, I could give people lifts! I'd pick up as many people as I could along the road to Mama Issara. Often, the people most vigorously asking for a lift were young people. As I drove along however, I saw more and more older people, men and women, usually carrying loads on their backs or shoulders and I could kick the youngsters out to give the older travellers a ride. I would tell the younger ones 'I don't want to be cursed by those old people'. Iraqw believe if you do bad things to people, they can get justice by cursing you and bad things will then happen to you. It became quite a joke and younger travellers started telling people 'forget it, she only gives lifts to old people' (laughter).

I have been very lucky to go back again and again over the years. In 2001, I went with my family and my two-month-old child for a year. It was great being able to take our child 'to work' but I quickly realized I could not get anything done—everyone totally ignored me to play with him and I couldn't get any news out of anyone (laughter). So I learned to leave him at home in Mbulu. Going back over the years has been great but it is also bittersweet. When I was on my own and on foot, I knew every path, I knew every stone, I knew every tree, houses of friends, etc. But when you have a vehicle and go for shorter periods of time, it is not really the same experience as living day to day for a long period. And, over the years, friends have died, moved away, gone to university, and many have started families and some are even now grandparents. The friendships I have made there continue and we pick up where we last left off whenever I turn up. I do miss the time I had as a student when I could sit around and just yak with people. That is how you really learn interesting stuff!

I was struck, in listening to Tina say she was not surprised by things when she worked in her home community. Recently, I have had a similar feeling of not only not being surprised, but thinking I could predict what people would say next! In interviews, as people were talking, I was thinking 'I know exactly what you're going to say now' (laughter) and sure enough, yup here it comes. While this familiarity has made it harder to find new things to write about, it is also a source of enormous comfort.

Sulle (Chapter 6)

I remember when Katherine was doing her studies and I had just joined primary school in 1991 the second year that she was there. And you could see this young white lady running and fetching rice from Mbulu town. And every time she passed we would stop in the class to watch her (laughter). It was really amazing and we were inspired that she could do things we could not do. And then she came with her boyfriend Sasha. He did not know how to dig with a hand hoe (laughter). It was really funny (laughter).

Throughout this time I did not really talk to her until I finished my primary school. And I did not know what I was going to study because the highest person who you could see who had achieved things was the head teacher who was smart in the standards of those days. The most important thing I remember from primary school is that I only studied hard because I did not want anybody to beat me at class. I just wanted to be number one. After that I got two admissions. I was admitted to seminary and to the government school. I did not go to seminary for a while because I did not have enough money but the priest convinced me to go and then I went to seminary.

So after I finished seminary I went home and the first plan was to build a house so that I could study and so that my last-born brother could study—I wanted him to go to secondary school. And then a messenger came to say that Mwalimu (teacher) Johnny was looking for me, he lived with Katherine in a compound. I went to this teacher and he said 'Katherine is looking for a research assistant.' And I said 'O, but that you know my English is not good' but we went to do interviews. There were four of us others from form 4, others from form 6, and some had diplomas.

So I got recruited and we started this work for seven months and when Katherine went to Dar es Salaam to do other studies she recommended me to a German anthropologist. And then this German anthropologist said you should go to the diocese director so that they can hire you. Then immediately when I get there the guy says 'Do you have form 6?' 'No.' 'Diploma?' 'No.' 'Well we don't need you!' (laughter). So I went back to Katherine and said 'I did not get that job'. I was so stressed because the job I was doing with her understanding democracy and development from the perspective of the rural people was so interesting. It was really empowering me in terms of writing and research was the first thing I wanted to do. And this German lady came back to Katherine and said to her 'He was not employed', and Katherine said 'You must get Sulle if you want your project to succeed'. So then this lady said 'I'm going to hire you using my own money', and I was sitting with colleagues with form 6 who were my elders.

Then she gave me questionnaires to see how they translated from English to Swahili and my first impression was that these guys did a direct translation. You won't get answers from the Iraqw. They were like 'Kuna ng'ombe ngapi?' ('There are how many cows?'—laughter). You do not ask the Iraqw like that, they will be annoyed and tell you another story and then you leave. This is a very important aspect and I have learned throughout my research really getting good questions for people.

So I started working with her and she was paying me and then I joined high school and I was working with Katherine whenever she returned to the village. And at home I had her book and was reading it. And then other people would tell me 'Sulle, do you remember the lady who wrote that book' and I would say 'Yes, yes. She knows Iraqw and our traditions more than we do. She knows about ways of dressing (ma'assay) that have now gone.' And when I went back to do interviews and focus group discussions, things that we lived have actually gone, some have really gone. There is no ma'assay, there is no metimani, which is when a girl gets pregnant when she is not married then she is chased out. Nowadays those things are off. The key question of the project is the methodology: how do you reconcile things that you do not know? Katherine knew these things were happening. I partially know them. But I did not live with them, they are gone. So reconciling these things is a really important aspect and documenting them. Because some of the things my daughter will not know at all. They are all gone. So it shows that the project we are doing is really important. For my group is key and I sense this is true others here. It is a really thoughtful project it gives us an opportunity to reflect back to see what is happening to us.

But I want to end with a note on my experience in other places and how they inform my current project. I did my first research project around the Serengeti. The first village was Rubanda. And these guys asked me 'Where are you coming from?' 'St Augustine University, Mwanza.' 'Do you have a car and a driver?' 'Yes.' 'O, it looks like you have been sent by the VIP' (laughter). 'I said what is the VIP?' They said 'You know it.' They started talking ki-iramba. They wanted to set me alight. Because there were some professors from the University of Dar es Salaam who did an environmental impact assessment and suggested that this village was inhibiting ecological systems and so it must be evicted.

So they started telling me all these stories, so I had to start my negotiations. I had to use a lot of diplomacy. I have no idea who are the VIP, I have just got a scholarship, and all this stuff. That was how I survived. And then my second visit was to Tarime. So I told my driver 'You stand here, I am going to interview people'. And I met this young lady. I greeted her and she said 'What are you looking for?' I was surprised. So immediately I started being interviewed (laughter) and she said 'How did you come here, where is your car? No, you want to take our land' (laughter). Literally, she chased me away so I could not do any interview. I could not do any interview in Tarime.

But after having all those hard times, I did research in other places in Tanzania and I never had any bad experience. In fact it's only now Katherine's project is taking me back so I have actually done nothing apart from Katherine's project in my own village. I have been immersed in Kilombero and other parts of Tanzania where people are so friendly. In fact you [overseas researchers] do not get more challenges than we do. So blending this type of experience from other groups in Tanzania brings out the lives in Tanzania and how they vary from one place to another.

Willie (Chapter 9)

Dan's account from Rukwa makes me want to say something about embeddedness in fieldwork. Before I went to Burunge I had done anthropological fieldwork in Marakwet, Kenya, together with my family, which at the time included two children under five. This experience came to influence my time in Burunge in at least two ways. One was the value of making 'the field' home, and the other was an openness to allow your research planning to be sabotaged.

When children make your paths into a society, you find yourself moving in directions you had not planned to go. The children take you to people you might not otherwise have chosen to socialize with. You also end up in situations, and conflicts, you had not in the least planned. It quickly became obvious that there are particular insights to be gained from undirected encounters.

This I conclude from practical experience. However, it could equally well be argued theoretically. Wittgenstein described his philosophical investigations as travelling criss-cross over a wide field of thought.[2] Following just one direction cripples one's thoughts, he argued. Anthropologists are used to changing research designs when realities change. What matters is being honest and allowing oneself to be taken by surprise.

I had a research grant to go to Marakwet to study a somewhat technical topic on the relation between ecological zones and demography. That was what I could get research money for, but my personal interests were broader, and more ethnographic. Planning for the fieldwork I read among many other things John Middleton's book The Study of the Lugbara.[3] In the introduction he writes that the brief for his work was to study the Lugbara. Full stop. That told of a time that seemed long gone already in the early 1970s, but it appealed to me, and having a reasonably long period of time in Marakwet ahead of me, more than two years,

[2] Wittgenstein (2009). [3] Middleton (1970).

I thought I should not miss this opportunity to make my study as comprehensive as possible. There was also another sentence in Middleton's book, already on page one in fact, that came to act as a loadstar to me. He wrote that 'what I did was decided very largely by the Lugbara themselves'. The time in Marakwet taught me to let what happens govern the field research more than the set research design.

I came to the village Goima (in the Burunge area) in 1985 by chance. I was evaluating a land rehabilitation project in the Kondoa Irangi Highlands.[4] This made me follow cattle herds expelled from the highlands into the surrounding plains to study if the conservation intervention had meant that the soil erosion problems had been exported elsewhere. Goima was one of the villages reported to have received livestock. Arriving there, I was captivated: a serene atmosphere, the blessed shade from fully grown trees in the middle of dry land, the white gorogoombimo flowers against red soil, the old primary court in its quiet decay, the slow pace of trade in the marketplace, which was but the space below a ficus tree in the middle of the village. The flowering jacaranda trees at the primary school, birds shining in metal-bright colours, and an unassuming but warm welcome at the village office, housed in an old grain warehouse dating from the colonial period. When I later, in 1991, was offered the possibility to make a study in the Burunge Hills, I instantly decided to make Goima village the home base.

People have different styles of fieldwork. Detached, objective research is a desirable ideal, of course, but we all have our personal inclinations and yens. Mine were to be involved, to get close. I liked being in Goima, and the Burunge Hills, despite its widespread poverty, the lack of water, the feeling of remoteness, and the harsh living conditions that most people there faced in the early 1990s. When I think of it, perhaps the relative remoteness was in fact more of a bonus than a liability. At home I live on an island, which creates its own mentality of both self-reliance and fellowship. When people talked about life in the hills, I could recall phrases and attitudes from home.

The fieldwork in Burunge was organized in shorter periods compared to Marakwet, a few months at a time, spread out over a three-year period. But having had the experience of living family life in Marakwet, I somehow ended up constructing a similar environment also in the Burunge Hills. Back in 1985, during the evaluation of the land rehabilitation programme, I had worked together with a then newly graduated forester, Joseph Mduma, and we got along well. In 1991, I made enquiries if he could join me also this time, and the Forest Department graciously released him for the entire period of fieldwork. So, there we were, two outsiders in Burunge, away from our respective families. We worked long days and spent the evenings on a small porch outside the house where we stayed, going through the day's experiences and contemplating all other things in life.

[4] Östberg (1986).

Our room was adjacent to the Catholic church in Goima. As it happens, we are both Lutherans but became close with the fathers and sisters of the Goima parish. We participated in the Sunday mass and got to know some of the parish members rather well. The weekday morning masses provided tranquil moments, observing the light entering the church hall while listening to the sisters' voices greeting the day. On Sundays, the compound was crammed with people. We made acquaintances and the parish became more and more of a family to us.

We made a survey of agriculture and livelihoods in Goima and the neighbouring village Mirambu during different times of the agricultural year. The farm survey provided us with valuable information for understanding natural resource management in the Burunge area, but when we became totally mesmerized with how the Burunge theorize about how soils form and change over time, we no longer found time to write up our survey. It was there in my notebooks, but that was all.

Two decades later the 'Longterm livelihood change in Tanzania' project came along. The question was put if I had primary data from the early 1990s which could be used for this project. For twenty-five years I had had a guilty conscience for having spent all that time—my time, Mduma's time, the farmers' time—on a survey which was never properly used. It was wonderful to be able to answer that I did indeed have such data, and that I would be thrilled at the prospect that they finally could come to good use.

The records were handwritten in Swedish. The process of turning the notes into a spreadsheet took weeks and weeks. Entering the figures into Excel columns turned out to be a slow process. As I plunged into my old notebooks, I was reliving the interviews, recalling the farmers we had met. The spreadsheets mentally took me back to the Burunge Hills.

But eventually the database was ready, and it became time to return to Goima and Mirambu for the re-study. Joseph Mduma, now a seasoned senior forest officer in Katesh, sacrificed his annual leave to return to the Burunge Hills. We had been back on short follow-ups a few times, but now we again had a chance to work properly in Goima and Mirambu. There we were joined by Olivia Howland, Cathbert Mwanyika, and Einhard Mwanyika, of the 'Longterm livelihood change' project, providing their expertise on organizing and conducting follow-up surveys.

Twenty-five years after our first study, Mduma and I could marvel at the changes the area had gone through, particularly the last ten years. In a chapter in this book we analyse the developments, but perhaps our very first impressions, noted down in a blog post,[5] best captures how amazed we were over the striking contrasts between the early 1990s and the mid-2000s.

[5] https://livelihoodchangeta.wixsite.com/tanzania/single-post/2016/11/08/Getting-to-Know-Goima-Anew-Tracing-Change-in-a-Tanzanian-Village-with-a-25-Year-Perspective.

Dan

From my point of view, with respect to turning the interviews into spreadsheets, I did not appreciate that Willie was not just turning Swedish longhand into English spreadsheets but was also re-living, re-remembering, re-thinking, and re-visiting the experience of the interviews. From my point of view, I think we had a contract (laughter). Willie sent me a sample of three written-up questionnaires and after a certain time period he was going to complete sixty-seven interviews. But I just remember that after three or four months I wrote to Willie and said 'How is the process going on?' and he said 'The mushroom harvest has been such a distraction' (prolonged laughter). I'm being unfair. It wasn't just the mushroom harvest; he was also planting potatoes (more laughter). So working with Willie has also meant that I've learned a great deal about the domestic economy of the island [Gotland] where he lives.

Vesa-Matti (Chapter 10)

Not being an anthropologist, I was more or less ordered by my supervisor: 'Do not live in the village that you are going to study. You will get too embedded, you will not be objective. You have to stay somewhere else.' So, I ended up in Katesh, 25km from the village, which meant I needed a car.

My supervisor also told me not to work with any corrupt people, so I had to ask Swedish aid workers in the area if they knew anyone who was not corrupt. They recommended the district forest officer, but being one of few that weren't corrupt, he was totally swamped with Swedish aid work, so he tried to find me someone who was not corrupt that I could work with. He connected me to the most corrupt person in the district council (laughter), the district planning officer. He recommended that I study Gitting village, which he considered fulfilled my criteria of a rich village with major problems of land degradation.

He assigned the district beekeeping officer and two more research assistants who had detailed knowledge of Gitting village to work with me, and that was how the study started. I came to the village in 1991 and asked for the village household register. The village officials said 'We don't have one. But we may have something from 1974.' It took two weeks and then I got a handwritten copy of all the names of heads of households that were allocated land in the villagization in 1974. However, many of them had died, some had moved, and a lot of names had changed. So, I spent three weeks with a very big air photograph of the village and twenty people around a table asking who lived where. I ended up with 632 names of household heads, most of them men, of families in the village.

After the compiling the roster I tried to communicate with the village government. I wanted to start the study by interviewing the chairman of the village. I was told he was not there that day, that he was travelling. Finally after four weeks someone said that he was in Endasaki (a nearby village). I asked 'what is he doing there?' and I was told he stayed at an illegal liquor bar (gongo bar). I said we must go there to interview the chairman and my field assistants were very unhappy with that. It was an interesting place because on the one side there was a long table where the brew was served and on the other side there were beds. People actually drank at the table and then went to sleep at the beds and more or less lived at the bar and the village chairman was one of those people. It was not possible to interview him because he was too drunk. Later however I could interview him and it was clear that he was a puppet for the rich farmers in the village without any ambition to function as chairman.

A village executive officer from a different village, who lived in Gitting, helped me out and we could start a wealth ranking. It was very difficult to work in Gitting because there was no functioning administrative structure. Everything was unregulated, there was no one with whom I could communicate. Finally I started to talk to ordinary middle farmers that were identified in the wealth ranking because they had good control and were serious and actually farming in a way that wasn't degrading their soils. It became very clear after the wealth ranking and some interviews that the problem in the village was not lack of knowledge or ignorance among farmers (which was a standard answer among politicians and subject matter specialists in the district at the time) but rather the lack of a supportive administrative structure. The 'socialist' structure had been replaced (if it ever existed) by a patriarchal structure led by the richest five households in the village that catered for the exploitation of the village majority.

I could do my study but it took three and a half years before I had the data that I needed. I had been known as somebody who defended the middle farmers from the local big shots and the rich farmers were quite aggressive against me. By using the wealth ranking I could randomly sample farmers of all categories, from the poorest to the richest. While doing the interviews it became more and more obvious that there existed a hidden local 'structure' that I failed to get information about using my research techniques. Therefore, I made a post-doc study where I traced Iraqw people from their core area in Mama Issara to the areas they had expanded to in Manyara Region with a historical perspective on how the Iraqw moved out from their core area. I visited sixty-five households and made a network analysis of each household as well as their clan genealogies stretching back up to fourteen generations. I also identified their network strategies as well as their natural resource management institutions. Unfortunately I got a position at the newly established Södertörn University before I had published my findings and much of these data are still waiting to be analysed and published. Instead I was totally swamped in building a new university, intriguing but exhausting! At Södertörn University I initiated an educational programme in development studies and initiated a fieldwork course for undergraduate students. In 2019, 421 students from my university had gathered data in Manyara Region for their bachelor's theses. Because of that I have had chances to revisit Manyara Region twice a year since my post-doc project. This also meant that I had a very long experience of the changes that have taken place in the Manyara area that was very useful when doing the longitudinal re-study of Gitting.

In 2012 Dan approached me about doing a re-survey in Gitting, I went to Gitting on my next trip (in 2013) and I could not recognize the village at all. I had not been there since 1994. To start with there were electricity poles going along the road (this was new). Coming to the village centre I could recognize the old lorry that was already broken down in 1994 and I could see the useless warehouse. And there were a lot of trees, which was a very big difference. In Gocho they had a commercial centre with a lot of shops and restaurants. The whole village was totally changed. And as far as I could tell there was much less erosion compared to the 1990s, when it was treeless. People took care of their land, people co-operated to stop water from flowing over the long slopes and creating erosion, it was indeed a totally different world!

When Olivia and I came back to do the re-study in 2015, I was amazed. I went to the village office and asked 'Do you have a register of the households?' They said 'Yes, when do you need it?' I said 'Well, as quickly as possible'. They said 'Well, come back tomorrow'. And that was quite a change from sitting for weeks with an air photograph asking who lives in each house. In 2015, the whole list just came up. Of course there were some discrepancies in the lists, but we managed to get 1,137 names of households. From 632 to 1,137 households in thirty-four years with very little in-migration but quite extensive outmigration from the village!

The alcohol business was very different. In the early '90s the women had to brew local beer called mangure to get some income. In those days, at 6 o'clock in the morning Gittingers walked to different mangure places to identify the best beer and it was mangure every day for many men. There was no regulation. This time I could not see a mangure place and women controlled that the stipulated pub times were adhered to.

I recognized a lot of people and they recognized me as well. Others had died, mainly the rich ones. I made a study of the farmers who had helped me with the ranking. One of the very nice things that came up there is that women are becoming more independent because they can control the income of pigs and chickens. They get a lot of income from that. The men are complaining because women have too much power. All in all, social stratification which was so extraordinary in 1991 was now much less. The rich had become poorer and the poor richer contrary to my and many others' expectations.

I have now, as I am retired, become involved in an NGO, 'Manyara Organic Farming Initiative', where two hundred farmers from ten villages in Hanang and Babati Districts are converting from conventional to regenerative organic farming. The project will run for the coming three years and will initiate organic certification, use internationally proven methods to increase production, and make agriculture more sustainable.

Monique (Chapter 5)

Like Dan we got banished to Rukwa, which felt a bit like Siberia. This was 1991. In my case, I had been working in Eyasi and my husband in Serengeti. There were, at that time, too many researchers in the Serengeti. They were fighting with each other over everything—from the implications of putting radio collars around hyena necks to the ethics of families luring each others' nannies away from each other to look after their respective growing broods of children. It all seemed so pathetic. This is Tanzania just after the 1980s 'dark age'—really, really poor. It was terrible. And here were these wazungu fighting over nannies (laughter).

So in 1990 the (then) Director of Wildlife looked at Tim [Caro, Monique's husband] and me, and suggested we could cope outside of Serengeti—which we viewed as a compliment. He flew us all over the country in his little Cesna. I remember well, he was so short he could not actually see out of the front of the aeroplane. As we came west of Rungwa the rain started and we were enclosed by thick cloud. He remarked, 'I cannot see anything'. He asked Tim 'You look out left' while I looked out right. I was breastfeeding a tiny baby who was turning blue because it was so high up (laughter), and we were looking for the Central Line railway tracks that would take us towards Mpanda, and (hopefully) the airstrip. So this was how we ended up in Katavi five years later, where I started working in the villages that lie south of the national park (in Mpimbwe, then part of Rukwa Region).

We got funding in place by 1995 and, now with a 5-year-old, we started living in the national park at a small ranger station, because of my husband's research in conservation biology and park-based research. From a professional perspective I didn't much like living there, despite the natural beauty of the Ikuu River. I felt like Malinowski, living at my lovely campsite, and toddling off to the village for brief sojourns. I also felt I was setting a bad precedent for my graduate students—commuting to the village and back. How would the local community, who suffered from the depredations of lions, elephants, hippos, and bushpigs, ever trust me? Finally thank goodness we got kicked out of living in the national park (a long story involving a dog, a horse in foal, hippos on the Ikuu flood plain, and a pregnant woman—you work it out (laughter)). So we ended up moving down to Mpimbwe, and settling in the village of Kibaoni.

Twenty years have passed with comings and goings from the site. It was fascinating to follow the fates and fortunes of families for so long. Like Tina, however, I also found that, after fifteen years, I knew exactly what was coming up, and I was becoming less curious, maybe a bit bored, and asking less carefully thought-out questions. That's one of the reasons why we finally left that study site, fatigue. Now we have moved to working on Pemba (Zanzibar).

What are my personal reflections on my times in Mpimbwe? This is something I have often asked other researchers working in the global south but now it's my turn to answer.[6]

For me going with my family was vital. Living as a professor in America, life is so pressurized. I watch my colleagues in the summer. They send their kids to camp and write papers or teach a summer course. We, on the other hand, would just pack up as a family on 1 June and spend three to four months in Mpimbwe as a family. It was just so fascinating to have a kid living with me in the villages. As he grew up he would do amazing anthropology, telling me for example whom he had heard was really related to whom, or what the local scuttlebutt was from a kid's perspective.

I loved to watch the freedom that he had, and the trust he could place in others. Arriving in the village after many months' absence, and fresh (or not so) from the four-day drive to Pimbwe (yes, from Dar, it took that long, and that's without car problems), we would sleep heavily and long. Our son however would shoot off into the village early the next morning to find his friends. We would have to go and sort out paperwork at the divisional office in Usevya, and I remember once seeing my son on the horizon with two of his friends, all on an old Chinese bike together, constantly falling off as they hit the matuta (cultivation ridges). It's so great to be able give your kid the freedom they don't have elsewhere (or at least in many parts of the world) because you're worried about security.

So for me the personal experience of doing fieldwork, together with the family experience and all the amazing stuff I've learned from people, has just made it all worthwhile. It's a wonderful lifestyle and I'm incredibly grateful to the people of Tanzania for allowing me to share life's adventures with some of them. I think we mentioned it before but some of us have made our careers on the basis of these studies we've done—we should never forget that.

We have tried in the last six or seven years in Mpimbwe to give back. We have worked with educational, environmental, and poverty alleviation programmes in Mpimbwe that are persisting now as vibrant grassroots campaigns. Some of these programmes I initiated, helping with finding external funding, in part because I felt guilty for my privilege, and in part because I was now in a position to give back and raise money and support community groups. I should also acknowledge that I did it in part because Mpimbwe is very poor, as you have seen in my work, and people were always asking me for help. It was killing me, and I was unable to respond to people individually. So I proposed we set up an organization—in fact a series of organizations and campaigns—to address the big challenges in the area.

[6] Borgerhoff Mulder, and Logsdon (1996).

Mistakenly, I thought by setting up the organization it would protect me from these demands (prolonged laughter). Yes, quite the contrary. I thought I was smart, but it just made things more and more complicated. Yet, as we have pulled away from Mpimbwe to Pemba the programmes have taken on a life of their own,[7] and although we still serve on the board and advise a lot on fund raising, it's really great to see people in Mpimbwe start to engage with the outside world on their own terms and to achieve their own personal successes.

Agnes (Chapter 11)

When I started my PhD I wanted to do long-term fieldwork in Zimbabwe. I was focusing on small-town urban growth, migration, and remittances. It was a very geographical project. In Stockholm University, where I was based, there was a group of human geographers who were inspired by anthropological and ethnographic approaches. I had come from Lund, which had a much more quantitative approach. And I came to Stockholm and they thought that I was incredibly backwards and square (laughter). And so I tried to take the anthropological route in terms of embeddedness and I was planning to spend a year in the field. But the process of getting research permits and all the formalities of going to Zimbabwe turned out to be very complex. I had started out by doing a pilot study in a small town in eastern Zimbabwe, but formalizing the research process for my main stretch of field work took a lot of time. While waiting for the process to be completed I went for one round of archival work staying in Harare. By the time all the permits were in place the political crisis had escalated and my time was running out. This was in the late '90s. I ended up having to do my fieldwork really quickly because my funding was running out and the political situation was difficult. I had done some basic language classes but nothing proper and so I felt a bit of an impostor. I ended up living in the township for about three months staying with this family that I had met—the lady who cleaned at the hotel where I had stayed the first time around took me in. In the end, no one, not even the war veterans and the party functionaries who wondered what I was up to asked to see the research permit! Living with the family in the township turned out to be the best way of handling any suspicions. And I was in between doing it properly (living on site) and having to handle the plan B that had been imposed on me. This is a golden thread through this collection, at least from the perspective of researchers from the global north working in African contexts. You set out to work in African contexts to do one thing and you end up doing something quite different.

[7] http://www.lcmo.or.tz/.

For my PhD I was interested in finding out about livelihood systems across space and the linkages between the rural and the urban from an urban perspective. So I had this idea of doing in-depth interviews to capture household structures and household functioning and food remittances. Some of these were things that I only realized were important while I was in the field. But I did not come back with the data that I was expecting to. It was also winter and rained a lot (laughter), and the sampling and interviewing were hard and so my fieldwork data were not sufficient. So I had to boost them with other data and I ended up doing quite a lot of archival work, including in the United Kingdom in London and Oxford. The particular town where I was based was originally a refugee camp for Polish refugees in the war. It had been a Red Cross camp for women and children and so I used the historical archival records to learn more about its background. My dissertation ended up being this weird thesis about the economic geography of this place combined with an exploration of how households function, how do they navigate food shortage and handle livelihood insecurities under economic and political pressures. There was also work on institutions and local government. It was a very eclectic approach (laughter) which suited the topic quite well.

And after that I thought I am never going into academia again. I want to do something completely different. I went to work for the civil service which I did for a couple of years and it was very boring (laughter). But then I was recruited into AFRINT.

I joined because there happened to be funding. This is the advice I give to students. Don't be too rigid in what you want to do. Don't turn down offers that could be good even if they are different from what you wanted to do. For me there happened to be funding around for this project and it was an opportunity. And there was no other funding—we don't have many departments to choose from. It's only Lund, Stockholm, or Gothenburg that have any development geography. It is a quite marginal sub-discipline in other departments.

I remember the first time I met with AFRINT colleagues I thought I had to be completely honest and told them I had never done any statistics in my life (laughter). So I was really starting from scratch. I had not worked on statistics or survey design. At first I was involved as a post-doc and then put in charge of the database. I just had to learn how to manage it and I did.

AFRINT was originally conceived initially as a cross-sectional study (funded by Sida) but an advisor to the project had said right at the start 'Prepare for a second phase'. I came on board in that second phase of AFRINT, which was also funded by Sida. We spent the first two years trying to get funding from SIDA for the third phase because they had funded the first two. And we thought now it is becoming really interesting so we tried to get a third phase from them but they did not have funding. So I had to apply elsewhere. I applied with four different grants to enable the third phase of the project and this was how Dan and I met through the DEGRP project.[8] This allowed us to return to Tanzania and Mozambique. I had already secured money for Kenya, Ghana, Malawi, and Zambia. Getting all this funding was a lot of work because it was so staggered and it took time.

But then other things evolved over time. I am now the primary questionnaire designer of this project (laughter). I do a lot of questionnaire design and research design. Sometimes it is frustrating having this mixed methodological background because I get the feeling that I am just a fraud in all these areas but at the same time you also learn from your shortcomings. Also since I joined AFRINT, under my leadership, we have added a lot of qualitative work. It's been possible to say more about the quantitative data because we have better qualitative data.

But the frustration has been the lack of fieldwork. I was excited about the prospect of doing fieldwork—I like to be in the field, which I do now myself, though a lot is managing the project. I have to get people in a good mood and the right humour. There is a great deal of team-building and being on the same page and ensuring we want the same things. It would have been very difficult if AFRINT 1 had not worked so well to start that all from scratch. That spirit has been very important when there have been challenges to the project. When there has not been funding—or funding is complicated—and there are unwelcome surprises, we need this spirit in the data-collection process. Even if you are not embedded in the field you need to be embedded in the team; otherwise it won't work. We also work very closely with the partners in each of the different countries. Aida (Isinika) was part of the founding team (so we must have met the first time in 2007). And that introduces more variety, and makes things more challenging, but also more interesting to manage.

There is a strength in having this overview and being able to pick up generic patterns, especially with AFRINT because it is a cross-country study and we have the same research design everywhere to allow comparison. We have developed the research design as a collective, both the design itself and the questionnaire. The grounds for comparison are really useful and if you write from a theoretical perspective it is also a strength because you can tease out patterns. There are some places I have been to several times, for example in Zambia, when even if I go for only two to three weeks I go back to the same places to pick up on change. This is also the case in Ghana.

In Tanzania it is really interesting because where we had seen considerable intensification, now it is looking as if intensification is declining and may have been a response to a particular set of conditions which, in the space of only a few years, no longer apply. And it seems that may have been a classic boom and bust

[8] DfID-ESRC Growth Research Programme: see https://degrp.odi.org/about/.

and a response to declining rice prices.[9] But because we have comparative data from Malawi and Zambia we can also see some intensification of staple food crops in Zambia which is heavily connected to really strong state support and subsidies. Whereas in Tanzania if I understand correctly the subsidies have been scrapped. You can see this directly in the data.

In Tanzania there is also considerable disparity between villages and regions. So longitudinal change by village varies a lot, even within a place like Kilombero. In terms of the other dynamics in Tanzania I remember from the workshop in Copenhagen we could see things like housing dynamics which have improved. I think I agree with Stefano who observed an egg-shaped distribution—that is also the feeling I'm getting. Another issue is that the transition to adulthood is being delayed in all three countries. This is being scuppered by a lack of land or by adults finding other things to do with their land.

It is really interesting in the project in this edited collection how many different ways we can measure longitudinal change, and the commonalities and differences between the study sites. And things always seem to be much more complex the more you explore things. This is a challenge across all social sciences. But it is even more so if you are returning to a place or returning to data over time. And if you scratch the surface you uncover things.

And if you look at the questionnaire from AFRINT 1 it is really basic compared to the subsequent phases. This is the challenge of doing a longitudinal study, you are constantly bound, you are limited by the restrictions of the first phase. You realize over time that things are much more complicated, that societies evolve and that you would like to have a much longer record of some things than you actually have. And you can't do anything about it. You become a victim of the longitudinal surveys in some ways. Whereas it can tell you a lot about things in other ways.

Torben (Chapter 15)

I think I will bring in the perspective of the research assistants. Because if I look back on my work and coming back to Tanzania (except for when I went to Rukwa, when I could not bring Mwanyika) I have always worked with Einhard Mwanyika. Esbern has worked with Mwanyika longer than me but I first met him in 1986 coming as a Master's student. I was staying in a village in Njombe. We were groups of students staying in different villages and Mwanyika and his wonderful wife Constancia were working with one of the groups of students, and that is how I got to know him then.

[9] Andersson Djurfeldt et al. (2020).

We got very close as a group, it was a very nice group and we had very good people to assist us and help us with translations, and we were young and very inexperienced. We were in very good hands. Before leaving Njombe we had this party and we got a little bit drunk and so on. Just a little bit, opening beers with our eyes (laughter), and funny things like that, it was a fantastic party [Torben demonstrates opening beers with his eye socket to more laughter]. That was my first time in Africa, my first time in Tanzania, opening beers with my eye—it could not get better.

But what I wanted to say was that we had a very good bond with our local assistants including Mwanyika. When we said goodbye, we were laughing and crying and we agreed that we would not say goodbye, because we may meet again. After the Master's I did my PhD in Zambia and Rukwa, and I passed by Njombe on the way down there to meet Mwanyika and his wife Constancia, so we kept the contact.

In 1994 we got the SASA research programme [Sustainable Agriculture in Semi-Arid Africa], and Mwanyika was chosen to be the manager of a trial farm in Ikuwala, managing all the local staff and people hired in to assist. Being a former agricultural extension officer, he was really doing a good job, and in addition he is extremely good with people.

Quickly questions were raised: should he manage the fields or should he work with us as a translator? In those days the soil scientist researchers had been coming in and out every day, and staying overnight in Iringa. However, this was not going to work for me. So I ended up staying in the best house in the whole village of Ikuwala. It was a small brick house with a tin roof built as storehouse for equipment needed on the trial farm—in those days it was the best house in the whole village. To avoid the daily trips to Iringa we cleared a room and slept there so we could actually be in the village twenty-four hours a day—experiencing the late afternoons when people come back and go drinking and talk. That is when all the stories are told. Mwanyika was like the filter in many ways. He would come to us slowly and say 'maybe we should do things like this'. I always listened to him because his advice was always sound. He opened many doors for me. I feel extremely lucky and privileged to have been working with him for so many years.

We had the SASA programme for many years: 1994 to 2000. Mwanyika left his job in the government, which his wife was not happy about, to work on the research projects—he was well employed for many years with us. We had another project that took me back to this area. I had a PhD student who was working on a project on climate change who chose to work in Ikuwala as well—based on my advice (laughter). So, we got to go back, and I went in the field with him and Mwanyika.

Later on, I got other projects—once we had a chance, together with a soil scientist interested in soil carbon, to go back to Ilambilole. I had data on a long historical development of land use from these villages. So, it was interesting to combine this with how long people have been farming in certain places, and investigate the impacts and consequences for carbon in soil. Therefore, we emailed Mwanyika (this being in 2001!), and of course he was ready and willing to help, and it ended up being the most efficient fieldwork I have ever done. We flew into Dar es Salaam, picked up one of the former research cars, and drove up the same day to Iringa. The day before Mwanyika had been in the village announcing that we were coming and setting up meetings. He met us in the evening in Iringa. The next day we went to buy shovels and hand hoes because we were doing soil sampling. And the next day we were in the village doing our work.

So, the feeling of coming back after twenty years or twenty-five years—it is amazing. It is wonderful particularly when you are received well. We have been building up this relationship. He is the same age as me, and it is a very close bond—it has been a long relationship since 1987 and still ongoing. When working with Mwanika now, it is so easy, because it is like there is a connection right away. You sit and explain the purpose of what we are going to do now, and he picks it up right away. So that is very easy. Everyone likes him no matter where he goes, and I think he has had the same pleasure that we have had going back to these places. The latest I heard from him is today when he sent me an email, knowing I was in Arusha.

He has worked with over twenty PhDs for more than thirty years now. The good thing about this story is that Cathbert, Mwanyika's son, is now helping us. Esbern helped funding the education of Cathbert, who has worked with so many of us in the present research project (presented in this book) in Mbeya, Morogoro, Dodoma, Iringa, Ruvuma, and Manyara. Cathbert has worked in thirty-two of the thirty-seven villages covered in the survey presented in this book.

To conclude I would like to bring us back to Ilambilole, and at night outside the dispensary. We were sitting there, just having finished our food. I took out a small bottle of whiskey, and we were having a small glass. I was looking up into the sky, and then I saw the Big Dipper. I said 'Are you aware, actually you can be sitting here watching the Big Dipper, and I can be in Denmark looking at it at the same time—so we are not further away even though we are far away. We can watch the same stars at the same time.' He was blown away, he thought wow, I never thought of that. I said 'Even though we are apart that is how close we are'.

Mwanyika has worked for so many foreign researchers, but by the end of the nineteenth had actually never been out of the country. The most mind-blowing thing he had been to was the seaside with Esbern at Dar es Salaam. So we invited him to join us for the closing SASA conference in Copenhagen. He was there for a month, he stayed two days with all the researchers with whom he had worked.

We took him around. I took him to a Viking Museum in Roskilde. We wanted to tell him the story of where we came from. Then I took him to a Danish pig farm run by my wife's uncle. We had to dress up in white clothes to enter the stable, and it was very different from anything he had seen or known in Tanzania.

After the visit in the stable we went back to the main house and sat in the kitchen, having coffee and Danish pastry. The two farmers (the Dane and the Tanzanian) were sitting at the table, and I ended up just watching them as they began talking about pig farming. It was so striking to see this highly commercialized and mechanized pig farmer and this former extension officer from the southern highlands of Tanzania link up so well simply because they were farmers.

When you first visit Africa and come back, you realize how different and dramatic the changes are, and that things in Denmark previously looking important are no longer important when you put them in perspective. Then you learn to jump in and out of these different realities and the transitions become easier. However, I realized when I saw these two people sitting there that maybe we are not that different. There are many commonalities. It also illustrates who Mwanyika is: he can walk in anywhere and start talking to people, and we have to appreciate the assistance that we, as foreigners coming in, have enjoyed.

References

Andersson Djurfeldt, A., O. Hall, A. Isinika, E. Msuya, and G. T. Yengoh (2020). 'Sustainable Agricultural Intensification in Four Tanzanian Villages—A View from the Ground and the Sky.' *Sustainability, 12*(20), 8304. http://dx.doi.org/10.3390/su12208304.

Borgerhoff Mulder, M. and W. Logsdon (1996). *I've Been Gone Far Too Long: Field Study Fiascoes and Expedition Disasters*. Oakland, RDR Books.

Brockington, D. (2002). *Fortress Conservation: The Preservation of the Mkomazi Game Reserve, Tanzania*. Oxford, James Currey.

Middleton, J. (1970). *The Study of the Lugbara: Expectation and Paradox in Anthropological Research*. New York, Holt, Rinehart, and Winston.

Östberg, W. (1986). *The Kondoa Transformation: Coming to Grips with Soil Erosion in Central Tanzania*. Uppsala, Scandinavian Institute of African Studies.

Wittgenstein, L. (2009). *Philosophical Investigations*. 4th edn. Hoboken, Wiley-Blackwell.

Index

Note: Tables, figures, and boxes are indicated by an italic '*t*', '*f*', and '*b*' following the page number.